Praise for *President Nixon*

"Those who feel they can't bear to read another word about perhaps the most peculiar man ever to occupy the White House should think again. Richard Reeves sifted mountains of evidence in an attempt to get inside the President's skin. This approach works wonders. Nixon haters will still hate him, but they and less-partisan readers will come away from the book feeling they have lived a portion of Nixon's life."

—*Time* magazine, voted #5 on Best of 2001 list

"Dick Reeves has found new lodes of information to mine in the endlessly fascinating character and behavior of Richard Nixon. New information, newly interpreted with great insight."

—Ben Bradlee, author of *A Good Life*

"Fascinating . . . I thought I knew everything there was to know or all I needed to know about Richard Nixon, and I've learned stuff from this book. . . . A terrific read."

—Bob Schieffer, *Face the Nation*

"An intimate and gripping portrait. Richard Nixon's brain was a mansion with dark chambers and twisted halls. Reeves leads us through all of them. He is unrelenting but also sympathetic and humane."

—David Brooks, *Bobos in Paradise*

"Remarkable . . . Mr. Reeves, with his gift for candor and piquancy, takes advantage of the huge repository of material pertaining to Richard Nixon's presidency."

—William F. Buckley Jr., *National Review*

"Successful [and] solid . . . using some good new sources. Reeves's narrative structure also works well for a president who tried so hard to pull every string from behind his desk. Holding the reader in that office, always seeing the world through the lens of a withdrawn, insecure president, Reeves depicts an atmosphere of constant manipulation and deception."

—Philip Zelikow, *Foreign Affairs*

"Intelligent, heavily researched, and well-written. . . . Reeves demonstrates no inclinations for pussyfooting. This guy is a major-league reporter and he left very little on the cutting room floor. His is an authoritative, close-up view of a desperately introverted, sometimes brilliant man whose ambitions often were way beyond his skills. There is no fawning here. . . . A great read about a controversial, complex, insecure, tormented man."

—Jerry Gladman, *The Toronto Sun*

ALSO BY RICHARD REEVES

President Kennedy: Profile of Power

Running in Place:
How Bill Clinton Disappointed America

The Reagan Detour

What the People Know: Freedom and the Press

Passage to Pehsawar:
Pakistan Between the Hindu Kush and the Arabian Sea

American Journey:
Traveling with Tocqueville in Search of Democracy in America

Jet Lag: The Running Commentary of a Bicoastal Reporter

Convention

Old Faces of 1976

A Ford, Not a Lincoln

RICHARD REEVES

PRESIDENT NIXON

Alone
in the White House

A TOUCHSTONE BOOK
PUBLISHED BY
SIMON & SCHUSTER
NEW YORK LONDON
TORONTO SYDNEY

This book is for my father,
the HONORABLE FURMAN W. REEVES

 TOUCHSTONE
Rockefeller Center
1230 Avenue of the Americas
New York, NY 10020

Copyright © 2001 by Reeves-O'Neill, Inc.

First Touchstone Edition 2002

TOUCHSTONE and colophon are
registered trademarks of Simon & Schuster, Inc.

For information about special discounts for bulk
purchases, please contact Simon & Schuster Special
Sales at 1-800-456-6798 or business@simonandschuster.com

Picture research and editing:
Alexandra Truitt & Jerry Marshall,
www.pictureresearching.com

Manufactured in the United States of America

10 9 8 7 6 5 4 3 2

The Library of Congress has cataloged the Simon & Schuster edition as follows:
Reeves, Richard.
    President Nixon : alone in the White House /
Richard Reeves
       p.   cm.
    Includes bibliographical references and index.
    1. Nixon, Richard M. (Richard Milhous),
1913–94 2. Presidents—United States—
Biography. 3. United States—Politics and
government—1969–1974. I. Title.
E856.R44   2001
973.924'092—dc21   2001034417   [B]

ISBN 0-684-80231-7
     0-7432-2719-0 (Pbk)

Contents

Introduction

A mind forever voyaging through the strange seas of
thought, alone.

—WILLIAM WORDSWORTH, *The Prelude,* Book 3

ON MAY 17, 2000, more than two hundred men and women got together
at the Capital Hilton hotel in Washington for a dinner to celebrate the
twenty-fifth anniversary of an organization they called the February
Group, named that because it had been organized in February 1975. It
was a prosperous crowd, not young, and many of those present looked
vaguely familiar, as if you had seen them on television once. And you had.
The group was an informal alumni organization of people who had
served the thirty-seventh President, Richard M. Nixon. Christopher Cox,
a grandson of the late President, led the group in pledging allegiance to
the American flag. Many of the men there wore flag lapel pins, as their
leader had done in the White House from 1969 to 1974. Christopher's
mother, Tricia Nixon Cox, a middle-aged woman now, but forever young
for millions of Americans who remembered her wedding in that house on
June 12, 1971, introduced the main speaker, former senator Robert Dole,
who was chairman of the Republican National Committee during part of
the Nixon administration.

"The second half of the century that just ended could be called
'The Era of Nixon,' " Dole said. "The most extraordinary thing about
his presidency was not the way it ended, but that it happened."

President Nixon would have agreed with that. His rise to the presidency was an amazing triumph of will and intelligence. He was not born
for the job. In fact, he sometimes described himself, quite accurately, as

an introvert in an extrovert's business. Most politicians, good and bad, are men who can't stand to be alone. Nixon did not like to be with people. One of the many odd little notes I came across in years of going through his papers was a memo, dated April 13, 1970, to his chief of staff, H. R. Haldeman, about a visit from his classmates at Whittier College, a small Quaker school in Orange County, California: "You might have them on an occasion where we have an Evening at the White House or a church service. . . . This would be better than a reception for them alone where I would have to get into too much conversation."

He was always a man alone. A strange man of uncomfortable shyness, who functioned best alone with his thoughts and the yellow legal pads he favored, or in set pieces where he literally memorized every word he had to say. Prepared and comfortable, he was a formidable presence, not the cardboard man many remember. The people at the Hilton talked a great deal among themselves about what made the boss tick, just as they had every day in the famous years.

John Price, who was head of Nixon's Domestic Council for a time and became a vice president of Chase Manhattan Bank, told me of a flight on *Air Force One,* seated in the back next to Mrs. Robert Finch, whose husband had worked with Nixon for almost twenty years and was considered the President's closest friend in politics, even called the son Nixon never had. "You know him so well," Price began. Carol Finch seemed surprised, answering, "We don't know him at all." Haldeman, who spent hours each day alone with the President, always claimed that Nixon did not know how many children he had, or their names.

Ann Whitman, who was President Dwight D. Eisenhower's personal secretary, kept a diary. One entry, made on August 30, 1960, told of Eisenhower visiting Vice President Nixon, who was in the hospital for treatment of a knee infection. She wrote: "He mentioned again, as he has several times, that the VP has very few friends. Of course the difference to me is obvious—the President is a man of integrity, and sincere in his every action, be it possibly wrong. He radiates this, everyone knows it, everybody trusts and loves him. But the Vice President sometimes seems like a man who is acting like a nice man rather than being one."

He had learned how to act. Nixon had memorized his lines, as he had memorized hundreds of pieces of music in order to play the piano—all of them in the key of G. He was not a natural; it was all hard, lonely work. He also memorized entire speeches, working alone from notes, then throwing away the paper. He did the same thing with conversations, working from little scripts he committed to memory. He once said of himself: "I've found a way to do it. I'm a reader, not a buller. Most of the boys at the law school had long bull sessions about cases. I studied my cases alone."

And, alone, as he thought or as he watched others, he studied their words and actions and he calculated their motives. Like most of us, he could judge them only by what he knew of himself. More often than not, he thought other people were like him. But they were not. The power and opportunity of the presidency sometimes brought out the best in him, but it brought out more of the worst because he trusted almost no one. He assumed the worst in people, and he brought out the worst in them. He was too suspicious, his judgments were too harsh, too negative. He clung to the word and the idea of being "tough." He thought that was what had brought him to the edge of greatness. But that was what betrayed him. He could not open himself to other men and he could not open himself to greatness.

I set out in this book, as I had before with President John F. Kennedy, a man whose grace and image tormented President Nixon every day, to reconstruct the Nixon presidency as it looked from the center. I was interested in what he knew and when he knew it and what he actually did—sometimes day by day, sometimes hour by hour, sometimes minute by minute. As before, I hoped to get close to knowing what it was like to be president, something only forty-two men have known. But Richard Nixon at the center did not look outward in the way of Kennedy and most other politicians. Nixon still looked inward, which is why this book begins with his dialogues with himself, the hopes and fears and calculations scrawled on his yellow pads in his hours alone in his hideaway offices and late at night in his study, the room where Abraham Lincoln once slept.

The words he wrote when alone are the outline of a restless, driven man's quest for achievement. At his best and most longing, he lived for what Niccolò Machiavelli said princes should live for: "Nothing makes a prince more highly esteemed than the assumption of great undertakings and striking examples of his own ability."

Nixon had great abilities. The testimonies of his men converge on his intellect and vision. Bryce Harlow, his first congressional liaison, said: "Firm instructions not to bother him would go out. . . . He would bring along memoranda, studies, and reports and lean back on a kind of lounge, half-supine, would read, study, make notes, and prepare an outline of it all on his pad. When through, he would throw away his notes. He was now master of that issue; it was engraved on his mind. That's Nixon. That gift enabled him to achieve more than less gifted people could."

Herb Klein, a San Diego newspaperman who worked with Nixon for more than thirty years, told me: "He could feel a raindrop here and another there, and know there was a flood coming somewhere." Elliot Richardson, who held three Cabinet positions under Nixon and resigned from the last rather than follow the President's orders to dismiss a Watergate prosecutor, said: "He had a sense of how everything fitted in. . . . He had a definite sense of architecture in both foreign and domestic fields.

"He wanted to be the Architect of his Times."

They were no ordinary times. The United States was at war with itself at the end of 1968. More than two hundred young men were being killed each week in the undeclared war in Vietnam. A new wave of civil rights unrest and reaction was breaking over busing plans to implement court orders requiring immediate desegregation of public schools. As the Nixon men moved into the White House, one of them, John Ehrlichman, was visited by a Stanford Law School classmate, Warren Christopher, deputy attorney general in the outgoing administration of President Lyndon Johnson. "He arrived in my office with a big package of documents and suggested we keep them on hand all the time," Ehrlichman recalled. "They were proclamations to be filled in. You could fill in the name of the city and the date and the President would sign it and declare martial law."

The new president knew that whatever else he did—and he had grand secret plans of his own—voters would judge him on whether he brought order to the streets at home. His Inaugural address, lifted stylistically from Kennedy's 1961 speech, was built on a sign held up by a young girl in Ohio as he campaigned there: "Bring Us Together." But Nixon could not do that. He saw people as groups, to be united and divided toward political ends. The architecture of his politics, like that of his foreign policy, was always based on manipulating groups and interests, balancing them or setting them against one another, whichever suited his purposes of the moment or his times. He had a tribal and genetic view of peoples everywhere. He gloried in cultural warfare, dividing the nation geographically, generationally, racially, religiously. He believed that was what all politicians did. His "silent majority," a resentful populist center of working and middle-class Christians, loved him not for himself but for his enemies.

President Nixon saw himself as an idealist, believing that his generation had proved itself capable of larger things because of its suffering in the Great Depression and its service in World War II. He thought he belonged to "The Greatest Generation"—long before the phrase was popularized in the 1990s. Because of that, he could not be categorized as a small-minded conservative. He was narrow-minded in the sense that he had few interests—foreign policy, campaign management, sports, and getting even were what he cared about—and his ideological instincts were right-of-center, but he believed in pragmatic, activist governance, because he was persuaded that Americans preferred action, good or bad, to inaction.

That said, he expected little of the people who elected him. He was more Machiavelli than the Prince, a modern counterpart of the unemployed political strategist who, in 1513, wrote:

> A prudent ruler, therefore, cannot, and should not, keep his word when keeping it is to his disadvantage, and when the reasons that made him promise no longer exist. For if all men were good, this precept would not hold, but since they are bad and would not keep their word to you, you do not have to keep yours to them. Nor is there ever a shortage of legitimate reasons to disguise your disregard. . . . Everyone understands how laudable it is for a prince to keep his word and live with integrity and not cunning. Nonetheless, experience shows that nowadays those princes who have accomplished great things have had little respect for keeping their word and have known how to confuse men's minds with cunning. In the end they have overcome those who have preferred honesty.

Nixon's White House of lies was no accident. As I have tried to show in this book, he attempted to govern by surprise, scheming to bypass the checks and balances built into the United States Constitution and the scrutiny of the people, the Congress, and the press. His most important achievements—the remaking of the national and world economy in 1971 and the opening to China in 1972—became public in dramatic television announcements. In a kind of coup against both the Constitution and his own government, President Nixon literally changed the world without any public debate or participation. That kind of surprise, eliminating argument, required extraordinary secrecy, and the secrecy required lie after lie. In the end, only a few people knew what was happening in the house of lies; sometimes Nixon himself lost track of what was true and what was not—which is what ultimately destroyed him. Winston Lord, who served as the principal assistant to National Security Adviser Henry Kissinger, told me: "They deliberately mirrored adversaries which were secretive. In China, only two or three people were involved in decision making. . . . Bruised egos were a small price to pay in terms of foreign policy."

Deceived and confused egos, though, eventually undermined the President. So many layers of lies were needed to protect the layers of secrecy that no one inside the White House knew whom or what to believe. There was a chaos of lies at the top. The rings of deception built around the President, Kissinger, Haldeman, and Ehrlichman to protect themselves against "The Establishment" as Nixon imagined it, gradually isolated his Cabinet and much of his staff. Colleagues became distrusted parts of the hated bureaucracy, enemies who must be kept away by bodyguards of lies. In the beginning, the idea was to make the President's world secure from outsiders; in the end, even the insiders themselves could no longer penetrate to reality. There are many lines in the many lies of Nixon's Oval Office tapes, but two that weave and twist through the plots are attempts to cover up past lies while trying to unravel them at the same time. The President and Kissinger sometimes seem lost trying to concoct truths to tell Secretary of State William Rogers and Defense Secretary Melvin Laird in order to undo the chaos of past lies, large and small. It comes as no surprise then to learn that all the principals were spying on each other, stealing each other's papers, tapping each other's telephones, bugging their own offices. It was hard to keep track of the deceptions, even for the deceivers. The same confusion emerged in the taped byzantine maneuvering of the President, Haldeman, and Ehrlichman as they tried to simultaneously find and cover up the hundreds of horrors that finally became known as Watergate. In the end, no one knew whether anyone was telling the truth, the whole truth, or any truth at all.

There was one more level of deceit that isolated the Oval Office. The President's men did not always follow his orders. Haldeman, particularly, ignored some of the more obviously foolish or dangerous of Nixon's verbal mandates, most of them said in anger, many of them about firing people or bombing countries. Harlow always remembered the first thing Haldeman told him when he came to the White House: "You must always do what Nixon tells you to do, but you must use judgment on the way in which you do it."

Most of it, the orders, the lies, and the truth, ended up on paper or on tape, though some of it may never be found. There was just so much of it, forty-four million pages in the National Archives alone. One of the ways the Nixon presidency was different from all others was in the extent to which it was recorded and preserved. The tapes made in the Oval Office, in the President's hideaway office in room 175 of the Executive Office Building, in the Lincoln study, and at Camp David are only part of it, a part that will take many more years just to hear, much less transcribe and understand. The first time we talked about this book, Kissinger said to me: "Remember, the story is not in the tapes. The real Richard Nixon can be found on paper." That could be dismissed as an attempt to diminish the meanness and vulgarity of the taped language, but it is also an important reminder that Nixon was a man who learned and constructed his pictures of the world with books, summaries, and memoranda—and that Bob Haldeman was something of a pre-computer organizational genius.

In Haldeman's White House, which organizationally it was, the presidency was documented with a compulsion that will probably never be repeated. The tapes were only part of it. Every encounter with the President had to be reported in detail by each staff participant. At times, there were six or seven versions of what happened inside the Oval Office or EOB 175. If the reports were not received within a specified time, a reminder would go out from the staff secretary, and that usually did the trick because the next step was the wrath of Haldeman, a man who believed fear was essential to efficiency. This was a standard reminder, one of thousands from staff secretary David C. Hoopes:

> It has been discovered that a Memorandum for the President's File was not made for this meeting with Former Attorney General John N. Mitchell on Wednesday, April 12, 1972 at 3:29 PM.
> Our records show that you were present during this meeting. Since the President desires that this important file be as complete as possible, I would like to ask you to prepare a summary of what transpired, what commitments were made (if any) and what kind of mood or atmosphere prevailed.
> Your Memorandum for the President's File need not be lengthy, but you should keep in mind the historical significance of your report and understand that its significance will increase greatly with time. We hope you will be able to write and return such Memorandum to this office within five (5) days.

In addition to the formal reports, there were extensive notes by Haldeman and Ehrlichman, who would fill dozens of pages each day. Then there were Haldeman's diaries (parts of which have been published, and parts that appear for the first time in this book), which he wrote, and later dictated, each night. Another running file of the President's mood and thinking was the daily news summary he received, ten- to fifty-page reports on the news of the day from newspapers, magazines, and the nightly news programs on television. Most days the President marked up the summaries with comments and orders—the orders being passed along to the staff by Haldeman as "action memos." Sometimes, too, one of the "anecdotalists" was sitting in a corner taking notes. That little corps, which included William Safire, Patrick Buchanan, Raymond Price, and other talented writers, was created because the President was convinced that other note-takers were not getting across his warmth and wit in anecdotes that could be passed along to correspondents and columnists.

In September 1972, as the election approached, Haldeman ordered that the White House files be culled to remove the most important and most sensitive or potentially embarrassing of the papers being produced each day, including all those with the President's handwriting. Those, designated "White House Special Files," were all filed separately, ready to be checked and probably removed if Nixon lost the election. He did not lose, of course, but those were the papers—the good stuff—seized by the Federal Bureau of Investigation during Watergate and then turned over to the National Archives for indexing. Many White House papers were destroyed or disappeared during the Watergate investigations, but much more survived for history than Richard Nixon ever intended.

This book is a narrative of what President Richard Nixon did at crucial points in his years in power. What I searched for was what he knew or heard, said, or read. In this account all of what he says, and what is said to him, is taken from tape recordings, documents, journals, notes, and interviews. In the instances where people's thoughts are mentioned, it is done because they told me what they had been thinking, or told someone else at the time, or because they recorded their thinking in journals or memoranda. In some cases, particularly in tape-recorded meetings and telephone conversations, I have edited out "uhs," repetitions, and confusing errors of grammar. I have ended the main section of the book on April 30, 1973, when the President realized that he had lost control over the events of Watergate. "When he told me it was over on April thirtieth, he meant his presidency," said press secretary Ronald Ziegler. "That was the lowest point."

Nixon knew then that his enemies had prevailed—confirming for him his own dark view of the way the world worked—but he struggled on, spending his time and energy in a lost cause. Reminiscing with the February Group all those years later, Bob Dole said that he once told the President he thought he was destined to be misunderstood because he was too complicated a man to be totally understood. Nixon had responded to that with enthusiasm, saying, "Aha! Now you're getting somewhere." He did not want to be understood. If other men thought he was unreadable, then they must think there was a great deal more inside him than just a powerful mind voyaging alone in anger and self-doubt. But he also said something to Dole that was far more simple: "I just get up every morning to confound my enemies."

PROLOGUE

August 9, 1974

At midnight on August 8, 1974, Stephen Bull, the personal assistant to the President of the United States, walked into the President's office, the Oval Office. It was quiet and dark in the West Wing of the White House. The television cameras were gone. The correspondents and the technicians had folded up their equipment and left after the thirty-seventh president, Richard Milhous Nixon, had announced, two hours before, that he would resign the office at noon on August 9. Bull decided not to turn on the lights. He could see enough in the dim light from the hallway. He went in, picked up Nixon's briefcase, put it near the doorway, and then began to pack away the things on the desk. The President was flying home to California the next day, and Bull decided to put everything on the desk there, just the way it was here, as if nothing had happened. He began with Nixon's reading glasses and a photograph of the President's two daughters, Tricia and Julie. As he picked up the appointment book, he bumped against the silver cigarette case the girls had given the President on the day he was inaugurated. The case was knocked off the desk onto the rug. It opened and the music box inside began to play its tinny tune, "Hail to the Chief."

Later, the President's secretary, Rose Mary Woods, who had spent twenty-three years with him in good times and bad, and an assistant named Marge Acker came in and began emptying the drawers into cardboard boxes. There were moving boxes in the hallways everywhere in the building. The place smelled of burnt paper, as some of the most powerful men in the country threw memos and files into their office fireplaces. The office of Nixon's last chief of staff, General Alexander M. Haig, was filled with giant clear plastic bags that held shredded documents. "Duplicates," he said. In the Oval Office the women packed up everything in the "Wilson desk," which Nixon used because he admired Woodrow Wilson. Then they moved on to his other two desks. The one President Dwight D. Eisenhower had used in the Oval Office, when Nixon was vice president, was in room 175 of the Executive Office Building, next to the White House; Nixon often worked alone there. The last one, which was smaller, was the "Lincoln desk" in the President's sitting room in the living quarters upstairs near his bedroom; Abraham Lincoln had used it in his summer retreat, a farmhouse only a mile away, north of Pennsylvania Avenue.

Miss Woods began with the center drawer of the Wilson desk. In it was a folder marked: "THE UNAUTHORIZED DISCLOSURE OF THE INFORMATION CONTAINED IN THE ATTACHED DOCUMENT(S) COULD BE PREJUDICIAL TO THE DEFENSE INTEREST OF THE UNITED STATES. . . . Please put in the middle drawer of the President's desk." Inside were Nixon's funeral plans, six rose-colored pages, photographs, and an Avis Rent-a-Car map, with a description of Rose Hills cemetery in Whittier, California, the town where he grew up. "Rose Hills is renowned as Southern California's most spacious and naturally beautiful Memorial Park." There was a list of honorary pallbearers, as well as a list of six musical selections, from "God Bless America" to "California, Here I Come." Next to the California song, the poor boy from Whittier who had become president had written, "Played softly and slowly."

Into a box it went, along with letters, stacks of newspaper clippings and polling summaries, the plastic belts of dictating machines, even a Halloween mask from a party. Most of what went into the boxes were the President's memos to himself, hand-written over five years on long yellow legal pads or dictated late at night and transcribed the next day. "To do" lists and "to be" lists—about what he wanted from history, what kind of president he wanted to be, what kind of man he wanted to be. American self-improvement lectures to himself—the most important dialogue in the White House, an introvert's dialogue with himself.

One of the first of the lists, from the Eisenhower desk, was written late at night on February 6, 1969, Nixon's seventeenth day as president. He was preparing for an interview with Hugh Sidey, who wrote a column called "The Presidency" for both *Time* and *Life* magazines, and he wrote three pages of resolutions to himself:

Compassionate, Bold, New, Courageous. . . . Zest for the job (not lonely but awesome). Goals—reorganized govt. Idea magnet . . .

Mrs. RN—glamour, dignity . . .

Open Channels for Dissent . . . Progress—Participation, Trustworthy, Open-minded.

Most powerful office. Each day a chance to do something memorable for someone. Need to be good to do good. . . . The nation must be better in spirit at the end of term. Need for joy, serenity, confidence, inspiration.

One drawer in Ike's old desk in that hideaway was stuffed with letters Nixon had read and kept for some reason, along with the Dictaphone belts. The letters were the same kind any man kept, the important ones, or those that inspired or just flattered him. The oldest one in the desk turned out to be important. It was from Claude Kirk, the governor of Florida, who wrote on May 31, 1969: "In regard to the replacement of Justice Fortas, I want to bring to your attention a Federal judge in this district who meets what I believe is your criteria for experience, philosophy, and personal character. His name is Judge Harrold Carswell. . . . To paraphrase the play entitled 'A Man For All Seasons,' I can tell you that Justice Carswell is a man for all 'regions.' . . ." There was flattery from Theodore H. White in June 1969, along with the first copy off the press of his book *The Making of the President, 1968*. True to form, the author's prose was rich: "This book whose hero is Richard M. Nixon . . . My previous reporting of Richard Nixon must I know have hurt. If I feel differently now it is not that there is a new Richard Nixon or a new Teddy White but that slowly truths force their way on all of us. . . . this book tries to describe the campaign of a man of courage and conscience."

In the first days of January 1970, alone in EOB 175, Nixon gave himself a pep talk, writing:

Add element of lift to each appearance. . . . Hard work— Imagination—Compassion—Leadership—Understanding of young—Intellectual expansion . . .

Cool—Strong—Organized—Temperate—Exciting . . . Excitement—Joy in Life—Sharing. Lift spirit of people—Pithy, memorable phrases.

Some time after that, on an undated page found in the Oval Office, he wrote:

Foreign Policy = strength. 1. War is difficult—But our successes are hidden—and ending war will be denied us. 2. Must emphasize—Courage, Stands alone. . . . Knows more than anyone else. Towers above advisers. World leader.

Restoration of Dignity. Family man—Not a playboy—respects office too much—but fun.

Extraordinary intelligence—memory—Idealism—Love of country—Concern for old—poor—Refusal to exploit.

Yet must be personal and warm.

On November 15, 1970, he wrote himself two pages of notes that stayed in the desk in EOB 175 until they were packed away by Bull. They began: "2 years less one week or 6 years less one week," and went on:

I have learned about myself and the Presidency. From this experience I conclude:

The primary contribution a President can make is on Spiritual lift—not material solutions.

1. The staff—particularly K & H*—with my active cooperation have taken too much of my time in purely material decisions which could be left to others—

2. Harlow et al. have dragged me into too many Congressional problems.

3. My speech & idea group is inadequate—but part of the problem is that I have spent too little time with them—

4. The Press, the Intellectual establishment, and the partisan Dems are hopelessly against—Better means must be found to go over them to people.

5. I must find a way to finesse the Cabinet, staff, Congress, political types—who take time, but could do their job sans my participation. Symbolic meetings should be the answer.

---

* The names and initials in President Nixon's private writings include: "H" for H. R. Haldeman, "K" for Henry Kissinger, and "Z" for Ron Ziegler. Last names only are used for Secretary of State William Rogers, Secretary of Defense Melvin Laird, Secretary of Labor George Shultz, and Elliot Richardson, who held posts in four departments: State; Health, Education, and Welfare; Defense; and Justice. "Harlow" is for Bryce Harlow, Nixon's congressional liaison. EOB refers to the old Executive Office Building, sometimes called OEOB.

Primarily—I must recognize responsibility to use power up to the hilt in areas where no one else could be effective—

Then he made a list of new resolutions:

1. Stop recreation except purely for exercise . . .
2. Need for more reading . . .
3. Need for more small social events . . .
4. Need for spiritual lift—each Sunday . . .
5. Need for optimistic up-beat psychology . . .
6. Need for more stimulating people to talk to—

So little time, so much that could be done. Alone by one of his White House desks or at Camp David, the presidential retreat in Maryland, or in the California and Florida homes he bought for himself and then called "the Western White House" and "the Southern White House," he gnawed at the same themes: the unfriendly press, his disobedient staff and inadequate speechwriters, people who did not appreciate how hard he worked or did not emphasize his courtesy, his warmth, his thoughtfulness when they talked of him to outsiders. There was pain, too, in his serial self-analysis. He could be happy, but he could find no joy.

In the last days of 1970, alone in the Lincoln sitting room, Nixon wrote:

Every day is the last. Make it count. Is there anything I failed to do today—I will wish I could do when I no longer have the power to do it?

That was piled in with a note from his brother, Don, a man who always seemed to have a business deal almost done, and who had been helped this time by Thomas A. Brady, an attaché in the United States embassy in Madrid. "A characteristic of the Spaniard is that he never forgets a favor or a friendly act," Brady wrote to the President's brother, saying that people over there always appreciated Richard Nixon's pursuit of Alger Hiss as a communist, because Hiss, then a State Department official, had successfully opposed the admission of Spain to the United Nations in 1945. On the bottom of Brady's note, President Nixon scrawled: "H—Let's see that Brady gets a promotion."

• • •

In March 1971, Nixon's approval rating dropped from 56 percent to 51 percent in the Gallup poll—his desk drawers contained sheets of advance numbers supplied privately by both George Gallup and Louis Harris, the country's biggest names in public opinion survey research, and by his own pollsters, paid from the many bank accounts and stashes of political cash maintained for him. Trying to figure why, he wrote:

> People crave a leader. . . . Our major failure is an obsession with programs. Competent, grey men. We lack color. . . . Maintain Mystery. RN is not going to be exhibitionist—his acts . . . his strength must be played up.

Not long after, Nixon tucked away a letter dated April 5, 1971, from a man with a gift for flattery, his old adversary Dean Acheson, secretary of state under President Harry S Truman. As a rising Republican star in California, Nixon had attacked the Democratic president as "a graduate of Dean Acheson's Cowardly College of Communist Containment." Acheson, who was in fact every bit as tough on communism as Nixon was, had reached out to Nixon, giving him support on Vietnam. Nixon reciprocated by sending him *The Turning Point,* a book about the early days of the Republic. Acheson thanked him, writing: "Jefferson to me is a baffling figure. . . . He had enormous talents—a real 18th Century man, even more gifted than Franklin. But he always seemed to be as much interested in words as in the reality behind them. The more solid, less glittering talents of George Washington is what it took to get the country started."

Nixon underlined "less glittering talents." Perhaps the President saved the letter because he read "Kennedy" and "Nixon" for "Jefferson" and "Washington"; that was almost certainly the way Acheson meant it to be read. Nixon wrote one word on the letter: "True."

Later that month he also annotated and kept a letter dated April 28, 1971, from a film publicist named David Brown, who wrote: "You have achieved in your own way what General De Gaulle achieved for France. . . ." The President underlined that and added in his own hand, "A good theme."

The President's notes to himself from the next year, the election year of 1972, dwelled on even greater frustration about his public image—usually at great length. Once again, at night, he was trying to define himself. On October 10, 1972, flying from his Florida home in Key Biscayne back to Washington, he worried, not for the first time, about how he would be remembered after all his elections were over, writing:

> "Presidents noted for—F.D.R.—Charm. Truman—Gutsy.
> Ike—Smile, prestige. Kennedy—Charm. LBJ—Vitality. RN—?"

One of his ideas was: "The national conscience."

Then, after reminding himself to send a gift of cigars to Marshal Tito of Yugoslavia, President Nixon wrote out this question for "K":

> Have we misjudged V.C.* from beginning—1. "Running
> to wire—exhausted." 2. "Stop U.S. dissent and they'll talk."
> 3. "Give them a jolt and they'll talk."

Then two weeks later, alone at 1 A.M. on October 23, 1972, in the Lincoln sitting room, he wrote this to himself:

> I have decided my major role is moral leadership. I cannot
> exercise this adequately unless I speak out more often and more
> eloquently. The problem is time to prepare. . . . I must take the
> time to prepare and leave technical matters to others.

On his sixtieth birthday, January 9, 1973, he wrote:

> Age—Not as much time. Don't spin your wheels. Blessed with
> good health. . . . Older Men—De Gaulle, Ike, Yoshida,
> Adenauer, Churchill, Chou En Lai, Hoover . . . No one is
> finished—until he quits.

*The VC were the Vietcong guerrillas in South Vietnam.

CHAPTER 1

January 21, 1969

RICHARD M. NIXON arrived at the White House just before 2 P.M. on January 20, 1969, a couple of hours after taking the oath as the thirty-seventh president of the United States. His first question, to his chief of staff, H. R. Haldeman, was: "Is the dog there?"

The dog, an Irish setter, was a gift from the staff. It was a big, photogenic, presidential dog to go with the Nixons' French poodle, Vickie, and a Yorkshire terrier named Pasha. All three were included in a Nixon-directed campaign to project himself as a warm man. The new president put it this way in a memo to Haldeman: "I would like for you to give me a full report on how adequately the records are being kept on the various meetings in which I participate. I am referring now not to the formal record requiring and noting decisions, but the account of conversations, background, color, etc."

"He was like a little kid," Haldeman recorded in his diary that night. Of the Inaugural itself, he recorded: "Expression on his face was unforgettable, this was the time! He had arrived, he was in full command, someone said he felt he saw rays coming from his eyes."

On his first full day as President, Nixon came down to his office at 7:30 in the morning after four hours of sleep. The schedule for the day was in a brown leather loose-leaf folder placed in the center of the great oak Wilson desk. The first formal appointment was written in for 7:50, a meeting with his national security adviser, Henry Kissinger.

The timing of their first conversation that day was symbolic of the new framework of foreign policy decision making the two men had crafted in the eleven weeks since the election. The key was National Security Decision Memo 2, issued during the inaugural parade the day before, eliminating a State Department–dominated committee called the Senior Interdepartmental Group. The function of SIG had been to review foreign policy options presented to the National Security Council—and thus to the President—and to act as the "executive agent" for national security decisions. Under NSDM 2 the NSC would prepare options and also execute decisions, the plain signal that the new president intended to centralize power in his office. So from day one there was a new architecture of decision; Nixon intended to use the former Harvard professor as his agent in foreign and security policy. The power of final decision had shifted to an odd couple, both of them secretive and suspicious by nature, both of them ready and anxious to isolate the old foreign policy establishment, symbolized by the cautious men and rituals of the State Department.

Nixon told Kissinger about the desk and said he admired Woodrow Wilson as a man of both thought and action, which was also the way he saw himself. Nixon had used the desk when he was vice president, from 1953 to 1961. Since then it had traveled to Texas. Nixon's predecessor, Lyndon B. Johnson, had taken it away to his LBJ Ranch office. Now it was back and it was almost bare, with an in-box in one corner and a four-button telephone more than six feet away on another.

The place was simpler than it had been during the LBJ years; Nixon had told his men to get rid of Johnson's forty-two-button phone, the three television monitors, the wires that had led to the system Johnson used to tape-record both telephone calls and conversations, and the speakers Johnson had used to listen to the daily briefing and questioning of his press secretary. Nixon was not much interested in listening to what reporters had on their minds.

"Where's the news summary?" he asked Haldeman that first morning.

There was none. During the campaign and the transition, a small staff headed by the President's political valet, Patrick Buchanan, a thirty-year-old former editorial writer for the *St. Louis Globe-Democrat,* had prepared a daily digest of the news in six newspapers and the three television networks. The first White House news summary, in a gold-imprinted blue leather loose-leaf book, was on the big desk the next morning. Only five other copies were made—two filed away for the record, one for Haldeman, one for Ehrlichman, and one for Kissinger. The top item that first day was a local story: crime in the President's new neighborhood. The *Washington Daily News,* in a front-page editorial, said fear was stalking the streets of the capital city. *The New York Times* that day said: "President Nixon awoke this morning in a city where during the last week an 81-year-old District of Columbia 'mother of the year' was mugged and thrown down a flight of stairs in a pocketbook snatching; Mrs. Gwen Cafritz, a well known society matron, was the victim of a $250,000 armed robbery. . . ."

The President scrawled his reactions across the pages, beginning with: "John Mitchell & John Ehrlichman. Let's get going with announcement in 48 hours of some action. . . . We are going to make a major effort to reduce crime in nation—starting with D.C.!! RN."

The next item was a *Washington Star* editorial denouncing demonstrators who threw curses and beer cans at the Nixons' car during the Inaugural parade; it ended: "Despite the presence of police, National Guardsmen and paratroopers, the hoodlums shouted obscenities and made obscene gestures towards the President and Mrs. Nixon. At that point, it appears, there were no arrests. . . ."

Nixon wrote: "Why not? I think an opportunity was missed—when people would have supported strong action . . . give me a report how it got screwed up." He also preserved his record as an obsessive minder of details, all the while complaining that he had no time to think. On that first day he dictated word-for-word texts for letters to be sent to people involved in the Inaugural parade and celebrations:

> One of our difficulties in the past is that our thank-you notes have been bogged down because of lack of staff and go out two or three weeks, if not a month later. We will be held to a different standard now, and I want these to get out in 48 hours since we have enough staff to do it. I am going to give a little guidance with regards to the form in the dictation now. To the Ministers: something like this: . . . Dear _____: I want to express my deep appreciation to you for participating in the _____ (whatever the morning prayer thing was). The problems facing the United States and the world are so serious that we shall all need Divine Guidance if we are adequately to meet the challenge. . . .

He also dictated a memo to his wife:

> To: Mrs. Nixon
> From: The President
> . . . With regard to RN's room, what would be most desirable is an end table like the one on the right side of the bed which will

accommodate TWO dictaphones as well as a telephone. . . . In addition, he needs a bigger table on which he can work at night. The table which is presently in the room does not allow enough room for him to get his knees under it.

At 6 P.M. the first day, Nixon and Haldeman crossed the small alley between the White House and the old Executive Office Building to look for a hideaway office in that ornate, hulking gray building built as War Department headquarters in 1888. The President chose EOB 175 for what he called "brainwork"—time alone with his thoughts and his yellow pads. "I must build a wall around me," he told his most important assistant, the forty-two-year-old advertising executive he and everyone else called Bob. Haldeman's job was to be the face and voice and muscle of Richard Nixon inside the White House. The President wanted to be alone—and being with Haldeman was, in effect, being alone. The chief of staff's most important job was taking notes during presidential dialogues and monologues, then dictating Nixon's thoughts and orders as "action memos" that ricocheted around the building, then around the government.

Nixon liked to be alone—an odd preference for an American politician. But his role model as a national leader was not an American, it was President Charles de Gaulle of France. For years, in political exile, Nixon had compared his fate and his destiny to de Gaulle's after the general stepped down as president of France in 1946. Reading de Gaulle's memoir *The Edge of the Sword,* Nixon had underlined this sentence: "Great men of action have without exception possessed in a very high degree the faculty of withdrawing into themselves."

He was obsessed with solitude, with the use of his own time, writing, "Time is a person's most important possession. How he makes use of it will determine whether he will fail or succeed in whatever he is undertaking." The night was good to Nixon. Sleep was an enemy, or a drug that lesser men used to avoid facing crises. Or so he told his men during periodic monologues on the subject, which often turned into action memos, like this one to a speechwriter, William Safire, with Nixon referring to himself in the third person, just before his Inaugural: "It has been suggested to me that we capitalize upon the work habits of the President-elect: long hours of work, delayed dinners, eighteen-hour days, late reading, no naps, perfunctory and very short lunch and breakfast times (frequently five or ten minutes)."

Only the part about quick meals was true. His men, particularly Haldeman—who had been with Nixon on and off for eight years, beginning as an advance man in his first campaign for the presidency—knew that fatigue was Nixon's real enemy; he could not focus for more than three or four hours at a time. He took naps and came back to work for a couple of hours more. But the naps were a secret, usually marked "staff time" on his daily schedules. Part of Haldeman's job, as he saw it, was to protect Nixon from himself. When the President got too tired, he could not sleep; he might take pills or a drink or two—he had trouble with liquor, sometimes slurring his words after only a single drink—and then be unable to concentrate the next day. But Nixon would never admit that, even to himself. He was a man of will, who sometimes persuaded himself that normal human limits were symbols of weakness. Sleep, and vacations, too, he considered a waste of time—or so he said. In fact, he needed EOB 175 for naps as well as brainwork. The hideaway office was a two-room suite without a reception area. He rarely saw anyone there, except for Haldeman; John Ehrlichman, who was a domestic counselor; and Henry Kissinger. The blinds were drawn. Usually the President sat in an old brown velvet easy chair he had brought from the study of the Fifth Avenue apartment he owned from 1963 to 1968, his years as a New York lawyer.

Most of the time, Nixon curled in the chair with his feet up on the settee. No one ever saw him there with his jacket off. Only a select few, Stephen Bull among them, ever saw him with his reading glasses on, or smoking one of his pipes, or sitting with a drink—a martini. One of his assistants, Alexander Butterfield, who spent a great deal of time running presidential errands, told other staffers who rarely saw Nixon that not only had he never seen the jacket off, he had never seen the boss there with the jacket unbuttoned.

On January 23, the White House news summary which included fifteen pages summarizing network television reports from the night before, was prepared by Buchanan and an assistant named Tom Charles Huston, who had been president of a conservative group, Young Americans for Freedom. It began with a report on a U.S. Navy court of inquiry into the seizure of the USS *Pueblo,* a spy ship that had been intercepting radio signals off the coast of North Korea. "Bucher comes off a decent and honorable officer," Buchanan and Huston wrote of the ship's captain. "All three networks reflected sympathetically on Bucher and adversely on the Navy." Nixon underlined those words, then scrawled: "To Laird. RN agrees—Don't let Navy make a fool of itself." *

---

* The USS *Pueblo,* a 906-ton electronic surveillance ship with a crew of eighty-three—armed with only two 50-caliber machine guns—was boarded and seized off the coast of North Korea on January 23, 1968. Commander Lloyd M. Bucher and his men were held in North Korea for a year and were released on December 23, 1968, after signing confessions of spying.

That was the first "action memo." The President wanted his marginalia translated into Haldeman memos to the rest of the staff, usually ordering them to have an answer or explanation within twenty-four hours. The second action memo was written beside an account of French students occupying offices at the Sorbonne in Paris and of youthful demonstrators in the streets of several cities around the world—including Tokyo, Cologne, Nairobi, and Dacca—at the same time American students were demonstrating or running wild at dozens of campuses, including San Francisco State, the University of Massachusetts, Penn State, Rice, and Howard. The President wrote: "K—I want to hear a C.I.A. analysis in depth of worldwide common factors of youth disturbances."

At nine o'clock most mornings Nixon buzzed for Haldeman, and a half hour after that for Kissinger, and those conversations, with Haldeman taking notes on yellow legal pads, would produce a second flurry of notes from on high. Within only a couple of days, members of the staff and the Cabinet began to suspect that "the Boss," as some called Nixon, intended to meet alone with very few of them, maybe only four: Haldeman and Ehrlichman with their yellow pads, Kissinger with his thick, overwritten briefing books, and Rose Mary Woods.

They were right. The Boss had already told Haldeman that his job was to keep other people away from his two offices. Haldeman memos were the President's preferred medium of communication. The chief of staff was to do the things Nixon disliked: confronting, criticizing, and disciplining. Haldeman would do the firing and the insulting—and if anyone wanted to actually see the President he had to see Haldeman first. "RN," as Nixon called himself on paper and often in conversation, sketched out a schedule that might include only a single large meeting in his "public hours," generally from 10 A.M. to 5 P.M., with a couple of hours set aside for his five-minute lunch, almost always alone, almost always cottage cheese—flown in every week from Knudsen's Dairy in Los Angeles—and a canned pineapple ring. Then came brainwork or a nap in the solitude of EOB 175.

The meeting of the day on January 23 was the first coming together of the Urban Affairs Council, which the President created as a vague domestic shadow of the National Security Council. The official record of the meeting began with the President signing an executive order creating the new entity and included this: "There was a very exciting atmosphere as the President . . . spoke of the need for innovation and for exercising judgment. . . . 'I'd like to see more decisions made by the responsible men. John Quincy Adams and Grover Cleveland read every bill and almost killed themselves. You won't build big men down the line unless you give them responsibility.' " Then Nixon introduced the director of the council, a stranger, Daniel Patrick Moynihan—a New Yorker, a Catholic, a Kennedy Democrat, and a Harvard professor. Moynihan, who was forty-one years old, was set up as a rival to Arthur F. Burns, a sixty-four-year-old Columbia University economist and old friend, who had run a domestic policy task force during the transition and expected to run domestic policy. The meeting minutes indicated that Burns had tried to put Moynihan on the spot and failed: "Dr. Burns and the Vice President asked if Dr. Moynihan could prepare some outline of a national urban policy, and the President agreed. Dr. Moynihan said that 'I would be glad to undertake such a task, on the condition that—and I realize that one does not ordinarily impose conditions on the President of the United States—on the condition that no one take it seriously.' Everyone roared, including the President, who first blinked, and then joined in the laughter."

The next day, January 24, it was the first meeting of a new Cabinet Committee on Economic Policy, a meeting held up for almost a half hour while John Ehrlichman calmly wrote out an executive order creating the thing as Nixon paced restlessly back and forth. The President was ready to get on with it, but in his White House procedure was by the book. Haldeman's book. The Urban Affairs Council had an executive order, so the economic group would have one, too. The new chairman of the Council of Economic Advisers was Paul McCracken, plucked from the conservative School of Economics at the University of Chicago. He was getting ready for his first testimony before the Joint Economic Committee of the Congress, and the President quickly suggested that he work with Safire, a forty-year-old New York public relations man, an old Nixon hand on the speechwriting staff. Safire took the President's suggestion as a signal that he was to make sure McCracken did not spend much time on praise of economic growth under two Democratic presidents, John F. Kennedy and Lyndon B. Johnson—particularly given Nixon's campaign criticism of the Kennedy-Johnson economic record.

McCracken said that the economy was currently growing at a healthy 3.5 percent, and would probably go up to 4.5 percent.

"Why?" asked Nixon.

"The bulge in the birthrate after World War II now going into the labor force means a big demand for capital," the economist answered. "The plateau of 1.5 million housing starts has been par for the course for years. This year it should be 1.7 million, and more by 1970. And housing takes a lot of money. . . . The Nixon years ought to be years of extremely rapid economic growth. And if we manage it right, they will be."

The new secretary of agriculture, Clifford M. Hardin, started to say something about hunger in America: "Millions of Americans—" The President cut him off, saying, "It is not constructive to say that people here are starving—our friends on the other side of the Curtain would eat that up." A trivial matter, but the answer revealed an important indicator: Nixon had limited interest in domestic affairs—"building outhouses in Peoria," he once called them—giving them his attention only if the press was focusing on matters at home or when such matters became foreign policy problems, as civil rights demonstrations had when film footage and still photographs were seen around the world during the Kennedy and Johnson administrations.

On January 25, his fifth day in office, the President dictated a series of memos to John Ehrlichman that he wanted converted into a political framework for the administration. The first step, he said, was never to mention politics—at least on paper. His thoughts, referring to himself in the third person, included these:

> The letter to the Cabinet with regard to third level employees should be changed to strike out any references to politics. . . . you must always assume that this kind of a memorandum will eventually get into the press. . . . The tendency of the Cabinet officer will be to take the course of least resistance and go along with a competent career man who is identified with the policies of the past. This is a grave mistake. . . . The Cabinet officers should fill at least 90 percent of all the available positions with new people regardless of the competence of the old people who are not frozen in by Civil Service Regulations. . . . This is exactly what Kennedy did when he came in and that is one of the reasons why he was able to present a picture of a new fresh Administration. . . . That is why I constantly get back to the Inaugural—the necessity to follow it up in every possible way so that the people eventually will look back upon it as a far more significant statement than it may have even been. Take a hard look at what they did with the Kennedy Inaugural Address. . . .

Nixon spoke of the Kennedys every day. He modeled his Inaugural address on Kennedy's 1961 speech, but Kennedy's words were a Cold War call to battle and Nixon was calling for peace and order. His lines did not ring. The best of them had to do with ending the noise: "The simple things are the ones most needed today if we are to surmount what divides us, and cement what unites us. To lower our voices would be a simple thing. In these difficult years, America has suffered from a fever of words: from inflated rhetoric that promises more than it can deliver; from angry rhetoric that fans discontents into hatreds; from bombastic rhetoric that postures instead of persuading. . . . We cannot learn from one another until we stop shouting at one another."

The new president held his first press conference on the morning of the seventh day, January 27. The second question, from Helen Thomas of United Press International, one of 456 correspondents and technicians facing the President, got right to the point of the campaign that made Nixon President: "Mr. President, now that you are President, what is your peace plan for Vietnam?"

He had no plan. He simply repeated a list of proposals that had been widely discussed during the last Johnson years: "The restoration of the demilitarized zone as set forth in the Geneva Conference of 1954; mutual withdrawal; guaranteed withdrawal by both sides; the exchange of prisoners. All of these are matters that we think can be precisely considered and on which progress can be made." A bit later, in answer to another question, he expanded the answer, saying, "I think at this point this administration believes that the better approach is . . . mutual withdrawal on a guaranteed basis by both sides."

Asked about his campaign pledge to maintain "clear-cut military superiority over the Soviet Union," he said that perhaps "superiority" was the wrong word. "I think," he said, " 'sufficiency' is a better term, actually. . . ."

Nixon's answers were cool. On inflation, which was running at almost 5 percent, he answered: "I do not believe that policy should be made by off-the-cuff responses in press conferences or any other kind of conferences. . . . We are going to have some fine-tuning of our fiscal and monetary affairs in order to control inflation. . . ." Then he specifically ruled out government wage or price guidelines under any circumstances. In private, meeting with his party's congressional leaders, he repeated Republican doctrine on inflation, saying, "The culprit is government." He broke up the meeting to go out to the Rose Garden, where photographers congregated to take the first pictures of the new White House dog, King Timahoe, the Irish setter named for the town in Ireland where Quaker ancestors of Nixon's mother had once lived.

The President's first strictly political meeting was on his tenth day in office, January 30, with Haldeman and two young assistants, Fred LaRue and John Sears. First, the President told them he wanted to set up a campaign committee for his reelection outside the Republican National Committee—with separate financing. Then he agreed to their recommendation of continuous year-round polling.

EVEN UP CLOSE, Nixon was rarely direct—a tough man to figure. After a week in office, he wanted to go to Florida for the weekend. He went through a psycho-ballet with Haldeman, who said to Ehrlichman: "He immediately starts trying to think up excuses and covers. He's constitutionally unable to say he's taking time off, has to appear he's working. . . . Then he starts worrying about whether Ziegler has gotten out the story of how hard he's been working. . . ."

Watching him in public, though, Haldeman realized that Nixon loved pomp and ceremony. On January 31, at a reception in the East Room for foreign diplomats—a white-tie affair heavy on flags and trumpets—Haldeman thought his boss looked like a wooden soldier with his arms stiff at his sides, trying to hide the fact that he was as happy as a little kid. Unfortunately, this little kid had a dog that did not like him. That day, like the days before, King Timahoe refused to come near the President's desk, even when assistants laid a trail of dog biscuits leading to Nixon.

By the first week of February, the dog was beginning to follow the biscuits, getting closer and closer to his master. He got too close during the first meeting between Nixon and his science adviser, Lee DuBridge, pulling down one of the big flags behind the President's desk. And then there was the little nick on the antique grandfather clock in the Oval Office. Trying to entice Timahoe, a couple of Nixon's merry men, led by Haldeman, ended up throwing biscuits at each other, hitting the clock instead. Luckily, the boss was in his swimming pool, determined to get some exercise, wearing a bathing cap because the White House barber had told him the chlorine in the pool was not good for his hair.

The White House seemed to be settling into an orderly routine, with Ehrlichman and Haldeman presiding over morning meetings: the first one at 7:30, when a dozen or so staffers would report in to Ehrlichman in the Roosevelt Room, and then a smaller one at 8:15 in Haldeman's office, where Ehrlichman; Kissinger; Bryce Harlow, the congressional liaison; and one or two others would brief the chief of staff for his first meeting of the day with "the Leader of the Free World," as Haldeman liked to call the President—half in jest, half in awe.

The chief of staff was the keeper of the body and of the image, taking notes for hours each day, then diffusing or distributing the President's momentary passions, threats, and tantrums into cool gusts of formal action memos over his own name. Nixon was angry many days and repetitive most days, saying the same things, usually about firing bureaucrats and cutting off reporters. Most of the staff knew none of that. Haldeman protected the President and the staff from each other. Sometimes he just forgot about the ramblings and foul language of the Leader of the Free World. Some of the President's orders became inside jokes, one of them a presidential outburst after a bad landing on one of his first flights in *Air Force One:* "That's it! No more landing at airports!"

"I want everyone fired, I mean it this time," was a staple. Nixon said it on February 5 when he read that the Office of Economic Opportunity was refusing to release records from the Johnson years to a congressional committee. The next day he was mad at Herbert Klein, his communications director—they had met when Klein was a local reporter covering his first congressional campaign in Southern California back in 1946—for telling a columnist of Nixon's intention to do regular polling.

"No polls. Not concerned by Press, T.V. or personal style." Nixon wrote that at the top of a page of notes, as he prepared for an interview that day with Hugh Sidey of *Life*. Nixon went on, writing out the points he wanted to make, beginning with "Zest for job" and continuing: "Strong in-charge President. Aggressive. Anti-crime measures . . . On the ball. Honest." After writing that the job was awesome and not lonely, he added that it also brought him "best friends—I've never met."

"Remarkable ease and sense of pleasure," Sidey wrote after the interview, calling Nixon "the power center." The President liked what he read that day, but still had a gripe in a scrawled note to Ehrlichman: "E— have we done adequate job on RN at work? (Begins in office at 7:45. Non-stop to 6:30 or 7 etc.)" Later he had more editorial thoughts in another memo to Ehrlichman: "I think one point which could be emphasized is to rebut the theme which I see running in several columns that RN has done pretty well and the sailing is smooth, but that he cracks in a crunch. A graceful, firm reminder that in a crunch—Caracas, Khrushchev, the heart attack—and when the tough decisions had to be made in the campaign the coolest man in the room was RN. . . ." That same day, he annotated his news summary, which he usually read before Haldeman came in after the 8:15 meeting, with one word, "Bravo!" next to a report that the *Chicago Tribune* had announced it would no longer publish news of student antiwar demonstrators.

The President met the press again on February 6, only ten days after his debut conference. He was somewhat more direct when asked about United States troop withdrawals in Vietnam: "I do not want an American boy to be in Vietnam for one day longer than is necessary for our national interest. As our commanders in the field determine that the South Vietnamese are able to assume a greater portion of responsibility for the defense of their own territory, troops will come back. However, at this time I have no announcements to make with regard to the return of troops."

This time there were questions about school desegregation and the attitude of blacks toward his administration. On January 29, the new secretary of health, education, and welfare, Robert H. Finch, had ordered a sixty-day extension of deadlines for termination of federal aid to five segregated southern school districts that had not produced court-ordered desegregation plans.

"I support the law of the land," Nixon said, but then added that he preferred local solutions to court orders. "Before we use the ultimate weapon of denying funds and closing a school, let's exhaust every other possibility to see that local school districts do comply with the law." It was a carefully considered and deliberately vague answer. Nixon told his interrogators that he was aware of black distrust but he hoped his actions as president would show him to be the president of all Americans.

The news summary the next morning began: "All networks lead with the President's press conference. . . . Reviews of the session ranged from 'great' to 'tremendous.' On ABC News, Frank Reynolds said that there is one quality that the American people want in their President and that is a man in charge: 'The President is such a man. . . . Self-confidence with no arrogance crackled in the East Room today. There was no band to play "Hail to the Chief" as he came in, but they should have played it as he walked out.' "

Nixon's response, written over that item in the news summary, was, "How about some non-obvious letters to editors . . . ?"

He was obsessed with generating letters—real or fabricated—to newspapers and magazines and the television networks. The idea was for the Republican National Committee and state and local committees to build up lists of loyalists who could be called on to spread the party line by mail or whose names could be used on letters dictated from the White House. Later, he needled Ehrlichman in a memo that touched on another obsession, the Kennedys:

> I still have not had any progress report on what procedure has been set up to continue on some kind of basis the letters to the editor project and the calls to TV stations. . . . it gives us what Kennedy had in abundance—a constant representation in letters to the editor columns and a very proper influence on the television commentators. . . . Individuals can express their own enthusiasm for the RN crime program in Washington, the RN press conference technique. Later on, letters can be written taking on various columnists and editorialists when they jump on us unfairly. I do not want a blunderbuss memorandum to go out to hundreds of people on this project, but a discreet and nevertheless effective Nixon Network set up.

The President was excited and exhausted after the press conference. He usually was after a day or two of solitary preparation for the sessions, reading stacks of staff and Cabinet memos on possible questions and suggested answers. By the time he said "Good evening," he had edited or rewritten and then memorized dozens of answers. He left the White House after this one, taking his first weekend trip—to Key Biscayne, where he had been going for twenty years, staying at the house of a friend, a businessman named Bebe Rebozo. Nixon was always a restless man, rarely sleeping under the same roof for more than a week at a time. He was in Florida this time for three days. The White House physician, Dr. Walter Tkach, was along, and he and his patient got into a long conversation when the doctor said he had read medical reports, which he did not believe, indicating that there were people who did not need sleep. The President was fascinated, saying he had always thought that most people used sleep to avoid facing problems and making decisions. He said it was better to be "up" than relaxed. He also told the physician that he had never had a headache. He seemed to think headaches were imaginary—excuses for weak men. Tkach nodded, but later he told Haldeman that he had never known or heard of anyone who did not get headaches.

DURING THE FEBRUARY 6 PRESS CONFERENCE, Nixon had answered a question about proposals for an international conference to resolve disputes between Israel and Arab nations in an evenhanded way, talking of "bilateral" consultation and "four-power talks," rather than signaling automatic support for Israel. That led to a February 13 visit to the White House by a bipartisan group of six House members, four of them from New York, carrying a three-page declaration that said they believed they represented the opinion of the majority of both the House and the Senate. "There is concern," the congressmen wrote, "that Middle East interests may be sacrificed as part of bargaining in global settlements. . . . It would not be in the best interests of the United States that Israel be requested to withdraw from territory she occupies"—referring to the West Bank and Sinai, occupied by Israel since the 1967 Arab-Israeli War.

The little delegation was surprised when they were greeted not by the President but by Henry Kissinger alone. They were surprised again by what the national security adviser said to them: "The President feels the U.S. has an interest in a settlement. What we are trying to do is to 'position' the issue so that the American people can understand it. In Vietnam we have put ourselves in a position where our involvement is explained in terms of issues which the American people do not support. In the Middle East, if it ever comes to involvement, we cannot be in a position of justifying intervention to preserve Israel's conquests. We want to be in a position to explain our policy in terms of preserving world peace. . . ."

The congressmen were among the first to see that foreign policy was going to be run from the White House. A couple of days later, Haldeman was dispatched to inform Secretary of State William P. Rogers that the department's services would not be needed when the President met with representatives of the Soviet Union. Nixon and Rogers were old friends—and that may have been part of the problem. They were once close enough that Vice President Nixon actually moved into Rogers's house during the crisis months of 1955 after President Eisenhower's first serious heart attack. When Nixon moved to New York after his humiliating defeat in the 1962 gubernatorial race in California, Rogers was one of the few important New York lawyers to welcome him. But there was also the usual resentment: Rogers was handsome, charming, and seemingly secure. Nixon was Nixon, wondering whether Rogers secretly looked down on him.

Nixon thought, too, that Rogers was shallow and a little lazy, and that he did not know all that much about foreign affairs. Rogers was Nixon's third choice; the job had been offered to Robert Murphy, who had retired as a diplomat to become chairman of Corning Glass, and to William Scranton, the patrician former governor of Pennsylvania. "I don't accept the chessboard theory that we gain countries or lose them," Rogers said on taking over State. "What I favor for the U.S. is a more natural role, befitting our character and capacities."

Nixon, however, was determined to make American foreign policy bend to his own character and capability. And chess was Kissinger's passion. State was being maneuvered out of the Cold War loop. The Defense Department, too, would be reduced to an advisory role, with the commanders and other pawns available to execute global strategy. In fact, the President did not bother to inform his secretary of state that Kissinger and Soviet ambassador Anatoly Dobrynin had already met in secret—and worked out a back-channel (or East Wing–door) arrangement for the ambassador to come, secretly, to the White House every week for meetings with the national security adviser.

The first official meeting between President Nixon and Ambassador Dobrynin was on February 17. Rogers was not there, but to placate the Secretary of State, Malcolm Toon, the department's director of Soviet affairs, sat in—for a while. Soon enough, Nixon dismissed Toon and told Dobrynin again that Kissinger was the one. The ambassador gave Nixon a seven-page letter from Moscow that essentially agreed with Nixon's proposals, delivered through Kissinger three days before, that the two great nuclear adversaries would attempt to go forward simultaneously on a range of superpower concerns that began with arms control and included Berlin, Vietnam, and the Middle East. "Linkage" was the word Nixon used to describe the informal agreement. The Russian hinted at Soviet willingness to talk about a summit meeting—an offer American presidents rarely refused. Nixon, in turn, hinted that if things did not go well in United States–Soviet relations, he could explore openings to "others," which Dobrynin understood meant China, the other communist giant.

"Henry, how did I do? What do you think?" the President asked Kissinger in four calls after Dobrynin left. Within hours, sometimes minutes, the adviser's assistants, friends, and chosen journalists were hearing of the President's insecurity—and the adviser's calming advice.

WHILE THE PRESIDENT was meeting with Dobrynin, Haldeman was handling a domestic matter: passing along instructions from Nixon to set up a secret political fund for the 1970 and 1972 campaigns. In a memo to Ehrlichman mentioning the President's friend Bebe Rebozo and the richest of oilmen, J. Paul Getty, Haldeman wrote: "Bebe Rebozo has been asked by the President to contact J. Paul Getty in London regarding major contributions. . . . The funds should go to some entity other than the National Committee so that we retain full control of their use. . . ."

That same day the President saw a memo from one of his speechwriters, James Keogh, a former editor of *Time,* who was passing along a comment from Leonard Garment, a former law partner of the President's, suggesting that he display as much art as possible in the White House as a way to reach out to creative communities around the country. Nixon wrote: "E and H. A small cost—let's do it—(But NO modern art in the White House!)"

Keogh also wrote: "Media treatment of the President is almost uniformly excellent. . . . The usual media characterizations are 'efficient' 'cool' 'confident' 'orderly.' "

Nixon, in the twenty-seventh day of his presidency, answered that with: "You don't understand, they are waiting to destroy us."

CHAPTER 2

ONE MORNING in the last days of February, Bob Haldeman came into the Oval Office with some papers ready for signing. The President was surrounded by briefing books and papers, as usual. But what he was reading was a plumbing catalog, open to a page of showerhead pictures and specifications. Nixon, it seemed, could not figure out how to work the complicated power shower put in the President's bathroom for President Johnson. The thing was like a fire hose; it almost knocked him down the first time he turned it on.

Time to redecorate. The President who swore he wanted to be involved in only the biggest decisions was talking about carpets and hardware. There were meetings every few hours for days, until the new President was persuaded to use the same furniture, lamps, and such made for Williamsburg, the re-created old colonial capitol of Virginia. "Great idea," Nixon said, "authentic reproductions."

Among the action memos he sent out that week were such orders as:

> Would you check to see whether Miss Burum, my 5th grade teacher, and Mrs. Dargatz, the daughter of the doctor who took care of me when I fell out of the buggy as a child, received answers to their letters. . . . The silver Parker Pen that was given to me on Election Day, November 5, 1968, is such a good one that I would

like to get one other exactly like it as a spare. . . . When the Oval Room is re-done I would like to have the coffee table in front of the fireplace replaced by one that does not block the view of the fireplace from the desk. . . . We need as a basic research document the names of all artists and orchestra leaders, etc. who supported us in the campaign.

Nixon wanted to use music to top one of the cultural events of the Kennedy years, the 1961 White House party in which the Spanish cellist Pablo Casals played before an American audience for the first time in almost thirty years. But Nixon wanted an American night and nothing that highbrow. He loved a suggestion that it be for a black American, for the seventieth birthday of Duke Ellington. "That's it," the President said, standing up in excitement. "We'll bring in all the jazz greats, like Guy Lombardo. . . ."

On February 22, 1969, he sent a memo to Secretary of State Rogers and Henry Kissinger on a subject he knew better, the Middle East:

I have noted in reading the papers prepared by the State Department and by the Security Council Review Board on the Mideast, references from time to time on "domestic political considerations." The purpose of this memorandum is twofold: (1) Under no circumstances will domestic political considerations have any bearing on the decisions I make with regard to the Mideast. (2) The only consideration which will affect my decisions on this policy will be the security interests of the United States. . . . In the future, I want no reference to domestic political considerations to be included in any papers. . . .

On one level the order was about Israel, and thus about the strong support of Israel by American Jews. Richard Nixon did not like "our Jewish friends" or "New York Jews" or "the fucking Jews"—phrases he regularly used in private, projecting a rhetorical anti-Semitism not uncommon to Republicans of his time, though in his case more vulgar. He sometimes called Kissinger "Jew-boy" or "my Jew-boy," usually when his associate in foreign policy was not in the room, but occasionally when he was. He had already told his national security adviser that the one area of the world where Rogers would have primary authority would be the Middle East. Nixon was determined to improve relations with the Arab countries equally determined to destroy Israel—Arab countries becoming more dependent on aid and weapons from the Soviet Union—and he thought there was little chance Arab leaders would welcome a

Jewish emissary from the United States. Also, Kissinger had never been in an Arab country. Besides, as the President would tell anyone who would listen, "The Jews voted 95 percent against me."

That Soviet influence, as always, was key to another level of Nixon's thinking. He hoped to create a new power balance in the Middle East, not only between Israel and Arab countries but between the United States and the Soviet Union. "The difference between our goal and the Soviet goal in the Mideast is very simple but fundamental," he said to Rogers. "We want peace. They want the Middle East."

In a dictated memo to Kissinger, discussing Prime Minister Golda Meir and her country's ambassador to the United States, Yitzhak Rabin, the President, referring to himself in the third person, laid out his own position and feelings about Israel:

> They must recognize that our interests are basically pro-freedom and not just pro-Israel because of the Jewish vote. . . . What all this adds up to is that Mrs. Meir, Rabin, et al., must trust RN completely. . . . He will see to it that Israel always has "an edge.". . . . But he must carry with him the 60 percent of the American people who are in what is called the silent majority, and who must be depended upon in the event that we have to take a strong hand against Soviet expansion in the Mideast. . . . We are going to stand up in Vietnam and in NATO and in the Mideast, but it is a question of all or none. It is time our friends in Israel understood this. This is going to be the policy of this country. Unless they understand it and act as if they understood it right now, they are down the tubes.

There was one other current flowing through the President's little note of February 23. He did not want domestic politics driving foreign policy. Quite the opposite. As he had told Theodore H. White in 1967, "I've always thought the country could run itself domestically without a president. . . . You need a president for foreign policy." His principal concern at home was order above all, because he believed dissent and unrest, particularly among students, reduced presidential power and influence around the world.

On the same day he told Kissinger and Rogers to ignore domestic politics, he sent a memo to his chief speechwriter, Ray Price, who was preparing a public letter to Father Theodore M. Hesburgh, the president of Notre Dame, to praise Hesburgh for ordering on-the-spot instant expulsion for demonstrating students after two warnings. In a memo to the President, Price mentioned a column by Tom Wicker that had appeared the day before in *The New York Times;* the subject was lowered voices and dialogue between power and students. Forget Wicker, Nixon said, and went on: "I would strongly question his brushing off some of the outrageous actions which have taken place with the idea that 'they are trying to tell us something' and 'listen to them and treat them as adults.' As you well know from the campaign, the extremists do not want to be listened to and do not want to discuss their problems rationally. Some simply want to disrupt and others want nothing less than complete capitulation to demands that would destroy the higher education system."

The White House had announced at the beginning of February that Nixon would be making his first foreign trip as president after only a month in office, going to Europe to meet the leaders of Great Britain, France, West Germany, and Italy. But before leaving, he sent his first message to Congress, surprising many members by greatly toning down his campaign rhetoric about eliminating antipoverty programs, beginning with the Job Corps, which he had called a "failure" only four months before. The fact was that the President was willing to give liberals much of what they wanted so that they could preserve the welfare state built by Democrats from Franklin D. Roosevelt to Lyndon Johnson—as a price for support or at least quieter opposition on foreign policy. But inside the White House, some smiled at such weighty explanations. "The Boss is in love again," said Bill Safire, then quickly added that Nixon's crushes were more affairs of the head than of the heart.

The object of Nixon's affections at the moment was Moynihan, the former Kennedy man. Nixon loved ideas and self-confident men, strong men. There always seemed to be one new face around, an intellectual backboard, someone who impressed him and whom he wanted to impress. Rogers had once upon a time been a "new flame"—Safire's phrase—a young congressional staffer when Senator Nixon asked him to travel with him during the 1952 vice presidential campaign. It was something like that when Nixon met John Mitchell at Nixon, Mudge, Rose, Guthrie, and Alexander, the Manhattan law firm he joined after being defeated in the 1962 California gubernatorial election.

Nixon had read some of Moynihan's work, particularly his disappointed analyses of Kennedy-Johnson antipoverty programs and a 1966 article in *The Public Interest,* a journal Moynihan helped create, in which he wrote, "The Republicans are ready to govern. . . ." The Nixon old guard, led by Arthur Burns, were inclined to try to destroy the newcomer, but the New Yorker was an old White House hand and, not incidentally, an even more accomplished academic flatterer than Kissinger. Moynihan's advice to his own staff of nine bright Ivy Leaguers on dealing with the press was, "Say one thing, say it again and again and say nothing else." He had given Nixon something the President dearly wanted: a rooted self-image, an intellectual niche. The President, despite the populist anti-intellectual drive that made him successful in politics—and made his crusades against men like Alger Hiss and Dean Acheson as personal as they were political—craved the respect of the stars he hated. He wanted to show off Moynihan and his bright young men as he did Kissinger and his bright crew. He got the idea one day that the press would take notice if National Security Council staffers were issued blue blazers with insignia on the breast pockets. Kissinger managed to divert that one.

Nixon had begun his conversations with Moynihan after the election by asserting that he was not really the kind of conservative people thought he was. He had grown up in the Great Depression, a poor boy with genuine sympathy for the down-and-out. His chief conviction in domestic affairs, he had told Moynihan, was that modern government was not working, and he was determined to make it work. He saw his own election as the end of the New Deal and the overpowering influence of Franklin D. Roosevelt on American opinion. Moynihan did not disagree, but he pushed back, saying that to dismantle the underperforming programs of the New Deal and of President Johnson's Great Society would create unbearable tension within American society—and Nixon would fail as president.

"Don't do it, Mr. President," said the professor, pacing—dancing, really—before his new patron. "All the Great Society activist constituencies are out there lying in wait, poised to get you if you try to come after them: the professional welfarists, the urban planners. . . . I'm terrified of the thought of cutting back too fast. The urban ghettoes will go up in flames. . . ."

Instead, Moynihan offered Nixon a compelling option: become the conservative reformer. Benjamin Disraeli was the model. Moynihan gave the President a copy of Robert Blake's biography of the mid-nineteenth-century British prime minister, the founder of the modern Conservative Party, who pushed forward great reforms in public health and welfare—reforms initiated by his Liberal predecessor, William Gladstone. History deemed that progress and honored both men.

In the Nixon White House's first Haldeman-rigid organization charts only three men had direct access to the Oval Office: Haldeman, Kissinger, and Moynihan. The President favored the New Yorker with his ultimate compliments, taken from sports: "He's a heavyweight. . . . He's a cleanup hitter."

The President had met with Moynihan's new Urban Affairs Council for an hour and ten minutes on February 17, before his first Dobrynin meeting. "I'm keeping the Soviet ambassador waiting," he said. A high compliment. "But I don't mind keeping him waiting for a little while." Watching Moynihan in action, Nixon was impressed; the breadth of the voluble New Yorker's intellect was fun, even if the man sometimes seemed to have more answers than there were questions. But substantively, what Moynihan was saying made sense to Nixon: liberal thinking and goals depended on more and more conservative means and values. Moynihan and Nixon also shared a desire to drive social welfare decision-making power down from Washington to the states, to municipalities, to individuals. Even if Nixon thought the country could run itself—leaving him to toss other countries around in long sessions with Kissinger—the President did have a passion for diminishing the power of the Washington bureaucrats he had always despised.

On February 19, four days before he was scheduled to leave for his first foreign trip, to the capitals of Europe, the President held his first joint meeting with Republican and Democratic leaders of Congress. He began with a fifteen-minute soliloquy, saying that as a matter of form he wanted to make his first round of foreign meetings with allies, rather than with adversaries. Then Everett Dirksen, the Republican Senate leader, asked how Nixon intended to deal with President de Gaulle. What would he say if the French leader publicly urged him to go to Paris peace talks on Vietnam? What if de Gaulle asked him how the Americans could criticize the Soviets for sending weapons into the Middle East when the United States was sending Phantom jets to Israel after the French had refused to sell them their Mirage fighters?

Nixon hesitated. The room was quiet. Finally, according to Buchanan's official meeting notes:

> The President said he would impress upon the French leader his views to the effect that . . . the threat of war in the Mideast does not come from a potential preemptive strike by Israel; war would not be in their interest; rather it comes from a potential attack by Arab countries inspired by revenge. To deter such an attack, to preserve peace, the President felt the balance of power in the Mideast should be in Israel's favor. And the President hoped that De Gaulle would be satisfied with that response.
>
> On the second question, the President said he would decline an invitation to attend the Paris talks. A head of government should not go into such talks until he knows what is going to come out of them. The Presidency was an office that had prestige capital and we ought not to waste it now on a fruitless venture. . . .

The President ended the meeting by repeating his hopes for quiet Soviet-American cooperation, and he added a warning: "All that should be kept within this room." Then Dirksen got in a last word, saying that on June 14, Flag Day, all Americans should be urged to wear small American flags in their lapels to show the world that once again the nation was united. The Democratic chairman of the Senate Foreign Relations Committee, J. William Fulbright, broke that spell, saying: "We are divided over issues, like misguided policy in Vietnam. The President would do more to unite the country if he eliminated this cause of division."

CHAPTER 3

March 17, 1969

AIR FORCE ONE took off from Andrews Air Force Base, twelve miles from Washington, at 7:58 A.M. on February 23 carrying the vanguard of the three hundred men and women attending the President in his eight days of European travel. The first stop would be Brussels—then on to London, Paris, Berlin, and Rome.

For all but a few minutes of the seven-hour flight, Nixon, wearing a maroon smoking jacket, sat alone reading and editing the trip papers, beginning with a folder marked "Statements: Brussels." He took only one break, calling Kissinger forward to discuss Vietnam, specifically to talk about North Vietnamese sanctuaries and supply lines in Cambodia, a few miles from that small kingdom's border with South Vietnam. Only a week after taking office, Nixon had received a report from General Creighton Abrams, the United States commander in Vietnam, that forty thousand North Vietnamese troops were near that border. Abrams wanted B-52 strikes. The military said there were no Cambodians living in that area—which was not so. The President had hesitated then, but now he told Kissinger to work out a bombing plan.

Alone again, the President had big things in mind, having to do not with democratic allies in Europe but with the realignment of relations between the United States and its communist adversaries in the Soviet Union and China. Even the hardest foes of "monolithic communism" had to notice that on the day Nixon left Washington a commentary in the daily newspaper published by the Soviet defense ministry compared the Chinese leader Mao Tse-tung with Adolf Hitler.

The President knew there might be a great opportunity coming, and his mind was racing. But he saw his first job as repairing the West's united front—or once-united front—anchored by NATO, the North Atlantic Treaty Organization. The military-political alliance had been forced to move its headquarters from Paris to Brussels in 1966 because President de Gaulle wanted to develop French nuclear weapons rather than depend on American will and weapons. The world leader Nixon most admired simply did not believe Americans would use NATO's nuclear weaponry to defend Western Europe—or, as some said, trade Chicago for Lyon or Hamburg in a nuclear exchange with the Soviets.

When the jet landed in Belgium and King Baudouin stepped forward, the President, without notes, began speaking the words of the statement written by Safire—but it was the departure statement. Safire paled, sweat suddenly bursting from him in the cold, afraid Nixon would end with thank you and good-bye. But it turned out the President just did not like the prepared arrival speech and he had decided to ad lib, using material from the departure text. Haldeman was proudly watching his boss, again noticing how much Nixon loved ceremony. The President was obviously thrilled by the long red carpet at the airport and the red-and-black-cloaked horse soldiers who flanked the motorcade all the way into the city. The chief of staff had plenty of time to think about such things, because Nixon stayed up past 3 A.M., working on schedules and statements in his pajamas, regularly knocking on Haldeman's door with small questions.

Nixon was duly deferential as he began his speech the next morning to the fifteen European ambassadors to NATO this way: "I have come for work, not for ceremony; to inquire, not to insist; to consult, not to convince; to listen and learn and to begin what I hope will be a continuing interchange of ideas and insight. . . ."

As Nixon spoke, Kissinger and his principal military deputy, an Army colonel named Alexander Haig, and Haldeman went back into *Air Force One* to finish off the plan for bombing Cambodia. It was called Operation Menu. The plane was the only place they were confident they could not be overheard electronically.

The next stop was in London, and there Nixon had two personal triumphs, both of them in private, or at least in rooms closed to the press. The first was a small stag dinner organized at 10 Downing Street by Labour Prime Minister Harold Wilson. A man of the left more comfortable with the politics of Lyndon Johnson than with those of Nixon, Wilson did not know that the White House had wired a guest list to the

United States ambassador, David K. E. Bruce. Such decisions were now the province of former campaign advance men, Haldeman and his old crew, who behind their backs were called "the balloon droppers." The ambassador had cabled back: "Surely the absurdity of telling the British Prime Minister whom he can invite to his own home for dinner requires no explanation."

The balloon droppers had a purpose: they wanted to keep out John Freeman, Great Britain's new ambassador to Washington, appointed by Wilson months before in anticipation of a second Johnson term. Freeman had edited the socialist *New Statesman* and was celebrated in England for ten years of regular and usually savage attacks on Nixon. He had characterized Nixon's defeat in the California gubernatorial election as a victory for decency in public office and, for good measure, had added: "The record suggests a man of no principle whatsoever except a willingness to sacrifice everything in the cause of Dick Nixon."

Safire, whose wife was British, kept up on such things. He wrote Nixon a small wordplay joke to use at the dinner, but the President used it straight: "They say there's a new Nixon. And they wonder if there's a new Freeman. Let me set aside all possibility of embarrassment because our roles have changed. He's the new diplomat and I'm the 'new statesman.' " The British thumped the tables in approval and, a few moments later, Wilson wrote a note on his menu and passed it to Nixon: "That was one of the kindest and most generous acts I have known in a quarter-century in politics. Just proves my point. You can't guarantee being born a Lord. It's possible—you've shown it—to be born a gentleman. . . . H."

Then the President met privately with a mixed group of nineteen prominent British citizens and student leaders, who were told they could ask any questions in the man-in-the-arena format Nixon had used during the 1968 campaign. All off the record this time. The questions were good. Nixon greatly enjoyed himself, and he laid out a good deal of his view of America and the world. He began by saying that he expected to see a less adventurous Soviet Union in the next few years, because of tensions with China and pressure from its own consumers, then he turned toward home, saying:

> In the U.S. today, there's a growing isolationism, a trend toward protectionism coming out of our experience in the Vietnam war. Tied into the trauma of our race problem, this has tended to make some people lash out. But it would be a mistake to assess the U.S. today only by the scenes of violence you may see on television. . . . As I look at the "student revolution" in the U.S.—back in the Thirties, the student rebel had a cause, a belief, a religion.

Today, the revolt doesn't have that form—it's more negative against the Establishment. . . . When a nation is at war, you fight to stay alive; in a depression you fight to make a living. But in a time of peace, we have to provide a way to help young people make the world a better place. . . .

The answer said something about the contradictory nature of the man. Richard Nixon, naval officer, graduate of Duke Law School, member of Congress, Wall Street lawyer, vice president then president of the United States, did not see himself as a member of the establishment. He had grown up poor and resentful and he still seemed to hate the privileged life, real or imagined, of men who had been educated in the best schools of New England and New York—a smoldering anger he often focused on institutions like Harvard, the State Department, and *The New York Times*. He also had no particular use for American youth, except for soldiers and the shiny-faced young Republicans who provided atmosphere at political events and photo opportunities. One of his fundamental misunderstandings was that most American young men, threatened with being drafted and taken to Vietnam, did not see themselves growing up in "a time of peace."

His news summary of February 27, which he received by telex in the next country on the tour, West Germany, included mention of a column by William F. Buckley Jr., the founder of the conservative magazine *National Review*. Buckley cited an idea by economist Milton Friedman on the subject of quieting down American students: "Called for a cut-off date after which the president would send no more draftees to Vietnam, and fight the war with volunteers. This, Friedman thinks, could take the wind out of much of the anti-war rhetoric." On the margin Nixon wrote: "Get Laird's comment on this intriguing idea."

In West Germany, during arrival ceremonies, a German honor guard clicked and whirled to perfection and Haldeman whispered to Safire: "How long do you think it will take me to get the White House staff shaped up like that?" Then Nixon went to West Berlin for a ritual visit to the Wall, the high concrete barrier separating the communist east side of the city from the west side, which was democratically governed but still occupied by American, British, and French troops. The streets were lined with cheering Berliners, many of them waving American flags, but Nixon came and went within a couple of hours. In his mind, it was Kennedy's city. Nixon did not want to invite comparisons with the triumphant welcome President Kennedy received there in 1963 when hundreds of thousands cheered his declaration: *"Ich bin ein Berliner!"*

Flying from Berlin to Rome, for another quick stop and more or less ceremonial sessions with Italian leaders, Nixon was talkative but angry. The presidential humor was not helped when Safire reminisced about the first time he had been in Europe with Nixon, in 1958. The speechwriter described Queen Elizabeth II and then vice president Nixon in St. Paul's Church with the choir slowly singing the "Battle Hymn of the Republic."

Nixon cut off the conversation, telling Safire and Kissinger not to mention that detail in any statement, sort of growling in his deepest baritone, "That's a Kennedy song." Then he began to complain about American diplomats appearing at airports and giving him photographs of himself, which he was to present as gifts to foreign leaders. "I want that knocked off," he told Rose Mary Woods. His voice got lower, growly again, as he talked about the pictures. "I don't care if they stamp their feet. The next State Department type who hands me a picture of myself to give to someone . . . I'll—I'll wrap it around his neck."

Nixon turned away, looking out the window into the gray European sky. Safire watched him and, a few moments later, saw Nixon lift an imaginary frame and smash it down, presumably over an imaginary head.

"Here we go—*Vive la France!*" Nixon said as he walked to the door to meet President de Gaulle at the bottom of the plane's steps. He saw that his host was wearing no coat in bitter cold and stripped his own overcoat off before he stepped out the door. He was nervous about meeting the man alone he admired so greatly, but he also had an agenda. He believed that the aloof and imperious French president was in a unique position to help the Americans find "peace with honor"—a phrase coined by Disraeli—in Vietnam, once the center of the Southeast Asian countries called French Indochina.

There was balloon-dropper nonsense in Paris, too, as Haldeman's travel agents tried to persuade the American ambassador there, Sargent Shriver, to put away all photographs of his late brother-in-law, President Kennedy. But the old advance men around Nixon also had their view of how the world worked confirmed later that night when Ehrlichman was folding himself into the backseat of a car on the Quai d'Orsay, outside the French Foreign Ministry. He felt something sharp prick his thigh. Bouncing up, he found a hat pin attached inside the lining of his trench coat. "What the hell is this?" he asked a Secret Service agent back at the U.S. embassy. "Looks like a remote microphone," the man said, telling Ehrlichman later that he and Haldeman should assume that the French were listening in on every conversation.

Nixon, the diligent student of the French leader's style, asked de Gaulle for his personal evaluation of the situation in Europe, then leaned forward for forty-five minutes as de Gaulle swept back and forth through history, description, and prediction. Nixon was the questioner, the listener, for two days, focusing on four subjects—the Soviet Union, China, European military strategy, and then Vietnam—taking notes himself. De Gaulle's words as recorded by Nixon were:

> The Russians are thinking in terms of a possible clash with China, and they know they can't fight the West at the same time. Thus I believe that they may end up opting for a policy of rapprochement with the West. . . .
>
> On China, I have no illusions about their ideology, but I do not feel we should leave them isolated in their rage. The West should try to get to know China, to have contacts, and to penetrate it. . . . It would be better for you to recognize China before you are obliged to do so by the growth of China. . . .
>
> We believe that the Russians know that the United States could not allow them to conquer Europe. But we also believe that if the Russians marched, you would not use nuclear weapons right away, since it would imply a total effort to kill everyone on the other side. If both the Russians and the United States were to use tactical nuclear weapons, Europe would be destroyed. Western Europe and the United Kingdom would be destroyed by Soviet tactical weapons, and East Germany, Poland, Czechoslovakia and Hungary would be destroyed by American tactical weapons. Meanwhile the United States and the Soviet Union would not be harmed. . . .
>
> I do not believe that you should depart from Vietnam with undue haste. . . . I recognize that France had some part in this as she did not give the Vietnamese freedom early enough and thus enabled the Communists to pose as the champions of national independence, first against us and then against you. But you Americans can make this kind of settlement because your power and wealth are so great you can do it with dignity.

It was one of the great experiences of Nixon's life. He had the power to do the things that de Gaulle was envisioning. Expanding on his Vietnam answer, de Gaulle added, with Nixon nodding, that the Americans had the capacity to negotiate political and military issues at the same time, while establishing a timetable for the withdrawal of American troops.

There was also some disappointment for Nixon and Kissinger in Paris. Back in Washington, the State Department was resisting the idea of bombing Cambodia, saying that they would be unable to explain or defend it. On the first day of March, Nixon gave in, canceling the B-52 raids. Kissinger sulked through the day. He was also disappointed that de Gaulle did not approve of assistants sitting in on meetings between heads of state, so Kissinger was in only one of three Nixon–de Gaulle sessions. At one point at a dinner, though, the French leader did call on the American assistant to answer one question: "Why don't you get out of Vietnam?"

"Because a sudden withdrawal might give us a credibility problem."

"Where?" de Gaulle said.

"The Middle East," Kissinger answered.

"How very odd. It is precisely in the Middle East that I thought your enemies had the credibility problem."

AIR FORCE ONE headed for home late on the night of March 2. "The press has been good back in the States," said Ehrlichman, who had been reading a telexed copy of the news summary. ·

"All first presidential trips get good press," said a tired Nixon. "These trips aren't important for the rhetoric, they're important for what follows a year from now." The President talked himself down with five of his men—Haldeman and Ehrlichman, Kissinger, Safire, and press secretary Ron Ziegler—and got angry for a bit, complaining about national-security types back in Washington, saying they were liars and leakers. Someone said that Robert Finch, the secretary of health, education, and welfare, was taking a trip to Israel. Nixon grunted and said: "I ain't going to Israel. Ireland, maybe. Not Israel. I've been there, twice. They're a great people, doing a hell of a job, but a visit there is pure domestic politics and I've got all the votes I'm ever going to get from there."

Back in Washington, the President was on a high, energized by the eight-day trip, briefing the congressional leaders of both parties at 8:30 on the morning of March 4 after only two or three hours of sleep. As he talked and took questions for almost two hours, the subject on his mind most of the time was relations between the Soviet Union and China. In England, he said, Prime Minister Wilson told him he had never heard insults more horrible than what Soviet premier Aleksey Kosygin had said to him privately about dealing with his Chinese allies.

The President also related some points that André Malraux, the French minister of cultural affairs, had made in a conversation. Malraux had first met Mao Tse-tung in 1930 and had visited the Chinese leader as recently as the previous year. "The United States can never destroy us,"

Mao had told him—but it had never occurred to Mao, Malraux said, that the United States did not want to destroy him. As for the Soviets and the Americans, according to Mao, there was only one difference: "The Russians 'are barbarians who come by land' to invade us and the Americans 'are barbarians who come by sea.' "

"Perhaps we should make some economic overtures to the mainland Chinese," said Senator George D. Aiken, the seventy-six-year-old Republican from Vermont, the ranking minority member of the Foreign Relations Committee. "This is not the time," Nixon said. He said that it was too early to recognize the Chinese communists or to trade with them or bring them into the United Nations. "How about siding with the Soviets against the Chinese?" the President asked himself, then answered, "No. That might be good for short-range policy, but it would be suicidal long-range policy."

He knew, though, that the time was coming, times were changing. Two headlines on the front page of *The New York Times* on the day Nixon returned home pointed in new directions, too:

SOVIETS AND CHINESE CLASH ON BORDER;
EACH LISTS DEATHS IN SIBERIAN ENCOUNTER

SOVIETS MAKING INROADS IN ARABIA,
WHERE WEST WAS ONCE STRONG

That night the President held a televised press conference, a good one for him, allowing only foreign affairs questions. There were more than thirty over a full hour and Nixon was at his best, not making news as much as explaining it and the presidency itself. Asked about public opinion and Vietnam, he answered:

Our objective is to get this war over as soon as we can on a basis that will not leave the seeds of another war there to plague us in the future. . . . It will not be easy. The American people, I can say from having campaigned the country, are terribly frustrated about this war. They would welcome any initiative. . . . On the other hand, it is the responsibility of a President to examine all of the options that we have, and then if he finds that the course he has to take is one that is not popular, he has to explain it to the American people and gain their support. . . .

The next question was: "Do you see this possibility of expectation of a stage-by-stage withdrawal as a practicality?" He answered:

There are no plans to withdraw any troops at this time or in the near future. . . . To the extent that South Vietnamese forces are able to take over a greater burden of the fighting and to the extent, too, that the level of the fighting may decrease, it may be possible to withdraw. . . .

"The press conference was a masterpiece," reported his news summary the next morning. "With perhaps fifty million television viewers as a captive audience, the President 'used' the national press corps as a foil to his strongest suits: knowledge, coolness, competence and depth. The major accomplishment was not in news. It was in etching the President more deeply into the American mind. . . ."

The press seemed to think more of the President than he thought of them. Editorial page headlines over the next couple of days included "Good Work, Mr. President" (the New York *Daily News*); "A National Good Deed" (*The Miami Herald*); "Nixon's European Success" (*The New York Times*); "Brings Home Sober View of Europe" (*The Charlotte Observer*); "Mission Accomplished" (*The Philadelphia Inquirer*); and "President Nixon's Successful Tour" (*The Christian Science Monitor*). *The New Republic's* ever critical Richard Strout, writing as TRB, said: "Dazzling . . . death-defying tightrope act. . . . He talked swiftly, deftly. . . . It was a brilliant performance."

Sidey was downright lyrical in *Life:* "Over the last decade the Presidency has been encased in such manipulation and mystique that those routine practices which go on every day in thousands of PTA meetings, business conventions and Elks luncheons across the country are hailed as genius when they are applied in the White House. . . . Washington seems to have rediscovered through Nixon that knowing what you are talking about is a pretty good idea even in the Oval Office. . . . The hunger in and around the capital for a return to normalcy has seized on his quiet approach and built it into the image of a man about to conquer all."

What Nixon could not conquer was himself. He was down again within forty-eight hours—waiting, impatient for them to turn on him again. It was a pattern Haldeman knew well. The chief of staff's bearing and tone after his first morning meeting with the President sent silent signals through the White House: the man in the Oval Office was up, or he was down, usually nasty down. On some days, the mood alerts changed from hour to hour as the President was thrown off or turned on by events great and small. It was an edgy place when the President tried to focus on domestic affairs and politics. He had great powers of concentration; the problem was what he concentrated on, indiscriminately pondering events and ideas great and tiny—and ignoring everything else. The chief of staff had already realized that Nixon was turning back internal reports and recommendations on continuing programs like Head Start or the Job Corps without even reading them. But at the same time, Nixon could spot a sentence in a briefing paper speculating on increased violence in colleges and high schools and scrawl, "Good! (Predict it?)." He wanted action—letters to NBC—protesting a line on *The Smothers Brothers Comedy Hour* on March 9. The President wrote to Ehrlichman: "They had one sequence in which one said to the other that he found it difficult to find anything to laugh about—Vietnam, the cities, etc., but 'Richard Nixon's solving those problems . . . that's really funny.' "

Reading news summaries, Nixon barred the use of the old word "mansion" for the living quarters of the White House, ordering staff to call it "the residence." He killed the appointment of a State Department professional, Philip Trezise, as ambassador to Canada, because in 1967 he had once seen an anti-Nixon cartoon in the man's home when Trezise was serving in Argentina. He noticed that an Ohio congressman, Paul Findlay, intended to enter into the *Congressional Record* the names of the more than thirty-three thousand Americans killed in Vietnam—a number greater than American deaths in the Korean War—then scrawled, "Harlow—Don't ask him to see me again." On an ABC News report that the President was considering air strikes in North Vietnam if there was no progress in the ongoing peace talks in Paris, his comment was, "Good . . . RN is for this." Items like that, accurate or not, fit in with what the President called his "madman theory." He believed there was advantage in persuading adversaries, foreign and domestic, that there was something irrational about him, that he was a dangerous man capable of any retaliation, up to and including the use of nuclear weapons.

Other patterns were developing. Above all, the President wanted order in the White House. Kissinger was providing that in foreign policy. Moynihan and Burns were not; they were fighting for control of domestic policy. "These two wild men are beating up on me," he told Haldeman. He wanted a domestic czar, a bookend to Kissinger—and Moynihan was not the right man for that kind of command work. Haldeman pushed Ehrlichman, and first Burns and then Moynihan had to go to Ehrlichman or Haldeman or get around them to get into the Oval Office. By the forty-fourth day of the presidency, Haldeman and Ehrlichman, the keepers of order, had begun the neutralization of Burns and Moynihan. Nixon was bored with Burns's lecturing and wanted him kept away. Burns was reduced to pleading with Ehrlichman, saying he had to make the President understand that Moynihan's grand welfare reform plans—basically the idea that poor people should be given money rather than social services—were not consistent with Nixon's conservative philosophy. Ehrlichman laughed. "Don't you realize the President doesn't have a philosophy?" he said.

"If this is true," Burns told Bryce Harlow, "our country is in serious trouble." The two men, Nixon loyalists for almost twenty years, were greatly disturbed; each of them had come to the conclusion that Ehrlichman and Haldeman were bullies and liars who cared only for the way things looked. Harlow had already decided that he would leave the White House the first chance he got, probably after a year. But he thought Burns would stay in the administration—Nixon had promised him the chairmanship of the Federal Reserve Board after a year—and that his heart was going to be broken.

On the forty-eighth day of the presidency, Sunday, March 9, Nixon was in Key Biscayne, Florida. He had paid $252,800 for houses at 500 and 516 Bay Lane right after the election. Kissinger was calling in high dudgeon, complaining that Rogers must not be allowed to see Dobrynin, telling Haldeman that he would have to quit if the President did not exercise control over Rogers. What the Secretary of State had told the Soviet ambassador was that the United States was open to both political and military talks, held simultaneously and immediately, with the North Vietnamese. To Kissinger, that was not White House policy at all; he wanted parallel negotiations and the President wanted no negotiations without an end to North Vietnamese shelling of Saigon—military action he considered a calculated communist test of his own resolve. The tension between Kissinger and Rogers continued in internal debates over whether to begin Operation Menu, the secret bombing of Cambodia postponed by Nixon in Berlin. Kissinger favored the attacks and Rogers opposed them, with Nixon changing his mind more than once as he was pressured separately by both for two weeks. On March 15, the President decided to go ahead, calling Kissinger at 3:35 that afternoon with the order, calling back minutes later to say, "State is to be notified only after the point of no return."

The President had sided with Kissinger, the internal tough guy. Then, the next afternoon, he called Rogers and Laird—the Defense Secretary favored the bombing but opposed secrecy—into the Oval Office for what amounted to a debate. "Gentlemen," he said, "we have reached the point where a decision is required: to bomb or not to bomb."

He told neither that the command, initiating the first phase of Operation Menu—a cable to Anderson Air Force Base in Guam saying "Execute Operation Breakfast"—was being transmitted as they talked and a system of phony records was being put in place to disguise the bombing of a neutral country. The idea was not only to give Cambodia's ruler,

Prince Norodom Sihanouk, no reason to protest publicly the violation of his country's neutrality—he was not happy with North Vietnamese troops operating within his country—but also to try to prevent protest and demonstration in the United States. The secrecy and the lying bought time—that is why people lie.

Sixty B-52 bombers took off for Vietnam on March 17, the first sorties to try to destroy weapons, men, and headquarters at the end of the North Vietnamese supply road called the Ho Chi Minh Trail through Laos and Cambodia.* The next day, Kissinger rushed in, saying, "Very productive!" and waving intelligence cables. At the next Cabinet meeting, two days later, the President flatly stated that the war would be over by the following year but said the public line had to be that the outlook was very tough; that was a way to retain public support for the war during secret negotiations.

Not for the first time, the North Vietnamese, the Cambodians, and, presumably, the Soviets and the Chinese knew a great deal more about what the United States was doing in the war than did either the American people or the body with the constitutional responsibility to declare war, the Congress. On domestic matters, Nixon was willing to pander to Congress. On foreign policy, he tried to deal with both the people and the people's elected representatives on a "need to know" basis. He did not trust them with the truth. He had more respect for old adversaries like Dean Acheson, whom he invited in early in March to talk about exploiting differences between the Soviet Union and China. The former secretary of state was against negotiating with either of the great communist powers, but he and Nixon did find agreement on the evolution of the war in Vietnam. Acheson said he thought President Johnson had made a mistake sending in large numbers of troops in 1965. Nixon agreed, saying he had supported Johnson, but he now saw he was wrong, it was a mistake.

The President did call in congressional leaders from both parties, not to consult but to inform. He told them he had decided to support a modified version of Sentinel, the $80 billion antiballistic missile system proposed in 1967 by President Johnson to try to protect as many as twenty American cities against Soviet or Chinese missile attacks. "Safeguard" was Nixon's name to describe much cheaper research and development of a more limited antimissile system, which he said was designed to protect the silos of American strategic ballistic missiles and bomber bases at only two sites, in North Dakota and Montana. Over time, Safeguard would be deployed near ten more missile fields in the United States.

---

* Menu continued until May 1970, with 3,875 B-52 sorties dropping 108,823 tons of bombs on Cambodia. The designations "Breakfast," "Lunch," "Dinner," and "Brunch" represented geographical areas inside Cambodia.

Senator Fulbright interrupted to ask about using submarine-fired missiles instead. "Couldn't we just double that Polaris fleet? We know it works and what it costs precisely. Wouldn't more of these missiles insure the credibility of the United States deterrent force?"

"No," the President answered. "Construction of more Polaris missiles might indicate we are thinking about a first strike. This ABM has no first strike capability. No first strike implications." Besides, he added, land-based missiles were cheaper.

The Republican leader in the Senate, Everett Dirksen of Illinois, pushed at the other end, asking why Nixon was abandoning the idea of ABM sites protecting cities rather than silos.

"If they had shown me a complete defense for our cities, I would have approved it," Nixon said. "At the current 'state of the art,' what we are talking about is a reduction of casualties in the first strike from 60 to 80 million to the neighborhood of 20 to 40 million; that's the best we could do with city-defense ABM. . . . This system is not a system with the seeds of growth. We have a limited objective—the protection of our Minuteman sites, the protection of our deterrent."

It sounded logical enough. The President argued persuasively that the United States had to respond to advances in Soviet missilery. "I do not believe a President of the United States can run the risk of leaving us naked to a Soviet missile strike. . . . This is not 1962 when we had a five-to-one advantage over the Soviets in missiles. We are strong today; but the situation has changed; not because of anything we did, but because of what the Soviets did; they determined to close the strategic gap in 1962; they have come very far along that road; they have widened their lead over us in conventional arms; they have developed and deployed the world's only ABM system; we have none; they have increased their submarine force in quantity and quality. . . . and as for the Chinese, all of our estimates of the Chinese forces have been understated."

A good performance, but the President did not tell them the whole truth by any means. Safeguard was a shield in more ways than being able to stop incoming missiles—if it was even possible to create an umbrella defense over cities or missile fields. What it was, in Nixon's mind, was a bargaining chip, never to be built, but to be traded off one day for Soviet arms concessions. From the beginning of the nuclear confrontation with the Soviets, the real protection of the United States missiles and bombers, in national security jargon, was MAD—mutual assured destruction. Minuteman missiles protected themselves because they could be fired as soon as attacking enemy missiles were spotted by U.S. satellites. Hundreds of B-52 bombers were in the air or ready on runways at all times. The Soviets could not attack the United States without being destroyed themselves. That, at least, was the theory. The real purpose of Safeguard, kept from the Congress and the American public, was to convince the Soviets that the United States was about to add a new level of nuclear weaponry that they had to match, if they could—or negotiate away in return for scaling back their own substantial upgrading of land and submarine missilery. It was a bluff, but the Soviets could not gamble on that, or so Nixon reckoned. The Soviet Union, burned and impressed by American technology for more than thirty years, could not ignore the possibility that the Americans might be able to do it one more time. Odds were, Nixon calculated, the Soviets would be willing to give up a great deal to stop any American ABM program.

Fulbright was not persuaded. He thought an ABM system was a provocation, unless the Soviets believed it could never work. One neophyte in these high-stake games of three-dimensional chess, Bill Safire, the meeting's note-taker, came out of that meeting and asked Kissinger an obvious question about the contradictions of new weapons systems and test bans: "Will ABMs work? How can you know if we cannot test it?"

"The Russians will never know either," said Kissinger. "It could have talcum powder inside, but if they don't know that, it will be a deterrent."

On March 18, the President met alone with the Republican leaders of the Senate to talk politics, asking them at one point about the potential for more violence at colleges and universities back home. Gordon Allot of Colorado began, saying, "The patterns are not too dissimilar from the Hitler patterns of the 1930's." Margaret Chase Smith of Maine thought that was an exaggeration, saying the problem was not the students so much as the weakness of faculty, trustees, and administration. Nixon nodded, saying that both Father Theodore Hesburgh of Notre Dame and S. I. Hayakawa, the president of San Francisco State University, told him the real troublemakers were junior faculty. "Fascist conduct," said the assistant Senate leader, Hugh Scott of Pennsylvania.

Kissinger, who had been part of a real faculty and had lived under real fascists in Hitler's Germany, was angry but less alarmed, telling Nixon many times that the problem in the United States was indulgent parents and spoiled children. After a similar meeting between the President and young House Republicans—the talk was of noisy demonstrations and vandalism on campuses across the country—Kissinger returned to his own office grumbling, "These fools think it's the first days of the French Revolution."

A week later, on March 24, the President hosted his first state dinner, for Prime Minister Pierre Trudeau of Canada. He complained to Haldeman about it the next morning: "We've got to speed up these dinners. They take forever. So why don't we just leave out the soup course?"

"Well . . . ," Haldeman began.

Nixon cut him off: "Men don't really like soup."

On a hunch, the chief of staff called the President's valet, Manolo Sanchez, and asked: "Was there anything wrong with the President's suit after that dinner last night?"

"Yes. He spilled soup down the vest."

The action memo went out: No more soup, ever.

On March 27, as a short meeting with officials of the National Association of Manufacturers was breaking up just after noon, Nixon suddenly called back the businessmen and said that he had gone to Walter Reed Army Hospital the night before and seen former president Eisenhower, who was heavily sedated, but who opened his eyes and exclaimed: "Oh, Dick, how are you? Good to see you! How's the Administration going?"

"We're going to do all right," was Nixon's stunned answer.

"You bet!" Eisenhower said and then dropped back into unconsciousness.

The President spent the better part of the next morning talking with Haldeman and others about obscenity and pornography—on the stage, in movies, in books and magazines. There seemed to be a morality item or two every day in the President's news summary, usually inserted by Buchanan. The young speechwriter had added his own comment that day: "The pollution of young minds . . . an extremely popular issue; one on which he can probably get a tremendous majority of Americans." One day it was a Swedish movie called *I Am Curious (Yellow),* the next a "Rally for Decency" in Miami, where thirty-five thousand people turned out to hear comedian Jackie Gleason and a popular singer, Anita Bryant, call for tamer entertainment. *Newsweek* said: "Sheer numbers tell the tale—there are more explicitly erotic films, more blunt-spoken novels, more nudity on the stage. . . . More than ever we need direction from mature leaders. . . ." (In case anyone missed the point, the magazine's cover was a photograph of a nude couple embracing.)

Nixon was ready to be that leader. "Prepare," he wrote on another Buchanan memo. Another day he wrote, "Pornography and filth are gut issues with millions of decent people." The President told Haldeman he had an idea: he wanted to go to New York to see the play *Hair,* which had a nude scene a flashbulb long—and dramatically walk out of the theater.

After that he went to a National Security Council meeting, where the subject was new Soviet-Chinese artillery exchanges along the Manchurian border. Just after noon he walked back to the Oval Office with Defense Secretary Laird. A moment later Haldeman walked in with

Dr. Tkach. "Mr. President," the doctor said, "President Eisenhower just died."

Nixon began to talk about funeral arrangements, not making much sense, then he walked to the window, looked out into the gardens, and began to cry. He was sobbing and walked toward his bathroom. He came back and said, "He was such a strong man." The others watched nervously, not knowing what to do.

CHAPTER 4

April 15, 1969

O<small>N THE EVENING</small> of the day Dwight Eisenhower died, President Nixon went to Camp David to write a eulogy for the great war hero who had changed his life in 1952. The presidential retreat seventy-five miles north of Washington, on Catoctin Mountain in Maryland, had been one of Eisenhower's favorite places. Franklin D. Roosevelt had loved it, too, calling it Shangri-La, after the setting of a popular book and movie about a magic land hidden in the Himalayas. It really was a camp then, two hundred rustic acres owned by the U.S. Navy on the nineteen-hundred-foot peak, with a few cabins heated by fireplaces. Eisenhower renamed it for his grandson, David, who was now Nixon's son-in-law. On the day the Nixon family moved into the White House, David had pulled back a rug in the living quarters looking for a slip of paper he had hidden there on his grandfather's last day in office, when he was eleven years old. "I will return," it said.

Ray Price, the most serious of Nixon's speechwriters, was there to help. He said that he thought Eisenhower had been the most loved man in the entire world. "Yes," Nixon said in reply. "Everybody loved Ike. But the reverse of that was that Ike loved everybody. . . . Ike didn't hate anybody. He was puzzled by that sort of thing. He didn't think of people who disagreed with him as being the 'enemy.' He just thought: 'They don't agree with me.' "

Then Nixon told Price, "In politics the normal reactions are to have strong hatreds. . . ." Or so he thought. Whatever Richard Nixon said in the sadness of his benefactor's death, he was a hater. And he thought most everybody else was like him. His view of the world was a bad mirror image of himself, of his own darkness. He did not like people because, more often than not, he distorted their motivations to match his own.

Ike's funeral on March 30, 1969, drew seventy-five world leaders to Washington. Beginning with Charles de Gaulle, at 10 A.M. on March 31 in the Oval Room of the living quarters—the room above the Oval Office—the President met with one after another until 6:30 the next evening. It was Nixon at his best, listening and engaging, at least intellectually. If de Gaulle was long-winded, Nixon was patient; he clearly wanted, once again, to seek out the old man's wisdom. The conversation focused on two topics: dealing with the Russians and getting out of Vietnam.

The President began by saying that he had never met the current rulers of the Soviet Union and would appreciate de Gaulle's impression of them. The Frenchmen said they seemed to be forthright and frank—and sincere, though that could be a pose.

"Should I meet with them?" Nixon asked.

"Most assuredly so," said de Gaulle. "The whole world is waiting. . . ."

On Vietnam, the official notes of the talk reported: "General de Gaulle said that the real key to this situation was what the President did, what the United States did. The U.S. was the master of the situation. . . . He felt that the sooner it was clear the U.S. was leaving, the greater would be the willingness of the Thieu regime and the NLF to get together and work out some sort of a solution. Conversely, the longer they believed the U.S. would remain, the less likely they were to arrive at some solution. . . . He repeated that the essential thing was for the U.S. to end the war. If we did so, the power and prestige of the United States would be vastly increased and confidence in it throughout the world would be renewed." *

The President nodded more than once, finally saying that by the end of the year there would be progress in reducing the American commitment, but that he would not specify any time limits or dates. After de Gaulle, a parade began: Süleyman Demirel, the prime minister of Turkey; foreign minister Josef Luns of the Netherlands; former prime minister Nobusuke Kishi of Japan; President Habib Bourguiba of Tunisia; Prime Minister Chung Il Kwon of South Korea.

Nixon already knew many of the leaders he saw over those two

---

* The NLF—the National Liberation Front—was the formal name of the Vietcong, who were South Vietnamese communist insurgents. The North Vietnamese, officially, were in the war as supporters of the NLF.

days. He had met Bourguiba in 1953, several years before his election as Tunisia's first president. Now the Tunisian leader was sixty-five, and he made a rather touching request. He said the current leaders of Arab countries were "little men"—leading their countries to humiliation and defeat, capable of mortgaging their futures to the Soviet Union. He asked Nixon to do all he could to preserve Tunisia after he was gone. "You can count on it," said the President as the two of them walked outside to the old man's waiting car.

Nixon's conversation with Chung was the most specific. The Korean leader talked tough, as recorded in official notes: "The surest way to bring the North Vietnamese to a peaceful settlement was to apply the pressure of force. If the resumption of bombing in the north is not desired, the port of Haiphong should be blockaded and mined, thus cutting off the preponderance of supplies from the Soviet Union. . . . Consideration should also be given to sending forces across the DMZ into North Vietnam. If the Chinese Communists threatened to intervene, the President should write a letter to Mao Tse-tung saying that if they did he would use the nuclear bomb against them."

Nixon said politely that he would think about it. Then, tired but a happy man, the President went back to the residence for a family dinner with his brother Don and his daughter. While the President was getting advice and ideas from world leaders, Haldeman and Ehrlichman had been negotiating with Don Nixon and Donald Kendall, the president of Pepsico, who had volunteered to give a job to Don, a hustler who sullenly lived off the family name. In his diary that night, Haldeman wrote: "E came in at 7 P.M. to report on problems with Don Nixon. Don Kendall had spent half the day on this. Don Nixon still holding out for more dough, plus extracurricular earnings and fees. A real jerk—and a real burden for the P."

The period of mourning for Eisenhower over, the President went to the ball game. Rearing back to throw out the first ball of the American League season—the Washington Senators playing the New York Yankees—Nixon dropped the ball. Newspaper photographs immortalized the scene as he knelt down to pick it up while the Senators' manager, the great hitter Ted Williams, watched. The great seal in front of the Presidential box spelled the key word "PRESIDNT."

The next day, Nixon met with King Hussein of Jordan, who came with messages from Gamal Abdel Nasser of the United Arab Republic (Egypt). The thirty-three-year-old king said that he and the Egyptian ruler had been polar opposites in the Arab world but had been drawn together by crushing defeat in the 1967 war with Israel and by the internal dangers and pressures of increasing Arab extremism in their countries since that defeat. He said he had been authorized by Nasser to tell Nixon that the United Arab Republic would like to reestablish diplomatic relations with the United States and that all Arabs were willing to negotiate a "just and honorable" settlement document with Israel—anything short of a formal peace treaty. "The Arabs have learned," said Hussein, whose country was home to more Palestinian refugees than Jordanian citizens since the 1967 war, "that Israel's right to exist is now unchallenged."

The President was interested. He said the United States wanted a settlement and asked Hussein to prepare informal proposals on borders in the area, with emphasis on what to do about Jerusalem, which had been divided between Israeli and Jordanian control before 1967, but now, along with all the territories of the West Bank of the Jordan River, was occupied by Israel. Nixon was greatly impressed with Hussein. As he waved good-bye outside the White House—when he liked the leaders of other nations he would walk with them right up to their cars in the driveway—he turned to a State Department official and said: "We've got to help the King. We cannot let the American Jews dictate policy."

That same day, a former New York police detective named Jack Caulfield was shown to his new office in the Executive Office Building by Ehrlichman. They had met during the campaign, when Caulfield was assigned as a security liaison to the Nixon entourage, and the two of them got along. Ehrlichman had approached Caulfield after the February 17 meeting at which the President said he wanted private political funds and intelligence. On March 26, the President approved an Ehrlichman plan for around-the-clock surveillance of Senator Edward M. Kennedy. Ehrlichman then went back to Caulfield and hired him to run political intelligence errands for the White House, working outside the view or knowledge of the FBI, the CIA, and the Republican National Committee. The idea was to pay the detective with unused 1968 campaign funds, but he insisted on a White House job—and he got it.

On April 15, the President's day began at 7:20 A.M. with a call from Kissinger telling him of unconfirmed reports that a slow-flying Navy reconnaissance aircraft had been shot down off the coast of North Korea. "We're being tested," Nixon and Kissinger repeated to each other. Nixon's thoughts tumbled out: "Meet force with force. . . . Murder . . . honor."

There was a certain political symmetry involved. A year before, the North Koreans had captured the USS *Pueblo* and candidate Nixon had attacked President Johnson for not retaliating, saying then, "When . . . a fourth-rate military power like Korea will seize an American naval vessel on the high seas, it's time for new leadership to restore respect for the United States."

But now there was a difference. In 1968, electronic intelligence intercepts seemed to indicate that the action was deliberate, authorized by the North Korean government. This time, National Security Agency radio intercepts—for the President's ears only—indicated that the shooting down might have been a mistake, that only one North Korean jet was involved and that the pilot may have fired because of communications errors between him and his immediate commanders.

The President kept to his morning schedule. He was presiding over a budget meeting with more than a dozen Cabinet members and other officials going over domestic funding requests, when Kissinger bustled into the room, ready to whisper to him. Nixon cut him off: "You can tell them what we know, Henry."

"At 1 A.M. this morning we lost a reconnaissance plane," Kissinger began. Buchanan was taking notes and recorded: "It was flying 'identical patterns' of planes in the past near North Korea. It was attacked ninety nautical miles at sea by two MIGs. First question we asked was about radar surveillance. The plane was under direct radar control at all times. A half hour before the attack occurred, we received information that two MIGs had scrambled on a North Korean field. A rescue plane is in the area with a fighter escort. . . . Two ships steaming toward the area; they are now believed to be Soviet. We are now making a study in the State Department as to what North Korean assets exist outside North Korea. No U.S. Navy ships in the area. This mission was approved by a board consisting of the intelligence community and the Attorney General—"

The President interrupted: "It was a sitting duck, it has no combat capability, it was flying an elliptical pattern." The plane was an EC-121, the military designation for a four-engine Lockheed Constellation—an old propeller-driven airliner—an electronic spy plane with six tons of listening equipment to monitor North Korean radio traffic. Thirty-one crewmen were aboard.

Nixon and Kissinger left the room as budget director Robert Mayo took over the briefing. The national security adviser was pushing for the bombing, baiting Nixon, "Weakling . . . they will think you are a weakling." Bombing was what Nixon wanted to do, but both Rogers and Laird, who initially did not know of the NSA intelligence, were opposed from the beginning; the two secretaries and their aides ridiculed Kissinger's notion of a "surgical strike." When the President said the United States could not appear to be weak, Rogers said that was what President Johnson had said about Vietnam and now we could not get out. Without telling the President, Laird suspended spy flights near the Korean peninsula. The Undersecretary of State, U. Alexis Johnson, said the

North Koreans might take bombing as the beginning of war and attack South Korea again. The ambassador to South Korea, William Porter, cabled that if the United States bombed there was a chance the South Koreans would take it as a signal to invade the North.

Even Haldeman and Ehrlichman lined up against retaliation, or at least against Kissinger. They saw the fuming national security adviser, in crisis for the first time, as a man out of control in their very cool White House. At one point, Kissinger asked Ehrlichman about domestic reaction to retaliation.

"What retaliation?" Ehrlichman asked.

"Knocking out the base where the planes came from," Kissinger answered.

"Okay, but what if they knock out something of ours?"

"Then it could escalate."

"How far?"

"Well, it could go nuclear," said Kissinger.

The President considered one idea after another, including capturing or sinking a North Korean asset—a ship on the high seas—but no ship was found. Finally, after three days, the President himself decided against direct retaliation. Instead he sent two aircraft carriers to show the flag in the Sea of Japan, cruising across the horizon off North Korea, and he announced fighter escorts for spy flights in the area—without knowing there were no flights to escort because Laird had cancelled them.

So nothing happened, at least militarily. But in fact Nixon was deciding he could not rely on Rogers or Laird to implement his orders. He was in a rage that night when he called Kissinger, slurring his words a bit, saying he was going to get rid of the two secretaries. His anger soared again when Rogers, appearing before the American Society of Newspaper Editors, answered a question about the incident by saying, "The weak can be rash. The powerful must be more restrained."

It was a critical moment—and a clear demonstration of the limits of presidential power. Whatever Nixon decided, the United States did not have ready force available. Even an air strike would have required five days of planning. "They got away with it this time, but they'll never get away with it again," he told Kissinger, who was telling him the world would see this incident as proof of moral decay in America.

That was the mood of the Oval Office. The news summary a couple of days before the EC-121 incident had included a summary of a report by the British Institute for Strategic Studies that read: "The U.S. has lost 'the desire and the ability' to be the dominant power in the world. In the past year Russia has become the 'full equal' of the United States in military and political terms and is likely to overtake America in Inter-

Continental Ballistic Missiles by mid-1969. . . . 'Recent experience at home and abroad has exhausted their confident sense of purpose and ability.' "

"H.K.—Very important & accurate," Nixon scrawled.

He was an angry and frustrated man. He could not even seem to find a way to get attention in Hanoi. He was still convinced that the road to North Vietnamese leaders led through Moscow and Beijing. He initialed a secret one-page memo for delivery to the North Vietnamese almost pleading for secret talks: "Peace is achievable. . . . The president is willing to explore avenues other than the existing negotiating framework." Kissinger delivered the paper to Soviet ambassador Dobrynin, who said he could guarantee that it would be in Hanoi within forty-eight hours—but he could guarantee nothing else. And nothing was what was happening.

"The maddening diplomatic style of the North Vietnamese," Kissinger called it. "Insolent." But what was most maddening was that the North Vietnamese were saying nothing, or saying the same things in private as they were in public: Yankees, go home. Hanoi wanted unconditional unilateral American withdrawal and the abolition of the South Vietnamese government.

Though he knew better, Nixon seemed to be reverting to the old anticommunism, acting as if all communism and geography were the same thing. In an April 18 press conference, three different times he said "South Korea" when he meant to say "South Vietnam," as his first crisis was fading away with no real action. The best he could do in retaliation for the EC-121 incident was secret and absurdly indirect, making little sense to anyone but himself. On April 19, he ordered more and heavier Menu bombings of suspected North Vietnamese positions inside Cambodia. This time the action was called Operation Lunch—still a secret protected by deliberately false Air Force record keeping.

With the bombs away, Nixon went to Camp David for the rest of the weekend—watching the film *Dr. Zhivago* with Attorney General John N. Mitchell and his wife, Martha—and then came back Monday, April 21, to the routine of being president. Some of it was a learning experience, even for a man who had spent almost all of his adult life in the game of politics. On the morning of April 22, he met with Representative Mendel Rivers of South Carolina, the very conservative Democrat who was chairman of the House Armed Services Committee. Nixon hoped to persuade him to allow his ABM proposal, Safeguard, out of committee before the Senate considered it. Rivers immediately said he had no intention of doing that because it would be embarrassing to have the Senate ignore House action. But . . .

Rivers paused and then offered to do it, if the President supported appropriating $3.8 billion for Navy modernization, if the President terminated federal employees identified as having worked on military systems analysis during Robert S. McNamara's tenure as secretary of defense, and if the President gave him advance notice of military and construction contracts in his district as well as any anticipated changes in desegregation guidelines relating to schools in South Carolina. Nixon said no, but only after Rivers had left.

The President got more satisfaction that day from "a Historic First!"—one of his favorite expressions—inviting the wives of Cabinet members to sit in on a meeting. Sitting between his wife and Mrs. Melvin Laird, the President called in photographers to record the event, saying, "It's only coincidental that we were discussing pollution when the press came into the room."

On that same day, his briefing paper for a meeting with Postmaster General Winton "Red" Blount read: "Purpose: Therapeutic—To give Red exposure . . . you rarely see him." Haldeman also told Nixon that both Vice President Spiro T. Agnew and Transportation Secretary John A. Volpe were asking for regular meetings. The Vice President—"He's driving me nuts," Nixon said—had a habit of telephoning the President at dinner time with "Urgent!" calls, like one with the name of a friend he wanted named to a space council. Then there was his secretary of housing and urban development, George Romney, the former president and chairman of American Motors and governor of Michigan, a man used to being listened to, who casually interrupted the President at meetings. Nixon instructed Haldeman about all three: "Just keep them away from me."

That was Haldeman's job. And he preferred to do it with cold precision. Arthur Burns, the domestic counselor who had known Nixon for twenty years, was in with the President that Wednesday. Leaving the Oval Office, he suddenly remembered that Blount had asked him to tell the President something about postal reform, so he turned to walk back in. Haldeman blocked his way, saying, "Your appointment is over, Dr. Burns." The economist moved forward a little and Haldeman blocked him again, saying, "Send a memo."

"Even John Mitchell has to come through me now," Haldeman said to an Ehrlichman assistant. "Put it in a memo and John or I can decide if it's important enough to take up the President's time. . . . The President's time is valuable. This is the system. It is the way the President wants it, and that's the way it's going to be."

• • •

THE PRESIDENT had brought order to the White House. But there was disorder outside. Tens of thousands of students and thousands of professors at hundreds of universities and colleges were chanting of revolution. A *Fortune* magazine poll reported that precisely 12.8 percent of the country's university students held political views that were "revolutionary" or "radically dissident." The president of Georgetown University, Father Edwin Quain, said, "The freshmen are much more radical than the seniors, and I'm told the high school students coming up are even more so." At Mills College in Oakland, California, twenty-year-old Stephanie Mills gave a valedictory speech entitled "The Future Is a Cruel Hoax," and she pledged never to bear children. Softer words, quoted in both *Time* and *Life,* came from the class speaker at Wellesley College in Massachusetts. "For too long, those who lead us have viewed politics as the art of the possible," said Hillary Rodham, who was headed for Yale Law School. "The challenge that faces them—and us—now is to practice politics as the art of making possible what appears to be impossible." In a commencement address at the University of Pennsylvania, the British economics writer Barbara Ward exhorted: "Please stay angry. I implore you to determine that you are going to give public officials no peace. I say, go out, bite them!"

In *The Wall Street Journal,* Max Ascoli, the editor of *The Reporter,* commented: "Even after Ho enters Saigon and every single GI is back from Vietnam, Lincoln should be kept constantly in mind. He took extreme liberties with the Nation's laws, but he saved the Union. President Nixon faces an even harder task, for he must save the Union not from a civil but a guerilla war." On the day's news summary, the President wrote next the Ascoli piece: "Mitchell, Finch, Ehrlichman—RN shares this view. We may have to face up to more than 'dialogue.' "

Indeed. Police had been called onto the campuses of both Columbia and Harvard universities during building seizures and violent student strikes in the previous two weeks. There were fires at several schools, including New York's City College. In fact, *The New York Times* instituted a front-page box called "Student Unrest in Brief," listing demonstrations and damages each day. *Time* led its coverage of that rowdy April week at universities by saying: "Little by little, U.S. campus protest comes closer to resembling the compulsive mania of the recent Chinese 'Cultural Revolution.' " At Cornell University, which had recently given its airplane to black students to fly to New York City to find a bongo drum to celebrate the birthday of Malcolm X, half the 250 blacks among a student body of thirteen thousand seized Willard Straight Hall one morning at six, chasing guests who were there for Parents Weekend into a chilly dawn by shouting, "Fire! Fire!" Demanding a black-run Afro-American College at the university, they held the building for two days before marching out holding rifles and shotguns, wearing bandoliers of ammunition across their chests.

After conversations at the White House, James Reston of *The New York Times,* noting that the voters of both black neighborhoods and university communities opposed Nixon, wrote on April 27: "The picture of the Negroes at Cornell . . . sent a shudder through this country, and the concessions by the faculties and administrators at Cornell and Harvard to the use of force by the campus militants have convinced officials here that justice is too serious a business to be left to university teachers and officials. . . . The students and faculty on the left, paradoxically, are encouraging precisely the thing they fear the most. . . . They are encouraging the political authorities they oppose to use the political power and police power they hate."

Reston, the most important columnist in Washington, concluded, "Some authority must oppose anarchy." That was the way Nixon saw it: a question of order versus anarchy. Ironically, the next day, one of the great champions of order, Nixon's hero Charles de Gaulle, resigned as president of France, keeping a pledge he had made to quit if French voters did not support a national referendum on a relatively routine question of the balance of power between the country's central and regional governments. In addition to official statements of regret, Nixon sent de Gaulle a personal note: "History will record that your resignation was a great loss to France and to the cause of freedom and decency in the world." De Gaulle's response after reading the note was: "He is a true comrade."

That same day the President had Haldeman send around a speech he had just read, with a cover note: "The most significant and I think perceptive analysis of what is wrong with our approach to higher education was made by Professor S. A. Tonsor of the University of Michigan in a speech in Washington on April 1. I am sure that 'the establishment reaction' to this speech will be 'Tut, tut, this is old hat.' However, this happens to be my view."

The speech began by comparing Mark Rudd, a leader of student demonstrations at Columbia, with George Wallace, the segregationist governor of Alabama: "Both . . . stand in the schoolroom door, and seen from the vantage point of the academy they both hold the same low view of reasoned discourse. They believe that force ought to be substituted for sweet reason, that power ought to replace persuasion and that only 'socially approved' voices and views should be heard. They believe that toleration is a weakness rather than a strength in intellectual enquiry and they are in the deepest sense of the word anti-intellectual. They aim at nothing less than the destruction of the life of reason. The university and the parent society have no alternative to repression."

The United States Information Agency reported to the White House that the Cornell photographs were republished around the world. In London, the *New Statesman* said: "The U.S. is on the brink of racial revolution." On BBC, Alistair Cooke commented that the pictures looked as if they came from the Congo a few years before and the words reminded him of the cries of German students whose agitation paved the way for Hitler. On the other side of the Cold War divide, the line in Beijing was: "The U.S. ruling clique . . . is scared out of its wits and is plotting still more frenzied suppression of the students."

The Chinese, on April 29, also added a description of Nixon as "a hypocrite priest, a gangster holding a blood-dripping butcher's knife." Nixon sent Kissinger that item, adding, "K—pretty colorful!" He was enjoying the day—and that night, Dick Nixon outdid Jack Kennedy. The party for Duke Ellington's seventieth birthday was the biggest Negro event in the history of the White House, a house where Ellington's father had been a part-time butler. Guy Lombardo had not been invited, but the array of musical stars included Dizzy Gillespie, Billy Eckstine, Cab Calloway, Richard Rodgers, Dave Brubeck, and Mahalia Jackson. The place rocked, Nixon beamed, Ellington kissed every man in the room on both cheeks. The party did not break up until 2 A.M., and maybe that was a Nixon record, too.

May 6, 1969, was Nixon's one hundred and seventh day as President. That night CBS News broadcast an hour-long special called "The Correspondents Report: The First Hundred Days of Richard Nixon." Like most of the print and television reports at the same time, it was generally favorable. The moderator, Walter Cronkite, turned most often to the network's White House correspondent Dan Rather, who said: "The manner is measured and deliberate, cool, calculated, calm, at least on the surface. An image of thought instead of motion. Candor and direction instead of wordiness and evasion. Great vigor in international affairs. . . . There's comparatively less vigor in domestic affairs. The President doing less, not more. A belief in the theory of constructive nonaccomplishment. . . . Surprising and refreshing."

The greater surprise came three days later in Key Biscayne on May 9. The secret bombings in Cambodia were no secret anymore.

"RAIDS IN CAMBODIA BY U.S. UNPROTESTED" was the front-page headline over a *New York Times* story by the paper's Pentagon correspondent William Beecher. The headline referred to the fact that Prince Norodom Sihanouk was saying nothing about Menu, which had been raining bombs on his country for two months. The story began: "American B-52 bombers have raided several Viet Cong and North Vietnamese supply dumps in Cambodia. . . ."

Henry Kissinger was beside himself at breakfast, shouting and jumping up, pacing at the pool of the Key Biscayne Hotel as Haldeman and Ehrlichman watched. They had seen him angry before, but this time he was almost apoplectic. "Outrageous! Outrageous!" he shouted, telling Haldeman he had to see the President immediately.

"We must do something!" Kissinger told Nixon, whose house was a few blocks away. "We must crush these people! We must destroy them."

He did not say it directly, but Kissinger really wanted to destroy Rogers and Laird, who he believed had leaked the story to discredit him. He had already called the Secretary of Defense off the Burning Tree Country Club golf course near Washington, opening with: "You son of a bitch." Laird hung up on him. Nixon was angry, too, but he said, "You should look at your own people."

"They're bad news," said Nixon, not for the first time, of the Ivy Leaguers who served Kissinger. The one the President most distrusted was Morton Halperin, who had taught with Kissinger at Harvard and was in Key Biscayne to help with the Vietnam speech the President planned to give in five days. By lunchtime Kissinger had talked to the FBI at least three times, using the President's name. The conversations were about wiretaps. FBI director J. Edgar Hoover took down Kissinger's words: "National security . . . extraordinarily damaging . . . dangerous . . . destroy whoever did this."

After lunch, Kissinger asked Halperin to walk with him on the beach. He told him of Nixon's suspicions and said he had an idea. He wanted to deny Halperin access to classified material, so that when there was another leak, he would be able to prove it was not Halperin. By the time Halperin called his wife back in Bethesda that evening, an FBI agent was listening and recording the call. The tap had been activated as he walked with Kissinger.

The next day, back in Washington, Kissinger's military assistant Alexander Haig went to the FBI with the names of three more men. "Just for a few days," Haig told a Hoover deputy, warning that there should be no written records of the taps. The new targets were Kissinger's assistants, Helmut Sonnenfeldt and Daniel Davidson, and Laird's military assistant, Colonel Robert Pursley. At the same time, Jack Caulfield got one of his first assignments, arranging the tapping of a private citizen, Joseph Kraft, a syndicated columnist with good foreign policy contacts who had been reporting that Nixon's Vietnam peace efforts were not going well in Paris. This time it was strictly illegal; there was no attempt to work through the courts, the FBI, or law enforcement of any kind. Caulfield called the fifty-five-year-old director of security at the Republican National Committee, John Ragan, who shinnied up the telephone pole outside Kraft's house in Georgetown. "The top guy wants this," Caulfield told Ragan, who had retired as the FBI's best wire-man to sweep telephone lines for bugs wherever candidate Nixon stayed during the 1968 campaign.*

The presidential party returned to Washington on Sunday, May 11, on the Air Force's Airborne Command Post, the top-secret jet on constant standby for use by the President if Washington were threatened in a nuclear emergency. At first, Nixon seemed distracted as officers explained the in-air refueling that would allow the plane to stay aloft indefinitely and began a test exercise in command control, for use if the United States was under missile attack. But then he clicked in and asked one question after another about nuclear capabilities, throw weights, and kill rates, falling silent as the numbers were recited: ten million, twenty million, fifty million, seventy million deaths. "Pretty scary," Haldeman reported. "The exercise proved to P that when the Russians appear to be launching an attack our options are pretty limited and our retaliatory strike power is pretty weak."

The White House was preoccupied with the Vietnam speech for the next three days. "The peace plan speech"—this was it. On Monday afternoon, after several sessions with the President, Kissinger called the two principal writers, Price and Safire, to his little basement office.

"The President feels you can be warm and human, Ray," reported Kissinger. "And Safire, you're tough and cynical. That's what we need for the lead. . . ."

"A warm, tough, human, cynical opening," Safire said—humor Kissinger did not appreciate.

"The President wants all the casualty figures to make the point that we have suffered in past wars, but we have always treated our enemies generously."

"We beat the Germans, we didn't beat the North Vietnamese," Safire interrupted.

"You have a point." Kissinger nodded. "We've been generous with the people we've defeated; now you've got no idea how generous we can be with people who defeated us."

On Tuesday, May 13, the President sat down for final discussions

---

* The Kraft tap produced nothing but the conversations of maids because the columnist and his wife, Polly, were in Paris. At Nixon's request, French authorities tapped the Krafts' hotel room.

on draft reform. An administration bill was scheduled to be introduced in the coming week. The idea that had been proposed to Nixon early on by Milton Friedman as a way to defuse student activism (President Johnson and Senator Edward M. Kennedy also had proposed it as early as 1967) was refined and pushed by Defense Secretary Laird. The key provisions would essentially reduce young men's Selective Service eligibility from seven years to one. That one year would be a man's nineteenth (rather than his being eligible from age nineteen to age twenty-six) or his first year after graduating from or dropping out of college. The order of calling those nineteen-year-olds would be determined by an annual lottery, with 365 numbers keyed to birth dates from January 1 to December 31. Whatever date was pulled first, men with that birth date would be selected first, and so on. Men with high lottery numbers—say, 250 to 365—would almost certainly not be called. Luck of the draw.

The Urban Affairs Council was next on the President's schedule. A group led by the Reverend Ralph Abernathy, the successor to Martin Luther King Jr. as head of the Southern Christian Leadership Conference, waited in the Roosevelt Room. The preacher read a nine-page statement crafted to echo the cadences of King's "I Have a Dream" speech. "I am concerned," he said at the beginning of each paragraph: concerned about Vietnam, about the ABM, about military spending, about jobs, about hunger, about school desegregation, about Title I school funds, about equal employment opportunities. . . .

Abernathy ended by quoting a Nixon appointee who said, "This administration owes nothing to blacks," and asserting that any administration owes justice to all Americans.

"You're right," Nixon responded, noting that the remark about owing nothing was only political commentary on the fact that more than 90 percent of black voters had voted against him. Then he went on: "You want peace. I want peace. We're going to get it. We're making progress. But I have to take responsibility for the *kind* of peace it is. I have to think of the *next* man who sits in this chair. I have to think about peace for the balance of this century."

He said he wanted Abernathy to know that although his men, the white men running the country, were wearing expensive suits and had impressive titles now, many had grown up poor. "What I am trying to say," he continued, "is that you have here a group of men who are really *trying* to find answers. Most of us haven't known the kind of poverty you have seen. We don't want other Americans to know it. We haven't known the prejudices you have seen. We don't want others to know it."

"You are our President, and you will have our support," Abernathy said. "We want to help you lead." He talked for ten minutes more—he was a hard man to stop—saying his people wanted individual meetings with Cabinet members.

"You have an hour, so have at 'em," said the President, gesturing at Secretaries and staff members on the other side of the big table. He got up and left.

The meeting went on for another three hours, with Pat Moynihan reporting the details to the President. It was quite a show. An Indian woman from Oklahoma said the government was planning to exterminate the last of her people. A black woman said: "Mr. Nixon leaves to avoid hearing our comments. . . . Mr. Nixon says we should go back to Africa." Then she added that stories of men going to the moon were all lies: "If you come up there God gonna destroy you. If God don't destroy you, we gonna destroy you. I better stop now before I say too much."

After the meeting, John Volpe and George Romney took Abernathy to the Indian Treaty Room to meet the press. When the television lights went on, the civil rights leader said: "It was the most disappointing and the most fruitless of all the meetings we have held in Washington."

The meeting's note-taker, Ray Price, concluded: "A pompous, tiresome charlatan. The poor deserve better." Moynihan went to the Oval Office to apologize to the President, saying: "He goes into the press room and pisses on the President of the United States. It was unconscionable and I promise you it will never happen again."

"The strongest dressing down of any President on his own doorstep in the memory of veteran White House correspondents," Walter Cronkite reported that night. Next to that line on the next morning's news summary, Nixon wrote: "E-H. This shows that my judgment about not seeing such people is right. No more of this!"

The President told Moynihan, too, that he was not surprised by what Abernathy had done, because black people simply thought he did not care about them. And he didn't. He had little political use for most blacks—a fact that came out again and again in White House meetings, including an economic meeting the next day.

The President opened the session of the Cabinet Committee on Economic Policy by proposing that inflation might be checked by cutting back on federal aid and loans for housing construction. "Sure, I know the need for more housing, but if we can get a gig in this price thing now, we would all be better off. We cannot cool it next year—politically, it's impossible. It has to be now. . . . Let's take the bad news now, don't wait. But we want a very good response next spring. . . . Get those nails pounding in July of next year"—an election year.

The President and two of his economists, Burns and Secretary of Labor George P. Shultz, went back and forth on the impact of trying to slow down home building, but the argument was turned and won by Vice President Agnew, who demonstrated why he had succeeded as a new kind of suburban politician. He said: "Any further stringent actions to cut down on this field would mean that you are thrusting against the young, white, middle-class factor, and you don't just affect them today, you affect them their whole lives. Politically, it's a very delicate thing to squeeze housing any more."

Nixon's response was telling. Economics bored him. Politics did not. Talking of recessions past and the congressional elections of even-numbered years, he had already told the men in the Cabinet Room: "I remember 1958. We cooled off the economy and cooled off fifteen senators and sixty congressmen at the same time."

So, this time, he was persuaded by the Agnew argument. "Okay," he said. "I see my hunch was wrong. I can see that if you go below 1.5 million housing starts, you are in trouble."

The subject shifted then to international trade and antitrust law at home.

"We recommend the repeal of the Fair Trade Acts," said Assistant Attorney General Richard McLaren. "Repeal would be a step in the war against inflation. Retail prices in fair trade tend to be 15 percent higher."

Nixon interrupted him. "The fair trade laws keep some businessmen going that would otherwise go under."

"Little retailers?" McLaren said.

"Yes," Nixon said. He did not say his father had been one and had failed. "Does it mean that Mom and Pop stores are on the way out—and supermarkets are all we'll have? There is a sociological problem here. We may be helping consumers, but we don't help the character of our people. This is an old-fashioned attitude, Dick, I know—but I would rather deal with an entrepreneur than a pipsqueak manager of a big store."

This he cared about. He went on: "The deeper question is—What should be the social policy? Unfortunately, through the years, the policies have reflected the selfish interests of the top people. Look at it from a Wall Street lawyer's viewpoint. I see the immense profits going to those who pull off these conglomerates. We represented Continental Banking and Stone & Webster. We were for conglomerates when it was our client taking over, and we were against conglomerates when someone was taking over our client. . . . I don't like leaving it to the lawyers in Antitrust. Every one of these decisions made at the lower level reflects one man's view of what kind of society he wants. . . . Supermarkets may be able to sell Wheaties at a cent less, but I just don't think we want a nation of supermarkets."

Treasury Secretary David M. Kennedy picked up the drift and said: "I hear the same people are there in Antitrust who were there before."

McLaren, stung, interjected: "But I am making the decisions."

"You go over them with Mitchell?" Nixon asked.

"He signs all the orders."

"Does he read them?" the President said. "I have signed things I didn't read."

AT 10 P.M. on May 14 Nixon gave his first Vietnam address from the White House. He had worked and reworked the speech by himself all day in the Lincoln sitting room of the residence, as Kissinger spent the day briefing columnists and commentators on what to expect and what it meant. When the television lights went on, the President talked tough, laying down his official line:

Reports from Hanoi indicate that the enemy has given up hope for a military victory in South Vietnam, but is counting on a collapse of will in the United States. There could be no greater error in judgment. . . . Our fighting men are not going to be worn down; our mediators are not going to be talked down; and our allies are not going to be let down.

The time has come for new initiatives.

He ticked off eight points, most significantly, "simultaneous withdrawal of foreign troops from South Vietnam."

There was no immediate reaction from the other side. The North Vietnamese did not consider themselves foreigners. The United States seemed to be on the verge of unilateral withdrawal, a retreat under fire. The President hinted as much that night: "The time is approaching when the South Vietnamese will be able to take over some of the fighting fronts now being manned by Americans."

Nixon was in a good mood the next morning, which began with a joint meeting of the Cabinet and the National Security Council. The men assembled applauded as he walked in to take his seat. He motioned to the director of central intelligence, Richard Helms, to cover reaction in North Vietnam. Helms began by saying, "The most important point is that we won't chicken out. . . . their theory is that domestic dissent will force the United States to pull out. . . . Pham Van Dong . . ."

Nixon interrupted him, giving away the showcase nature of the session. "When you use names like that, you ought to give some identification so everyone knows who you are talking about."

Right. "Pham Van Dong is Prime Minister of North Vietnam," Helms said. "You might say he's the young Ho Chi Minh of the North Vietnam government. . . ."

"Oh, you mean he's their Finch," Nixon said. The laughter all around included Robert Finch, the secretary of health, education, and welfare, the former lieutenant governor of California, who had probably known Nixon longer than anyone in the room.

Helms also noted that a North Vietnamese spokesman had, as usual, called the South Vietnamese "puppets and lackeys" and Ambassador Henry Cabot Lodge, who was also in the room, an "odious neo-colonialist."

"Well, Cabot," Nixon interjected, "you may be a neocolonialist but you are not odious."

Then he got serious, laying out his own view, more directly than he had the night before, of what was at stake in Vietnam:

What is on the line is more than South Vietnam. It's a question of what happens to the balance of Asia and to the rest of the world. If we fail to end the war in a way that will not be an American defeat, and in a way that will deny the aggressor his goal, the hawks in Communist nations will push for even more and broader aggression. . . . If a great power fails to meet its aims, it ceases to be a great power. When a great power looks inward, when it fails to live up to its commitment, then the greatness fades away. The road to peace will be difficult, but we aim to get there.

His men stood and applauded again.

CHAPTER 5

June 19, 1969

AT THE END of the joint meeting of the Cabinet and the National Security Council on May 15, the President confirmed what a few of the men in the room already knew. Supreme Court Justice Abe Fortas, the man President Johnson had wanted to be chief justice, was resigning. Under fire. A year earlier, Fortas had withdrawn from a confirmation fight for the appointment as chief after questions were raised about his personal finances. Now a new charge had been turned up by the press and seized on by Republicans: it seemed he had been receiving twenty thousand dollars a year from a foundation run by a convicted stock swindler named Louis Wolfson. Nixon suddenly had the opportunity of a presidential lifetime: with Chief Justice Earl Warren scheduled to retire at the end of the Court's spring term, the new President could nominate two justices, one of them a new chief justice.

The President had followed Fortas's troubles closely for months for a couple of reasons more personal than political. The structure of foundations interested him greatly. He considered himself an accomplished tax lawyer—a specialist in minimizing clients' taxes—and had thought of creating a foundation to pay for and hold the title to a house he was negotiating to buy on the Pacific Ocean at San Clemente, California.

The politics of appointments to a federal judiciary still dominated by appointees of Roosevelt and Truman was laid out in a seven-page memo Nixon had kept in his desk since receiving it on March 25. The author was Tom Charles Huston, who wrote: "Through his judicial appointments, a President has the opportunity to influence the course of national affairs for a quarter of a century after he leaves office. . . . The growing popular disillusionment with the courts can most likely be traced to recent Supreme Court rulings on crime and segregation. The man in the street believes the courts are 'soft' on criminals and blacks. To the more thoughtful critic of the courts, however, the problem is more fundamental: the courts have opted for active combat in the political arena."

The memo stated that Presidents rarely involved themselves in lower federal court appointments—a process traditionally controlled by individual senators—and argued that Nixon should find a way to take back that power. Two days after it was written, the President wrote across the cover page: "RMN agrees. Have this analysis in mind in making judicial nominations."

There was also the fact that such appointments were coin of the realm. A president could use judicial nominations as bargaining chips. In fact, Nixon was already trying to play that old game to win a single vote on Safeguard, telling his congressional liaison, Bryce Harlow, to see whether he could make a deal to trade an appointment for a vote by a Republican senator, Marlow W. Cook of Kentucky: "I noted that Howard Baker is concerned that his Tennessee candidate for a vacancy on the 6th Circuit Court of Appeals is being pushed by a candidate from Kentucky sponsored by Cooper and Cook. . . . Unless we can get Cook to swing over to us on ABM, the appointment should go to Baker's man. . . ."

Nixon went to Camp David for the weekend, but he turned angry and restless as he read the Sunday morning newspapers. There were no long, analytical pieces about his Vietnam speech, no serious mention of it—positive or negative. Haldeman was sitting by the swimming pool, having lunch in the warm spring sun when he got a call telling him that the President wanted to go back to Washington immediately. Back in the White House, Nixon called Haldeman into the Oval Office and went on for two unhappy hours, saying that 98 percent of foreign comment acclaimed the speech; that if Kennedy had given it, American comment would have been ecstatic. "De Gaulle was right," he continued, "there's no point in being chummy with the press."

No one in the press thought Nixon was chummy. The current issue of Newsweek offered free advice in an article about reporters complaining they had no access to Pat Nixon, saying, "The ironic thing is that if there is one thing the Nixons need, it's humanizing. . . . Pat says she wonders why people don't know about Dick's sense of humor. Well, here we are panting on their doorstep and they are shutting the door in our faces." Reading that in his news summary, Nixon wrote, "RN does not agree—I would just as soon keep the society reporters away altogether if we could get away with it."

The President also wanted Haldeman to figure out an excuse to cancel a speech scheduled for early June at Ohio State University, because the FBI was warning of major antiwar demonstrations being organized there. In the morning, Nixon had his own answer. He told Kissinger to schedule a meeting with the President of South Vietnam that week in California. Even Haldeman thought that was funny, saying: "The big news will be the important meeting, when actually the whole thing came about as an idea to get out of Ohio State."

Then it turned out that President Nguyen Van Thieu wanted the meeting to be in Hawaii instead of California. "He has a girl in Hawaii," Kissinger told the President. Whether that was true or not, Nixon did not want to go to Hawaii, because Thieu had conferred there with President Johnson in July 1968. They compromised on a plan to meet June 8 on Midway, a U.S. naval base more than a thousand miles northwest of Hawaii; then Thieu, if he wanted to, could go on to Hawaii for a vacation. *The Washington Post* had the date in a story on Tuesday, May 20, the day the two presidents were supposed to announce it simultaneously.

Nixon was furious. He ordered Haldeman to ban all communication with the *Post*. The day before, he had ordered bans on *The New York Times* and the *St. Louis Post-Dispatch*. Pacing the office in frustration, he compared the White House correspondent of the *Times* with the Premier of the Soviet Union, saying: "I know our guys will say Bob Semple is a nice guy, and Kosygin is probably kind to his mother, but all that is totally irrelevant." Then Nixon said he was not going to tell anyone, including his spokesman Ron Ziegler, about his choice for chief justice of the Supreme Court. Finally, he let Haldeman go home.

At 10 P.M., Nixon called the chief of staff back to the White House. The President was still pacing the office, wearing a blue velvet smoking jacket. He wanted to talk about his choice for Chief Justice, Warren E. Burger of the District of Columbia Court of Appeals, who had given a law-and-order speech that was reprinted in *U.S. News & World Report* and found its way into the news summary. "Get me *Who's Who*," he told Haldeman and then read aloud the Burger entry as well as his own.

Burger's was short. Warren E. Burger, age sixty-one, had earned his law degree at night in St. Paul, Minnesota, worked in the 1952 Eisenhower campaign, come to Washington as an assistant attorney general, and been appointed to the federal bench in 1956. The key sentence of the speech Nixon read was: "The right to be safe on the street, in the home, and to be secure in one's person is an individual right of high order entitled to protection." Like Chief Justice Earl Warren, Burger was a big man with spectacular white hair. He looked the part, and he costarred with the President in a prime-time television announcement of the appointment on May 21. For the moment, the President was a happy man; his secret held this time as Burger was brought into the White House through a tunnel from the Treasury building next door.

The reviews were good. The governor of Florida, Claude Kirk, wrote to say: "Mr. President: Your selection . . . has met with resounding acclaim here in Florida. . . . In regard to the replacement of Justice Fortas, I want to bring to your attention a Federal judge in this district who meets what I believe is your criteria for experience, philosophy and personal character. His name is Judge Harrold Carswell. . . ." Nixon underlined the name and put the letter in the middle drawer of his desk.

There was additional good news the next day—from a distance. Apollo 10 astronauts had come within 9.4 miles of the moon before starting back for earth in the first and final rehearsal before Apollo 11 astronauts would attempt the dream of centuries, actually landing on the moon. But the President was grouchy on the weekend, despite a small personal triumph. He went to Camp David for the weekend with his wife, Pat, and Bebe Rebozo, then went off to bowl alone on the presidential alley. He came back to Aspen Lodge happily declaring he had rolled a 204 game, his best ever.

The President was just as restless when he returned to the White House, spending hours alone or with only Haldeman, complaining once more about the staff not getting out stories about how hard he worked—and, as always, about how the press was trying to ruin him. "A new phase," Haldeman told anyone who asked. Nixon was rambling a bit in meetings, sarcastic. On May 28, at a meeting of the Cabinet Committee on Economic Policy, he challenged Paul McCracken, the chairman of his Council of Economic Advisers, as numbers were bounced around the table, saying: "Perhaps statisticians are inherently dishonest people. Paul, are there any inherently honest people? You don't have to answer that." Later, in discussing foreign aid, he cut off the discussion by quoting Senator Allen J. Ellender, a Louisiana Democrat: "Same old shit!" Then he said: "I have supported foreign aid for twenty-two years. But I heard the same programs and same fallacious arguments back in 1956—more technical assistance, more private enterprise. Isn't it time for new approaches? Don't just look at programs, break the organization into pieces, throw it up in the air and put it into new bundles."

Nixon had a hard eye for the details of government programs, but most of the time he ignored them because he thought it was futile to try to change them. Seeing a report on federal summer job programs funding 861,000 jobs for "disadvantaged youth"—at a cost of more than $750 million to keep kids off the streets—he asked: "Is this huge amount really worth what it accomplishes? It's a pretty big bribe unless it leaves some permanent results."

The presidential mood was not helped at all when on June 3, *The New York Times* broke the story of secret negotiations to return political control of Okinawa to Japan—but leave more than forty-five thousand U.S. military personnel and numerous U.S. bases there. Under the byline of Hedrick Smith, the *Times* revealed details of a secret National Security Council decision memo that included plans to announce the turnover, and the removal of American nuclear weapons from the island, during Japanese Prime Minister Eisaku Sato's scheduled visit to Washington in November.

Kissinger, who had worked out the Okinawa plan to defuse rising anti-American sentiment in Japan, immediately came in with a new list of new wiretaps, beginning with Smith. That would make eight, the original four placed on May 9 and 12, plus two NSC assistants, Richard Moose and Richard Sneider, added on May 20, and Henry Brandon of *The Sunday Times* of London, added on May 28—the last of these, recommended earlier by J. Edgar Hoover, was done after Nixon, looking for Kissinger, found him at a dinner party at Brandon's home.

By the next day roles were reversed. Kissinger was calming down. He told Haldeman there could be "kickbacks" if the taps were revealed. But Nixon was getting madder and madder. He was flying across the country in a remodeled *Air Force One*—"New configuration is great," Haldeman said, "Puts the press way in back"—for a speech at the Air Force Academy in Colorado Springs, Colorado. Nixon blew up when Haldeman told him that the evening *Washington Star* and *The New York Times* both were reporting that there would soon be a joint U.S.–South Vietnamese announcement of the first U.S. troop withdrawals since six years of buildup put 550,000 Americans in South Vietnam. Nixon not only wanted the *Times* cut off this time, he told Kissinger to stop holding NSC meetings—the two of them would work alone and in secret.

At the academy, the President expressed more calculated anger: "In some of the so-called best circles in America . . . military programs are ridiculed as needless, if not deliberate waste. Patriotism is considered by some to be a backward fetish of the uneducated and the unsophisticated."

Then he questioned either the judgment or the courage of his political adversaries: "My disagreement with the skeptics and the isolationists is fundamental. They have lost the vision indispensable to great leadership. They observe the problems that confront us, they measure our resources, and then they despair. When the first vessel set out from Europe to the New World, these men would have weighed the risks and they would have stayed behind. When the pioneers set out from the East Coast colonies into the interior, these men would have counted the costs, and they would have stayed behind."

The so-called best circles reacted on cue. Columnist Joseph Kraft wrote: "For my money, the President has been showing his worst side—the side that earned him the name Tricky Dicky. . . ." When Nixon read that in the news summary and saw quotes from unnamed White House staffers quoted in *Time* magazine saying that some of the language was "unfortunate," he scrawled: "E. 1. On an urgent basis I want the whole staff to be questioned on this. 2. Tell them to pipe down if they can't be loyal."

In fact, Nixon felt good after the speech. He had said what he wanted to say, telling Safire: "Put yourself in the Russians' position. All they hear in the U.S. is 'No' to the ABM and MIRV; 'cut the defense budget by fifteen billion'; 'pull out of Vietnam'; 'the arrogance of power.' . . . Now if all they were to hear from the Administration is comments from me about how we really want peace, then they'd be likely to interpret it as weakness. We can't let that happen."

The planes of President Nixon and President Nguyen Van Thieu arrived at Midway within fifteen minutes of each other on the morning of June 8. Nixon, traveling with his family and a party of five hundred assistants and newsmen, had spent the day before at the Hilton Hotel in Honolulu meeting with military men, telling them, in effect, that their commander in chief intended to withdraw gradually from an undeclared war in which thirty-six thousand of their troops had been killed over the past five years. The United States was beginning a slow retreat covered by bombing and new rhetoric. There would be no more talk of a threat to the national security of the United States.

Midway was a set piece, but Nixon was tense. He hated personal confrontation and could not be sure how Thieu would play his part. The South Vietnamese leader, a general himself, was a proud man in an impossible position—and he believed, as he had for more than two years, that if he defied the Americans he would be assassinated by them. Like the American generals and admirals in Honolulu, he knew the decision he had come to talk about had already been made. The American mission, under the banner of "Vietnamization," was changing from victory to buying time for the President to construct "peace with honor." When Thieu walked into the newly painted and refurnished house of the commandant of the U.S. base he saw that Nixon's chair was bigger than his. Without a word, he walked into another room, found an identical large chair, and carried it into the negotiations himself. Then he sat down to face his patron.

It was an odd meeting, lasting five hours in total, with a break after the first hour and a half to announce the preprogrammed results. A joint statement, timed to meet newspaper and broadcast deadlines seven time zones away in New York and Washington, announced the immediate withdrawal of twenty-five thousand American troops of the half million and more in Vietnam, to be followed by more withdrawals at "regular intervals." Nixon controlled the fiction, saying that he was acting on the recommendation of President Thieu and the American commander in Vietnam, General Creighton Abrams.

In fact, inside the house, Thieu did choose to act as if the whole idea was his. He spoke of the American withdrawals—which he called "redeployments"—as necessary to confirm regular statements in Saigon and Washington that the war was going well. His greatest concerns seemed to be political ones—that the United States would agree to a coalition government in Saigon or would secretly negotiate a military settlement with North Vietnam, consulting with Saigon only after the deal was done.

When Thieu said that there was a sagging of spirit in Saigon because of speculation that the Americans were prepared to make political concessions to the National Liberation Front, Nixon responded that political enemies and the press were trying to drive a wedge between the two of them. The American memorandum of the conversation had Nixon saying: "Unless President Thieu heard something from him directly, he should disregard it. There is currently a lot of speculation regarding American pressures for a coalition government and it is entirely unfounded. . . . There can be no reward for aggression. . . ."

The notes concluded: "The President mentioned that we have a difficult political problem in the U.S. and that he appreciated Saigon's understanding for his domestic problems. . . . President Nixon described the Congressional situation and the importance of the 1970 elections. The U.S. situation is a weapon in the war. (At this point the President asked Henry Kissinger to explain the Cambodian strikes.)"

Then the presidents went their separate ways. Nixon was jubilant at first. Thieu had been more accommodating than he had expected; there had been no confrontation. In fact, the South Vietnamese leader seemed resigned to his nation's fate, saying at one point: "I know that you are going to go, but before you go, you have to leave something for us as friends. Leave something to help me out." What he wanted, he said, was money, training, and equipment to create two new elite army divisions mobile enough to counter North Vietnamese attacks from Cambodia or Laos. What he visualized, he told his own men after the conference, was a Korean solution for his country, a demilitarized zone between South and North Vietnam, with two divisions of American soldiers—forty thousand men—staying in the South to deter Northern aggression.

Thieu flew home by way of Taiwan where he met with Chiang Kai-shek, the Nationalist Chinese leader driven from the mainland in 1949, whom he considered a friend and something of a mentor. "So," said Chiang, "the Americans are going to leave Vietnam. Why did you let them do it?"

"When Nixon decides to withdraw, there is nothing I can do about it," Thieu answered. "Just as we could do nothing about it when Eisenhower, Kennedy and Johnson decided to come in. Once you know that you cannot change the American decision, it is better to make the best of it."

Chiang asked Thieu about Nixon and he answered: "He told me he had a domestic problem . . . a hostile Congress, the press, demonstrating students. . . . He promised me eight years of strong support. Four years of military support during his first term and four years of economic support during his second term. He spoke of military Vietnamization in the first term and economic Vietnamization in the second. By the time most of the Americans have withdrawn, so will the North Vietnamese; by then Saigon should be strong enough to carry on its own defense with only material support from the United States."

Chiang had a warning for Thieu. He told him that the Americans had an inclination to solve military problems with political means, saying that in the past the Americans had tried to pressure him into a coalition government with the communists of Mao Tse-tung.

Nixon left Midway believing that he had gained control over future events in Vietnam and that his strategic retreat would neutralize the antiwar movement at home. Reading a *Boston Globe* report on Midway's "unresolved questions," Nixon wrote across a news summary: "Henry—Virtually all press are crying in their beer because their dire predictions of RN–Thieu troubles did not surface!"

BACK IN WASHINGTON, Nixon began spending more time alone again, dictating action memos. On June 16, he stayed in the Lincoln sitting room of the residence and sent out one after another—all negative—including these:

Before the Inauguration I ordered a one-third cut in USIA, AID, military personnel except in combat zones like Vietnam and Korea and Western Europe. Nothing whatever has been done. . . . I know that everybody on the staff disagrees with my approach here but this is something I feel very strongly about and I want action on it immediately. . . . I think we should have Hatfield as one of our speakers at the Sunday services. This would be a nice ploy in the direction of the "bitch" groups. . . .*

"Mitchell—go after him," he wrote to the Attorney General after seeing a *Wall Street Journal* story on a Louisiana Teamsters Union official named Edward Partin who had testified against the union's president, Jimmy Hoffa, and was "something of a hero to men who worked for Robert Kennedy." On a news summary report that Cuba was replacing Argentina on the United Nations Economic and Social Council, he scrawled: "K—Pull the U.S. out of this council." On a *New York Times* report that his administration was in danger of not getting its $2.6 billion in foreign aid requests, Nixon ordered: "Harlow—Don't try too hard."

There had been a mean, frustrated edge to Nixon for a couple of weeks. His response to a *Christian Science Monitor* article praising Interior Secretary Walter J. Hickel was this note to Ehrlichman: "E—This worries me—He may be caving in too much to his critics." The Baltimore *Sun* reported that the United States might withdraw its consular mission to Rhodesia to protest white-minority rule and he wrote: "K—no—I disagree—If we have a mission in Hungary we'll have one here. This is an order." On a *Miami Herald* headline, "NIXON TO BOMB AGAIN IF REDS STEP UP WAR," he wrote: "K—Good!" On an inflation story, he wrote of himself: "There is no more chance that Pres. Nixon will ever seek a wage-price freeze than there is of Hades icing over. . . ." A briefing memo on a bipartisan group of Senators demanding closer scrutiny of military spending was marked: "E—Can't we infiltrate this group?"

On June 19, he spent the day in the same room, preparing for his sixth press conference, an evening affair to be televised nationally. The first item in his news summary concerned an article written by President Johnson's last secretary of defense: "All today's papers report Clark Clifford's call for a pullout of all U.S. ground troops from South Vietnam by the end of 1970. . . ."

The first question at the press conference followed that lead: "Mr. President, former Defense Secretary Clark Clifford has suggested that

---

* USIA stood for United States Information Agency, which included the Voice of America and libraries around the world. AID was the Agency for International Development, which administered foreign aid. Senator Mark Hatfield of Oregon was an antiwar Republican.

100,000 American troops ought to be out by the end of this year and we ought to say that all ground troops will be out by the end of 1970. I wonder if you think that is a realistic timetable?"

Nixon was ready and waiting, clearly angry: "For five years of the administration in which he was Secretary of Defense in the last part, we had a continual escalation of the war, we had 500,000 Americans in Vietnam; we had 35,000 killed; we had over 200,000 injured. . . . In the year, the full year, in which he was Secretary of Defense, our casualties were the highest for that five-year period. . . . He did have a chance in this particular, and did not move on it then. . . . I would hope we could beat Mr. Clifford's timetable. . . ."

Nixon was happy with the performance, staying up for hours and calling Haldeman and a dozen others to ask how he did. At 7:30 in the morning he appeared, smiling with King Timahoe on a leash, walking on the White House grounds, through the Executive Office Building, even out along Pennsylvania Avenue. He brought the dog into Haldeman's 8 A.M. staff meeting, not saying much, just grinning. Several days later, John Osborne in *The New Republic* noted some of those events and wrote an analysis of what he thought had happened over the past few weeks—the most prominent piece yet probing the President's psyche. Osborne signaled that this was not normal political commentary by writing that the most difficult thing about covering Nixon was remembering he was "human."

"That is not easy," Osborne wrote. "Most of the people who work for him at the White House do their witless best to conceal the fact, making him out to be a President who never—but never—succumbs to the pressures of the office and who in all other conceivable ways is without fault or foible . . . in his calm mastery of himself and of his job. . . .

"I was told, and was astonished at being told within the disciplined precincts of the Nixon White House, that the President fell, some weeks ago, into a passing phase of extreme frustration. 'Depression,' it was said, would be too strong a word for the mood that he then exhibited. . . . It was at about this time that the President's habit of withdrawal for hours of lone cogitation began to be emphasized in the press."

Osborne, though a relentless critic, seemed to have better sources inside the White House than any of his colleagues and competitors. Certainly the man from *The New Republic* had a cooler eye than most. He concluded that the President snapped out of it—whatever *it* was—by venting some nastiness at the Air Force Academy and more during the June 19 press conference. "Sneered" was the word Osborne chose to describe the President's characterization of both Clifford and the so-called best circles.

"A reasonable conclusion to be drawn is that Nixon, like other men, needs to be himself from time to time," the writer concluded. "Not the whole self, of course, but the meaner self that he has been in the past and will be again, in the Presidency. I suggest that it's a form of therapy, good for him if not always good for the country."

A week later, the Osborne piece was abstracted in the President's news summary. Nixon underlined a sentence about his blowing his cool, which ended, "Assistants who observed it were troubled and temporarily dismayed." Then he scrawled: "E&H—Here we go again. Certainly we should be able to find out who on our staff talks to this character."

"E," Ehrlichman, was actually among those who speculated in conversation with Osborne and others about what went on in the mind of Richard Nixon. Such musings were bound to slide into public dialogue, and such voices were raised again when *Look* magazine published a long article under the headline "PRESIDENT NIXON'S FORMER DOCTOR WRITES ABOUT THE MENTAL HEALTH OF OUR LEADERS."

Dr. Arnold Hutschnecker was an internist on Park Avenue in New York when he began treating Nixon in the early 1950s. Later he changed his practice to psychiatry and came to consider himself an expert on leadership. In *Look,* he did analyze Nixon—and Caesar, Napoleon, Hitler, and Lyndon Johnson, too—but he was careful to say that his only professional treatment of Nixon was physical. Between the lines, though, he seemed to be agreeing both with some of the more observant Nixon watchers in the White House and with the idea that this was a "New Nixon."

Hutschnecker framed his thoughts with the work of Hippocrates and of Ivan Petrovich Pavlov (who studied humans as well as dogs) and wrote:

> Pavlov called them 1) the strong, excitatory type; 2) the lively; 3) the calm-imperturbable; 4) the weak, inhibitory. . . .

> Men of type two represent the most desirable leaders because they show a controlled reaction when exposed to stress. . . . Type-one men, who are driven by hostile-aggressive impulses, make up the majority of leaders in all areas of life. Types one and four are the most likely to break down under stress. Therefore they become a risk in social and certainly political situations of responsibility. . . .

The doctor then turned specifically to his former patient, focusing on Nixon's 1962 blowup—"You won't have Nixon to kick around anymore!"—after losing the 1962 election for governor of California. Hutschnecker tried to pull it all together:

> It is one thing for a man to suffer a personal defeat that seems to end all hopes for his political future and to react to it emotionally. But it is quite another thing for a man in a position of power to be confronted with a crisis that is impersonal. . . . With the help of time and advisers, he can weigh the problem objectively. . . . During the North Korean plane incident in April, Mr. Nixon made an objective evaluation of the facts and consequences and exercised restrained judgment and control. . . . His behavior indicates that, as President, he may turn out to be a type-two leader, the controlled, adjusted personality, moving with strength through negotiations toward peace.

His example of a type-one leader who learned such self-control was Abraham Lincoln. The doctor's final words read like the midnight yellow-pad ruminations of his former patient, the President:

> The change can take place in a man who may have felt himself driven by ambition but is able to relax after having reached his goal.

CHAPTER 6

July 20, 1969

I N LATE MAY, an American astronaut, Frank Borman, had represented the country at a meeting of the International Committee on Space Research, held in Czechoslovakia. It was a rare visit by a prominent American to a communist country, particularly one that had been in open revolt against Soviet domination only a year before—a revolt ended by Soviet invasion and occupation. The astronaut's visit was not covered on controlled Czech television or newspapers, but the word was out—some of that thanks to Radio Free Europe—and the American was mobbed and cheered everywhere he went from the moment he stepped off a United States Air Force plane at the airport in Prague. Seeing a paragraph on that excitement in his news summary of June 6, Nixon scrawled: "K—I believe we could needle our Moscow friends by having more visits to Eastern Europe.... Cabinet members?... It's time we start causing them some trouble."

On June 28, the White House surprised the press and probably a lot of Nixon voters by announcing that the President himself had accepted an invitation to visit Romania, a rigid communist police state trying to assert some independence from Moscow, during an around-the-world trip scheduled to begin at the end of July. Privately, he explained the stop in Eastern Europe and a good deal more to congressional leaders of both parties in a breakfast meeting in the State Dining Room of the White House:

We must show the 150 million people in that ancient part of the world that the United States has not written them off. . . . We do not go there to antagonize the Soviets or to create a revolutionary situation which we could not ever assist; we go there to offer hope to the people of Eastern Europe.

Then he revealed something of the product of all his hours alone with yellow pads, showing himself more than a few steps ahead of the other politicians at his table. The meeting notes continued:

With regard to the Sino-Soviet situation, the President said that some people, of course, urge the United States to join some sort of informal alliance with the Russians to contain Communist China. The President said again that he felt this to be a brilliant short-range strategy, but disastrous long-range strategy. He said it would pit the white world against the non-white world in Asia, and Communist China would be the natural inheritor of the support of the non-whites, some of whom are our friends. "We must play a role in Asia if we are to avoid being dragged into future wars in Asia," he said. "Our role essentially should be to provide a nuclear shield for the Asian countries. . . . We have put ourselves on the line for dramatically increased population control programs in the underdeveloped countries. Without this kind of program, our aid to these countries is worthless. . . ."

It was the thing Nixon did best, seeing the world whole, thinking and acting at that architectural level. He went on, analyzing one country, then another, but he did not reveal the end point of his thinking about West and East. In fact, he believed that one day there would almost certainly be a race war between the whites of the world and the people of color, with the Soviet Union breaking down into its European and Asian halves—and the way to avoid that kind of war for as long as possible was through economic growth, population control, democratization where possible, and American military presence.

Most other parts of the job Nixon had fought for most of his life left him unsatisfied. There was little of the joy he wrote of in his solitary dialogues with himself. Only eight months after his election he was often melancholy or angry. Restless. He was often bored, too, especially by the complexities and irrationalities of domestic policy and relations with Congress. He shuttled back and forth between the White House and Camp David, planning his trips as escapes from Washington and grumbling on about the press and his staff. The more he complained that he did not have enough free time to think about such great things as wars of races and cultures and the immediate prospect of men walking on the moon—Apollo 11 was scheduled for liftoff on July 17—the more he sent out flurries of trivial action memos through Haldeman.

Before and after a state dinner on July 8 for Haile Selassie, emperor of Ethiopia, the President had fired off one separate little memo after another on the new dictation machine by his bed:

> In the future I would like to see the musical selections planned for the state dinners submitted to me. . . . There is an excellent musical group at Chez Vito. They are not ultra sophisticated but they are in a class of their own and would give an audience a good lift.

> Regardless of who happens to be the guest, the President is served first. I do not like the custom and hereby direct that it be changed. The following rules will apply. 1. If it is a stag dinner or lunch, with no guest of honor, the President is served first. 2. If it is a stag affair, with a guest of honor, the guest of honor will be served first and the President next. 3. If it is a mixed dinner, with no guest of honor, Mrs. Nixon will be . . .

After the July 8 dinner, Nixon went to Camp David, which was beginning to look like a construction site. The President had ordered millions of dollars of work to upgrade the mountain retreat. The President's cabin, Aspen Lodge, had once been a barracks for young Civilian Conservation Corps members clearing fire trails, a rough log building gradually upgraded over the years. In his first six months in office, Nixon spent almost $2 million to move trees around and to add such amenities as the bowling alley and a new $550,000 swimming pool next to his cabin. The astounding cost of the pool, replacing a small one in the woods, included more than $150,000 to reopen an old quarry to make sure the new stone around the pool would match the stones around Aspen and $261,000 to reinforce Orange One, the presidential bomb shelter. The new heated pool, placed exactly where Nixon had casually directed—pointing to a spot as he toured the grounds with Haldeman—was built directly over the shelter, which then had to be rebuilt. No one ever told the President that. He gave the order to Haldeman, who did what he was told, ignoring the arguments of Navy engineers. All the money for the work came from secret military funds, as did $418,000 to build a presidential helicopter pad near the President's new Florida retreat on Key Biscayne.

Nixon was using Camp David three or four times a month. This time he was working on what really interested him, war and peace. He was reviewing a secret National Security Council plan called "Duck Hook" being put together quickly from old contingency plans by Kissinger and his bright young man, Alexander Haig, who had impressed both Nixon and Kissinger by collecting the old plans from the Pentagon without alerting or alarming Secretary Laird. The NSC team had quickly slapped together a plausible plan to bring North Vietnam to its knees if there continued to be no progress in the Paris peace talks and no response to back-channel feelers being sent out by Nixon and Kissinger. The President had a deadline in mind; he wanted to punish North Vietnam militarily if there was no progress before November 1, the first anniversary of the bombing halt President Johnson had ordered just before the 1968 election. The old contingency plans included intensive bombing of Hanoi and Haiphong, of rail lines into China, and of the country's system of irrigation dams and dikes. Haiphong harbor and the country's principal rivers would be mined. One Duck Hook option was the use of nuclear weapons to try to block the Ho Chi Minh Trail, the north-south tangle of mountain passes, roads, tunnels, and paths used to move troops and supplies from the north to the Mekong Delta south of Saigon.

The President crafted an ultimatum for delivery to North Vietnamese President Ho Chi Minh, saying: "I realize that it is difficult to communicate meaningfully across the gulf of four years of war.... I wanted to reaffirm in all solemnity my desire to work for a just peace ... to move forward toward an early resolution of this tragic war." Nixon also wanted Ho to be told that if no progress was made by November 1 the United States would institute "measures of great consequence and force." On July 15, in the White House, Nixon handed the letter over to a former French delegate-general to Hanoi named Jean Sainteny, whose wife, Claude, had met Kissinger at Harvard during an international seminar in 1953.

In the mountains, Nixon was forever plotting, planning revolutions great and small, sometimes to build a better world, more often just coups against his own staff and Cabinet. He saw himself as a man of ideas, and of surprise moves, his real work done alone with his yellow pads, or with Haldeman and Ehrlichman, his agents of control and organization, whom he saw as his two arms. Haldeman was the gatekeeper; calls to the President went through him and the short conversations usually ended with him saying something like "Can you call me back later, Senator? If I'm tied up, my assistant's name is ..." Haldeman and Ehrlichman, who had become friends in college, were more than just an extension of the President; the two, along with Kissinger, were becoming Nixon's environment.

So Haldeman and Ehrlichman were with him at Camp David the

long weekend that began on Thursday, July 17—and they had an agenda: to continue the implementation of the President's still-vague plans to reorganize domestic decision making in the White House along lines similar to Kissinger's foreign affairs shop.

The President had become more and more irritated by the confrontation and untidiness of the constant push and pull between his old friend, Arthur Burns, and his innovative flame, Pat Moynihan, both of whom wanted to be seen as deputy presidents in charge of domestic affairs, as Kissinger saw himself as deputy president for foreign affairs. On the foreign affairs side, the new man, Kissinger, had already outmaneuvered the President's old friend, Secretary of State Rogers. As Nixon viewed it: "Rogers feels that Kissinger is Machiavellian, deceitful, egotistical, arrogant and insulting. Kissinger feels that Rogers is vain, uninformed, unable to keep a secret and hopelessly dominated by the State Department bureaucracy." Both men were right. But Kissinger had prevailed by playing to the President's penchant for secrecy and his old hatred of the bureaucracies of State.

Ehrlichman, with Haldeman's backing, was promising conflict resolution on the domestic side, providing the order and quiet Nixon wanted. Ehrlichman, who had become an advance man, a balloon dropper, because he was bored practicing real estate law in Seattle, had already impressed Nixon by synthesizing the friction between Burns and Moynihan into the kind of crisp policy papers the President preferred to oral argument—or even to plain old conversation. If Nixon listened to Moynihan, as he enjoyed doing, he had to balance that with interminable monologues by Burns. "I can't stand listening to Arthur anymore," Nixon said, and Haldeman and Ehrlichman went into action.

The vehicle of Ehrlichman's takeover was a paper on executive branch organization prepared for Nixon by Roy Ash, the president of Litton Industries. A document carefully tailored to the President's preferences, it included this assessment: "The many departments involved and the multi-faceted programs to achieve domestic goals preclude the same personal role in domestic affairs as he plays in foreign ones. The President cannot and should not also be the 'domestic desk officer.' "

Haldeman and Ehrlichman seized on those words as a way to shift control and responsibility for urban affairs and the rest of domestic policy into their own hands. Haldeman, who cared little for the substance of policy, wanted control; Ehrlichman wanted responsibility and power. Burns and Moynihan and Labor Secretary Shultz, a University of Chicago economist who had caught Nixon's ear by arguing that what the country most needed was "a bridge from welfare to work," would become staffers and idea men reporting to Ehrlichman rather than to the President. Before the weekend was over Nixon agreed that Ehrlichman would give up the title "Counsel to the President" to take over a new "Domestic Council," moving the noise of domestic policy friction out of the President's earshot. Moynihan was being marginalized. Burns could sit and wait until January 1970, when Nixon intended to keep a promise to make him chairman of the Federal Reserve Board.

That was the way the President wanted it. Nothing was announced and neither Burns nor Moynihan was told what had happened. Burns knew something was wrong when he got past Haldeman to see the President with a carefully drawn update of an old Republican idea, "revenue sharing"—giving states unmandated federal aid rather than telling them how to spend each and every dollar—and Nixon listened for only a minute or so. Barely looking up, the President said, "Yes. Give it to Ehrlichman."

Burns, about the last to know, was stunned to realize that Nixon did not give a damn about the details or even the idea itself. What the President wanted were dramatic domestic announcements to quiet critics in Congress and the press who were saying that his interests at home concerned politics, not governance. And the criticisms were accurate.

Unlike Burns, Moynihan was not totally opposed to the creeping Ehrlichman takeover. The energetic Democrat from New York was not interested in administration. He was a perpetual thought machine. He got along well with Ehrlichman, who knew that sooner or later Moynihan would get bored and realize that his work was done.

Moynihan had spent his energies crafting a program, a bold one, to replace Aid for Families with Dependent Children, the principal New Deal welfare plan, which essentially provided monthly checks to out-of-work mothers with children. When politicians or people complained about "welfare" or "relief," AFDC was usually what they meant. Moynihan's scheme was called Family Security System, a combination of old liberal ideas (reworded by Moynihan to suit Nixon's love of surprise and novelty) including a guaranteed annual wage for both the welfare poor and "the working poor"—a Shultz phrase. The President jumped on those words, thinking they could be used to mobilize the working-family constituency he hoped to wean away from the Democratic Party and George Wallace, who had won 13 percent of the 1968 presidential vote as a third party candidate. What was taking shape in his mind was a new political majority. The President asked Shultz to be more specific on the work-related requirements and Shultz came back with two ideas: healthy welfare recipients would have to get jobs or job training, and low-income workers would be eligible for the same money and benefits as welfare recipients.

Nixon's attitude toward government relief had something to do with the fact that his poor family had rejected government help when he was a boy; he had contempt for traditional custodial welfare and he hated social workers. His parents had refused to send his brother Harold, dying of tuberculosis, to a free public hospital because they believed accepting government help was demeaning—and they wanted to "keep up appearances." But his goal was presidential in the sense that all the presidents back to the man who created the social welfare system wanted to get rid of the damned thing. "What I am seeking is the abolition of relief altogether," wrote President Franklin D. Roosevelt in a 1934 letter. "I cannot say so out loud yet, but I hope to be able to substitute work for relief." Nixon, fascinated still with the Disraeli comparison, was ready to say it out loud. He even thought of a new word to use: "workfare."

Moynihan, a Rooseveltian liberal himself, had primed Nixon with hours of engaging tutorial and pounds of paper highlighting statistics like these: under state-administered relief a three-person family could receive anything from $39 a month to $263 depending only on where the family happened to live; 69 percent of welfare births in New York City were out-of-wedlock; 93 percent of welfare homes had no father in residence, partly because AFDC went only to women alone and their children.

"Will FSS get rid of social workers?" Nixon asked Moynihan.

"Wipe them out," came his answer with a smile.

Moynihan elaborated on that in a memo to the President: "The service-dispensing groups in the society—teachers, welfare workers, urban planners, nutrition experts etc. etc.—are preoccupied with the black problem and almost at times seem to resent hearing there are whites who are in difficulty. . . . The black poor seem to be favored over the white near-poor, the loud mouths get louder and temperatures rise."

As Nixon rearranged the chairs in his White House, the most amazing thing happened in the house of his enemies. Senator Edward Kennedy, President Kennedy's youngest brother, the man Nixon expected to be his 1972 opponent for the presidency, disappeared for more than eight hours after driving a car off a wooden bridge on a little island called Chappaquiddick, just off Martha's Vineyard in Massachusetts. More than ten hours after the accident divers found a dead body in the submerged car, a twenty-eight-year-old former secretary in the office of Senator Robert F. Kennedy. The woman's name was Mary Jo Kopechne. The President of course wanted to know every detail. Bill Safire told Nixon he thought the incident would be forgotten in the excitement of the landing of the *Eagle,* the name of the lunar module on the Apollo 11 mission, which was already circling the moon. "No," said Nixon. "It'll be hard to hush this one up; too many reporters want to win a Pulitzer Prize."

"He was obviously drunk and let her drown," Nixon said. "He

ran. There's a fatal flaw in his character." Ehrlichman sent his on-staff detective, Jack Caulfield, to Martha's Vineyard to pose as a reporter. "We want to be sure Kennedy doesn't get away with this," he told the ex-cop. Caulfield took along another former New York policeman hired by Ehrlichman, Tony Ulasewicz, who was being paid twenty-two thousand dollars a year out of a secret Nixon political fund being handled by the President's personal lawyer in California, Herbert Kalmbach:

Nixon was wrong on the press and the mysterious death of Mary Jo Kopechne—at least at first. The original story in *The New York Times* ran under a two-column headline: "WOMAN PASSENGER KILLED, KENNEDY ESCAPES IN CRASH." Spanning eight columns above that was:

ASTRONAUTS SWING INTO MOON ORBIT
IN PREPARATION FOR TODAY'S LANDING

The next day, the story of the landing of the *Eagle* was not only the entire front page of the paper, it was the only story in the entire front section, beginning with the largest headline type the *Times* ever ran:

MEN WALK ON THE MOON

ASTRONAUTS LAND ON PLAIN
COLLECT ROCKS, PLANT FLAG

VOICE FROM MOON: "EAGLE HAS LANDED"

On Sunday night, July 20, 1969, sitting in the small private office behind the Oval Office with Haldeman and astronaut Frank Borman, the President watched Neil Armstrong, commander of the spacecraft, step out on the surface of the moon, at a place mapmakers called the Sea of Tranquility. There were television cameras in the formal office to record Nixon, in the longest-distance telephone call ever made, congratulating Armstrong and his crew, saying, "This certainly has to be the most historic phone call ever made from the White House. . . . As you talk to us from the Sea of Tranquility, it inspires us to redouble our efforts to bring peace and tranquility to earth."

He was attacked for that. *The New York Times,* in a nasty little editorial, pronounced that a call from Nixon was "unseemly" and would waste the precious time of the astronauts—and that the President was trying to steal the glory of his predecessors, John Kennedy and Lyndon

Johnson, who had each pledged that an American would be first to the moon.

Nixon was an angry man that night. Watching the film *West Side Story,* a musical version of *Romeo and Juliet* updated as a story of love and hate among Italian-Americans and Puerto Ricans in modern New York City, the President walked out before it was finished, grumbling, "I can't stand any more of this propaganda."

Four days later, on the deck of the aircraft carrier USS *Hornet* in the Pacific south of Hawaii, with a Navy band playing "Columbia, the Gem of the Ocean," the President was bouncing with excitement when he actually saw the astronauts, two hours and five minutes after they splashed down. He talked to Armstrong, "Buzz" Aldrin, and Michael Collins through the glass of a quarantine chamber on the *Hornet,* beginning with a bad joke about his call being collect. Nixon was no good at small talk, but he loved to say big things, and he did: "This is the greatest week in the history of the world since the Creation!"

Whoops! A Nixon friend, Billy Graham the evangelist, immediately said there were greater times: "1. The first Christmas. 2. The day on which Christ died. 3. The first Easter." Seeing that in his news summary, Nixon scrawled: "H—Tell Billy RN referred to a week not a day."

The news summary had become news itself, with one syndicated columnist, Marquis Childs, reporting rumors that it was the only thing the President read and it was only one page a day.

Well, as a matter of fact, the news summary often ran to more than twenty pages and the President may have been getting more than he needed or wanted. He sometimes complained about both the content and his suspicion that too many people were seeing the same pages he saw each day. "As I pointed out in a previous memo—in the future editorials and columns from the *N.Y. Times* and *Washington Post* need not be included in news summaries," Nixon wrote on his copy the day the *Times* attacked his call to the astronauts. More and more, the news summary was central to White House days. On the day the question about the President's isolation was asked, he scrawled a note on his summary saying: "H & E: Be sure that the distribution of the news summary from now on is limited to RN & H & E—Not to Klein, Keogh, Ziegler, or anyone else."

Haldeman suggested that perhaps that was going too far and the next day circulated a memo from the President to Ehrlichman, Ziegler, Klein, Kissinger, and Harlow: "As each of you is aware, the President reads quite closely his daily news summary and . . . issues daily instructions on the basis of stories and articles within that summary, instructions for action on the part of the White House Staff. After this memorandum is received, the President will assume that you have read

Buchanan's news summary by 10:00 o'clock and that you have taken action on issues affecting your department, by at least noon."

That day's summary also mentioned a speech by the Republican mayor of New York, John V. Lindsay, an antiwar liberal, who had said to great applause: "Nine billion dollars of New York money goes every year into the work of death. Our resources do not belong in Vietnam. The money belongs in the streets, in the homes and in the hopes of this city." Nixon's note on that was: "E—Let's put a freeze on the silly ventures we've been in helping this guy." Reading a report on a syndicated column by Roscoe Drummond saying that unless he gets out of Vietnam "popular opinion will roll over him as it did LBJ" Nixon wrote: "E & K—Tell him that RN is less affected by press criticism and opinion than any Pres in recent memory."

After the splashdown of Apollo 11, *Air Force One* went on its way around the world. In flight the next day, the President looked at some of the reviews—journalistic report cards—of his first six months in office. The wisdom was conventional: good grades on foreign affairs, incompletes or failing grades on domestic affairs. *Life* magazine said:

> FOREIGN POLICY: Nixon's determination to phase out of Vietnam is now clear. His effort to negotiate with the Communists, to bring the Thieu government around, and to withdraw troops over a two-year period in any case is an intricate maneuver which has been conducted so far with considerable skill. . . . Less evident, but also on his mind, is his commendable resolve to reach some kind of an arms limitation agreement with the Soviet Union, and even if possible an understanding with China. . . . if it can be done at all, it is conceivably best achieved by a Republican.
>
> INFLATION: He has pursued a hard line and steady course, except for a few verbal wobbles. . . . The trick is to avoid a recession and too much unemployment. Good marks so far.
>
> DOMESTIC UNREST: . . . With Negroes he gives the impression he's not much involved; regards them politically as not to be won over and only hopes they won't be too troublesome while he assembles his Middle America majority. He has retreated on school desegregation and voting rights.
>
> CONGRESS: The President has asked for little and got less.

They got it right on "Negroes." A news summary that week included an article reporting that Governor Richard B. Ogilvie of Illinois wanted the federal government to cancel ultimatums on school desegregation in Chicago. Nixon's response: "Why can't we let up in such a case?"

Time gave Nixon better grades. In commenting on the flight to the moon, the weekly newsmagazine presciently laid out analysis that evolved into strategy. What the mission represented, said *Time,* was "the solid, perhaps old-fashioned American virtues . . . an accomplishment of 'middle America' of whom the President was the soul." Then Time-Life's White House correspondent, Hugh Sidey, was quoted: "He has given a voice to the majority that did not know it was a majority. . . . They have fastened upon RN who goes to ballgames . . . and follows space flights with the enthusiasm of a small boy. He is the president of the Jaycees, the Kiwanis booster, the cheerleader flying around the world, glorying in what middle America has wrought."

So began Nixon's around-the-world trip. The first stop after the early-morning excitement on the *Hornet* was Guam, an island that usually was only a routine military refueling stop. It was a place without television and, in Boston, Senator Edward Kennedy was on television trying to explain what had happened at Chappaquiddick. Haldeman sat at a telephone—in the White House one of his men held the phone at the other end of the line up to a television set—taking word-for-word notes, which he immediately read to Nixon. The President took a few questions from traveling reporters, answering one on Vietnam by saying, "We must avoid that kind of policy that will make countries in Asia so dependent on us that we are dragged into conflicts such as the one we have in Vietnam."

Reporters jumped. They live on change, ever alert to difference or contradiction. "Dragged into" was not the phrase usually used by Nixon in connection with the war. He elaborated by revealing the essence of hours of conversations he and Kissinger had been having about the three kinds of Asian conflict: first, internal subversion or civil war; second, attack by a neighbor; third, attack by China or the Soviet Union. "As far as the problems of military defense," he said, "except for the threat of a major power involving nuclear weapons, the United States is going to encourage and has a right to expect that this problem will be increasingly handled by, and the responsibility for it taken by, the Asian nations themselves."

Within an hour, as Nixon slept, those words were being broadcast and published around the world as the "Guam Doctrine"—in shorthand, that the United States would provide small allies with matériel but not men, supplies but not soldiers. The interpretation was that the Truman Doctrine—restated by President Kennedy as the American determination to "bear any burden" in the worldwide fight against communism—was now a thing of the past. On July 26, *The New York Times* headlined: "NIXON PLANS CUT IN MILITARY ROLE FOR U.S. IN ASIA."

Kissinger was stunned by Nixon's sweeping indiscretion, figuring the President had just been too tired to fend off the press. Haldeman's reaction, on the President's orders, was to inform members of the administration that they should do whatever they could to have the "Guam Doctrine" instantly renamed the "Nixon Doctrine." And so it was, by accident, the kind of PR triumph RN so coveted.

The next morning, the presidential entourage flew on to Manila, then Indonesia, Thailand, and South Vietnam. After a pro forma meeting with President Thieu in Saigon, Nixon was flown by helicopter to the U.S. First Army base at Di Nam, twelve miles outside the city. He walked and talked with dozens of American soldiers, asking where they were from and then switching to conversations about sports. It was easy to make fun of his stilted man-to-man style, but the day had real impact on him. He called Haldeman into his flying office, saying he was overwhelmed by the character of the young men in uniform. Then he said, "Never let those hippie college-boys in to see me again. . . ."

The next stops were New Delhi, in India, and Lahore, in Pakistan. The party was moving too fast for much more than sight-seeing. Flying into New Delhi, Haldeman sat down next to Kissinger and handed him the three-page statement prepared for the President's arrival. "The President says this is too long—hold it to two pages," Haldeman said. Kissinger glanced at him, handed the papers to a typist, and said: "Put this on two pages."

Flying from Lahore to Bucharest, in Romania, Nixon told Kissinger and Haldeman how much he was impressed by Pakistani president Agha Mohammad Yahya Khan, the former army commander who had taken over the country in 1969. He was a hearty fellow who liked to carry a riding crop under his arm—a hard-drinking, straight-talking, barracks optimist. "A real leader," said Nixon, "very intelligent." He thought Khan had showed insight into relations between the Soviet Union, an ally of India, and China, which maintained closer relations with Pakistan. As Yahya Khan saw it, Russian leaders had a great fear of China, because so much of the Soviet population was Asian and might prefer to be part of China if given a chance. "He could be a valuable channel to China—maybe to Russia, too," Nixon said to Kissinger as they left the country.

As a private citizen two years earlier, Nixon had met, cordially, with President Nicolae Ceausescu of Romania. He was also one of the few Eastern European leaders who had reached out to the Chinese communist leader Mao Tse-tung, much to the displeasure of the Soviets. Nixon and Ceausescu talked then about tensions between the Soviet Union and China. The day he had left Washington, Nixon described that 1967 visit to Kissinger: "By the time we get through with this trip the Russians are going to be out of their minds that we are playing a Chinese game."

That was part of it. Ceausescu also had good relations with North Vietnam, and Nixon wanted a message passed. He rephrased the message he had sent Ho Chi Minh, repeating his secret deadline: "We cannot indefinitely continue to have two hundred deaths a week in Vietnam and no progress in Paris. On November first this year . . . if there is no progress, we must re-evaluate our policy."

The crowds in Bucharest were tremendous; it was the first visit by an American president to a communist country since World War II. Hundreds of thousands of people waited in the rain, waving Romanian and American flags provided by the government, and dancing in the streets and chanting, "Oora! Oora!"

"Historic! . . . Historic!" Nixon used the word over and over again, puffing a cigar as he walked in the gardens of his guest villa in the Romanian capital. The same thing happened the next morning, a Sunday, as he and Ceausescu toured the city, stopping at markets and just about every new building in town. Nixon was euphoric. He relived the moments again and again with Haldeman before heading for the airport and the trip home. Haldeman saw Kissinger and said, "You know, he actually seriously intends to visit China before the end of the second term."

"Fat chance," said Kissinger.

The national security adviser was not on the flight home. The press was told that he was flying to Paris to brief French officials on Nixon's trip. His place on *Air Force One* was taken by Ehrlichman, who had just flown from Washington to brief Nixon on the final draft of the Family Security System legislation.

The Kissinger announcement was a ruse. The real reason he was going to Paris was to attempt to set up back-channel negotiations with the North Vietnamese, separate from the official talks being conducted by David K. E. Bruce at the city's International Conference Center. On August 4, Kissinger went to the rue de Rivoli apartment of Jean Sainteny, the courier for Nixon's original deadline letter to Ho Chi Minh. A half hour later, Xuan Thuy, a low-level official of the North Vietnamese foreign ministry, came into the apartment. The two men talked for more than three hours. Kissinger, through interpreters, laid out scribbled plans for mutual withdrawal of "outside forces" from South Vietnam. Xuan Thuy, also through interpreters, methodically repeated Hanoi's position, that they were not outsiders and would fight on until the last American withdrew. There was vague agreement on the possibility of future contacts. If there was any advantage, it was to the North Vietnamese: they probably understood that the Americans were going to withdraw with or without an agreement—but then they had always believed that anyway.

In Washington, the President stepped off *Air Force One* in a heavy rainstorm at Andrews Air Force Base, cheered by three thousand officials. Prominent among them, shaking Nixon's hand, was Senator Edward Kennedy. The President was "buoyant" the next morning—that was the word used in the official minutes of his breakfast briefing of the legislative leaders of both parties on August 4. It was Nixon at his best again, forward-looking, knowledgeable, and more candid than usual. House and Senate leaders, including Senate Majority Leader Mike Mansfield and the chairman of the Foreign Relations Committee, Senator J. William Fulbright, applauded the President again and again.

"American policy in Asia is in a transition stage," Nixon began. "The U.S. must move away from a monolithic approach to a country-by-country approach." Then he said it was worth going halfway around the world to see Yahya Khan in Pakistan and Ceausescu in Romania because the United States did not always have intelligence agents in such places. Speaking of Vietnam, he said history would vindicate American efforts, that if the United States had not intervened, the 115 million people of Indonesia would now be under communist rule. As for President Nguyen Van Thieu, he said, "He is the most impressive South Vietnamese leader I've met." But then he added, "That isn't saying a great deal."

Then he elaborated on the doctrine he had quickly pronounced on Guam, now being promoted as the Nixon Doctrine: "If a major power should move in across a border openly, this would be a different ball game, but since that would involve a confrontation of some kind with the United States, the likelihood of that is small. . . . In the event that the difficulties in an Asian country arise from an internal threat, these countries will be called upon to handle it entirely on their own. In the event that the aggression within is subsidized from the outside, we will provide them with American assistance in the form of arms and matériel, but we will not provide the troops."

According to the minutes, he also gave the leaders a quick glimpse of his thinking on global racial interactions. "He said that every Asian leader did ask him about a Soviet proposal of a collective security pact for Asia. His answer was a categorical no. . . . An anti-Chinese security pact would leave the Chinese in the position of charging that the Soviets and Americans had joined together in a white alliance against the colored races and enable the Chinese to take the leadership of non-white peoples. . . . We have to find a way to communicate with the Chinese."

"What about East-West trade?" asked House Majority Leader Hale Boggs.

"Nixon said," according to the notes, "he used to hold the opinion that every time you trade with a communist country you strengthen its hold on down-trodden people. Now, he said we should trade with them to open these countries up . . . adding consumer goods to these economies would tend to leaven their society."

"Have you thought about foreign astronauts in American spaceships?" asked Ross Adair, a congressman from Indiana.

"Great idea," said the President.

The man certainly seemed to know what he was doing. "RN is riding high," he said in a memo to Haldeman and Ehrlichman telling them to make sure to send favorable poll ratings to congressmen, "who may have thought it will now be safe to give in to their deepest desires and kick us in the teeth."

After the meeting, the President asked Ted Kennedy into his office. Haldeman, sitting in the corner, recorded: "He told him he understands how tough it was, etc. Said he was surprised to see how hard the press had been on him, especially because they like him, but you have to realize they are your enemy at heart, even if they do like you, because their prime motivation is the story."

CHAPTER 7

August 8, 1969

IN HIS BIOGRAPHY OF DISRAELI, Robert Blake wrote: "The social measures passed in 1874–80 did something to make a lot of the urban masses less unhappy, less precarious and less unhealthy. Disraeli was at the head of the Administration that brought this about even if he did not concern himself with the details."

"It is the Tory men with liberal policies that have enlarged democracy," said the President. Or at least that is what Pat Moynihan went around telling people Nixon was saying. Moynihan promoted President and program, saying, "The Family Security System is a genuinely new unmistakably Nixon program . . . likely to reverberate through the society for generations."

The liberal *New Republic* seemed to agree, commenting: "It embodies two revolutionary principles. One is that the federal government is obligated to guarantee to welfare beneficiaries, families and individual adults, a minimum national standard of support. The other is that family heads who work for a living and earn less than a declared minimum (below 'the poverty level') are entitled to a federal payment sufficient to bring their family incomes up to that minimum. A third principle, basic to the program, is not revolutionary at all. In the opinion of many critics, including some officials who contributed importantly to the Nixon concept, it is reactionary and self-defeating. This principle is that employable beneficiaries of welfare should be made to work."

The "Tory" president did not have to believe in the program or agree with much of anything about it to decide to go with it. The appearance of public equality, he had concluded, was essential to the public order—particularly in maintaining peace in urban black ghettoes—and the appearance of domestic calm and concern was essential to his own political standing. Actually, he believed black people were genetically inferior to whites. Talking about welfare reform with Moynihan out of the room, Nixon told Haldeman and Ehrlichman: "You have to face the fact that the whole problem is really the blacks. The key is to devise a system that recognizes this while not appearing to. . . ." In private he would assert that there had never in history been a successful or adequate black nation. "Africa is hopeless," he told Ehrlichman. "The worst is Liberia, which we built. . . ." *

But those were not views for public consumption. On August 6, he assembled his Cabinet at Camp David to promote the Family Security System, saying: "What we are trying to do here is to break that deadly cycle in which generation after generation knows nothing but welfare. A big point in this plan is to give the family a little dignity. I remember that in the Depression a lot of families would not go on welfare. The psychology has now changed, particularly among the group that we are talking about here. We are not sure that we can restore that kind of pride. But

---

* On May 24, 1969, Haldeman had written: "Went through his whole thesis re: blacks and their genetic inferiority and the hopelessness of any early change in the situation. Have to wait for in-breeding—in the meantime just take care of them and help the few good ones to rise up. I firmly believe he's right." That entry was excised before publication. The President, however, obviously understood that whatever he personally believed, his obligations were of a different order. In a long memo to Haldeman on February 28, 1973, he wrote: "I am very distressed about the failure to follow through on my firm directives with regard to the employment of the ethnics and other minorities in the new administration. . . . I think sometimes we go too far in insisting on a very competent person when someone else who might not be quite as competent could do the job with adequate backing at lower levels. I recently told you that one out of five such appointments should be from the minority groups. It probably ought to be two out of five. Set that as a goal and then we might end up with one. Basically what I want are more Poles and Mexicans. . . . Certainly we don't want to be in a position where we are not putting qualified Negroes into jobs, particularly since we are removing so many from positions in OEO. However the first priority should go to the groups I have mentioned above. The Blacks already have a disproportionate representation as far as minority groups are concerned and no matter what we do in this area we seem to get very little credit." Finally, nine years later, in 1982, during a two-hour conversation, Nixon told me that he thought "yellow" Asians were genetically superior to Caucasians, at least in intellect, and that blacks were markedly inferior to both Asians and Caucasians. He said, then, that he expected Asians to dominate the world by the middle of the twenty-first century. At home, he offered these thoughts: "What people resent is this business of some colleges pushing blacks too far for their own good, making them doctors and everything else. . . . The racism has receded, I think, but it's there and it always will be there. . . . A lot of people are just as racist now, but it's not fashionable anymore—and I think that's damned important. You can't talk about blacks like you once did."

what we are trying to do is provide the best new plan that is possible and hope that it will work."

The briefing on the details of FSS was given by Robert Patricelli, one of Robert Finch's deputy assistants at the Department of Health, Education, and Welfare. Patricelli was a twenty-nine-year-old Harvard Law School graduate. When he finished, Nixon thanked him and said, "How do you get that smart?"

The meeting lasted four hours. Vice President Agnew led the opposition, saying that forty of the fifty state governors would oppose the plan. "This adds 13 million people to the welfare rolls. Isn't it possible to fix the deficiencies of the present system—with regard to work incentives and day care—without adding these 13 million people to the rolls?"

But Agnew could not stay to argue his point. He had to get back to Washington for critical Senate votes on amendments designed to kill funding for Safeguard missiles. The administration expected a tie vote, which would have killed the anti-ABM amendments, and the Vice President was dispatched in case his no was needed to keep the program alive. Seeing Agnew's frustration, the President tried to make a joke: "I guess we can count on your vote."

Agnew answered in kind: "Mr. President, if there's a tie, I may call you to see if you've changed your mind on FSS."

Most of the Cabinet sided with the Vice President. HUD Secretary Romney, like Agnew a former governor, repeated several times that he thought middle-income people would resent such help to the working poor, as that group had always resented the people on welfare. Bryce Harlow, the Congressional liaison, seemed to be the only staff member involved who comprehended what the President was doing. In a memo to Ehrlichman the week before, he had written: "If it is the President's object to loft this program without regard to (1) Republican resentment or (2) likelihood of Congressional approval, I of course understand and readily acquiesce. . . . If however he desires to *enact* the FSS rather than merely propose it, then I consider the present plans inadequate."

Nixon had long ago decided to propose dramatic welfare reform—and the drama was more important to him than the specifics of reform or the possibility of enactment. As far back as mid-April, he had sent a Moynihan memo on to Ehrlichman with the notation: "E—in confidence—I have decided to go ahead on FSS. Don't tell Finch & Moynihan."

At the end of those four hours, even the densest must have realized that the consultation was—in the word Haldeman favored—nothing more than "therapy." They were getting time with the President, but he did not much care what they thought. In fact, he rather enjoyed the sensation of being a leader who could not be swayed by the arguments of his titled advisers. He calculated that an honest vote of the Cabinet would go against him by 14 to 11. This reminded him of a story told about Abraham Lincoln and the Emancipation Proclamation: when every member of his Cabinet voted against it, Lincoln supposedly said, "The ayes are one, the nays are nine, the ayes have it!"

What Nixon said was: "I know that the welfare road we have been on is the wrong road. It is a total disaster. I don't just want to patch it up; we must move in a new direction. We don't know that the program we have decided upon will solve the problem, but I like the balance between work and security. And now that the decision has been made, I ask that everyone join in the process of selling this as a very exciting new domestic program. . . ."

Two nights later, on August 8, the President told the nation about the plan in a television address. At the last minute the name was changed to Family Assistance Plan. It was a negative income tax scheme guaranteeing welfare families of four members sixteen hundred dollars a year in cash from the federal government. But before explaining that, Nixon attacked the welfare state: "A third of a century of centralizing power and responsibility in Washington has produced a bureaucratic monstrosity, cumbersome, unresponsive, ineffective. . . . A colossal failure."

Then he proclaimed a "New Federalism" built on "revenue-sharing," with the federal government ending some grants to state and local governments for specific programs such as road construction and, instead, sending those governments the cash collected as federal taxes—$1 billion the first year, rising to $5 billion after five years—which could be used for existing programs, or used to create new ones, or remitted to taxpayers. "Power and responsibility have flowed toward Washington, and Washington has taken for itself the best sources of revenue. We intend to reverse this tide."

Most of the speech centered on FAP and its work or job-training requirements. "The present system often makes it possible to receive more money on welfare than in a low-paying job," he began. "I therefore propose that we will abolish the present welfare system. Its benefits would go to the working poor, as well as the non-working. . . . a basic Federal minimum would be provided, the same in every state. . . . Everyone who accepts benefits must also accept work or training. The only exceptions would be those unable to work and mothers of preschool children."

The President concluded: "Abolishing poverty, putting an end to dependency—like reaching the moon a generation ago—may seem to be impossible. But in the spirit of Apollo, we can lift our sights . . . toward a new birth of independence."

A quick Gallup poll reported that 65 percent of Americans supported the idea. Ninety-five percent of newspaper editorials were favorable. "Mr. Nixon has taken a great step forward," wrote James Reston in *The New York Times*. "He has cloaked a remarkably progressive welfare policy in conservative language. . . . He has insisted that poverty in a prosperous country must be eliminated." *

THE NEXT DAY, the President and his family took off for Southern California to spend a month in the fourteen-room, forty-five-year-old house overlooking the Pacific Ocean that he had bought in April. La Casa Pacifica, "the House of Peace," Nixon called it, though a more accurate translation would have been "the Peaceful House." It was about halfway between Los Angeles and San Diego, near the town of San Clemente, within the sound of the gunfire of Marines at Camp Pendleton being trained to go to Vietnam. He had big plans for the place, designating it the "Western White House."

By the time Nixon got there it was exactly that. Helicopter pads, temporary office buildings, grass, and flowers were put on what had been a Navy radar facility four hundred yards from Nixon's house. The President drove a Cushman golf cart—unofficially called Cushman One— back and forth. The government had already spent more than $1 million at San Clemente, including more than $500,000 for the offices and improvements of the thirty-acre property and adjacent land owned by the Navy and the Coast Guard. The work included a new heating system for the house, office furnishings, windscreens, and new bulletproof windows, all listed as security requirements. The same kind of home improvement was happening at the "Southern White House" at Key Biscayne, where the government spent more than $625,000 for capital improvements and equipment, including $621 to replace an ice-making machine because, according to White House Mess records, "The President does not like ice with holes in it." The cost of flying staff members and other officials back and forth between Washington and the two houses was more than $7 million a year.

Nixon had never much liked Washington or its people, and now he was creating a hideaway White House three thousand miles away, just

---

* Under the plan, a welfare family of four would receive $1,600 from the federal government and states could supplement that as they wished. Family members could keep up to $60 a month in earnings if they worked. They could also keep 50 percent of earnings above that. Working poor families would also receive direct federal payments calculated on a complicated scale. President Nixon used two examples: a family of five earning $2,000 a year would receive a federal supplement of $1,260; a family of seven earning $3,000 a year would have its income raised to $4,360.

as he had done seventy-five miles away at Camp David and a thousand miles away on Key Biscayne. In Florida, the government had joined with two of the President's best friends, Rebozo and Robert H. Abplanalp, a wealthy inventor and marketer of the aerosol valve used on spray cans, to purchase the four houses near Nixon's to insure his privacy and security. There was little public attention to the bicoastal White House construction work, although while Nixon worked at San Clemente that summer, the *Washington Evening Star* ran a short "Washington Beat" item that read: "Inside Washington political salons, the curious and the gossips are trying to figure out how President Nixon could possibly afford all the money he is lavishing on himself and his family."

The White House press office responded reluctantly to such questions, answering with half-truths and minimum estimates, saying that the President paid $340,000 for La Casa Pacifica and six acres of property— a cash down payment of $100,000 and the assumption of a $240,000 mortgage. But in fact the property, sold as a single package, included a total of twenty-eight acres. The actual price, hidden in trust documents, was at least $1.4 million. The President, who had a net worth of just over $300,000 when he took office, had borrowed $450,000 from Abplanalp, then used $400,000 of the loan as a down payment and took out a $1 million mortgage.*

Now, after only seven months in office, Nixon was withdrawing from Washington, from the press, from his Cabinet, and from most of his

---

* Details of who actually held the title to the San Clemente house and property were hidden from the press and public in the files of trust companies and an investment partnership owned by Abplanalp. Some details on the financing of Nixon's California and Florida homes became public during congressional investigations in the spring of 1973. The total figure for capital expenditures, equipment, operating costs, and maintenance for the homes at San Clemente and Key Biscayne was $3,350,688.87. That included a little more than $34,000 for security arrangements at the home of Julie Nixon Eisenhower in a Bethesda, Maryland, a home owned by Bebe Rebozo; and apartments in Cambridge, Massachusetts, and New York City used by Tricia Nixon Cox after her marriage in 1971. At about the same time, the *Santa Ana Register* reported that the congressional investigators also had evidence that 1968 campaign funds were used in the purchase of La Casa Pacifica, but that report has never been documented. Some of those leftover campaign funds were used for personal purchases, including $4,562.38 for diamond earrings the President gave his wife for her sixtieth birthday. The Abplanalp loans were later forgiven by the lender. In addition to providing gifts and loans, Abplanalp spent more than $1 million to build a helicopter pad and other facilities near his home on Grand Cay, a coral island he owned in the Bahamas, to facilitate presidential visits. By the time Nixon left office, his net worth had risen to more than $1 million, but he was then assessed about $467,000 in back taxes, principally for taking illegal deductions, many of them having to do with the renovations to his two new homes in the sun. One final note: William Gulley, who was director of the White House Military Office under four presidents and ordered and paid for many of the improvements from a secret military contingency fund, ended an interview with me by saying: "I don't think money was what Nixon was about. Compared to some of the others, he was a real straight arrow."

staff. The day after the President headed west, Haldeman issued a new housekeeping memo: "The President wants his phone redesigned; he would like to have a direct dial line (an outside line) on the phone so that he can dial numbers directly when he wants to. . . . He also wants direct lines to Ehrlichman, Kissinger, and Haldeman."

Outside the President's fences and walls, the country was relatively quiet. There had been fewer than 100 racial disorders in cities around the country, compared with 135 in 1968 and 138 in 1967. While British troops were moving into Northern Ireland to try to end riots and violence between Protestants and Catholics, and Israel and its Arab neighbors seemed close to another war, *U.S. News & World Report* was saying of the United States: "The war is being phased out; violence in the cities has simmered down; campuses may be quieter; space had brought more respect for the nation; business is good, and most of all, people are living amazingly well."

The opening essay in *Time* began: "For a rare moment, most of the U.S. seemed to be soothed and quiet. . . . In California, President Nixon golfed and tended to minor matters of state with equal equanimity. . . . U.S. campuses were largely empty for the summer, and the questing young—more than 400,000 strong—gathered in upstate New York for a weekend rock festival (called Woodstock) that unfolded without violence in an Aquarian instant of communion and discovery. . . . The ghettos stayed quiet. . . . Vietnam is no less of a morass, and the flag-draped coffins continue to come home to Oswego and Oakland; yet the nation has decided, without the President's saying precisely so, that it is all over except for a bit more shooting."

In fact, the President was never an easy man to soothe. Haldeman was spending a good deal of time almost forcing his boss out of the new Western White House for golf or a walk on the beach, sometimes tagging along and reflecting on Nixon's silence and occasional observations. "Good grief!" the assistant reported to his wife after Nixon looked up the seventy-five-foot-high cliffs on which his house was built and said it would be lovely to see hotels and condominiums up there.

The President began his days with long morning briefings, usually by Kissinger and Mitchell. The national security adviser reported on an Army announcement that the commander of Special Forces in Vietnam, Green Beret Colonel Robert B. Rheault, might be charged with murder, along with several of his men, in the disappearance of a South Vietnamese civilian working for U.S. forces. Also, there were more reports of American units, up to the size of companies, refusing to follow orders sending them into combat.

When Mitchell was in, the conversations were about possible

Supreme Court nominees. After Burger was confirmed as chief justice, Nixon was determined to appoint a southerner to the Fortas seat, and those talks almost invariably turned into bull sessions on the politics of the South, past and future. Nixon believed he could make that future Republican, reversing the tide of a century of Democratic control of the politics of the seven states of the old Confederacy. He had already had some success, carrying five of those states—Virginia, Florida, Tennessee, North Carolina, and South Carolina—in the 1968 election. The times were changing: in 1950, the Republicans had two senators, seven House members, no governors, and 263 state legislators in the South; by 1970 the numbers were eight senators, thirty-six House members, six governors, and 477 state legislators.

The racial integration of southern school districts, segregated by law since the rise of southern Democrats in the late 1870s, was the subject of many of the political conversations above the Pacific and hundreds more in Washington. Nixon, once considered a Republican liberal on race issues, had tailored his views like a suit for warmer climes, most famously in a closed meeting with southern delegates at the Republican National Convention in Miami on August 6, 1968, when his nomination was threatened by southerners and other conservatives enamored of a new California star, Ronald Reagan, elected governor in 1966. At a closed meeting, a North Carolina delegate asked: "On the racial problem in the South, can you say that you favor forced busing of schoolchildren for the sole purpose of racial integration?"

Nixon rambled a bit but told them what they wanted to hear, and Senator Strom Thurmond of South Carolina, who had carried four southern states running for president as a segregationist in 1948, circulated Nixon's answer throughout the South during the general election campaign:

> This is a problem in the North, too. . . . I don't believe you should use the South as a whipping boy or the North as a whipping boy. My feeling is this: I think that busing the child into a strange community . . . I think you destroy that child. . . . And there is another thing that I would say with regard to the courts of this land. . . . I think it is the job of the courts to interpret the law, and not make the law. . . . I don't think there is any court in this country, any judge in this country, either local or on the Supreme Court . . . that is qualified to be a local school district and make the decision as your local school board.

Before and after his election, Nixon continued to promote the favorite southern reaction to now-illegal segregation laws: "freedom of choice." The words rang better than the results. Students, whatever their race, could go to any school in their county or district. In fact, almost none of them did change schools; the whites would not go to black schools and blacks were afraid to go to white schools. "Freedom of choice" produced so little desegregation that the Supreme Court had ruled it "inadequate" in May 1968. The ruling read: "The burden on a school board today is to come forward with a plan that promises realistically to work, and promises realistically to work *now.*"

The word "now" was italicized in the Court's ruling. Under President Johnson, the Department of Health, Education, and Welfare produced guidelines saying that "now" ended, at the latest, with the beginning of the 1969–1970 school year in September 1969. But many southerners, and Nixon, too, pretended that freedom-of-choice plans were still an option. They agreed, too, as did many of their countrymen, that the worst of options—worse than drawing new school district lines or "pairing" schools in white and black neighborhoods—was "busing" white children to black schools and black children to white schools.

Lords of the South, politicians and educators—not all but many of them—read Nixon's Miami answer as a pledge that a Nixon administration would end or try to end busing—would go easy on the South. So did black Americans. In 1960 Nixon had received 20 percent of the black vote when he ran against John F. Kennedy, but in 1968 that dropped below 12 percent when he ran against Vice President Hubert H. Humphrey.

From the beginning of his first term, President Nixon had done what he could to keep his bargain with the South. Five school districts in North Carolina, South Carolina, and Mississippi, which had not filed court-ordered desegregation plans, had been scheduled to have federal funding cut off a week after Nixon's inauguration. Robert Finch's HEW ordered a sixty-day delay and Senator Thurmond issued a statement asserting that the postponement represented assurance that Nixon would keep his campaign commitments to the South. The Senator's administrative assistant, Harry Dent, was appointed to the White House staff and the President passed the word that "nothing should happen in the South without checking with Dent." In a private meeting with Finch on May 15, the President laid down the law, as recorded in a one-page memo. The President said that he expected Finch or his executive assistant, L. Patrick Gray, to personally monitor desegregation plans to ensure they were "developed in method and content in such a manner as to be inoffensive to the people of South Carolina"—and every other Southern state. On a news summary item reporting that a Texas congressman, Republican James Collins, believed the administration was opposed to antibusing laws, the President wrote: "I am not opposed to this kind of bill—call the dogs off."

The man circled by dogs was Finch, who had served as Nixon's executive assistant during the vice presidential years. HEW was a huge civilian army, guardian of the American welfare state. Those troops were not about to surrender because a new president wanted to play games with the laws they were dedicated to enforcing. The President was on the wrong side of the law and of history. He knew that, but he saw a unique opportunity to get on the right side of the politics. Perhaps he could manipulate racial issues, just for now, to realign presidential politics by winning over George Wallace's voters to his side before 1972. He had become president with only 43.4 percent of the vote, but the combined Nixon-Wallace total in 1968 represented 57 percent. Nixon could send the same kind of messages as Wallace did.

The permanent bureaucracies at HEW and in the Justice Department were resisting the White House's attempts to look the other way on race. So were federal courts. Judges, all with lifetime appointments, were following Supreme Court mandates to desegregate southern schools as quickly as possible. The President's strategy was to do as little as possible to enforce those decisions—while blaming the courts for desegregation. But the unruly and idealistic troops of HEW and Justice were fighting him in his own name. The most visible of the fighters was a thirty-year-old California Republican named Leon Panetta, who Finch appointed to head HEW's Office of Civil Rights. And then there were the civil rights organizations. In July, at the annual convention of the National Association for the Advancement of Colored People, Roy Wilkins, the group's executive secretary, accused the White House of deliberately breaking the law by violating court orders. "It's almost enough to make you vomit," Wilkins said.

Panetta immediately responded to the questions Wilkins raised, telling reporters Nixon was committed to civil rights and the rule of law. Two hours later the White House called. It was Ehrlichman, saying, "Cool it, Leon!"

Later Ehrlichman added: "Blacks are not where our votes are, so why antagonize the people who can be helpful to us politically?" When the assistant attorney general for civil rights, Jerris Leonard, told a reporter that Nixon in 1972 might follow a "Northern Strategy" writing off the "Deep South," the President scrawled across his news summary: "Get me a report. This is utterly stupid!"

"This line is to be used by all Administration spokesmen from now on," the President wrote across a memo. "We are opposed to segregation in any form, legal and moral, and we will take action where we find it, and where it amounts to a violation of an individual's rights—but our opposition to segregation does not mean we favor compulsory or forced integration; and we remain opposed to the use of federal funds to bring about some arbitrary racial balance in the public school system."

The strategy on desegregation—of saying one thing but doing nothing about court orders—began coming apart that summer. Among the first documents sent to the Western White House was a four-page single-spaced personal letter teletyped to the President from Senator John Stennis of Mississippi, the sixty-eight-year-old conservative Democrat who was chairman of the Senate Armed Services Committee. Stennis had been the floor manager on the ABM legislation and was ensuring its placement in the final omnibus military authorization bill. The subject was a ruling by the Fifth Circuit Court of Appeals ordering desegregation of thirty-three Mississippi school districts when the new school year began on September 11—and ordering that plans for the desegregation be submitted to the court by August 11. Stennis wrote: "The plan now proposed will, as a practical matter, destroy our public school system. . . . As chairman of the Armed Services Committee I have major responsibilities here in connection with legislation dealing with our national security, but I will not hesitate to leave my duties here at any time to go to Mississippi to do whatever else must be done to protect the people of Mississippi and to preserve our public school system. While I have not yet spoken to Senator Symington, I am sure that as the ranking member . . . he will be glad to assume those committee responsibilities if I am called away. . . ."

It was a threat. He did not spell it out, there was no need. Senator Stuart Symington of Missouri, who would then take over management of the Safeguard authorization fight, was against ABM funding.

The President responded by ordering HEW and the Justice Department to go to court to appeal the desegregation order. The federal government would argue against desegregation for the first time since 1954, when the Supreme Court had unanimously ordered the end of legal school segregation with "all deliberate speed." The same government attorneys who had argued for immediate implementation of orders one day came back into court the next day and argued the opposite. At least one quit on the spot. Although HEW had already approved Mississippi's desegregation plans, Finch, without informing his Office of Education, wrote a letter to the Fifth Circuit asking for more time, until December 1, to consider the matter. He asserted that the plans would create "chaos, confusion and catastrophic educational setback to the 135,700 children, black and white alike. . . ." The court granted the stay—which in effect meant delaying desegregation for at least a year—and the NAACP Legal Defense and Education Fund immediately appealed to the Supreme Court.

The day the NAACP went to court, August 18, happened to be the day the President announced his choice to fill the Supreme Court vacancy created by the resignation of Justice Fortas. Attorney General Mitchell had compiled a list of 170 candidates, and Nixon chose one who met his informal criteria: southern, strict constructionist, a sitting judge. The chief judge of the Fourth Circuit Court of Appeals, Clement Furman Haynsworth, a fifty-six-year-old, fifth-generation South Carolina lawyer, a graduate of Harvard Law School and of Furman College (which had been founded by his family), fit the mold shaped by Nixon at the Republican National Convention: "Men who are for civil rights but who recognize that the first civil right of every American is to be free from domestic violence."

THE SUMMER REMAINED CALM, but Nixon received a warning note from Defense Secretary Laird, who wrote: "I believe this may be an illusory phenomenon. The actual antipathy for the war is, in my judgment, significant and growing." At the same time, Tom Charles Huston got another long memo through to the President. This time, in more provocative words than Laird used, he predicted trouble on college campuses when the fall term began: "I am willing to state unequivocally that we will witness student disorder in the fall which will surpass anything we have seen before. Student militancy will sweep major campuses and flow into the streets of our major cities. . . . You will see it most likely by October 15, certainly by November 15. . . . People will insist on prompt action to quell it, and we will be faced with the sole alternative of repression once the crisis is at hand. . . . Action is required, and time is running out."

The dates were not picked at random. Antiwar groups, led by young veterans of Eugene McCarthy's 1968 campaign for the presidency, had created a Vietnam Moratorium Committee. The hope was that a significant percentage of the seven million American college and university students, and faculty, would leave university classrooms on October 15 to demonstrate against the war—and they would protest again each month after that until peace was at hand.

Nixon saw protesters for the first time as president on August 21, when he left the Western White House to travel north to San Francisco for a state dinner and meetings with President Park Chung Hee of South Korea at the St. Francis Hotel. Six thousand people outside in Union Square chanted antiwar slogans for three hours as 238 invited guests were entertained by the United States Marine Band and the Army's Strolling Strings, all flown in from Washington. "It is a little noisy outside," Nixon told the Korean leader and the crowd, "but please remember that 98 percent of the American people are Korea's friends. . . ."

The President told Park privately that if there was no progress in talks with the North Vietnamese in Paris he intended to resume bombing—the plan that was called Duck Hook—probably on November 1. He kept whispering that threat to foreign leaders, apparently expecting each of them to pass the word to Hanoi. But the American people knew nothing of a deadline.

The next morning the two presidents met again. Nixon brought up the EC-121 incident of four months before, this time saying that he had made a mistake in not retaliating militarily. It would not happen again, he continued; any similar incident would be met with "massive retaliation."

Then he laid out his view of American aims in Park's part of the world:

> It is also important for us in Asia to notice the possible damage which will result from the Soviet domination of Communist China. This will temporarily remove the threat of Communist China, but we must consider a bigger threat of the Soviets backed by the enormous population of China. . . . We are thinking ahead of what will happen 25 years from now, not two or three years hence. I do not want to give the impression to the 800 million people of Communist China that they have no choice but to cooperate with the Soviet Union. . . . There are many strategies to keep our enemy divided.

On August 25, the Urban Affairs Council was flown out to San Clemente for a long, rambling meeting with the President about the New Federalism package. "We must sell this program and constantly resell it," Nixon began. "We must remind the country the program is ours and not someone else's. The liberal wing of the Democratic Party will come in with their own bills. . . . All this is like a campaign." Then he wandered off into the kind of ethnic analysis he favored in private. He told them he had just met with Cardinal James Francis McIntyre, the Archbishop of Los Angeles.

> McIntyre tells me the Mexican Americans are worse off than the Negroes. With the natural Latin volatile temperament they are supposed to have, if they blow, it will make the Negro thing look mild. There is the same problem in Arizona and Texas. . . . Working with Justice, and using L.A., check marijuana use of

blacks and browns. It is a depressant. Don't overlook the Mexican problem. I'd hate to have it blow up on us. . . .

Speaking of other areas, I've never assumed that education is the sacred cow some believe it is. It is so goddamn ridiculous to assume everyone should go to college. I'm not suggesting that there be more manual laborers. I am suggesting that, in terms of violent frustration, far more than black, white or potentially Mexican, the frustration of a man or woman with a college degree, having nothing he is prepared for, is the greatest. There is nothing for him or her to do but join the revolution.

After that, the Secretary of Commerce, Maurice Stans, opened up a discussion of "negative budgeting"—searching for government programs to eliminate or cut back. "In eighteen months," he said, speaking of his service in the Eisenhower administration, "we succeeded with only one—a program of $50,000 a year to eliminate weeds on Indian reservations."

"What are the poor Indians going to eat?" cracked Nixon.

Eyes rolled. But a couple of weeks later, working on his press conference briefing book, Nixon wrote all over a page with a question about Indians protesting discrimination by occupying Alcatraz Island, the prison in San Francisco Bay, saying, "A small political problem, but a great moral problem . . . a national disgrace . . . for 100 years."

Figuring out Nixon was a growth industry. Left to its own devices by a slowdown in news processed and distributed by the White House, the press corps began looking in other directions, using other voices to say what correspondents were thinking. The White House they knew was empty and some set up shop inside the President's head, as John Osborne of *The New Republic* had been doing.

Joseph Kraft, in his syndicated column, wrote that the great problem in the White House was Nixon's isolation, his bent toward "sweet sessions of solitary thought and reading." He offered a list of national security types who had quit or were looking for jobs for the most basic White House reason: they could not get to see the President, which meant no one in power was much interested in seeing or hearing them.

The search for the "real Nixon" led *The New York Times* and *Time* magazine to a paper presented at the annual convention of the American Political Science Association convention. The author was a thirty-nine-year-old Yale professor named James David Barber. The *Times* on September 4 and *Time* a few days later published chunks of Barber's thesis, which was that Richard Nixon was a dangerous man with wild, but predictable, mood swings. The magazine led with a quote from the paper: "The danger is that Richard Nixon will commit himself irrevocably to some disastrous course of action."

In studying Nixon and four other Presidents, Barber evolved a labeling system that types each man according to his character (positive or negative) and his way of life (active or passive). Barber listed Nixon under the heading of "active-negative."

Nixon's problem, Barber says, is failure to communicate; it stems from "a very strong drive for personal power—especially independent power—which pushes him away from reliance on anyone else." In council, Nixon listens attentively and then "retires to his chambers, where he may spend hours in complete solitude" before he "emerges and pronounces the verdict."

The flaw in style is compounded, in Barber's view, by a major character deficiency—Nixon's tendency to lapse into unguarded behavior after periods of great stress. . . . Barber even provides a scenario for future situations brought on by Nixon's "crisis syndrome"; the Administration is defeated on a key issue. . . . at a press conference, he is badgered about it and lashing out, takes an exaggerated policy stand. It is, says Barber, the stuff of "tragic drama: the danger is that he might refuse to revise his course of action in the light of consequent events."

The *Times* used many of the same quotes in its article and added this one: "When Nixon begins to feel pleasantly relaxed or playfully enjoying, I think, some danger sign goes up, some inner commandment says no, and he feels called back into the quest for worlds to conquer." *

ON SEPTEMBER 7, the Western White House began its move back to Washington. There had been little criticism of the President's absence from the capital city, though the *Newark Evening News* published a Bill Canfield cartoon showing the President on a White House tour with a guide saying, "And in here, Sir, you'll find your desk." And *The Miami*

---

* Another study, this one by psychologists Richard E. Donley and David G. Winter of Wesleyan University, published in 1970, rated modern presidents on their "need" for power or achievement. Analyzing words used in Inaugural addresses, they concluded that Nixon did not like the "power game" of accumulating influence but was driven toward visible substantive achievement. Donley and Winter rated Theodore Roosevelt as the most power-hungry president, with a numerical rating of 8.3, compared with Harry S Truman at 7.3 and Lyndon Johnson at 6.8. On the need-for-achievement scale, Nixon ranked first at 8.5, compared with Johnson at 7.5, Kennedy at 6.8, and Teddy Roosevelt at 6.2.

Herald did editorialize about the expense of it all and an "uneasy feeling. . . . we have a part-time President." But that was dismissed as Key Biscayne envy.

On its way home to Washington, *Air Force One* stopped first in Del Rio, Texas, where the President dedicated a bridge across the Rio Grande with the President of Mexico. Then the plane circled over areas damaged by the winds and rains of Hurricane Camille in Louisiana and Mississippi before landing at the municipal airport in Gulfport, Mississippi, for a ten-minute stop.

That was the plan—until the President saw the largest and most enthusiastic American crowd he had ever seen. *Time* said it was the most excited political reception correspondents had seen since Robert F. Kennedy began his presidential campaign. There were at least thirty thousand people—locals said seventy-five thousand—waiting in the hot and humid night. The number depended on which newspaper did the counting, but the reason so many came out seemed to be racial: the crowd was virtually all white. One sign read: "NOT MANY REPUBLICANS HERE, BUT LOTS OF NIXONOCRATS." They mobbed the President and Mrs. Nixon, too. He stayed there for an hour and a half, grinning and sweating—the dark dye in his hair began to run, revealing that his modest sideburns were actually gray—and glorying in the kind of cheering and touching he had missed during his long life in politics.

Alone in his seat that night as *Air Force One* flew through the night, Nixon pulled out a legal pad and began to write:

H—Tricia job

K—Hijacking plan for Cuba

Most powerful office

Each day a chance to do something memorable for someone

Need to be good to do good

Need for joy, serenity, confidence, inspirational

Goals: Set example, inspire, instill pride

1. Personal image of Presidency—Strong, compassionate, competent, bold—Joy in job

2. Nation is better in spirit at end of term

CHAPTER 8

October 15, 1969

ON SEPTEMBER 12 in Washington, the President spent the morning with Kissinger and the three top Americans in South Vietnam, Ambassador Ellsworth Bunker, General Creighton Abrams, and Admiral John S. McCain, the U.S. commander in the Pacific. The subject was troop withdrawal. Nixon wanted to bring home another 35,000 Americans before Christmas, which meant that 60,000 would have been withdrawn in Nixon's first year in office, with 484,000 still on the line. During a break, Kissinger sounded out General Abrams about stopping the scheduled court-martial of the group of Green Berets who had been charged with murdering a Vietnamese interpreter accused of spying for the North Vietnamese. He said that the President thought a court-martial would be bad for both the military and the country. The General said he wanted the men to go to trial, that Colonel Rheault, the Green Beret commander, had directly lied to him during the investigation of the case.

The day's official business done, the President, back from California less than seventy-two hours, left for Camp David with "HEHK," the latest staff system he had worked out with Haldeman. Haldeman-Ehrlichman-Harlow-Kissinger. The idea was that those four would be the only members of the staff to see the President under normal circumstances; the addition of Harlow was an attempt to get the President to spend more time focusing on congressional business and domestic affairs in general.

The plan was to spend the evening talking about White House organization and congressional relations, particularly the confirmation of Judge Haynsworth, which the President had pretty much ignored since the announcement the month before—after all, no Supreme Court nominee had been rejected in the past forty years. Attorney General Mitchell, who had selected Haynsworth, had told the President not to worry. Nor did Mitchell worry. He left the job to two conservative senators from the South, James O. Eastland of Mississippi and Ernest F. Hollings of South Carolina. It was a mistake. The judge from South Carolina was almost unknown in Washington; he had no friends but had significant adversaries, beginning with civil rights groups and organized labor. Roy Wilkins of the NAACP knew the judge's work very well, particularly a 1963 decision that equal protection under the law was not violated in Prince Edward County, Virginia, when all schools, black and white, were closed to prevent desegregation. White children had gone back to their classrooms in public schools that were now called "private" and seventeen hundred black children went without schools. George Meany, president of the AFL-CIO, said the judge was "not fit," citing his rulings in favor of a South Carolina company called Darlington Manufacturing in a long and bitter 1963 dispute with the Textile Workers of America. The judge was a small, dignified man of the old school, a wealthy pillar of the community, who casually traded small amounts of stock in companies involved in Fourth Circuit cases. The opposition seemed pro forma at first except for a handful of liberal Democrats, led by Senator Birch Bayh of Indiana, who ignored the judge's old-fashioned southern legal credentials to pick away at matters of financial disclosure.

The phone started ringing as soon as the President and his men arrived at Camp David. The press was asking more and more questions about the Green Beret affair. "A big PR problem," Nixon called it, fodder for the antiwar types. Kissinger tried to call Admiral McCain to get his private views on the case, but the answering call was from Laird, angry that the White House was going behind his back to military commanders.

"How do you suppose he knew that?" said Ehrlichman with a wicked grin. The President shook his head. "He's a sneak," Nixon said. The Army Signal Corps operated the White House Communications Agency, and J. Edgar Hoover had warned him on inauguration day that they listened in on presidential calls.

The Green Beret story, which had first surfaced in early August, became front-page news a week after the Camp David meeting. On September 19, *The New York Times* headlined:

ARMY TO TRY 6 OF 8 BERETS IN VIETNAM MURDER CASE

"TROUBLE AHEAD!" was the heading on the President's news summary that morning. The item, written by Buchanan, began: "The decision to court-martial the six Green Berets for murder is one that offers us nothing that we can see that would be to the benefit of the Administration, the Green Berets, the United States Army, or the American effort in Vietnam—and a great potential for damage to all four."

Nixon slashed two lines across the page in an unusually large hand: "K—We _must_ have a delay—work out with Mitchell, E, and Laird—a device."

Thai Khac Chuyen, officially "Agent SF7-166," had been on the payroll as an interpreter for Special Forces headquarters at Nha Trang. On May 10, after a battle in Phuoc Long province, a South Vietnamese soldier had taken a roll of film from the pocket of a dead Vietcong fighter. It was developed at Nha Trang and showed a meeting of North Vietnamese officers in a jungle clearing, and one of them was or looked like Chuyen. For weeks, Green Berets questioned Chuyen, using polygraph machines and "truth serum"—sodium pentothol—but they were unable to get him to admit he was a double agent or to prove he was the man in the photo. Finally, Colonel Rheault, the commander of the 4,500 Special Forces in country, sent three of his men to CIA headquarters in the United States embassy in Saigon. The CIA men told the Green Berets, unofficially, that they had only three options: fire Chuyen, put him back on duty, or "Get rid of him."

The Green Berets got rid of him. On June 12, Chuyen was injected with a huge dose of morphine and three officers checked out a small boat for a midnight ride into the South China Sea. Captain Robert Marasco shot him twice in the head with a CIA-designed long-barrelled .22 caliber pistol with a built-in silencer. Then they chained truck tire rims to the body and dropped it into the sea.

The next morning at 5 A.M., Rheault received a cable from Theodore Shackley, the CIA station chief in Saigon, talking about what the agency called "termination with extreme prejudice": "This is not a solution for the problem. It is immoral and has the highest flap potential. . . . Unless you can give us assurance nothing will happen to this agent, we will have no alternative but to bring it to the attention of command levels in MACV, including General Abrams."

The agent of course was already dead. Rheault cabled back that Chuyen could not be reached because he was on a mission. Shackley did not believe that and went to Abrams and Bunker. The general called Rheault, a forty-three-year-old West Point graduate from a prominent Boston family, to MACV headquarters, and the colonel repeated that he did not know anything about Chuyen. When he left, Abrams turned to an assistant and said: "He lied to me. He said they did not kill this man, but I'm sure he was lying. . . . This is murder."

By the last week of August, the press was filled with stories that Rheault and seven others were being held in a military prison and were conferring with civilian attorneys from the United States. One of the lawyers, Henry Rothblatt, appeared on ABC News, saying: "I don't intend to compromise the democratic rights of these great officers. . . . People in high places made a mistake and are refusing to admit it. . . ."

Reading that in his news summary, Nixon wrote: "K—I think Helms should be made to take part of this rap." He followed that up with orders to Haldeman, whose notes read: "Get a letter from the CIA saying they will refuse to provide witnesses for the CIA trial—executive privilege." That was the fallback plan—cite "national security"—because he and Kissinger had failed to persuade either Abrams or Secretary of the Army Stanley Resor to end the investigation and let the men go. The two men had been friends since 1944 when they first met as young army officers at the Battle of the Bulge. In fact, Lieutenant Resor's platoon, trapped by German tanks, was rescued by American tanks led by Major Abrams. They would not yield to the White House and Resor told Kissinger and Ehrlichman: "The CIA and the U.S. Army simply do not do business as the men in this case did. Spies are not taken out and killed without due process of law."

"Who'll believe that?" Ehrlichman said later.

That same day, with one eye on the beginning of the college year and the other on the "Moratorium" scheduled for October 15, the President announced a fifty-thousand-man cut in draft calls. He added that calls scheduled for January and February of 1970 would be reviewed later and might be revised depending on the progress of continuing "Vietnamization" of the war.

The principal organizers of the Moratorium were a couple of young men, Sam Brown and David Hawk, who had worked together in Gene McCarthy's presidential campaign. Hawk, a Cornell graduate, had gone to work for the National Student Association and persuaded 253 student body presidents around the country to say they would refuse induction if they were drafted—and then asked President Nixon to meet with the group. That did not happen, but Hawk and some of the students were invited to the White House and had met with Ehrlichman and Kissinger in April. The national security adviser gave them a lecture on foreign policy and credibility. Then he left and Ehrlichman said: "If you people think you can break laws just because you don't like them, you're going to force us to up the ante to the point where we're handing out death sentences for traffic violations." Then he slammed his fist on the table and walked out.

On Saturday, September 20, Nixon did meet with student leaders, 225 student council presidents, most of them from small colleges, most of them accompanied to Washington by the presidents or deans of their colleges or universities. They were about the most scrutinized and sanitized group of students in the history of the country. Months of preparation and screening went on before the 225 were selected from the thirteen hundred member institutions represented in the Association of Student Governments. Then they were invited to the capital for a conference titled "Evolution Not Revolution: A Time for Constructive Activism."

But even on that Saturday there was a good deal of tension about the scheduled meeting with the President in the East Room. The chosen 225 were coming after a day and night of roughing up administration officials, particularly Education Commissioner James Allen, with questions and angry assertions about Vietnam and the draft, drugs and racism. But inside the White House they politely listened as the President delivered his message, described by *The New Republic* as "The way to be effective is to be quiet."

"Useless," said the President to Haldeman after an hour and forty minutes of listening to the students, one of whom quietly lectured him on how to be president. "It was a mistake to even invite them." He went off to Burning Tree Country Club for a round of golf with his funniest friend, Bob Hope.

There was no secret about the purpose of the meeting or of the draft cuts. In the *New York Post,* Max Lerner, a liberal columnist, wrote: "For probably the first time ever, an Administration's military-political strategy is geared to the opening of the schools. . . . the President hopes that this combination of troop withdrawal and draft suspension will give him a longer spell of freedom from domestic confrontation."

Seeing a quote from the column, Nixon wrote: "H—Just to confuse the Libs—put him on a W.H. guest list (with Alsops et al.)." Perhaps he had a soft spot for the straightforward New York liberalism of the *Post*. Two days later, a younger *Post* columnist, Pete Hamill, praised the intelligence of the Republican candidate for the office of mayor of New York, John Marchi, who had defeated Mayor John Lindsay in the Republican primary. Nixon wrote of Hamill: "H—This fellow is a Moynihan Liberal—I still think he might be a good addition to our staff."

Instead, three men from politics, not journalism, were added to the staff. The new Nixon men were Franklyn (Lyn) Nofziger, forty-five, who had been Ronald Reagan's press secretary in California; Jeb Stuart Magruder, a thirty-four-year-old cosmetics executive who knew Haldeman, and Charles (Chuck) Colson, a thirty-eight-year-old Washington lawyer who had worked for Senator Leverett Saltonstall, a Massachusetts Republican. "We've got a tiger on our hands," said Harlow, who had seen Colson operate in the halls of the Senate. "This Colson will chew some people up."

The day of that announcement, September 23, Nixon got the White House press corps—noisy, nosy, and sloppy—out of the West Wing lobby, where they had worked since Theodore Roosevelt invited them into the building during a freezing rainstorm one day in 1901. In the early days of the Nixon administration, the press had protested and frustrated a scheme to move them to the Executive Office Building next door. This time the plan was to cover over the drained swimming pool— "Kennedy's pool," Nixon called it—and give correspondents little cubicles and a briefing room lit for television. With Haldeman tagging along, Nixon personally took the dean of the White House press corps, Merriman Smith of United Press International, and two other reporters on a tour to talk about the new plans. Smith liked the idea of larger quarters. "A fait accompli," Haldeman happily reported.

Two days later Haldeman had another piece of good news, noting: "K feels he finally has the Green Beret problem under control. The CIA has been ordered to refuse to let their men testify as witnesses. Helms really dragged his feet, but finally gave in. Now Laird has to get Resor to cancel the trial for lack of case. . . ." The CIA had caved and Nixon was sure Resor would: When Mendel Rivers called the White House that day, saying the wife of one of the accused Green Berets was in his office, the president said: "Tell her not to worry. The men will be released."

On September 26, Nixon held his first full-dress televised press conference in more than two months. Predictably, the first question was on Vietnam, the second on Judge Haynsworth.

Frank Cormier of the Associated Press asked about cutoff dates for the U.S. military in Vietnam and the President circled the question in his own way, saying that such dates might prolong the war. Using proposals for withdrawal by mid-1971 as his straw man, Nixon said: "That destroys any chance to reach the objective that I am trying to achieve, of ending the war before the end of 1970 or before the middle of 1971." Reporters piled on after that, pushing Nixon to go further than he intended. In answer to a question from Herb Kaplow of NBC News he said: "Once the enemy recognizes that it is not going to win its objective by waiting us out, then the enemy will negotiate and we will end this war before the end of 1970."

Of Haynsworth, he said: "I do not intend to withdraw the nomination. . . . I have also noted the various items that have been brought up during the course of his hearings in the Senate. I still have confidence in Judge Haynsworth's qualifications, in his integrity."

Nixon was asked about the story that led the morning newspapers. "NIXON SEEKS LINK IN SOCIAL SECURITY TO COST OF LIVING" was the *New York Times* headline. In a most un-Republican but very political move the President had called on Congress to raise Social Security payments by 10 percent and provide annual automatic cost-of-living raises. Paul Healy of the New York *Daily News* asked whether he could persuade Congress to do that when historically the idea had been rejected because it was considered a sure way to trigger inflation. Nixon replied, "I'm going to try." The President was asked, too, about school desegregation, particularly in Mississippi, and about reports he had made a deal with Senator Stennis during the summer. He answered: "Senator Stennis did speak to me. . . . But anybody who knows Senator Stennis and anybody who knows me would know that he would be the last person to say: 'Look, if you don't do what I want in Mississippi, I am not going to do what is best for this country.' He did not say that, and under no circumstances, of course, would I have acceded to it."

But, of course, that was what Stennis had said—and what Nixon did.

Finally he was asked about the October 15 Moratorium. "As far as this kind of activity is concerned, we expect it," he said. "However, under no circumstances will I be affected whatever by it." It was a bad answer. The press piled on again, accusing the President of ignoring the will or the sentiments of the people.

On September 29 Haldeman's final diary note read: "K got his Green Beret trial turned off, with Resor dropping the charges because no CIA witnesses." The news was in the papers the next morning. This time the headline in *The New York Times* was "ARMY DROPS BERETS' CASE AS C.I.A. BARS ITS AGENTS FROM TESTIFYING AT TRIAL." Secretary Resor issued a short statement: "I have been advised today that the CIA, though not directly involved in the incident, has determined that in the interests of national security, it will not make available any of its personnel as witnesses. . . . It is my judgment that under these circumstances the defendants cannot receive a fair trial. . . ." At the White House, press secretary Ron Ziegler stated: "The President had not involved himself either in the original decision to prosecute the men or in the decision to drop the charges against them." In Santa Monica, California, Daniel Ellsberg, a research analyst at the RAND Corporation, the Defense Department's favored think tank, was sure the Secretary of the Army was lying when he stated there was no pressure from the White House to drop the charges. He was angry, and his anger focused on a top-secret government study on the origins of the Vietnam War. He knew that one of the fifteen copies of the seven-thousand-page report was in a safe at RAND. He called a friend, Anthony Russo, and asked, "Tony, can you get a Xerox machine?" The two of them began to copy the study, ordered by Robert Mc-Namara when he was Secretary of Defense, page by page late that night.

THAT WEEK the President called together the first meeting of what he called the "Political Group for 1970." The Republican congressional leaders, Senator Hugh Scott of Pennsylvania and Congressman Gerald R. Ford of Michigan, were invited to Camp David along with Harlow, Dent, Nofziger, and Buchanan. "Absolutely off the record," the minutes began, then quoted the President saying: "For eight years the Democrats talked about draft reform; we have done something about draft reform. For eight years the Democrats talked about welfare reform; we have done something about welfare reform. . . . on and on down the line with postal reform, revenue sharing, etc. We have to put our party on the side of being for something rather than being on the attack which is easier and which we have been doing for so long it is a habit."

Nixon went on to say: "I do not intend to be the first American President to lose a war. We have 'turned it around' as far as world opinion is concerned. . . . By the 1970 elections, one way or the other, it is going to be over with. . . ." Then he asked Buchanan about the moratorium and the speechwriter said the President should not get involved. Nixon smiled and said, "It might be well to estimate that the opposition would get twenty-five million. . . . When they don't get it, we'll call the thing a failure."

They all had a good laugh at that one and the session broke up after two hours.

The President met with Republican leaders two days later in the White House to discuss the Haynsworth nomination. Senator Robert P. Griffin of Michigan had been delegated to deliver the bad news. He said he was speaking for several Republican senators. He began by using the name of Bobby Baker, a Lyndon Johnson protégé driven from his position as secretary of the Senate on corruption charges; Baker and Haynsworth, though they had never met, both had small investments in a South Carolina real estate deal. "Mr. President," said Griffin, "you have nominated a business partner of Bobby Baker to the United States Supreme Court. . . . Let's face it, Mr. President, Haynsworth is not above suspicion. It is not as important how things are as how they appear to be."

Griffin, who was the minority whip, then assured the President that he and Minority Leader Hugh Scott would be the last to leave the ship. "The captain will still be on the bridge," the President said. "I will not retreat."

Then, as usual, he shifted the talk to foreign affairs. The subject was Soviet nuclear missiles, and the President said: "In megatonnage the Soviet Union is now ahead of the United States, and, in total number of missiles, they have pulled abreast of the U.S. If they move as they have been moving with MIRV, they will be substantially ahead of us in a year or two. . . ."

Nixon turned to Kissinger to compare the missile balance to the situation at the time of the Cuban missile crisis at the end of 1962. The national security adviser said that the Soviets had only thirty-five strategic missiles at that time, compared with the United States' four hundred—a 15-to-1 imbalance. The President took over again, saying that when he had met with Israel's Prime Minister Golda Meir the week before, she had assumed that if the Soviet Union tried to smash Israel, the United States would move against the Soviets. "The President said perhaps we would have done that a while ago," wrote Buchanan, who was taking notes. "But that has to be doubtful now."

The congressional leaders were shaken by all that. Representative John J. Rhodes of Arizona, the deputy leader of House Republicans, said the public had to be told of Soviet gains. "There's a problem with that," said Nixon. Using the upcoming West German elections as an example, he argued that if the Socialists had an inkling of American inferiority, they would have an incentive to join with parties further to the left and win control of that government.

The last item was Vietnam, and the President made fun of the "bug-out resolutions" of Republican members, particularly Senator Charles E. Goodell, the New Yorker appointed by Governor Nelson Rockefeller after the assassination of Senator Robert Kennedy, and Representative Donald Reigle of Michigan. "That's all right. Occasionally we have to take these little boys and lead them a bit." Of Reigle, he added: "I knew he was naive, but I didn't know he was that naive."

The President left after that for a long weekend at Key Biscayne. On Friday, October 3, he called in Haldeman and Ehrlichman. Sitting in swim trunks and a sport shirt, he told them he wanted to concentrate on foreign affairs for the next six weeks. "You handle domestic without me," he said, treating the two men as co-presidents for a time. He said he needed more free time to think about Vietnam.

In fact, Kissinger had been telling him that "Vietnamization" could not work, that the only two options he had were "bug out" or "accelerate." The national security adviser wanted to accelerate. At breakfast the next morning, Kissinger sat with Bill Safire, sharing his frustrations about the war with the speechwriter.

"Are we getting anywhere?" asked Safire.

"You want my official or my private opinion?"

"Private."

Kissinger shook his head and said, "No."

On Monday, both *Time* and *Newsweek* seemed to be confirming that judgment. Reporting on Haynsworth, students and the war, and the victory of an antiwar Democrat in a special House election in a normally Republican district in Massachusetts, *Newsweek* used the cover line "Nixon in Trouble!" Inside, an anonymous Republican politician was quoted saying: "The main thing is that people are sick and goddamn tired of the war." The line over *Time*'s "National Affairs" section was "Nixon's Worst Week." In *U.S. News & World Report* it was "Nixon Staff in Disarray." In *The Washington Post* of October 6, the headline over David Broder's column was "The Breaking of the President." Broder wrote: "It is becoming more obvious with every passing day that the men and the movement that broke Lyndon B. Johnson's authority in 1968 are out to break Richard M. Nixon in 1969. The likelihood is great that they will succeed again. . . ."

Smaller things were not going all that well either. Haldeman's weekly orders from on high that week included this memo to one of his assistants, Lawrence Higby: "The President is concerned by the fact that an increasing number of birds seem to be plummeting to their death against the windows of his Oval Office; specifically, the door out to the portico. He wonders if there is some device. . . . give me a report as quickly as possible."

On Monday afternoon, Senator Edward Brooke, the Massachusetts Republican who was the only black in the Senate, announced he intended to vote against the confirmation of Judge Haynsworth. Then Senator Griffin jumped ship, sending the President a letter informing him that he would vote against confirmation. Nixon responded by sending Harlow over to try to change his mind, then telling Haldeman that Griffin had to be destroyed. Senator Griffin came into the President's office later in the day as part of the Republican congressional leadership. Not a harsh word was said. "Honest disagreement," Nixon said, smiling in the Senator's direction. Later he told the leaders: "I will stick by Haynsworth if there is only one vote left for him in the Senate. . . . If we cave in on this one, they will think that if you kick Nixon you can get somewhere. . . . I didn't get where I am today by running away from fights."

"Divert attention" was Nixon's written order to Haldeman in a Moratorium memo on October 10. Ehrlichman had just sent him a memo by Jack Caulfield, the detective in the Executive Office Building. Caulfield was spying on Moratorium planning and reported in: "The heaviest outlays of funds for mailing lists, leaflets and transportation, has come from the Socialist Worker Party. The Communist Party has maintained a background identity, but it is known to have supplied mailing lists in support of the coalition effort. . . . A very secretive meeting between nine leading governmental figures and leaders of militant organizations took place in New York City within the last 48 hours. U.S. Senators Javits and Goodell are alleged to have been present. . . . They asked for, but apparently did not receive, a commitment from the militant leaders present that there would be no violence."

"Priority: Get this out to all columnists," Nixon wrote after underlining parts of the memo. Later that day, the White House announced one diversion: the President would deliver a major policy address on Vietnam on November 3. Announcing it just before the Moratorium seemed an obvious ploy, but the President did still have the one-year anniversary of President Johnson's election-eve bombing halt in mind—and his secret July ultimatum to Ho Chi Minh. But Ho was dead at the age of seventy-nine on September 3, and the American people did not know of any deadline. Even Kissinger, pushing for a military step-up in Vietnam, was saying he learned of the Ho letter only by accident, having overheard Nixon talking about it to President Yahya Khan of Pakistan during a state visit in August.

What Kissinger did know all about was Duck Hook, the "Top Secret—Sensitive," plan to attack North Vietnam if nothing happened before November 1. "Savage, punishing" were the words he used to whip up his own staff as they crafted the plan—a scheme to destroy as much as possible in the country in four days. "We need a plan to end the war, not only to withdraw troops," Kissinger had told Nixon early in the summer. This was it: bombing of North Vietnamese cities, mining of harbors, destruction of irrigation dikes, even a ground invasion of North Vietnam and the use of tactical nuclear weapons. "I can't believe that a fourth-rate power like North Vietnam does not have a breaking point," Kissinger told his staff.

Kissinger was an extremely difficult man, brilliant, charming when it served his purpose, but harsh, moody, and duplicitous inside the White House—and vicious, too. "Our drunken friend," Kissinger would say to his staff, holding his hand over the receiver when Nixon called and was slurring his words after a drink or two at night. But he was already the indispensable man. It was not that he and the President agreed on everything—Kissinger feared that phased troop withdrawal was a sure road to defeat. What mattered was that Kissinger, like Haldeman, had become the system through which this president operated.

Whatever Kissinger knew about Nixon's ultimatum, the American public knew nothing about it—or about Duck Hook. Secretary of

State Rogers did not know and neither did Secretary of Defense Laird, who continued diligently pushing "Vietnamization" as the only way out of Vietnam. It was also not clear how much North Vietnamese leaders knew. Finally realizing that the ultimatum and the attack plan meant nothing if all of this was only in his own head, the President himself leaked some of the details of Duck Hook—or he told nine senators about it, which amounted to the same thing. Just before the Moratorium (and two weeks before his speech) those details appeared around the country in the syndicated column of Rowland Evans and Robert Novak. Kissinger's plan to bring the North Vietnamese to their knees evolved from Nixon's big secret to his big bluff. The President activated part of Duck Hook in mid-October, ordering the nuclear bombers of the Strategic Air Command on full alert to attract the attention of spies around the world. The idea was that someone, presumably the Soviets, would alert and frighten the North Vietnamese.

Nixon's "madman theory." He wanted leaders in Hanoi to fear him as a madman capable of reducing their country to ashes rather than be seen as a loser. But the men running North Vietnam either did not notice or did not care. They were busily issuing statements to cheer on the Moratorium organizers. The last one ended: "The struggle of the Vietnamese people and U.S. progressive people against U.S. aggression will certainly be crowned with total victory. May your fall offensive succeed splendidly."

Time seemed to be running out for Nixon. Sixty-four members of Congress were publicly supporting the Moratorium. The national Gallup poll in June had shown that 47 percent of respondents backed the President's Vietnam policies and 45 percent opposed them. The September numbers were 35 percent in support and 57 percent in opposition. One factor in the decline was a summer issue of *Life* that ran the photograph of almost every one of the 251 young Americans killed in Vietnam in one week, and said: "We must pause to look into the faces."

In those pre-Moratorium struggles over public perception, the President countered with an open letter to a student. The student, selected by his speechwriters, was a Georgetown University sophomore named Randy J. Dicks, who had written a letter to the White House saying: "Your statement at your recent press conference that 'under no circumstances' will you be affected by the impending anti-war protests, in connection with the 'Viet Nam Moratorium' is ill-considered to say the least. It has been my impression that it is not unwise for the President of the United States to take note of the will of the people."

Stating that he was the one on the road to peace, the President, in words written by a Kissinger assistant named Anthony Lake, answered:

"To listen to public opinion is one thing; to be swayed by public demonstrations is another. . . . Whatever the issue, to allow government policy to be made in the streets would destroy the democratic process. . . . It would invite anarchy." The press predictably descended on Georgetown, finding Dicks in a French class. He repeated his criticism of Nixon, then offered some criticism of democracy, too. It turned out he was president of the Student Monarchist Society.

ON MORATORIUM DAY, October 15, 1969, more than twenty thousand people demonstrated in Washington, at one point forming themselves into a field of candles flickering on the Mall from the Washington Monument to the fence at the back of the White House grounds. Hundreds of thousands more demonstrated in cities around the country—a hundred thousand in Boston, thirty thousand in New Haven, at least fifty thousand in New York. Martin Luther King Jr.'s widow, Coretta Scott King, spoke in Washington. Senators Eugene McCarthy and Charles Goodell and entertainers Shirley MacLaine and Woody Allen spoke in midtown Manhattan. On Wall Street the speaker was Bill Moyers, who had been Lyndon Johnson's press secretary. The television networks ran ninety-minute prime-time specials, asking Sam Brown and David Hawk and other Moratorium figures respectful questions about their views and goals. Walter Cronkite of CBS News said that night: "Historic in its scope. Never before had so many demonstrated their hope for peace."

Of Cronkite, Nixon wrote on his news summary: "A nothing!"

The White House was a tense place, prepared for war, but not for the singing and candle-lighting of thousands upon thousands of well-dressed, well-spoken Americans asking the President to give peace a chance. Kissinger's moods were as up and down as the President's, so much so that Nixon ordered Haldeman to talk to the national security adviser and tell him that his gloomy overreaction to any criticism was dragging down the morale of staffers reading his face for news of war and protest. Ehrlichman was below the White House in the bomb-shelter war room, listening in on the walkie-talkie conversations of the young organizers. Reporting to him by walkie-talkie was the Justice Department's man on the street, John Dean, a Mitchell assistant, who began, "They seem to be nice people."

Two of Ehrlichman's children were demonstrating at their schools. Haldeman's daughter Susan was demonstrating at Stanford in Palo Alto, California, along with Ehrlichman's son Peter. Vice President Agnew's fourteen-year-old daughter Kim wanted to join the crowds, but he was able to stop her. William Watts, a Kissinger assistant working on the November 3 speech, came up from his National Security Council office for fresh air and saw his wife and daughter walk by outside the White House fence holding their candles.

"The Moratorium was a success," Pat Moynihan reported to Nixon in a candid memo. "In style and content it was everything the organizers could have hoped for. The young white middle-class crowds were sweet-tempered and considerate, at times even radiant. . . . I believe the administration has been damaged. . . . If we are going to get through this period, we are going to have to act a lot smarter than we have done lately."

Near the other end of the White House's political spectrum, Pat Buchanan wrote to Nixon: "The war in Vietnam will now be won or lost on the American front. . . . Americans are confused and uncertain and beginning to believe that they may be wrong and beginning to feel themselves the moral inferiors of the candle-carrying peaceniks who want to get out now."

This period on the American front was going to continue. The idea was to demonstrate again every month, on the fifteenth day. November 15 was next. The President walked through October 15 as a business-as-usual day; he spent the afternoon in a two-hour meeting, discussing the 1970 budget with a dozen of the economic advisers he regularly tried to avoid. But he was shaken, thinking that he had been beaten this day, believing his secret ultimatum to the North Vietnamese and Duck Hook were both dead. If he moved militarily, the hundreds of thousands in the streets might be millions.

THE NEXT DAY the political counterattack began. The President convened a secret group he called the "Middle America Committee." Its self-description was as follows: "This committee is composed of White House staffers who understand politics and are very much interested in reaching the Middle America group for the President and the long-range advantage of the Republican Party. The members are: Pat Buchanan, Clark Mollenhoff, Martin Anderson, Tom Huston, Bud Krogh, Lyn Nofziger and Harry Dent. We will ask for assistance from outside sources and others within the White House from time to time, but this will be done in a way that will not reveal the committee's existence or compromise candid discussions within the committee. . . ." *

---

* Anderson, a conservative Stanford professor, was an Arthur Burns assistant. Mollenhoff was a former reporter for *The Des Moines Register,* and Egil "Bud" Krogh was an Ehrlichman protégé.

Notes of the first meeting defined the constituency: "The large and politically powerful white middle class is deeply troubled, primarily over the erosion of what they consider to be their values. They believe that as individuals they have lost control of a complicated and impersonal society which oppresses them with high taxes, spiraling inflation and enforced integration, while rewarding the very poor and very rich. . . ."

Three days later, on October 19, at a $100-a-plate Republican fund-raiser in New Orleans, Vice President Agnew, delegated by the President but reading words he had mostly written himself, began the hard-hitting rhetorical phase of Nixon's dividing of America, saying, "The recent Vietnam Moratorium is a reflection of the confusion that exists in America today. . . . A spirit of national masochism prevails, encouraged by an effete corps of impudent snobs who characterize themselves as intellectuals."

Agnew went on, to repeated applause, hitting a dozen hot buttons within his reach: "The hardcore dissidents and the professional anarchists within the so-called 'peace movement' . . . refused to disassociate themselves from the objectives enunciated by the enemy in Hanoi. . . . We seem to be approaching an age of the gross. . . . Those who claim to speak for the young overwhelm themselves with drugs and artificial stimulants. . . . Education is being redefined to suit the ideas of the uneducated. . . . The lessons of the past are ignored and obliterated in a contemporary antagonism known as the generation gap."

The next night, at another $100-a-plate dinner that drew twenty-four hundred guests in Jackson, Mississippi, he continued, this time with help from Safire and Buchanan back in the White House: "For too long the South has been punching the bag for those who characterize themselves as liberal intellectuals. . . . We have among us a glib, activist element . . . nattering nabobs of negativism . . . snobs for most of them disdain to mingle with the masses who work for a living. . . . Americans cannot afford to divide over their demagoguery—or be deceived by their duplicity—or to let their license destroy liberty. We can, however, afford to separate them from our society—with no more regret than we should feel over discarding rotten apples from a barrel."

THE PRESIDENT had begun working on his own speech, the November 3 national address on the Vietnam War. Alone in his EOB hideaway, he wrote across the top of his legal pad: "Don't Get Rattled—Don't Waver—Don't React."

Nixon took great pride in the fact that he wrote his own most important speeches—or edited speechwriters so much that their work became his—something fewer and fewer modern politicians did anymore. In fact, like his hero Woodrow Wilson, Nixon believed writing—clarifying and transferring ideas into enlightening and persuasive rhetoric—was the most important part of the presidency. That was something James Barber, the Yale political scientist, had caught. "In assaying Nixon's personal style the easiest place to begin is with the elimination of personal relations as a primary focus for his energies in adapting to political roles," he had written. "Nixon has been a very hard worker but with very few exceptions this has been hard work in preparing and delivering speeches. His conscious investment in rhetorical calculations has been immense. . . . Nixon has devoted his intelligence to figuring out how to speak and act in such a way as to convey a desired impression. He attends his own performances carefully."

So it was this time. The President was spending twelve-hour days and sleepless nights in Washington and at Camp David working through his own thinking about the war—he wrote at least twelve drafts of the speech—asking basic questions of staff, of friends, of political enemies. Mostly, though, he asked himself. The others, including Kissinger, did not know what he was thinking or exactly why he was asking. Outsiders, and his own staff, too, assumed that the President had two principal options: in the most dramatic of choices, an all-out effort on the secret Duck Hook model to force North Vietnam to negotiate—or just get the hell out of there.

Much of the advice he solicited was polar or contradictory. "What would you think if we decided to escalate?" he asked Sir Robert Thompson, the British general credited with defeating communist insurgents in Malaya in the 1950s. Thompson answered that he thought protests at home and abroad would destroy Nixon's administration. But then he added that he thought the United States could win the war over two years with "Vietnamization," building up the South Vietnamese military as the South Korean military had been built up to hold off North Korea in the mid-1950s.

"We should see it through?" Nixon asked.

"Absolutely," Thompson answered. "In my opinion the future of Western civilization is at stake in the way you handle yourselves in Vietnam."

At the other end of the spectrum, Senate Majority Leader Mike Mansfield told him in a memo: "The continuance of the war in Vietnam, in my opinion, endangers the future of this nation. . . . Most serious are the deep divisions in our society to which this conflict of dubious origin and purpose is contributing."

President Nixon was in his element. Alone. Alone with his yellow pads and his thoughts. Those closest to him still did not know what he was going to say, did not know which way he was going. One of the few breaks he took from his task was to sit for an hour, an angry hour, with the Soviet ambassador, Anatoly Dobrynin. The meeting was important because the ambassador was delivering the news that his superiors in Moscow were ready to go ahead with Strategic Arms Limitation Treaty talks to limit production and tests of strategic nuclear weapons. SALT talks—first scheduled for late 1968 by President Johnson but cancelled when Soviet troops invaded Czechoslovakia—would now begin again in mid-November in Helsinki, Finland. The American team was to be headed by Gerard C. Smith, head of the Arms Control and Disarmament Agency, and among its members were Llewellyn Thompson, the State Department's ranking Soviet expert, and Paul H. Nitze, a former deputy secretary of defense, with whom Nixon had worked over the years. The President called in Nitze and told him that he did not trust Smith and he did not trust Secretary of State Rogers either. He asked Nitze to report to Kissinger on what was happening in Helsinki, saying Kissinger would pass the reports on to him. Nitze said he thought that would destroy the delegation. "Well," Nixon said, "I've described the back-channel communications available to you. If you see something going wrong, contact Kissinger, or me through Kissinger."

The talk with Dobrynin quickly turned to Vietnam. The written instructions the ambassador carried included this line: "Moscow feels the President should be frankly told that the method of solving the Vietnam question through the use of military force is not only without perspective, but also extremely dangerous. . . ."

Nixon pushed a yellow pad across his desk and told the Russian to take notes. He launched into a monologue, talking about his own disappointment that there seemed to be no Soviet-American cooperation on any issue during his nine months in office—beginning with Vietnam. He said he believed that the Russians did not want the war to end.

"You may think you can break me," Nixon continued. "You may believe that the American domestic situation is unmanageable. . . . All you have done is repeat the same tired old slogans that the North Vietnamese used six months ago. You know very well they can lead nowhere. It is time to get discussions started, because I can assure you, the humiliation of a defeat is absolutely unacceptable to my country." There was more. Finally the President said, "Let me repeat that we will not hold still for being diddled to death in Vietnam."

When Dobrynin tried to respond, Nixon stood up, walked around the desk, shook his hand, and walked him to the door. Kissinger, sitting in, was excited, speaking as soon as the door closed: "Extraordinary . . . No President has ever laid it on the line to them like that."

Soon enough, Kissinger himself got a bit of the same treatment. The national security adviser was opposed to withdrawal schedules and worried that Nixon might bow to the antiwar protests. The President already knew that, and he interrupted Kissinger's regular morning briefing on October 27 by standing up and saying, "Well, that's all for today, have to get to work."

He did not want to talk. He was focused on the speech, sending two brief memos to Kissinger:

> I would like one brief paragraph, 100 words or less, on the reason we intervened in Vietnam in the first place. I am not sure that I will cover this point but I want a paragraph or two submitted to me for my consideration. . . .

"Is it possible we were wrong from the start in Vietnam?"

Nixon was a man capable of iron discipline. He wrote alone. He was not thrown off at all by the destruction of his anti-busing schemes and deceptions. On October 30, the Supreme Court shocked most of Washington with a decision on the NAACP Legal Defense Fund's challenge to the desegregation delay he had personally ordered—after Stennis threatened to abandon the fight for an ABM system—in the case of the thirty-three Mississippi school districts still not in compliance with court orders. The decision was unanimous, the first major decision handed down since Warren Burger took over as chief justice: the court ordered the Mississippi districts and every other district with a dual school system to desegregate "at once." It was the legal end of "all deliberate speed," the language of the Warren court in 1954.

The New York Times interpretation read: "The decision was a stinging setback for the Nixon administration. The Justice Department had argued less than a week ago that delays were permissible in some districts. . . . The effect of today's decision is to write a legal end to the period during which courts have entertained various excuses for failure to integrate Southern schools. Its basic message was integrate now, litigate later."

The principal White House response was a statement from press secretary Ziegler: "The administration will carry out the mandate of the Court. . . ." The President did not comment, perhaps thinking that now the White House was finally out of it. When Haldeman told him of the decision, Nixon smiled and said, "Now let's see how they enforce it."

That night, he was alone in the pre-dawn, writing: "They can't defeat us militarily in Vietnam. They can't break South Vietnam. Include a paragraph on why we are there. They cannot break us." At eight o'clock in the morning on November 1, Nixon called Haldeman from Camp David and said, "The baby's just been born."

He stayed out of Washington for a day more, memorizing the speech. It was a matter of great pride to Nixon that he could do that—like Winston Churchill, like Charles de Gaulle. He enjoyed quoting from a conversation he had with Churchill's son and biographer, Randolph Churchill, who said: "My father spends the best hours of his life writing out his extemporaneous speeches." Leonard Garment, one of Nixon's assistants and a former law partner, who had once been a professional musician, told others in the White House that he thought Nixon had learned to memorize at the piano. The President could not read music and had memorized the finger movements and tempos of hundreds of pieces beginning with "Home on the Range."

In his last meeting with congressional leaders before the speech, the President sat patiently through a Kissinger briefing on strategic missile construction and testing by the Soviet Union. "I am astounded and shocked by their progress," Kissinger began, then reeled off a half-hour recital of numbers. But as soon as the subject turned to Vietnam and the speech, Nixon took over, beginning by saying that the day before was the first day since 1965 that not one American had been killed there. Then he said there would be no advance copies of the text of the speech for anyone, including them. "It will be candid," he added toward the end of the meeting. "The American people are going to hear the truth."

THE "TRUTH," as Nixon presented it on the three television networks at 9:30 P.M. on November 3, was this: "Let us understand that the question before us is not whether some Americans are for peace and some Americans are against peace. The question at issue is not whether Johnson's war becomes Nixon's war." Then he did make it Nixon's war.

"There were some who urged that I end the war at once," he said. "This would have been a popular and easy course to follow. . . . But I had a greater obligation than to think only of the years of my administration and the next election. I had to think of the effect of my decision on the next generation and the future of peace and freedom in America and in the world. . . . This first defeat in our Nation's history would result in a collapse of confidence in American leadership, not only in Asia but throughout the world."

Then the President laid out, in significant detail, a list of American settlement initiatives—including his letter to Ho Chi Minh—and asserted that if there was no peace it was because Hanoi did not want peace. And he outlined again the Nixon Doctrine. The United States would back its friends economically and militarily but would not fight their wars. Kneading history a bit, he said that was what Vietnamization and withdrawing American troops was about. He added: "If I conclude that increased enemy action jeopardizes our remaining forces in Vietnam, I shall not hesitate to take strong and effective measures to deal with that situation."

Finally, he got to the hardest part, the words he had worked over and over. He began by saying he was addressing young people: "I respect your idealism. I share your concern for peace. I want peace as much as you do." Then he continued, trying actually to isolate young people and other antiwar activists:

> Let historians not record that when America was the most powerful nation in the world we passed on the other side of the road and allowed the last hopes for peace and freedom of millions of people to be suffocated by the forces of totalitarianism. And so tonight—to you, the great silent majority of Americans—I ask for your support. . . . The more support I can have from the American people, the sooner that pledge can be redeemed.
>
> Let us be united for peace. Let us be united against defeat. . . . North Vietnam cannot defeat or humiliate the United States. Only Americans can do that.

Seventy million Americans watched him call on the "silent majority" to silence the noisy minority. One correspondent among the many who offered live television analysis after the President concluded provided an accurate understanding of what had happened. Tom Jarriel, the White House correspondent of ABC News, said: "The President tonight perhaps has polarized attitude in the country more than it has ever been into groups that are either for him or against him."

The President was not sure how well he had done. As the television lights were being carried out of the Oval Office, without even glancing at post-speech analysis on the networks, Nixon told Haldeman to make sure one hundred letters complaining about that analysis were sent out by Republican state committees and the letters-to-editor writers in the bowels of the Executive Office Building. "I want dirty, vicious ones to the *Times* and *Washington Post* about their editorials," he added—this before the editorials were written.

He needn't have bothered. The gamble was determining whether or not he had a majority. He did.

A quick national Gallup poll by phone indicated 77 percent approval of the President's message. A few days later Gallup's overall approval rating for the President had climbed from 52 percent before the Moratorium to 68 percent. Congressional resolutions expressing bipartisan support for the President's position were signed by 300 of the House's 435 members and 58 of the 100 senators. The President pulled a surprise, going to the Capitol without notice to tell members in joint session: "When the lives of our young men are involved, we are not Democrats, we are not Republicans, we are Americans."

More than fifty thousand telegrams and, a bit later, thirty thousand letters came to the White House, almost all of them praising the President. The White House, with the help of Republican state committees, some unions, and the American Legion and Veterans of Foreign Wars had organized letter-writing campaigns, but the numbers were great enough to indicate that most came from real people out there, citizens who respected and trusted their president. The next day, the chairman of the Federal Communications Commission, Dean Burch, called the networks and asked them to send transcripts of their analysis to the commission so they could be judged for fairness—just an unfriendly reminder that the government regulated the industry and had the power to renew or refuse station licensing.

"The euphoria continues," Haldeman wrote in his diary. The next day, the Republicans won close gubernatorial races in New Jersey and Virginia after the President had campaigned in both states. Secretaries were still bringing in telegrams and piling them on the President's desk and they stayed there for several days before Nixon would let anyone remove them. "Fifty years ago at this very desk, President Woodrow Wilson spoke words which caught the imagination of a war-weary world," Nixon had told his war-weary nation. He did not know that the Wilson who used the desk was Henry Wilson, a shoemaker by trade who became a senator from Massachusetts and then President Ulysses S. Grant's vice president. No matter. Nixon had his feet up among the telegrams, telling anyone who came in: "We've got those liberal bastards on the run now!"

CHAPTER 9

December 8, 1969

Richard Nixon made a mistake when he chose Governor Spiro T. Agnew of Maryland as his running mate in 1968. The governor looked good and seemed impressive enough to people who did not know him very well—a group that included Nixon. "There's a mystique about this man . . . ," said Nixon. "You can just look at him and see he's got 'It.' " Agnew, the son of a Greek immigrant, worked his way through college, was an infantry company commander in World War II, came back home to finish law school at night—and left the Greek Orthodox Church and the Democratic Party to become an Episcopalian and a Republican in the process. He drifted into electoral politics from a PTA presidency in the suburbs of Baltimore at just the right time, when those suburbs were shifting toward Nixon's party. He became a county executive and was elected governor of a state balanced between South and North in 1966, when the Democratic candidate turned out to be a racist or did a pretty good imitation of one. Then there were race riots in Baltimore in April of 1968 and Agnew gained some national attention by calling in moderate black leaders, the ministers and NAACP types, and literally reading them the riot act, saying they were silently complicit with the "circuit-riding, Hanoi-visiting, caterwauling, riot-inciting, burn-America-down type of leader."

He did not look good to those who watched a bit more closely or a bit longer than Nixon had. That included *The Washington Post,* which covered Maryland politics closely. In an editorial written by one of the paper's stars, Ward Just, the *Post* offered this opinion as the 1968 campaign unfolded: "Nixon's decision to name Agnew may come to be regarded as perhaps the most eccentric political appointment since the Roman emperor Caligula named his horse a consul."

Agnew was a quick study, but essentially an ignorant man. His nomination was a stunning surprise and Nixon loved that. But Nixon had talked to the man only a couple of times. Within weeks of the nomination, Agnew was campaigning by using the phrases of the red-baiting 1950s, the era of Joseph McCarthy, calling Vice President Hubert Humphrey "squishy-soft on communism." In Chicago, explaining that he was without prejudice, he used the word "Polack." Asked why he did not campaign in poor neighborhoods, he said, "If you've seen one slum, you've seen them all."

At that point, concerned Nixon assistants leaked the uncheckable, saying that their man had a tested IQ of 135. One of the campaign aides dispatched to watch Agnew, Stephen Hess, was asked about the mystique and "It." He answered, "Whatever 'It' is, I hope it's not catching." Democrats had a definition. One of their last television commercials in the election campaign was a thirty-second spot with the words "President Agnew" on a black screen; the sound track was laughter.

President Nixon did not quite know what to do with Vice President "Ted" Agnew. But he did sympathize; he had suffered his own hurts as President Eisenhower's unseen vice president. Nixon liked underdogs; he always saw himself as one. Also, Agnew was a pretty aggressive fellow, showing up whether or not he was asked. Pat Buchanan and Bill Safire, the speechwriters, both liked working with Agnew; the man did not take himself as seriously as the President did and he would say most anything they wrote for him.

Then Pat Buchanan came to the President with an idea. He primed "the Old Man" with quotes from the networks' live analysis after the November 3 Vietnam speech. "He doesn't seem to be any different from Mr. Johnson or Secretary Rusk," said Eric Sevareid on CBS. The network's diplomatic correspondent, Marvin Kalb, offered the opinion that the President misunderstood the North Vietnamese response to the Ho Chi Minh letter. "No new initiative, no new proposal, no announcement of any new troop withdrawals," said Frank Reynolds on ABC before he turned to a guest analyst, W. Averell Harriman, who had been an aggressive architect of the war policy of Presidents Kennedy and Johnson.

"Let Agnew go after these guys!" Buchanan told Nixon.

At the beginning of the summer the Vice President had turned down an invitation to speak at the Midwestern Regional Republican Conference, scheduled for November 13 in Des Moines, Iowa. Two days before the event, the White House called and said the Vice President was coming—and he was going to talk about television news. Buchanan wrote the speech and Nixon personally edited it. The text was sent to the three networks with a request for live coverage. This paragraph was underlined:

> A small group of men, numbering perhaps no more than a dozen anchormen, commentators and executive producers, settle upon the film and commentary that is to reach the public. They decide what forty or fifty million Americans will learn of the day's events in the nation and in the world.

"This small and unelected elite," Agnew called them, and went on: "Whether what I've said to you tonight will be seen or heard at all by the nation is not my decision, it's their decision." All three networks decided to carry the speech live. "The purpose of my remarks tonight is to focus your attention on this little group of men who . . . wield a free hand in selecting, presenting and interpreting the great issues of our Nation," Agnew began, putting them in their place on the American map. "To a man, these commentators and producers live and work in the geographical and intellectual confines of Washington, D.C., or New York City . . . they talk constantly to one another, thereby providing artificial reinforcement to their shared viewpoints."

As for their role, Agnew reached a bit.

> When Winston Churchill rallied public opinion to stay the course against Hitler's Germany, he did not have to contend with a gaggle of commentators raising doubts about whether he was reading public opinion right, or whether Britain had the stamina to see the war through.
>
> The American who relies on television for his news might conclude that the majority of American students are embittered radicals, that the majority of black Americans feel nonregard for their country, that violence and lawlessness are the rule. . . . As with other American institutions, perhaps it is time that the networks were made more responsive to the views of the nation and more responsible to the people they serve. . . .

The speech was a sensation. Agnew had said, "They can elevate men from local obscurity to national prominence within a week," and his new eminence certainly proved the point. The President loved it. "This really flicks the scab off," he said to Buchanan after his first reading of the text.

On November 20 in Mobile, Alabama, Agnew made a second speech attacking the press. This time he focused on the two newspapers most read by national political leaders, *The Washington Post* and *The New York Times*. His tone was milder and his points resonated: the Post Company not only had the biggest newspaper in town, it also controlled *Newsweek* magazine, a Washington television station, and the city's all-news radio station; the *Times* practically had "diplomatic immunity" from criticism coming from politicians.

Reporting to the President after the Mobile speech, Buchanan said: "Those who were laughing three weeks ago are now writing columns about the danger of Agnewism . . . he has become the acknowledged spokesman of the Middle American, the Robespierre of the Great Silent Majority. . . . Another positive is that the Veep succeeded in knocking the Mobilization off the front pages of both national news magazines."

"Right!" the President wrote on the memo. *Time*'s cover was a photograph of some of the fifteen thousand clean-cut young people and the many American flags at the Washington Monument—not on Mobe day but on Veterans' Day, November 11—and the headline was, "COUNTERATTACK ON DISSENT." At the same time, a $500,000 advertising campaign, financed by a young Dallas millionaire named H. Ross Perot, the founder of a data-processing company, urged Americans across the country to send letters of support to the White House.

The New Mobilization Committee to End the War in Vietnam, called "the Mobe" by most everyone, was organizing the second of the planned monthly antiwar demonstrations. The Moratorium had been run basically by veterans of Senator Eugene McCarthy's antiwar presidential campaign. There was a rougher edge to Mobe planning, because it involved such groups as Students for a Democratic Society, the Socialist Worker Party, and the Weathermen, an SDS spinoff intended to "lead white kids into armed revolution." The demonstrations, starting with another candlelight march around the White House—the "March Against Death"—happened to begin a couple of hours before Agnew spoke in Des Moines. Even though there were more protesters in Washington—more than three hundred thousand this time by White House counts done on aerial photos of the crowd—Senators Edward Kennedy, Edmund S. Muskie, and Jacob K. Javits, who endorsed the Moratorium, refused to do the same for the Mobe. Chants included "Two, Four, Six, Eight—Organize and Smash the State!"

Coverage was different, too; there was no live network television coverage of demonstrations over the weekend. *Time,* accepting Nixon's assertions, reported: "The week's activity nationwide served to emphasize that those who want an immediate end to the war, regardless of consequences, still represent a minority."

The President himself divided his time between bowling, watching the Ohio State–Purdue football game on television, and, at one point, visiting with Haldeman, who was coordinating activity in the bomb shelter deep below the White House. Nixon said it was like watching a movie, wondering what would happen next. He suggested using helicopters to blow out the demonstrators' candles. Then he went to Cape Kennedy, Florida, on board his own helicopter, *Marine One,* to watch the liftoff of Apollo 12, man's second flight to the moon, leaving behind a White House surrounded by a barrier of empty buses.

There was some violence. More than a thousand young people led by Weathermen and other declared revolutionaries charged the Embassy of South Vietnam, throwing rocks before being driven away by police and volleys of tear gas. At the Justice Department, where there were a few hundred people, some pulled down the American flag and ran up a Vietcong banner before being driven back.

But that was a sideshow. On the Mall hundreds of thousands of Americans of all ages were singing the Beatles' "Give Peace a Chance" to drown out SDS obscenities, then chanting like college cheerleaders: "What do we want?" *"Peace!"* "When do we want it?" *"Now!"*

Despite the size of the crowd, the Mobe came and went in forty-eight hours. On the second day, coincidentally, the story surfaced of an incident in Vietnam more than a year and a half earlier, while President Johnson was still in office. A reporter named Seymour M. Hersh, who had left the Associated Press to become Eugene McCarthy's campaign press secretary in 1968, distributed a story, published in only thirty newspapers around the country, about a massacre of civilians, of women and children, by a U.S. Army unit on March 16, 1968. The details were not clear—there was even confusion about the name of the village, which the U.S. military called "Pinkville" and designated a "free-fire zone," but others called My Lai 4, a hamlet within a village area called Son My. Hersh's story asserted that 350 to 500 Vietnamese had been killed by soldiers of C Company, First Battalion, Eleventh Infantry of the Americal Division. At the time, My Lai was reported as a victory in the Army newspaper *Stars and Stripes,* which headlined: "U.S. Troops Surround Reds, Kill 128." The action also made the front page of *The New York Times,* which reported: "American troops caught a North Vietnamese force in a pincer movement on the central coastal plain yesterday, killing 128 enemy soldiers in day-long fighting."

Hersh's accounts charged that the Army had covered up the incident until a soldier named Ronald Ridenhour wrote letters to newspapers in April. Though the public did not know about the charges, the Army did investigate and, without releasing any details, on September 5 had ordered the court martial of Lieutenant William L. Calley Jr. of Miami, a twenty-six-year-old platoon commander in Company C. The court martial charges connected Calley to 109 "unlawful" civilian deaths. Defense Secretary Laird said he had informed the President of the investigation while he was at San Clemente in August, and that Nixon had said go ahead. *The New York Times* picked up the story two days later, reporting from Vietnam that villagers said the death count was 567, including women and children. Within a few days, Secretary of the Army Resor was appearing before a joint meeting of the Senate and House Armed Services Committees, a closed meeting, showing colored slides, collected by the Army, of the incident at My Lai. Some members came out looking ill; one of them, Senator Daniel K. Inouye of Hawaii, who had lost an arm in combat during World War II, said, "I thought I would be hardened, but I must say I'm sickened."

The first Gallup poll after the Mobe showed Nixon at new highs, with a 68 percent approval rating. But those numbers had not helped Haynsworth. On November 21, the Senate voted fifty-five to forty-five against his confirmation as a Supreme Court justice. The President was as angry as he was newly popular. During one of several tantrums over the courts and Haynsworth and also over the increasing coverage and investigations of the My Lai killings, the President slammed his desk and said, "It's those dirty rotten New York Jews."

Actually, if anyone was to blame for the Haynsworth defeat, it was Mitchell. Trusting in Senators Eastland and Hollings, the Attorney General turned the core of Haynsworth's defense over to the head of his Office of Legal Counsel, a forty-five-year-old Arizona lawyer named William H. Rehnquist. "The clown," Nixon called Rehnquist because of his bright shirts (usually pink), and scraggly sideburns. But Mitchell thought the young man was as smart as lawyers come. Rehnquist's major effort was a sixteen-page brief rebutting the conflict-of-interest charges, a legalistic defense against a political attack. The brief, citing precedent and criminal codes, was sent to John Ehrlichman at the White House, who gave it to the President in mid-October. Nixon marked it up before putting it in the middle drawer of the Wilson desk. The President's principal effort for his nominee was to call forty reporters into his office after reading Rehnquist's brief. The most notable thing about that session was not what Nixon said but the fact that the official transcript was casually doctored to change the President's words and meanings. He made a joke about Haynsworth's real estate holdings, saying he should buy next to a

Coast Guard station—as Nixon had done in San Clemente—and then said that he would not let Haynsworth withdraw before the vote. The joke and the pledge, which might have been marginally embarrassing, were simply edited out of the transcript.

The President wanted revenge after the vote, particularly against the seventeen Republican senators who joined Democrats in rejecting Haynsworth or in voting against funding the ABM. On November 24, he sent a three-page memo to "HEHK"—Haldeman, Ehrlichman, Harlow, Kissinger: "With regard to all those who opposed, I want one general rule followed without deviation. You are undoubtedly going to have instances where people like Griffin, Schweicker, Percy et al."—Robert Griffin of Michigan, Richard Schweicker of Pennsylvania, and Charles Percy, Republican senators who sometimes voted against the White House line—"may contact members of the White House staff indicating their willingness to support us in the next nomination or on some other issue which may be coming up. They will, of course, when we are sure to win it. I want the answer in each case to be along these lines: 'Thank you very much but the President wants you to feel free to vote your politics on this issue. He doesn't need you on this one.' . . . I think the best line to follow in the future with them is not to discuss anything with them and if they complain simply say we wanted to honor their request that we not exert White House pressure. . . . None of them should get in to see me."

ALL IN ALL, though, Nixon was in a pretty good mood, in his own way. A couple of days after Haynsworth was rejected, Kissinger came into the Oval Office to say that he had received a number of telegrams from Harvard praising a November 25 presidential statement announcing that the United States intended to destroy its stores of biological weapons and lethal chemical weapons. Nixon looked up with a half smile and said, "Henry, the wires would really pour in from Harvard if I surrendered the United States to Kosygin." Then on Thanksgiving Day, November 27, he hosted a White House lunch for 230 invited old folk, some in their nineties, with all of his family and President Eisenhower's son John and his wife and children. As Pat Nixon and daughters and the Eisenhowers sat down with their guests, the President went upstairs to the residence and ate alone, his usual cottage cheese.

He flew to Key Biscayne for the holiday weekend with his family later that afternoon, then was back in Washington four days later for another historic first of sorts. The first lottery under the new Selective Service Act he had pushed was held on December 1. A huge glass bowl filled with 365 blue capsules was set up and the capsules were drawn and opened one by one. The first date pulled was September 14, the next April 24, then December 30; nineteen-year-olds born on those dates in 1951 would be the first drafted. Most, if not all, of the men whose birth dates were drawn after the halfway mark of 182 would almost certainly never be called.

On the day he returned, the President sent Haldeman his first marching orders for the new year, an election year: "One of our most important projects for 1970 is to see that our major contributors funnel all their funds through us. . . . we can see that they are not wasted in overheads or siphoned off by some possible venal types on the campaign committees. . . . we can also see that they are used more effectively than would be the case if the candidates receive them directly."

Haldeman; Secretary of Commerce Maurice H. Stans, who was an experienced political fund-raiser; Harry Dent; and Dent's assistant, John Gleason, met in the White House to set up a secret fund-raising operation designed to bypass the Republican National Committee. The idea was to deliver 1970 campaign funds to Republican candidates favored by the President and to keep the money away from "bad Republicans," the kind who had voted against Haynsworth. "The Town House Project" was the name they chose early in December because the project had to be in private offices. The first list of potential contributors included W. Clement Stone, a Chicago insurance tycoon; Donald Kendall of PepsiCo; and H. Ross Perot. The project was one of several secret money-drop operations controlled by the President. One was run by Bebe Rebozo and included fifty thousand dollars delivered to Key Biscayne in mid-September by an employee of Howard Hughes.

The President scheduled the eighth and last news conference of his first year in office for December 8. He went to Camp David for the weekend to prepare, then came back on Monday and worked alone for six hours in his EOB hideaway office. The first question that evening was about why he held so few news conferences—the real answer was that he took so long to prepare—and then not surprisingly there were questions on the three subjects that dominated the news of the past month: Agnew and the press; the Supreme Court and the South; and the Army and My Lai.

Q.—Vice President Agnew, in recent weeks, has made two speeches in which he has criticized the news media, broadcasting in particular. What, if anything, in those speeches is there with which you disagree?

A.—The Vice President does not clear his speeches with me. . . . However, I believe that the Vice President rendered a public service in talking in a very dignified and courageous way about a problem that many Americans are concerned about.

Q.—Before the Supreme Court ordered immediate school integration, you said you preferred a middle-of-the-road policy, that is, between segregation forever and instant integration. What is your policy now?

A.—To carry out what the Supreme Court has laid down. I believe in carrying out the law even though I may have disagreed as I did in this instance. . . . But we will carry out the law.

But the question that dominated the news the next day was on My Lai. *Life* had run ten pages of horrific color photos, the ones shown privately to members of Congress, taken by an Army photographer named Ronald L. Haeberle, showing the corpses of women and children, and old men and old women, in grotesque piles. Douglas Cornell of the Associated Press asked whether the President thought the killing was a massacre or a military matter.

"What appears was certainly a massacre, and under no circumstances was it justified," Nixon answered.

One of the goals we are fighting for in Vietnam is to keep the people of South Vietnam from having imposed upon them a government which has atrocity against civilians as one of its policies. We cannot ever condone or use atrocities against civilians in order to accomplish that goal. . . . I would only add this one point: Looking at the other side of the coin, we have 1,200,000 Americans who have been in Vietnam. Forty thousand of them have given their lives. Virtually all of them have helped the people of Vietnam in one way or another. They built roads and schools. They built churches and pagodas. . . . Now this record of generosity, of decency, must not be allowed to be smeared and slurred because of this kind of an incident. That is why I am going to do everything I possibly can to see that all of the facts in this incident are brought to light and that those who are charged, if they are found guilty, are punished.

"His most successful press conference," said *The Atlanta Constitution*. "An impressive performance," said *The Boston Globe*. Quick CBS News polls showed that Nixon's approval rating had shot up to an astounding 81 percent nationwide—86 percent in the South.

"Very significant," the President wrote across his news summary. "Another evidence of the T.V. credibility gap." The same day, reading the summary of a *Christian Science Monitor* report—"North Vietnam is showing itself to be acutely sensitive to charges that it has ill-treated U.S. POWs . . ."—Nixon scrawled: "H—Get a massive campaign going on this. . . ." George Wallace, along with California's Governor Reagan and several other Republicans responded to the My Lai charges by blaming the press for "profiteering" and using "unverified photographs." Seeing those quotes in his news summary, Nixon wrote: "Bravo!"

So the year was ending not so badly. No matter how large antiwar demonstrations were becoming, there was no doubt that the President still had most of the nation with him, and that the antiwar movement was hardly monolithic. The President passed around a summary—with the annotation "K—Very perceptive"—by a liberal columnist, John Roche, who wrote on December 18: "The Democratic Party has . . . a vested interest in a U.S. catastrophe in Vietnam. . . . If the American people ever recognize that liberal Democrats are rooting for a U.S. defeat in South Asia, the Democrats will be through politically for the rest of the century." David Broder of *The Washington Post* concluded that "the breaking of the President" had failed and Nixon had "restored confidence in government's ability to govern." In his year-end review, John Osborne said he had always been repelled by Richard Nixon, then wrote: "Nixon the President seems to me to have become a stronger man, a more decent and credible man. . . ."

Inside the White House Pat Buchanan's news summary covering the last days of the year concluded: "We continue to roll steadily along on a high and comfortable plateau. . . . The unnamed Eastern Establishment press fellow who moaned, 'We never laid a glove on him' while emerging from the news conference has been quoted and re-quoted. . . . The Vice President's choice as the third most respected man in America in the Gallup Poll is proof enough that he remains enormously strong with large segments of the American public. . . . Evans-Novak report that the President is stronger than Wallace in the South as a whole, the Vice President is running him into the ground. . . ."

Buchanan, who had a Nixonian knack for finding new enemies, noted that Defense Secretary Laird was becoming a press favorite— "A hard-liner with a heart of gold . . . playing the dove for the liberal press." Nixon's suspicious comment on that, ironic in its destination, was, "K—note—we must watch this!"

Buchanan's conclusion was: "All in all, the President gets his highest grade from the press for the handling of the war, and the politics of the war. The constant dropping of U.S. casualties is having its impact; it is widely covered on the networks—each week's reduced casualties."

By the end of the year, Nixon had reduced the number of Ameri-

can troops in Vietnam by 115,000. He was commanding that most difficult of military maneuvers, a retreat under fire—leaving 435,000 men
there, rolling the calendar back to the level of mid-1967. There was also
another numerical first. The President had gone to fourteen countries already, logging 75,443 air miles, three times the previous high logged by
President Johnson.

One week into January of 1970, Richard Nixon, alone with his
yellow pad, wrote down his New Year thoughts:

> Goals:
> Personal: 1. Make people have a memorable experience each
> day—2. Be worthy of 1st man in nation and in world—3. Make
> use of each day
> National: 1. Progress toward peace: V. Nam—Soviet—
> China—Europe—Latin—Mideast . . . Armament control
> 2. Progress on National goals: Environment—Welfare—
> Inflation—Crime—Organization of govt.
> Spiritual: Add element of lift to each appearance. . . . Hard
> work—Imagination—Compassion—Understanding of young—
> Intellectual expansion
> Cool—Strong—Organized—Temperate—Exciting . . .

CHAPTER 10

January 22, 1970

During the holidays, the President spent some time with his family in California. While he was there, his youngest brother, thirty-nine-year-old Edward Nixon, talked to him about the popularity of auto racing, telling him it was the biggest spectator sport in the country, bigger than baseball or basketball or football. A lot of the drivers, Ed told him, were big Nixon supporters, particularly two of racing's biggest names, Andy Granatelli and Mario Andretti. On January 9, the day after Nixon returned to Washington from San Clemente, Haldeman sent around a memo saying: "The President requests that we think about a way to recognize auto racing as a sport, and Granatelli and Andretti particularly, as a way for the President to identify with millions of people who find this a happy way to spend their Sunday afternoons."

Many of those millions, particularly in the South, were George Wallace's people. They were the people—men, mostly—who Nixon wanted in his "silent majority." In fact, the President's major domestic goal was to pull together under his banner the 57 percent of American voters who chose him or Wallace in 1968. If Wallace did not run again as a third-party candidate in 1972, Nixon saw the possibility of getting that kind of big majority, rather than the 43.4 percent he got in 1968, with Wallace in the race. He was thrilled by a Republican National Committee poll, done in January, that indicated that 73 percent of all voters in both parties considered themselves part of the silent majority. "Significant," he marked the numbers in a memo to Haldeman. "Should be read by all. . . ."

Wallace understood what was happening, too. He was publicly urging southern governors to defy federal school desegregation orders and at the same time predicting that Nixon would be a one-term president if he did not satisfy the South, the white South. "The so-called Southern Strategy has been all talk," said the man who inspired it. "The Administration has done more to destroy the public school system in one year than the last administration did in four."

The line was picked up in a January 13 editorial in the Charleston *News and Courier* in South Carolina: "Wallace charges that the Administration says one thing and does another and he has a strong case. . . . The President is risking loss of those Southern states he carried in '68 if he doesn't stop HEW from wrecking public school systems."

Reading of Wallace's statement and the *News and Courier* editorial, which appeared in his news summary a week apart, Nixon scrawled similar messages, this one on the editorial: "E—I would like to know what I can do on this. Can't we do or say something to bring some sense into the dialogue? I just disagree completely with the court's naive stupidity. I think we have a duty to explore ways to mitigate it. . . . I don't give a damn about the Southern Strategy—I care a great deal about education and I know this won't work. Give me a plan. . . ."

Harry Dent, whose job at the White House was the Southern Strategy, had just come back from a series of meetings with southern Republican chairmen, and he reported in with a skeptical memo to the President: "Achieve total desegregation in the South in 1970 with the major burden being borne by the state Democrat leadership on orders of the Federal courts and without blame being attached to this Administration, then we will have achieved the miracle of this age."

The President's view of such events was more complicated than it seemed. Nixon was in every respect a true national politician—he had no distinct geographic base even in California—who knew that "selling out to the South," the phrase of the moment, was a guarantee of national defeat in 1972. The same was true, to him, of "selling out" to black demands. The last thing he wanted was to win over blacks. During a week in which officials at HEW and Justice were defending the administration's record on school desegregation, the President wrote: "Our people have got to stop bragging about school desegregation. We do what the law requires—nothing more. This is politics, and I'm the judge of the politics of schools; believe me, all this bragging doesn't help. It doesn't cool the blacks. They must not—they will not—be sucked into praising our great record."

Later, in a meeting with his speechwriters, he added: "The nation is at a historic moment. . . . You're not going to solve this race problem for a hundred years. Intermarriage and all that, assimilation, it will happen, but not in our time. Desegregation, though, that has to happen now. . . . Somewhere down the road I may have to carry out this law. I can't throw down the gauntlet to the court."

He had no choice, he told them: "There is no mileage doing the right thing here, there's only mileage for demagogues. Put it this way: There's mileage for anyone who wants to be governor, no mileage for anyone who has to be President." He was talking about George Wallace, of course. He hoped to keep Wallace from running for president again— or in some way persuade him to run as a Democrat—and the best way to do that was by building a strong enough Nixon base in the South to persuade Wallace he would risk humiliation in the states of the old Confederacy if he ran against the President. In fact, Nixon's Postmaster General, Winton Blount, who was from Alabama, had told the President that he believed Wallace was open to a deal of some kind to stay out of the President's way in 1972.

Over a *New York Times* story about the possibilities of blacks supporting Nixon, the President wrote: "H—Be sure our PR types make it clear we aren't adopting policy for the promise of being 100% Negro and winning their vote—We know this is not possible." When he saw a *Savannah News* headline that read, "DESEGREGATION DEADLINES WON'T BE ENFORCED," he noted: "Excellent job." When he saw a news summary report on civil rights leaders calling for Congress to declare Martin Luther King Jr.'s birthday a national holiday, he wrote in letters twice as big as his usual writing: "No! Never!" He told Haldeman: "That would be like making Nero Christ." There was one black political idea he liked, however. Reading of the formation of a black-led political party in Alabama, which would inevitably take votes from Democrats, Nixon wrote to Haldeman: "H—Get this subsidized now." There was a double underline under "now."

Nixon's hope was for a bigger miracle than Dent envisioned; he wanted to do what Franklin Roosevelt had done, unite the white working men and families of both North and South. Part of that drive was to embrace the cultural strategy Pat Buchanan was writing into Agnew speeches. Buchanan showed the President *Newsweek* polls and analysis by Richard Scammon, a former director of the Census bureau who was writing a book on political demographics, and wrote in the magazine: "Statistically, Mr. Nixon registers 'highly favorable' rating among about one-third of the people of Middle America. . . . All these groups did not vote Republican in November, 1968. . . . the new GOP target is very obviously the manual worker."

"We need to study Agnew's upsurge," Nixon told his speechwriters in his first meeting with them in 1970. What Nixon, who had just told Haldeman to keep the Vice President away from him, wanted to talk about were the ideas in play. In the news summary of January 13, Buchanan inserted the full text of an unsigned editorial published the day before in *The Wall Street Journal*. The headline was "Assaulting the Aristocracy."

> The heart of the Agnew phenomenon is precisely that a class has sprung up in this nation that considers itself uniquely qualified ("the thinking people") and is quite willing to dismiss ordinary Americans with utter contempt ("the rednecks").

"Excellent! . . . Very perceptive," Nixon wrote next to that line. The editorial continued:

> Mr. Agnew's targets—the media, war protestors, rebellious youth—are representatives of a class that has enjoyed unusual moral and cultural authority through the 1960s. Seldom before has such wide influence been wielded by the highbrows, the intellectual–beautiful people–Eastern liberal elite. Yet how well have the members of this elite discharged this authority? Has the economy been well managed? Have the cities prospered? . . . Whose theology culminates in the death of God? Whose artistic advice culminates in pornography? Whose moral advice culminates in "anything goes" with sex and drugs? Whose children sack the university?

Nixon ordered the editorial copied and distributed throughout the White House. He also told Haldeman, "See if you can get this editorial writer (probably a young staffer) for our staff." The writer, a young *Wall Street Journal* staffer named Robert Bartley, declined.* At the same time, reading a column by William S. White on a possible connection between violence on television and street crime, Nixon noted: "A good subject for possible attack by Agnew. TV and movies are vulnerable."

On January 19, the President announced his new nominee for the Supreme Court seat vacated by Abe Fortas and denied Clement Haynsworth. "Find a good Federal judge further South and further to the right," Nixon had told Harry Dent in the days after Haynsworth was re-

---

* Bartley stayed with the *Journal*—later winning a Pulitzer Prize—and became a leading voice of movement conservatives through the 1990s.

jected. The idea was, win or lose, a message would be delivered in the old Confederacy. That judge's name was the one in the President's desk drawer for the past year, Judge G. Harrold Carswell of the Fifth Circuit, the friend of Florida's Governor Kirk. Nixon had nominated Carswell for the circuit court judgeship in May, seven months earlier, and the Senate had confirmed him without anyone paying much attention. He was young enough, forty-nine, and had enough southern credentials to please Dent, but his first qualification was that he did not seem to have conflict-of-interest problems. Refighting the Haynsworth battle, the White House asked for and received Carswell's old bankbooks. Bud Krogh waved checks and FBI records in the hallways of the EOB, saying, "We know everything about him, we vetted every one of his checks. He's clean as they come."

He was wrong. Within forty-eight hours, it was revealed that on August 2, 1948, when he was a twenty-eight-year-old candidate for the Georgia state legislature, Carswell had said in a speech, which was reprinted in a newspaper he edited himself: "Segregation of the races is proper and the only practical and correct way of life. . . . I have always so believed and will always so act."

Carswell immediately renounced those words, saying they were "abhorrent" to him now. Actually, the old speech was not the big problem. After going door to door to senators' offices with the nominee, Bryce Harlow unhappily reported back to the President: "They think Carswell's a boob, a dummy. And what counter is there to that? He is."

Nixon ignored Harlow's warnings. He was preparing for his first State of the Union address, scheduled for January 22. He had tremendous concentration at times, usually before major speeches and press conferences. Ray Price had completed the first draft of the address on January 9. Nixon wanted his schedule cleared for the next thirteen days, and during much of that time he did not come down to his office from his study in the old Lincoln bedroom. He locked himself into EOB 175, then finally retreated to Camp David. He was alone with his yellow pads, which ended up pushed into desk drawers when he returned. At Camp David on January 14, he wrote: "Lift spirit of people. . . . Pithy, memorable phrases. Need for a name—Square Deal, Fair Deal, New Deal, New Frontier, Great Society." Then on January 16 it was: "Most important (1) Must be zest—Joy—welcome the work—the challenge of speech or press conference."

His obsession with time and solitary internal dialogue did not make the President an efficient man. Quite the opposite—as Haldeman and Ehrlichman believed. Ehrlichman guessed that Nixon spent half his time on what he called "non-substantive areas." "I have watched Nixon spend a morning designing Walter Cronkite's lead story for that evening, then send Ron Ziegler, Henry Kissinger or me out to the press briefing to deliver it in such a way that Cronkite couldn't ignore it," Ehrlichman said. Haldeman added: "He spends as much time discussing the problem he has of shortage of time as he does doing the things he says he doesn't have time to do. . . . He really needs crises . . . not good on self-initiated momentum." In the days leading up to the State of the Union address, Haldeman's notes read: "Limited schedule to provide time to work on speech, but he didn't use any of it for that" (January 12); "Another day supposedly cleared . . . but no work done" (January 13); "Nothing on schedule today, so frittered away" (January 14). So it went day after day. Just after midnight on January 17, as Nixon worked on the speech, there was a fire alarm in the White House triggered by smoke from the Lincoln sitting room. Nixon had tried to light a fire in the fireplace. He stayed in the smoke—"I love the smell"—writing until 2:30 A.M.

The President prepared for news conferences with the same intensity. He hated the conferences, not so much because of his problems with the press, but because they exhausted him. He edited, reedited, and memorized much of the big answer book prepared by staff—with as many as 178 possible questions and practiced answers by the end of 1969—before his fifteen- or twenty-question confrontations with the press. Then it took him a day or two to come down, working off the tension that grew inside him before each performance. Typically he would go through cycles of exhilaration, doubt, and then anger, no matter how well he did—and he usually did quite well. He told Haldeman in a memo that he had decided to do only five or six a year, writing: "I have now reached the conclusion that with the amount of effort and the enormous exposure and risk involved in having to be prepared to answer so many questions that cover so many fields . . . It simply isn't worth all the effort that goes into it. . . ."

The President finished his draft of the State of the Union address on January 21 and called in Haldeman and Kissinger for a reading that afternoon. Then he called Haldeman back, asking him to see if the speechwriters or the Library of Congress could find a Thomas Jefferson quote that went something like "not for ourselves but for the whole human race." The best that the researchers could find was a complicated paragraph that made the point. "No, no," Nixon said. "Keep checking." He told the researchers to look for letters, saying that Jefferson often refined his thoughts as he went along—until he got it right.

The speech on January 22 lasted only thirty-six minutes, but Nixon touched all the bases, stealing a couple the Democrats saw as theirs. The four-column New York Times headline read:

NIXON, STRESSING QUALITY OF LIFE,
ASKS IN STATE OF THE UNION MESSAGE
FOR BATTLE TO SAVE ENVIRONMENT

He had surprised his adversaries again, seizing the initiative on such issues as air and water pollution, the "quality of life" issues, which had been pretty much a liberal preserve. Nixon, who had called for several polls during the two weeks he worked on the speech, made notes on the fact that public concern on environmental issues had risen from 25 percent in 1965 to 75 percent at the end of 1969. And the Democrat he thought might be his 1972 opponent, Senator Edmund Muskie, was a leading figure in an upcoming national rally, called "Earth Day," scheduled for April. It was hard to say how deep Nixon's new commitment was. Like many Californians, he had been shocked by the January 1969 blowout of a Union Oil well off Santa Barbara that spread black gunk and dead birds and fish along two hundred miles of beach. But in private with Ehrlichman, who considered himself an environmentalist, the President had remarked: "In a flat choice between smoke and jobs, we're for jobs. . . . But just keep me out of trouble on environmental issues."

His first State of the Union address sounded like a campaign speech. "The prospects for peace are far greater today than they were a year ago," he said. "Controlling inflation"—which was at 6.1 percent, the highest in ten years—was now his first priority. Then, imitating in writing the rhythms of Martin Luther King Jr.'s "I Have a Dream" speech of 1963, Nixon promised to spend $10 billion on "clean water," which had never been one of his priorities in the past. He began: "I see an America in which we have abolished hunger, provided the means for every family in the nation to obtain a minimum income, made enormous progress in providing better housing, faster transportation, improved health and superior education. I see an America in which we have checked inflation and waged a winning war against crime."

Near the end, he quoted a letter that Thomas Jefferson had written to a friend in 1802. We act, Nixon said, "not for ourselves alone, but for the whole human race."

"Inspiring exhortation," pronounced the New York *Daily News*. A consistent critic, Richard Dudman of the *St. Louis Post-Dispatch*, offered a backhanded compliment: "The blandness and optimism was another step in President Nixon's already successful effort to pacify the people." In the CBS News post-speech analysis, White House correspondent Dan Rather said: "What it boils down to is that the President has caught the Democrats bathing and he's walked away with their clothes."

The day after the speech, alone with Haldeman, Nixon talked

about crime again, particularly crime in Washington, which had a black mayor, appointed by President Johnson in 1967, named Walter Washington: "What about a white mayor? A white Alabama coon-killer?"

A couple of days after the State of the Union address, Democrats and the press finally got a chance to mock Nixon. The occasion was a state visit by Prime Minister Harold Wilson of Great Britain—and the official unveiling of new White House police uniforms, inspired by the honor guards Nixon had seen in Europe. The cops were wearing double-breasted white tunics with starred epaulets, gold piping, draped braid and high black plastic hats decorated with a large White House crest. "They look like old-time movie ushers," said *The Buffalo News*. "The Student Prince" said the Chicago *Daily News*. In the *Chicago Tribune*, a Nixon friend, columnist Walter Trohan, was more serious, saying the uniforms belonged onstage, calling them "frank borrowing from decadent European monarchies, which is abhorrent to this country's democratic tradition."

The President shot out instructions on the news summary. "H— Have Klein take the offensive on the slovenly White House police we found. . . . I want our staff to take RN's position on this regardless of their own views. . . ." The uniforms lasted two weeks.

On January 30 the President had no schedule; he spent the day studying for an evening press conference. "Mr. President," began an inevitable question, "if you had known about the speech in which he advocated white supremacy, would you have nominated Judge Carswell to the Supreme Court?"

"Yes, I would," Nixon said. "I am not concerned about what Judge Carswell said twenty-two years ago when he was a candidate for a State legislature. I am very much concerned about his record of eighteen years—as you know, he had six years as a U.S. Attorney and twelve years as a Federal District Judge—a record which is impeccable and without a taint of any racism. . . ."

The next day's *Washington Post* reported that during his years as a trial judge, more than two-thirds of Carswell's civil decisions had been overturned in higher courts.

There were four questions on the economy at the press conference, the first by Douglas Cornell of AP, who began by reciting a series of headlines, including: "Balance of Trade Makes Slight Progress in 1969"; "Big Firms' 1969 Profits Down"; "Dow Average Hits New Low for 3 Years"; "GNP Rise Halted"; "U.S. Steel Will Raise Sheet Prices February 1." Then he asked, "How, sir, do you assess the possibility that we may be in for perhaps the worst possible sort of economic conditions—inflation and a recession?"

"The major purpose of our economic policy since we came into office a year ago has been to stop inflation," Nixon began. "Now, as a result, we are now in a position, the critical position, in which the decisions we make in the next month or two will determine whether we win this battle. . . . I would simply say that I do not expect recession to occur." Later he was asked what were the critical decisions he mentioned. He answered that he expected his 1970–1971 budget would persuade the Federal Reserve Board to loosen up the money supply before recession took hold. "I am not saying what the Federal Reserve ought to do; I do know, though, that if monetary supply remains too restricted too long, we have a recession, and monetary policy will remain restricted unless the Federal Reserve and those in charge of monetary policy are convinced that fiscal policy is responsible."

Nixon's idea that the government itself was responsible for inflation was one of his few economic convictions. He did not like talking about money—or business, for that matter. He had been put off during his New York years by all the conversations swirling around money, but he did know the language just well enough to fend off questions in press conferences. In private, he would invariably go back to his year of service as a federal bureaucrat, with the Office of Price Administration between his wartime Navy service and his first run for Congress, saying: "Controls? Oh my God, no! I was a lawyer for the OPA during the war and I know all about controls. They mean rationing, black markets, inequitable administration. We'll never go for controls."

There was argument about that at the next Cabinet meeting, an unusually lively one, with Nixon listening as Romney of HUD and Postmaster General Blount argued for an open effort to control prices and wages, against Paul McCracken, chairman of the Council of Economic Advisers, Treasury Secretary David Kennedy, and Labor Secretary George Shultz, who favored the existing policies.

"Our policies worked in a slower way than expected," said Kennedy, who had been president of Continental Illinois National Bank in Chicago. "But they are working. We will work this out without a recession. . . . As profits go down, companies get tougher at the bargaining table and reach sounder settlements."

"We can see some very inflationary wage settlements coming this year," said Romney, who had been president of American Motors before going into politics in Michigan. Shultz joined Kennedy in promoting patience. But Romney would not bend, finally saying, "We must have a wage-price policy."

Then the President interrupted, asking, "What wage-price policy ever worked?"

"The British plan."

"Oh, no. Now, George, don't tell me about British wage-price policy. I know about that. It didn't work. And anyway, the situation here is quite different."

Then the President said he wanted to talk about the politics of economic policy, beginning with his first principle: "Inflation has never defeated an Administration—but recession has."

He went on, saying that corporations are not really concerned about recessions, because hard times bring labor into line. "I suppose I would feel the same way in their place, but . . . If the Administration comes into the election with a recession and fear-of-recession psychology abroad in the country, then candidates in the marginal districts will fall. . . . If our candidates are defeated and we can't hold our own in the House and Senate, we will not have enough responsible members to carry on the fight against inflation. . . . So what we must do is avoid fear of a recession. We must combat what will be a desperate effort by the other side to show that this Administration has plunged the country into a recession."

Then Nixon shifted to race and the questions of North and South, trying to point out just how fine was the high wire he wanted to walk on school desegregation, but separating the politics of the issue from the merits. "Talking politics, now," he said, "we must understand what our Democratic friends are up to. Here's Senator Ribicoff, former HEW Secretary, a great liberal, who is calling for nationwide application of the same integration policy. . . . He is trying to force this Administration to visit the troubles of the South on the North. . . . The cynical Northern liberals who don't have any problems with the civil rights issue in the coming election will try to needle this Administration to enflame the situation."

He continued: "Segregated education is inferior, therefore, there cannot be any more dual systems," and added that he thought the Supreme Court was right in 1954. But he was equally certain that busing was harmful to education. "It is wrong to pick up a child and bus him fifteen miles to another school just to achieve racial balance."

The "fifteen miles" was not a random number. Otto Passman, a pro-Nixon Democratic congressman from Louisiana, had been in the Oval Office complaining about busing, and he took out a photograph. "Here's my little golden-haired granddaughter," he said, "being bussed right past her neighborhood school." She had been assigned to a formerly all-black school fifteen miles across town.

Nixon had also been impressed by an article in *The New Republic,* shown to him by Buchanan, in which Yale law professor Alexander

Bickel also tried to separate race, politics, and education. "There must be a better way to employ the material and political resources of the federal government," Bickel argued. "Massive school integration is not going to be attained in this country very soon, in good part because no one is certain that it is worth the cost. Let us therefore try to proceed with education." Quoting that line in a memo to Ehrlichman, Nixon wrote: "I have decided to reverse this process. We will take heat from the professional civil-righters—but education comes first. . . . This is my decision. If there are those in the Administration who disagree they can resign."

In case Ehrlichman did not understand what he meant, the President added: "I want Panetta's resignation on my desk Monday as a starter."

It was not the first time that the President had said he wanted the young director of HEW's Office of Civil Rights out of there. Ehrlichman, Haldeman, and Finch had ignored the same order more than once—for different reasons. Ehrlichman and Haldeman expected a press firestorm. Finch, the President's protégé, was being crushed, in a very personal way, trying to satisfy his mentor and keep the approval of all the young Republicans like Leon Panetta who believed in integration just as deeply as the Democrats who had sat in the same chairs only a year or so earlier. Finally, on February 17, Panetta got the word—on the front page of the *Washington Daily News:* "Nixon Seeks to Fire HEW's Rights Chief for Liberal Views."

As he rushed to Finch's office to find out what was happening, Ron Ziegler was telling reporters at the White House's morning briefing: "It is my understanding that Mr. Panetta has submitted his resignation to Secretary Finch. . . . I think it has been accepted." Panetta himself was sitting in the lounge of Finch's office when a secretary told him his wife was on the phone. He punched a flashing button, saying, "Sylvia—" But the voice on the other end was that of a *Washington Post* reporter, Peter Milius, asking if he knew this was going to happen.

"Hell, no," Panetta answered. "I'm trying to tell my wife about it now."

The next day, six people in the Office of Civil Rights quit. On CBS News that night, Daniel Schorr reported that others at HEW were angry, too. Reading that in his news summary, Nixon wrote: "Fire them." His mood was not helped that day by another item reporting that a black Georgia legislator named Julian Bond, visiting in Amsterdam, had said during an interview on Dutch television: "If you could call Adolf Hitler a friend of the Jews, you could call President Nixon a friend of the blacks." Panetta gave some interviews, in which he said that Haldeman, Ehrlichman, and Harlow had been out to get him because they were anti-integration. Ehrlichman's private reply was: "The poor bastard doesn't know that it was the President who was out to get him."

Nixon was trying to move on and away. He released a 160-page "First Annual Report to the Congress on Foreign Policy for 1970," his first "State of the World" message. It began: "The postwar period in international relations has ended. . . ." The idea of the report was new—part of Nixon's determination to confront what he considered a new birth of American isolationism—and *The New York Times* gave it a five-column lead headline and printed the forty-thousand-word document in a special ten-page section on Thursday, February 19. It was the purest Nixon, a product not of committees but of contemplation, alone and with Kissinger.

The style was architectural, the content pragmatic—"framework" and "structure" were among the most used words—but there was a personal undertone, one that perhaps revealed the man himself. The argument was thought out as if nations were individuals. The President came to "one certain conclusion":

> Peace must be far more than the absence of war. Peace must provide a durable structure of international relationships which inhibits or removes the causes of war. . . . The insecurity of nations, out of which so much conflict arises, will be eased, and the habits of moderation and compromise will be nurtured. Most important, a durable peace will give full opportunity to the powerful forces driving toward economic change and social justice.

On a canvas so large, Vietnam was inevitably a small subject, or so Nixon obviously preferred to think. It was as if he now knew the answer to the question he had asked Kissinger four months before: "Is it possible we were wrong from the start in Vietnam?" Words like "victory" were no longer part of the rhetoric. "We seek a just settlement" was as far as he went in the report.

He identified not Vietnam but the Middle East and Soviet weaponry advances as the greatest immediate threats to global peace. The seemingly endless conflicts and confrontations—bombing raids, aerial dogfights, and shelling most every day in what amounted to undeclared war between Israel, supported and supplied by the United States, and its Arab neighbors, particularly Egypt and Syria, increasingly turning to the Soviet Union for equivalent support—constituted an almost daily threat of Big Power confrontation as the Israelis traded fire with Syria over the Golan Heights and Egypt on both sides of the Suez Canal.

He had laid out his own thinking on the Middle East quite directly the day before, in a private briefing on the message for Republican congressional leaders. In the briefing he had specifically stated that American policy was no longer based simply on the survival of the state of Israel, thus actually elevating the American view of the Jewish state from moral obligation to strategic ally: "U.S. policy in the Middle East is designed to advance United States interests. . . . Those interests involve vital stakes in the Mediterranean and Iran; they involve oil interests in the Arab world. . . . We intend to see to it that Israel is not overrun for the reason that Israel is the current most effective stopper to the Middle East power of the Soviet Union. . . ."

His take on Europe was similar, he told the leaders: "We do have a new attitude. We must remember we are there in Europe not to defend Germany or Italy or France or England; we are in Europe to save our own hide."

Finally, in the message, he directly addressed the reasons the United States needed arms control agreements beyond the Nuclear Nonproliferation Treaty negotiated by President Johnson, then signed by Nixon and Soviet President Nikolai V. Podgorny three months before. The Soviets, said Nixon, had caught up with the United States in nuclear missilery. These were his numbers: in 1965 the United States had 932 intercontinental ballistic missiles and the Soviet Union had 234; by the end of 1970, the United States would have 1,054 and the Soviets, 1,290; in 1965, the United States had 464 submarine-launched ballistic missiles and the Soviets had 107; by the end of 1970, the United States would have 656 and the Soviets 300.

On communist China, the President stated the American interest as: "a more normal and constructive relationship with the government in Peking."

Those were more than idle words. The President's secret courtship of communist China was progressing in Warsaw, where American and Chinese diplomats had begun meeting in mid-December after years of ignoring each other. And Kissinger had told Nixon in December that Soviet-Chinese relations were so bad that he expected the Soviet Union to invade China before mid-April. On January 8, the national security adviser had told the President, according to Haldeman's notes: "The Chinese are less dangerous than the Russians. . . . Russian leaders are thugs with a vested interest in foreign war or threat because . . . the country is dull, dreary, people will come to need stimulation. Chinese leaders are smart and sophisticated and less likely to blunder into war or stupid action—for internal consumption. . . . Real fear in Russia is that their 'Kennedy' might emerge and urge let's get moving. The question is how much time do we have. The new leader would now have some military areas of superiority over the U.S. and might be tempted to try to use it."

Two days later, a commission headed by a former secretary of defense, Thomas S. Gates Jr., came in to tell Nixon something he wanted to hear on another subject. The President's Commission on an All-Volunteer Armed Force recommended that Selective Service be eliminated on June 30, 1971, and replaced by a professional army, navy, and air force. "We unanimously believe that the nation's interest will be better served by an all-volunteer force, supported by an effective standby draft," the report began. No more draft. Military compensation competitive with civilian salaries and benefits. Maybe no more young men protesting on campuses and in the streets.

The President's good mood ended on February 26. "This is as mad as I've ever seen him," Haldeman told Ehrlichman that day. The President was pacing in the Oval Office cursing Jews because of demonstrations across the country against Georges Pompidou, the president of France. The French leader was on an eight-day state visit and had spent the first two days at Camp David and in Washington, talking with Nixon before going on to dinners and speeches in San Francisco, Chicago, and New York. At every stop, Pompidou and his wife were booed and jeered by angry crowds protesting a French decision to sell 110 Mirage jet fighters to the new revolutionary government of Libya, headed by a twenty-seven-year-old army colonel named Muammar al-Quaddafi, while refusing to sell 50 of the planes to Israel. In Chicago the demonstrators got close enough to rough up Pompidou and spit on his wife.

"This is unconscionable," raged Nixon. "The fucking Jews think they can run the world. Well . . ." And on and on. He decided right there to postpone the sale and delivery of twenty-five U.S. Phantom jets and eighty Skyhawks to Israel—a sale that he had secretly approved only two weeks before in meetings with Prime Minister Golda Meir. Turning to Kissinger, he said, "I don't want any more Jews in here to talk about the Middle East."

Then he read that both Governor Nelson Rockefeller and Mayor John Lindsay were boycotting the France-America Society dinner honoring the Pompidous at the Waldorf-Astoria in New York City. "I'm going then, goddamn them," he said. As for the city and its mayor, the President signed off on a long memo to Ehrlichman that began with an order: "Cut all federal projects you can find which provide aid for New York City. . . . Discontinue or delay programs with discretionary funding which directly aid the City government, concentrating on three departments vital to the City's needs—HEW, HUD and Transportation."

The President flew to New York on March 2 for the French-American dinner. Protesters were chanting outside the hotel and Nixon used them to get a couple of laughs. Toasting the French president, Nixon said: "When I learned that President and Madame Pompidou were coming to the United States, I wanted them to see our country, the United States, as a President of the United States saw it. . . ."

He paused. The audience of seventeen hundred paused, too, for a second and then broke into laughter and applause. Nixon picked up, "And I must say, we overdid it a bit, as we usually do." More laughter. The front page of *The New York Times* the next morning included four separate stories on the dinner. The headline across the top of page one began: "NIXON OFFERS HIS APOLOGY." Below that was a story with the headline "JEWS AFFRONTED," reporting on Pompidou's canceling a planned meeting with American Jewish leaders.

On the receiving line at the earlier White House dinner for the Pompidous, John B. Connally Jr., the former Democratic governor of Texas, who had declined Nixon's pre-Inaugural offers to be secretary of defense or the treasury, held Nixon's attention for a long moment, saying he was ready to do something for the administration if Nixon was still interested. In a March 2 memo to Haldeman, Nixon wrote: "He is a top property and he would be excellent in the Cabinet or in any other position of significant importance. . . . He has the subtlety and the toughness and the intelligence to do a very good job."

There was another of Nixon's memo flurries on that day and the next. He sent Ehrlichman a list of entire states that, like New York City, he wanted punished for one reason or another. "In your budget plans . . . ," he wrote, "I want Missouri, New York, Indiana, Nevada, Wisconsin and Minnesota to get less than they have gotten in the past. New York is the only place where you must play a slightly different game because of Rockefeller. . . . the message can get across that states with Republican Senators are going to get a better audience at the White House than those with Democratic Senators who are constantly chopping at us."

He wrote Haldeman: "In thinking about the finance situation, I think what you ought to do is to get the names of 20 men in the country who can give $100,000 or more. We should concentrate on them. Have them in for a small dinner, let them know that they are RN's personal backers. . . . Clem Stone, possibly Elmer Bobst, John Rollins, the South Carolina textile man." In another memo he wrote: "I would like for you to set up a procedure whereby telephone polls can be taken on immediate issues so that we can get an immediate response." And in another: "Billy Graham tells me that a group from Texas, Arizona and several other states is considering the possibility of raising funds which would enable them to get control of CBS."

Then he sat down for more quiet explaining—into a Dictaphone—his thoughts on organizing his own time and priorities, saying in a memo to Haldeman, Ehrlichman, and Kissinger:

> After a great deal of consideration of our performance during the first year, I have decided that our greatest weakness was in spreading my time too thin. . . . What really matters in campaigns, wars or in government is to concentrate on the big battles and win them.
>
> In the field of Foreign Policy, in the future all that I want brought to my attention are the following items:
>
> 1. East-West relations.
>
> 2. Policy towards the Soviet Union.
>
> 3. Policy towards Communist China.
>
> 4. Policy towards Eastern Europe, provided it really affects East-West relations at the highest level.
>
> 5. Policy towards Western Europe, but only where NATO is affected and where major countries (Britain, Germany and France) are affected.
>
> At the next level . . . policy toward the Mid-East and then finally in the last is policy with regard to Vietnam and anything that relates to Vietnam, Laos, Cambodia, etc.
>
> In the future, all that I want to see with regard to what I consider the lower priority items would be a semiannual report indicating what has happened; and where a news conference is scheduled, of course, just enough information so that I can respond. . . .
>
> With regard to domestic affairs, I want to take personal responsibilities for the following areas:
>
> 1. Economic matters, but only where the decisions affect either recession or inflation. I do not want to be bothered by international monetary matters.
>
> 2. Crime: I feel that we have really failed in this area, not perhaps so much in what we have done but in publicizing it adequately.
>
> 3. School integration: I must assume the responsibility here because it will be the major issue of controversy for the foreseeable future.

You will note that I have excluded the environment. I consider this to be important. . . . I don't want to be bothered with the details. Just see that the job is done.

I have also not included family assistance, revenue sharing, job training, the whole package making up the "New Federalism." I consider this to be important but . . . don't bother me.

Nixon, the politician, meant that. A couple of days later, he looked at a brief memo on environmental problems and dismissed it, writing, "I think interest in this will recede." At a Legislative Leadership meeting on March 3, according to Buchanan's notes: "Ford talked about the parliamentary problems of taking up the Labor and Education Bill. It was an involved thing, and the President cut it off by saying, 'Look Jerry, this thing has been beating around long enough. . . . Whatever you decide on this issue, you can say you have our support.' "

"Let me explain something to you quietly . . ." was one of the President's favorite openings, generally followed by a well-thought-out exposition. After saying again that he wanted more time alone, he called in Haldeman to explain, quietly, attitudes he wanted distributed to Cabinet members and staff. The subject was "leaks," and Haldeman's notes included these lines:

If important leaks do occur this will inevitably result in the President acting in a detrimental way. The prime example of this is the LBJ syndrome where he took the position that if something leaks he automatically reversed the impending decision so as to make the leak untrue. . . . The President's reaction will be different, but might also be quite detrimental; that is, he will usually react by refusing to talk about things which might leak, and this would mean that we can't have the kinds of meeting that we have been having.

The President generally thinks that the meetings he is required to sit in are a waste of time. . . . If anything leaks, there will be no more meetings. The President is perfectly capable of making the decision alone, and prefers to do so. . . .

CHAPTER 11

April 8, 1970

O N MARCH 6, more than two thousand Department of Health, Education, and Welfare employees petitioned their boss, Secretary Robert Finch, stating, "We are gravely concerned and indeed confused about the future leadership role of HEW in civil rights. . . ." Finch was in California, where he was spending long weekends trying to drum up support for a Senate race—or just trying to escape the pressures generated by the contradictions in the administration's talk and action on racial issues. In the Oval Office, Nixon said of another appointee working on school desegregation issues: "What he can't understand is that the confusion is deliberate."

So it was. That same morning, twenty-one civil rights leaders joined to denounce Pat Moynihan, now called "counselor to the President"—Ehrlichman had taken over the domestic affairs staff—after a 1,650-word memorandum to the President that had somehow gotten into *The New York Times.* "The time may have come," wrote the new counselor, "when the issue of race could benefit from a period of 'benign neglect.' . . . Negro problems have been too much talked about . . . too much taken over by hysterics, paranoids and boodlers on all sides." The newspaper, however, did not get the original of the memo, which had the President's written comment: "I agree."

Nixon was not distressed by the leak; it helped confuse what he wanted confused. He was much more concerned about the news that

Lawrence O'Brien, an old Kennedy hand, had agreed to become chairman of the Democratic National Committee. Nixon was, as always, afraid of the Kennedys, and he thought O'Brien was the party's most effective operative. He called in Haldeman and told him to have Murray Chotiner, an old Nixon operative with a base reputation, put together an "Operation O'Brien" to try to discredit the man. "Start with his income tax returns," the President ordered.

That day at noon a town house at 18 West Eleventh Street, one of the best streets in New York City's Greenwich Village, disappeared in flame and smoke. The cause was believed to be a gas leak, but investigation showed that the elegant house that was no more had been a bomb factory for the Weathermen, the underground group trying to foment the violent radicalization of young white antiwar activists. In the rubble, police found the body of a young man named Theodore Gold and a woman's torso without head or hands, riddled with nails, the shrapnel of homemade antipersonnel bombs. There was not enough of a third body to identify. Several other Weathermen survived and disappeared into the streets in the smoke and confusion. One of them was Cathy Wilkerson, the twenty-five-year-old daughter of the house's owner, a businessman named James Wilkerson, vacationing with his wife in the Caribbean. The police also found sixty sticks of unexploded dynamite.

On March 12 the front page of *The New York Times* carried stories on the town house bombing investigation; the bombings of a courthouse in Cambridge, Maryland; three early-morning bombings of office buildings in midtown Manhattan; and a progress report on government efforts to design devices to detect explosives in luggage at airports. On March 13, there were three more midtown bombings and more than three hundred bomb threats—telephone calls to police and newspapers—in New York City alone. In Manhattan, fifteen thousand people were evacuated from office buildings before police bomb squads began searches.

That day, Huston had a memo titled "SUBJECT: REVOLUTIONARY VIOLENCE" on the President's desk. It warned: "In the last 48 hours, we have had five separate incidents involving bombings. . . . New York bombings occurred in the offices of three large corporations—a new target of the revolutionaries as witnessed by the attack on the Bank of America. . . . You should be aware that the most logical target at some point in time for these people is the President and the White House. . . . ask yourself how difficult it would be for a 23 year old beauty to place her handbag with 5 sticks of dynamite in the ladies room of the Residence while going through on a White House tour. . . . Those kids had a bomb factory."

There were a lot of kids. More than one-third of Americans between the ages of eighteen and twenty were in colleges and universities— 7.8 million young men and women. Some of them were burning books in campus libraries, setting fire to ROTC buildings. Some threatened to organize two hundred thousand demonstrators if the President dared to attend his daughter Julie's graduation from Smith College. Nixon was outraged. One item that made him mad was a wire service report that students from the University of Wisconsin had stolen an Air Force ROTC training plane and used it to drop three homemade bombs on an Army ammunition plant outside Madison. The bombs did not explode, but the university's student newspaper praised the bombers, saying that theirs had been a legitimate protest that failed.

The New York Times seemed almost as understanding, suggesting in a front-page analysis that the violence was partly a response to the undermining of antiwar passions: "The galvanizing appeal once provided by the Vietnam war . . . appears to have been blunted by President Nixon's pullout of troops, the advent of the draft lottery, the general psychic release provided by last fall's Moratoriums and a general feeling that antiwar protest has become futile."

"Forget them," Nixon told Haldeman when the aide passed on suggestions for reaching out to young people. He read a news summary paragraph the next day on a Wall Street Journal report that a minority of young Americans returning from Peace Corps service were complaining that the Corps was just another part of the country's foreign policy apparatus, "a graduate school for imperialism." The President wrote: "K & H—I have decided that a quiet phasing out of Peace Corps and Vista is in order. The place to begin is to get the appropriations cut—get Harlow to work quietly on this."

The President spent more than an hour that day playing the piano—with another living-room pianist, the Vice President. Nixon had an idea for the annual dinner of the Gridiron Club, scheduled for the next night, March 14. Each year since 1885, one hundred newspaper correspondents and their guests had put on a roast of the powers of the day, beginning with the president—and usually the president responded with a humorous after-dinner speech. Nixon had done it many times going back to 1950, but that did not mean he enjoyed it. This time he had cooked up the idea of a piano duet with Agnew. No one knew what he was going to do after the show, which featured jokes and ditties about the White House's Southern Strategy. One line went, "Nobody knows the trouble I've seen; / Nobody knows but Haynsworth." The lights came up, and the President was gone, his seat empty. Then the audience heard the familiar low voice and turned toward the stage again. There were Nixon and Agnew at two pianos.

"Mr. Vice President," said Nixon, "I would like to have your candid responses to a few questions. First, what about this 'Southern Strategy' we hear of so often?"

Agnew clicked his heels, saluted, and said in an elaborate southern accent, "Yes suh, Mister President, Ah agree with you completely on yoah Southern Strategy."

Nixon sat down at his piano and said he would play the favorite songs of past presidents, beginning with Franklin D. Roosevelt's "Home on the Range." After a couple of notes, Agnew sat down and started to bang out "Dixie." Nixon began Harry Truman's "Missouri Waltz"; Agnew started "Dixie" again. Then came Lyndon Johnson's "The Eyes of Texas Are Upon You." More "Dixie." The crowd was roaring with laughter and cheers.

"Hold it! Hold it!" Nixon called out. "Now we'll play my favorite." He began playing "God Bless America." Agnew joined in and the audience stood and sang along. They cheered and cheered. "I'll never top that," Nixon told Haldeman that night. "So that was my last Gridiron dinner."

The President had been in Key Biscayne on the day of the explosion in Greenwich Village. He was working over an eight-thousand-word statement, prepared by Kissinger and his NSC staff, explaining B-52 bombings in Laos, where more than six thousand North Vietnamese were in action against the Royal Lao Army. The bombings had begun, in secret, on February 16 and were reported in American newspapers as early as February 19. The reports led to a series of speeches by antiwar senators, both Democratic and Republican, demanding to know whether United States troops were in the country. The President's statement concluded, "There are no American ground combat troops in Laos. . . . No American stationed in Laos has ever been killed in ground combat operations."

Within hours, the press began excavating details of a decade of United States operations in Laos. First there was a *Los Angeles Times* account of the death of Captain Joseph Bush, killed in a firefight with Pathet Lao commandos on February 10, 1969. NBC News followed with an interview with an American pilot in civilian clothes, then reported that there were fifty or sixty U.S. military installations, including several airstrips. "Laos: The Same Old Shell Game" was the *Washington Post* headline. According to a *Philadelphia Inquirer* editorial, "To say that a credibility gap is developing with regard to Administration statements on U.S. involvement in Laos is to understate the case."

Americans, in uniform and out, had secretly been observing, training, and sometimes fighting in Laos since the early days of Kennedy's presidency. And though the country had never been declared a combat zone, American military men there had been receiving combat pay since 1966. *Newsweek* gave a clearer picture than the President did, focusing on Air America, an airline with 150 planes, six hundred $25,000-a-year pilots, and one customer, the United States government: "It is an operating arm of the CIA. . . . Air America came into the spotlight when it flew several hundred into Laos to help the CIA-sponsored 'secret' army of Gen. Vang Pao defend the outpost of Long Cheng from Communist attack. . . . The bulk of the line's work is in Laos, where it drops tons of rice to Meo tribesmen under a contract with the Agency for International Development, carries troops to the front and evacuates refugees. . . . pilots wear thick gold bracelets which they can barter for food and medicine in case of forced landings in remote regions."

Within forty-eight hours the White House conceded that at least twenty-seven Americans had been killed in action in Laos during the past six years. Nixon was furious. But this time his target was not the press alone. He blamed Kissinger and the NSC. "Keep Henry out of here," he told Haldeman, and Kissinger was literally blocked at the door.

"Henry's going crazy," Haldeman reported back. Kissinger blamed Rogers and Laird, saying they had fed him false information. Anyway, he said, the Americans killed in Laos, military and civilian, were actually "stationed" in Vietnam.

"You know, he's like a psychopath about Rogers," the President complained to Haldeman. And for a couple of days, Nixon was free of Kissinger's daily, sometimes hourly complaints about the Secretary of State's preeminent position in attempts to get negotiations going in the Middle East and his opposition to the Laotian bombing.

Two strange men linked. Kissinger could not exist without President Nixon. President Nixon could not do what he wanted—build what he called a structure of peace—without Kissinger. The national security adviser was living a double life. As he fought turf wars at home, he had been secretly flying back and forth on weekends and holidays since February 20 for negotiations in Paris with Le Duc Tho, a member of the North Vietnamese politburo who was also traveling secretly. Rogers knew nothing of the talks. Neither did Laird, at least officially. Kissinger was flying on a White House Boeing 707—on flights officially recorded as training missions—making unrecorded landings at a French air base at Avord in the center of the country and then transferring to President Pompidou's private jet for the flight to Paris. He would be driven to a small house in a working-class suburb called Choisy-le-Roi—and then come back the same way. But there still was no real progress on any kind of settlement.

On March 11, the President let Kissinger back in the Oval Office, trying to reassure him. It took all day. The President's other appointments and staff meetings were pushed back and back. Late that night at home, Haldeman told a bit of the story in his diary: "K finally got in. He's still shook up about Laos. . . . in pretty bad shape, feels he goofed and thus let P down, and was taken in by both Defense and State, and has lost P's confidence. The lecture was designed to undo this, and get him back in gear, but I don't think it worked."

He was right. For another week, several times a day, Kissinger stormed around the White House, in and out of the Oval Office, raging two or three times a day that Rogers was out to get him. "Stabbing me" were his words. During that week—as the President, through Haldeman, urged Kissinger to take a vacation and get himself together—twenty thousand young demonstrators in Phnom Penh, the capital of Cambodia, attacked the embassies of North Vietnam and of the South Vietnam Provisional Revolutionary Government. On March 11, the rioters broke into the buildings, threw furniture out windows, and burned any cars they found around the compounds. Cambodian soldiers and police stood by, leaving no doubt that the demonstrations had been organized by the government.

The head of that government, Prince Norodom Sihanouk, was in Paris for medical treatment and his annual high-living holiday. From there he intended to go on to Moscow and Peking. The rallies were prelude to a coup against Sihanouk, who in 1945, at the age of eighteen, had been crowned king by the French colonial authority. With one title or another, he had run the country in one way or another since the French colonialists were defeated in Vietnam in 1954. The king become prince become prime minister become chief of state had been brilliantly and unpredictably inconsistent in preserving as much independence as possible for his small and weak country, avoiding the clutches of both the traditional enemy, the Vietnamese, and of the Americans. Declaring himself and the seven million people of his nation "neutral," he had cunningly played each side against the other for years. But the price of the game was high; North Vietnamese soldiers were operating freely in "sanctuaries" along the border between Cambodia and South Vietnam, and American B-52s were trying to find them with daily Menu bombings—3,630 secret sorties in a year. One result was that North Vietnamese troops were moving away from the border and into larger villages and towns, coming closer and closer to Phnom Penh.

While the Prince was away—he had been out of the country since January 7—his prime minister, a general named Lon Nol, was in charge at home. According to the book kept on foreign military leaders by the United States Defense Intelligence Agency, Lon Nol was "a friend of the

West . . . cooperative with U.S. officials during the 1950s." Many took that wording to mean he was an American intelligence "asset"—a paid agent. Sihanouk's public reaction to the anticommunist riots, which had actually begun three days earlier in provincial areas, was a statement from Paris that began: "This was organized by personalities aiming at destroying beyond repair Cambodia's friendship with the socialist camp and at throwing our country into the arms of a capitalist, imperialist power."

The "friendship," to Sihanouk, was necessary for national survival. The reason for going to the capitals of world communism—which greatly upset General Creighton Abrams—was to ask Soviet and Chinese leaders to pressure North Vietnam to pull back a significant number of its tens of thousands of troops operating deeper and deeper in Cambodian territory. On March 12 Lon Nol moved on those troops—rhetorically. He ordered all North Vietnamese troops—sixty thousand men, according to his estimate—to leave Cambodia within seventy-two hours, then announced the closing of the port of Sihanoukville on the Gulf of Siam, which the North Vietnamese used as an essential part of their military supply line.

The CIA station in Saigon sent to Washington that day a cable that began, "Indications of possible coup in Phnom Penh." It said that Lon Nol and First Deputy Premier Prince Sisoweth Sirik Matak had decided "to adopt a showdown policy against Sihanouk's followers." It continued: "The demonstration had support from all the anti-Sihanouk elements who had been without a leader for the past two few years. . . . The Army has been put on alert to prepare for a coup . . . against Sihanouk if Sihanouk refused to support the current government or exerted pressure on the government."

At the same time, Cambodian informants with access to Lon Nol told Defense Intelligence Agency operatives they expected the continuing demonstrations to quickly escalate into a coup d'etat, because Lon Nol believed that Sihanouk intended to dismiss him when he came home after the Moscow and Peking visits. The seventy-two-hour ultimatum to North Vietnam came and went without anything much happening. The North Vietnamese pledged to continue to respect the independence of Cambodia. The new government closed down the country's high schools and colleges, trained ten thousand students and peasants on a golf course for a couple of days, and then dispatched them, some without uniforms or weapons, on Coca-Cola trucks to regions held by the North Vietnamese and Vietcong.

On March 18, communication lines between Phnom Penh and the outside world were shut down. Two hours later a CIA message from outside the country was received in the National Security Council's Situation Room in the White House: "According to monitored broadcasts of Radio Phnom Penh, both houses of the Cambodian Legislature met in closed session . . . at the request of the government. The legislature then voted unanimously to withdraw its confidence in Sihanouk as Chief of State."

The Prince learned the news in Moscow, from Soviet premier Aleksey Kosygin, who disliked the vain and volatile little Cambodian leader as much as Abrams did. Kosygin drove to the airport with Sihanouk. Only as the limousine pulled up to the plane waiting to take Sihanouk to Peking did the Soviet leader tell Sihanouk what had happened. Back in Cambodia, there were angry pro-Sihanouk demonstrations outside Phnom Penh. In the market town of Kompong Cham, fifty miles from the capital city, peasants who believed their royal family were gods found a brother of Lon Nol and killed him. They ripped out his liver and went to a Chinese restaurant and forced the chef to cook and slice it for them, and then they went back into the streets to offer the slices to the crowd.

The next day, March 19, the top of the front page of *The New York Times* carried a three-column photograph of Kosygin and Sihanouk shaking hands at the plane, under the headline "SIHANOUK REPORTED OUT IN A COUP BY HIS PREMIER; CAMBODIA AIRPORTS SHUT." A second story, from Washington, began: "The United States government appears to have been surprised by the overthrow . . ."

In the White House, President Nixon asked Secretary of State Rogers about the CIA: "What the hell do those clowns do out there in Langley?" On a memo from Kissinger that day, Nixon wrote: "Let's get a plan to aid the new government. . . . I want CIA to develop and implement a plan for maximum assistance to pro-US elements in Cambodia. Don't put this out to the bureaucracy. Handle like our air strike." But Kissinger was having trouble focusing on the job at hand. The presence of the Secretary of State in the White House was enough to throw Kissinger into new fits of rage. Rogers had come to Nixon's office to argue against Kissinger's demands for more bombing in Laos. Then the President called in Haldeman and told him to tell Kissinger to go ahead with new bombing without telling State, keeping it secret from both the public and Rogers's men—"those impossible fags over there," as Nixon sometimes called the men of State. "Tell him to just do it," said the President. "Skip the argument."

The lead story of the *Times* that day was not about Southeast Asia but much closer to home. A four-column headline read: "MAIL SERVICE HERE IS PARALYZED BY POSTAL SYSTEM'S FIRST STRIKE: BUSINESS BEGINNING TO FEEL PINCH." Two hundred thousand of the country's 750,000 mail carriers and clerks were in the streets, most of them in Northeastern cities. They had not had a raise since 1962. The starting salary was a miserable $6,167 a year; after twenty-one years, a mail carrier could get $8,442. For its part, the administration wanted to make a new salary scale part of a deal to transform the Postal Service from a government agency into a public corporation.

"Fire them all!" was Nixon's first reaction in private. "If troops can be moved, move them."

Within forty-eight hours, the strike was national. Banks and stock exchanges were talking about closing down because checks and securities were somewhere in giant piles of canvas mailbags. On March 20, the President called a press conference in his office—no cameras, no microphones—and began: "We are prepared to negotiate . . . but under no circumstances will any grievances be discussed with any government employees when they are out on an illegal strike. . . . On Monday I will meet my Constitutional obligation to see to it that the mails will go through."

At 2 P.M. on March 23, the President went on national television with a seven-minute statement announcing that he was sending 2,500 regular Army troops, 12,000 Army and Air Force National Guard members, and 15,500 Navy and Marine reservists into New York City to restore essential mail service. "What is at issue," he told the nation, "is the survival of a government based on the rule of law."

Haldeman had never seen Nixon happier. He had come to learn that his leader came fully alive only in a crisis. "Completely cool, tough, firm and totally in command . . . and loving it." The first eight hundred soldiers, sailors, and airmen began work in New York's General Post Office at 11:30 P.M. Monday, sorting stacks of mail by the first three numbers of zip codes. They were supposed to root out and send on medical supplies and prescriptions; Social Security, pension, and salary checks; and financial and legal documents, and letters to Vietnam.

The President was engaged, shuttling back and forth between strategy sessions on the postal strike and a speechwriters' meeting to prepare a presidential statement on school desegregation. The last line of Haldeman's daily diary on the day the troops began sorting mail was: "Poor K, no one will pay attention to his wars. . . ."

The next day Kissinger went, reluctantly, to the Bahamas for the vacation the President had ordered him to take. He was not missed—at least not right away. Nixon was impressed with daily briefings by Kissinger's assistant, Colonel Alexander Haig, who talked him out of ordering a raid on surface-to-air missile sites near Hanoi until Kissinger had talked with the North Vietnamese one more time in Paris. The President was also meeting regularly with Rogers, and he realized that

Kissinger had distorted the secretary of state's positions and those of Defense Secretary Laird on a pretty regular basis.

IN FACT, the only war the President was concentrating on was Rogers's war in the Middle East. Israel, striking and defending itself against Egypt and Syria almost every day, had continued to press for the plane delivery that Nixon continued to delay. He was balancing the pressures on one of the structures that always seemed to be in his mind. On January 31, he had received a letter from Moscow that he considered a threat. President Kosygin wrote: "We would like to tell you in all frankness that if Israel continues its adventurism, to bomb the territory of the United Arab Republic and of other Arab states, the Soviet Union will be forced to see to it that the Arab states have means at their disposal, with the help of which a due rebuff to the arrogant aggressor could be made." Six weeks later, on March 12, Nixon had received a personal letter from Prime Minister Golda Meir, who wrote: "It is true that our pilots are very good, but they can be good only when they have planes. Lately some rumors have reached me that your decision may be negative or at best postponed. I absolutely refuse to believe it. If, God forbid, this were true, then we would really feel forsaken."

The rumors were true. On March 23, Rogers announced that the President believed Israel had sufficient airpower for the moment and the decision to sell the Phantoms and Skyhawks would be "held in abeyance for now." This was an "interim decision," Rogers said, adding that the United States had approved $100 million in new short-term credit for Israel.

The Secretary of State and the President had laid out their thinking, privately, at a full Cabinet meeting on March 18, as recorded officially:

Rogers said that Israel has the superior force in the Middle East, that it could win a Middle East war, and that this situation was likely to continue for years. The reason the Arabs cannot catch up, Rogers said, is because "they can't handle the equipment." So, if the United States were to supply now the planes that the Israelis have requested, the Administration could be justifiably accused of escalating the arms race and the Soviets then might supply more to the Arabs. So the intention is to supply no more planes at this time but to consider replacements of planes the Israelis lose and to grant more economic aid.

The President added that . . . the policy that Rogers had outlined would surely bring "a considerable broadside from the Jewish community." He told the Cabinet to be prepared for criticism of the policy—since many of the media are heavily weighted to the Jewish point of view. "If they don't get at you directly on this, they will be on you about a lot of other things because of this, so get your bomb shelters up."

In a memo to Kissinger, dictated that same day, the President said he wanted a political message delivered personally to Mrs. Meir and her ambassador in Washington, Yitzhak Rabin:

> Israel is relying on the peace-at-any-price Democrats. . . . What they must realize is that these people are weak reeds. When the chips are down, they will cut and run. . . . On the other hand, their real friends (to their great surprise) are people like Goldwater, Buckley, RN et al. who are considered to be hawks on Israel. Our interests are basically pro-freedom and not just pro-Israel because of the Jewish vote. . . . What all this adds up to is that Mrs. Meir, Rabin et al. must trust RN completely. Unless they understand it and act as if they understood it beginning now they are going down the tubes.

THE ATTENTION OF PRESIDENT and press shifted back to Southeast Asia on March 27. Exercising what the White House called "the inherent right of self-defense," small units of the Army of the Republic of Vietnam (ARVN) began attacking North Vietnamese positions inside Cambodia. Next across the border came a South Vietnamese Ranger battalion covered by American helicopter gunships. B-52s and South Vietnamese aircraft were also bombing targets ten miles inside Cambodia. On the ground, outside Phnom Penh, a civil war was going on; in Kompong Cham, pro-Sihanouk peasants attacked Lon Nol supporters, killing at least two members of the National Assembly. On March 29, thirteen Americans were killed in Cambodia, fighting in the eastern region of the country called the Parrot's Beak, near the border with South Vietnam. On April 3, in that area, which jutted into Vietcong-controlled areas in South Vietnam, three North Vietnamese battalions attacked Cambodian military installations—the first major military confrontation between the two countries.

By April 7, the President felt he had to go on national television to repeat, "Vietnamization has succeeded." Kissinger, who felt he was fighting for his own survival, handed Nixon a note: "Before you go on tonight I want you to have this note to tell you that—no matter what the result—free people everywhere will be forever in your debt. Your serenity during crisis, your steadfastness under pressure have been all that has prevented the triumph of mass hysteria. It has been an inspiration to serve."

THE FINAL VOTE on the Supreme Court nomination of G. Harrold Carswell came on April 8. He was rejected by a 51-to-45 vote, with thirteen Republican senators voting against the judge, some because of the open racism of his younger years. But the killer issue was the almost routine reversals of Carswell's decisions by higher courts. One of his last champions, Senator Roman L. Hruska of Nebraska, defended Carswell by saying that mediocre people had as much right to representation on the high court as other groups.

The final vote was something of a surprise to the White House. The day before that vote and after a flurry of telephone calls from the President and a couple of meetings with uncommitted Republicans, the Senate had killed a motion to recommit the nomination to the Judiciary Committee by a vote of 52 to 44. But the White House, it turned out, had lobbied on the wrong vote. Despite Nixon's eleventh-hour lobbying, sometimes because of it, the White House lost several moderate and uncommitted Republicans, most importantly Margaret Chase Smith of Maine and Marlow Cook of Kentucky.

Senator Smith voted in cold anger after learning that Bryce Harlow had told other senators that she was a yes vote. The President had personally asked for Cook's vote during an hour-long meeting over coffee—a very rare move for Nixon—on April 2 and then invited him to the White House two days later for a ceremony honoring Medal of Honor winners who had died in Vietnam. Driving back to the Capitol, Cook thought about the deaths of those young men—"men of excellence," the President had called them—heroes cut down, and then thought of Carswell, a man of no excellence, and decided he could not vote for him.

When it was over, the President was both angry and bitter—"He's like a demon over this," said Haldeman—and it showed in a prepared statement he read on television:

Judges Carswell and Haynsworth have endured with admirable dignity vicious assaults on their intelligence, their honesty and character. In my opinion neither would have been rejected had he not been born in a Southern state. . . . I will not nominate another Southerner and let him be subjected to the kind of malicious character assassination accorded both Judges Haynsworth and Carswell. . . . I understand the bitter feeling of millions of Americans who live in the South about the act of regional discrimination that took place in the Senate yesterday.

"Washington woke up startled today by this remarkable change in the President's style," wrote Max Frankel in *The New York Times*. "His decision to abandon the role of conciliator and the manner of respectful argument with his critics evoked an urgent stream of both political and psychological analysis."

"THE SEVENTH CRISIS OF RICHARD NIXON" was the headline over the story in *Time*. The magazine's cover line was: "THE CARSWELL DEFEAT— NIXON'S EMBATTLED WHITE HOUSE." The President's approval rating in Gallup polls had dropped eleven points in just two weeks—to a new low of 53 percent. Haldeman, who usually delivered polling messages, decided not to tell the President unless he asked directly. Instead, he told Nixon that he thought he was not going on television enough, that people had to see a president regularly to believe he was really in charge. Nixon argued with Haldeman more than once on that subject, saying that there was no gain in being on television with little to say. The idea, said the President, was to attach himself to big events, the moon landing, for one, and the war, segregation, and the economy. "Show leadership when it counts," he said. "You should go see *Patton*, the movie," said Nixon, who had just seen the film, a heroic take on George S. Patton, the flamboyant World War II general. "He inspired people, charged them up, Bob, that's what a chief of staff should do."

Nixon himself was fighting several battles. His problems, as analyzed by *Time* magazine, were: "The continued toll of inflation . . . The fear of recession is prevalent. . . . Unemployment rate rose to 4.4 percent. . . . Labor turmoil in eleven major industries . . . Conflict over school integration . . . Crime continues to increase inexorably. . . . New fighting in Cambodia threatens an expansion of the war. . . . At home, dissent against the war is blooming once again. . . ."

The most important labor problem was still the postal dispute. Workers turned down one offer after another and refused to negotiate details of the administration's plans to turn the U.S. Postal Service from government agency into public corporation. In the end, the government agreed to one of the highest wage increases in recent times: 14 percent, with the first 6 percent retroactive to the end of 1969. The 6 percent raise was also applied to all 5.6 million federal employees, civilian and military—5.75 percent more than the President had proposed in his 1970 budget message. Secretary of Labor Shultz was among those who knew the President might have traded labor peace now for inflation later. But the President declared victory in the agreement to privatize the service.

As the post office crisis was winding down, the International Brotherhood of Teamsters won a contract raising the pay of 450,000 truckers by 27.5 percent over two years. A sixty-day strike by 2,000 tugboat operators and employees working in the Port of New York won them a pay increase of more than 50 percent over three years.

Time heard "the toll of inflation." The President said the same, in public. But in private it was recession he feared. He repeatedly interrupted Cabinet discussions to go over the history of Republican defeats when the economy was in slow growth or decline, usually ending with a discussion of the party's 1954 and 1958 congressional defeats. In one of those meetings, during the Carswell fight, George Shultz got the President's attention when the subject of Arthur Burns and the Fed came up again. Shultz said: "Arthur has a way of holding the money supply as a hostage—saying that 'if you don't behave, I'll tighten up on money,' and in that way he's trying to run the whole executive branch with the Federal Reserve."

With that, the President slammed his hand on the table and said: "When we get through, this Fed won't be independent if it's the only thing I do in this office." Then Nixon offered a political economic theory: holding down the federal budget really had little direct effect on inflation. But it affects the thinking of the Fed, he said, and they react to budget imbalance by tightening money supply. "In 1954," he said, "the Federal Reserve waited too long to loosen up with the best of intentions—and great stupidity."

In mid-April, the White House sent a memo giving Cabinet members and department heads these instructions: "A careful line on economic policy predictions should be developed and followed by all Administration spokesmen. Keep the blame on 1965–1968 for our present troubles. Keep insisting we are doing what is right. . . ." To Shultz, Nixon said: "On monetary policy, however, I believe it would be a mistake to tell Arthur to be 'moderate' in moving to less restrictive policy. He will tend to be too cautious. Urge him to do more and he will end up doing a moderate amount. . . ."

NIXON'S THIRD CHOICE for the Supreme Court seat vacant for almost a year was announced on April 14, less than a week after Carswell's rejection. The President had toyed with the idea of naming Senator Robert C.

Byrd of West Virginia, a conservative Democrat. Then he asked Chief Justice Burger for advice and Burger recommended Judge Henry A. Blackmun, another Minnesota judge, a member of the Court of Appeals for the Eighth Circuit—who had been, in 1933, the best man at Burger's wedding. The announcement was made by press secretary Ron Ziegler, with no comment whatever from the President.

Nixon was preoccupied—to say the least. Like much of the world, he awoke on April 14 to a deadly drama, the plight of Apollo 13, the third American mission taking men to the moon. Just before midnight on April 14, Kissinger had telephoned Haldeman at home to tell him that an explosion in an oxygen tank and a fire had crippled the spacecraft five hours before it was scheduled to go into orbit around the moon—and could doom the three astronauts to the nightmare of being lost in space forever. "A technical problem, no decision required" said the chief of staff, refusing to wake the President.

In the matter-of-fact back and forth between the spacecraft and Mission Control in Houston, the controllers had a better overview of the situation than the astronauts. Mission Control summed up the situation this way: "We have an apparent serious problem with a leak in the oxygen in the service module which provides electrical power coming out of the fuel cells and also breathing oxygen for the crew. We're now in the process of manning the lunar module. Under this alternative mission, the lunar module would serve as a lifeboat to bring the Apollo 13 crew back to earth—that is, its consumables, oxygen, electrical power."

"Okay," came the answer from the commander, Navy Captain James Lovell, 206,000 miles away. "Didn't think I'd be back so soon."

The oxygen needed in the fuel cells and for breathing in the main craft, the command module, was leaking badly, and the three men had crawled into the lunar module, called *Aquarius,* the craft that was supposed to take two of them to the surface of the moon as the third man orbited in the command module. There were forty-eight pounds of oxygen in the lunar module, enough to get them back to earth in their little space lifeboat—if nothing else went wrong. The plan was to take the attached modules into orbit around the moon and use the orbiting momentum as a slingshot to propel the modules back toward earth. The trajectory home would depend on using the small rockets intended to guide the smaller craft to the moon and back to the command module. The trip would take sixty-two hours and the astronauts would crawl back into the command module before entering the earth's atmosphere. The smaller module did not have heat shields to protect the men against the heat generated by reentry at twenty-five thousand miles per hour. If they did not get back they would suffocate; if they reentered in the lunar module they would burn to death.

There was no margin for error. Finally, at 4 A.M., Haldeman decided to call Nixon—and then call Ziegler, to make sure the press was told that the President was in personal charge of the crisis all night. In space, Lovell was turning his ship around, telling Houston: "*Aquarius* is coming in."

CHAPTER 12

April 30, 1970

Apollo 13 seemed cursed from the beginning. Six days before the scheduled liftoff in the afternoon of Saturday, April 11, engineers at Cape Kennedy in Florida had discovered a leak in the helium tank. Then an astronaut on the backup crew, training with the three-man mission crew commanded by Jim Lovell, began to run a fever and NASA doctors discovered he had rubella, the contagious childhood disease usually called German measles. Blood tests of the three men set to board the lunar capsule atop the S-4B rocket showed that Lovell and Fred Haise had had the disease as children and were thus immune. But the command module pilot, Ken Mattingly, had never had the disease, and NASA officials decided to replace Mattingly less than twenty-four hours before liftoff with the backup crew pilot, John Swigert.

Now, with the crippled ship trying to make it back to earth, the President was pacing, talking with Haldeman, Ehrlichman, and Kissinger. "You could go to Houston," said Ehrlichman. Former astronaut Frank Borman, who was in Houston, recommended against the trip. There was nothing the President could do there.

"Cancel everything," Nixon said, including plans for a televised announcement of new troop withdrawals from South Vietnam. Then he was told that the prime minister of Denmark, Hilmar Baunsgaard, was on his way to the White House. Nixon flew into a rage, cursing Haldeman for having invited the Dane at all. As Nixon talked with Baunsgaard, Haldeman learned that Vice President Agnew, who was on a Midwest tour, was at the airport in Des Moines—ready to take off for Houston. Haldeman ordered him not to move until he talked to the President.

The Vice President sat on the runway for more than an hour, until he got the order to head back to Washington. He was angry, too, which did not bother Haldeman a bit. The chief of staff was still mad about an Agnew meeting with the President almost two weeks before, on March 31, because he had thought once again that the Vice President was bothering Nixon with trivia. This time it was a complaint about how the General Services Administration, in charge of most federal buildings and building, was awarding construction and maintenance contracts in Eastern states. "Our friends are being discriminated against," Agnew said, and added that someone had to take over such patronage. "Incredible," Haldeman told Ehrlichman, when he realized Agnew had already gotten away with ordering GSA to clear all contracts in Maryland, Virginia, Pennsylvania, and the District of Columbia through his office.

After lunch on April 15, with encouraging reports coming in from Houston, the President decided to drive, unannounced, thirteen miles to the Goddard Space Flight Center in Greenbelt, Maryland—where tracking information from seventeen NASA stations around the world was collected and transmitted to Houston—for a series of briefings. Then he had to go back to the White House for the state dinner for Prime Minister Baunsgaard.

"Farewell, *Aquarius,* and we thank you," were the words from Mission Control in Houston as Lovell and his crew crawled back into the command module with handheld oxygen bottles for the reentry into the atmosphere. The astronauts disconnected the lunar module and the little lifeboat tumbled off into space. The crippled spacecraft splashed down safely in the Pacific Ocean at 1:07 P.M. Eastern Daylight Time on April 17. The whole world was watching; European television networks calculated the viewing audience worldwide as the largest in history. Church bells rang out across the United States and in many other countries as well.

The President stood by the small television set in Alexander Butterfield's office next to a speaker box with an open line to NASA. He was with two former astronauts, William Anders and Michael Collins. "Cigars!" he shouted, having found out that cigars were passed out in Houston after successful landings. He immediately called the wives of the three astronauts and then waited while the astronauts themselves were patched in to their wives. But Nixon couldn't contain himself, telling White House telephone operators to connect him to one person after another—

and having one drink after another—saying the same thing over and over again: "Isn't this a great day! Isn't this a great day!"

One of his calls was to Jerry Ford, the House Republican leader. Nixon was so excited that he told Ford he should call Supreme Court Justice William O. Douglas with the good news. He had forgotten that four days before he had persuaded Ford to call publicly for the impeachment of Douglas, the most liberal justice—as revenge for the rejection of Carswell. By 4:15 that afternoon, the President was drunk, falling asleep on the couch in EOB 175.

The next morning the President flew to Houston to meet with the wives of the Apollo crew in an awkward little ceremony and then to congratulate the NASA officials and staffers in the Manned Spacecraft Center control room in Houston. Then it was on to Honolulu to greet the astronauts in a magnificent photo opportunity with Diamond Head in the background. Haldeman handled the arrangements, which involved Navy bulldozers working through the night to move huge mounds of dirt piled up during airport renovation because they blocked the perfect angle. With mountain and sea where Haldeman wanted them—at a cost of more than twenty thousand dollars billed to the Navy—the President presented each of the astronauts with the Medal of Freedom. "Greatness comes not simply in triumph but in adversity," Nixon said. "It has been said that adversity introduces a man to himself."

On Sunday, April 19, in Hawaii, the President decided to have breakfast with Admiral John S. McCain Jr., commander of United States forces in the Pacific. McCain—whose son, a Navy pilot, was a prisoner of war in Hanoi—was considered the most energetic and persuasive briefer in the Navy. For an hour and forty minutes he had the President pretty much to himself, telling him that both General Abrams and Ambassador Ellsworth Bunker in Saigon believed that the Lon Nol government in Cambodia was facing certain defeat by the North Vietnamese. He said "Vietnamization" could collapse if the remaining United States troops were attacked from the safety of Cambodia—with the highest casualties in a long time. Nixon knew those arguments, of course, but he seemed to come back from Hawaii with a new determination to finally hit back hard against the communists. He had been President for more than a year and a frustrated one for most of that time. The North Vietnamese had shelled Saigon early in 1969 and he had done nothing; the North Koreans had shot down the EC-121 and he had done nothing. The Soviets were moving into the Middle East and the United States had been unable to stop them. The Paris peace talks were going nowhere, and the communists were having their way in Laos and were now threatening to take Cambodia, too. This was the time and this was the place to show the world that he could meet force with force. "This is what I've been waiting for," he told Kissinger.

If he had made up his mind to go ahead with a United States invasion of Cambodia, which was what McCain and Abrams were urging, he did not show it that day as he flew east to San Clemente. In fact, the business of the moment was a television statement, rescheduled for Monday night, on future troop withdrawals. But Admiral McCain was aboard *Air Force One* because the President had asked him to brief Kissinger, who was flying west from Washington.

On Monday, as Nixon was editing the speech in San Clemente, Kissinger and McCain came into his study with reports that the communist forces were attacking two Cambodian cities, Snoul and Takeo, and had already taken Saang, a provincial capital only twenty miles from Phnom Penh. There was no fight; the Cambodians withdrew without firing a shot. The first thing the combined force of North Vietnamese and Vietcong did was to distribute AK-47 rifles and ammunition to ethnic Vietnamese residents of the place—to protect themselves. Cambodians, both soldiers and peasants, were turning on resident Vietnamese—four hundred thousand lived in Cambodia—driving them into the jungle or killing them. Bodies were floating down the Mekong River, most of them Vietnamese civilians beaten to death by their neighbors. In one place, called Prasaut, eighty-nine Vietnamese villagers were killed; the official story was that they were caught in a crossfire during a North Vietnamese attack, but it was clear that they had been massacred by Cambodian troops.

Ironically, the United States was preparing to distribute AK-47s, too—to Cambodian soldiers. The United States was flying in six thousand of the semiautomatic rifles from captured stock and also sending ten thousand old American carbines to Phnom Penh, a move approved by Nixon personally on the recommendation of General Abrams. In Jakarta, American agents were putting together a plan with the Indonesian leader, General Suharto, to fly in Indonesian army weaponry, which was to be replaced later by the United States. Finally there were some American-trained and -controlled ethnic Cambodian units in the army of South Vietnam—a few thousand men called Khmer Krom and Khmer Serai—whom the United States was preparing to airlift to Phnom Penh.

As the Vietcong patrolled Saang, Cambodian troops rounded up Vietnamese being held in a refugee camp near Phnom Penh, packed them in trucks that drove the twenty miles back toward Saang, and stopped on a road two miles from the town. Then soldiers with sticks beat the refugees toward Saang as their own officers threw rocks at their men to keep them moving. Cambodians with bullhorns were behind the officers, ordering the Vietcong troops to go back to Vietnam. "Psychological warfare," said the Cambodian commander. As the ragtag procession neared Saang, shooting began and dozens were killed—most shot in the back.

Some of that, but not all by any means, was being reported back to the White House. A National Intelligence Analysis prepared by the CIA, "Stocktaking in Indochina: Longer Term Prospects," was blocked by the agency's director, Richard Helms. The report had concluded that Lon Nol was incapable of stopping the Vietnamese. That could only be done, said the paper, by "sustained and heavy bombing and large numbers of foot soldiers, who could only be supplied by the United States and South Vietnam." Helms knew that was exactly what the President was considering. But the analysis concluded: "But, however successful, it probably would not prevent them from continuing the struggle in some form." Helms sent the analysis back, writing, "Let's take a look at this on June 1st and see if we would keep it or make certain revisions." Within the agency, that was assumed to mean that this was not the time to deliver bad news to the President.

The military, too, was calculating its institutional interest. The Army chief of staff General William C. Westmoreland cabled General Abrams in Saigon on April 21: "As you are certainly aware, there is highest-level concern here with respect to the situation in Cambodia. The threat to Phnom Penh and the present concern of higher authority may be conducive to some relaxation of some of the restraints under which we are operating. If this happens we should be prepared to take advantage of the opportunity."

THERE WERE other stories, too, getting attention back in Washington, a couple of them pretty surprising. In Washington, Sam Brown, the original organizer of the Vietnam Moratorium, was announcing the end of the effort, saying that the movement was obviously having no effect on administration war policies and that demonstrations, though smaller and smaller, were providing cover for radicals intent on organizing revolutionary violence. In Miami, G. Harrold Carswell retired from the Fifth Circuit bench and announced he would seek the Republican nomination for the Senate. The President heard about Carswell—"He's tickled," said Haldeman—just before he went on the air from California on April 20.

The speech proved to be a triumph of an unusual sort: Nixon fooled the press and fooled the nation, too. He had promoted leaks to both *The New York Times* and *The Washington Post* that the next withdrawal would be between 40,000 and 50,000 troops, but he announced a cut of 150,000 of the 434,000 men in Vietnam—changing the numbers and their impact by simply expanding the time. The 150,000 would be withdrawn over a full year, with no specified timetable. The reason there was no timetable was that the President intended to make no withdrawals at all for at least two months, because Abrams in Saigon said he needed the men there to defend against or attack the North Vietnamese sanctuaries in eastern Cambodia.

Nixon finished the fifteen-minute speech just before 5 P.M., California time, and decided he wanted to fly back to Washington. Haldeman was surprised, because Nixon did not like to fly at night, so he guessed he had already decided to move on Cambodia. As *Air Force One* flew east, Nixon said, "Cut the crap on my schedule. I'm taking over here." Then he added, "Troop withdrawal was a boy's job. Cambodia is a man's job."

The plane landed at 1:26 A.M. at Andrews Air Force Base. The President was in his office less than seven hours later, saying he wanted to see Kissinger and CIA director Richard Helms. But before they came in, he dictated a series of memos that his secretary, Rose Mary Woods, sent on to Haldeman with the notation: "Quite a few of the attached memoranda might well be classified 'BURN AFTER—IF NOT BEFORE—READING.' Until we are able to stop the leaks of our confidential memoranda it seems rather dangerous to have some of these floating around. . . ."

The first of the memos was about a leak of a letter from Doctor Hutschnecker to HEW concerning early education programs. Nixon ordered Haldeman to execute what he called "the German option":

> You first are to find out how many people the letter was sent out to. You shall then call Bob Finch and ask him who are the most likely people in his shop who are not on Civil Service who had copies of the letter. . . . There will probably be six people involved. He is then to tell them that they have 48 hours for one of them to come up and say that he leaked the letter. If they do not, he is to ask for the resignation of all six. This is the battle plan. Execute it.

The next were a string of complaints about the press:

> I would like for you to execute a freeze (orally, of course) applying to all White House staffers who might conceivably be called by Maxine Cheshire"—a *Washington Post* society reporter—"return no calls whatever to any *Post* reporter. . . .

> When RN made his statement on Carswell on television *The New York Times* reported that he was "bitter." We had scores of letters

from all over the country saying that they had seen me on television and that the *Times* was completely wrong in that assessment. . . . This will be a notice to them that they can't get away with characterizing how the President looks when he says something, particularly when the President is on live or on film just before or after they say it.

With the exception of Sidey and in his case only when he is trying to get something for his column I want a complete freeze put on *Time* for the next 60 days or until I direct otherwise. . . . I have reasons that I do not want to put in this memorandum or to discuss orally. Just execute the freeze. . . .

One thing you might lean on is the utter silliness of youth using the V signal. Point out that this is old hat. After all, this is a relic of Churchill and World War 2. . . . As far as haircuts are concerned you can really demolish them on this. Point out that they are 25 to 50 years behind the time. Old Tom Connally, Mendel Rivers, Senator Clyde Hoey of North Carolina and conservatives like Les Arends today have worn their hair long for the last half a century. Make it "out" to wear long hair, smoke pot and go on the needle. Make it "in" to indulge in lesser vices, smoking (cigars preferably non-Castro!) and alcohol in reasonable quantities. . . .

On a more important subject, he sent a memo to Kissinger:

I think we need a bold move in Cambodia, assuming that I feel that way today (it is five A.M., April 22) at our meeting as I feel this morning to show that we stand with Lon Nol. I do not believe he is going to survive. We have really dropped the ball on this one due to the fact that we were taken in with the line that by helping him we would destroy his "neutrality" and give the North Vietnamese an excuse to come in. Over and over again we fail to learn that the Communists never need an excuse to come in. . . .

That day, Wednesday, April 22, hundreds of thousands of Americans marched in cities across the country not for or against the war but because of a new cause: Earth Day celebrated the new environmental movement. Across the globe, South Vietnamese troops were positioned on the border of Cambodia, across from the Parrot's Beak. United States troops and more South Vietnamese units were moving into position at another jutting area to the south, this one called the Fishhook. Walking into an NSC meeting that afternoon, the President grinned and nodded toward Kissinger and said: "He's having fun. . . . Playing Bismarck."

The President was not smiling after the meeting. He called Kissinger into the Oval Office and shouted at him in almost uncontrolled rage. He blamed the national security adviser because Vice President Agnew, who usually said nothing at such meetings, had suddenly brushed aside nuanced arguments and said, "Let's stop this pussyfooting and do what we have to. . . ." It was the second time in two weeks Agnew's blunt words had embarrassed the President, made him look soft. When Nixon said he had decided not to attend the graduation of his daughter Julie from Smith College because of antiwar demonstrators and the possibility of violence, Agnew had said, "Don't let them intimidate you, Mr. President. . . . You're her father and a father should be able to attend his daughter's graduation."

Kissinger went back to his task of the moment, creating a system to have messages about Cambodia circulate only in a new loop of a dozen or so men in Washington. "Nodis / Khmer" was the designation— "Nodis" meaning "no distribution," as outlined in a memo to Kissinger from one of his assistants, William Watts, on April 24: "There will be only nine officers in the State Department who will receive these messages including the Secretary. Such messages will be sent directly to Dick Helms on an Eyes Only basis. None will be sent to Defense. . . ."

In fact, Laird and Nixon, through Kissinger, were locked in silent struggle over the President's contradictory cuts in the defense budget and his determination to inflict more punishment on the North Vietnamese. On April 17, Kissinger had signed a "Top Secret / Sensitive / Nodis" memo to Laird stating: "The President has directed . . . there should be no further reductions in levels of tactical air and B-52 sorties and average loadings in Southeast Asia." On April 29, one of Kissinger's men, Lawrence Lynn, sent his boss a memo with the same classification. This one read: "Secretary Laird's response ignores your memo. . . . Faced with Secretary Laird's insubordination, you can: (1) have General Haig call Laird's office and tell them to try again to come up with an acceptable reply; (2) write to or call Laird yourself; (3) report Laird's answer to the President and get him to sign a new directive."

Later that day, a "Nodis / Khmer" message to the U.S. stations in Phnom Penh and Saigon established a pattern of reverse reality: statements from the field were to be crafted to match news briefings in Washington, rather than the other way around. The first memo from Washington read: "Following are relevant excerpts from transcripts of today's White House and Department briefings relating to April 23 NY Times story concerning shipment of AK-47 rifles to Cambodia." In the excerpts, Ziegler and a State Department briefer asserted that the shipments were arranged between the governments of South Vietnam and Cambodia. "You are instructed to seek appointments soonest with GVN and Cambodian officials at appropriate levels . . . to request that GVN and GOC not say anything publicly which would be inconsistent with above . . . and request that in their public statements GVN and GOC not go beyond what US spokesman said. Embassies Phnom Penh and Saigon should, of course, conform any comments to press on this subject along above lines."

The final line of another cable added: "White House instructions emphasize that U.S. statements are to be rigidly adhered to, allow for no additional comment, explanation or speculation whatever."

As for the man in the White House himself, Nixon was spending a good deal of time alone or talking with members of the Joint Chiefs of Staff. He was playing Patton, or so it occasionally seemed to the few White House staffers who knew he was watching the movie again. "Americans have never lost a war and will never lose a war because the very thought of losing is hateful to Americans" was a favorite *Patton* line. Now the President was pacing back and forth in the office and outside in the Rose Garden with his hands locked behind him, the same way actor George C. Scott did playing the general. Standing by the French doors leading to the garden, looking out as Haldeman walked in one morning, the President said, "Damn Johnson, if he'd just done the right thing we wouldn't be in this mess now."

When Nixon talked about Johnson and the right thing, he meant the bombing of North Vietnam, which President Johnson had ordered stopped before the 1968 election, and which Nixon had not resumed because of continuing peace talks, public and private. Ironically, though, the area being fought over since the overthrow of Sihanouk was among the most bombed in history. More than thirty thousand tons of American bombs had been dropped on the Fishhook and the Parrot's Beak, the sanctuaries at the end of the Ho Chi Minh Trail, in the past thirteen months.

On Friday, April 24, the President began the day meeting with Kissinger; Helms; General Robert Cushman, who was deputy director of the CIA; and Admiral Thomas H. Moorer, who was scheduled to become chairman of the Joint Chiefs in May. Nixon told the admiral that he was present only as an adviser to the commander in chief and he was not to tell Defense Secretary Laird of the meeting. By midday it was clear that the President was ready to go ahead with an invasion of the Parrot's Beak by South Vietnamese troops with American advisers and air cover in two days, on Sunday, April 26. After that session, Kissinger met with WSAG, the Washington Special Action Group, which included Helms, Moorer, and deputy secretaries of State and Defense. The group, formed after the EC-121 crisis the year before, was modeled after the special group of advisers President Kennedy had convened during the Cuban missile crisis of October 1962—with a critical difference. Kennedy had included his secretaries of state and defense, while the Nixon-Kissinger group was specifically designed to bypass Rogers and Laird from the final planning of military options.

The WSAG dialogue had escalated in just a few days from sending rifles to Cambodia to a surrogate invasion of the country. After the meeting, Kissinger telephoned Laird to fill him in on some of the President's thinking and orders, and asked for old contingency plans for a Parrot's Beak invasion. Laird suggested that Congress should be consulted. At that point, the national security adviser said the President himself would handle that. Nixon talked by telephone with only a single senator, John Stennis, chairman of the Armed Services Committee. By then it was after 2 P.M. and Nixon left for Camp David with Bebe Rebozo. Kissinger, alone now with Haldeman, told him he thought the President would probably decide against Fishhook options using United States troops on the ground, but that if he decided to go ahead with American troops the war would be won or lost in a year, depending on how the North Vietnamese reacted.

That evening, April 24, Kissinger called together his young staff. There were five of them: William Watts, Winston Lord, Anthony Lake, Roger Morris, and Lawrence Lynn. Every few minutes the phone would ring. It was Nixon barking orders into the phone and then hanging up. Kissinger rolled his eyes each time, finally telling his men, "Our peerless leader has flipped out."

It was a long night. The President called again after watching *Patton* once more. His words slurred together as he gave Kissinger orders—with Watts listening in on an extension. Finally Nixon said, "Wait a minute. Bebe has something to say to you."

"The President wants you to know if this doesn't work, Henry," said Rebozo, "it's your ass."

Still the national security adviser did not tell his young men what was actually happening in Cambodia, talking only of a South Vietnamese operation aided by Americans in spotter planes. All of Kissinger's assistants argued against the idea, saying, sometimes shouting, that it would be a military disaster and it would bring peace activists back into the streets at home. When the meeting was over, Kissinger asked Watts to coordinate NSC staff work on the invasion. Watts refused.

"Your views represent the cowardice of the Eastern establishment," Kissinger told him. Watts moved toward him menacingly, as if he were going to hit him, then wheeled and walked out of the room, went to his desk, and wrote out a letter of resignation. Haig found him there and said: "You can't resign. . . . You've just had an order from your commander in chief."

"Fuck you, Al," Watts said. "I just did."

Lake and Morris talked, then decided they, too, would resign. "As you know we have grave reservations about the value of using U.S. troops in Cambodia," they wrote in a joint letter. "But the reasons for our resignations, involving an increasing alienation from this administration, also predate and go beyond the Cambodian problem. We wished to inform you now, before public reaction to our Cambodia policy, so that it will be clear that our decision was not made after the fact and as a result of those consequences."

They gave the letter to Haig and suggested he deliver it after the invasion began. It was a suggestion he took, not wanting to upset Kissinger more until the deed was done. When Moynihan heard about the decision, he, too, talked of resigning, but stayed after Nixon told him there would be no Family Assistance Plan without him. Moynihan's twenty-two-year-old personal assistant, Arthur Klebanoff, quit, telling his boss that he felt he was on the wrong side of the barricades. "I wish I had an argument to talk you out of this," Moynihan said. "But I don't."

The next day, Saturday, April 25, Kissinger spent the morning going over General Abrams's plans for a joint American–South Vietnamese attack on the Fishhook area, flying by helicopter to Camp David for lunch with the President—with Rebozo sitting in silently. Then the three men flew back to Washington on *Marine One* for an evening cruise on the presidential yacht, the *Sequoia*. Back at the White House by 8:30 that night, the President watched *Patton* again.

On Sunday, April 26, the President spent almost three hours alone in EOB 175, preparing for a National Security Council meeting at 5:30 P.M. It was only then that Secretaries Laird and Rogers realized that the President had made or was about to make a decision to send American troops into Cambodia within the next seventy-two hours, the time General Abrams said was necessary for deployment along the border. Until that session, Laird and Rogers had been cut out of the debate and decision making, even though their deputies had sometimes been part of Nixon's secret planning and debates. Laird was not actively opposing action but he continued to warn the President that American casualties could be as high as five hundred dead a week—and protests at home might be beyond control. The press knew nothing or very little of what was actually happening—most stories focused on the sending of rifles to

Lon Nol—a happy condition for Nixon that he felt had justified the decision to cut Laird and Rogers out of the loop.

Finally, Laird and Rogers were in the President's hideaway office. Agnew was no longer invited. The meeting lasted three hours, with Rogers continuing to argue against involvement of American troops. "High casualties, low gain," he said. He also argued against the repeated use of the phrase "the COSVN operation." "COSVN" stood for "Central Office for South Vietnam," believed to be a complex of concrete emplacements and underground caverns in a bamboo forest five or ten miles inside the Cambodian border. The North Vietnamese insisted the thing did not exist. It did, but as Rogers had told the President and as foreign intelligence sources and journalists confirmed, the communists' command complex was mobile. "The damn thing moves all the time," said the Secretary. "We'll never get it."

Laird would not commit himself either way. His anger was focused on WSAG, saying that the White House, meaning Kissinger, was usurping military authority in implementing the President's decision. The President deflected that by changing the word "implementation" to "coordination," then saying he had not yet made his decision. That was almost certainly untrue, and Laird probably knew that, but he continued to push against using American troops, saying General Abrams was against it. That was not true either, but Nixon responded by ordering Kissinger to ask Abrams specifically about that. So Kissinger, a man of many wordings, sent this query to the commander in Saigon: "Can you assure success using only South Vietnamese troops?"

The President ended the meeting by postponing the attack for twenty-four hours. The reason was that Rogers was scheduled to testify the next day at a closed meeting of the Senate Foreign Relations Committee. Rogers said he would not lie if he were asked about invasion, but he could say there was still no decision. Then he brought up the possibility of demonstrations and campus violence. Nixon said: "I want to hear that now, but if I decide to do it, I don't want to hear of it again. If I decide to do it, it will be because I have decided to pay the price."

Then the President was alone in EOB 175 with his thoughts and his yellow pad, making lists of plusses and minuses. The first plus, the first words he wrote were: "Time running out . . ."

He continued: "Aid to Cambodia can only be symbolic. . . . Provoke move on to Phnom Penh? . . . If they don't move now and we don't either the Cambodian government may fall under Communist control or influence. This may make it impossible to close Sihanoukville or to launch later air attacks on sanctuaries."

He refined the lists as he went along, considering the impacts of using United States troops along with the South Vietnamese army, writing:

> Pluses:
>
> 1) Reduce impact of sanctuaries in Vietnamization.
>
> 2) It may divert Communists from attack on Phnom Penh.
>
> 3) It may undermine leadership of North Viet Nam, or it may lead Hanoi or the Soviets to negotiate.
>
> Minuses:
>
> 1) It could provoke an attack by the Communists on Phnom Penh.
>
> 2) It will create deep divisions in the United States.
>
> 3) It might lead to a cut-off of the Paris talks.
>
> 4) It might provoke a Communist attack across the DMZ. . . .

The President showed the list to Kissinger, who had prepared a similar list, and then Kissinger showed it to columnist Stewart Alsop of *Newsweek*. On the top of his notes, Alsop wrote: "HK—ground rules: Any direct quotes to be checked with HK, HK himself not to be named. . . ."

That was the Kissinger style. Alsop's notes continued:

> HK (not to be used) first saw these yellow sheets on the morning of April 26th, when he briefed Nixon at 8 A.M., said that he never offered views on domestic matters, but that he did have a certain knowledge of university life, and he feared that if the President moved against Cambodia with US troops, some universities would be burned, and the whole academic community would be up in arms.
>
> The President said, "Believe me, I've considered that danger," then produced his yellow sheet and pointed to his second minus item. . . .

Alsop continued, quoting Kissinger in his notes:

> The downfall of Sihanouk was entirely unpredictable, and changed the whole ballgame. Suppose the President had done

nothing, and both Cambodia and Laos had fallen by midsummer. Then the reaction of the opposition would be wholly predictable: Why kill Americans for South Viet Nam when Cambodia and Laos have already gone? "It would have taken one big Communist attack on the lines of Tet to make our whole position untenable." Now we have time, flexibility, we can move in any direction, with some sort of ground rules, we can get out very fast. . . . If we have two years . . .

SA: "Henry, you haven't got two years."

HK: "No, but we have to act as though we had."

Our problem is that the whole establishment, which detests Nixon, has turned against him at the very moment that he is trying to save the establishment. Nixon is not a fool. He is perfectly aware that there is no way to leave South Vietnam with all the banners flying. "But we have to get out as a matter of policy—American policy. We cannot be shoved out. If we are shoved out by the North Vietnamese this would have terrible effects abroad and it would tear this country apart, and hand it over to the hard hats. This is why Nixon is in the curious position of trying to save an establishment which despises him."

Then Kissinger compared Nixon's thinking with de Gaulle's actions in withdrawing French troops from Algeria in 1962, calling the French leader a great illusionist who staged a retreat from North Africa in a way that made France look more powerful than it actually was. Alsop responded, according to his own notes:

"Great minds think alike—I've compared Nixon on Viet Nam to the Wizard of Oz, his great clouds of rhetoric designed to conceal the fact that he has embarked on the greatest retreat in history." HK smiles and nods agreement. The trick, he says, in effect, is to stage a great retreat and emerge at the other end still a great power, reasonably cohesive at home. . . .

In the middle of writing out his yellow pages, Nixon paused and telephoned Haldeman to say that he had decided the solarium of the White House living quarters was too small for a pool table he wanted, telling his assistant to find a room for the table in the EOB. "Absolutely astonishing," wrote the chief of staff in his diary that night. "He could get into trivia on the brink of the biggest step he's taken so far."

On Monday afternoon, Rogers was questioned for two and a half hours in a closed session of the Senate Foreign Relations Committee;

later, he reported to the President that the questions focused on military aid and arms shipments to Lon Nol's government. When the doors opened, the committee chairman, Senator William Fulbright, told waiting reporters that the committee was unanimously opposed to sending weapons to Phnom Penh. Neither he nor reporters mentioned the use of American troops.

The President was on his own. He had already decided that if American troops were part of Fishhook, they might as well join the Parrot's Beak operation. He told this to Rogers and Laird and Attorney General Mitchell in a twenty-minute meeting on Tuesday, April 28. Mitchell prepared the report of the meeting, writing: "The President further stated that, in arriving at his decision, he had taken into consideration the positions taken by the Secretary of State and the Secretary of Defense in opposition to the use of U.S. forces. . . ."

The President noticed that Mitchell seemed distracted, as he often had recently. In a dictated memo to Haldeman, the President said: "As I am sure you have noted, Martha Mitchell gave an exclusive interview to Myra McPherson of *The Washington Post* and got chopped up again. . . . see if he can exert any pressure on her press adviser to keep her from sticking her neck out." Mrs. Mitchell was a heavy drinker who spent days and nights on the telephone, alternately amusing and abusing the people on the other end of the line. The White House military assistant, William Gulley, had gotten a 4:30 A.M. call that was mostly silence on her end punctuated by screamed lines like: "Don't you go back to sleep you little son-of-a-bitch. Remember that my husband is the fucking Attorney General of the United States of America."

The order to enter Cambodia was sent by cable on Tuesday night to General Abrams in Saigon by General Earle Wheeler, chairman of the Joint Chiefs: "Higher authority has authorized certain military actions to protect U.S. forces operating in South Vietnam. Authorization is granted for a combined US/GVN operation against Base Area 352/353."

At 10:09 that night, the President called Kissinger to ask whether the South Vietnamese—with American support troops—had entered the Parrot's Beak. "Yes, Mr. President" was the answer. The South Vietnamese government planned to make no announcement until the next morning. Using the "Nodis" channel, a "Top Secret / Sensitive" cable from Rogers to the embassy in Saigon directed: "Avoid picturing this as a major operation but rather handle publicity from Saigon in the pattern of the shallow border penetrations that have thus far taken place. . . . An attempt will be made to prevent media representatives from accompanying the forces and it is suggested that Cambodia do what it can to prevent or discourage correspondents in Cambodia from entering the area." Within an hour, the answer came back from Lloyd Rives, the American chargé d'affaires in Phnom Penh: "Government of Cambodia will take steps see that journalists do not rush Parrot's Beak too quickly. I gather that ferry at Neak Leung may have breakdown." Cambodian soldiers would prevent reporters and photographers from using the ferry so they could not get to the action.

Cambodia was not in the news the next morning. That day *The New York Times* reported that the American Bar Association had issued a statement on the nomination of Judge Blackmun for the Supreme Court, saying he met "high standards of professional competency, temperament and integrity." Another front-page story, under the headline "DEMOCRATS PRESS FOR PARTY REFORM," reported that a twenty-eight-member party commission headed by Senator George McGovern of South Dakota was stating: "We believe that popular control of the Democratic Party is necessary for its survival." "Popular control" was a euphemism for greatly reducing the influence of local and state party leaders in the selection of delegates to the 1972 Democratic National Convention.

That night, Wednesday, Nixon wrote alone until midnight in the Lincoln sitting room, drafting the speech he intended to give after the entrance of United States troops into Cambodia. He called Kissinger a dozen times—barking orders like "Fire Rives!" and hanging up—and also called Governor Nelson Rockefeller of New York and the Reverend Billy Graham. He told Rockefeller that Defense Department recommendations amounted to "a little nit-picker," then said: "If you are going to take the heat, go for all the marbles. . . . I have made some bad decisions, but a good one was this: When you bite the bullet, bite it hard—go for the big play."

HE WAS UP AGAIN at 1:15 A.M. after an hour's sleep—it was Thursday, April 30, now—and worked on the speech until 4:45 A.M. before going back to bed. By then the South Vietnamese in Saigon had announced their entry into the Parrot's Beak. His press secretary, Ron Ziegler, was reciting the line Nixon had dictated the day before: This was the same as the South Vietnamese border crossings of the past couple of weeks—just bigger, that's all. The *New York Times* headline that morning reflected the line:

U.S. AIDS SAIGON PUSH IN CAMBODIA
WITH PLANES, ARTILLERY AND ADVISERS;
MOVE STIRS OPPOSITION IN SENATE
NIXON TO SPEAK ON TV TONIGHT
ACTION IS TERMED LIMITED

The President spent most of April 30 by himself, continuing to work on the television speech scheduled for 9 P.M. At about 3 P.M., he read his latest draft to Kissinger and Haldeman in the small study off the Oval Office. Both men approved—although the President was not really consulting them or anyone else. When Kissinger left the room, Nixon told Haldeman to give him a lecture that his job at press backgrounders was not to perform but to sell. "Make sure he understands that, Bob," he said.

At 6 P.M., the President sat down with congressional leaders of both parties in the Cabinet Room to tell them that United States troops would be crossing the border at the Fishhook in less than three hours. One congressman, apparently trying to embarrass Nixon, asked why, if the border crossing was as limited as he was telling them, the code name was "Operation Total Victory." Kissinger took that one, saying "Total Victory" was the South Vietnamese code name—the United States designation was "Rock Crusher"—and that they called every action "Total Victory."

"This one," he said, "is 'Total Victory 42.' "

The President left after twenty-five minutes. Later he told Haldeman that the only intelligent question had come from Senator Edward Kennedy, who quietly asked where the money was coming from as the other leaders stood and applauded when Nixon started to walk out. Nixon stopped at the doorway. He walked back into the room and said that after he lost to John Kennedy in 1960, a woman came up to him at a dinner in Illinois and said she had voted for him, adding: "Mr. Nixon, it's just too bad for television that you can't do something about your face." The leaders laughed and applauded again.

Then Haldeman and Kissinger presided over a briefing in the Roosevelt Room for the White House staff. The chief of that staff handed out a one-page paper titled "Points on the Cambodia Military Action," which began: "For the past ten days the enemy has enormously increased its activities in the 'Cambodia pocket.' " It ended: "Only the President has all the facts in this situation. He must act in what he considers to be the best interests of our country and our troops."

Kissinger's presentation was more confrontational. There were questions about domestic reaction, which the national security adviser shrugged off, saying, "We'll get paid off if we end the war, not if we get the doves off our backs. The point is we won't play the game by the communists' rules. Anyone who wants to negotiate a peace has to hang tough. If we get through this, we should have a negotiation by July or August."

Donald Rumsfeld, the head of the Office of Economic Opportunity, interrupted: "We shouldn't say this is not an expansion, that's not credible." Kissinger flushed and snapped back: "That is what makes me personally as well as institutionally impatient. Here the North Vietnamese have 40,000 troops marching on the capital of Cambodia, and a lousy fifty U.S. advisers go in last night, and you hear Senators say we're the ones who are escalating."

As the meeting broke up, Bill Safire asked Kissinger if the use of American troops was a kind of violation of the Nixon Doctrine. The answer was: "We wrote the goddamned doctrine; we can change it." At the end of that session, Ehrlichman, half-joking about a Black Panther murder trial in New Haven—the city was surrounded by ten thousand federal troops ready to move in—and the possibility of trouble at Yale after the speech, said in a German accent that mocked Kissinger's: "Tomorrow, right here, a briefink on der operations around New Hafen."

"We" did not write the specch. Nixon had, and he revealed a good deal about himself and his view of the war and his Presidency. He exaggerated the crisis at home and abroad. He also lied a couple of times, saying, "For five years, neither the United States nor South Vietnam has moved against these enemy sanctuaries because we did not wish to violate the territory of a neutral nation." Unmentioned was the thirteen months of secret bombing.

The President rejected Secretary Rogers's advice not to emphasize COSVN, the secret communist superheadquarters. There was a large map behind Nixon as he came on national television that night. He said:

> The sanctuaries are in red. . . . These communist-occupied territories contain major base camps, training sites, logistic facilities, weapons and ammunition factories, air strips and prisoner of war compounds. . . . Tonight, American and South Vietnamese units will attack the headquarters for the entire Communist military operation. . . . This is not an invasion of Cambodia. The areas in which these attacks will be launched are completely occupied and controlled by North Vietnamese forces. Our purpose is not to occupy the areas. Once enemy forces are driven out of these sanctuaries and their military supplies are destroyed, we will withdraw.

Then he changed his tone and the subject, describing a war at home:

> We live in an age of anarchy. We see mindless attacks on all the great institutions which have been created by free civilizations in

the last five hundred years. Even here in the United States, great universities are being systematically destroyed. Small nations all over the world find themselves under attack from within and from without. . . . If when the chips are down, the world's most powerful nation, the United States of America, acts like a pitiful helpless giant, the forces of totalitarianism and anarchy will threaten free nations and free institutions throughout the world. . . . I would rather be a one-term President and do what I believe is right than to be a two-term President at the cost of seeing America become a second-rate power and to see this nation accept the first defeat in its proud 190-year history. . . . It is not our power but our will and character that is being tested tonight.

In this room, Woodrow Wilson made the great decisions which led to victory. . . . Franklin Roosevelt made the decisions that led to our victory. . . . Dwight D. Eisenhower made decisions that ended the war. . . . John F. Kennedy, in his finest hour, made the great decision. . . .

It is customary to end a speech from the White House by asking support for the President. What I ask is far more important. I ask for your support for our brave men fighting tonight halfway around the world.

In Phnom Penh, Lloyd Rives learned that the invasion was a full-scale American operation only when he heard the President's speech on Voice of America radio. He rushed to Lon Nol's home, later cabling the Secretary of State: "FLASH..TOP SECRET: Unable discuss with Lon Nol prior president's speech. Lon Nol received me at 0900. . . . I expressed regret at inability alert GOC. Cambodians were all extremely interested and grateful for information and actions being taken by USG. Lon Nol was receiving the press including NBC television and New York Times immediately. . . . We discussed his proposed answers to obvious questions. He would stick largely to past scenario, explaining ignorance of events occurring . . . but also generally approving actions leading to removal enemy forces from Cambodian soil."

General Lon Nol also told the press, as a joke, that the Americans reminded him of the Vietcong—both were uninvited guests in Cambodia. Rives told him the number of Americans was being announced as five thousand. In fact, there were more than thirty-one thousand U.S. troops (and more than forty-three thousand South Vietnamese) in the invading force. They met little resistance. Three U.S. helicopters were shot down the first day, but the casualty report listed only six men wounded.

The first waves of calls and telegrams to the White House praised the President by a ratio of 6 to 1—that was the first announcement made by Ziegler the next morning, May 1. He had been called into the Oval Office by the President and given the line for the day: "Cold steel, no give, nothing about negotiation. . . . Stay strong, whole emphasis on 'back the boys,' sell courage of President."

As Ziegler began his briefing, the President was on his way to the Pentagon, to personally emphasize the "back the boys" message. He was cheered in the hallways—"God bless you, Sir!" "Right on!"—and a young secretary whose husband was in Vietnam came up to him there and said, "I loved your speech, Mr. President. It made me proud to be an American."

"I wrote that for those kids out there," Nixon replied. "I have seen them. They're the greatest."

Then he gave his opinion of antiwar kids. "You see these bums, you know, blowing up the campuses. Listen, the boys that are on college campuses today are the luckiest people in the world, going to the greatest universities, and here they are, burning up the books, storming around about this issue . . . you name it. Get rid of the war and there will be another one."

In a closed meeting with Pentagon briefers, going over maps of Cambodia, the President asked about four areas besides the Parrot's Beak and Fishhook, which were marked red, indicating heavy concentrations of enemy troops. "Could we take out all those sanctuaries?" he asked.

The officers began to talk about larger antiwar demonstrations, but the President interrupted: "Let me be the judge as far as political reactions are concerned. . . . I want to take out all those sanctuaries. Make whatever plans are necessary, and then just do it. Let's go blow the hell out of them. Knock them all out so that they can't be used against us again. Ever."

It was a warm and sunny spring day in Washington. After he left the Pentagon, the President decided to take a cruise on the Potomac with his wife; his daughter Julie and her husband, David Eisenhower; Bebe Rebozo; Rose Mary Woods; and one of his military attachés, Marine Colonel John V. Brennan. Woods, who had known Nixon for twenty years, thought she had never seen him so exhausted—or so exuberant.

After a couple of drinks, the President said to Brennan in a deliberately gruff voice: "Do you approve of what I said last night?"

"It was one of the proudest moments of my life," he answered. "I only wish I were over there to help carry out what you've ordered."

"I do too," said the President. "I think I'll resign and we'll go together."

When the yacht approached Mount Vernon, where naval vessels always salute George Washington's tomb by playing the national anthem, the President ordered the captain: "Really blast it out!" He stood at rigid attention there in the bow of the yacht, then he turned to the crew with a wide smile and shot his right thumb into the air.

At five o'clock he helicoptered to Camp David and sat down to watch *Patton* again.

CHAPTER 13

May 4, 1970

PRESIDENT NIXON was on the phone with Haldeman much of Saturday, May 2. "Good numbers," reported the chief of staff, 65 percent approval of the speech in a Chilton poll done for the White House. The Gallup poll put the approval at 51 percent, disapproval at 35 percent. Nixon told Haldeman he should let everybody go home, get some rest.

"No," was the answer. "Not now when we've got things rolling. I'll let up on them later."

That night the President watched *Patton* again, then early on Sunday he came back to Washington and walked into a meeting of Haldeman's Cambodia Action Group and talked for ten minutes. "This will buy the time we need for Vietnamization. . . . It took ten months to build up this complex, and we're tearing the living bejesus out of it," he said. "Anything that walked is gone after that barrage and B-52 raids. . . ."

He went on: "Don't play a soft line—no aid and comfort here. Big game is to pull this off. Bold move, imaginative, none of this screwing around. Congressmen, really put it to them, some of them are cowards— sticking the knife in the back of U.S. troops, not supporting the President. . . . Giving aid and comfort to the enemy—use that phrase. Don't worry about divisiveness—having drawn the sword, don't take it out— stick it in hard. . . . Hit 'em in the gut."

That morning *The New York Times* revealed new secret bombing of North Vietnam. The lead story by William Beecher, who had revealed the secret and continuing bombing of Cambodia, reported the first heavy bombing of the north since President Johnson had suspended heavy raids before the 1968 elections. The three-column headline read:

128 U.S. PLANES CARRY OUT
ATTACK IN NORTH VIETNAM;
SUPPLY LINES ARE TARGETS.

Hearing of the questions Beecher was asking around Washington, Kissinger had called Max Frankel, the *Times*'s Washington bureau chief, on Saturday to request that the story be held in the interests of national security. Beecher was listening on an extension. The *Times* went ahead, and among those who learned of the bombing from the paper was Defense Secretary Laird. Nixon, through Kissinger, had dealt directly with the new chairman of the Joint Chiefs, Admiral Thomas Moorer.

Before the *Times* was on the street, Alexander Haig had formally notified the FBI of a "serious security violation" and asked for four new wiretaps: on Beecher; on Laird's principal assistant, Colonel Robert Pursley; on one of Secretary of State Rogers's assistants, Richard Pederson; and on Deputy Assistant Secretary of State William H. Sullivan, a former ambassador to Laos.

Below Beecher's story, a two-column headline read: "ALLIED SEARCH IN CAMBODIA YIELDS FEW SIGNS OF FOES." In the Fishhook area, American and Vietnamese troops had driven twenty miles inside Cambodia without encountering significant numbers of North Vietnamese or Vietcong. Eight Americans had been killed and thirty-two wounded. The invaders had found large stores of ammunition and equipment, but the enemy was gone, having moved westward into Cambodia.

On Monday, May 4, the President announced that the raids on North Vietnam had been "terminated." That same day, the presidents of thirty-seven of the most prestigious universities in the country—Columbia, New York University, and Notre Dame among them—sent the White House an "urgent" open letter warning of new campus demonstrations. Student strikes had already closed down some schools and were scheduled at more than one hundred universities and colleges. Students were rampaging at Stanford, Princeton, and the University of Kansas. Their favorite targets were ROTC buildings and offices.

In Ohio, two or three thousand students from Kent State University had surged through the town of Kent on Friday night, May 1, breaking shopwindows and battling with police who tried to clear the streets. The next night, a fire was set at the school's old wooden ROTC building, which burned to the ground as dancing, cheering students watched. Governor James A. Rhodes, who had already ordered National Guardsmen onto the campus of Ohio State University in Columbus, called in troops of the 145th Infantry, Ohio National Guard, saying their mission was to "eradicate the communist element." "Brownshirts . . . worse than Brownshirts," Rhodes called the demonstrators, comparing the Kent State students to Hitler Youth. On Monday, May 4, about two thousand of Kent's twenty thousand students gathered on campus, some of them taunting the guardsmen, men their own age in gas masks. Thousands more were gathered at a distance watching the confrontation. The soldiers tried to break up the crowd of demonstrators by firing tear gas. Students threw the steaming canisters back. Then the soldiers, kneeling in a firing line, tried to bluff the students, but did not fire. The troops then withdrew to another line on a small hill, as some students kept after them. This time they fired. There was a fusillade of sixty-seven shots in thirteen seconds as the front lines of the demonstrators turned and ran.

The President was in EOB 175 alone when Haldeman hurried over just before 3 P.M., saying: "Something just came over the wires about a demonstration at Kent State in Ohio. The National Guard opened fire and some students were shot."

"Are they dead?" Nixon asked.

Four students were dead, eleven wounded.

Nixon was stunned. "Is this because of me, of Cambodia? . . . How do we turn this stuff off?"

"I hope they provoked it," he said. Probably not, Haldeman told him, there was just some rock throwing. The White House issued a statement from the President:

> This should remind us all once again that when dissent turns to violence it invites tragedy. It is my hope that this tragic and unfortunate incident will strengthen the determination of all the nation's campuses, administrators, faculty and students alike, to stand firmly for the right which exists in this country of peaceful dissent and just as strongly against the resort to violence as a means of such expression.

The next morning almost every newspaper in the United States used the same photographs over front-page reports. One showed Guardsmen in gas masks, bayonets unsheathed, advancing on the students behind a cloud of tear gas. The other showed a kneeling girl, arms outspread over a dead student on a campus walkway. The father of one of the dead students was quoted as saying, "My child was not a bum."

There was tear gas in the air across the country, with new student demonstrations breaking out in every state. One school, Boston University, simply shut down, informing its commencement speaker, Senator Edward Kennedy, that there would be no ceremony.

The President's formal schedule on May 5 began and ended with closed meetings with congressional committees on Cambodia: breakfast with the Senate and House Armed Services Committees; a 5 P.M. session with the House Foreign Affairs Committee and the Senate Foreign Relations Committee. His talking papers, prepared by the NSC, reported more than two thousand enemy killed, 837 bunkers captured, 27 tons of ammunition and 395 tons of rice seized, but at the same time drastically scaled back presidential rhetoric, emphasizing limits and lowered expectations: "Our principal target is not personnel but the enemy's logistic infrastructure. . . . Limited measures—they should only last six to eight weeks, at which time allied forces will be withdrawn. . . ."

In the meetings Nixon went further, pledging his "firm commitment" that American troops would be out of Cambodia in three to seven weeks. He then said that no troops would go more than twenty-one miles into the country. He also had a legal justification for the entry into Cambodia, a fourteen-page brief written after the fact by Assistant Attorney General William Rehnquist.

Outside those meetings, political battle lines were being drawn, even within the administration. The next day's *New York Times* reported the results of calls and lunches across Washington in a story headlined "ROGERS AND LAIRD TERMED DOUBTFUL." Max Frankel wrote: "There is increasing evidence of . . . serious misgivings about the use of American troops in Cambodia. . . . an atmosphere of confusion, as well as dissent." The story also questioned the President's COSVN statements, reporting that officials in the State and Defense Departments had reported to him that the headquarters complex had been moved into South Vietnam in late March because of communist fears that the Cambodia sanctuaries would be attacked before the rainy season began in June.

Once again, this time on Nixon's order, Kissinger called in Stewart Alsop of *Newsweek*. The columnist's notes of this meeting read:

> Much exercised by statement p. 32 NWeek, to the effect that Laird was "not wired in" on the Viet Nam decision; that he was by-passed when K delivered orders direct to JCS. "That is a total untruth—I don't know how to put it more strongly than that." . . .
>
> Kissinger no Nixon idolator. But you had to give him credit for doing what he thought in the natl interest. There was nothing to

gain for him—if he had decided just to slide out, the establishment—Clifford, Vance, Gardner, Bundy, etc.—would have applauded him—at least until things went wrong. . . . HK very bitter about "establishment's" feebleness—"they are mounting an attack on the authority of the Presidency just to provide a catharsis for their own failure." *

Between his meetings with the congressional committees, the President spent more than an hour with a half-dozen of his economic advisers to discuss another immediate effect of the move into Cambodia. The Dow-Jones industrial average of securities prices on the New York Stock Exchange dropped 17 points in two hours after the news of the Kent State shootings was sent out in an Associated Press bulletin—the largest one-day drop since the assassination of President Kennedy on November 22, 1963.

So far, on Nixon's watch, the Dow had dropped from 985 on December 3, 1968, to under 700, a seven-year low, and was still declining at the fastest rate since 1938. Prices were up, rising at a rate of almost 6 percent, unemployment had gone from 3.3 percent to 4.8 percent; gross national product had dropped 3 percent on an annual basis in the first quarter of the year. Newspapers were mocking the single line on economics from his Inaugural address: "We have learned at last to manage a modern economy to assure its continued growth." A survey by Louis Harris reported that 78 percent of corporate executives blamed the market decline on Nixon's policies—or ignorance—and particularly on his inability to end the war. Liberal economists and Democratic politicians were hitting him almost daily from the other side. Senator Edmund Muskie, considered the front-runner for the 1972 Democratic presidential nomination, said, "In the 1920s it took Republicans eight years to go from prosperity to unemployment and now they've learned to do it in one year." Economist Paul Samuelson of the Massachusetts Institute of Technology, in his column in Newsweek, linked the crisis on Wall Street and the war: "If Mr. Nixon were to announce defeat in Viet Nam and cutting of our losses, the market would jump 50 points. People are distrustful. . . . They want the peace without victory that we are going to get in two years, but they want it now."

The country was diving into recession in an election year. The President considered himself an economic conservative, but he was in

* Former defense secretary Clark M. Clifford, former undersecretary of state Cyrus R. Vance, Common Cause president John W. Gardner, and former national security adviser McGeorge Bundy all had served in the Johnson administration.

fact a politician with a single goal: to do whatever was necessary to hold off a recession until after the 1970 congressional elections. The purpose of the meeting with his economic advisers was to pressure Arthur Burns, now at the Federal Reserve, to forget his own conservatism in service to that goal. A meeting memo to the President concluded: "Dr. Burns . . . will agree that a small deficit is acceptable as long as expenditure levels are kept in the $197.9 billion area." That was for the fiscal year 1970 budget, which Nixon had pledged to balance but now wanted to use to try to stimulate the economy before November. Burns reported that he had persuaded the Federal Reserve Board to reduce the margin requirement for stock purchases from 80 percent to 65 percent—which might drive the Dow up a few points. "It's heresy," Burns told Nixon later, "but I'm even thinking about wage and price controls."

The next day, Wednesday, May 6, with the number of closed universities reaching eighty, Secretary of the Interior Walter J. Hickel, a former governor of Alaska, sent the President a letter saying, "Youth in its protest must be heard," and invoking the names of great American "youths"—Patrick Henry, Thomas Jefferson, James Madison—to charge Nixon and the administration with failing the young people of the country. Nixon read the letter before it reached the White House; the text, which closed with "Faithfully yours," was on the front page of the afternoon *Washington Star*. The President was furious; his first order was to immediately break up the White House tennis court, regularly used by Hickel and other Cabinet members.

By the end of the week, there were National Guardsmen on twenty-one campuses in sixteen states and the number of closed colleges and universities had reached 448. There had been demonstrations on more than 1,100 campuses and two million students were on strike. And there was a counterattack, at least in downtown New York City, where hard-hat construction workers in the Wall Street area charged into an antiwar demonstration; they were waving flags and swinging fists, lead pipes, and crowbars, injuring at least seventy of the young protesters. Another group of construction men stormed City Hall, demanding that the American flag flying at half-mast to honor the four students killed at Kent State be raised to its full height. In Washington, more than two hundred Foreign Service officers and other State Department employees signed a petition condemning the Cambodia action. Nixon responded to that with a 1:30 A.M. call to Undersecretary of State U. Alexis Johnson: "Fire them all!"

The President was elated by the charge of the hard hats. It seemed to validate his views of a new kind of politics, a shadow of the realignment he hoped to create. Union leaders were being quoted as saying they supported the President not because he was pro-labor—"Because he isn't for labor," said Peter Brennan of New York's Building Trades Council—but because he was the president. A twenty-seven-year-old electrician named James Lapham, who was working on a graduate degree in European history, put it this way: "This is not the 1930s. Labor is middle-class and has middle-class attitudes. We don't like students coming to tell us that everything that has made us that way is rotten. . . ." Wallace Butenhoff, a forty-three-year-old sheet metal worker and a World War II veteran, said: "Some of them spit on our flag. . . . Don't think we're for the war. No one is . . . I don't want the war. But we elected Nixon and we have to back him."

Nixon could not say it better, though he tried many times. In one of the great ironies, the President's New York hard hats marched behind a hand-painted sign that read: "GOD BLESS THE ESTABLISHMENT." Speaking from Chicago, though, the hugely popular radio commentator Paul Harvey, whose antiestablishment conservatism was something like Nixon's, told millions of his listeners across the country: "America's six-percent section of the planet's mothers cannot bear enough boy babies to police Asia—and the nation can't bleed to death trying."

A true voice of the elites Nixon so hated, The New Yorker magazine, abandoned wit for alarms in its urbane "Talk of the Town" section: "The two-hundred-year-old American system is under its most serious attack in modern times, not from the poor, the blacks, or the students, but from the White House. . . . Disregard of the Constitution, the tempering strictures of our history, and the principles of the American democracy . . . an act of usurpation . . . War by fiat . . . Our democracy is not an elective dictatorship. . . . The President has now declared himself superior to the people, to the legislature, and to the laws."

ON THE NIGHT OF FRIDAY, MAY 8, after a day and a half alone at Camp David, the President returned to Washington for a televised news conference, his first in three months. He was visibly nervous, sweating as he began. There were twenty-six questions, one about the stock market, one about the still-pending sale of jets to Israel, and twenty-four about Cambodia, the war, and demonstrations:

"Mr. President, have you been surprised about the intensity of the protest?"

"Mr. President, what do you think the students are trying to say?"

"Mr. President, some Americans believe this country is headed for revolution . . . ?"

"Mr. President, Vice President Agnew is quoted . . . ?"

"Mr. President, on your use of the word 'bums' . . . ?"

"Mr. President, what have we accomplished in Cambodia? Was

it worth the risk, and what do we do when they reestablish those sanctuaries?"

"Sir, without asking you to censor the Secretary of the Interior . . . ?"

"Mr. President, in light of the Kent State incident . . . ?"

To the question about what the Cambodian operation had accomplished, Nixon answered:

> I will say that it is my belief, based on what we have accomplished to date, that we have bought at least six months and probably eight months of time for the training of the ARVN, the Army of South Vietnam. We have also saved, I think, hundreds, if not thousands, of Americans. . . . Rockets by the thousands and small arms ammunition by the millions have already been captured and those rockets and small arms will not be killing Americans in these next few months. And what we have also accomplished is that by buying time, it means that if the enemy does come back into those sanctuaries next time, the South Vietnamese will be strong enough and well trained enough to handle it alone.

Of the students, he said:

> They are trying to say that they want peace. They are trying to say that they want to stop the killing. They are trying to say that they want to end the draft. They are trying to say that we ought to get out of Vietnam. I agree with everything that they are trying to accomplish.

When the President went upstairs to the residence, staff members stayed until a half hour past midnight answering calls from ordinary citizens. Walking out into the hot night—the temperature was still above eighty degrees in the early hours of Saturday—the secretaries and operators passed through hundreds of combat-ready troops of the Third Army. The soldiers were jumping from trucks to take up hidden positions inside the Executive Office Building. The orders from the Department of Defense read: "They should be capable of rapid response; however, minimum visibility should be the key." Buses were being maneuvered to form a wall outside the wrought iron fence around the White House grounds. Five thousand more troops were moving into government buildings around the city as the first of tens of thousands of antiwar demonstrators began congregating in the night, gravitating toward the lawns and lights around the monuments visible from the back of the White House.

• • •

In the Lincoln sitting room, the President was making one phone call after another to talk about the news conference—forty-seven calls between 9:22 P.M. and 1:55 A.M. He talked to Kissinger seven times, Haldeman seven times, Rose Mary Woods four times. He called two of the most famous clergymen in the country, Billy Graham and Norman Vincent Peale, and two reporters, Helen Thomas of United Press International and Nancy Dickerson of NBC News.

"I really love those kids," he said to Dickerson at 1:30 A.M. "I've told Haldeman and Ehrlichman to bring them in. I want to see them all."

He even called Hickel. He returned a call made by Safire, who was in Atlanta with Vice President Agnew, and rambled on for seven minutes, saying, "All this business up here, it'll work out okay. If the crazies try anything, we'll clobber them—relax, whenever I say anything like that it drives people up the wall, I know. . . . What are you doing in Atlanta? . . . You know, my father's grandfather is buried down there. My father's father was born after his father was killed in the Civil War. . . . My mother's grandfather ran an underground railroad. . . . This Southern Strategy stuff—all we're doing is treating the South with the same respect as the North. But your friends in New York won't see it that way. . . ."

And on and on. Nixon went to bed a little after 2 A.M. but was up again at 3:24, calling Paul Keyes, a producer of the television show *Rowan & Martin's Laugh-In,* and then Kissinger again. He put Rachmaninoff's second piano concerto on the record player and then called his valet, Manolo Sanchez, at 4:22 A.M.

"Have you ever been to the Lincoln Memorial at night?" he asked Sanchez, a Cuban who had just become an American citizen. "Get your clothes on, we'll go!"

At 4:35 A.M., the President and his valet walked outside, startling Secret Service agents. "Searchlight"—Nixon's code name—"Searchlight is on the lawn," crackled through security speakers.

"Oh, my God!" said Bud Krogh, who was on night duty in the war-room operation collecting and coordinating information on demonstrations. Then the speaker behind him kicked on again: "Searchlight has asked for a car." Krogh called Ehrlichman at home, asking him what to do. "Go out there and introduce yourself," Ehrlichman said. "Ask him if there's anything you can do."

But by the time the young assistant got outside, Nixon was gone. Krogh ordered another car and headed for the Lincoln Memorial. When he got there a few minutes later, the President was on the steps of the monument talking quietly with eight or ten young men and women. It was a very quiet scene, hazy in the first glimmering of dawn. The President did not seem awkward to Krogh, even though he was surrounded by young men with wild hair. The people who were most obviously and nervously out of their element were the Secret Service men. The demonstrators-in-waiting were respectful, bewildered at first. Nixon, tired and wired, was doing almost all the talking—an introverted man avoiding the risks of interaction.

Some of the students, who had driven through the night to protest the war and this man, seemed to be in awe when the man himself showed up. Krogh felt proud to serve Nixon.

The President asked where they were from, how old they were. Then he asked if they had heard the news conference. No. He said he had tried to make the point that his goals were the same as theirs, to end the war and stop the killing. "I know that probably most of you think I'm an S.O.B., but I want you to know that I understand just how you feel. . . ." Then he talked about being poor when he was young, about being a Quaker and not wanting to go to war or into the military, thinking that Neville Chamberlain was a hero for seeking peace with Hitler. "I thought Winston Churchill was a madman. . . . But I was wrong. . . ."

He spun on, talking of the importance of travel, as he always did with young audiences: See the great United States, see the world while you can. Pat and he borrowed money to see Mexico when they were young. Somehow that led him to talk about the mistreatment of American Indians—"We have to find ways to bring them back into decent lives"—and he urged the white students to learn to communicate with blacks, not separate from them. Something pushed the environment button and he said he had ordered the Marine Corps to allow surfing on the beaches off Camp Pendleton near San Clemente. He began to describe world cities, beginning with the grayness of Moscow, saying he hoped to see China and bring its seven hundred million people back into the world.

The group around him had grown to a couple of dozen, including Ron Ziegler, who was trying to pull him away, urging Sanchez to tell him there was an urgent call on the car telephone. One of the newcomers, wearing an Army surplus jacket, the ironic uniform of the day, said, "I hope you realize we are willing to die for what we believe in."

"Certainly I realize that," said Nixon. "Do you realize that many of us, when we were your age, were also willing to die for what we believed in, and are willing to do so today? The point is that we are trying to build a world in which you will not have to die for what you believe in."

After a half hour, the President said he had to go, turning to say, "Don't go away bitter." A young man with a red beard walked down the steps, taking pictures with a small camera. The President asked him for the camera and motioned to Dr. Tkach, who had come with Ziegler, to take a photo of him and the young man. He stopped to shake hands with three young women, asking where they were from, where they went to school. "Syracuse University," one said, and Nixon said he knew the city and asked her how the football team was doing.

Back in the car just before 6 A.M., the President asked Krogh how Ziegler and Tkach knew where he was. "I called Ehrlichman," Krogh said. Nixon looked at him for a moment and said, "It's wrong to wake people up like that in the middle of the night."

"Let's go to the Capitol," the President said. They entered the building on the Senate side—shocking the night guards and watchmen—and Nixon tried to get into the office he had used as Vice President in the 1950s. But it was locked. On the other side of the building, a custodian named Frazer had a key to the chamber of the House of Representatives and let them in. Nixon went to the seat he had when he came to the House in 1947 and sat down. "Manolo," he called, and sent Sanchez to the podium used by the Speaker of the House.

"Speak, speak," the President said. Sanchez said he was proud to be an American now. Nixon applauded in the empty chamber.

As Nixon and Sanchez left the chamber, three cleaning women came up to the President. One, Carrie Moore, asked him to sign her Bible. "Most of us don't read it enough these days," he said as he wrote his name.

"Mr. President, I read it all the time," Mrs. Moore said.

He took her hand, held it, and said, "You know, my mother was a saint. She died two years ago. She was a saint." Krogh thought he was about to cry. Then he said, "You be a saint, too."

"I'll try, Mr. President."

The White House gang, led by Haldeman, were waiting outside the Capitol when the President came out. It was 6:40 A.M. The chief of staff knew about this; he had spent many long nights during campaigns walking strange streets looking for candidate Nixon in strange cities. The candidate would disappear for hours after midnight and Haldeman usually found him huddled in the corner booth of a café, drinking coffee alone. This time Nixon wanted to do the same thing, saying he was hungry and wanted to go for breakfast at a place he knew on Connecticut Avenue. It was closed, so they walked into the Rib Room of the Mayflower Hotel on the same street, a few blocks from the White House. It was the first time the President had been in a Washington restaurant since his election. He ordered a poached egg and corned beef hash, telling flabbergasted waitresses that the last time he had hash was on a train five years earlier.

The President wanted to walk to the White House, but the Secret Service finally got their way and drove him back through the White House gates at 7:30 A.M. One reporter, Garnett Horner of the *Washington Star,* a favorite of Nixon's, happened to arrive a few minutes later. "You're not going to believe this," Ziegler began, figuring he could brief Horner and then Horner could write out a pool report for the rest of the press. But as the press secretary began, the President walked in and began to tell the story himself, saying, "They were fine kids from all over the country."

At 8:30, Nixon was still roaming the White House talking to anyone he saw. Haldeman took him into the EOB to shake hands with some of the soldiers hidden there. Some crawled out of sleeping bags and tried to snap to attention as the commander in chief suddenly appeared. The President asked the first man he saw how bad the snoring was, then he asked men where they were from.

"Burbank, Sir!"—and Nixon repeated the nightly joke used by Johnny Carson on *The Tonight Show*: "Are you really from beautiful downtown Burbank?"

"Texarkana, Sir!"—and Nixon said he served with a guy from Texarkana in the Pacific during World War II. "Best scrounger in the whole Navy, I hear he opened a bar when he got home."

Then, as he started to leave, he turned, his fists clenched, and said, "It's a good country."

"The weirdest day yet," Haldeman dictated for his diary. "I am concerned about his condition. . . . he has had very little sleep for a long time and his judgment, temper and mood suffer badly as a result. . . . He's still riding on the crisis wave, but the letdown is near at hand and will be huge."

At the same time, Nixon was dictating a memo to Haldeman:

> For the next two months when I will be deeply immersed in the Cambodia situation and problems of the economy, I would like you to take responsibility with regard to the news summary. . . . I am not going to take the time to read the summaries myself. . . . What I would like to suggest is that you read the summaries each day and bring to my attention when we have our morning meeting items in the news summary, either foreign or domestic, that you conclude should have my attention. . . . This will save me a great deal of time. . . .

CHAPTER 14

June 30, 1970

T HE SUMMARY QUOTE chosen by the wire services and many newspapers on the President's early morning ramble through Washington came from a Syracuse University student whom reporters found among the more than sixty thousand people gathered on the Ellipse that hot Saturday. "I hope it was because he was tired, but most of what he was saying was absurd," she said. "Here we had come from a university that was totally uptight—on strike—and when we told him where we came from, he talked about the football team. And surfing."

"It's too bad all he could talk about was sports," said John Ehrlichman a couple of days later. Nixon was so mad when he heard that remark that he sat down and dictated an eight-page memo recounting his version of what had happened, beginning with a cover note to Haldeman:

I can understand why John Ehrlichman got the idea from the news report that I was tired and all I talked about was surfing and nonsensical things. This, of course, reflects on two points—even when I am tired I do not talk about nonsensical things and also more fundamentally, I am afraid that most of our staff, to their credit, are enormously interested in material things and what we accomplish in our record, etc. etc. but that very few seem to have matters that are infinitely more important—qualities of spirit, emotion, of the depth and mystery of life which this whole visit really was all about. . . . We seem to lack on the staff any one individual who really understands or appreciates what I am trying to get across in terms of what a President should mean to the people.

He followed that call for depth and mystery with a long and cranky memo, saying that he wanted stories planted detailing the violence and expense of the demonstration in Washington: "Injuries to policemen, the number of windows broken, the fact that $5,000 in damage was done to the Washington Monument, etc." He also wanted to find a columnist who would say that some of the student leaders were trained in Cuba and were moving from campus to campus organizing riots. On May 12, he responded to the news that the Senate had confirmed Judge Blackmun's Supreme Court nomination by a 94-to-0 vote, writing: "I want the facts brought out that Blackmun insofar as being a strict constructionist is concerned was exactly in the same tradition as Haynsworth and Carswell. The purpose of this column is to get it widely circulated in Southern states. . . ."

The President was alone, talking and talking into his Dictaphone. "He's in love with the machine," Haldeman said as he brought in more secretaries to transcribe the gripes and ideas. "The President himself," said the President, "has finally reached the conclusion which should cause the media some concern. He realizes that he does not have to have their support. . . . This is a subtle point to get across but I think it is one that can have considerable effect on the press and news media if they finally realize that they are losing their most important listener and viewer—reader—the President of the United States."

"Get me the information with regard to the distribution of Department of Defense research funds to major colleges and universities," he said in another memo. "Two hundred million dollars, I think is the total package. . . . I believe that no DOD funds for research should be provided to any university unless the faculty by a majority vote approves receipt and use of the funds for those purposes. . . . Put the faculties, not the university presidents, on the spot."

Whatever the President's mood, he was directing a rather effective campaign on two fronts, Cambodia and in the United States. Each day the White House announced high yields and low casualties, issuing daily reports on the capture of thousands of rifles, grenades, and mortar shells stored along with tons of rice in wood and earth bunkers, and each day repeating that American troops would soon be out of the country. American casualties—110 killed in action between April 30 and May 13—were not as high as anticipated. Nixon was also redefining his terms and downgrading his decisions. The "invasion" became the "incursion" and there was no longer any mention of finding or even looking for "COSVN," the jungle headquarters of the communists. The official line had become "buying time" to train more South Vietnamese troops and bring home American boys.

Congress was a third front. In the Senate there were energetic bi-partisan efforts to cut off funding for the Cambodian operation and even for the war in Vietnam. John Sherman Cooper, a Kentucky Republican, and Frank Church, an Idaho Democrat, were sponsoring a bill barring funds for U.S. troops in Cambodia after June 30. George McGovern of South Dakota and Mark Hatfield, an Oregon Republican, introduced an amendment to the military appropriations bill that set rigid timetables for withdrawal of all American forces from all of Southeast Asia. In both houses, there was a drive toward lowering the voting age from twenty-one to eighteen, the argument being that if young men were old enough to die in Vietnam they should be old enough to vote. "Give someone direct orders and responsibility to stop this: Highest priority," the President wrote Ehrlichman. He knew that if a bill got to him, he would almost certainly have to sign it.

That did not mean the American people were embracing their young. After the initial shock of the killings at Kent State faded, students themselves became the issue—and most of the country did not like them, did not like their ingratitude, their arrogance, or the way they dressed and grew their hair. "Fuck Richard Nixon!"—a common battle cry—was not winning over parents who paid tuition, not to mention parents who could not afford tuition for their children.

In *Life* magazine, on a week when the cover story was a shattering photo-essay, "Our Forgotten Wounded," done in veterans' hospitals and showing broken young Vietnam veterans, Hugh Sidey wrote in his column "The Presidency": "Democratic political analyst Richard Scammon took his own cab-driver poll and found the nation turning against the students. In a lighter moment he suggested that a march be led from the seamy wards of Cambridge into Harvard Yard, the students evicted and their rooms turned over to the poor families. The gesture, Scammon opines, should certainly satisfy both the wishes of those needing housing and the inner distress of the young who want to do something for the good of mankind. . . ."

Letters to the editor on the Kent State killings in the magazine's next issue, dated June 5, included these:

It was a valuable object lesson to homegrown advocates of anarchy and revolution, regardless of age.—PHILIP A. SCHLOSS JR., ALEXANDRIA, VA.

They were a part, however passive, of a riotous mob which repeatedly refused to disperse upon the direct orders of a legally
constituted authority. . . . One might just as well say that a Marxist, shot while robbing a gas station of money with which to further his cause, was killed for his political beliefs.—RALPH
MILLERTON, MEMPHIS, TENN.

The President's approval rating was going up again. A Gallup poll
done for *Newsweek* showed that 58 percent of respondents blamed the
Kent State students for what had happened and only 11 percent blamed
National Guardsmen. The cultural divide revealed in polls also was creating a growth industry: the making of American flags. The flag boom
had begun the year before when *Reader's Digest* sent small flag decals to
its eighteen million subscribers—and received mail requests for thirty-
one million more. Gulf Oil made a similar offer and distributed another
twenty-two million. "America—Love It or Leave It" bumper stickers
began appearing on car bumpers a little later, along with flag stickers on
construction workers' helmets and flag patches on the sleeves of most of
the country's policemen. Three new flagpoles were built on the Capitol of
the United States, so more flags could be flown for a few seconds and then
distributed by congressmen to patriotic constituents. In the White House
during the Cambodian operation, members of the President's staff began
wearing small flag lapel pins.

In *Newsweek,* Stewart Alsop wrote a column under the headline
"NIXON AND THE ANTI-KID VOTE," saying: "In what he used to call his
'rocking, socking' campaigns, young Mr. Nixon consistently used the
same political technique. This was to identify the opposition with a minority that was a) widely hated, b) virtually powerless in terms of voting
strength and c) unanimously opposed to him in any case. . . . Might this
old technique, in modern dress, be even more effective than it was a generation ago? Might not 'flag-burning college radicals' fill the old Communist role, while two other detested minorities, the black militants and the
'left-wing media,' fill the subsidiary roles? . . . There have been hints—
like his spontaneous crack about college 'bums'—that this thought has already occurred to him."

On Thursday, May 14, the President presided over a ceremony
for past winners of the Congressional Medal of Honor in the morning,
had a meeting with economic advisers after lunch, and then flew to Key
Biscayne. Bebe Rebozo met him there and Nixon asked his friend if his
girlfriend, Jane Lucke, could do some sewing for him. The medal ceremony had given him the idea of giving medals to Haldeman, Ehrlichman,
and Kissinger. The "Blue Heart" was awarded to the three men on the

flight back to Washington. Nixon called them into his cabin and said, "I have devised a new award, a Blue Heart for those who are true blue."

"This will be our secret," he said, giving each a little cloth heart sewn by Miss Lucke. "I wanted you to know how much I appreciate what you have done."

By June 4, the President felt confident enough to go on television again for a report on the Cambodian operation. By then United States casualties in Southeast Asia had begun to drop again—142 Americans were killed the week of May 27, down from 217 the week before—and the Dow-Jones average was up to 700 again after bottoming out at 631 on May 26. The President had also been welcomed by more than eighty thousand cheering young people in the football stadium of the University of Tennessee—at a Christian revival meeting, a crusade run by Billy Graham. Nixon told aides it proved he could go anywhere in the country, even to college campuses.

On television that night, the President pledged again that every American would be out of Cambodia by the end of the month. Then he showed Army film of crates and piles of arms, ammunition, and rice captured in Cambodia, saying, "Here also you will see a few of the over 15,000 rifles and machine guns captured. They will never be used against American boys in Vietnam. . . . I can now state that this has been the most successful operation of this long and difficult war."

He tried to write off Cambodia as an issue and succeeded to a great extent, rewriting intent and history as he went along, saying seventeen thousand of the thirty-one thousand Americans who entered that country were already back in Vietnam. In fact, his principal goal since the Kent State shootings had been to calm dissent at home. The most important fact of the day was that college students were going home, looking for summer jobs.

FOR A FEW DAYS, the President was free to focus on domestic affairs. He had been trying to prevent the election of George Wallace as governor of Alabama. Early in the year, the situation had looked good to Nixon—that is, Wallace's chances looked bad. He had served two two-year terms in Montgomery from 1963 to 1967. He had run in four Democratic presidential primaries in 1964, losing but getting about three times as many votes as expected. Then, in 1966, prevented from running by the state's antisuccession law, he managed and did the talking for the campaign that made his wife, Lurleen, his successor. There was never any doubt that he continued to run the state and was planning his 1968 run for president. Lurleen Wallace died of cancer in May 1968, as her husband was campaigning across the country as the candidate of the American Independent Party. Lieutenant Governor Albert P. Brewer, a loyal Wallace man, became governor and Wallace pledged not to run against him in 1970. But he did, even though statewide polls showed Brewer running well ahead of him.

Those polls persuaded the President that there was a chance Wallace could lose and that defeat might knock him out of the 1972 presidential race, leaving Nixon as the candidate of the center and the right everywhere in the country. On March 25, the President had told Haldeman to get $100,000 to Postmaster General Winton Blount, an Alabama Republican, who would work out a way to get the money to the Brewer campaign. On April 1, a former *Montgomery Advertiser* political columnist named Robert Ingram flew to New York and approached a man sitting with a briefcase in his lap in the lobby of the Sherry Netherland Hotel.

"Are you Mr. Jensen of Baltimore?" Ingram said, as he had been told to do.

"No, I'm Mr. Jensen of Detroit," said the man, who was actually Herbert Kalmbach, the President's personal lawyer. He handed Ingram a manila envelope with $100,000 in hundred-dollar bills removed that morning from a safe-deposit box controlled by Nixon.

At the same time, the President, through Haldeman, ordered Clark Mollenhoff to investigate the Wallaces, concentrating on Gerald Wallace, George's brother and, some said—in fact, many said—his bagman, the guy who handled the cash in Alabama. Mollenhoff then turned over the tax information to Murray Chotiner, who handled the President's Jack Anderson account, leaking to Anderson, who was evenhanded in helping and hurting Nixon and his enemies. Within three weeks, Jack Anderson's syndicated national column, which was widely circulated in Alabama, began to publish details, accurate ones, about an Internal Revenue Service investigation of Gerald Wallace.

On May 5, in the first round of the Alabama Democratic gubernatorial primary, Brewer defeated Wallace by eight thousand votes, but did not win the necessary majority. For the second round, the President authorized Kalmbach to deliver $300,000 in cash to the Brewer campaign. A Brewer man named Jim Bob Solomon picked up $200,000 at the Sherry Netherland and another $100,000 from Kalmbach in Los Angeles. Solomon was so worried that the plane back from Alabama might crash, and the one thousand $100 bills in his briefcase be found, that he pinned a note to his underwear saying that the money was not his, he was only delivering it for the President of the United States.

Wallace dubbed Brewer "the candidate of three hundred thousand niggers" and won the runoff by 32,000 votes. The President's first call the morning after that election, from the residence, was to Haldeman. He did not ask for results. The night before, after he had asked for and gotten the numbers from a handful of Jefferson County, Alabama, precincts he knew well, he had gone to bed sure Brewer was beaten. What he wanted to know was how the secret $400,000 had been spent.

So Wallace was going to be a factor again in 1972. All the talk of southern strategies and new majorities came down to combining the Nixon and Wallace votes of 1968—43 percent for Nixon and 13.8 for Wallace—into a dominating vote reelecting the Republican president in 1972. Nixon had hoped that a Wallace defeat in Alabama would leave himself as the only choice for the nation's center-right voters. He told Haldeman that morning that he wanted all Republican comment to try to marginalize Wallace by calling his victory racist.

For his part, Wallace declared: "Alabama still keeps her place in the sun. . . . We'll see all you national newsmen again." The next day, as Nixon spoke to the nation about Cambodia, Wallace was asked by reporters if he was planning to run for president again. He answered: "If Nixon don't give us back our schools."

On the morning of Friday, June 5, the President met with J. Edgar Hoover of the FBI, Richard Helms of the CIA, and the heads of the National Security Agency and the Defense Intelligence Agency to discuss putting together a new domestic intelligence system. His talking paper for the meeting, prepared by young Tom Charles Huston—who some staffers called "Secret Agent X-5" behind his back—began: "We are now confronted with a new and grave crisis in our country—one which we know too little about. Certainly hundreds, perhaps thousands, of Americans—mostly under 30—are determined to destroy our society. . . ."

The President went on a tear, complaining, with some evidence, that the intelligence agencies seemed to be at war with one another rather than with forces trying to overthrow the established order at home and abroad. With all the money they were spending, with all their resources, why could they not connect the antiwar forces in the streets of Washington with Marxists in Paris or Hanoi? What were the connections to communists? In Cuba. In North Korea. In Algeria. How could an organization like the Black Panthers be formed by young men receiving federal salaries from the Office of Economic Opportunity? Policemen were being targeted. There were bomb factories. Plane hijackings. He told the men in the room that they would be constituted the Interagency Committee on Intelligence. He demanded a "threat assessment" and a range of options to deal with the threats to domestic security. The President asked Hoover to chair the ad hoc committee. Huston would act as the White House liaison. He left them with this presidential thought: The real problem was that American parents could not face up to the fact that some of their children were trying to destroy their country.

The elevation of Huston, a fourth-level White House aide, into the company of Hoover and Helms was a calculated insult. Nixon was convinced that both the FBI and the CIA had failed to find the links he was sure bound domestic troubles and foreign communism. But bringing them to the White House was also part of a larger Nixon plan. He was determined to exert presidential control over the parts of the government he cared most about—the agencies dealing with foreign policy, military matters, intelligence, law, criminal justice, and general order. "Keep us informed," in many agencies, was code for consulting with the White House, usually with Kissinger or Ehrlichman, before decisions were announced and before hires and promotions were made. The National Security Council, responsible only to the President, was not only a tribute to the bureaucratic skills of Nixon and Kissinger, it was a model for centralization and a tightening up of executive control.

The President's view of the danger had personal aspects. The next day, Saturday, June 6, was graduation day for Julie Nixon Eisenhower at Smith, but she could not be there because there would be demonstrations attacking her father. So the Nixons and some of the Eisenhowers were at Camp David. Bebe Rebozo appeared at dinner carrying academic robes borrowed from George Shultz, who had accepted an honorary degree from Notre Dame the week before. The President put on the robe and read a little "commencement address" Pat Buchanan had written for Julie; for her husband, David, graduating from Amherst; and for David's sister, Susan Eisenhower, who was graduating from high school in Pennsylvania.

Three days later, the President was discussing executive control again, this time for three hours with Haldeman, who ended his record of the meeting in his diary: "Sure has no interest in domestic programs per se, which gives E a wide open field if he wants to use it." More often than not, Nixon was interested in domestic policy only if it directly impacted domestic politics; racial issues and national concern over air and water pollution were examples of that. But, issues aside, he was obsessed with responsiveness and loyalty in the executive branch. He had approved one of Roy Ash's recommendations and created a new Office of Management and Budget, which centralized the budget-writing functions of the Bureau of the Budget and brought extensive new powers into the White House, particularly ongoing oversight of all executive agencies. The President named George Shultz as its first director and Caspar Weinberger, the chairman of the Federal Trade Commission, as Shultz's deputy. At the same time, in mid-June, Finch was moved over to the White House as a counselor and Elliot Richardson was named to replace him at HEW. The President also had a hit list of Cabinet members he wanted to remove, beginning with Hickel at Interior. The others he wanted to get rid of were David Kennedy at Treasury, John Volpe at Transportation, and George Romney of HUD. The former governor of Michigan, a national figure in his own right, quickly fell out of favor with the President, because like most former governors, Walter Hickel among them, he was used to being listened to and used to making his own decisions. In late May, Romney, who had grown rich as chairman of American Motors in Detroit, had reacted to the Washington balanced-budget fervor that usually accompanied rising inflation by issuing a press release announcing that he was voluntarily taking a salary cut to reduce the budget. "That does it," Nixon told Ehrlichman. "An ineffective grandstand play. He's got to go."

Two weeks later, on June 9, the President sent Ehrlichman a memo asking whether it was possible to cut his own salary from $100,000 a year to $75,000 a year. He added that Ehrlichman should also check to see if he could get the $25,000 back later as pension.

The President's mind was turning to money, as it always had to as elections approached. The 1970 congressional campaigns were beginning. The memos began moving as fast as Republican candidates in town for ritual photos with the President. Nixon's role was described in a memo: "The candidates will be brought into your office individually, where a picture will be taken of the candidate seated at the yellow chair to the left of your desk talking with you. . . . The candidates will have been briefed that time does not permit the usual social amenities of shaking hands and extending greetings."

That same day, the President's lawyer and bagman, Herbert Kalmbach, forwarded a list of sixty-four individuals and couples identified as Nixon's "angels," major donors to his campaigns. It was an impressive list, including the names of men (and one woman) who controlled many of the nation's great fortunes and corporations. It included many well-known Americans, among them W. Clement Stone, Walter Annenberg, Richard Mellon Scaife, Henry Salvatori, Arthur K. Watson, J. Howard Pew, Max Fisher, Robert H. Abplanalp, Mrs. Helen Clay Frick, Robert O. Anderson, Willard F. Rockwell Jr., William J. Casey, DeWitt Wallace, F. K. Weyerhauser, A. C. Nielsen, Elmer Bobst, John Hay Whitney, John Olin, and Charles Payson. The last name on the list was Thomas Pappas, a Greek-American businessman from Boston, who was reported to have delivered $549,000 to the 1968 Nixon-Agnew campaign from the intelligence service of the military dictatorship ruling Greece.

On June 25, the President flew to the Western White House for a two-week "working vacation," stopping in St. Louis on the way for an enthusiastic rally sponsored by the Missouri Jaycees. Before leaving Washington, he unhappily signed an extension of the Voting Rights Act of 1965, one of the most important civil rights laws passed during the Johnson presidency. It was another bill he opposed until it was obvious it could not be stopped and then took credit for as it became law. This one was different, though, because Senator Edward Kennedy had managed to attach a rider reducing the voting age in federal elections from twenty-one to eighteen, effective January 1, 1972—empowering eleven million new voters without going through the long process of amending the Constitution. Republicans were angry, knowing many states would also adopt the new age and fearing the young voters would favor Democrats. After signing the bill, the President called for a court challenge to the constitutionality of the provision he had just made law. He was for the idea, he asserted, but against the way it was done. Afterwards, he met privately with Republican congressional leaders. "I had to do it because of the Voting Right Acts and the possibility of trouble from blacks this summer," he began. "But there is no doubt in my mind that it is unconstitutional. . . ."

His last conversation that day was with Kissinger, who spent most of the time talking about newspaper stories speculating that he was seriously involved with a young movie actress, Jill St. John. Yes, he had dated her, Kissinger said, but the stories implied more, a lack of seriousness on his part. He told the President he was sure the stories were being planted by Secretary of State Rogers to destroy him.

In San Clemente on July 26, Nixon began the day with elaborate Cambodia briefings for forty reporters, editors, and news executives, among them the presidents of the news divisions of the three television networks. "At the White House," the paperwork read, which meant a small auditorium in one of the temporary buildings put up a few hundred yards from La Casa Pacifica. Nixon began by repeating that the information was embargoed from public use until after the withdrawal of United States troops from Cambodia, scheduled in five days. "The basic question is, 'Was it worth it?' " the President began. "Some would say, 'Was it worth it, even though it might have been successful, speaking in strictly military terms, was it worth it from the standpoint of the effect on the people in the United States?' "

He argued, as before, that the operation would reduce American casualties and help end the Vietnam war sooner. He mentioned seeing "PEACE NOW" signs in St. Louis and said: "Everyone in this room wants peace now. . . . The great question—and it is the great question that

Americans had to answer in World War II, in Korea—is not the question of peace now, it is the question of peace that will last."

Then he made his principal point, rambling a bit:

> If the United States shows weakness; if we show a tendency to retreat from a position which we have taken . . . when the pressure is put on us; if we show weakness at home . . . the real problem is: It may buy us trouble someplace else because whether the leaders of the Soviet Union or China—and this is not Cold War rhetoric, this is simply a statement of fact—there are other leaders in the world, other people in the world who want to expand their systems. . . . The only reason that any other nation could afford the luxury of neutrality if it were not, in the present world, for the power of the United States.

> That is a fact. The people of India know it. The people in Indonesia know it. . . .

On June 30, the White House issued a seven-thousand-word "Report to the Nation" titled: "CAMBODIA CONCLUDED: Now It's Time To Negotiate." It stated that American and South Vietnamese troops had captured more than twenty-two thousand individual weapons, fifteen million rounds of ammunition, and fourteen million tons of rice, and had destroyed 11,688 bunkers and buildings. Enemy troops killed in action were listed as 11,349, and 2,328 men were captured. The President did not mention the 344 Americans or 818 South Vietnamese killed in Cambodia. COSVN also went unmentioned, though the battle Pentagon of the North Vietnamese had been brought up during the San Clemente background briefings by a "senior official," as usual Henry Kissinger. The exchange was friendly. "Where is COSVN now?" an editor began.

Looking over at press secretary Ron Ziegler, Kissinger answered, "Ron has kept me from mentioning a five-sided wooden structure we found. . . ." When the laughing stopped, Kissinger said that finding the communist headquarters would have been a bonus but was never a goal of the invasion. He ignored the fact—and reporters did not press him—that the President had called it a principal goal in announcing the invasion on national television two months before.

Back east, the press was tougher. A four-column headline over a front-page "News Analysis" in The New York Times read: "CAMBODIA INCURSION BY U.S. APPEARS TO UNITE FOE." The piece quoted foreign diplomats who argued that the American move had brought the communists of Vietnam, Cambodia, and Laos together after decades of hostility and had also brought all of them closer to alliance with their historical enemy, China. Still, Nixon was more relaxed than usual. He liked being in California. He spent some time reading parts of presidential biographies, recommended by Moynihan; then he told Haldeman: "The whole trick in this business is to do something different, the difference now is you have to do it for television."

In Washington that same day, the Senate, by a vote of 58 to 37, passed the Cooper-Church Amendment to the Military Sales Act; the amendment prohibited the authorization or expenditure of funds to maintain United States troops in Cambodia. It could have no immediate effect—and the House was expected to reject it—but it was an astonishing challenge to the powers of the commander in chief.

The next day the President drove to Los Angeles for a one-hour joint television interview on foreign policy by the anchormen of the CBS, NBC, and ABC networks. Asked whether United States troops might reenter Cambodia, he said, "We don't plan on it." Asked about Cooper-Church and Hatfield-McGovern, he said no president could accept such restrictions. He used President Kennedy's actions during the Cuban missile crisis of 1962 as an example of the kind of individual leadership needed inside the White House. He also added a warning about the increasing Soviet presence in the Middle East, which involved supplying weapons and advisers in Egypt and Syria: "Once the balance of power shifts where Israel is weaker than its neighbors, there will be war. . . . Therefore, we will do what is necessary to maintain Israel's strength vis à vis its neighbors."

CHAPTER 15

September 23, 1970

THE REPORT OF THE "Special Interagency Committee on Intelligence (Ad Hoc)" was forty-three pages long and Tom Charles Huston got it to the President in less than three weeks. It began: "The movement of rebellious youth known as the 'New Left,' involving and influencing a substantial number of college students, is having a serious impact on contemporary society with a potential for serious domestic strife. The revolutionary aims of the New Left are apparent when their identification with Marxism-Leninism is examined. . . ."

Huston attached a memo to the President recommending six of the options covered in the report: (1) increased domestic electronic surveillance, (2) monitoring of international communications by Americans, (3) relaxation of restrictions on opening mail, (4) planting informants on college campuses, (5) lifting restrictions on "surreptitious entry," and (6) creation of a new Interagency Group on Domestic Intelligence and Internal Security, to be controlled from the White House.

Most of those options were extensions of government activity instituted during World War II but gradually phased out in the postwar years. Of "surreptitious entry" by government agents, Huston wrote in the memo to Nixon: "Use of this technique is clearly illegal: it amounts to burglary. It is also highly risky and could result in great embarrassment if exposed. However, it is also the most fruitful tool and can produce the kind of intelligence which cannot be obtained in any other fashion. . . ."

This technique would be particularly effective if used against the Weathermen and Black Panthers." The intelligence services and military agencies signed off on the report, with one condition: Presidential approval should be required for such actions as break-ins.

The President approved the plan on July 14.

"The recommendations you have proposed . . . have been approved by the President," Haldeman wrote Huston, ordering him to prepare a formal decision memorandum to the directors of the FBI, the CIA, and the five intelligence agencies in the Defense Department. "He does not, however, want to follow the procedure you outlined . . . regarding implementation. He would prefer that the thing simply be put into motion on the basis of this approval." *

Huston was told to channel all communication to Haldeman rather than to the President. The first memo to the chief of staff began with plans to use the Internal Revenue Service to harass think tanks and other tax-exempt research or charitable institutions considered unfavorable to the White House, beginning with the Brookings Institution and the Ford Foundation.

"Making sensitive political inquiries at the IRS is about as safe a procedure as trusting a whore," said the Huston memo. "With the bark on, the truth is we don't have any reliable political friends at IRS. . . . We won't be in control of the Government and in a position of effective leverage until such time as we have complete and total control of the top three slots of the IRS. . . . If we reach the point where we really want to start playing the game tough, you might wish to consider my suggestion of some months ago that we consider going into Brookings after the classified material which they have stashed over there. There are a number of ways we could handle this. There are risks in all of them, of course; but there are also risks in allowing a government-in-exile to grow increasingly arrogant and powerful as each day goes by."

On July 26, Hoover invited Huston to his office. Looking down at the young man from his desk on a platform at one end of his huge office, the FBI director read out the extensive notes he had written on the margins of the decision memo. The old man began by stating that the "old ways" were now "too dangerous." Then, after reading each of his notes about the specifics of the plan, he looked up, deliberately getting the young man's name wrong as he asked: "Do you understand, Mr. Hoffman? . . . Is that clear, Mr. Hutchison?" The next day, Hoover went to his nominal superior, Attorney General Mitchell, and told him that the

---

* The agencies involved were the Central Intelligence Agency, Federal Bureau of Investigation, Defense Intelligence Agency, and National Security Agency, along with the intelligence and counterintelligence units of the Army, Navy, and Air Force.

times had changed, there were more policemen and security guards everywhere, and secret intelligence agents would, sooner or later, be caught—and such arrests would bring in civil liberties groups and "the jackals of the press" and reveal a history of long-past and recent incidents of illegal or embarrassing government surveillance of its own citizens. He objected to sharing FBI information with other agencies and said that he would not authorize actions he considered illegal without specific written orders from the President.

The next day Haldeman ordered Huston to collect all copies of the decision memo. The "Huston Plan" was withdrawn after fourteen days. The President did not have the political guts to fire the most revered of American lawmen, even if Hoover at seventy-five was failing and becoming more irrational.

The President was still obsessed with subversion and the dangers of youthful dissent. "We have to find out who controls them," he said to Haldeman after pulling back on the Huston Plan. "Get our guys to rough them up at demonstrations." About that, he was the irrational one. In fact, the Selective Service lottery and Vietnamization was working, at least in defusing mass dissent at home. Overseas was a different story. In Paris, Le Duc Tho confronted Kissinger with the obvious: "How can you expect to prevail with the South Vietnamese army alone when it could not win with the assistance of 500,000 Americans?" The North Vietnamese, blunt and harsh, continued to say the same thing publicly and privately: If the Americans wanted to end the war they should get out—and take Thieu with them.

On July 1, the second draft lottery was held. Capsules with birth dates in 1951 were pulled from a rotary drum, and the first date pulled was July 9, 1951. Nineteen-year-olds born on that day would be drafted first. The great majority of American young men were no longer at risk of going to Vietnam. Young men whose numbers were above 195 were considered safe from involuntary induction, and most of those drafted would serve in Europe or the United States.

"We are ending the war," the President said at a news conference on July 30 in Los Angeles during another San Clemente working vacation. "We will bring the draft to an end and have a volunteer armed service. We are going to clean up the air and the water. . . . We are reforming government to make it more responsive to the people, more power to the people. . . . But once all those things are done, still the emptiness and shallowness, the superficiality that many college students find in college curriculums will still be there . . . that is not a problem for government—we cannot solve it—it is a problem college administrators and college faculties must face up to."

The next question was, "Do you have any concern, Mr. President, that your staff might have you isolated, as has been charged in some news columns?"

"Well," he began, "*I* isolate them"—which was true. "No, as a matter of fact, I not only see my staff, but I see a great number of people who come in representing all points of view. . . . And some members of my staff believe that perhaps I have been having too heavy a schedule. . . . I am generally, incidentally, a very good listener, except in press conferences."

With the midterm elections little more than three months away, the President was listening more to domestic advisers and reading more polls. Early in July, he had redeemed his State of the Union pledge by creating, by executive order, a new Environmental Protection Agency. But only the name was new, as he took 5,650 current employees and $1.4 billion in existing budget lines, principally from the departments of Agriculture, Interior, and Health, Education, and Welfare. But there was an important difference: the new EPA reported directly to the White House rather than going through the Cabinet. When he asked for the opinion of Secretary of Transportation Volpe, who was also losing some employees to EPA, Volpe answered, "Is it all right for a Cabinet member to say, 'No comment'?"

"Yes," Nixon said. "And it's about time."

The environment was big news now, driving many domestic-dissent and racial stories to back pages or out of the news altogether. School desegregation stories, in fact, had evolved in the way John Mitchell had planned from the beginning: the action had shifted from the White House and Justice Department to federal courts.

Nixon told his men once more: "Our people have got to quit bragging about school desegregation. We do what the law requires—nothing more. This is politics, and I'm the judge of the politics of schools. . . . We cooperate with local officials; we don't coerce them. 'Mixing Marshals' will not be sent into the South. Southerners will not be treated as second-class citizens. . . . All Administration people who discuss the school problem must say flatly that we oppose busing; otherwise they will be fired." In the specific case of a private college, Bob Jones University in South Carolina, he signed off on a staff recommendation that said: "There is little doubt that Bob Jones is in clear violation of the law. . . . I propose that we keep reviewing and studying for a while."

ON THE DAY the last Americans left Cambodia, the administration's "senior official," Henry Kissinger, held a backgrounder at the White House, telling reporters that Southeast Asia was no longer the nation's main foreign policy problem. The Middle East was. The rationale for that statement, spread without attribution in newspapers and on television, was direct Soviet involvement in equipping and training the armed forces of the Arab countries surrounding Israel. The American concern, Kissinger said, was no longer the sovereignty and survival of Israel but fear that Moscow was radicalizing Arab governments, particularly those of Egypt and Syria, and might be attempting to establish control over the region's oil-producing countries, including American allies Saudi Arabia and Iran. The senior official went so far as to say the goal of United States policy was to "expel" the Soviets from Egypt.

Kissinger went too far. In a July 20 news conference, which had been held in the Oval Office without television cameras, the President tried to clarify Kissinger's remark by saying that the word "expel" had nothing to do with using armed force. Then he said: "It is important to maintain a military balance so that no state in the area would be encouraged to launch an offensive against another state or be driven to launch a preemptive strike. . . . I have indicated that the Soviet movement of not just weapons but men to Vietnam"—he meant Egypt—"to man the weapons causes us concern. . . ." Nixon's concern was that an arms race in the Middle East would draw Americans into supplying more weapons and, for the first time, draw American military men into Israel. "That is why," he said, "we have not announced any sale of planes or delivery of planes to Israel at this time. . . ."

"They're testing us" was the line that Nixon and Kissinger invariably used in private in discussing the Soviet Union. The President believed that the leaders of the communist world would continually press at any point where they thought the United States might be vulnerable—"soft" was Nixon's word. He believed that the Soviets would withdraw or revert to the status quo, the balance, if the United States and its allies showed resolve. "Being belligerent is beside the point," he said during a July meeting about missile systems. "The Russians, simply and only, understand conviction and strength."

Nixon believed that it was possible to deal with the Soviets—in fact, he overrated their influence on their allies in many places, beginning with Hanoi—and so he had used Dobrynin and other channels to begin talks with Moscow on a number of subjects. The most important of those was strategic arms limitation. Both sides had an economic interest in reducing the extraordinary cost of missile development, and SALT (Strategic Arms Limitation Treaty) talks had begun in Vienna in mid-April. At the end of July, the United States had presented its first formal proposal, basically an overall limit on intercontinental missile systems—preserving the current balance of strategic weapons—and restricting the development of new ABM (antiballistic missile) defense systems to one to protect Moscow and one to protect Washington.

In terms of projecting strength, the President needed congressional approval of Safeguard, his modified antiballistic missile system, if for no other purpose than to use it as an example of American resolve and a bargaining chip in arms negotiations. By July 23, his congressional liaison, Bryce Harlow, reported a Senate vote estimate of 50 to 48 for Safeguard; it was too close to call. Nixon called in his two closest allies on that issue, Senator John Tower, a Texas Republican, and Senator Henry ("Scoop") Jackson, a Washington Democrat. "Why is it so difficult to convince some of these Senators of facts that are so obvious to us?" Nixon asked.

Jackson answered that many senators were in fact pro-Russian. "One came up to me and said," he told Nixon, " 'It just can't be true that the Russians continued building SS-9s and SS-11s after they said they would not.' " "Senators are socializing with Russian embassy people, talking to them every day," Tower added. The three men agreed that the FBI should be checking this—and the President called in Colson and told him to make sure that happened.

As they broke up, Nixon wanted to know whether he should personally ask for the vote of Senator Clinton P. Anderson, a New Mexico Democrat. Jackson said that was a good idea but it had to be done just before the vote because otherwise Anderson would not remember. Nixon smiled. Men with failing memories were a regular problem among the elders of the Senate. The next day Nixon pushed for the vote of another conservative Democratic senator, Robert Byrd of West Virginia. His background paper for that meeting read: "Byrd has expressed no concern about the substance of ABM. . . . He indicated that there are two basic things he would like to discuss—(1) where we are going on integration and (2) appointments to the Court. . . . For your information, we have just gotten a job for his son-in-law with the Naval Research Laboratory. . . ."

The Soviets were probably not ready to test the United States in the Middle East. In historical terms, they had just gotten there. But it was a heady time for the national descendants of the czars. The Russians were there by invitation in Mediterranean ports and desert oil fields for the first time in history. That was an unanticipated result of Israel's total victory in the Six-Day War of 1967. The Soviets had been invited in by President Nasser of Egypt (the United Arab Republic) when Arab leaders realized they were helpless against the modern American weaponry and technology available to Israel. The Arabs learned a bitter lesson in those six days: their overwhelming advantage in manpower had been useless after the Israelis gained absolute control of the air with a massive pre-emptive strike that destroyed the Egyptian air force on the ground. Now, with as many as ten thousand Soviet advisers, trainers, and technicians in his country, Nasser was regaining confidence to match his determination to regain the Arab lands lost in that war. Three Israeli Phantom jets had been shot down by improved Soviet SAM-2 missiles within the week before Nixon's July 20 news conference. Israeli ambassador Rabin told the White House that Israeli jets had encountered advanced MIG 21s piloted not by Egyptians but by Russians, and that fourteen SAM-2 sites had been moved within thirty miles of the Suez Canal. The SAM-2 sites, he said, were being guarded by three more sophisticated SAM-3 sites—and those sites were manned by Russian crews.

The White House and the Defense Department insisted that the Israelis were exaggerating the threat. But it was not the first time Israel had asked for this kind of help. In March, when Rabin had come to plead his nation's case, he told the President that for the first time Russians were on site. Nixon had startled him by saying, "Have you considered attacking them?"

There was a speechless moment.

"Attack the Russians?" asked Rabin, the commander of Israeli forces during the 1967 war.

But despite the tough talk that always punctuated his private conversation, the President was acting with secret restraint, replacing Israeli losses and supplying F-4 parts, ammunition, and advanced communications equipment, keeping the number of combat-ready Phantoms at about forty. Whether or not the Israelis were right about the seriousness of the threat from Egypt on their western borders, they were threatened on their eastern borders by the possibility of civil war in Jordan, where King Hussein, the most moderate of the Arab rulers, was reluctantly, in the name of Arab solidarity, hosting at least 1.2 million Palestinian refugees from the wars of 1948, 1956, and 1967—this in a country with a total population of only 2.2 million. At least twenty thousand of the Palestinians were fedayeen fighters, determined to use Jordan one day as a base to begin the holy war that would destroy Israel, with or without Hussein's help.

On the American side, the game was complicated by Nixon's determination not to give in to pressure from American Jews to give Israel whatever it asked for, and by the corrosive contempt and suspicion between Kissinger and Secretary of State Rogers. From the beginning, the President had given Rogers control over Mideast policy, because of Kissinger's ignorance of that part of the world and because he did not like the idea of an American Jew dealing with Arabs fighting Israeli Jews. In fact, American policy in the area was called the "Rogers Plan"—the Sec-. retary's proposal for a return to something like the region's pre-1967 borders in exchange for Arab recognition of Israel's sovereignty—the Jewish state's right to exist. Land for peace.

The President knew what was happening, of course. He told Safire: "Henry thinks Bill isn't very deep, and Bill thinks Henry is power-crazy. And in a sense, they're both right."

Kissinger—"He's almost psycho," said Haldeman—was upset because Rogers was enjoying high visibility, traveling through Europe, and meeting comfortably with the leaders of the new Conservative government of Prime Minister Edward Heath in London, all the while promoting his own temporary peace plan for the Middle East. He was calling for a ninety-day cease-fire in place along the Suez Canal, the de facto border between Israel and Egypt since 1967. Suez was the focus, but in essence the Secretary of State was proposing a three-month cease-fire in place across the Middle East—halting the sporadic fighting between Israel and Egypt across the canal. Since the beginning of 1970, Israeli jets, sometimes for days at a time, had been bombing sites under construction on the Egyptian side, trying to disrupt deployment of the new Russian missiles and artillery. During the cease-fire, the United States would promote United Nations mediation based on the Rogers Plan.

On July 23, President Nasser, after consultations in Moscow, announced that Egypt was ready to accept the Rogers's cease-fire. In Tel Aviv, the Israelis debated, convinced that Nasser would use the three months to continue building up Arab forces without threat from Israeli planes or the possibility of Israeli land invasion. Secretly, Nixon was offering the Israelis four Phantoms and four Skyhawks per month if they would agree. Within forty-eight hours, Jordan accepted as well. The small kingdom was undergoing a kind of civil war, with small firefights between King Hussein's army and Palestinian combat units based in refugee camps. Syria announced its rejection, but that was dismissed as more propaganda than decision. On August 7, Rogers announced a cease-fire between Egypt and Israel along the Suez Canal under United Nations supervision.

But fighting continued on other fronts. Two days after the announcement, Palestinian guerrillas based in Syria attacked Israeli outposts on the Golan Heights, and Israeli jets were bombing Palestinian bases in Lebanon. In Amman, the capital of Jordan, Al Fatah, the largest of the Palestinian groups, led by a former engineer named Yasir Arafat, announced that it would intensify guerrilla actions against Israelis during any cease-fire in an attempt to destroy the peace process.

Before the end of August, Mideast peace talks were under way at the United Nations in New York. But the agreement brokered by Rogers was already in some trouble. A right-wing Israeli party, Gahal, led by Menachim Begin, had withdrawn its six members of the Knesset from Prime Minister Meir's governing coalition, and the government itself was complaining, with some photographic evidence to back it up, that Egypt was continuing to expand its missile sites on the east bank of the canal. On August 15, a Saturday, Kissinger met with Rabin, who told him Mrs. Meir was "in desperate straits" and wanted to come to the United States to meet with the President. It was a meeting Nixon did not want, because he did not want to do anything publicly that might give the Soviets a rationale for sending even more military aid into Arab countries.

When Kissinger came into the Oval Office to report on the Rabin meeting, he quickly changed the subject and startled the President by saying, "The Soviets are massing to attack China."

The adviser and his staff, following intelligence reports of small clashes and artillery barrages along the Manchurian border between the communist allies, had charted troop locations and railheads on both sides—and realized that the Soviet troops were all near the end of Russian railroad lines, while the Chinese were hundreds of miles from their own railheads and roads. The Soviets were moving; the Chinese were responding. Kissinger's conclusion: The Soviets intended to use nuclear weapons to destroy Chinese missile installations and were positioning troops to defend against the possibility that the Chinese would retaliate with a land invasion. The idea seemed preposterous to Nixon.

The next day, Kissinger discovered that the President and Secretary Rogers had helicoptered to Camp David to spend the rest of the weekend there together. Unloading his anger and suspicions on Haldeman, he let slip his disdain for the President, which Haldeman recorded in these words: "Says P problem is his reluctance to understand that tactics turn into strategy, and you can't let things go along and then try to save them with brilliant maneuver. Feels the real stake (in the Mideast) is Nixon credibility with Soviets."

"Weird," Nixon responded, telling Haldeman he worried about whether Kissinger had about reached the end of his effectiveness. "He's worth it, I guess. . . ." But the President was also convinced Kissinger was feeding information to the Israelis. "He's purposely trying to screw up the peace proposal," the President told Haldeman. He was doing it, Nixon thought, because he was obsessed with the prospect of Rogers getting credit for a deal and maybe he thought that deal was not good for the Israelis.

Nixon tried to get both Haldeman and Haig to persuade Kissinger to leave the Mideast negotiations alone—with no luck. They came back to the President with a typed set of demands from Kissinger: "1. Attacks on Henry Kissinger, direct or indirect, must cease. An attack on Kissinger is an attack on the President. . . . 2. All cables with policy implications, including especially the Middle East, must be cleared in the White House. . . . 3. All contacts with Dobrynin must be cleared ahead of time."

KISSINGER WAS ALREADY on his way to Paris for secret meetings with the North Vietnamese, who had returned to the French capital after a nine-month boycott and had appeared again at official negotiating sessions with the American delegation led by David K. E. Bruce, who knew nothing of the separate Kissinger negotiations.

It was a White House organized for deception. There were secrets large and small—beyond the double books hiding the bombing of Cambodia for thirteen months and beyond Kissinger's trips to Paris to meet the North Vietnamese. The President's briefing memo from Kissinger for an August 17 meeting with Secretary of Defense Laird and General William Westmoreland after a Westmoreland visit to Vietnam included: "A copy of General Westmoreland's trip report . . . is at Tab A. Secretary Laird should not know we hold this report." At the same time, Nixon and Kissinger thought they had a secure back channel to General Creighton Abrams in Saigon in the run-up to the Cambodian invasion, but Secretary of Defense Laird saw every word and talked to Abrams before the general answered White House queries. At the same time, the Joint Chiefs of Staff installed a spy on Kissinger's staff, a twenty-eight-year-old Navy yeoman first class named Charles Radford, officially a stenographer. But his real job, as explained to him by Admiral Rembrandt Robinson, the liaison officer between the Joint Chiefs and the NSC, was to copy and send on every piece of paper he saw to the Joint Chiefs of Staff.

There were double books and phony memos, too, on the political meetings that had begun on July 22 for the run-up to the congressional elections. The President met for two hours on that day with Haldeman, Finch, Harlow, Harry Dent, Murray Chotiner, and Donald Rumsfeld, a former Illinois congressman who ran the Office of Economic Opportunity before being called to the White House. The three-page report to the President's File, prepared by Dent, concerned such things as a presidential visit to the South and campaign schedules for David and Julie Eisenhower. The real memo, kept under lock and key in Dent's office, was a record of the President's orders determining the initial distribution of secret campaign funds collected during the first two years of the administration, including: "Alaska: We are to give $10,000 now (the $3,500 already given is included therein) and probably go as high as $25,000. . . . New Jersey: We are to give $25,000 now and perhaps go as high as $200,000 depending on Dent's assessment of this state at a later time. . . . New Mexico: Chotiner is to see that a poll is conducted before too long and if necessary go as high as $200,000. . . . Nevada: $200,000 . . . North Dakota: $200,000 . . . Tennessee: $200,000 . . . Utah: No more than $50,000 is to be put into Utah at this time. The total allocation will be $100,000. It could be more later."

And so it went, state by state. The President decided that no money should go to Michigan, New York, and several other states. In Michigan, the winner of the Republican primary for senator was Lenore Romney, George's wife. "She's not one of us," said the President. In New York, the Republican incumbent was Charles Goodell, once a conservative House member, who had transformed himself into one of the country's most visible and vocal antiwar liberals after being appointed by Governor Rockefeller to complete the Senate term of the assassinated Senator Robert F. Kennedy. "We are dropping Goodell over the side," said the President of a three-way race with a liberal Democratic Congressman named Richard Ottinger and the Conservative Party's nominee, James Buckley, best known for being the brother of William F. Buckley, Jr. Nixon wanted to help Buckley, but that was difficult to do without publicly betraying a Republican, something he had never done before. One idea Nixon had was to send Vice President Agnew into New York, telling him that he could not use Buckley's name—or Goodell's—but that he should repeat and repeat the line "Vote for people who will support the President."

The Buckley race fascinated the President because he had been playing with the idea of a third party or a new name for the Republican Party to bring in conservative Southern Democrats. On September 8, sitting alone in front of the burning fireplace—with the air conditioning on full blast—in his EOB hideaway office, Nixon had filled a legal-size page with political thoughts, including: "Need for new party name, poll Conservative-Liberal. . . . Need to handle Wallace . . . Wallace proves fallacy of Southern gains—unless race and power of race issue. . . . Hang race-liberal-student tag on Demos. . . ."

That same week the President pushed those ideas in the comments he scrawled alongside items in his news summaries. "Cambodia and Kent State led to an overreaction by our own people to prove that we were pro-student, blacks, left." "We must get turned around on this before it is too late—Emphasize—anti-Crime—anti-Demonstrations—anti-Drug—anti-Obscenity." Reacting to an item on network coverage of a Department of Housing and Urban Development official named Robert Affeldt, who said the administration was "encouraging and perpetuating racial discrimination," the President wrote one word: "Good."

Those were not idle thoughts. Attorney General Mitchell had one too many at a cocktail party in the Women's National Press Club and was overheard and quoted by a *Women's Wear Daily* reporter named Kandy Stroud as saying: "This country is going so far right you are not even going to recognize it. . . . These stupid kids . . . And the professors are just as bad if not worse. They don't know anything. Nor do these stupid bastards who are running our educational institutions."

The story was played as an embarrassment. But the President's reaction was, "John—Good Job—Don't back off." The President knew Stroud—"that kike girl," he called her. The next day, though, he wasn't quite so happy when the summary reported that Mitchell's wife, Martha, had called Helen Thomas of UPI to yell about the press picking on her husband as college professors were turning kids into communists. Nixon's note: "Again!" In private he was saying, sadly, that his friend would have to go if he could not control his wife's drinking and calls to reporters and staffers.

The Attorney General's musings were, in fact, the Nixon party line—whatever you called the party. Like almost every politician in Washington, the President was reading *The Real Majority*, a new book by Richard Scammon, the former Census director, and Ben J. Wattenberg, a moderate Democratic analyst. The numbers and the thesis of the book were compelling: the real American political majority was "unpoor, unyoung, and unblack"; it was "middle-income, middle-aged, middle-educated, and white." Scammon and Wattenberg put a face to their findings: the real American voter was "a 47-year-old housewife from the outskirts of Dayton, Ohio, whose husband was a machinist."

The Dayton housewife, according to the authors, divided the politics of 1970 into two issues, the economic issue, which had basically favored Democrats since the days of Franklin Roosevelt, and the social issue, the perceived threats of crime-in-the-streets, chaos on campus, hippies, drugs, pornography, and, for many whites, the rising of blacks. For an issue featuring a cover story on "the hottest candidate in either party"—conservative Ronald Reagan, running for reelection as governor of California—*Life* magazine found a forty-seven-year-old machinist's wife from a Dayton suburb, Mrs. Bettye Lowery, a registered Democrat, who said such things as: "The U.S. made a commitment in Vietnam, and I very much regret we'll have to fulfill it. . . . Dissent is one thing, violence another, if students break the law they should be disciplined. . . .

Agnew? You have to like the man in a way. He does say what he thinks." *

On September 16, the President went to Kansas State University and told a wildly cheering audience of fifteen thousand—and millions watching or listening on nationwide television and radio—exactly what he thought of the state of the nation in the election year of 1970.

> Consider just a few items in the news . . . in the last five weeks: A courtroom spectator pulls out a gun . . . gives arms to the defendants . . . moves to a waiting getaway van . . . four die, including the judge. . . . A man walks into the guardhouse of a city park, pumps five bullets in a police sergeant sitting quietly at his desk. . . . A Nobel Prize winner working on a cancer cure returns to the cages of his experimental rats and mice . . . to find them vandalized . . . some thrown out the windows. . . . A police patrolman responds to an anonymous emergency call. . . . He finds the house deserted, but a suitcase is left behind. . . . It explodes, blows off his head. . . .
> Those who bomb universities, ambush policemen, who hijack airplanes . . . deserve the contempt of every American. . . . There have always been among us those who would choose violence or intimidation to get what they wanted. . . . What is new is their numbers, and the extent of the passive acquiescence, or even the fawning approval, that in some fashionable circles has become the mark of being 'with it.' . . . The blood is on the hands of anyone who encouraged them . . . hinting that the cause is right all the same.

Then the master crafter of political messages turned it:

> There is a growing, dangerous attitude among millions of people that all youth are like those who appear night after night on the television screen shouting obscenities. . . . One of the greatest disservices that the disrupters have done in fact is precisely that, to reflect unfairly on those millions of students, like those in this

---

* The idea of the typical "Middle American" was not totally new to Nixon's men. On August 18, two White House staffers had been sent into the public rooms of the East Wing of the White House to "find a 'Proper' family to be named for millionth visitor for 1970 . . . (by) acceptability rather than the precision of counting." They chose Mrs. Leon Sheldon of Webster City, Iowa, who was visiting Washington with her husband and four children. They were brought into the Oval Office for a photograph with the President.

room, who do go to college for an education, who do study, who do respect the rules.

The "hijacking" in the news was international. On September 6 and 9, the Popular Front for the Liberation of Palestine—headed by George Habash, a rival of Al Fatah's Yasir Arafat—took over five airliners with more than four hundred passengers and forced three of their crews to land on an abandoned World War II airfield on a desert plateau in Jordan not far from Amman. The hijackers were demanding the release of Palestinian terrorists held in European jails. But the immediate effect was on the shaky cease-fires between Palestinian military units and the government of King Hussein, and between Israel and Egypt along Suez.

All of the planes had been headed for New York and there were dozens of Americans among the hostages. The President's first reaction was to order fighter-bombers on aircraft carriers in the Mediterranean to strike Palestinian bases in Jordan and Lebanon. Defense Secretary Laird ignored the order, repeatedly blaming bad weather conditions. His first call was to Admiral Thomas Moorer, the chairman of the Joint Chiefs: "Tom, I've gotten this order . . . We're just going to have terrible weather out there for the next forty-eight hours."

On the day of the first hijacking, Israel walked out of United Nations peace talks in New York, demanding that Egyptian missiles be moved back to the positions they occupied when the talks had begun in August. Three days later, fighting erupted again in Jordan, as government troops and Palestinian units exchanged small-arms and artillery fire all across Amman. That same day, in Chile, Marxist Salvador Allende finished first in presidential voting with 36.3 percent of the vote; his party won eighty of the two hundred seats in the country's congress. The United States ambassador, Edward M. Korry, appointed by President Johnson, cabled Washington:

> Chile voted calmly to have a Marxist-Leninist state, the first nation in the world to make this choice freely and knowingly. . . . There is no reason to believe that the Chilean armed forces will unleash a civil war or that any other intervening miracle will undo his victory. It will have the most profound effect on Latin America and beyond; we have suffered a grievous defeat; the consequences will be domestic and international. . . .

Reading that, Nixon underlined the last sentence. He knew Korry and disliked him, thought of him as a Kennedy man. But the ambassador hated and feared Allende and was at least as unhappy as the President. His cable, two days later, began: "There is a graveyard smell to Chile, the fumes of a democracy in decomposition. They stank in my nostrils in Czechoslovakia in 1948 and they are no less sickening today. . . ." Korry, arrogant and outspoken, was already telling politicians and businessmen in the country's capital, Santiago: "Not a nut or a bolt will be allowed to reach Chile under Allende. Once Allende comes to power we shall do all within our power to condemn Chile and Chileans to utmost deprivation and poverty. . . ."

Tough as he was, the ambassador did not think the United States had the means or the power to derail Allende. That judgment made him ever more suspect back in Washington, where the White House, prodded and alarmed by corporations heavily invested in Chile (led by Anaconda Copper, PepsiCo, and International Telephone and Telegraph Corporation), was pushing the CIA to find some way to get rid of Allende. In March the CIA had been allocated $1 million for "spoiling operations," but that effort was smaller than in the past two Chilean elections, when the United States had secretly spent as much as $20 million to support anticommunist candidates. The CIA told the President that during the 1970 campaign Cuba secretly provided Allende with $350,000, which happened to be the same amount spent by ITT's anti-Allende operations. But the overall 1970 effort was uncoordinated and sloppy; perhaps the Americans had become used to Allende's rhetoric of "solidarity with the Cuban Revolution," of ending "imperialist exploitation . . . American monopolies . . . aggression in Vietnam." After all, this was a country of only 9.5 million people, a democracy far from the principal battlefields of the Cold War.

The post-election analysis of the Interagency Group—which included representatives of State, Defense, and the CIA, plus the National Security Council—stated: "The Group concluded that the United States had no vital interests within Chile, the world military balance of power would not be significantly altered by an Allende regime and an Allende victory in Chile would not pose any likely threat to the peace of the region. The Group noted, however, that an Allende victory would threaten hemispheric cohesion and would represent a psychological setback to the U.S. as well as a definite advance of the Marxist idea."

That and the concerns of ITT and other American companies, including PepsiCo, which was run by Nixon's friend Donald Kendall, was enough for the President. And for Kissinger. They wanted to find a way to prevent Allende from being ratified as president by the Chilean congress on October 24, even though, in Chilean tradition, losing parties had always stepped aside so that the top vote-getter could be elected president. Kissinger set the tone for a covert CIA campaign, saying privately, "I don't see why we need to stand by and watch a country go Communist due to the irresponsibility of its people."

The President called in Kissinger, Haldeman, and John Mitchell, who had done legal work for ITT in Chile, on September 15. After a while, he called CIA director Helms into the meeting. Helms was there for less than twenty minutes. His notes read: "One in ten chance perhaps, but save Chile! . . . Not concerned risks involved. No involvement of embassy. $10,000,000 available, more if necessary. Full time job—best men we have. . . . Make the economy scream. 48 hours for plan of action."

It was the first time the CIA director had ever been exposed to Nixon in heat. He went away understanding that American investors were afraid that Allende would nationalize their industries and properties, and that his job was to do whatever it took to overthrow Allende. Back at CIA headquarters, Helms called in senior officials. The official minutes of that meeting reported:

> The Director told the group that President Nixon had decided that an Allende regime in Chile was not acceptable to the United States. The President asked the Agency to prevent Allende from coming to power or to unseat him. The President authorized ten million dollars for this purpose, if needed. Further, the Agency is to carry out this mission without coordination with the Departments of State and Defense. . . . The Director said he had been asked by Dr. Henry Kissinger to meet with him on Friday, 18 September, to give him the Agency's views on how this mission could be accomplished.

In a separate State Department operation, the President signed off on $250,000 to be sent to the United States embassy in Santiago to try to buy votes in the Chilean congress to vote against the Marxist on October 24. The first CIA move was to offer $50,000 to Chilean military officers willing to kidnap their own chief of staff, General René Schneider, who opposed a military coup, to get him out of the way for a few days. The embassy plan was referred to as Track I. The CIA planning was called Track II and was kept secret from the State Department. Neither seemed to be having any impact, and conservative political leaders friendly to the United States told American diplomats and agents why: Chileans were less afraid of Marxism than of losing their democracy. Ambassador Korry's "eyes only" cables carried stronger warnings. When he realized that CIA agents were approaching Chilean military leaders without his knowledge he wrote: "I think any attempt on our part actively to encourage a coup could lead us to a Bay of Pigs failure. I am appalled to discover that there is liaison for terrorists and coup plotting. . . . this would be an unrelieved disaster for the United States and for the President. Its consequences would be to strongly enforce Allende now and in the future, and do the gravest harm to U.S. interests throughout Latin America, if not beyond."

AFTER HIS SPEECH IN KANSAS on September 16, the President flew to Chicago. At 2 A.M., September 17, Kissinger called Haldeman at the President's hotel. He wanted to tell Nixon that street-to-street fighting had begun in Amman between Jordanian troops and Palestinian units—and Israeli and British intelligence were telling him that Syrian tanks were massed at the border of Jordan. Left unsaid was that the National Security Council had no way to confirm that intelligence because Nixon, with Kissinger's help, had cut American intelligence agencies, both military and civilian, out of the decision-making process. Haldeman, ever protective, saw no need to wake the President, but he did tell Kissinger to go ahead and say he had spoken to the President—allowing Kissinger to operate through the night in the President's name. That meant he could avoid notifying Rogers or Laird. Let them sleep, too, while Kissinger ran the war room. Then, at 8 A.M., he called Chicago again, and began by repeating what he had told the President before he left Washington: "It looks like the Soviets are pushing the Syrians and the Syrians are pushing the Palestinians." Nixon's first reaction on this morning was, "There's nothing better than a little confrontation now and then, a little excitement."

Six hours after the first reports, Kissinger, still relying on the Israelis and the British for intelligence, told the President that Jordanian troops and tanks seemed to be taking control of Amman in bloody encounters with lightly armed Palestinian fedayeen. Then the national security adviser switched crises, repeating something he had told the President a week earlier: there seemed to be increased numbers of Soviet personnel in Cuba, especially around a small naval base at Cienfuegos. Increased Soviet naval activity and harassment of United States spy-plane flights had just about convinced Kissinger that the Soviets wanted to use the base as a refueling station for nuclear submarines cruising off the east coast of the United States.

Nixon was in Chicago for informal meetings with the editors and editorial boards of the city's four newspapers, followed by a briefing for sixty midwestern editors and broadcast executives—part of his endless quest to reduce the dominance of the Washington, D.C., and New York press. Kissinger flew out to meet him there and give the editors a "senior official" backgrounder. Kissinger emphasized "American credibility," which was his way of linking all issues to Soviet-American confrontation and to the war in Vietnam. Then he gave them an earful about a world at risk, some of it secret, some just speculation or threat. "The Egyptians and the Russians violated the cease-fire along Suez, literally, practically from the first day onward. . . . I don't think we should delude ourselves that an Allende takeover in Chile would not present massive problems for us. . . . If the Russians start operating strategic forces out of Cuba, say, Polaris-type submarines, that would be a matter we would study very carefully. . . . The deepest rivalry which may exist in the world today is that between the Soviet Union and China. . . . A great deal of the peace and stability in the world depends on the confidence other people have in America's credibility."

On the Middle East, the President had interrupted to say, "We will intervene if the situation is such that our intervention will make a difference."

The President's words were supposed to be off the record, but the *Chicago Sun-Times* printed them. Kissinger's thoughts were printed, too, as anonymously sourced White House warnings to the Soviets, the Egyptians, the Cubans, and the Chileans. Within twenty-four hours, newspapers across the country were crying alarms and warnings—which was the point of the Nixon-Kissinger exercise. In fact, the President was not convinced by Kissinger's evidence of what, if anything, the Soviets were doing in Cuba. But the next day, Kissinger, at least, became totally convinced he was right about new dangers when a CIA photo analyst reported that new spy-plane photographs indicated a soccer field was being built at Cienfuegos. To him, that meant Russians were involved, because Cubans played more baseball than soccer. He rushed into the Oval Office, where Nixon was waiting for the arrival of Israeli Prime Minister Golda Meir, and handed the President a one-page memo that began: "TOP SECRET / SENSITIVE / EYES ONLY—Analysis of reconnaissance flight photography over Cuba has this morning confirmed the construction of a probable submarine deployment base in Cienfuegos Bay. . . ."

Mrs. Meir's message was simple and brief. To Nixon's great discomfort, she said the United States had gotten her country into the cease-fire and it was up to the United States to make sure it worked for Israel. The American record of the session went on:

> The Prime Minister said . . . the Israeli Cabinet had been split on the acceptability of the U.S. initiative. In fact, they had decided not to accept the proposal. . . . But after this decision to reject the U.S. initiative was made, President Nixon's letter arrived urging Israel to accept. On the basis of the President's letter, the Prime

Minister was able to assemble a majority of votes. . . . No sooner had Israel accepted the U.S. initiative, the Prime Minister continued, than the other side undertook to violate the provisions of the cease-fire by the forward movement of SAM missiles into the cease-fire zone.

Then Ambassador Rabin rolled maps out onto the carpet, covering part of the bright yellow Great Seal of the United States. The maps showed six SAM-2s and two SAM-3s inside the cease-fire zone on August 11, eight SAM-2s six days later, and thirty-one more SAM-2s and one additional SAM-3 within thirty miles of the Suez Canal on September 13.

Mrs. Meir said the reason for Israel's original opposition to the cease-fire was that it was linked to the Rogers Plan and her country could not accept going back to pre-1967 borders, because they could not defend themselves against Syria in the area of the Golan Heights. "Defensible borders" was the Israeli term. According to the American record of the session, she stated that

> Israel's problems were not a result of the Arabs but due entirely to the Soviet Union. Russia, she stated, was not concerned with the interests of either the Arabs or the Israelis but only her own interests in expanding Red influence in the Middle East. It was Soviet military equipment and Soviet presence which had changed the situation. Egyptians cannot operate SA-3 missiles. Soviet personnel were interspersed at all levels of decision within the Egyptian military and Soviet pilots had been active over the Canal. . . . While the Israelis favor peace in the area, they cannot accept the situation as it now stands nor can they enter into negotiations with a Russian pistol in the form of SAM missiles at their head.

Then the President asked the others to leave the room and delivered bad news, saying that she should not expect much withdrawal of the weapons; it was too late now. But there would be an expansion of American aid and credits, both military and economic.

After the Israelis left, Nixon talked with Kissinger about Cuba, saying he was still not persuaded by the spy-plane photographs. He said the Defense Intelligence Agency had reported that the water at Cienfuegos was too shallow for Soviet subs. He told Kissinger to order more spy flights, but added that he did not want a Cuban crisis interfering with a European trip scheduled to begin in a few days. He felt that even if the worst were true, it would be easier to persuade the Soviets to back down in secret. Besides, he added, the last thing he needed was some "clown senators" demanding another invasion of Cuba.

On the matter of Jordan, Kissinger was more persuasive, and he changed Nixon's mind on an important point. The President had said at the beginning of the crisis that he would use American planes and men— for the first time in the Middle East—before he would allow Jordan to fall to Arabs backed by the Soviet Union. Kissinger had argued all along for using the Israeli military if King Hussein's army was in trouble, and Nixon finally agreed to that in a Saturday telephone call from Camp David. So far, the Israelis knew nothing of that two-man American plan.

EARLY ON SUNDAY, September 20, Kissinger called Camp David, and got Haldeman. The news was that Syrian tanks, some painted with Palestinian insignia, had crossed the Jordanian border, rolling through several villages and penetrating more than fifteen miles. But they withdrew after the Jordanians counterattacked, reportedly destroying thirty of the Syrian tanks. "They're testing us," Kissinger said. The problem, he said, was Rogers. He was worried because the Secretary of State was in New York and might go to the United Nations or might meet with Soviet ambassador Dobrynin, who also happened to be in New York. He told Haldeman that Rogers had to be stopped. "We are pissing away all we've gained in eighteen months," he said. "Maybe that's the reason why there's no reply to the summit offer and for Dobrynin's insolence regarding Egyptian violations." He told Haldeman he was worried that if King Hussein fell, the Israelis would move. If there were a meeting between the Secretary of State and Dobrynin, the Russian would realize, in Kissinger's words, "Rogers is a patsy." Then, said Kissinger, "he will refuse to deal with me."

As the day wore on, more and more conflicting reports of Syrian activity, most from Israeli intelligence, clattered in on teletypes. As Nixon stayed in touch by telephone from Camp David, Kissinger told him Israeli or American troops would have to respond. An airborne brigade was on alert in Germany, a move that had more to do with warning the Soviets than helping the Jordanians. Nixon returned to the White House before 8 P.M.

By then, pilots and agents of three countries, Israel, Britain, and the United States, reported or estimated that more than two hundred Syrian tanks had reentered Jordan. Kissinger telephoned Israeli ambassador Rabin, who was in New York at a United Jewish Appeal dinner with Mrs. Meir, and told him that King Hussein would welcome Israeli help against Syria—an idea Rabin had trouble believing. The ambassador asked whether the United States was advising Israel to intervene. "Yes," Kissinger said. The next morning Rabin gave his government's answer: the Israelis were considering air strikes against Syrian positions, and would use ground troops at the same time. Then Kissinger went back to Nixon. "Tell them to go," the President said. "I've decided. . . . Bomb the bastards!" Then it was Kissinger who backed off, not passing along that answer to the Israelis.

There were no bombs. The next day, as Israeli tanks took positions along Israel's borders with Syria and Jordan—the Golan Heights and the Jordan River—and United States reconnaissance planes skirted the Mediterranean, King Hussein said he did not need or want the help of Israeli ground forces and he was not sure he wanted their planes over his country, either. In fact, his men were driving the Syrians back, destroying half their tanks, many from the air, as the Syrian air force never appeared to cover their ground forces. By the early morning hours of September 23, Hussein was in control of his country.*

After a long National Security Council meeting that morning, in which the President and everyone else talked in disciplined language about the multiple crises, the President walked back to the Oval Office with Kissinger and Haldeman. When that door was closed, he sat down behind his desk, put his feet up, and started talking. There were still real problems around, but he could barely restrain his excitement, saying it looked like the Syrians were out for good and Hussein had a cease-fire. He said that Rabin had called him before the NSC meeting and said things had worked out well because of: "First, the tough U.S. position; second, the Israeli threat; third, Russian pressure on Syria and Iraq as a result of the U.S. position; fourth, superb fighting by Jordanian troops."

Taking notes as always, Haldeman wrote: "Another crisis handled darn well—with P very strong & cool on top—& K's system, WSAG etc. functioning very well in spite of Rogers' ineptness—& Rogers' role also a constructive one in forcing caution."

Kissinger seemed to think, however, that this was the beginning, not the end. He told Haldeman the United States was now confronting the Soviet Union, and he was convinced the Soviets were ready for what amounted to a global showdown. He was almost frantically warning of a new Cuban missile crisis, as recorded by Haldeman: "K has a real plot building—re: whole Soviet plan. Feels they have been using summit and

---

* By cutting out U.S. intelligence agencies, the White House, on its own, did not seem to know that Syria had its own problems, involving an internal power struggle. The Syrian air force was commanded by General Hafez al-Assad, who two months later would become the country's ruler in a coup d'etat.

Egypt missiles as covers for their Cuban operation. Following same pattern as in '62. Thinks this will surface in ten days. Can't hold until after elections, which is what P wants. . . . Soviets will lose all their fear of RN—then P will have to go violently the other way. . . . Russia may well be heading for a showdown. Egypt was smokescreen. . . . Cuba is real kick in teeth to RN."

Nixon's reaction was that if the Soviets were actually attempting to put a nuclear submarine base at Cienfuegos, a U.S. blockade of the port was probably the only solution. Kissinger said he thought that the situation would surface soon and that there were no contingency plans for any action—because Rogers was stalling at State. The President told him to convene WSAG again and get a plan. Nixon was separating himself from the details of the ongoing crisis—Kissinger was reporting them regularly and often the President would only nod or even seem to look through him—and the style impressed the adviser. This was not the Nixon rearranging place settings minutes before a state dinner. During the Mideast crises, Kissinger found him slow and uncertain in committing to action, but his timing seemed extraordinary and he was resolute after coming to a decision. The President seemed calm but joyless, open to argument—not at all the impetuous, shouting man of more ordinary days.

So the President had time again for domestic matters, announcing that one thousand new agents would be trained by the FBI—while Kissinger lined up and briefed columnists, Joseph Alsop, Joseph Kraft, and Hugh Sidey among them, to report that Nixon's leadership and his own quick decision making on both American and Israeli mobilization had prevented another Middle East war. Sidey was then shuttled from Kissinger's office to the President's for a thirty-minute visit, preceded by a Kissinger memo that said, "Mr. Sidey will have no substantive questions for you; he is simply interested in seeing the scenes, and getting the feel of your working routine during the past two weeks."

Time's cover that week was a heroic portrait of Nixon under the headline "Facing the Middle East. When to Use or Not to Use Power." Inside the magazine, along with the President's practiced talk of winning a generation of peace, there was a revealing paragraph: "Nixon ordered that neither his time nor his mind was to be cluttered with the details of how many ships should be moved where. 'It is very important to take the long view,' he cautioned. 'I am not going to get bogged down in the details.' "

That was how the President wanted to see himself. It was also a key to Kissinger's growing power. Though Rogers and Laird were still the ones getting their pictures in the papers and sitting in the chairs of television talk shows, it was the national security adviser (whose German accent kept him off television—President's orders) who was moving ships around. Kissinger sent the aircraft carriers *Independence* and *Saratoga* into the Mediterranean, flew C-130s into Turkey, and even mobilized the Eighty-second Airborne in North Carolina, using the moves as public signals to augment the cables to Moscow warning of "gravest consequences."

Two days later, on September 25, the Cienfuegos story did break in newspapers across the country because no one had passed the President's word to Jerry Friedheim, the Defense Department's chief spokesman. At his daily morning briefing, Friedheim responded candidly to a reporter's vague question about whether anything was happening with Cuba these days. Kissinger was angry. The "senior official" in the White House—Kissinger, of course—immediately called reporters in for a background briefing, saying the Soviets had been warned that building a submarine base was a violation of the 1962 settlement of the Cuban missile crisis. To clarify that point, he read a November 1962 statement by President Kennedy: "If all the offensive weapons are removed from Cuba and kept out of the hemisphere in the future, under adequate verification and safeguards, and if Cuba is not used for the export of aggressive communist purposes, there will be peace in the Caribbean." But in fact there was little reaction to the story, partly because a lot of important people, including the President, simply did not believe Kissinger's warnings. In the third paragraph of a front-page story, *The New York Times* reported: "In Washington, United States officials, including members of the intelligence community, have expressed puzzlement over the charges, noting that these have been based on dubious and dated information."

On September 27, the last of the hostages held in the Jordanian desert—thirty-two Americans—were released by the Palestinians, who had won the release of hundreds of their own men in European and Israeli jails. The next day King Hussein and Palestinian leader Yasir Arafat, brought to Cairo by President Nasser, signed a cease-fire agreement, with other Arab leaders signing as witnesses. The agreement emphasized that Israel was the real enemy of all and guaranteed both the King's throne and a continuing Palestinian presence in Jordan. At the same time, Kissinger called Israel's Ambassador Rabin with official thanks from President Nixon: "The United States is fortunate to have an ally like Israel in the Middle East. These events will be taken into account in all future developments." It was a statement that Rabin took to mean that the United States now saw Israel as more than a moral obligation; to him the words meant a new strategic alliance, a Cold War bond that seemed more solid than the old sense of obligation and paternalism.

• • •

NIXON'S REWARD to himself was a European trip. He left the United States on September 27, heading first for Rome and a meeting with Pope Paul VI. The highlight was going to be a visit with the Sixth Fleet in the Mediterranean for naval maneuvers, a big, noisy fireworks display designed to show that the Russians might be in the neighborhood now, but this was an American lake. On the eight-hour flight from Andrews Air Force Base to Rome's Ciampino Airport, he sat with Haldeman for a time, saying that he wanted to create a "campaign attack group"—Colson, Buchanan, Huston, Chotiner, and Lyn Nofziger—to begin negative research and harassment of possible 1972 Democratic opponents. He named Edward Kennedy, Edmund Muskie, and Hubert Humphrey, and wanted the group to begin by collecting income tax returns at the Internal Revenue Service. Then he switched to the constant battle between Rogers and Kissinger—the Secretary of State was on the plane and Kissinger was in Paris—asking Haldeman if he thought the time had come to get rid of one of them. "No," Haldeman answered. "Okay," Nixon said. He added that if one had to go it would be Kissinger; he could be replaced by Alexander Haig.

The President arrived by helicopter aboard the aircraft carrier USS *Saratoga* on the evening of September 28. "It's been a hard two or three weeks," he told the forty-seven hundred men of the great ship's crew. "The fact that we were successful is the fact that you were there. When power is used in such a way that you do not have to go the ultimate test, then it is really effective." Then he sat down for dinner with the ship's officers and the Cabinet members who were traveling with him. He went to his cabin to rest for a few minutes. There was a quick rap on the door and Haldeman came in to tell him: "Nasser is dead!" The fifty-two-year-old Egyptian leader had died of a massive heart attack in Cairo. The President asked for information on the Egyptian vice president, Anwar Sadat, and then went to bed while the staff and Cabinet members prepared the appropriate statements.

On October 6, the day the President returned to Washington—after stops in Yugoslavia, Spain, England, and Ireland—Ambassador Dobrynin came to the White House with a Soviet statement denying that there had ever been a plan to build an offensive base in Cuba and saying that the Soviet Union repeated its commitment to the rather informal agreements made with President Kennedy after the Cuban missile crisis. Kissinger, meanwhile, was meeting with columnists. He said the President believed that White House firmness—"unmistakable steel," he quoted as the President's words—had prevented communist expansion or another United States–Soviet Union confrontation in the Caribbean. A week later, on October 13, under the headline "U.S. NOW DUBIOUS ON SUB BASE," *The New York Times* reported: "The Defense Department today said that new evidence from Cuba made it now appear less likely that the Soviet Union was planning to build a submarine base there. . . ."

On Friday, October 9, Ambassador Korry in Santiago was told to come to Washington the next week. After reporting in to Kissinger, he was taken to see the President. When the door to the Oval Office opened, Nixon was there, saying: "That son-of-a-bitch! That son-of-a-bitch! . . . Not you, Mr. Ambassador. I know this isn't your fault and you've always told it like it is. It's that son-of-a-bitch Allende."

Korry had met Nixon in Ethiopia in 1967 and the two of them had talked long and frankly then. Now Korry spoke frankly again. The President carefully avoided talk of coups and such, but he did say the United States could bring down Allende in one way or another.

"You're dead wrong, Mr. President," Korry said. He wanted to try to work with Allende, saying there was no other choice. Then the ambassador brought up the activities of the coup plotters, saying, "There are madmen running around." The President was calm, Kissinger was glaring—and Korry was sent on his way. He had no doubt the President was even more angry than Kissinger.

In Chile, two days later, the CIA station chief in Santiago, Henry Hecksher, cabled Washington: "General Schneider is the main barrier to all plans for the military to take over." The reply from CIA headquarters began: "Constant pressure from White House . . . more important than ever to remove him." That was backed up by more than words. Another cable to Hecksher that day read: "IMMEDIATE SANTIAGO (EYES ONLY) SUB-MACHINE GUNS AND AMMO BEING SENT BY REGULAR COURIER LEAVING WASHINGTON 0700 HOURS 19 OCTOBER. . . ." The machine guns, with their serial numbers filed off, were sent in a U.S. diplomatic pouch. A cable from Washington to the military office of the embassy read: "High authority in Washington has authorized you to offer material support short of armed intervention to Chilean Armed Forces in any endeavors they may undertake to prevent the election of Allende on October 24."

Attempts to kidnap General Schneider failed on October 19 and on October 20. At 8 A.M. on October 22, Schneider's car was stopped in traffic and he was shot to death. In the United States it was reported as another botched kidnap attempt with the general shot in a misunderstanding when he raised his own pistol. But in Santiago, the official police report stated: "His car was surrounded by five individuals, one of whom, making use of a blunt instrument similar to a sledgehammer, broke the rear window and then fired at General Schneider, striking him in the area of the spleen, in the left shoulder and in the left wrist."

Forty-eight hours later, on October 24, the Chilean congress accepted the country's election results and confirmed Salvador Allende as president. Eight days before, after sending secret supplies of machine guns and other weapons into Chile to be used in coup attempts, the CIA in Langley, Virginia, had cabled Hecksher:

> It is firm and continuing policy that Allende be overthrown by a coup. It would be much preferable to have this transpire before 24 October but efforts in this regard will continue vigorously beyond this date. . . . It is imperative that these actions be implemented clandestinely and securely so that the United States government and American hand will be hidden.

CHAPTER 16

November 3, 1970

Have you all read the Scammon-Wattenberg book?" the President asked in a meeting with his political attack team on September 26. "All the Democrats are reading it. All Democrats are trying to blur their image—toward crime, toward students. . . . Hit them for being rubber stamps for the ultra liberal left. Hang it on them."

They all nodded. *The Real Majority* was quickly becoming the conventional wisdom of the political class as the 1970 campaign began. But Dent, Safire, Colson, and the rest of Nixon's political team had heard most of the same ideas time and again from Nixon. The "New Majority" or "New Party" born on his yellow pads over the past year or so was a political strategy crafted from the same poll numbers Scammon and Wattenberg had collected. In the book, they put it this way:

> Just as Democrats must move on the Social Issue to keep in tune with the center, so the Republicans must move on the Economic Issue to capture the center. . . . A Republican Party perceived as go-slow on the problems of unemployment or the cities or transportation or pollution, or against Medicare or Social Security, will be vulnerable. Americans of the center in the seventies will want activist problem-solving government. Republicans must offer up such an image or face trouble; they cannot keep the image of the party of the small-town banker. There aren't

enough small-town bankers to elect a President. . . . Republicans must prove they are the party of Middle America and not of fat cats. Nixon's party must capture that "little man" feeling if they want to win the Presidency. The Democratic Party can remain credible in that role, particularly so if there is a recession, a rise in unemployment, or continuing inflation.

In other words, voters in the middle gave the benefit of the doubt to Democrats on pocketbook issues, as they had since Franklin Roosevelt ran against President Herbert Hoover in the early years of the Great Depression almost forty years before. In its "Business" section the first week of October, *Time* began a wrap-up of the week's news with a new word, "stagflation"—a stagnant economy with growing inflation—then continued: "The many aches that the U.S. economy has suffered for more than a year have been noticeable less for their severity than for their variety. The nation has had a bad case of pernicious inflation, sagging production, swelling unemployment and choking interest rates. Fortunately, relief seems to be on the way. . . ."

Perhaps. But even so, it might be too late for Nixon's purposes in 1970. A *New York Times* survey of the thirty-five Senate races—ten seats held by Republicans and twenty-five by Democrats, which meant that the Republicans could control the upper house by taking seven Democratic seats—ran under this deck of headlines:

TWO PARTIES PICK DEFINITIVE ISSUES FOR SENATE RACE

DEMOCRATS STRESS INFLATION AND REPUBLICANS DISORDER
IN FIGHT TO WIN CONTROL

POLITICIANS GIVE 10 to G.O.P. AND 22 TO
ITS RIVALS, WITH 3 CONTESTS UNCERTAIN

The story below included: "Vice President Agnew stated the Republican case. . . . The overriding question, he said, is 'whether the policies of the United States are going to be made by its elected officials or in the streets.' For the Democrats, Lawrence F. O'Brien, the national chairman, and other spokesmen have been deriding 'Nixonomics.' . . ."

But Nixonomics was shot down by Nixon—and by some bad luck. The "Nixon Game Plan," as it was called in the beginning, was pretty basic Republican economics. "Gradualism" was the word used by his advisers. The idea was to hold down federal spending while the Federal Reserve Board restricted money supply enough to cut demand enough to raise unemployment enough to moderate wages and prices enough to stabilize inflation.

Nixon had seen the Republicans burned by recession in the 1954 and 1958 congressional elections, and he had been pressuring the Fed to push out a little more money on the theory that inflation was less of a danger to incumbent presidents than recession. Nixon had reluctantly approved a big trend-setting wage settlement with the postal workers as part of the price for an old Republican dream, privatizing postal service. The United Auto Workers, with 344,000 members, struck General Motors in mid-September 1970, taking $12 million a day in wages, $200 million a week in supplier sales, and $2 billion a week out of the gross national product (GNP).

So, wages and prices were going up, but the economy was not growing. Also, with all the power of the presidency, Nixon could not control his old friend Arthur Burns. Back on January 1, as he had sworn Burns in as chairman of the Federal Reserve, and the crowd applauded, Nixon had smiled and said, with embarrassing candor: "That's a standing vote of appreciation in advance for low interest rates and more money. . . . I respect Arthur's independence. However, I hope that independently he will consider my views are the ones that should be followed."

But Burns was more independent than that. In June, the President had tried to act on his own—and deflect Democratic demands for wage and price controls—by doing something he had said, in his first presidential press conference, that he would never do: he announced a voluntary wage and price scheme, "Inflation Alerts," a program to focus attention on what the government considered excessive wage and price demands. But at the same time he repeated the pledge he had made since his service at the Office of Price Administration in 1945, that he would never advocate mandatory controls on either business or labor. Never. The voluntary idea failed, as Nixon had always predicted. In fact, meeting with advisers just before he asked for restraint, he said: "People don't want to be good. They want to make money. We can't ask them to make economic decisions on anything but economic grounds."

For a time, Nixon focused his frustration on meat prices, maybe because he was a grocer's son. When meat prices rose, he issued one of his wilder orders, this one to Secretary of Agriculture Clifford Hardin, telling him he wanted meat prices reduced by the next Monday—or else. Nothing happened, of course, so he ordered the Council of Economic Advisers to give him a report on "profiteering or collusion" by supermarkets. When the council's chairman, Paul McCracken, reported back that there was no evidence of price-fixing, Nixon angrily told an aide,

Peter Flanigan: "I think you will find that the chain stores who generally control those prices nation-wide are primarily dominated by Jewish interests. These boys, of course, have the right to make all the money they want, but they have a notorious reputation in the trade for conspiracy."

To press what they saw as their political advantage, the Democratic majorities in both houses of Congress voted to grant the President, against his wishes, standby authorization to impose wage and price controls. He vowed again that he would never use the authorization. Never. *The Wall Street Journal*, accurately, accused the loyal opposition of hoping for the worst: "For Democratic politicians, happiness is higher unemployment, shrinking overtime pay, rising prices, lofty interest rates and tight money." The President told Ehrlichman the real goal was not 1970: "I really want the economy to boom beginning in July '72."

By October the numbers looked bad for the White House. Since Nixon took office, inflation had increased from an annual rate of 3.3 percent to an annual rate of 5.5 percent in September, and the figure for the fourth quarter of 1970 was 7.5 percent. The GNP was flat, about the same at the end of 1970 as it had been at the beginning of 1969.

Ironically, in the next couple of weeks economists, liberal and conservative, realized that most of those indicators had begun moving in the right direction: a mild recession had bottomed out sometime in October. But the housewife in Dayton did not know that. The upticks did not seem to be having any effect on "Economic Issue" voters. *The New York Times* did not have a resident housewife, but the paper did follow a teamster from Akron named Mike Mangione in the weeks before the election; he told them that he hated antiwar demonstrators, that he thought the National Guard was right to fire at Kent State, but that his overtime was way down.

The President himself was the Republican campaign manager. More Machiavelli than the prince; he knew more politicians and precincts than any man in the country, and it was one of the things, along with football and foreign affairs, that he genuinely liked to sit around and talk about. He spent hours in the office recounting old campaigns, restating old lessons, and grumbling that all would still be well if his own men would listen and then get off their butts. They certainly listened. Day after day, Nixon would call in the boys—usually Colson or Haldeman or Harry Dent—and begin a monologue, sometimes playing the part of a candidate, expounding on his favorite game as they all took notes:

> The Democrats are trying to move over to the center, keeping us on the defensive on the economic issue. Even a screwball like McGovern is racing towards the center. We have to force them to repudiate the left or else to take the left—get them on the defensive,

say: "I don't question his sincerity—he deeply believes this radical philosophy." . . . Permissiveness is the key theme. All this permissiveness started with the goddamn Supreme Court. . . . Seventy-eight percent of the American people think the courts have gone too far towards permissiveness. Kick 'em on this.

Agnew should be very square, like Lombardi, like Meany. . . . We want to avoid the litany of "Agnew attacks this man and that man." . . . Say: "These are not bad men. This particular candidate—I knew his father. They deeply believe in the left. They are sincere, dedicated radicals!"

Now, about Agnew himself. He doesn't have the energy for that kind of campaign. Don't work him too hard. Don't press him too hard. Give him a chance to look good and feel good. . . . If the Vice President were slightly roughed up by those thugs nothing better could happen for our cause. If anybody so much as brushes against Mrs. Agnew, tell her to fall down.

On the kid thing—strong against bomb throwing. . . . Let others say that life is hard for the little bastards, that we should listen to them. . . . Find ways to talk of the dignity of work and pay respects to our Catholic friends. We could have had a mass at the Labor Dinner and 80 percent of the people would have hit the rail.

On abortion—get the hell off it. Just say it's a State matter and get the hell off it. And stay the hell off Israel. Not a goddam vote in it. . . . You can tell your Jewish friends privately all the right things, but the country is 3 to 1 against us on it. The country doesn't want to get into a war on Israel.*

Buchanan, Safire, do a speech on the courts. Praise them as I did, but judges who bend the law go too far. There have been some horrible decisions in the courts. Don't mention civil rights—Southerners will get the point.

---

* Nixon did not believe everything he read about Israel. Reading a September 14, 1970, Louis Harris poll reporting that 46 percent of respondents said their sympathies were with Israel while only 6 percent expressed sympathy for the Arabs, he wrote on his news summary: "This is absolutely a fraud." Reading, in the same poll, of a 38 percent to 38 percent split over approval of the use of American troops if Israel were threatened by the Soviet Union, he wrote: "Our poll shows 3-to-1 against."

Now, about the press . . . Please don't try to please the press by saying something new all the time. Keep saying what works. Tom Dewey told me you have to tell people something at least four times before they remember it. We all have "the" speech. Lincoln made the House Divided speech a hundred times before Cooper Union. Bryan made the Cross of Gold speech 259 times before the convention. . . .

Take a walk. Great TV. It's true you are the cutting edge, but also let them see the warm, human man. Don't appeal just to the people at $500-a-plate dinners. . . . If radicals show up, stand right in front of the sign with the worst obscenity on it. . . . If the Vice President sees a sign like "Fuck Nixon," he should go right up to it—and talk to the individual holding it and let him have it.

Fund-raising audiences are the flattest of all. They're rich and fat and drunk and dumb. You want to get on TV with the real people, not those sodden-looking old bastards. Walter Judd, the congressman, used to say, "You have got to make love to the people." It's always been a very difficult thing for me to do, but you must plunge into the crowds. You have to show you care, and you must care.

At the same time in those late summer and early autumn weeks, targeted political "groups" were marching in and out of the Oval Office for photos and a few presidential words as memos on strategy and tactics flowed out. Colson brought in the forty members of the Supreme Council of the Sons of Italy and the President told them how proud he was to have ordered the Justice Department to discontinue the use of the words "Mafia" and "Cosa Nostra" to describe organized crime. When the applause died down, the Supreme Venerable, Americo Cortese, thanked the President for his moral leadership. "You are," he said, "our terrestrial god."

Among the memos coming out was the President's signing off on a Tom Charles Huston project described this way: "He has established an organization that ostensibly endorses the radic-lib candidates and puts out a brochure of some kind that can be slipped under doors in the right areas of states praising the candidate (our opponent) for his outstanding liberal voting record and his solid opposition to all of the programs of the Nixon Administration re: law and order. . . ."

And then, as always, there was campaign money. On October 5, during the long flight back from Ireland, the last stop on his European tour, the President had talked alone with Haldeman, not about the enthusiastic crowds everywhere or his talks with Yugoslavia's Marshal Tito and Spain's Generalissimo Francisco Franco, but about a short private conversation with Joseph A. Mulcahy, the master of Kilfrush, a manor house in Ireland. Mulcahy, the president of Quigley Steel, a division of Pfizer Corporation in New York, had entertained the President the night before at a lavish six-course dinner punctuated by Irish song and drink. After coffee, the host asked Nixon into his library and told him he was willing to give the campaign between $1 million and $2 million—in cash—for whatever was needed.

A return gift for Mulcahy was made the responsibility of a Haldeman assistant, a friend from UCLA named Alex Butterfield, a former Air Force colonel who won a Distinguished Flying Cross as a fighter pilot in Vietnam. "Top priority," said Haldeman when he got back. But the President's priorities were making Butterfield a little crazy. He was, at the moment, still working on Haldeman's Action Memo P-562, which read: "The President would like to try '61 and '64 vintage years of French Bordeaux, both Lafite-Rothschild and Haut-Brion. . . . Let's get a reading again as to what really are the good years. Include in your reading a check with the gal from La Côte Basque where the President had dinner last week. She seems to have some views on the subject which he is impressed by."

The President took wine very seriously—memos about vintages were part of what Butterfield called "these beaver patrol projects"—and he drank the best. Nixon was often served wine from bottles wrapped with napkins to hide the label from guests offered California ordinary. Gifts were serious business, too. He kept a small loose-leaf binder in the center drawer of his Oval Office desk with lists of the prices of the gifts he thrust awkwardly into visitors' hands—with bad jokes to men: "Give this to your wife. Or girlfriend. We won't tell." Women's compacts were $14.50, key chains were $4.40, ashtrays were $4.00. Presidential cuff links cost $24.50. Ballpoint pens embossed with the presidential seal were listed as $.39 in a box, $.15 in cellophane. The most expensive gifts in the drawer were diamond pins, which cost $212.00 each. He had given out three, to Madame Chiang Kai-shek, to Mamie Eisenhower, and to President Johnson's widow, Lady Bird Johnson.

BY THE TIME the President came back from Europe, the Vice President had been on the road for thirty-five days, campaigning against "radical liberals," most particularly Senator Albert A. Gore in Tennessee and Senator Charles Goodell in New York. The Vice President did not go so far as to endorse James Buckley, the Conservative Party candidate in New York, but he said vote for the man who supports the President—and said Goodell did not. "The Christine Jorgensen of the party," he called Goodell, using the name of a young man who had become famous after going to Denmark for a sex-change operation. That prompted Governor Rockefeller to call the White House to say he wanted Agnew kept out of his state. Republican leaders in other states, including California, were saying the same thing.

Agnew had worn out his welcome. The Democrats had adjusted to the "Social Issue." Their candidates were denouncing student violence, too, and loudly sponsoring dozens of tough-sounding anticrime bills in Congress. Across the country, liberals were giving virtually the same "law and order" speeches as their Republican opponents and making television commercials shot in cruising police cars or in police stations.

What Nixon really wanted to do was get out there and campaign himself. But first he rested for a long weekend at Key Biscayne, polishing yet another Vietnam speech, this one for October 7. This time he proposed a standstill cease-fire, which was immediately rejected by Hanoi. On the flight back from Key Biscayne on October 10, the President wrote out a query to Kissinger, questioning whether the two of them really understood the war and, in this case, the thinking of the Vietnamese communists, listing theories that had failed: "Have we misjudged V.C. from beginning—1. Running to wire—exhausted. . . . 2. Stop U.S. dissent & they'll talk. . . . 3. Give them a jolt & they'll talk." Two days later, reading the news summary, he saw a long diplomatic analysis by Peter Kumpa of the Baltimore *Sun,* saying that the newest Nixon plan was reasonable enough but it never had a chance because "Hanoi's leaders are driven by passion and faith." The President underlined those words, writing: "K— The real problem."

Nixon's first campaign trip, only a day, was to Connecticut, with a brief and purposeful stop at the Westchester Airport north of New York City. The President stepped out of the plane for a moment, a crowd waving big "BUCKLEY FOR SENATE" signs ran out onto the tarmac, photos were taken, and the Conservative Party candidate had a no-words-spoken endorsement from the Republican president. The crowd was good in Hartford and Nixon happily pointed out a couple of young demonstrators waving Vietcong flags.

Those flags and other manifestations of dissent, in manageable numbers, were useful props. At the airport in Green Bay, Wisconsin, John Osborne of *The New Republic,* waiting for the President to appear in the doorway of *Air Force One,* was standing next to two local patrolmen when a sergeant appeared with orders from the White House advance men. "The minute the President steps out on the ramp, turn the lights on this bunch," he said, nodding toward the chanters of "One, Two, Three, Four. We don't want your fucking war!" The patrolmen were surprised, so their boss continued: "That's what they want us to do—*now do it!*"

As Nixon campaigned, the White House announced the withdrawal of 40,000 troops from Vietnam before Christmas—part of the 150,000 he had announced at the beginning of the year—and Defense Secretary Laird held a news conference to declare that he expected the draft to be ended by the summer of 1973. But the war itself, as opposed to antiwar demonstrators, was fading as an issue, at least according to polls. It was coming down to law and order on one side and the economy on the other. On October 16, a state grand jury indicted twenty-five people in the riots and killings at Kent State in May; all were students and university officials. Jurors found that the National Guardsmen could not be held liable because they fired into the crowd only because they sincerely believed their lives were in danger. Then five days later, on October 21, the Labor Department released September consumer price index statistics that showed a half-percent rise in the cost of food, clothing, housing, and other essentials.

In the week before the election, dozens of national leaders were in New York for the opening session of the United Nations General Assembly. Nixon invited only two of them to Washington, an odd couple. He hosted state dinners for his favorite unelected president, Yahya Khan of Pakistan, and for his favorite communist, President Ceausescu of Romania. He liked and trusted Yahya Khan, whose country had good relations with communist China and knew that the Pakistani leader would be visiting Peking in November. When they were alone after dinner, the President asked Yahya Khan if he would pass a message to Chinese leaders that the United States—Nixon personally—was interested in discussing more normal relations with Peking. The next night, October 26, toasting Ceausescu, Nixon referred to China as "the People's Republic of China." It was the first time an American president had ever used the name the communists had made official in 1950.

But the headlines stayed focused on bad economic news. On October 27, front pages featured Labor Department statistics indicating that eighteen metropolitan areas, including Los Angeles County and most of New Jersey, were being added to a "Substantial Unemployment List"—a list with only six places at the end of 1969—which meant unemployment had reached 6 percent in those areas and was expected to continue rising. The next day various economic indicators for September and October were released, and all the news was bad for the White House. The GM strike was blamed for some of the sagging indicators, including the wholesale price index and unit labor costs in manufacturing.

The President, meanwhile, was studying polls and political reports every day, often ordering that Cabinet members be dispatched to states or districts where they might help, or ordering White House money sent to Republicans in close races. "H—Put in 200Gs immediately," he scrawled on a report that Republican John Wold was within 12 points of Senator Gale W. McGee in Wyoming. "H—Go all out. 200G," he wrote on a poll report showing Republican Lowell P. Weicker 4 points behind Democrat Joseph Duffey in Connecticut. He was on the road for the last two weeks of the campaign, scheduled into twenty-three states from October 12 to Election Day.

On October 29, the President swept across the country, from Chicago and Rockford, Illinois, to Rochester, Minnesota, and then to Omaha, Nebraska, and San Jose, California. Haldeman picked up the story there, laying out exactly what the President wanted to do:

> The real blockbuster. Very tough demonstrators shouting "One, two, three, four, etc.," on the way into auditorium. Tried to storm the doors after we were in, and then really hit the motorcade on the way out. We wanted some confrontation and there were no hecklers in the hall, so we stalled departure a little so they could zero in outside, and they sure did. Before getting in car, P stood up and gave the "V" sign, which made them mad. They threw rocks, flags, candles, etc., as we drove out, after a terrifying flying wedge of cops opened up the road. Rock hit my car, driver hit brakes, car stalled, car behind hit us, rather scary as rocks were flying, etc., but we caught up and all got out. Bus windows smashed, etc. Made a huge incident and we worked hard to crank it up, should make a really major story and might be effective.

Nixon was on a high. His car was dented and broken glass and rocks were all around him as the Secret Service went into an assassination alert. The police chief said it was an act of God that the President escaped. The leader of the local Peace and Freedom Party, which had organized two thousand demonstrators, said: "He's a war criminal and he's not welcome in California. . . . After dropping that many bombs on the Vietnamese people how can anyone associated with the government claim to be upset about people throwing some eggs and rocks at Nixon? What's so precious about Nixon?"

The presidential party flew on to San Clemente, and Nixon almost burned his own house down starting a fire in the fireplace in his den. When Haldeman and others arrived, the house was filled with smoke and firemen were pulling hoses through the rooms. Wandering around in a bathrobe and slippers, a laughing Nixon said he loved the smell of smoke and was going to sleep in the house. It was 1 A.M. before he calmed down—he was showing how he gave the "V" sign back in San Jose—and finally went to bed in the early morning hours in a guest house.

Two days later, the presidential cavalcade came into Phoenix, Arizona, for a rally in a hangar at Sky Harbor International Airport. "A thousand haters," he called the demonstrators in San Jose, and the words reverberated around the huge metal building. So did the cheers of the noontime crowd bused to the airport. "Those who carry a 'peace' sign in one hand and throw a bomb or a brick with the other are the super-hypocrites of our time. . . . Let's recognize these people for who they are. They are not romantic revolutionaries. They are the same thugs and hoodlums that have always plagued the good people. . . . They increasingly terrorize decent citizens. . . . When you permit an imbalance to exist that favors the accused over the victim, you are inviting more violence and breeding more bullies."

When he stepped down from the platform, to the cheers of the bused-in faithful, Nixon told Haldeman that he wanted a tape of the speech to be shown on all three national television networks on election eve. That was a mistake. The tape, cut to fifteen minutes, was grainy; the sound boomed and dropped, as it had in the hangar. The President looked manic. Watching in Washington, Attorney General Mitchell said to friends, "My God, he looks like he's running for sheriff."

It all looked even worse by comparison when the Democrats were given free time to respond and the party chose Senator Edmund Muskie, who opened up his summer home in Kennebunkport, Maine, and spoke quietly and calmly from a rocking chair about "the politics of fear." The Democrat looked positively Lincolnesque. Almost immediately he was running ahead of Nixon in quickie one-on-one 1972 presidential polls.

On Election Day, November 3, the President voted in San Clemente, drove around for an hour or so, and then went home to make telephone calls. In Akron, Ohio, *The New York Times*'s model teamster, Mike Mangione, voted Democratic, telling the paper that he did it because his wife was going to have to go back to work, for the first time in twenty-two years, to pay the tuition of their three children in Catholic schools.

Nixon's first call was to Bill Buckley, indirectly wishing Buckley's brother well, saying: "I don't know how you mackerel snappers look at others, but if a quiet Quaker prayer will help, you've got it. Tell Jim to go to the bar with the warm beer and relax a couple of hours after the polls close."

Buckley provided Nixon one of his few satisfactions the next morning. *The New York Times,* the paper in his chosen state, carried an eight-column headline:

ROCKEFELLER AND BUCKLEY ELECTED,
DEMOCRATS RETAIN CONGRESS CONTROL
AND MAKE GAIN IN KEY GOVERNORSHIPS

Most of the candidates the President campaigned for lost, beginning with George H. W. Bush in Texas and George Murphy in California. The Republicans did gain two Senate seats—incumbent Democrats Albert A. Gore of Tennessee and Joseph D. Tydings of Maryland were losers—but lost nine seats in the House and eleven governorships. So the new House would be Democratic, 254 to 181. The Senate would also be Democratic, 55 to 45. There would be twenty-nine Democratic governors and twenty-one Republican ones. In terms of total votes, even with the lower turnout in a nonpresidential year, the overall Democratic margin in House elections increased from 1.1 million voters in 1968 to 4.5 million in 1970.

CHAPTER 17

December 31, 1970

T HE PRESIDENT TRIED TO declare victory after the midterm elections. The public line from the White House was that most other presidents had done even worse in past midterm elections, which was true, and that he had won an ideological majority of Republicans and conservative Democrats, which was not true. The results of the President's obsessive campaigning were pretty much a standoff. "A missed opportunity," he told Ehrlichman as he retreated to Key Biscayne on November 7 for a six-hour meeting on how to prepare for the 1972 election. The chosen few for that session were Mitchell, Finch, Harlow, Haldeman, Ehrlichman, Colson, and Rumsfeld.

The meeting began with the usual presidential monologue. Nixon repeated campaign themes and cited local numbers that made him feel good. But when the others began to talk, an unofficial list of problems was drawn up, and this became public because someone in the room passed his notes along to columnists Evans and Novak, who published the main points: "1. The President . . . The image of the hermit leader, walled off from the people, antagonistic to the nation's youth, possessed by foreign affairs, must be changed; 2. The Economy . . . Greater changes than the President had been willing to consider; 3. The Program . . . The President had to be shown to favor something besides the antiballistic missile and G. Harrold Carswell; 4. The Cabinet . . . Hickel, Romney, Kennedy had to go; 5. Congress . . . new lobbyists, a softer line; 6. The Vice President . . . must be toned down."

When Ehrlichman, responsible now for a domestic agenda, urged the President to spend more time working with Congress, Nixon snapped at him: "Don't keep saying that, John. I know I have to—I'll work twenty-two hours a day instead of twenty."

He was more enthusiastic about Cabinet changes. He wanted Romney out at Housing and Urban Development; if he would not quit, the idea was to let him continue to talk about integrated housing and then fire him and get credit for it in the South and some of the Northern industrial states. He wanted Hickel out at Interior, David Kennedy out at Treasury, Volpe out at Transportation. He wanted Mitchell to manage the 1972 campaign. He wanted to move Moynihan to the United Nations. And at the end of the year, he said, he wanted Rogers out and Nelson Rockefeller in as Secretary of State. He wanted John Mitchell to handle Romney, Hickel, and Kennedy. Colson could tell Volpe to go.

Most of all, Nixon wanted the economy to be booming by July 1972. He talked on, saying that advocating a program was more important than actually changing the law. "Sink FAP. . . . It's lost," he said of the Family Assistance Plan. Someone said that the welfare budgets of states and large cities were increasing by 20 to 50 percent a year. "Yeah," Nixon said, shifting gears, saying maybe they should push FAP, so that when it failed and welfare rolls continued to grow, they would get credit for trying. The President had a final idea, a value-added tax—a national sales tax—that would raise $30 billion a year which could be distributed to states and cities as block grants, eliminating more than a few federal agencies.

On November 9, Charles de Gaulle died. Nixon decided to go to Paris for the great man's memorial mass at Notre Dame, arriving in the early morning hours of November 12 and then returning to Washington the next evening. In between, he said, he wanted to go to a good restaurant for a Parisian lunch, but Kissinger and the Secret Service talked him out of that. He sulked. "I never get to do anything that's fun," he told Haldeman. "I have to always do what's right."

Back in the office on November 15, he was upset when he caught up with the Evans and Novak column reporting on the marathon Key Biscayne meeting, particularly the line about being a hermit. In the same news summary, there was an excerpt from a Marquis Childs column that read: "It appears that the President has no associates with whom he freely exchanges ideas and he is said to get his news in digest form on a single sheet of paper. . . . No matter how many times White House spokesmen deny it, this isolation is patently a fact."

"Knock it down," wrote Nixon in the margin.

Childs was wrong about the summary, which was twenty-nine

pages that day, but in his solitary way Nixon confirmed the columnists' facts that night. Alone upstairs in the Lincoln sitting room, he wrote about himself, beginning with a count of his days left in office. The next morning he put the pages in his desk downstairs:

> 2 years less one week or 6 years less one week. I have learned about myself and about the Presidency. From this experience I conclude:
> The primary contribution a President makes is on Spiritual lift—not material solutions.
> 1. The staff—particularly K and H—with my active cooperation have taken too much of my time in purely material decisions which could be left to others.
> 2. Harlow et al. have dragged me into too many Congressional problems.
> 3. My speech & idea group is inadequate—but part of the problem is that I have spent too little time with them.
> 4. The Press, the Intellectual establishment, and the partisan Dems are hopelessly against—Better means must be found to go over them to people.
> 5. I must find a way to finesse the Cabinet, staff, Congress, political types—who take time, but who could do their job sans my participation. Symbolic meetings should be the answer.
> Personally I must recognize responsibility to use power up to the hilt in areas where no one else could be effective.
> Stop recreation except purely for exercise—and on a regularly scheduled basis . . . Need for more social events . . . Need for optimistic upbeat psychology.
> Need for more stimulating people to talk to . . . Need for dignity, Kindness, drive, Youth, Priority, Spiritual quality.

Whatever his desires, the President was caught up in rounds of meetings for the next couple of days. He met first with senators-elect, at least the ones he liked. He was most impressed by James Buckley and by Lloyd M. Bentsen, the Texas Democrat who had beaten one of his Republican favorites, Congressman George H. W. Bush. But Bush was fine. The President was considering him for several consolation prizes, including a White House staff position or chairman of the Republican National Committee. Bush had hoped to be ambassador to the United Nations, but Nixon decided to give that post to Moynihan, who accepted and then informed Harvard that he would not be returning. But that one got screwy when *The Boston Globe* reported the appointment, not yet announced—the story was a total surprise to the man in the job, Ambassador Charles W. Yost. He was a veteran foreign service officer, and that, of course, triggered an anti-Moynihan campaign by the State Department and its traditional allies at the Council on Foreign Relations, based on the argument that the professor-turned-presidential-counselor had little experience in international affairs. Besides, Moynihan's wife, Elizabeth, said she had no intention of living in New York. Within a week, Moynihan reversed his acceptance.

In the middle of the day set aside for meeting new senators, the President saw Pearl Bailey, a singer and actress who had impressed him when she entertained at a state dinner for Chancellor Willy Brandt of West Germany. Awkward around strangers, Nixon required thorough talking papers even for minor appointments. Bailey's took three sheets, in part:

Points That May Be Raised by Miss Bailey

During Miss Bailey's performance at the White House the President crowned her "Ambassador of Love...." Somehow this action brought forth a request for Diplomatic license plates. (1) Diplomatic plates are only issued to foreign diplomats. (2) U.S. Diplomats in Washington, D.C., do not receive Diplomatic plates. (3) No American, regardless of position, receives Diplomatic plates within the United States. (4) Miss Bailey's car is not registered in Washington. (5) Vehicles bearing Diplomatic plates are exempt from police action. (6) If this were done, we should be setting a precedent and opening the door for future difficulties. Take, for example, Bob Hope, who is probably a bigger celebrity . . .

Miss Bailey is performing at Ford's Theatre on November 18 in what is called "Salute to American Music." At one time both the President and Mrs. Nixon were to attend. At the present time they are not going to attend. The reason for not attending is political. The program is sponsored by Andy Williams (a strong Democratic supporter). . . . The public line that is being used is as follows: "The President had to severely disrupt his schedule to attend the funeral services of General De Gaulle and, as such, his schedule obligations now are extremely heavy. . . ."

The President and Miss Bailey spent thirty minutes talking, mostly about drug problems among American young people and the possibility that she might perform in Eastern Europe and the Soviet Union.

Neither brought up the subject of license plates. Nixon had a less pleasant encounter a couple of days later when he was walking through a ceremony awarding Young American Medals for bravery to four teenagers and one of them, named Debra Jean Sweet, greeted him by saying, "Mr. President, I find it hard to believe in your sincerity in giving out these medals until you get us out of Vietnam."

That same day, *Newsweek* appeared with a column by Stewart Alsop, who challenged assertions by Senator Fulbright and others who were saying that Nixon was actually expanding the war. But Alsop's commentary, under the headline "Vietnam: Out Faster," was no comfort to the commander in chief. Reporting on drug use among American troops in Vietnam and telling of soldiers refusing to fight and threatening to kill officers and sergeants who ordered them into combat situations, he wrote: "No one wants to be the last man killed in a war. Any army, moreover, reflects the home front and the home front has lost stomach for the war. . . . The combat forces in Vietnam three or four years ago were highly professional, and very impressive. Now the combat forces are manned by bitter draftees. Almost nine out of ten infantry riflemen are draftees. . . . they get killed at nearly double the rate of non-draftee enlisted men. Is it any wonder that they do as little fighting as possible? . . ."

Mitchell failed on two of his three firing assignments. Only Treasury Secretary Kennedy was willing to go quietly. Romney asked for an appointment with the President. Wanting to keep his job, he told the President what he wanted to hear, that he would stop pushing suburban integration. Nixon's private reaction was predictable. "He talks big, but folds under pressure." In private, Romney told friends: "I don't know what the President believes in. Maybe he doesn't believe in anything." That left Hickel, still hanging on six months after his letter to the President. "Wally," said Mitchell, sitting down in Hickel's office at Interior, "we've been talking this over, and it would be better if you just quietly resigned."

"John," said Hickel, "the only man who could ask me to quit would be the President. John, anytime the President wants my hat, he can have my hat."

On Thanksgiving eve, November 25, the President played an elaborate hat trick. At 4 P.M., George Shultz called Hickel and asked him to come to the White House for a meeting on the Interior Department's budget. When he arrived, Shultz was not there. John Whitaker, the White House liaison with Interior, was in an office with three budget officials. Hickel refused to talk numbers with them, saying he would wait for Shultz. After a few awkward minutes, the phone rang. Whitaker answered, said "Yes," hung up, and said to Hickel, "The President wants to talk to you."

As Hickel left, Whitaker turned to the others and said, "The Secretary won't be back."

Nixon was pacing nervously in the Oval Office. Ehrlichman was there to take notes. He had given the President a five-page typed script of arguments for Hickel's departure. It ended: "To insure Secretary Hickel fully understands . . . All comments should be simple and uncomplicated. . . . It must be assumed that every word will be repeated by Hickel to the press. . . ." A military band was practicing on the South Grounds, so it was done to music.

"I've decided to make a change," the President said.

"I understand," said Hickel. He did not stop there, however, telling Nixon of his boyhood, how his family left Kansas when he was a boy because their area was run by oil companies. He went on—the meeting lasted forty-five minutes—and finally said that he would leave on January 1.

"No, it should be effective immediately," the President said. He told Hickel that he would be succeeded by Congressman Rogers Morton, the chairman of the Republican National Committee. When the Secretary arrived back at his office, microphones had been set up for his public announcement. He talked a bit, then looked at the floor for a long moment and walked out. It was the lead story of the next day's *New York Times,* under a three-column headline, pushing aside the photographs of the President's reception for the leaders of a daring U.S. Army helicopter raid on a North Vietnamese prisoner-of-war camp at a place called Sontay, only twenty-five miles from Hanoi. The raid, personally approved by Nixon, was perfectly executed, but the camp turned out to be empty because the ninety prisoners had been moved a few days before.

On the Saturday of Thanksgiving weekend, Nixon was alone at Camp David, making another list of resolutions, generally positive ones, under the heading "Goals for '71–'72." He began: "1. President as moral leader—conscience of the nation . . . bring nation together . . . End war. Arms control or increase Defense budget . . . New approach on 3d world . . . New tax program . . . Restore Law and order. . . . Restore pride in American faith, hope and charity—upward and onward. . . . Courage, hard work etc. etc. . . . Listen to new visions. . . ."

He also dictated a calm memo that seemed to indicate he knew the White House midterm campaign may have gone too far. Contradicting his tough talk inside the Oval Office during the campaign about Republican liberals—and looking ahead to 1972, when his own name would be at the top of the ballot—now he said of the Republican liberals in the Senate:

We have people like Ed Brooke (Massachusetts) and Cliff Case (New Jersey) and Chuck Percy (Illinois) who are coming up this year, and regardless of what they may do to us, our primary goal is to avoid any action or words which may be harmful to them in terms of their re-election. . . . There is a tendency for us not to recognize that people like Brooke, Case, Schweiker (Pennsylvania), Saxbe (Ohio), Cooper (Kentucky), Percy, even Javits (New York), et al., have their constituencies, but try to be with us when they can, and when they are against us do not try to make a virtue out of being against us. . . . Don't read people out of the Party at this point when we're going to need every one of them with us in 1972.

As ALWAYS, the next campaign began the day after the votes were counted. Both Muskie of Maine and McGovern of South Dakota were setting up campaign organizations for the coming Democratic presidential primaries. And Murray Chotiner was already receiving reports from the first Nixon spy inside the Muskie campaign, a person called "Chapman's friend" in White House memos. Actually there was no "Chapman"; the name came from Republican legend: Thomas E. Dewey used it when he placed long-distance calls because he was afraid operators might listen in if they knew a presidential candidate was on the line. In the Nixon operation, Chapman had many friends. The first message from the first one working for Muskie reported that the Senator had decided to run for president, a fact already known to any newspaper reader in the country.

Ten days later, on December 8, the President was up late in the Lincoln sitting room, writing again: "Candor, Glamour, Courage, Dignity . . . Ambition not to win but to do great things . . . 'Fill the Canvas.' . . . 'Lead up the Hill.' . . . 'Every day is the last, make it count.' . . . 'Is there anything I failed to do today—I will wish I could do when I no longer have the power to do it?' "

And, as always, "warmth." The President had an idea and it was transmitted to Dwight Chapin, the appointments secretary, who then sent around a memo creating a new job and word: "The President has stated that for virtually all meetings which he holds, except naturally those that are private head-to-head sessions, and absolutely for all public sessions, all dinners, etc., there is an assigned 'anecdotalist' in attendance. You should plan on sitting in on the meetings to which you are assigned but obviously should not speak unless called upon. The President has asked that you not take notes but should be very alert to the opportunities for a warm human interest story coming out of the meeting. . . ."

"The anecdotalists"—speechwriters Price, Buchanan, Safire, Lee Huebner, and John Andrews were the stars—were assigned each morning to sit in various nooks and corners wherever the President went. Their mission was listening for "flavor, tone, warmth and color"—Nixon's words—to be passed on to reporters and history.

The memo was part of his night work. During the day the President was focusing on personnel and organization, tightening the circle he wanted around him. He was fascinated by the last of the thirteen reports of the President's Advisory Council on Executive Reorganization, the study group headed by Roy Ash, of Litton Industries. This one proposed breaking up several Cabinet departments and agencies dealing with domestic and economic matters into three super-departments—with fifteen hundred executives compared with the current four thousand—called Department of Human Resources, Department of Community Development, and Department of Productivity, Employment, and Growth. At a two-hour session with Ash's group and a dinner afterward, the President was most impressed by one council member, John Connally, the former governor of Texas, a Democrat who was practicing law in Houston. In the meetings, Connally made the kind of political argument Nixon appreciated. "Win or lose on the proposal," he said, according to the meeting minutes, "you would be on the side of change—while opponents have to argue that the status quo was fine."

"The President's in love again," said anecdotalist Safire. First Nixon told Kissinger he wanted Connally on the Foreign Intelligence Advisory Board. Then, on December 4, at a morning meeting with Connally, the President began to talk about his Cabinet problems—and said maybe he ought to be thinking about Connally himself for Treasury. By the afternoon he had decided that he would ask Billy Graham to call Connally and persuade him to take the job. Then he changed his mind and told Haldeman to call, telling him exactly what to say: The President wants you as not only Treasury Secretary but as counselor, adviser, and friend—someone to talk with, a peer, who would be involved in everything including foreign policy. He would be a member of the National Security Council. Also, he told Haldeman to assure Connally that he did not have to switch parties, and that the President considered him the only Democrat capable of being the next president. In fact, the President's regular musings on a new party or a new coalition had quite suddenly begun focusing on the possibility of a Nixon-Connally ticket in 1972—a combination geared to Republicans and conservative Democrats, giving shape and voice to the new American majority he was sure existed. The idea, Nixon told Ehrlichman, would be to call a convention of conservative and moderate elected officials of both parties and try to win control of Congress and, perhaps, a few state legislatures.

Both the idea and Connally, too, were more attractive to the President because he had lost all faith in Agnew. Nixon paced and plotted in the Oval Office, telling Ehrlichman: "I've got to get rid of this guy. . . . He's terrible. He wants to come in here all the time and bother me."

Connally was interested. He told Haldeman he would have to make some financial adjustments, sell property because he was paying eighty thousand to ninety thousand dollars a year in interest on loans, and you can't do that on a government salary. He also suggested that the President find a job first for George Bush—Connally had appeared in anti-Bush television commercials for Bentsen—because Nixon could not hire a Texas Democrat before he took care of his local Republican. The President made the formal offer to Connally at breakfast three days later. Not mentioning Bush this time, Connally said, "The earlier the better, so the press has less time to cut me up."

Bush could take care of himself. The President decided to make him chairman of the Republican National Committee. When Bush was called in by Haldeman on December 9, he said he had hoped for the United Nations. So the two of them went into the Oval Office and Bush made his pitch. According to Haldeman's notes: "He explained that the reason for his interest in the U.N. was his feeling that for too long the President had not been represented there by anyone who was a strong advocate . . . there was a dearth of Nixon advocacy in New York City and the general New York area—that he could fill that need in New York social circles. . . ." Bush got the job.

The conversations about Bush's future and other personnel moves were going on when Colson came in with photographs obtained by a private detective he had hired to follow Senator Edward Kennedy, who was in Paris at the time of the de Gaulle funeral. The pictures showed the Senator dancing and carrying on with someone who was purported to be an Italian princess of some sort. The President decided that copies of the photos should be sent to Senator Muskie and other Democrats who might be running for president in 1972, so they could use them against Kennedy if he ran.

The job of Republican National Committee chairman finally went to the only man who wanted it, Senator Robert Dole, a freshman from Kansas who was Nixon's most consistent defender on the Senate floor.

That settled, the President called in Haldeman and said he had figured out a way to screw NBC for its lousy campaign coverage. He liked correspondent Nancy Dickerson and told Haldeman to offer CBS an exclusive presidential interview on one condition, that it be done by Dickerson. Haldeman did not have the guts to tell Nixon that Dickerson did not work for CBS. She had worked for NBC and then moved over to PBS, the Public Broadcasting System. Then Kissinger came to Haldeman's office to say, once more, that he might have to quit. This time it was because he had just found out he was not invited to a meeting between the President and Israel's defense minister, Moshe Dayan—and Rogers was going to be there.

A few minutes before six o'clock that evening, Kissinger went back to his own office to meet with Agha Hilaly, the Pakistani ambassador to the United States, who had telephoned the day before and said he had a message from his president, Yahya Khan. The White House had heard nothing from Yahya Khan since Nixon had approached him about China back in October. The President and Kissinger assumed that nothing had happened, and that he had been preoccupied with cyclones and tidal waves that had ripped through East Pakistan—killing hundreds of thousands of people living in the Ganges Delta—and by provincial elections there that had been won by a separatist party, the Awami League. Hilaly unfolded a handwritten letter from Yahya Khan—his president's notes of a conversation with Premier Chou En-lai of China on November 15. He read slowly, saying finally, "A special envoy of President Nixon's will be most welcome in Peking."

After more than twenty years of silence and hostility, leaders of the most powerful country in the world and the most populous were going to speak to each other again. Chou had specified that the meeting should be about "the vacation of the Chinese territories called Taiwan." But he went on to say that Chairman Mao Tse-tung, Defense Minister Lin Piao, and himself—the three most powerful men in the People's Republic of China—had all approved the idea of a meeting. They had received and understood some of the messages sent out from Washington— through Pakistan, through Romania, through Poland—and now: "This is the first time that the proposal has come from a Head, through a Head, to a Head." Mao through Yahya Khan to Nixon. The English was stilted but the words were clear: this was the breakthrough Nixon had envisioned for more than two years, when he sat alone for hour after hour thinking about the triangular lines of power between the United States, the Soviet Union, and the People's Republic, when he had brainstormed for hours and days with Kissinger about how to approach the Chinese. It was never far from mind. In the middle of a September interview with Hugh Sidey about the Middle East wars, Nixon had suddenly said: "If there is anything I want to do before I die, it is to go to China. If I don't, I want my children to."

Kissinger walked down the hall to the Oval Office. The President and he talked for an hour, most importantly agreeing that the reference to Taiwan was no more than a starting point. In fact, Yahya Khan had added his own note at the bottom, saying that he was certain the reference to Taiwan was for domestic consumption and that Chou fully expected to discuss a range of issues involving the two great countries. Nixon and Kissinger began crafting an answer that night to Chou's initiative. The key phrase of the answer was, "the broad range of issues which lie between the People's Republic of China and the United States, including the issue of Taiwan."

It was a moment of triumph for Nixon. This was what he had been thinking about on his twelfth day as president, February 1, 1969, when he had written a memo to his national security adviser, saying: "I think we should give every encouragement to the attitude that this administration 'is exploring possibilities of rapprochement with the Chinese.' " And Kissinger had imitated his boss before his own new staff, saying: "Our leader has taken leave of reality. He thinks this is the moment to establish normal relations with Communist China. He has just ordered me to make this flight of fancy come true. . . . China!"

But watching him now, Kissinger saw no joy. Nixon was a man who had learned to contain or control his own hopes. Deep inside, Kissinger thought, Nixon always expected to lose, always expected his rewards to be snatched away, always believed his enemies would prevail. He was conditioned for rejection or failure, confused by success. As Nixon and Kissinger talked about the note, which Chou had dictated to Yahya Khan, fewer than a dozen people in the world knew of its existence. Nineteen days earlier, on November 20, the United States had, as usual, used parliamentary procedure to once again deny the People's Republic a seat in the United Nations General Assembly—even as, for the first time, the Assembly members voted for admission by 51 to 49, with 25 abstentions. The United States was able to block that by winning a majority vote for a resolution declaring that a two-thirds vote was necessary for the admission.

IN A PRESS CONFERENCE the next day, the President's first since July, there was a China question that the President answered in a way that eluded his questioners.

Q.—"Mr. President, since the United Nations vote on China, have you found it expedient for the United States to review our policy toward mainland China?"

A.—"No, our policy wouldn't be based on expediency. It would be based on principle. We have no plans to change our policy with regard to the admission of Red China to the United Nations at this time. However, we are going to continue the initiative that I have begun, an initiative of relaxing trade restrictions and travel restrictions and attempting to open channels of communication with Communist China, having in mind the fact that looking long toward the future we must have some communication and eventually relations with Communist China."

There was no disguising the genuine hostility between the President and the press in the days before the December 10 conference, only his twelfth on television and eighteenth overall in two years—in contrast to between twenty-two and twenty-seven a year during the Kennedy and Johnson presidencies. Twenty-five reporters, organized by Stuart Loory and Jules Witcover of the *Los Angeles Times,* had met two days before to try to develop a plan to pressure Nixon to hold more conferences. Then on the morning of the tenth, *The New York Times* ran a long "News Analysis" by Max Frankel, listing thirty questions on subjects ranging from how long Americans would be fighting in Vietnam to whether Nixon had secret commitments for an increased money supply from the supposedly independent Federal Reserve Board.

A first-time visitor to the news conference, author Allen Drury, was sitting among White House correspondents when Ziegler called, "Ladies and gentlemen, the President of the United States!" Drury heard a reporter mutter, "Unfortunately."

A number of questions were phrased negatively, among them: "Do you think it's fair to say your economic policies haven't worked?" and "Would you comment on speculation that you might be a one-term President?"

Robert B. Semple Jr., White House correspondent of *The New York Times,* asked: "There seems to be a feeling in some quarters, not just among blacks and students . . . that you have yet to convey a sufficiently sharp and clear sense of directions, vision and leadership on many matters to end the divisions in this country as you said you hoped to do two years ago. . . . Do you recognize this as a problem for yourself and, if so, what can you do about it and what will you do about it?"

A question that appeared on the Frankel list got an interesting answer without follow-up. Asked whether he considered Soviet submarine activity in the Caribbean to be a threat to national security, the President gave his shortest answer of the tense night: "No, I do not."

Afterward, Ziegler told the President that a number of reporters had told him that they disapproved of the Loory meeting and of the kind of questions asked that night. Nixon passed that along in a memo to

Haldeman and then wrote: "This, of course, is simply the prostitute attitude of the press. They want to play both sides and Ziegler should never forget that and should not be fooled by this sort of sickening apologetic attitude to him at a later time. This is what any pimp will do when he knows he has to play another line. . . . Everyone knows that after the conference they were shaking their heads and saying, 'This is a lousy conference, we didn't embarrass the Son-of-a-Bitch. . . .' "

The President sat alone that night and the next dictating long, intricate letters to editors about the conference, telling Haldeman to find people to sign and send them. The first was to John Osborne of *The New Republic*. Suggesting that it be signed by a graduate student from Yale or Georgetown, Nixon dictated the text: "Your scathing attacks on President Nixon have delighted me beyond belief. . . . I don't know when I looked forward more to a television program than the press conference. . . . I thought this was really the time the press would get to this S.O.B. . . . It was a shocking disappointment. Can't you do something to get smarter people in the press corps? . . . He chopped his questioners to bits." "Copy it to Max Frankel," Nixon added. One to James Doyle of the *Washington Star* said: "I write this letter, not in any sense of anger but simply one of sorrow . . . that you and your colleagues had utterly struck out when you tried to take the President on in his press conference."

John Connally's appointment as Secretary of the Treasury was announced on December 14, a perfect surprise. "A bold stroke," in one of Nixon's favorite phrases. It was a wonderful morning for the President, who coveted surprise, seeing it as a key to maintaining power over people. "Absolutely stunned," was the self-description of Arthur Burns. Nixon did not bother to explain, telling Burns later: "Only three men in America understand the use of power. I do. John Connally does. I guess Nelson Rockefeller does."

Acting Secretary Connally showed his style the next day at his first Cabinet meeting. The subject was revenue-sharing. Nixon said: "Let's not kid ourselves into thinking it's a bold new program. Or that it will pass. . . . And it doesn't trim down the bureaucracy—it just shuffles them around a bit." Connally interrupted: "The Great Society gave hope for change, but hell, if you'll pardon my saying so, Mr. President, the average person doesn't even know revenue sharing was ever proposed. And what difference does it make if no one knows it? I say let's run the risk. If you lose, you lose big—but what's the sense in losing small?"

Watching from a chair along the side of the Cabinet Room, Safire, the speechwriter working on the State of the Union address, saw how much Nixon loved that kind of talk. He was sure that the President was now going to accept a phrase Safire had coined—"the New American Revolution"—to describe stringing together the same old programs and calling it revolution. He knew his man. In his yellow-pad musings at Camp David that month, the President wrote: "Our major failure is an obsession with programs—competent gray men. We lack color, only Mitchell and Connally are big-league in public mind. . . . Richardson and Shultz, able . . . Moynihan—a blizzard of programs but no focus."

Revolutions were colorful. As he had been by Moynihan's blizzards of ideas, Nixon was charged up a bit about domestic issues and he wanted to transcend the gray men. Later that day he met with one of the grayest, Burns. For the first twenty minutes or so, the economist filled the air with statistics, most of them designed to show that the Fed was allowing the money supply to grow at some of the fastest rates in history, close to 6 percent, by his estimate. Only in four years, he said—1951, 1965, 1967, and 1968—had the money supply been increased by more than 5 percent. He said the country's economic stagnation was not a money problem, but a confidence problem, Americans were not sure there really was a recovery coming soon and they were afraid of inflation. "Risk," he said, "is on the side of inflation and monetary policy must be responsible."

Then the President made a single point: he wanted the economy growing in the summer of 1972, his reelection year. Ehrlichman, the note-taker, wrote: "The President then told Dr. Burns that at all costs we must err on the side of a too-liberal monetary policy rather than too conservative with relation to domestic matters. The President is willing to risk inflation."

Nixon repeated the idea: "Err toward inflation." Then he walked out.

The President was talking like a Democrat, a Democrat who wanted to be reelected. His big-picture economic adviser was now a Democrat, Connally, while his numbers man was George Shultz, the head of OMB, who was smart enough to know policy was usually in the details and who chose to pay more attention to actual statistics and performance than to ideology. The former dean of the temple of modern conservative economics, the University of Chicago's Department of Economics, privately was talking more like Walter Heller, President Kennedy's chief economic adviser, than like his friend and former colleague, Milton Friedman, an advocate of tight money. Shultz was advocating a "full-employment" budget—the old liberal scheme, heresy to most Republicans, for justifying budget deficits by saying they would not exist if unemployment was at a rate of 4 percent or less. Since unemployment was actually above 6 percent, that theory, in effect, gave the President as much as $20 billion in deficit spending to spread around in the run-up to 1972.

The President liked it. "Psychological recession" was the phrase he used in private to explain the stagflation phenomenon of both slow growth and inflation. If that deficit spending would entice more private spending, by both corporations and consumers, then the Republican president was now ready to buy into the pump-priming theories of John Maynard Keynes, the British economist, patron saint of liberal economists and big-spending politicians. But that did not change the fact that most of the men around him were still conservatives who had always seen inflation as the true devil. There was also another devil, another heresy on the table inside the White House: wage and price controls. On that subject, Milton Friedman had come to the Oval Office to try to straighten up the President's ideological spine during a meeting after the congressional election, and had said, "The Democrats are saying, 'We tried guidelines and they failed; why shouldn't Republicans try guidelines and fail too?' "

It was not only Democrats anymore. Burns, who had been against controls his entire career, was now publicly calling for a federal wage and price review board, just a step short of mandatory controls, because he was so afraid that increasing money supply, along with the President's re-election anxiety, would produce higher and higher inflation—and he preferred anything, controls included, to more inflation. Shultz was against mandatory controls, as Nixon was, but did favor trying to hold down wages and prices by "jawboning" and eliminating government supports that were essentially inflationary—such things as import quotas and, especially, the forty-year-old Davis-Bacon law, the New Deal legislation that required union wages to be paid on all federal and federally assisted construction projects. That meant almost one-third of all the construction in the country. It also meant that construction wages were escalating by 18 percent a year. The President's hard-hat silent majority had every reason to wave flags.

Donald Rumsfeld was the leading White House champion of jawboning—that is, trying to use presidential rhetoric to persuade or shame corporations and unions into holding down prices and wages in the national interest. Rumsfeld, like Connally, knew what it was like to run for office, and he was a master of political argument as the key to opening the President's mind. On December 2, he told Nixon in a memo: "If the economy turns around and we deal with unemployment and inflation effectively in the next two years, jawboning would help RN get credit. If the economy fails to turn around ; . . . jawboning can help to prevent him from taking full blame."

Kissinger was saying similar things to the President about a different subject: Vietnam. The President had begun to talk privately about ending the war in the spring of 1971. In a long diary entry on December 15, Haldeman wrote: "Henry was in for a while, and P discussed a possible trip for next year. He's thinking about going to Vietnam in April, or whenever we decide to make the basic end of the war announcement. His idea would be to tour around the country, build up Thieu and so forth, and then make the announcement right afterwards. Henry argues against a commitment that early to withdraw all combat troops because he feels that if we pull them out by the end of '71, trouble can start mounting in '72. . . . He favors instead a continued winding down and then a pullout right at the fall of '72, so that if any bad results follow they will be too late to affect the election. . . ."

"He's a devious bastard," the President said after Kissinger left, not without a touch of affection. He told Haldeman he was worried about Kissinger's energetic building of back channels, thinking that no one knew about them but him. "There's going to be trouble one of these days with Rogers or someone else. . . . Tony Lake knows all about this," Nixon said, referring to one of the National Security Council aides who had left because of the Cambodia invasion. "And now he works for Muskie."

December 21 was a big day in the world. In Poland, a new secretary of the United Workers Party, Edward Gierek, took over after an increase in food prices led to six days of rioting, beginning with dockworkers in the northern port city of Gdansk. But inside the White House the news was Elvis. A limousine pulled up the gate and a driver delivered a handwritten note to the guards there. It ended up on the desk of Bud Krogh, who was now charged with coordinating the administration's narcotics policy. He read:

> Dear Mr. President,
> . . . I am Elvis Presley and I admire you and have great respect for your office. The drug culture, the hippie elements, the SDS, Black Panthers, etc. do not consider me as their enemy or as they call it the establishment. I call it America and I love it. Sir, I can and will be of any service that I can to help the country out. . . . I wish not to be given a title or an appointed position. I can and will do more good if I were made a Federal Agent at Large and I will help out by doing it my way through communication with people of all ages. . . . Sir, I am staying at the Washington

Hotel. . . . I am registered under the name of Jon Burrows. I have done an in-depth study of drug abuse and Communist brain-washing techniques and I am right in the middle of the whole thing. . . .

Presley had added a P.S., saying that he had a gift for the President. It turned out to be a chrome-plated Colt .45 automatic with a clip of silver bullets, and the Secret Service took it from him as he walked though the halls wearing sunglasses, tight dark velvet pants, and a cape to match, his white silk shirt open halfway down his chest, against which bounced a gold medallion. Secretaries were peeping out of every doorway. "The King" walked into the Oval Office with Krogh, then stopped, uncertain for a moment. The President stood up and came around his desk with his hand out, saying, "It's very good to meet you, Mr. Presley. I appreciate your offer to help us with the drug problem."

"Mr. President, thank you for seeing me," Presley said. "I'd like to show you some pictures of my family and some of my badges. . . . I have a collection of badges from police departments around the country." He laid out the badges on the desk, explaining how he got each one. Nixon was nodding, saying nice things about police. Then Presley said: "The Beatles, I think, are kind of anti-American. They came over here. Made a lot of money. And then went back to England. And they said some anti-American stuff when they got back."

"You know," the President said, "those who use drugs are the protesters. You know the ones who get caught up in dissent and violence."

Presley talked a bit about brainwashing and drugs, then said: "I can go right into a group of hippies and young people and be accepted. . . . Mr. President, can you get me a badge from the Narcotics Bureau?"

"Bud, can we get him a badge? . . . See that he gets one."

Presley reached his left arm around the President and hugged him. Nixon walked behind the desk to take out tie clips as a gift. Presley followed him and they rummaged through the drawer together.

As Nixon and Presley chatted about American youth, the United States Supreme Court changed what the young were permitted to do. In a 5-to-4 decision, the Court ruled that Congress had no power to reduce the voting age in state and local elections, but did have jurisdiction over federal elections. Beginning in 1972, eighteen-, nineteen-, and twenty-year-olds would be eligible to vote for a president and for members of Congress.

The administration's official summary of President Nixon's first two years had been issued the day before, on December 20. The document was deliberately understated—the White House was trying to back away from the overheated rhetoric of the 1970 campaign—and the title was, too: "Balance, Direction, and Forward Thrust." It began with a report on Vietnam: "When Richard Nixon took office . . . there were 542,500 American troops in Vietnam with no plans for bringing them home. Casualties in 1968 had averaged 280 a week and were going higher. . . . There were 340,000 by year's end. . . . There were only 26 casualties per week. . . ."

The inside report was given at an end-of-year Cabinet meeting on December 21. Secretary of State Rogers and OMB director Shultz spoke of foreign and domestic achievements and problems, and then, as the year before, the program was turned over to "the clean-up hitter," Pat Moynihan, who was finally leaving the White House to go back to Harvard:

> Just two years ago, it seemed the worst of times. It was the habit then to speak of the nation as divided and to assert that the situation was grave beyond anything since the Civil War itself. This was misleading—the country was not so much divided as fragmented. It was coming apart. . . .
>
> The agony of war was compounded by and interacted with the great travail of race, which once again not so much divided as fractured the society. Racial bondage and oppression had been the one huge wrong of American history. . . . Government was not believed, nor was much to be expected of it. Government had begun to do utterly unacceptable things, such as sending spies to the party conventions in 1968.
>
> Since that time, mass urban violence has all but disappeared. Civil disobedience and protest have receded. Racial rhetoric has calmed. That great symbol of racial subjugation, the dual school system of the South, virtually intact two years ago, has quietly and finally been dismantled. All in all, a record of some good fortune and much genuine achievement.
>
> Be of good cheer and good conscience. Depressing, even frightening things, are being said about the Administration. They are not true. This has been a company of honorable and able men, led by a President of singular courage and compassion in the face of sometimes awful knowledge of the problems and the probabilities that confront him.

It was also time to release information on the President's annual physical examination and Nixon wanted to handle the programming of that himself, writing to Ron Ziegler: "Let Dr. Tkach give them the results. . . . He should then say that his major concern about the President's health is that he does not get enough recreation, does not have the relaxations of others in the office. He does not play bridge, he has played golf only four times in the last year, he bowled five times. . . . He should say that the President's daily work schedule is the most back-breaking that he has ever observed in a public figure. He should point out, nevertheless, that the President remains in excellent health due to very spartan habits. . . . I think Tkach could do it with complete credibility. . . ."

Finally, in the last days of 1970, the press took a skeptical look at the thirty-seventh president. The news summary team sent the President their report of the CBS News broadcast. Walter Cronkite began by asking correspondents what they considered the most important event of the American year. Nixon read the answers:

> Dan Rather named the Calley trial.* It symbolized much of what made up America this year: mixed emotions, confusion and complexities over where we're going, who we are, what is our leadership.
>
> Young John Lawrence named Kent State—Middle America was shown that the penalty for protest can be death.
>
> Dan Schorr felt that the key event was the first decline in the real production of goods and services in twelve years.
>
> Roger Mudd called the Carswell nomination a "watershed for the Administration" in that it took away any statesmanlike posture of RN with Congress.
>
> Eric Sevareid noted the national mood of belt-tightening and consolidation; a desire not to spend so much abroad.
>
> Cronkite said the key event was the 1970 election—not for what happened, but for what didn't happen. The country didn't go "right."

At the end of the hour, Eric Sevareid offered a summation:

> The war is winding down; peace is holding in the Mideast; inflation shows signs of slowing; political extremism is waning. There's lots of bad news but we forget sometimes what people are doing—they're raising children, traveling, holding down jobs. They assume a future. Only the intellectuals have the time to consider the apocalypse. In perspective, how can this complex society unsurvive? It's easier to survive.

* The court-martial of the leader of the troops accused of massacring South Vietnamese civilians had begun on November 12.

The President hosted a small New Year's Eve party for, of all people, the few reporters still hanging around the press room at six o'clock. There were only six: Frank Cormier of the Associated Press, Helen Thomas of United Press International, Herb Kaplow of NBC, two photographers, and a radio technician. Nixon mixed martinis at the small bar in his EOB hideaway and Helen Thomas joked, "Now I know why you spend so much time in here." The President took questions for more than a half hour.

Haldeman reported: "Ziegler was particularly amused by P's statement that I, and the other key members of the staff, had the highest IQs of any White House staff people at least since Roosevelt, and that as a group, E, Shultz, Weinberger and I were the most brilliant. Ron, for some reason, thought that was very funny."

CHAPTER 18

March 29, 1971

Presidential Nixon loved football and watched a lot of it on television, usually with the sound off so that he could do paperwork and make telephone calls at the same time. On New Year's Day, like millions of his fellow Americans, he would begin watching the college bowl games after lunch and continue through to the end of the Rose Bowl at nine o'clock or so Eastern time. On the first day of 1971, the President was at Camp David with his family and Haldeman and Ehrlichman and their families. It was a crystal-and-white day; more than a foot of snow had fallen during the day and night before. But the President was unhappy. He called Billy Graham and Bob Hope to announce that for the first time he was rooting against the West Coast team in the big game from Pasadena. He told them that he was for Ohio State over Stanford because he had seen a story in *The Washington Post* saying that the Stanford quarterback, Jim Plunkett, had posed for photographs with topless dancers in San Francisco.

Two days later, he spotted an item in his news summary that said: "Don Larrabee writes in the *Greenville News* in S.C. that RN may have set some kind of Presidential record during the holiday season for numbers of hours spent in front of the TV watching football. RN's interest in sports puts him on comfortable common ground with most males. . . . White House aides have been astounded by RN's statistical knowledge of sports. . . ."

RN himself did not take that as a compliment, sending a rocket to

Colson: "Get out fast I missed both games on Jan 2. I never allow T.V. to interfere with state business. . . . Submit a report on action taken by tomorrow 8 A.M. . . ."

On January 4 he came down from Camp David for an interview with correspondents from the three networks and public television. He talked of progress in ending the war and of his hopes for a summit meeting in Moscow sometime during the year, but he concentrated on problems and programs like a good gray man until he was asked what had happened to his goal of a "driving dream," a constant of the 1968 campaign. His answer was both defensive and sweeping, but not gray:

> We have to get rid of some of the nightmares we inherited. . . . If we can get this country thinking not of how to fight a war, but how to win a peace—if we can get this country thinking of clean air, clean water, open spaces, of a welfare reform program that will provide a floor under the income of every family with children in America—a new approach to government, reform of education, reform of health . . . then we will have the lift of a driving dream.

The White House's official "Year-End Review" for 1970 pointed in those directions: "The President reordered spending priorities. The budget for Fiscal Year 1971 was the first in two decades in which human resource spending was greater than defense spending. In FY 1968 the ratio was 32–48, now it is 41–37." All that sounded suspiciously like the lift of a liberal dream, at least to Pat Buchanan, the house conservative, a young man whose beliefs were true enough to give him the freedom to criticize "the Old Man"—and he did in seven single-spaced pages.

> Neither liberal nor conservative, neither fish nor fowl, the Nixon administration . . . is a hybrid, whose zigging and zagging has succeeded in winning the enthusiasm and loyalty of neither the left nor the right, but the suspicion and distrust of both. . . . Rather than draw up our own yardstick of success and failure, we have willingly invited judgment by the old measures of the old order. Thus, we proudly point out that we are spending more on "human resources" than for "defense resources." . . . We publicize statistics on how much "integration" has taken place. . . . The open embrace of an "expansionary deficit" . . . The President is no longer a credible custodian of the conservative political tradition of the GOP. . . . Truly, the liberals went swimming and President Nixon stole their clothes—but in the process we left our

old conservative suit lying by the swimming hole for someone else to pick up.

Near the end, Buchanan added angrily: "Conservatives are the niggers of the Nixon administration." The political right, Buchanan thought, was getting nothing but rhetoric. Nixon scrawled a short answer on the last page of Buchanan's screed: "You overlook RN's consistent hard line on foreign policy."

Buchanan was right and obviously Nixon knew it. But the President was confident that he already had the political loyalty of the old Republican right; he was trying to win over old-fashioned conservative and centrist Democrats and drive the Democratic Party itself farther left. He also had a secret: he did not much care whether or not this new agenda passed. The idea was to make it look and sound good enough to keep Congress and the press busy so that he could concentrate on his own driving dreams: the realignment of American politics and of world power structures. Stewart Alsop captured part of that in a *Newsweek* column with a clever headline, "Nixon to the Left of Himself." President Nixon, Alsop argued, was going to run into trouble in one way or another because he was more liberal than Mister Nixon. "President Liberal," as Alsop called Nixon in the column, was proposing a guaranteed wage for the poor and a $12 billion universal medical insurance plan, and had "Ordered a withdrawal of American troops from Vietnam. . . . Announced a new 'doctrine' designed to reduce U.S. global commitments— except in the Middle East. . . . Adopted an economic policy of pure Keynesianism. . . ."

The Keynes reference was the talk of Washington. The big news of the television interview was something the President had said off the air. Howard K. Smith of ABC News remarked that he was surprised to hear a Republican president saying that an unbalanced federal budget was acceptable in slow times. Nixon smiled and said: "I am now a Keynesian in economics."

Smith was surprised enough to say: "That's a little like a Christian crusader saying, 'All things considered, I think Mohammed was right.' "

The President flew to San Clemente the next day and there celebrated his fifty-eighth birthday on January 9. Ziegler, who was being pressed by photographers, persuaded Nixon to take a birthday stroll along the beach—and he did. Newspapers around the world showed the President, in a blue windbreaker decorated with the presidential seal, dipping his toe into the Pacific. He was wearing black wing-tipped shoes.

He did have a triumph of some economic importance out there, though, jawboning Bethlehem Steel when the company announced, on

January 11, a price rise of 12 percent on many of its products. On January 18, after a week of White House and administration attacks, Bethlehem announced it would hold the rise to 6.8 percent. The President returned to Washington for his State of the Union address, scheduled for January 22. The draft of the speech, which covered only domestic issues, was completed, leaving Nixon in a pretty good mood. That was good for Richard Moore, a speechwriter who was the assigned anecdotalist that day for the President's "Open Door Hour," a series of brief scheduled encounters that was a Friday ritual when Nixon was in residence. There were a few laughs this time. Moore began:

> All but one of the visits involved persons who work for the President at a low or middle level. When anyone claims that the President is unconcerned and impersonal toward people around him . . . this is a pretty telling response.
>
> 1. Seven nervous staff members working on the budget came in for photographs. The President took over, lined them up, saw they all looked grim and cracked: "Look as if you just found something to cut in the budget." Laughter all around.
>
> 2. Two young staffers about to be married, Debbie Murray and Hugh Sloan, came in and Nixon asked if she planned to continue working. When she said "yes," he said: "Married women can work here. I've read all about women's lib. I know all about these things."
>
> 3. Dr. William Pecora, chief of the U.S. Geological Survey, presented the first copy of the new National Atlas to the President. "How much does it cost?" Nixon asked. "One hundred dollars," Pecora answered. Nixon said, "Take it back."
>
> 4. Larry Higby, Haldeman's go-fer, was invited in because the President had heard that his wife just gave birth to their first child. When Higby looked nervously at the floor during the picture-taking, the President said, "C'mon. Look at the camera. You have to learn to do this."

In the State of the Union address, the President said that he intended to try to eliminate one-third of federal grant programs, including more than one hundred Great Society programs, but that they would be replaced by revenue sharing. More than $16 billion in federal income and sales tax revenues would be returned to the states and the cities with few strings attached. Then he outlined a wide range of essentially liberal programs, fashioned by Ehrlichman's pragmatic Domestic Council. "What this Congress can be remembered for," he declared, "is opening the way for a New American Revolution—a peaceful revolution in which power was turned back to the people. . . ." Nixon proposed "six great goals for the American nation and the American people: welfare reform; full prosperity in peacetime; restoring and enhancing the natural environment; improving health care and making it available more fairly to more people; strengthening and renewing state and local government; and a complete reform of the Federal government"—the last a reference to the Ash reorganization plan. It was more rhetoric than revolution; some of it, like welfare reform, had already been rejected.

Nixon had indeed stolen some of the Democrats' clothes, particularly on health care and the environment. But it was mostly talk. "Just a holding action," he told Haldeman after the speech. The President, the Congress, and the economy, too, seemed in stalemate. Nothing was moving. The war and the debate over it, waxing and waning, was still taking most of the country's political energy. Now Nixon had a domestic program on paper for the run-up to the 1972 campaign—and he was not greatly concerned with whether it became law or not. If the revolution actually happened he could take credit; if the revolution failed, he could blame the Democrats. The President's approval rating in Gallup and Harris polls was at about 50 percent. He was running statistically even with the Democratic presidential front-runner, Senator Muskie, in the first matching-up polls for the 1972 election. In a January poll of the most admired Americans, Nixon scored only 9 percent, trailing three fallen leaders: John F. Kennedy at 34 percent, Martin Luther King Jr. at 19 percent, and Robert F. Kennedy at 15 percent.

THE PLANNING for the campaign was already well under way, with most of the focus on the press and raising money. A substantial amount of the action was moving into the offices of Chuck Colson, whose staff had increased to twenty-three people. Beginning on January 25, one of those new assistants, George Bell, began to work on implementing an old Nixon idea: organizing the staff to prepare lists of friends and enemies. The first three came in within three days. One was from Mort Allin, the editor of the news summary, who did his in two categories: "The first includes those who have on occasion written good material but who, in my view, can't be trusted and who would prefer not to see Richard Nixon in the White House in 1973. The second is made up of the definitely hostile type." The not-to-be-trusted category was led by Hugh Sidey and John Osborne, and included columnists Jack Anderson, Rowland Evans and

Robert Novak, Joe Kraft, David Broder of *The Washington Post,* and CBS's Dan Rather, Eric Sevareid, and Harry Reasoner. Allin's hostiles category, eighteen names, included Marquis Childs, Garry Wills, Max Lerner of the *New York Post,* Mary McGrory of the *Washington Star,* and Peter Lisagor of the Chicago *Daily News.* The second list, much longer, came from Tom Huston, and it included most any man or woman who had ever said a discouraging word about Nixon—from actors Gregory Peck and Carol Channing to the usual list of politicians, from Teddy Kennedy to John Lindsay. The third one, from Colson's office, listed "enemy" organizations, including the Brookings Institution, the Ford Foundation, Common Cause, the National Association for the Advancement of Colored People, and the AFL-CIO.

The lists were so numerous that Alexander Butterfield sent a memo to Haldeman that said: "I received a copy of the very sensitive Eyes Only 'Opponents List' put together by Messrs. Colson and Bell. I do not see in the media section of that list the names of Kandy Stroud of *Women's Wear Daily,* Judith Martin or Maxine Cheshire of *The Washington Post,* who, according to my understanding, are on the current 'Freeze List.' At the same time, I do note the names of others on the 'Freeze List'—namely, Senators Nelson, Kennedy, and Muskie, Congressman Robert Kastenmeier and Sandy Vanocur of PBS. Am I wrong to assume that the 'Freeze List' is something over and above the 'Opponent List'? . . . If you will straighten me out on this matter, I will pass the word to Colson, Bell, Rose Mary Woods . . . and others who have a need to know."

While the lists were being circulated at lower levels, the President was back on the mountain, preparing a radio address to discuss his State of the World report. On a Sunday morning, he called speechwriter Bill Safire to Camp David to work on the address. They chatted for a while in the little office in Aspen Lodge and the President offered a couple of thoughts on Vietnam that were not going to be part of any speech:

> To get out in a way that would vitiate the purpose of an effort that cost 45,000 lives would be a great tragedy; it would gnaw at the conscience of the nation for years to come. I'd like to do something in terms of looking back one day and saying, "That was a fine hour for America." Of course, you can't say that now, people would go up the wall. But we can't cast this speech as "We're doing our best to slink out." . . . Here's a line: our purpose was not to conquer North Vietnam, our purpose was to give both South and North Vietnam a right to live in peace without being dominated by the other. . . .

Now, on the Mideast. Let's brag a little. I know how Henry feels about this. He doesn't think it is going to work, he thinks we're selling out the Israelis, and let's face it, he's a little jealous that it's a State Department project. . . . I just don't like the stuff about partnership. I know it's Henry's idea, but it's just not true. We're not in partnership with these other countries. . . . God, I hate spending time with intellectuals. There's something feminine about them. I'd rather talk to an athlete.

When they finished working on the speech, Nixon asked Safire what he thought of it. "Thoughtful," he said. "But there's no news lead, so it won't set the world on fire."

The President replied: "The whole object of our foreign policy is *not* to set the world on fire."

THAT SAID, Nixon was spending most of his time on another strike plan in Southeast Asia. The Cambodia incursion had succeeded in cutting the supply line from the port of Sihanoukville to communist units in the Mekong Delta south of Saigon, and now the President was showing new interest in an old plan, a thrust into Laos to cut the enemy's main land supply route, the Ho Chi Minh Trail, at a point twenty miles to the west of, and just below, the border between North and South Vietnam. On January 18, during a three-hour session designed primarily to brief Secretary of State Rogers on another decision already made in secret—the meeting was called to avoid the public differences that surfaced during the Cambodian adventure—the President had specified that all the troops used must be South Vietnamese. Ten thousand Americans would be involved, providing artillery support from inside South Vietnam and air support for twenty thousand of the Army of Vietnam's best troops.

Actually, the President may have had no choice but to hold Americans back. The Cooper-Church amendment and other congressional measures passed on the last day of the Cambodian operation prohibited funding for the use of any American ground forces in Cambodia and Laos. The plan as outlined that day to Rogers was similar to one proposed four years earlier by General William Westmoreland, then the commander in Vietnam. But he had recommended using four American divisions, sixty thousand men, to cut the dirt trail, which was not a single road but many, weaving together over four hundred miles on roads and trails of hard-packed dirt in the dry season, covered by bamboo canopies, cutting through valleys and around mountains in a cratered jungle landscape that had been bombed day after day for years. Listening to Rogers's fading objections over the three hours, Nixon realized that Rogers did not understand that the real purpose of the exercise was to prevent the North Vietnamese from using the dry season to transport enough equipment south to sustain an offensive during the 1972 presidential campaign.

After the meeting, Nixon told Haldeman that although Kissinger was driving him crazy with his constant whining about Rogers, if it came to a choice he would get rid of Rogers. Haldeman asked why. "Vanity" was the word the President used to describe Rogers. "Loyalty" was one of the words he used to describe Kissinger. Nixon said Kissinger would fall on a sword for him, but Rogers would not. "I agree," Haldeman said. "But he would do it with loud kicking and screaming and make sure the blood spurted all over the place so he would get full credit."

On January 26, the President called in Kissinger, Haig, and the chairman of the Joint Chiefs of Staff, Admiral Moorer, for the real planning, going over the details of the four phases of the plan, code-named, in Vietnamese, Lam Son 719.

In phase one, the United States Fifth Mechanized Brigade would clear and repair the highway from Khe Sanh in South Vietnam to the Laotian border. At the same time, U.S. artillery units would establish fire bases along the border and other American units would take blocking positions along the demilitarized zone (DMZ). In phase two, forty-eight hours later, ten thousand ARVN troops would cross the border heading for the provincial town of Tchepone, population two thousand, an important way station for most branches of the Ho Chi Minh Trail. ARVN's First Airborne Division would be airlifted in by American helicopters to take the Tchepone airport. In phase three, the ARVN forces would surround Tchepone and begin the destruction of local infrastructure—the roads, bridges, and communications centers—and destroy trucks and supplies in the area. Phase four was the withdrawal after four to six weeks.

"If the enemy fights, and it is likely that he will, U.S. air power and fire power should inflict heavy casualties which will be difficult to replace," said Admiral Moorer. "The current flow of matériel versus manpower through the Ho Chi Minh Trail confirms that a large bulk of supplies and materials will be in the Tchepone area during the period of ARVN attack."

Rogers was not at the January 26 meeting, but the President had decided to put him out front. Nixon intended to stay away from cameras and microphones on this one. On January 29, in a press conference, Rogers stated that the United States was prepared to provide air support if South Vietnamese forces decided to attack supply bases in Laos. Actually, phase one—and bombing—was already under way. B-52s had been bombing, heavily, in southern Laos for weeks. Secrecy, if there ever was any as U.S. and ARVN units moved toward the South Vietnam–Laos border, was totally lost when *The New York Times* of January 31 carried the front-page headline "U.S. SILENT ON SPECULATION ABOUT AN INVASION OF LAOS. . . . NEWS BLACKOUT IS REPORTED."

After January 29, U.S. officials in both Washington and Vietnam refused to discuss conditions in the northern sector of South Vietnam— and American correspondents were denied seats on military aircraft flying north from Saigon. Inside the White House, the debate continued in a series of National Security Council meetings over whether to launch phase three, with the President stating that this was the last chance for the United States to assert its power because, by the dry season of 1972, October to May, there would not be enough U.S. personnel in Vietnam to make a difference on the ground.

On February 3, Nixon canceled an NSC meeting and called in Kissinger, Haldeman, Mitchell, and Connally. After more than an hour, the President went into the small study off the Oval Office and stripped to his underwear, listening to the others as his chiropractor, Dr. Kenneth Riland, manipulated and massaged his back. Then he came back into the discussion wearing only underpants and sat down, telling Kissinger and Haldeman to issue the order: phase two, the ARVN invasion, was "Go."

The next day, at 4:30 P.M. in Saigon (3:30 A.M. in Washington), the U.S. military command announced that nine thousand American troops and twenty thousand ARVN troops were on the Laotian border, but it refused to confirm that they were ready to cross that line in the jungle. However, the military did allow photographers up to the border so that they could photograph signs on the South Vietnamese side that read: "WARNING—NO U.S. PERSONNEL BEYOND THIS POINT."

THE OPERATION IN LAOS was running behind schedule. So the President had hours of free time, which he filled largely with political discussions, including a two-hour meeting with Mitchell and Haldeman. The conversation rambled a bit, then focused on two subjects: the futures of J. Edgar Hoover and George Wallace. The President wanted to replace the aging FBI director before the 1972 election—because if he lost that election a Democrat would almost certainly be in the White House and have the chance to name his own head of the agency. And there was another reason: Hoover was getting crankier and crankier about carrying out the internal security measures Nixon thought essential; his blocking of the Huston Plan in July 1970 was only one example. More and more, the director was worrying about his men being caught in illegal activity by local police or the press.

Nixon told Mitchell that day to go ahead on his own and activate as many as he could of the internal security schemes—essentially reinstituting the Huston Plan bit by bit—that Hoover was opposing. And if the FBI director found out, the President continued, a confrontation, in private, might create circumstances that would force Hoover to step aside. Then the subject turned to Wallace, once again installed as governor of Alabama. The President said he had the sense, from people who knew Wallace (a reference that usually meant Postmaster General Blount), that the governor might be willing to make a deal and not run in 1972. "I don't want him in. . . . We should work this out," Nixon said. Then he said he had also heard that Richard Daley, the Democratic mayor and political boss of Chicago, might be interested in a deal, too. The idea would be for Daley not to push too hard against Nixon in 1972, if the President could stop his largest contributor, W. Clement Stone, the big-money Chicago insurance man, from raising money for the Republican candidate for governor of Illinois.

The situation in Laos was still in the hurry-up-and-wait stage, so the President decided to go to Camp David for the weekend, leaving by helicopter with Kissinger and Haldeman. On the ride he leaned over and asked Haldeman, sitting closest to him, if he could handle the care and feeding of Kissinger over the weekend. The national security adviser had been threatening, all week, again, to quit, telling Haldeman and Safire: "If Rogers doesn't knuckle under, I go. You . . . don't think I'm serious about it, but I mean it!" That done, the President dined and bowled alone.

PHASE TWO began on February 8 at 7 A.M. South Vietnamese troops jumped off at that hour, and in Saigon, President Nguyen Van Thieu announced the operation, using almost the same words President Nixon had used nine months before when the Americans invaded Cambodia. "This will be limited in time as well as in space," Thieu said. "South Vietnam does not have any territorial ambitions whatever."

The next morning, at a meeting with the Republican congressional leadership, the President launched into a long and sometimes angry monologue on the Laos operation, telling some of his own men more than they had ever heard about his view of the war. Buchanan was the note-taker: "He said according to CIA estimates since 1965 more than 630,000 North Vietnamese troops have come down the Ho Chi Minh Trail. These troops have inflicted 45,000 American deaths and a

quarter of a million American casualties. . . . He said what it's all about is
not just getting out of Vietnam, we are going to get out in a way to justify
the investment we've made so far. . . . In this operation, the North Vietnamese are going to have to stand and fight because we are cutting their
lifelines. Eventually we can look back and say we accomplished
America's objectives in Vietnam. . . . The possibility of freedom in countries like Thailand is immeasurable."

Lam Son 719—the United States role was code-named Dewey
Canyon II—went well for a week. ARVN units rolled sixteen miles into
Laos without meeting heavy opposition, but after ten days they were
stopped as the North Vietnamese sent entire divisions from the area
around Saigon, counterattacking from the south as American and South
Vietnamese troops faced north, expecting counterattack from across the
DMZ. Within a couple of weeks, with forty thousand North Vietnamese
troops pinning down most ARVN units, Nixon passed the word through
Haldeman, telling him, "We still need to build up Presidential leadership
in Laos. We must claim victory regardless of the outcome." Under American pressure, Saigon finally sent in reinforcements, raising the number of
ARVN troops inside Laos to about thirty thousand. They were still out-
numbered and were being outfought by North Vietnam's best troops.

United States B-52s, F-100s, and F-4 Phantoms were turning jungle into wasteland, but in that wasteland the South Vietnamese were
being slaughtered. *Time* chronicled the days of a regiment of ARVN's
"crack" First Division, which advanced twenty-two miles into Laos; of
five hundred men who went in, thirty-two came out on U.S. rescue helicopters. The magazine reported on another regiment: "One unconscious
soldier had one arm wrapped around a machine-gun mount, while his
comrades held him from inside the chopper; as the aircraft touched
down, they let go, and he fell to the ground in a heap. A young U.S. adviser, watching from a jeep, held the latest copy of *Stars and Stripes,*
which carried the headline 'Rogers: Laos Drive a Success.' He folded the
paper and said: 'Sure, and here come the victors.' "

In the end, the President himself, on February 25, came up with
the idea for an endgame, telling Kissinger and Moore, "It would be a
great public relations coup if the ARVN actually reached Tchepone." On
March 7, two thousand ARVN men were airlifted to the town, on U.S.
helicopters. It was deserted. Thieu did claim victory, proclaiming that the
destruction of the town, which had been leveled by American bombing,
was the objective of Lam Son 719. Most of the press bought the trick:
"MAJOR VICTORY BY SOUTH VIETS," headlined the *Chicago Tribune;*
"VIETS OVERRUN KEY LAOS BASE," said the New York *Daily News;* "THE
HUB OF THE HO CHI MINH TRAIL," said the *Washington Star.*

But an almost continuous flow of men and matériel continued to move along the many branches of the trail and the South Vietnamese were pinned down or retreating all along their line of attack. The North Vietnamese had zeroed in on ARVN radio frequencies and used them to call in American artillery barrages on South Vietnamese troops, and to lure U.S. helicopters into the range of communist antiaircraft emplacements. More than two hundred American helicopters were shot down in three weeks. ARVN casualties were climbing toward two thousand dead and six thousand wounded. Then began the twenty-mile retreat, only some of it disciplined. American television cameramen caught horrifying and unforgettable footage of panicked South Vietnamese soldiers clinging to the skids of U.S. helicopters already overloaded in a massive aerial evacuation of Vietnamese units trapped in Laos. Reality was worse than the film: many of those soldiers were ripped to shreds as the helicopters flew home at treetop level to avoid North Vietnamese fire. On the other side of the border, two platoons of U.S. infantrymen refused orders to advance toward the Laotian border to cover the ARVN retreat. The lead of one *New York Times* story on the retreat, reported by Iver Peterson on the South Vietnam side of the border, read: "The last four miles of Route 9, down which exultant South Vietnamese troops moved unopposed to the Laotian border six weeks ago, have become a daily ordeal for the American tank crews that are covering their retreat under heavy fire. . . . a hail of Communist bullets and rockets."

At home, there were no mass demonstrations. But on March 1, at 1:32 A.M., a bomb exploded in a public rest room of the Capitol. A half hour before, an anonymous male caller had told a congressional telephone operator: "This building will blow up in thirty minutes. You will get many calls like this, but this one is real. Evacuate the building. This is in protest of the Nixon involvement in Laos."

WATCHING THE FILM of American helicopter crews pushing away terrified South Vietnamese soldiers, Nixon understood immediately that television had done him in once again—even as he tried to use it himself, appearing for an hour with Howard K. Smith of ABC News, saying that the Laos operation had met its key goals. During the early days of Lam Son he had been angry with Kissinger for spending so much time with James Reston of *The New York Times* and other columnists. "Tell Henry the columnists don't matter," Nixon told Haldeman. "Television is what matters."

The politician Nixon was correct. The professor Kissinger knew those columns were first rough notes of history. Television was becoming

.the medium of politics. Print was still the medium of history. In fact, during the Lam Son meetings, as Nixon watched Kissinger, Rogers, and Laird play their endless games of taking credit and avoiding blame, the President began to think that he had made a mistake in taking out President Johnson's taping system. He told Haldeman that he needed a record of his decision making to protect himself in the eyes of history. He wanted Oval Office and Cabinet Room meetings recorded, preserved on tape—tape only he would know was running.

Haldeman turned the job over to Lawrence Higby and Alex Butterfield, telling them the President wanted a voice-activated system in the Oval Office and a switch-activated system in the Cabinet Room. And he did not want the job done by the Army Signal Corps, because he believed they would report back to the Pentagon. He wanted it done by the Secret Service, which had a technical security division. The work was done at night. Five small microphones were embedded in the President's desk, and two more were put in the wall light fixtures on either side of the fireplace near the arrangement of a couch and chairs where Nixon often greeted visitors. Taps were placed on the three phones in the office. It was done and ready by February 16, using hidden microphones and $199 Sony reel-to-reel machines hidden away in a Secret Service locker room in the basement of the West Wing. Each five-inch reel could record almost six hours and thirty minutes of conversation. Secret Service agents changed the reels every day, putting the used ones in a small, locked room in the Executive Office Building.*

Even with tapes running, the President's favorite medium was his yellow pads, on which he continued to write new lists in the early hours of four mornings in March, the sixth, fifteenth, sixteenth, and seventeenth, including his thoughts on friends and foes—and on "Nixon the Man" as he sometimes called himself:

> Above all don't let them break through and see what kind of man new RN is—Maintain mystery—don't be common. . . . Best qualities: 1. guts to stand alone, 2. intelligence, 3. leadership—world experience. . . . Great need is to stand firm for American values. Don't give way. . . .
>
> H—speak to Connally about VP. . . . Failure to go to auto races= bad . . . TR had boxing—people loved it. . . . Must quit playing to elite. . . . Common Cause= Desperate last stand of the establishment. . . .

---

* During the next four months, microphones and taps were also placed in EOB 175, the Lincoln sitting room in the residence, and Aspen Lodge at Camp David.

In his rambling conversations with Haldeman, Nixon had said he intended to ask Agnew to resign as vice president and then appoint Connally—as soon as he thought he could get congressional approval in confirmation hearings. The "love affair," in Safire's words, was still going strong. Hour-long weekly meetings with the Treasury Secretary were a fixture on the President's schedule and one of their favorite topics of conversation was "the New Party," the coalition of Republicans and conservative Democrats that would be introduced in 1972 with a Nixon-Connally ticket and then nominate Connally for president in 1976.

Two pieces of business were occupying the President as spring came, the trial of Lieutenant Calley in Georgia and the trials of Pakistan's Yahya Khan. Pakistan, hastily created by the British masters of India in 1947, was on the verge of disintegrating. Pakistan was essentially two countries carved out of British India as a haven for Muslims hostile to, or afraid of, the far greater numbers of Hindus who dominated the subcontinent. West Pakistan bordered Iran, Afghanistan, and China along the great peaks of the Himalayas and the Hindu Kush. East Pakistan was a thousand miles to the east on the Bay of Bengal, in the lowland region historically dominated by Calcutta.

There had been separatist movements in East Pakistan since partition, united under the political banner of the Awami League. Yahya Khan, under increasing pressure of his own hearty promises to return all of Pakistan to civilian rule, had thought he could quiet vocal turmoil in West Pakistan and real rebellion in East Pakistan with an election in December 1970. The Awami League, led by Sheikh Mujibur Rahman, won 167 of the 169 contested seats in East Pakistan, gaining not only local control but a majority of the 310 seats in the National Assembly. "Mujib" almost immediately declared independence and Yahya responded by sending in the army. Forty thousand soldiers and American-made tanks were flown in beginning on March 26. The army arrested Mujib as a traitor, cut the telephone lines, and expelled foreign journalists—and the killing began. A secret radio transmitter hidden in the U.S. consulate in Dacca transmitted hundreds of horror stories; one was the killing of female university students driven from dormitories by fire and then calmly gunned down by West Pakistani soldiers. The dead were estimated at one hundred thousand in the first three days. The American ambassador in New Delhi, Kenneth B. Keating, a former Republican senator from New York, was also cabling home reports of genocide in East Pakistan: "Reign of military terror . . . Promptly, publicly and prominently deplore this brutality."

On March 29, at Fort Benning, Georgia, the longest war crimes trial in American military history ended. After thirteen days of deliberation, a jury of six officers found Lieutenant William Calley Jr. guilty of premeditated murder of civilians during the My Lai massacre of 1968. The jurors, all of whom had served in Vietnam, rejected the lieutenant's defense and testimony: "They were all the enemy. They were all to be destroyed. . . . That was my order, sir. That was the order of the day, sir." Calley said that he had been told that even the children of the hamlet were considered Vietcong sympathizers and had thrown grenades at Americans. On March 31, the court-martial sentenced Calley to life in prison. There were more than five thousand telegrams at the White House by then, and they were running 100 to 1 in favor of clemency. A quick White House national poll indicated that 79 percent of respondents disapproved of the verdict.

The President spent the day at home in La Casa Pacifica discussing the Calley case with Haldeman, Ehrlichman, Connally, Finch, and Kissinger. He also made call after call to Washington for reaction. One of those he called was Representative Olin E. Teague, a Texas Democrat who was chairman of the House Veterans Affairs Committee. Teague told Nixon, "Calley's a pathetic case, he never should have been an officer in the first place. But I was always against the court-martial."

"Well, then," Nixon said, "why don't you get out and talk that up with other members."

"Let's keep our eye on the ball," Nixon said to his aides in San Clemente. The "ball" was not military justice, it was not even maintaining military morale, which he thought was important; it was maintaining public support for the war. "Let's see if this time there isn't a way that we can be on the side of the people for a change, instead of always doing what's cautious, proper, and efficient."

In fact, the President had already thought a good deal about what he would do when the Calley verdict came in. He wanted to make two points at the same time: Americans do not condone this kind of action, but men who serve their country must be given the benefit of the doubt unless there is a clear breach of orders. He followed his first instinct, which was to get Calley out of jail, and he did it immediately because he wanted to dominate stories and analysis in Sunday newspapers and in the newsmagazines, which went to press on Sundays. He ordered Admiral Moorer to have Calley released from the stockade at Fort Benning and allowed to live in his apartment on the base, given the freedom of the base, while the trial and verdict were under appeal. When he hung up the phone, he said, "That's the one place where they say, 'Yes, Sir,' instead of 'Yes, but . . . ' "

The next day, the President announced from the Western White House that as commander in chief he would personally review the Calley case before a final sentence was carried out.

That was the people's choice. White House polls indicated a 96 percent "awareness" level on the Calley verdict. One of the first visitors to the lieutenant's apartment was George Wallace. When he came out he told reporters that because of the verdict, "Every time a soldier seeks out the enemy, he will be tried for murder." Then he added, "Anyone killed is a direct result of the North invading South Vietnam." By the end of the weekend, Nixon's approval rating in his own polls jumped by 13 points.

The day after the Calley verdict, Nixon was looking out over the Pacific during a long interview on larger subjects with Allen Drury. The questions were broad, rather sweeping ones about being president, and so were some of the answers:

> I would like to leave a renewed conviction in America that the system does work, that democratic government is better than the alternatives, that reforms can be made through peaceful change. . . . In a sense it's all right here in this room—right here in this chair. Whoever is President of the United States, and what he does, is going to determine the kind of world we have. His leadership must be strong—and firm—and, we hope, wise. . . .
>
> You ask about my comment . . . that this would be "the last war." I meant, of course, the last general war, the last big conflict. Of course, there will be brushfire explosions, things like Pakistan, Nigeria, things like that. But any Soviet leader who comes along—or any Chinese leader, for that matter—will know what I know: that if he begins a major war, he almost instantly kills seventy million of his own people. The same applies to me and my successors. I don't think that kind of national suicide is feasible any longer, for any sane man.

The next night the President had trouble sleeping and was up at 1:30 A.M., thinking about his down-and-up polls: "Laos blackout raised credibility issue . . . played as escalation, shook confidence in RN's war plan." Then he switched momentarily to affairs at home, writing: "Dilemma—Need for a simple understandable domestic goal."

PART OF THE DILEMMA was that Nixon's own goals involved foreign policy and his reelection—and the money needed for the campaign. On a single day in March, in a series of phone calls and private meetings with milk producers, the President personally traded higher federal milk production subsidies for more than $2 million in secret campaign funds for 1972. The money was to be passed through a farmers' cooperative called Associated Milk Producers, Inc. AMPI had forty thousand members, most of them in the Midwest and Southwest, producing about 12 percent of American milk. The organization had traditionally supported Democrats; in 1968, AMPI had contributed more than $150,000 to Hubert Humphrey's race against Nixon. Now they wanted access to Republican power and they had retained Murray Chotiner as soon as he left the White House staff. In 1969 and 1970, AMPI officers had delivered at least $235,000 in cash to Herbert Kalmbach for use in the Townhouse Project and other secret Nixon operations. The milk lobby's goal was to increase the price the federal government guaranteed milk producers from $4.66 per hundredweight to $5.21; in the jargon of the trade, that meant raising parity from 79 percent to 90 percent. But on March 12, Secretary of Agriculture Clifford Hardin announced that the support price would remain at $4.66, which was actually a reduction of support if inflation was taken into account.

With John Connally as their friend at court—and the $2 million already promised—AMPI officials were invited to the White House on March 23 and spent fifty minutes with the President. "Let me start by saying I have been very grateful for your support," he began. "I know you are a group that's politically very conscious. . . . I don't have to spell it out. . . . some others keep me posted as to what you do. . . . Tell us what you want."

The conversation revolved around 85 percent parity, or a support price of $4.92. The President rambled off into a long discussion of marketing milk as a sedative: "If you get people thinking that a glass of milk is going to make them sleep, I mean, it'll do just as well as a sleeping pill. It's all in the head." When the subject got close to money, how it would be delivered, Nixon cut it off. "Don't say that while I'm sitting here. Matter of fact, the room's not tapped. Forgot to do that."

There was a big laugh. But, of course, the room was wired and the tapes were spinning on downstairs in the basement.

At five o'clock that afternoon, the President sat down with Connally, Hardin, Ehrlichman, and Shultz to work out the details of revising the $4.66 decision the Department of Agriculture had announced ten days earlier. "I don't want to go over the economics of it—" Connally said.

"How about the politics?" Nixon interrupted.

"Looking to '72 . . . You're going to have to be strong in rural America."

Nixon asked how much the raising of the support price would cost the government. "About $100 million," Hardin answered.

That was that. Ehrlichman stood up and said: "Better get a glass of milk. Drink it while it's cheap."

That night the President spoke at a Republican fund-raiser at the Washington Hilton. After that, at midnight, Harold Nelson, the president of AMPI, went to the Madison Hotel with Chotiner. They woke Kalmbach, then worked out the transfer of the $2 million to the secret funds controlled by the President's lawyer.

A week after he intervened in the Calley case, on April 8, the President received a four-page letter from the young Army officer who had been the prosecutor in Lieutenant Calley's court-martial. Captain Aubrey W. Daniel III wrote: "How shocking it is if so many people across this nation have failed to see the moral issue . . . that it is unlawful for an American soldier to summarily execute unarmed and unresisting men, women and children, and babies. But how much more appalling it is to see so many of the political leaders of the nation who have failed to see the moral issue or having seen it, to compromise it for political motives. . . . You have subjected a judiciary system of this country to the criticism that it is subject to political influence. . . ."

The next night the President went on television to announce that another 100,000 U.S. troops would be withdrawn from Vietnam by December 1, leaving a total of 184,000 men there at the end of 1971. He concluded that the South Vietnamese operation in Laos had been as successful as the joint American–South Vietnamese operation in Cambodia. Then he said: "Consequently, tonight I can report that Vietnamization has succeeded."

CHAPTER 19

June 12, 1971

T HIS MEMORANDUM IS NOT TO BE HANDED TO ANYONE TO READ — IT IS FOR TALKING PURPOSES OF HRH AND RMW" was the line across the single copy of the four-page memo the President dictated on March 31 to Haldeman and Rose Mary Woods. Allen Drury had asked to interview the two of them on the personality of "Nixon the Man," and that man was telling them what to say:

"Drury asks some general questions with regard to my personal habits," Nixon began, and then went into his use-of-time routine—five minutes for lunch, five minutes for breakfast, no exercise. The second question was more of the same and he said: "The question about 'getting away from the Presidency' has never been one that particularly concerns me. I have no desire to get away from the burdens of the Presidency. As a matter of fact, when I feel most frustrated is when I am spending time doing something that I may really enjoy, but which I feel takes me away from what I really ought to be doing to do the job of the Presidency adequately. Polk once said that no one who really does the job of the Presidency adequately has any time for leisure—and this was 100 years ago."

Drury wanted to interview Mrs. Nixon, so the President dictated a memo from "RN" to "PN" suggesting what she might tell Drury. She followed the script: "He is so thoughtful of all of us. He is always planning little surprises and little gifts for us. He is not a cold man. I have never seen anyone more thoughtful than he is. . . . He does the little things that mean so much. He also is very thoughtful of our feelings about the criticisms he receives. When he gets some good editorials or comments in the morning, he will frequently have them Xeroxed and sent over to the house to us so that we can have a bright spot in the day, too. . . .

"Dick has a marvelous sense of humor—what you might call a situational humor. He always begins his speeches with some little note on something that has happened. I remember when we had the Republican National Committee reception over here, he spoke and cracked jokes. . . . He does this all the time but sometimes it doesn't appear in the newspapers. . . . And also some people just don't want to write about it because they think it makes him seem more human and likable. . . . He sat down and played the piano at the Christmas party for the children that we gave here—played Christmas carols. He always thinks like that"—she snapped her fingers—"about spontaneous things that he can do. . . . the children gathered around him and put their arms around him. Children know."

The "Nixon the Man" campaign was in full voice, with many voices coming straight from the White House, including the President's own. He appeared with Barbara Walters in a long interview on *The Today Show* on NBC. Walters rather tentatively asked him about his "stuffy image." He replied, "I don't worry about images." Meanwhile, his anecdotalists were filling pages of presidential color, some of it charming, if exaggerated a bit by the corps of anecdote Boswells. John Andrews reported that during an awards ceremony the President had digressed from the script to point out the tulips in the Rose Garden, saying, "You can admire them or you can tiptoe through them if you like." Alexander Butterfield filed this one after an event honoring a committee on employment of the handicapped: "Although no special words were spoken in this brief meeting, I noticed something again which I think is very much worth reporting. The President is always remarkably at ease when mingling and conversing with physically handicapped persons. . . . The truth is that the President is especially thoughtful of others. The truth should be better known."

Reading his news summary on a boat near Key Biscayne, Nixon spotted an Associated Press story by Frank Cormier that began, "President Nixon is making a determined effort to bridge the gap between his rather stiff public image and the 'real Nixon' whose private life has always been exceedingly private." The real Nixon wrote: "Z should knock down idea that RN has P.R. buildup for image." A memo to the President from Jeb Magruder outlined the presidential drill for a session with Fred Maroon, the photographer taking "inside" White House pictures for the Drury book *Courage and Hesitation*. Scheduled Oval Office poses in a fifteen-minute session included: "1. You and Messrs. Haldeman, Ehrlichman and Kissinger standing in front of your desk talking informally, but seriously, as though a meeting had just concluded. . . . 3. You and Dr. Kissinger standing by the door leading out to the patio, engaged in conversation. . . . 6. You, Mr. Klein and Mr. Ziegler. You will be seated at the desk. Messrs. Klein and Ziegler will be standing behind you, looking over your shoulder at newspapers on your desk. . . . Seated at your desk being served coffee by Manolo."

He always wanted a script, but the real Nixon did often demonstrate the awkward charm of the shy. Butterfield had been impressed by the President's joking with a pair of twins badly crippled by muscular dystrophy, and seeing him lift a friend, Harvey Firestone, out of a wheelchair and stand by him for a picture, waving away a nurse who was rushing up with a walker for the old man. "He doesn't need that damn thing."

His daughter Julie Eisenhower also sat for an interview about him with Helen Thomas. Julie said: "He's just a very human, warm person. . . . I think he is such a sensitive person." She also talked about students returning to their studies—"There isn't too much they can really get worked up over"—and the fact that casualties in Vietnam had dropped from hundreds a week under President Johnson to dozens under her father.

"To Julie—Great Job!" he wrote on the news summary account of the interview. A side note to Haldeman said, "H—You can see what a waste it was not to have this on T.V."

The charm offensive included the cover story of the May 1971 issue of *McCall's* magazine: "THE NIXONS NOBODY KNOWS—A Surprisingly Private View of a Public Marriage" featured photos, without eye contact, of husband and wife petting King Timahoe and walking along the beach on a nasty, rainy day. His wife may have overrated his sense of humor, but Nixon did try. At a demonstration of a new police "sniffing device" designed to detect the presence of humans—presumably to find people hiding—the President clapped his hands when the thing went off as it got close to him. "See," he said. "My critics are wrong!"

The Wall Street Journal caught the "Nixon the Man" blitz under the headline "THE PERIL OF PAINTING NIXON AS 'ONE OF THE BOYS.' " John Pierson wrote: "The humanizing of Richard Nixon, as it might be called, is not likely to be a fruitful effort. First, it won't work: Mr. Nixon is simply not a very humorous, relaxed, fun-loving man. Second, it will backfire: people resent being told something they know isn't so. Third, it's irrelevant: whether a President is one of the boys or not isn't remotely as important as his policies and ability to lead."

True. But often Nixon did want to be seen as one of the boys. And whether he expressed it well or not, he was very proud of his family. He enjoyed telling Tricia and Julie long stories of his courtship of their mother—even if, as with many other things in his life, he had found excitement in the chase but little joy in victory. Outside the family, he saw himself and the men of his generation, the men who fought World War II, as perhaps the last American innocents. In a dictated evaluation of Don Rumsfeld, the President said: "I think Rumsfeld is still too program oriented. . . . He is part of the new, pragmatic, post-war college group who are no-nonsense types and frankly lack the basically idealistic and romantic attitude. . . ."

He was a sentimental man, maudlin sometimes. A few days after Julie's interview, he read a news summary item about a karate enthusiast named Billy Corbett who broke a world's record by breaking 2,056 bricks with his hand, hoping people would donate a dollar for each brick for children with kidney diseases. Unfortunately, he also broke his hand and raised less than three hundred dollars. The President scrawled: "RMW—Send $100 to this cause—and inform this man."

Pat Nixon herself was a mystery to most of the men around the President. She seemed to regard being First Lady as a full-time professional job, and she put in long hours of detailed work. She insisted on answering letters by hand and protecting her small staff against the efficient and organizational passions of the President's staff—a euphemism for Haldeman. The chief of staff despised the former Thelma Catherine Ryan—Mrs. Nixon's maiden name—and he regularly brought what he called "Thelma" problems into the Oval Office. And Nixon brought "Mrs. Nixon" problems to Haldeman. "Pretty hard when PN won't help and yet won't let someone else take over," Haldeman wrote in his diary. "He wants to change lousy food but PN approves the menus." Most of the time the President just listened to whoever was complaining, deflecting what he could, avoiding confrontation.

Mrs. Nixon, of course, usually got her way—most notably when Haldeman, in a preemptive strike, brought interior decorators in from New York to shape up the dowdy precincts of Camp David.

"When are we going to get to the furnishing of the cabins?" Mrs. Nixon asked the camp commandant the next time she was in residence. He answered that the work was all done. "Oh?" she said. "I'd like to see it." The Marines began carting away the stuff from New York the next day. The First Lady took over, starting from scratch.

March 17, 1971, was an important day in the Nixons' life, and not just because it was St. Patrick's Day and the couple had Irish roots. The President said that his wife had always been called Pat because she was born on another St. Patrick's Day.* On this one, during the White

---

* Mrs. Nixon was actually born on March 16, the day before St. Patrick's Day.

House's "Irish Celebration," the Nixons happily announced that the elder of their two daughters, Tricia, twenty-five, was to be a June bride. A doll-like little blonde who shared her father's iron will, Tricia had avoided reporters and pretty much everybody else after she got into the newspapers for writing a friendly letter to Lester Maddox, an Atlanta restaurant owner who was refusing to serve Negroes. She had suggested that he make the restaurant a private club so that he could turn away folks he did not like. In the privacy of the family, she could be an exceedingly difficult young woman, often forcing the President of the United States to change family plans because she would not leave her room for one event or another. Her fiancé, Edward Ridley Finch Cox, was a second-year law student at Harvard. A young Republican from New York City—and the Social Register—Cox had worked a summer for Ralph Nader, a liberal crusader for consumer causes. Mrs. Nixon, naturally, intended to play the full role of the mother of the bride, an intent that caused hours of huddling together by Nixon and Haldeman to figure out ways to use the nuptials as a showcase for "Nixon the Man." The President's idea was that people needed "great events" to take them out of "their humdrum existence"—and what better than a state wedding with a beautiful young bride and her tall handsome groom?

The President was in the midst of a great courtship himself, the object of his attention being the country he used to call "Red China." "A diplomacy of smiles" was the phrase used in *New Times,* the Soviet Union's leading foreign affairs journal. The Kremlin was wary about a series of Nixon administration decisions relaxing or eliminating some of the trade and travel restrictions the United States had imposed on Peking since the early 1950s. The Soviets gave no public indication that they knew of Nixon's private overtures to Chou En-lai, even though Leonid Brezhnev was denouncing "imperialists . . . trying to sow dissent between China and the USSR." And, in fact, the private channels between the Americans and the Chinese were quiet again as Peking denounced South Vietnamese actions in Laos—Premier Chou En-lai visited Hanoi during Lan Som 719—just as the January 1970 Warsaw initiatives had ended with the invasion of Cambodia later that year. Then, on April 6, Washington, Moscow, and much of the world were startled by the simplest of invitations: at the end of the World Table Tennis Championships in Japan, the captain of the Chinese team asked the American captain to bring his team to China for a week of exhibition matches. None of the players, or anyone except Chinese Premier Chou En-lai, knew the invitation came from Mao Tse-tung.

The visit of fifteen players, the first group of Americans to visit China since the early 1950s, became a worldwide sensation because the

Chinese government allowed a number of American newspeople, print and television, to come with the team. American journalists had been banned in China for the past twenty-two years, but "Ping-Pong diplomacy" instantly became headlines and fascinating entertainment. Reporters and cameras were recording every word and move of the young Americans and the Chinese they met. Hundreds of people followed the Americans wherever their guides took them through the streets of Peking, Shanghai, and Canton. The Americans saw the Great Wall. They saw Premier Chou En-lai, who said, in words headlined, repeated, and studied back in Washington: "You have opened a new chapter in the relations of the American and Chinese people. I am confident that this beginning again of our friendship will certainly meet with majority support of our two peoples."

The exhibition match, played in Peking, was an exercise in Chinese tact. Instead of using their best players, who were far superior to America's best, the hosts used younger and lesser players. They defeated the American men five matches to three, and the American women by five to four.

In Washington on April 16, the President answered China questions for almost an hour at the annual meeting of the American Society of Newspaper Editors. He guarded the truth of American contacts well, using phrases like "long process" and saying that he had told Tricia and her fiancé that China would be a great place for a honeymoon.

The private and the public diverged sharply when Nixon appeared before the editors at the Shoreham Hotel. In private, he was plotting to force the resignation of J. Edgar Hoover as director of the FBI after forty-seven years, scheming to make an event of it on the director's seventy-seventh birthday, January 1, 1972. Many of his staff agreed, including Buchanan, who told the President in a memo: "Mr. Hoover has already passed the peak of his national esteem. At one point I would guess that 95 percent of the nation thought he was doing a phenomenal job. . . . To young people, especially, who do not have anything near the esteem for him as do their parents, he is increasingly becoming a villain, and he is tied totally to us." That take fit with something Nixon was hearing from Moynihan, who was back in private life making a little money as a consultant to leaders of big business and high finance, and was astonished to find them hostile to Nixon—particularly on issues of dissent and civil liberties—finally concluding, "They are mostly getting this attitude from their children." But in public, when the panel of questioners asked whether charges by congressional Democrats that the FBI was bugging their phones would hasten the director's resignation, Nixon answered "No," and then defended Hoover against "unfair . . . malicious criticisms." He did the same thing when the editors asked about criticisms of Agnew, saying, "This old game . . . of having the President disagree with his Vice President goes on and on, but I am an expert at it and I'm not going to get into it. I defend my Vice President." In private, he was still trying to figure out a way to dump Agnew and team up with Connally. Driving back to the White House, he joked about the first question of the session, an editor asking him what he thought about when he wakes up at 3 A.M. "A generation of peace," he answered, and went on at length. In the car, he said the real answer was, "Going to the bathroom."

In publicly defending Agnew, the President had also told the editors that they should get to know the Vice President better, spend time with him. Nine of their reporters did just that three days later in Williamsburg, Virginia, where the Vice President was attending the spring meeting of the Republican Governors Conference. After the last session of the conference, Agnew invited the reporters back to his room at 12:30 A.M. and talked for three hours—off the record. What he talked about was his disagreement with any opening to China and his disgust with the press for giving the communists a propaganda victory with its euphoric, unquestioning report of the Ping-Pong team's visit. The early-morning session stayed off the record for less than twenty-four hours. The nine reporters told the story to colleagues, who were not bound by the "off the record" agreement, and the story was all over the front pages on April 20.

Agnew was out of the loop on China policy and out of bounds on his backgrounder. Press secretary Ziegler came into the Oval Office before his daily briefing to tell Nixon he intended to say that Agnew's thoughts were just his opinion. The President said that was not enough. He told Ziegler to put out a statement saying that the Vice President "fully supports" administration initiatives to improve relations with the People's Republic. "Tell him that the job of the Vice President is to support the President." In *The New York Times* that story ran below the announcement that the State Department was issuing tourist visas to the Chinese table tennis team to visit the United States.

The lead story that day ran under a three-column headline:

SUPREME COURT, 9–0, BACKS BUSING
TO COMBAT SOUTH'S DUAL SCHOOLS'
REJECTING ADMINISTRATION STAND

The unanimous decision, written by Chief Justice Burger, effectively ended the White House's official opposition to busing. But it also was the final and successful step in the President's strategy of letting the courts take the political heat. Edward Morgan, an assistant to Harry Dent, laid out that line in a memo to the President: "If we can keep the liberal writers convinced that we are doing what the Court requires, and our conservative Southern friends convinced that we are not doing any more than the Court requires, I think we can walk this tightrope until November, 1972."

"Good, keep it up," was the President's written comment on that.

THE LAOS OPERATION in February had reinvigorated some elements of the antiwar movement. A new group calling itself the National Peace Action Coalition was organizing a mass demonstration in Washington and other cities during the last week in April. But demonstrators were having more and more trouble getting attention. They had become part of the capital's routine, like the blossoming of the cherry trees. There was, however, one group was engaging the press and scaring the White House, Vietnam Veterans Against the War. "Dewey Canyon III"—a mockery of the American code name for the Laos campaign, Dewey Canyon II—was led by a charismatic former Navy lieutenant, a Yale graduate named John Kerry.* In case anyone missed the meaning of the code name, the veterans issued dispatches written in military jargon and in imitation of Nixon's Cambodia and Laos arguments. The first one read, in part:

> The incursion . . . will penetrate into the country of Congress for the limited purpose of severing the supply lines currently being utilized by the illegal mercenary forces of the Executive Branch. . . . We would like to make it perfectly clear that our primary concern, and the only reason the incursion was ordered, is to ensure the safe withdrawal of our limited force of Winter Soldiers from the countries of the District of Columbia.

On April 23, after camping on the Mall for a week—a Federal court denied a Justice Department request for an injunction against the encampment—seven hundred veterans stood in line and one by one threw the medals and combat ribbons they had won in Vietnam over a temporary fence that had been erected around the Capitol. The Purple Hearts, Silver Stars, and commendations remained there through the weekend, as more than two hundred thousand coalition demonstrators marched through Washington and hundreds of thousands more marched in other cities. The President, at Camp David, received a new White House poll that day showing a 3 percent drop in support for the war.

---

* John F. Kerry was elected to the United States Senate from Massachusetts in 1984.

"We'll probably have to crank the Vice President up again," he told Haldeman.

It was a crowd of liberals, mainly. They listened to speeches by members of Congress. There were few arrests. The next day, though, April 25, things began to get ugly. Members of a loose coalition of radical groups calling themselves the Mayday Tribe began to arrive, with the announced intention of "shutting down the government" on Monday, May 3. The Mayday plan had been worked on for months—and had been discussed with North Vietnamese diplomats in Paris by the thirty-year-old chief organizer, Rennie Davis. By April 27, *The Washington Post* was reporting hit-and-run incidents all over the city, including "guerrilla theater" in the halls of Congress. The *Post* reported that screaming demonstrators dressed as Vietnamese peasants ran into a senator's offices, followed by men in American combat gear. "Seventy people died in Vietnam last week," one shouted. "So seventy people are going to die here." Two hundred twenty-four protesters were arrested the next day at HEW. Three hundred seventy were arrested at the Department of Justice on April 30.

The President flew to San Clemente that day. His mind was on China. On April 27, after all the signals—from Ping-Pong diplomacy to a *Life* magazine article saying that Chairman Mao was open to a meeting with Nixon as president or tourist—Ambassador Hilaly of Pakistan had hand-delivered another note from Chou En-lai. This one said: "The Chinese government reaffirms its willingness to receive publicly in Peking a special envoy of the President of the United States (for instance Mr. Kissinger) or the U.S. Secretary of State or even the President himself. . . ."

Ironically, the greatest problem in the note was the word "publicly." Nixon wanted to send an envoy secretly to make preparations for a spectacular public visit by the President himself. For a couple of days, he had more or less tortured Kissinger by analyzing the merits of potential envoys—perhaps David Bruce, perhaps Nelson Rockefeller. Then he told Kissinger he was the one.

On May 1, the President held a news conference at the Western White House and, commenting on the demonstrations going on in Washington, said, "We are going to see to it that the thousands of Government workers who have a right to go to work peacefully are not interfered with by those militants, those few militants, who in the name of demonstrating for peace abroad presume that they have the right to break the peace at home."

That peace was indeed broken on Monday, May 3. Before dawn, crowds of protesters moved out to try to block streets and bridges. They came in waves, using their bodies, trash cans, tree limbs, and anything else they could get their hands on to stop cars and trucks, but they were arrested in waves, too, as the government and police outwitted them time and again. Federal workers were called in at 5 A.M. The police problem was what to do with the disorganized mobs once they got them out of the roadways. Seven thousand demonstrators were arrested on Monday without being charged. Most of them ended up in concentration pens, without food or sanitation facilities, behind eight-foot-high cyclone fences in the parking lots and fields around Robert F. Kennedy Memorial Stadium, normally home to the Washington Redskins football team. As night fell, cold and rainy, they were moved indoors onto the cement floor of the Washington Coliseum, a basketball arena. Their only real victory that day was forcing the closing of the Capitol to visitors.

Another 2,680 were arrested the next day, as protesters surrounded the Justice Department, with Attorney General Mitchell watching impassively, puffing his pipe, from the balcony outside his office. The President was back in the White House, reading detailed half-hourly reports from observation teams coordinated by his young counsel John Dean. The noon report the second day, May 4, read, in part: "Demonstrators gathering in vicinity of Franklin Park (14th & I); May Day coalition speakers are urging mass march to Department of Justice for nonviolent civil obedience. . . . Two thousand gathered. . . . Total Arrests: 232 (majority for disorderly conduct); now being processed for arraignment . . . There are approximately 1500 demonstrators who were arrested yesterday and are still detained at the Coliseum and have not been arraigned because they have refused to cooperate with the court officials in the necessary processing."

At 1:30 P.M., Dean reported: "Four thousand on the route of march from Franklin Park and/or on the sidewalks of 10th Street at DOJ . . . 685 arrests (majority: disorderly conduct and misdemeanors, i.e., jaywalking and failure to move). Live bomb found suspended underneath Taft Street Bridge; deactivated by military bomb squad." At 3:30 P.M.: "A confrontation has occurred between the police and demonstrators at 12th and Pennsylvania Avenue. . . . Troops moving back onto bridge to monitor evening bridge traffic."

At 7 P.M., Dean reported to the President: "Latest estimates indicated that 2,000–2,100 demonstrators were arrested at DOJ, most of whom were charged with unlawful assembly; this is in addition to the 685 people arrested at other points in the city this date. . . . The evening rush hour traffic was normal and without incident. Chief Jerry Wilson feels that the demonstrators have been broken in strength and spirit. Included in those arrested in yesterday's demonstrations were notables

"The most extraordinary thing about his presidency was not the way it ended, but that it happened," said one of Nixon's men, Senator Robert Dole. In a business of men who could not stand to be alone, Richard Nixon wanted people kept away. In the words of another aide, Elliot Richardson, his ambition was as extraordinary: "He wanted to be the Architect of his Times."

He was obsessed by history and the Kennedys. "Anecdotalists" were assigned to follow him, crafting quotes and anecdotes to show "Nixon the Man," walking the beach in the Kennedy manner—in wingtips.

The real man, though, was alone, collecting his thoughts and hopes on yellow pads: "The Press, the Intellectual establishment, and the partisan Dems are hopelessly against—Better means must be found to go over them to people . . . I must find a way to finesse the Cabinet, staff, Congress, political types—who take time, but could do their job sans my participation. Symbolic meetings should be the answer."

4

5

America was at war with itself over race and Vietnam. "Cultural revolution," said *Time*. "The nation is shuddering at this photograph," wrote *The New York Times*, when armed black students took over buildings at Cornell. Students at Kent State University were shot down by National Guardsmen during antiwar protests. In the South, George Wallace, his campaigns partly financed by Nixon, was leading white opposition to school integration—and then was gunned down himself.

6

"We are seen as gray men," said Nixon, organizing a buttoned-down administration run by his former advance men, H. R. Haldeman and John Ehrlichman, shown here with appointments secretary Dwight Chapin. On his third day in office, Nixon posed with some of his men: George Shultz, Robert Mayo, John Mitchell, Arthur Burns, John Volpe, Robert Finch, Vice President Spiro Agnew, Clifford Hardin, George Romney, Daniel Patrick Moynihan, and Maurice Stans.

After only a month he began traveling, first to France meeting with his role model, President Charles de Gaulle, a master of the politics of secrecy and surprise, along with Ehrlichman, Haldeman, National Security Adviser Henry Kissinger, and Secretary of State William Rogers. He was not greatly interested in domestic governance—"Building outhouses in Peoria," he called it— except for bringing order to a divided America, delegating much of that job to Attorney General Mitchell, FBI director J. Edgar Hoover, and Ehlichman.

"Vietnamization" was Nixon's exit strategy—a retreat under fire leading to "Peace with Honor"— gradually withdrawing the 550,000 Americans there when he took office. Aboard *Air Force One*, on his way in the summer of 1969 to explain the policy to South Vietnamese officials, he traveled with Rogers, Defense Secretary Melvin Laird, Generals Paul Harkins and Creighton Abrams, Admiral John McCain, Kissinger, and Henry Cabot Lodge and Ellsworth Bunker, who both served as ambassador to Saigon.

One of his problems that summer was the pending court-martial of Green
Beret Colonel Robert Rheault, accused of ordering the execution of one of his
own Vietnamese spies suspected of being a double agent—a case dropped
when Nixon and Kissinger persuaded the CIA to declare that an investigation
would threaten "national security." The successful cover-up of the killing fore-
shadowed the unsuccessful Watergate cover-up three years later. In 1970,
Nixon ordered troops into Cambodia, triggering demonstrations across the
country, but also triggering an avalanche of supportive telegrams from what
he called his "Silent Majority."

"The hardest thing about covering Nixon is remembering that he is human," wrote an important White House correspondent. Regular "Nixon the Man" charm offensives were designed to make that point. He posed for *McCall's* magazine with his wife, though he often communicated with her by memo. He broke his rule about dancing in public at his daughter Tricia's White House wedding and posed with the family each year at Christmas: Tricia and her husband, Edward Cox; Pat Nixon; and their daughter Julie and her husband, Ensign David Eisenhower, grandson of Nixon's political patron, President Eisenhower.

17

Nixon and Kissinger were an odd couple, with the National Security Adviser alternately hysterically predicting war and threatening resignation—"They are calling you a weakling, Mr. President!" was one of his more effective lines. But working in secret, throwing lies to the winds, they surprised the world and confounded their real and imagined enemies. In February 1972, Nixon flew to China for meetings with Premier Chou En-lai and Chairman Mao Tse-tung, ending almost twenty-five years of hostility between the richest and the most populous of nations.

Three months after his China trip, Nixon, with Kissinger, was walking again where no President ever had—inside the Kremlin. The principal achievement of the summit with Soviet leader Leonid Brezhnev was a treaty banning the deployment of new antiballistic missiles by either country. The ABM treaty was signed in Moscow on May 26, 1972—with Pat Nixon who had sneaked into the grand Kremlin hall watching from behind a column.

"The boss is in love again," said speechwriter William Safire when John Connally, a former Democratic governor of Texas, was appointed as Secretary of the Treasury.

On the second weekend of August 1971, the President, Connally, and a dozen assistants met secretly at Camp David and changed the politics of the 1972 election and the economics of the world, putting together a New Economic Policy that included wage and price controls at home and the end of the post–World War II monetary system that tied world currencies to a dollar backed by all the gold at Fort Knox. Among the dozen were Safire, Shultz, and Herbert Stein, chairman of the Council of Economic Advisers, all shown here with Kissinger outside the Oval Office. Inside, Nixon was trying to get rid of Agnew and nominate Connally for vice president, then create a new party of the center that would nominate Connally for president in 1976.

After carrying forty-nine states in the 1972 election, the President demanded the resignation of his Cabinet and staff, plotting alone at Camp David to centralize government decision making in his own office and mind. But it was not to happen. Agnew arrived to say he was being investigated for fraud. And John Mitchell's wife, Martha, already famous for drunken late-night calls to officials and reporters, was talking of dark doings in the White House, hinting her husband was being set up to take the rap for unnamed "horrors." To himself, Nixon wrote: "Don't get rattled—Don't Waver—Don't React."

The "horrors"—surveillance of the Kennedys, wiretaps, and burglaries paid for with cash from White House safes and campaign offices—began to come out during the investigation and trials after police arrested seven men during a break-in at the offices of the Democratic National Committee in the Watergate office complex. The President himself was ordering the paying of hush money to the Nixon men who organized that break-in—G. Gordon Liddy, a former FBI agent who was counsel to the finance committee of Nixon's reelection committee, and E. Howard Hunt, a former CIA agent, reporting to Ehrlichman.

After generally ignoring the Watergate story for almost a year, the press rose up against the President, trying to link Nixon to the horrors. The man in the White House, who wanted more and more time alone to think and scheme on his yellow pads, now found himself spending almost all of his time responding to charge after charge, saying once: "I am not a crook!"

30

31

32

By the spring of 1973, the Senate was putting together a Select Committee, chaired by Senator Sam Ervin, to investigate presidential abuse of power. The star witness was the President's counsel, John Dean, who had been assigned to keep the scandal away from the Oval Office. The presidency went into a free fall of investigations, resignations, indictments, confessions, and accusations. It was revealed that cover-up meetings had been recorded by a secret White House taping system. Nixon appointed Elliot Richardson (*right*) as attorney general and he, in turn, appointed Archibald Cox as a special prosecutor for Watergate.

Nixon retreated to the loneliness of Camp David, where he called in Halde-man and Ehrlichman on Sunday, April 29, 1973, to tell them to resign—"This is like cutting off my two arms," he said—in a desperate, doomed attempt at saving himself. He was crying and said he had prayed before going to bed the night before, hoping he would not wake. "You and Bob," he said to Ehrlich-man, "you'll need money. I have some . . . you can have it."

35

After Haldeman and Ehrlichman left, Nixon stood at the window of Aspen Lodge as the daylight faded. Press Secretary Ron Ziegler came in quietly. The President did not turn, just said: "It's all over, Ron, do you know that?" Speechwriter Ray Price came in next, and Nixon said: "Maybe I should resign, Ray. If you think so just put it in." Then Nixon walked outside, toward the heated swimming pool he had ordered built just outside his door. Price stayed a few steps behind. He was afraid the President might try to kill himself.

Abbie Hoffman (YIPPIE), Dr. Benjamin Spock, Rennie Davis, and Al Hubbard (VVAW leader)."

The next day, May 5, there were demonstrations around the country—in both New York and San Francisco, more than a hundred thousand people gathered. In Washington, there were 1,146 arrests at the Capitol, where a few thousand people gathered to present a "People's Peace Treaty." In the end, the government stayed open. Twelve thousand people were arrested, many of them illegally—and there was criticism of that—but the Nixon White House scored it as a victory. The President and Haldeman laughed when Dean informed them that Chuck Colson had sent a crate of oranges to the prisoners penned up in RFK Stadium. The label read: "Best of luck, Senator Edmund Muskie."

"He's got the balls of a brass monkey," Nixon said.

"He's going to get caught at some of these things," Haldeman said. "But he's got a lot done he hasn't been caught at."

As WASHINGTON RETURNED to normal, the President went to the annual dinner of the White House Correspondents Association, an affair designed to distribute awards to members and show a certain Washington camaraderie between the people who run the country and those who regularly cover them. This one left the President in a rage and the next morning he dictated a long memo to Haldeman:

> Every one of the recipients was receiving an award for a vicious attack on the Administration—Carswell, wiretapping, Army surveillance, etc. I had to sit there for 20 minutes while the drunken audience laughed in derision as the award citations were read. . . . The dinner, as a whole, was probably the worst of its type I have attended. . . . I don't want any of our naive staff members to give you any impression that as a result of my going there and sitting through three hours of pure boredom and insults, I thereby proved I was the "good sport" and therefore may have softened some of the press attitude towards the President. On the contrary, the type of people who are in the press corps have nothing but contempt for those who get down to their level and who accept such treatment without striking back. That's one of the reasons they have some respect for Agnew. . . . They are truly a third house supporting the Democratic candidates.

Then a couple of days later the President discovered a fourth house. He turned on television to watch a ball game and saw it was rained out. So he clicked around the dial to see what else was on and stopped on WTOP, a CBS affiliate, which was broadcasting the most popular situation comedy in the country, *All in the Family.* He was shocked, telling Haldeman about it the next morning, as the chief of staff busily took notes. "Star of show—square type—named Arch. Hippy son-in-law. . . . The show was total glorification of homosex. Made Arch look bad—homo look good. Is this common on TV?—destruction of civilization to build homos. Made the homos as the most attractive type. Followed *Hee Haw.*" That was filed with a memo to Haldeman complaining about a guest at a White House dinner honoring volunteerism: "Typical of the group was a fellow who came through the line from California who said he was a Quaker. . . . he was an obvious, roaring fag. It was disgusting to even pass him down the line to Pat."

The first poll the President saw after the demonstrations reported that 32 percent of Americans approved of VVAW's Operation Dewey Canyon III and 42 percent disapproved. The numbers for Mayday were 18 percent approval and 71 percent disapproval. More than 75 percent approved of the mass arrests. "Fortunately, they're all just really bad-looking people," Haldeman said to Nixon of the Mayday Tribe.

But that was not true of former lieutenant Kerry, who was invited to testify before the Senate Foreign Relations Committee, and touched on a Nixon fear when he said: "The country doesn't realize it yet but it has created a monster in the form of thousands of men who have been taught to deal in and to trade in violence and who are given the chance to die for the biggest nothing in history. . . . Each day to facilitate the process by which the United States washes her hands of Vietnam someone has to give up his life so that the United States doesn't have to admit something that the entire world knows . . . that we have made a mistake. . . . How do you ask the last man to die for a mistake?"

The returning men were a major concern for the President. More and more young men were coming back angry and bitter about the war. Sometimes they were also addicted to heroin or other drugs cheaply available most everywhere in Vietnam. "As COMMON AS CHEWING GUM" was the headline on a *Time* magazine story on drug use by American soldiers. The problem came to the White House at the end of April when a Republican congressman, Robert W. Steele of Connecticut, just back from a visit to Vietnam, told Bud Krogh that he believed as many as forty thousand young Americans there were addicts. In some units, he said, one out of every four men was a drug user. Steele told Krogh that the problem was so bad that the only solution might be to withdraw all American servicemen from Vietnam before it was too late. John Ehrlichman, responding to Krogh's memo, thought that was a little extreme—and refused to pass the warnings on to the President.

What Nixon was seeing were tough-talking reports from the Defense Department and from the Bureau of Narcotics and Dangerous Drugs that the drug problem was under control. There were more investigations, more seizures, more arrests. So, the President was being told, whatever the government was doing must be working.

It was a *New York Times* headline on May 16 that got through to the President: "G.I. HEROIN ADDICTION EPIDEMIC IN VIETNAM." Nixon told Krogh that what worried him most was the effect on Middle American support for the war if clean-cut young men were coming back to their mothers and their hometowns as junkies. Suddenly drug use was a national security crisis. "This is our problem," wrote Nixon on a news summary report of a *Washington Post* story that quoted the mayor of Galesburg, Illinois, saying that almost everyone in that conservative town wanted their sons out of Vietnam. The stories had a momentum of their own: NBC reported that a survey of 120 soldiers returning home to working-class Boston indicated that half of them had drug problems. The *San Francisco Chronicle* reported that the 250 Vietnam returnees arriving in that city by ship each day were bringing in duffel bags full of drugs for their own use or to sell when they got back home.

THE PRESIDENT went to Key Biscayne for a long weekend in mid-May, then returned to Washington by way of a little speechmaking in Alabama, stopping in Mobile and then Birmingham. The most notable thing about the trip was that Governor George Wallace was along. Other Southern governors were on the plane, but the press had eyes only for Wallace. Reporters were more than a little surprised by what seemed to be an easy relationship between the governor and the President. In fact, the meeting had been set up by Winton Blount, who had brought back a conciliatory message from Wallace a week earlier. "He and the Nixon administration have a common interest—to keep a liberal Democrat out of the White House."

Holding on to the White House would cost money—and that subject was a constant in Oval Office conversation. On May 13, the President told Haldeman and Ehrlichman that International Telephone and Telegraph Corporation, already a major donor to his campaigns, was going to be even more of a target of opportunity. "Kleindienst has the I.T.T. thing settled," he said, referring to Justice Department antitrust action against the conglomerate. "He cut a deal with I.T.T. We give them Hartford, which they badly need. . . ."

The President, who considered most antitrust action to be bureaucratic harassment of business, had already talked about the case with Deputy Attorney General Richard G. Kleindienst, complaining about the aggressive stance of the head of the department's Antitrust Division, Richard McLaren: "I don't know whether I.T.T. is bad, good or indifferent. But there are not going to be any more antitrust actions as long as I am in this chair. . . . I want something clearly understood, and, if it's not understood, McLaren's ass is to be out of there within one hour. The I.T.T. thing—stay the hell out of it. Is that clear? That's an order. . . . I do not want McLaren to run around prosecuting people, raising hell about conglomerates, stirring things up. . . . I don't like the son-of-a-bitch."

Despite McLaren's efforts, a sweetheart deal of some sort was in the making between the White House, the Antitrust Division of the Justice Department, and the twelfth-largest company in the country. ITT had grown by purchase and takeover, buying 110 companies in seven years, and Justice had filed charges in three of those acquisitions, the Hartford Fire Insurance Company; Grinnell Corporation, a manufacturer of fire alarm equipment; and Canteen Corporation, a vending machine company. Kleindienst was supervising the cases because Attorney General Mitchell had represented ITT when he was a New York lawyer.

"They give us Grinnell and one other merger they don't need and which they've been kind of sorry they got into, apparently," said Nixon on May 13. "Now this is very very hush hush and it has to be engineered very delicately and it'll take six months to do properly. . . ."

"Does I.T.T. have money?" Haldeman asked.

"Oh God, yes," Nixon answered. "That's part of this ball game. . . . But it should be later. It should not be right now. . . . Nothing done until the deal is over."

As for Wallace, a few days after his ride on *Air Force One* he told his chief fund-raiser, Tom Turnipseed: "I'm tired of these kooks in the third-party business. It's crazy. I'm thinking about going back into the Democratic Party"—running for president as a Democrat in 1972. It was the second big surprise that Turnipseed had in a week. The governor's brother, Gerald, who seemed to be in depression, had told him, "Those damn IRS boys, Tom. I think they've got me this time." Then Turnipseed saw Gerald again after the Nixon trip and he seemed a new man, implying that his tax troubles were over.

Hoping his own troubles with Wallace were over, too, Nixon came back to Washington in time for his weekly meeting with Connally. But the President had Haldeman call the Treasury Secretary to tell him the President was behind schedule and he would call back to set a time. Actually, the President just wanted to play a little joke on his new friend. He walked across the South Lawn to the Treasury building and took an elevator to Connally's office. He walked in with a big smile, to the shock of both Connally and his secretaries. The two men talked for an hour, then went out together and shook hands with some of the crowd that had gathered when word got out that the President was inside.

At 3:45 P.M. on May 18, the President was in the Oval Office talking politics with Haldeman and Colson—working out a plan to have agents follow Muskie and Kennedy around-the-clock—when Kissinger burst in saying, "The thing is okay!" He and the President then went into a kind of double-talk routine that made no sense to Colson, until Haldeman gave him a nod to leave. The "thing" was a "breakthrough" in Strategic Arms Limitation Treaty talks with the Soviet Union. The formal talks, announced to the public, had gone through seventy-four separate sessions with the Soviets in Helsinki and Vienna since November 1969. But like the official peace talks in Paris, those meetings were technical sessions, or elaborate frauds. The real negotiations had been going on all that time between Kissinger and Ambassador Dobrynin. Very few people knew about those "back-channel" negotiations. Among those who did not know were Secretary of State Rogers and the chief American negotiator, the director of the Arms Control and Disarmament Agency, Gerard Smith. Nixon and Kissinger had gotten the business of the national security of the United States down to a two-man operation.

Nixon invited Haldeman and Kissinger to come with him for a dinner cruise on the *Sequoia*—and then invited Colson and Ehrlichman to join the celebration. But those two did not know what they were being invited to celebrate. They found out during dinner on the Potomac when the President told his national security partner to read the agreement aloud. Kissinger began:

> The Governments of the United States and the Soviet Union, after reviewing the course of their talks on the limitation of strategic armaments, have agreed to concentrate this year on working out an agreement for the limitation of the deployment of antiballistic missile systems (ABMs). They have also agreed that, together with an agreement to limit ABMs, they will agree on certain measures with respect to the limitation of offensive strategic weapons. The two sides are taking this course in the conviction that it will create more favorable conditions for further negotiations to limit all strategic arms.

The President's mood did change a bit when the conversation turned from that triumph of secrecy to the press leaks that continued to plague the administration. After a few celebratory glasses of wine, the President, talking to Colson and Kissinger, said: "One day we will get them—we'll get them on the ground where we want them. And we'll stick our heels in, step on them hard and twist—right, Chuck, right? Henry knows what I mean—just like you do it in negotiations, Henry— get them on the floor and step on them, crush them, show no mercy."

The world would hear the words of the joint statement in thirty-six hours, in a joint announcement from Washington and Moscow. That did not give Nixon and Kissinger much time to tell Rogers and Smith that they had been deliberately deceiving both of them for the past seventeen months. Haldeman was delegated to tell Rogers that the reason he knew nothing was that the breakthrough came suddenly with an extraordinary letter to the President from Leonid Brezhnev. A lie.

The Secretary of State was shattered, saying he was willing to re-sign if that was what the President wanted. "A laughingstock" was the way he described himself after Haldeman said, as he had been told to, that he had known nothing because arms control cut across all depart-mental lines; this had been handled at the highest level and it was essen-tial that no one take any credit for this except the President himself. By the time Haldeman returned to the White House, Rogers had called and asked for "the party line," wanting to know what to say to his depart-ment and to congressional leaders. The President returned that call, re-peating much of what Haldeman had said. When he hung up, Nixon spun his chair toward the windows looking out to the Rose Garden, sighed, and said, "This would be an easy job if you didn't have to deal with people."

Kissinger had to tell Smith that his agency and his negotiations had been a shadow play—a necessary one, he said. The Helsinki and Vi-enna meetings had had almost nothing to do with the agreement, which Smith believed was basically translated from the Russian. Literally. Throughout the negotiations, after all, the Soviets had wanted an ABM agreement, because they could never match American spending potential for the development and deployment of such a system, and the Ameri-cans had wanted limits on offensive weapon production and deployment to maintain United States missile superiority without beginning expen-sive new programs. Smith knew, as Kissinger did, that the Soviets were focusing most of their resources on building submarine missile systems and MIRVs, multiple independently targeted reentry vehicles—neither of which were mentioned in the 106-word breakthrough statement. The hu-miliated arms negotiator considered the "breakthrough" an agreement to continue talking—on Russian terms. But he took it and kept his mouth shut.

Rogers and Smith—and Defense Secretary Laird, who had been blindsided, too—sat with the President the next morning, mouthing the party line to a joint meeting of the Cabinet and congressional leaders.

Rogers, Smith, and Laird each spoke briefly before the President took over. At the end of an hour the President repeated that this was neither a treaty nor even a detailed plan, but it was a commitment that had been made at the highest level of the two governments. "Today," he concluded, "may be remembered as the beginning of a new era—an era in which nations can increasingly devote their energies and resources not to weapons of war but to works of peace."

The men in the room stood to applaud. Two hours later, the President went on national television to announce the agreement. In Moscow, the two paragraphs were read on the radio at the same hour.

Dictating his thoughts for a memo the next morning, the President laid out points he wanted "pounded home," including these three: "The deadlock was broken by an initiative taken by the President on his own. . . . The President is personally assuming responsibility for achieving the goal of an agreement this year. . . . This is by far the most important foreign policy achievement since the end of World War II."

Some of that was true, but some was not. Exactly a month before, at a Republican leadership meeting, the President had said: "We are engaged in difficult negotiations around the world, especially in the SALT talks. Some think the simplest thing we could do would be to negotiate only on ABM, but we must look at the whole picture. Let's analyze just where we are now in national strength. We are ahead in conventional power. We are roughly equal in air power. With regard to nuclear punch they have approximately 1,500 ICBMs—we have 1,000. They have bigger warheads or throw weight. By 1974 they will catch up to us in nuclear subs. We must negotiate on the broad picture."

That was then. Now there was a new party line.

Ten days later, on May 31, Ambassador Hilaly was in Kissinger's office with a cable from Yahya Khan, still the messenger of choice between Peking and Washington: "There is a very encouraging and positive response to the last message. . . . Level of meeting will be as proposed by you. Full message will be transmitted by safe means."

The next day, June 1, Nixon spent almost the entire day alone in EOB 175, preparing for a prime-time televised press conference scheduled for 8:30 P.M. That evening, most of the questions were about Vietnam, national drug policy, and police tactics during the Mayday confrontations in Washington. He was asked about whether he intended to visit Europe. No. Then would he visit Vietnam? No. The only question about China was whether the United States was reconsidering its opposition to United Nations membership for the People's Republic. He answered that the matter was under study, but that the study would not be completed for at least six weeks.

The full message from the Chinese, two sheets of paper hand-carried by Hilaly, arrived the next evening. A state dinner for President Anastasio Somoza Debayle of Nicaragua was just breaking up and Kissinger, flushed and out of breath, caught the President on his way to the residence. He handed the paper to Nixon, who read:

> Premier Chou En-lai has seriously studied President Nixon's messages . . . and has reported with much pleasure to Chairman Mao Tse-tung that President Nixon is prepared to accept his suggestion to visit Peking for direct conversations with the leaders of the People's Republic of China. Chairman Mao Tse-tung has indicated that he welcomes President Nixon's visit and looks forward to that occasion. . . .
>
> Premier Chou En-lai welcomes Dr. Kissinger to China as the U.S. representative who will come in advance for preliminary secret meeting. . . .

The word "secret" was the idea of the Americans, not the Chinese, who originally resisted the idea, fearing, as it were, that it meant that the Americans were ashamed to be seen with them. But in fact Nixon wanted to maximize the surprise at home when the visit was announced, and did not want other Americans, particularly Democratic leaders, to upstage him with earlier visits. He also did not like the idea that Kissinger would be in Peking before he was—even if secretly—and had tried to have the preliminary meeting in some other city, or even better, in Pakistan.

Kissinger was beaming. "This is the most important communication that has come to an American President since the end of World War II," he said. Nixon invited him upstairs to the Lincoln sitting room and went to the kitchen and found an unopened bottle of brandy, Courvoisier. He walked back with the bottle and two snifters for a victory toast. The two men talked for almost an hour, choosing July 9 to 11 for the Kissinger visit, to be masked in some way by his sneaking off while on a fact-finding mission to Asia. The fact-finding diversion was a problem in itself, because he had never traveled abroad alone as national security adviser; his earlier trips had always been planned and staffed by the State Department. Once again, the two of them began to plot some way to deceive Rogers—and most everybody else in the world.

Among those who knew nothing of the China plan was the Vice President. Three days later, Agnew called Haldeman and said he needed to see the President. The appointment was set up for 5 P.M. and Agnew came in and said he had a great idea. He was going to South Korea for the inauguration of a new president there and he, of course, planned to stop in Taiwan to see President Chiang Kai-shek. Then he thought he would go to the mainland, to Peking—like the Ping-Pong players. The President said no—no Peking and no Taiwan, either—without telling Agnew why. That weekend at Camp David, the President called in Haldeman and said he wanted him to have another conversation with John Connally about being vice president—"Ask him if he thinks we can pull it off."

ON SATURDAY, JUNE 12, the day of Tricia's wedding, the President, like any father of the bride, had been shunted aside, left to be nervous on his own. He was wandering around the White House in the morning and he ended up sitting down with Haldeman, ever the sounding board. Nixon said he was worried about what to do with Bill Rogers. The Secretary of State, he thought, had looked more than a little foolish during a dinner cruise on the *Sequoia* two nights before when he confronted Ehrlichman after the domestic chief said State Department officials had told him they favored economic sanctions on drug-producing countries like Turkey. "I don't believe that. Who said that?" Rogers asked angrily. Ehrlichman hesitated, then said, "Alex Johnson"—U. Alexis Johnson, the Undersecretary of State for Political Affairs, was the number-three man in Rogers's department.

Nixon kept looking out the window as he talked. It was raining. He knew Tricia wanted an outdoor wedding, but his wife and his younger daughter, Julie, were both pressing to move the ceremony indoors. Nixon wanted outdoors, too. There had been White House weddings before, but this would be the first outdoor ceremony in the history of the 171-year-old house. The commander in chief was in regular touch with the Air Force, which told him at 4:15 P.M. that there should be fifteen minutes of clear weather over the Washington area at 4:33 P.M. Taking orders from the bride, and ignoring a month of protocol decisions about who should sit where, he ordered military aides to wipe the seats and seat the crowd. He escorted his daughter down the South Portico stairway and into the Rose Garden, where she became Mrs. Edward Cox at 4:48 P.M., just as the misty rain began again. Fifty-nine million Americans watched the ceremony on television.

At the reception, the President danced with his wife, which he had never done in public during all his years in public life. There were those who said they had never seen him happier.

The next day's *New York Times* carried a deep two-column picture of the bride and her father at the top of the front page. Next to it was a three-column headline that read:

VIETNAM ARCHIVE: PENTAGON STUDY TRACES
3 DECADES OF GROWING U.S. INVOLVEMENT

The newspaper had been given a 2.5-million-word official history of United States involvement—titled "History of U.S. Decision-Making Process on Viet Nam Policy" and classified "Top Secret"—under four presidents from Eisenhower to Johnson. The Pentagon Papers included seven thousand pages of official documents. The story, by Neil Sheehan, began:

A massive study of how the United States went to war in Indochina, conducted by the Pentagon three years ago, demonstrates that four administrations progressively developed a sense of commitment to a non-Communist Viet Nam, a readiness to fight the North to protect the South, and an ultimate frustration with this effort—to a much greater extent than their public statements acknowledged at the time.

CHAPTER 20

June 30, 1971

T HE NAME RICHARD NIXON did not appear in the forty-three volumes of classified documents on Vietnam obtained by *The New York
Times*. The study and its attached compendium of cables and meeting
memoranda had been completed on January 15, 1969, five days before
his Inaugural. Looking over the *Times*'s second segment, headlined
"VIETNAM ARCHIVE: A CONSENSUS TO BOMB DEVELOPED BEFORE '64
ELECTION, STUDY SAYS," Nixon told Haldeman, "This is really tough
on Kennedy, McNamara, and Johnson.... Make sure we call them
the Kennedy-Johnson papers. But we need to keep clear of the *Times*'s series.... the key for us is to keep out of it."

"Top Secret" classification did not impress Nixon. He knew and
did not at all like the fact that hundreds of thousands of men and women
in and out of the government had clearance to see "Top Secret" documents—the best rough estimate was five hundred thousand people in the
Defense and State Departments and more than two hundred thousand
employees of defense contractors and suppliers. But he did think it was
criminal for someone to turn "Top Secret" documents over to the press
and that it would hurt his own war efforts, at least for a time, but probably do him more good than harm because it showed that the Democrats
had led the country into Vietnam. It was history, he said that day.

No one else seemed much concerned, either. Defense Secretary
Laird had been on NBC's *Meet the Press* that Sunday, June 13, and the

subject of the papers did not come up. He had heard about the *Times*'s plans on Saturday and had called Kissinger, who had been a consultant to the project. The project director was a former student of his at Harvard, Leslie Gelb, who had been deputy director of the Pentagon's Office of Policy Planning during the Johnson administration.

Nixon thought Gelb had given the report to the *Times*, particularly when he heard that he had joined the Brookings Institution after leaving the government in May 1969. Nixon could not have been more mistaken. Gelb had always worried that the papers would be destroyed, erasing evidence that might prove embarrassing to the men who made the war in the first place. There were only fifteen copies. Five were in Laird's safe at the Pentagon, and the Secretary occasionally referred to them for background on bombing decisions. There were copies at the Kennedy and Johnson presidential libraries. Seven had gone to former Johnson administration officials, including Robert S. McNamara and his successor as secretary of defense, Clark Clifford. Two copies, under the control of Gelb and Morton Halperin, who had quit Kissinger's staff to go to Brookings, were in safes of the RAND Corporation in Santa Monica. Nixon told Haldeman that it might have been someone on Kissinger's own staff, or just some group of "fucking Jews."

Kissinger thought at first that the leak consisted of a few pages and probably was done by Laird, his administration rival as a master of the care and feeding of the press. But when Laird told him there were seven thousand pages—sixty pounds of paper—Kissinger knew immediately it could have been only one man, Daniel Ellsberg. Kissinger's acquaintance with Ellsberg began in the 1950s, when Ellsberg was a doctoral candidate at Harvard. The professor invited the student to lecture on his thesis subject, "The Political Uses of Madness"—a thesis remarkably similar to Nixon's "madman theory." Ellsberg was a brilliant student who served as a Marine captain in Vietnam and then came back as a civilian assistant to General Edwin Lansdale, a famous CIA operative in both the Philippines and Vietnam, the model for a dashing or demented principal character in two best-selling novels, *The Ugly American*, by William Lederer and Eugene Burdick, and *The Quiet American*, by Graham Greene. Back home, Ellsberg worked briefly for Kissinger in the early days of the Nixon administration and then went on to RAND. By late in 1969, he was as zealously antiwar as a scholar as he had been prowar as a Marine. He had decided to try to copy the papers and find some way to make them public on the morning of September 30, 1969, when he saw, on the front page of the *Los Angeles Times*, that Army Secretary Stanley Resor had dropped charges against the six Green Berets charged in the killing of Thai Khac Chuyen, the supposed double agent whose body was dumped in the South China Sea. That was when Ellsberg telephoned his friend Anthony Russo, looking for a Xerox machine. Their night time copying took several weeks. Then Ellsberg spent months trying to persuade someone in Congress—he approached Senators Fulbright, McGovern, and Goodell—to make the papers public, thinking that doing it that way might get him congressional immunity. In February 1971 he approached *New York Times* reporter Neil Sheehan, whom he had first met in Vietnam.

Kissinger, who was in California that June weekend, called Nixon, talking for almost fifteen minutes and firing up the President: "It shows you're a weakling, Mr. President. . . . these leaks are slowly and systematically destroying us. . . . It could destroy our ability to conduct foreign policy. If other powers feel we cannot control internal leaks, they will not agree to secret negotiations."

Secrecy above all. China above all. Kissinger was supposedly on vacation, but in fact was preparing for his secret trip to Peking, scheduled for July 1. The national security adviser flew back to Washington on June 14. He asked Attorney General Mitchell to begin a study of possible criminal liability in the case, though he set no deadline on that project. After that he went to the Oval Office, and once again turned up the presidential rage. "The two of them are in a frenzy," Haldeman told Ehrlichman. At 7:30 P.M., Tuesday, June 15, Attorney General Mitchell called the *Times* and officially asked the newspaper to cease publication of the documents as a matter of national security. The *Times* refused—and the third segment of "Vietnam Archive" was on the streets under the headline "Study Tells How Johnson Secretly Opened Way to Ground Combat."

President Nixon now told Haldeman, once more, to cut off all contact with *The New York Times*. Warming to the subject the next morning, he talked about the *Times* and its Washington bureau chief, Max Frankel, adding conversationally: "Don't give them anything . . . because of that damned Jew Frankel all the time—he's bad. . . ."

Meanwhile, Assistant Attorney General Robert C. Mardian had ordered the United States attorney for the Southern District of New York to file for a court order temporarily restraining the *Times* from continuing publication of what people were beginning to call the Pentagon Papers. At 4:09 P.M. that day, June 15, the President was meeting with Mitchell on another matter when Ziegler came in to say that a federal district court judge in Manhattan, Murray Gurfein, had granted the restraining order to allow the government to consider espionage charges against the *Times* and persons unknown, the newspaper's source of the classified documents. The *Times* accepted the order. Its lawyers would argue against prior restraint but not publish until the judicial process was complete. The first argument in Judge Gurfein's court was set for Friday, June 18.

When Mitchell left, the President and Kissinger met with Soviet ambassador Dobrynin, who had come to deliver a proposal for a five-power nuclear conference, which would include the Americans, the Soviets, and the British, French, and Chinese. Nixon was not really interested and the subject turned almost inevitably to secrets and leaks. "The way our two governments can make the most progress is through the talks that you and Kissinger have been having," Nixon said. "They are completely confidential with nobody leaking. Your government has confidence in you; Kissinger has a special relationship with me. The real issue is the two-power relationship. . . . We will make a formal reply. Then you have a little talk with Henry Kissinger."

"What do you think of Soviet-American relations in general?" Dobrynin asked.

"We can make a breakthrough on SALT and Berlin, and then our whole postwar relations will be on a new basis," Nixon answered. "The press last week spoke of the failure of Berlin. You know better. We are at the point where we should make some agreement. If we culminate one, it will have a massive effect."

By Thursday, June 17, talk of the Pentagon Papers was consuming most of the President's time as one meeting after another broke down in attacks on the *Times* and speculation about the newspaper's source. When Daniel Ellsberg's name finally came up, Kissinger's response was savage: "He was always a little unbalanced. . . . drugs . . . sex . . . shot at peasants in Vietnam. . . . married a wealthy girl." Nixon listened, then offered, "Yeah, well, we don't know who the hell it is, but maybe it's him, or maybe it's Gelb, one of the two, either's a radical. Somebody's got to go to jail for that."

Haldeman was taken aback by Kissinger's vehemence. He thought the national security adviser was trying to protect himself, trying to divert Nixon from moving toward the conclusion that it had been Kissinger's men and friends, Halperin, Ellsberg, Gelb, and Anthony Lake, who had plotted to surface the classified documents.

The President was wondering whether there might be information in the papers that could be used for his own purposes. Was there anything in there that tied President Kennedy to the killing of South Vietnamese president Ngo Dinh Diem during a coup in Saigon on November 2, 1963? "I want that out," he told Colson. "I said that he was murdered. . . . I know what those bastards were up to." Was there anything that showed that President Johnson's bombing halt just before the

1968 election was just a political ploy to try to stop Nixon from winning?

"You can blackmail Johnson on this stuff and it might be worth doing," Haldeman said. Then Nixon asked Haldeman and Kissinger, not for the first time, why they could never come up with something on that halt. "Goddammit, I asked for it. . . . I said I needed it. . . ."

"Bob and I have been trying to put the thing together for three years," Kissinger said. "We have nothing here, Mr. President."

". . . But there is a file on it," Haldeman said.

"Where?" Nixon asked.

"Huston swears to God there's a file on it at Brookings," Haldeman replied.

Nixon sat up. "Now if you remember Huston's plan . . ."

"Yeah, why?" Haldeman said.

Kissinger said: "But couldn't we go over? Now, Brookings has no right to classified—"

The President cut him off, saying, "I want it implemented. . . . Goddammit get in there and get those files. Blow the safe and get them."

The President also had an idea for the Pentagon Papers and the courts. He would argue the case himself when it reached the Supreme Court. But the biggest action the next day, June 18, was not in the courts of Manhattan but on press in Washington. *The Washington Post* had obtained part of the papers and published them under the headline "Documents Reveal U.S. Effort in '54 to Delay Viet Election." Ten hours later, government attorneys in Judge Gurfein's courtroom were shocked when *New York Times* attorneys announced what had happened at midnight in Washington and asked whether the Justice Department intended to take legal action to block future publication by the *Post*. After a few minutes, the answer came back: "Yes."

The next afternoon, Gurfein, a Nixon appointee who had called the *Times* "unpatriotic" during arguments, shocked government lawyers by ruling that he was dissolving the temporary restraining order. He surprised both sides with his passion when he said, "The security of the Nation is not at the ramparts alone. Security also lies in the value of our free institutions. A cantankerous press, an obstinate press, a ubiquitous press must be suffered by those in authority in order to preserve the even greater values of freedom of expression and the right of the people to know. . . ."

The government appealed in New York. And in Washington, the Justice Department asked for a restraining order against the *Post*. That was denied by Judge Gerhard Gesell, another Republican, who said the government had provided no evidence of why the reports were a danger to national security. Gesell was overruled hours later by a three-judge panel of the Court of Appeals. But by then the *Post* had printed its second installment and distributed it to the 345 newspapers that subscribed to its national news service.

On June 21, in Washington, and June 22, in New York, federal appeals panels found for the government and remanded the cases to the original judges to hear more evidence. But that day *The Boston Globe* published excerpts from the papers. Day after day there were new publications of papers, in the *Los Angeles Times, The Philadelphia Inquirer,* the *Chicago Sun Times,* the *Detroit Free Press, The Miami Herald, The Christian Science Monitor,* the *St. Louis Post-Dispatch.* The government, seeking one injunction after another, was being surrounded. Ellsberg was traveling from town to town, secretly peddling the news. The FBI could not find him, even when he was interviewed by Walter Cronkite for an hour on *The CBS Evening News* and on a prime-time special on June 23.

That same day the President invited Senate Majority Leader Mike Mansfield to the White House for breakfast and threats. A day earlier, the Senate had voted 57 to 42 for a Mansfield amendment to the Selective Service reorganization bill which required the withdrawal of all American troops from Vietnam within nine months if American prisoners of war were released. Nixon said he was in the middle of negotiations on Vietnam and on arms control and by the end of the month he would know whether those talks were ruined by congressional action. If they collapsed, he intended to go on television and blame Congress generally and Mansfield specifically. He would also begin massive bombing. Later in the day, he warned Speaker of the House Carl Albert that if the House passed a similar resolution, he would call home Ambassador Bruce from the Paris negotiations with the Vietnamese—the "public" negotiations—and put the blame on Congress.

In the Oval Office after the congressional meetings, the subject turned back to the Pentagon Papers and then drifted on to gossip, with Haldeman taking notes: "K has reported to him that Teddy Kennedy is now in the position of practically being a total animal. At the opening of the Kennedy Center, he went to work on Christina Ford, whom he had also propositioned at the Carlyle. . . . He walked up to her door, said he wanted to screw her, and she said that they couldn't because of the press, and he said the press will never touch me. He pulled the same thing on Edgar Bergen's daughter. . . . So we need to take advantage of this opportunity and get him in a compromising situation if we can."

In the days of waiting for court rulings on the Pentagon Papers, Nixon and Kissinger spent hour after hour talking about Kissinger's solo world trip, which would begin on July 1 and would take him secretly to Peking to make plans for a Nixon trip in 1972. Nixon said a presidential trip to Peking would be the greatest piece of history since World War II. No, no, said Kissinger, since the Civil War. The President told him it was critical to get a guarantee from Premier Chou En-lai that no Democrat would be invited to China before the President's trip. But there was still a Rogers problem: how to tell the Secretary of State just enough—true and untrue—so that he would not speak out when he discovered he had been lied to so systematically. They came up with another lie, saying the Chinese were afraid to deal secretly with the State Department, especially after the publication of the Pentagon Papers.

At noon on June 24, subject to an eighth day of temporary restraining orders as arguments continued in courtrooms in both New York and Washington, *The New York Times* appealed directly to the United States Supreme Court to resume publication of the Pentagon Papers. Nixon expected the court to rule against the government, and there was nothing he could do about it except yell at people—his own people. At 10 A.M. on June 28, with the cracks and booms of a summer thunderstorm as background, he read the riot act to a meeting of his economic advisers, including Connally, Shultz, and Stans. But the subject was not the economy, it was talking about the economy to the press. He asked Haldeman and Kissinger to attend. Haldeman took notes: "The decisions on the economy are final; we will not have a wage-price board. We will have jawboning, but his way. . . . There must be one voice. . . . There will be no more of this crap. There must be a united front. . . . We have a plan, we will follow it. . . . No guidance is to be provided to the press. . . . If you can't go along with the administration decision, then get out. . . ."

Then Nixon stood up, turned his back, and walked out. Haldeman kept writing: "Henry was ecstatic afterwards and made the comment that it was one of the great moments here."

At a full Cabinet meeting the next morning, the chatter over coffee was about Ellsberg, who had surrendered to federal authorities in Boston, admitting he had given the Pentagon Papers to *The Times* and then to a dozen other newspapers. Then the President came in to continue his lecturing of the day before on loyalty and secrecy, saying angrily: "From now on, Haldeman is the lord high executioner. Don't come whining to me when he tells you to do something. . . . you're to carry it out. . . . We've checked and found out that 96 percent of the bureaucracy are against us; they're bastards and they're here to screw us. . . . You've got to realize that the press aren't interested in liking you; they're only interested in news or in screwing me. . . . I get a lot of advice on PR and personality and how I've got to put on my nice-guy hat at the White House, so I did it, but let me make clear that's not my nature. We're going to go forward on Ellsberg and prosecute him. . . .

"Haldeman has the worst job that anybody can have in the White

House. I remember poor old Bedell Smith"—President Eisenhower's chief of staff—"who had to carry out a lot of tough decisions for Eisenhower. In his later years, he started to drink a lot, probably to try and forget the things he had to do in his early years. He was at my house one night, and he started to cry and he said, 'All my life I've been Ike's prat boy, doing his dirty work.' Well, Haldeman is my prat boy; he'll be down the throat of anyone here regarding leaks if they affect the national interest. . . ."

Then, again, he stood up, turned his back, and walked out.

On June 30, at 2:30 P.M., the Supreme Court ruled in favor of the press by a 6-to-3 vote. The majority opinion stated: "Any system of prior restraints of expression comes to this Court bearing a heavy presumption against its constitutional validity. . . . The Government thus bears a heavy burden of showing justification for the enforcement of such a restraint. . . ."

The President was in the Oval Office with Colson when he heard of the decision. He began a countdown of the people he blamed, calling Justice Potter Stewart, an Eisenhower appointee, "a weak bastard . . . overwhelmed by the Washington-Georgetown social set." He told Colson: "We've got a counter-government here and we've got to fight it. I don't give a damn how it is done. Do whatever has to be done to stop these leaks. . . . I don't want to be told why it can't be done. This government cannot survive, it cannot function if anyone can run out and leak. I want to know who is behind this. . . ."

Nixon called in Mitchell, Kissinger, and Haldeman. As he had been doing on and off for days, he compared Ellsberg to Alger Hiss, the State Department official imprisoned for perjury after investigations driven by a young congressman named Richard Nixon.

"Don't worry about his trial," the President said of Ellsberg. "Just get everything out. Try him in the press. Try him in the press. . . . leak it out. We want to destroy him in the press. Press. Is that clear? . . . I want somebody to take it just like I took the Hiss case. . . . This takes— this takes eighteen hours a day. It takes devotion and dedication and loyalty and diligence such as you've never seen, Bob. I've never worked as hard in my life and I'll never work as hard again because I don't have the energy. But this thing is a hell of a great opportunity because here is what it is. . . . We won the Hiss case in the papers. We did. I had to leak stuff all over the place. Because the Justice Department would not prosecute it. Hoover didn't even cooperate. . . . It was won in the papers. . . . I leaked out the papers. I leaked everything. . . . I leaked out the testimony. I had Hiss convicted before he ever got to the grand jury. . . . Go back and read the chapter on the Hiss case in *Six Crises* and you'll see how it was done.

It wasn't done waiting for the goddamn courts or the attorney general or the FBI. . . ."

Brookings was the next thing on his mind. Again he talked about breaking into the place: "They have a lot of material. . . . I want Brookings, I want them just to break in and take it out. Do you understand?"

"Yeah," Haldeman said. "But you have to have somebody to do it."

"That's what I'm talking about," Nixon said. "Don't discuss it here. You talk to Hunt."

"Hunt" was E. Howard Hunt, who had retired as a CIA operations officer two months before, and was doing some investigative work for Colson. "Helms says he's ruthless, quiet, careful," Haldeman told the President. Colson added: "He's kind of a tiger. . . . He spent twenty years in the CIA overthrowing governments."

The President said: "I want the break-in. Hell, they do that. You're to break into the place, rifle the files, and bring them in. . . . Just go in and take it. Go in around eight or nine o'clock. . . .

"Clean it up. These kids don't understand. They have no understanding of politics. They have no understanding of public relations. John Mitchell is that way. John is always worried about is it technically correct? Do you think, for Christ sakes, that *The New York Times* is worried about all the legal niceties? Those sons of bitches are killing me. . . . We're up against an enemy, a conspiracy. They're using any means. *We are going to use any means.* Is that clear?"

The next day, Nixon asked Haldeman: "Did they get the Brookings Institute raided last night? Get it done. I want it done. I want the Brookings Institute's safe *cleaned out.* . . ."

CHAPTER 21

August 12, 1971

O N THE DAY before the Supreme Court ruling on the Pentagon Papers case, the President met with members of another of the new bodies he had created to try to shift decision making from the departments and bureaucracies of the executive branch to the White House itself. This one, the National Productivity Commission, was a mix of his own staff and business and labor leaders. The agenda of the commission reflected the broad ideas of John Connally and, to a lesser extent, of another new recruit, Peter Peterson, who left his job as president of Bell and Howell, a Chicago manufacturer of camera equipment, to become the first director of still another White House creation, the Council for International Economic Policy. Connally and Peterson were cut from different cloth— Peterson was a promising scholar turned innovative businessman—but both had the gift of packaging economic issues in Nixonian strategic and political terms. And both had spotted the challenge and opportunity of a new American problem: the trade deficit.

In April, Peterson had reached Nixon with a confidential report asserting that the United States was losing its position as the dominant world trader. Peterson's charts showed that although United States exports had increased by 110 percent since 1964, West Germany's had increased by 200 percent and Japan's by more than 400 percent. Half of the new television sets and sewing machines sold in America were being made overseas, Peterson told Nixon. So were 70 percent of the radios and 100 percent of the 35-millimeter cameras. In Los Angeles, 20 percent of new automobile sales were of cars made in Japan, but only 0.1 percent of Japanese buyers bought American cars. "Japan Inc.," as Peterson called it, had a $3 billion trade surplus with the United States. He told the President that by the end of 1971 Americans would have spent more money buying foreign goods and commodities than foreigners spent buying American products—the first American trade deficit since 1893.

Peterson handled the research, Connally closed the sale. The Secretary of the Treasury had a simple and direct view of the situation, telling one of his assistants, "My philosophy is that all foreigners are out to screw us, and it's our job to screw them first."

"The Japanese are still fighting the war, only now instead of a shooting war, it is an economic war . . . ," Connally told the President. "They have built up tariff arrangements, they have built up trade restrictions against U.S. goods . . . and they expect us to like it. . . . The people themselves, frankly, are more industrious than we are, and they work harder than we do. . . . The simple fact is that in many areas other nations are out-producing us, out-thinking us and out-trading us."

Nixon's response, in private, was as direct as Connally's challenge: "We'll fix those bastards." He cleaned up his language for the first meeting of the Productivity Commission on June 29. Before beginning, he asked Jerome Rosow, an assistant secretary of labor, why he was leaving the administration to go back to work in New York City for Standard Oil of New Jersey.

"They're doubling my salary," Rosow replied.

"Not enough," said the President. "They could never pay me enough to live in that jungle of Manhattan again."

Then Nixon began a monologue, the economic version of his polished tours of the world's political and diplomatic horizons. He paused, leaned on his elbows, put his head in his hands, and spoke with his eyes closed:

> Without putting it in too melodramatic terms, let me tell you what the world will look like in five or ten years. After World War II, our position was this: We produced 50 percent of the world's steel. The American economy position was so dominant we were concerned about the dollar gap. The Soviet Union was prostrated. Western Europe had had it. Japan was a defeated nation. . . . Then I remember a visit I had in Latin America in 1958 with the President of Colombia. He took me to his house, a humble home, and said, "The problem is like a great poker game. The rest of the world can't play. You must give chips to others around the table so they can play."
>
> Now here we are a generation later where for the second

month in a row, the United States of America has had an unfavorable balance of trade. This doesn't mean we have to paint our tails white and run with the antelopes. It does mean that a strong, free labor movement—and a strong management movement—must work together, with government, to build the kind of economy that can compete in today's world.

Nixon was in his element, engaged in economic policy as foreign policy:

> Look to the future. There you have Western Europe, with Britain in the Common Market. Three hundred million people, people like us—we will see all those nations as tough competitors. . . . Then look at the Soviet Union and China. We're entering a new phase of relations. Agreements may come—in SALT, in mutual troop reductions, to the point that we may reach a live-and-let-live detente. This is not because the Russian people and the American people are finally going to understand each other—but the danger of not getting along is just too great for both of us to accept. . . . Put yourself in the position of the man in the Kremlin. He knows that if I push the button, I will kill 70 million Americans and 80 million Russians, and if he pushes the button, he will kill 80 million Americans and 70 million Russians. . . .
> Turn to China: You might say, "Boy, 800 million people, what a wonderful market." Of course that is not true at this point. In the future, the U.S. and China will be competitors—so will China and the Soviet Union. Five to ten years from now, China, in spite of the Communist system, will be a major economic force in the world. You cannot take 800 million Chinese, even putting them in slave camps, without having them amount to something. And as detente develops, economic competition increases.
> Take Japan—they're knocking us out of the box with textiles and transistor radios. . . . Japan is an economic giant and a military pygmy.
> . . . Now the U.S. looks at low labor rates around the world and its immediate reaction is, "Boy, we better put up some quotas." Congressional pressure along these lines is enormous. But the U.S. cannot build a fence around itself and expect to survive as a great nation. . . . This morning, in the Cabinet meeting, Secretary Rogers saw a period of five to ten years from now when 75 percent of our foreign policy would be economics. We either have to come to the mark, or we will be number two economically.

Then he got to the bottom line, as he saw it:

It's terribly important we be number one economically because otherwise we can't be number one diplomatically or militarily. You hear a lot of stuff around that the U.S. is not to be trusted with power. You hear that our Presidents lie us into wars. You hear that the U.S. is imperialistic and aggressive. But we build up our enemies after wars, and we ask for not one acre. What will we get for ourselves out of Vietnam? Nothing.

If we retreat from the world scene, who's left? With all our stupidity, with all our impetuousness, what other nation in the world is more idealistic than the United States? . . . For the next quarter century, let us see to it that we do play this role. . . . The future of the economy is in our hands—and also the future of peace.

One of Peterson's charts asserted graphically that every $1 billion increase in American exports produced sixty thousand to eighty thousand new jobs at home—a figure many economists considered ridiculous. But it was also a number a politician could hardly resist, particularly with Connally telling Nixon he could diminish organized labor's enthusiasm for Democratic candidates in 1972 by showing that what he really cared about was American jobs.

On July 3, the Bureau of Labor Statistics announced one of the largest drops ever recorded in monthly unemployment numbers, from 6.2 percent to 5.6 percent. But *The New York Times*—under the headline "JOBLESS RATE OFF SHARPLY, BUT DOUBT IS CAST ON DATA"—reported it this way: "The nation's unemployment rate dropped substantially in June but part of the reason was a statistical aberration, the Labor Department reported. . . ." In the third paragraph, the story quoted Harold Goldstein, the assistant commissioner of labor statistics, saying that the rate would go up again when high school and college students came home looking for summer work.

Nixon's reaction was explosive: "That little Jew cocksucker is the same guy who screwed us in the Eisenhower administration. . . . He's a radical left-winger who hates us." He took off from there, telling Haldeman and Colson, not for the first time: "Washington is full of Jews. . . . Most Jews are disloyal"—he excepted Kissinger, Safire, and Leonard Garment—"Bob, generally speaking, you can't trust the bastards. They turn on you. Am I wrong or right?"

Haldeman said, not for the first time, he was right. Colson added: "You just have to go down the goddamned list and you know they are out to kill us." The result was a transfer of Goldstein, a civil service employee, and a presidential order to a White House staffer named Frederick Malek to find out how many Jews were in the bureau. Malek's answer came back in a memo: "Thirteen of the 35 fit the demographic criterion which was discussed."

As the President flew to San Clemente on July 6, newspapers ran short dispatches from Saigon, reporting that Kissinger had been there for two days of meetings, part of an Asian fact-finding trip. His next stop was Bangkok, Thailand, and then he flew on to Islamabad, Pakistan, supposedly to discuss Yahya Khan's bloody attempt to subdue East Pakistan. On July 7, Yahya surprised Kissinger with the news that he had received the invitation from Chou En-lai; the American could leave secretly for China in a few hours. The official story would be that Kissinger had been taken ill—a "stomachache." *The New York Times* thought that was worth one paragraph in its "Notes on People" column: "Fleeing the hot, humid air of the plains around Rawalpindi, Henry A. Kissinger, President Nixon's national security adviser, spent the day at Nathia Gali in the cool hills of northern Pakistan. He was described as feeling 'slightly indisposed.' "

The President called in Rogers to tell him what was happening, once again using the "sudden . . . surprise" story. The Secretary of State did not seem angry—as long as he would not be embarrassed in public— so Nixon set up a meeting between Rogers and Haig so he could tell him, for the first time, about Kissinger's secret negotiations with the North Vietnamese in Paris. When Rogers left, Bryce Harlow came in with more news Nixon wanted to hear. He said he had talked with Agnew and thought there was a three-in-four chance that the Vice President would agree to step down in 1972 and say that he wanted to return to the private sector—and become a rich man. That sounded good to Nixon. Agnew could not be pushed out, he thought, because the party's conservatives might react by uniting around Ronald Reagan—and try to push the President out.

On July 11, the President was handed a coded cable from Kissinger in Tehran, Iran. The message was, "Eureka." Nixon was going to China.

To maintain the extraordinary secrecy, Kissinger, code-named "Polo," had cabled the President on a secure CIA line. But more people knew what was happening than either the President or his emissary knew. One of the National Security Council staffers on the Asian trip was Navy yeoman Charles Radford, the spy planted by the Joint Chiefs. The sailor, officially a stenographer, had been copying NSC documents and Kissinger's memos for ten months, making an extra copy of most everything that went to a Xerox machine, working at night and searching burn bags, sending White House paper to the Pentagon each morning. After Kissinger returned to Islamabad, Radford went through his room and briefcases, finding and taking notes on the first draft of the adviser's long report to the President, which began:

> We have laid the ground for you and Mao to turn a page in history. . . . They will be tough before and during the summit on the question of Taiwan and other major issues. My assessment of these people is that they are deeply ideological, close to fanatic in the intensity of their beliefs. . . . The process we have now started will send enormous shock waves around the world. . . . With the Soviet Union we will have to make clear the continued priorities we attach to our concrete negotiations with them. Just as we will not collude with them against China, so we have no intention of colluding with China against them. . . . If we can master this process, we will have made a revolution.

The President was waiting on the helicopter pad when Kissinger touched down at El Toro Marine Corps Air Station near San Clemente at 7 A.M. on Tuesday, July 13. At the President's house the two men went over each of the 109 words in the communiqué Kissinger and Chou had worked out. There was no mention of issues in the document, but with the President interrogating him on every detail down to facial expressions, Kissinger said that only when he assured Chou that the United States would never support independence for Taiwan—as Chou was torturing him by saying he had a stack of invitation requests on his desk from other American politicians—did the Premier finally smile and say, "Good, these talks may now proceed." *

The President asked for time on the three networks at 10:30 P.M., Eastern Standard Time, on July 15, taking a helicopter from San Clemente to the NBC studios in Burbank. He began: "I have requested this television time tonight to announce a major development in our efforts to build a lasting peace in the world. . . . In pursuance of that goal, I sent Dr. Kissinger. . . ."

His introduction lasted only a minute or so, and then he read:

> Premier Chou En-lai and Dr. Henry Kissinger, President Nixon's Assistant for National Security Affairs, held talks in

---

* The Taiwan commitment was never made public. In his 1977 memoirs Kissinger avoided the subject in a single misleading sentence: "Taiwan was mentioned only briefly during the first session." After the transcripts of those conversations were released in February 2002, he conceded: "It's possible I didn't give a full accounting of everything."

Peking from July 9 to July 11, 1971. Knowing of President Nixon's expressed desire to visit the People's Republic of China, Premier Chou En-lai, on behalf of the Government of the People's Republic of China, has extended an invitation to President Nixon to visit China at an appropriate date before May 1972. President Nixon has accepted the invitation with pleasure. The meeting between the leaders is to seek the normalization of relations between the two countries. . . .

The President closed by saying, "It is in this spirit that I will undertake what I deeply hope will become a journey for peace. . . ."

"I'm flabbergasted," was the reaction of Senate Majority Leader Mike Mansfield. So was most everyone else. The *New York Post*'s Max Lerner wrote: "The politics of surprise leads through the Gates of Astonishment into the Kingdom of Hope." When the President and Kissinger briefed Senate leaders of both parties, John Stennis of Mississippi stood to say, "The President has made a good move. . . . I'm going to support him." Then Mansfield stood and said, "We're moving out of an old era to a new one. . . . As for me, I'll follow the Stennis line." An antiwar Republican congressman from California, Paul "Pete" McCloskey, had chosen that day to announce that he planned to run against Nixon in the 1972 Republican primaries, but he was ignored as the tide of China news swept through Washington.

Nixon and Kissinger did briefings all day long. The President would begin by saying China was ready to end its isolation, but secrecy was the key to this opening. Then they would take questions. During the briefing of White House staff, Paul McCracken, the chairman of the Council of Economic Advisers, asked: "What was your impression of their interest in politics as opposed to economics?"

Kissinger replied: "Their interest is one hundred percent political. . . . Even as we arrived at the airport, one of them commented to me, 'We are being overwhelmed by your businessmen. In due time, we'll do business, but in our own time.' . . . This generation didn't fight for fifty years and go on the Long March for trade."

That was too much for George Shultz, who said, "In Marxist theory, economics is paramount and all else is superstructure."

"In Marxist practice, politics is paramount," Kissinger retorted, as if the two of them were at a faculty meeting.

"Then this is ideological impurity," countered Shultz.

The next day, July 20, the President called Haldeman in for a progress report on a pet project, the political jawboning of television executives. Haldeman began with a couple of memos from Colson summarizing White House meetings with the president of CBS, Frank Stanton, and the president of NBC, Julian B. Goodman. Nixon laughed when he heard that Stanton was accompanied by his new Washington counsel, Alexander Lankler, who happened to be the Republican state chairman of Maryland and who happened to have been suggested by the President himself in an earlier meeting with CBS chairman William S. Paley.

Colson's memo of the meeting began: "Stanton . . . was contrite, apologetic, almost obsequious. There was none of the typical explosive arrogance. . . . I proceeded to point out recent illustrations of CBS 'screwing us.' " The CBS boss, said Colson, began to agree with him, talking about the "bad journalism . . . dishonest journalism" of the network's stars, naming two, Roger Mudd and Robert Pierpoint. "The upshot of the hour-and-a-half discussion," said Colson, who may have been exaggerating some, "was that Stanton has promised that he is taking steps to try to straighten out the acknowledged CBS News bias against the Administration; that he will report to me on the steps he has taken. . . ."

Attached to those notes was Colson's account of a meeting between the President and Goodman on June 9:

> The President, very quietly smiling and looking very calm, explained that he understood fully that most of the commentators and the reporters were biased, that their bias was quite obvious, but that this didn't bother him a bit. . . . This seemed to stun Goodman. . . . The President said: "Most of my staff have come to me from time to time and said why don't you call Stanton or Paley or Sarnoff . . . ? I told my staff that it won't do any good. They only own the networks but they can't control what the newsmen or commentators do and they can't change their bias." Goodman, with his hand visibly trembling said, "I'm very sorry you feel that way, Mr. President; we try very hard to be objective and professional. . . ." Goodman used the word "repression." The President laughed very loudly. . . . The President said, "When you look at Brinkley, Chancellor and others, they hardly look like they are repressed. . . . You don't feel repressed, do you, Julian?"

Back to China planning, the President, as happy as he had ever been, dictated a detailed memo to Kissinger about press briefings, saying: "One effective line you could use in your talks with the press is how RN . . . has similar character characteristics and background as Chou. . . . (1) Strong convictions; (2) Came up through adversity; (3) At his best in a crisis; (4) . . . Tough, bold, willing to take chances . . . (5) A man who takes the long view . . . (6) . . . A philosophical turn of mind; (7) A man who works without notes—in meetings with 73 heads of state and heads of government . . . (8) A man who knows Asia . . . (9) Steely but who is subtle and appears almost gentle. . . . You could subtly get this across by describing Chou En-lai and go into how RN's personal characteristics are somewhat similar."

ON THE HOME FRONT, which was the election front, the President met with Connally and Shultz to chart a political strategy on dealing with organized labor. The subject triggered a monologue on the President's own brand of populism: "Two-thirds of our society are working people, the other one-third is the so-called governing elite, editors, business leaders, academicians, etc. . . . The working two-thirds offer their backs and their brawn; these are the people who really stand up for their country in its times of need and give the country its great strength. . . . The elite have been showing signs of decadence and weakness; the more people who are educated the more likely we are to become brighter in the head but weaker in the spine. . . . The thing I despise most is the new arrogance of the young. . . ."

He told them, again, one of his favorite stories, about a father and son on a White House reception line, saying: "The boy was a graduate of one of our better Eastern colleges. The father was a working man. . . . I could tell as he spoke briefly to me that he had not had the benefit of a college education, or even of a high school education. . . . As I spoke to him, I saw the boy standing there, embarrassed. The boy was ashamed of his father. . . . I was ashamed of the son. My father grew up in a very poor family. He quit school in the sixth grade because his mother died three years earlier. He worked, when we were growing up, as a carpenter, as an oilfield worker, as a streetcar motorman, as a grocer, and as a service station operator. He raised five boys, and every one of them got a better education than he did, because of how he worked. . . . I was proud of him to the day he died."

Ehrlichman came in alone that afternoon with a progress report on finding a team to hunt leaks and investigate Ellsberg. Taking time off from his duties as the White House chief of domestic policy, he said he had created the Special Investigations Unit the President wanted to handle secret business, which was often illegal business that the FBI and CIA were refusing to do without written presidential orders. The first candidate for the job, Buchanan, refused it. Then Ehrlichman rejected Colson's candidate, E. Howard Hunt—although the former CIA man was given an office in the Executive Office Building and a $100-a-day stipend. Instead Ehrlichman chose his protégé, Bud Krogh, and Kissinger's former personal assistant, a thirty-two-year-old New York lawyer named David Young, as the "Special Investigations Unit." Their first job was investigating Daniel Ellsberg in particular and leaks in general. Ehrlichman jammed the two of them into a small office, room 16, in the basement of the White House—along with a three-combination safe and "sterilized" telephones. Their papers were to be stamped with the classification "ODESSA," but the young leak-stoppers immediately got a new name, "the Plumbers," when Young, whose grandfather had been a plumber, put a sign on the door: "D. YOUNG—PLUMBER." Their first hire, on July 19, at twenty-six thousand dollars a year, was G. Gordon Liddy, a former FBI agent and former prosecutor in Dutchess County, New York. By most accounts, Liddy was a wild man who was being pushed out of a Treasury Department job because he had given a speech to the National Rifle Association attacking administration gun control policy.

Code names and security classifications had become an obsession in the Oval Office. So were lie detectors; the President wanted a program of regular polygraph tests for officials with access to national security documents of any kind. One of Krogh and Young's first assignments was to track the leak of United States proposals and fallback positions in the SALT talks published July 23, under the byline of William Beecher, in *The New York Times*. The leak-busters pointed to William Van Cleave, special assistant to the assistant secretary of defense for international security affairs.

"He spent two hours with Beecher apparently this week," Krogh reported to the President. "He had access to the document. He apparently had views very similar to those which were reflected in the Beecher article. . . ."

"I don't care if he's a hawk or a dove," said Nixon. "If the son-of-a-bitch leaked, he's not for the government. . . ."

Then Nixon, Krogh, and Ehrlichman got into a round-robin about classification.

"Don't use 'Top Secret' for me ever again. I never want to see 'Top Secret' in this goddamn office," the President began.

"We used 'Presidential Document' before," said Krogh.

"How about 'Privilege'?" said Ehrlichman.

" 'Privilege' is, is not strong," said the President.

"Too soft. Too soft," said Ehrlichman.

On July 25, Apollo 15, another mission to the moon, lifted off from Cape Kennedy at 9:34 A.M. The President watched from the White House, or so it said in the newspapers. But in his diary that night, Haldeman wrote: "The Apollo shot was this morning; the P slept through it, but we, of course, put out an announcement that he had watched it with great interest." The day before, the chief of staff had made note of a presidential comment during a discussion of intelligence gathering: "The CIA tells me nothing I don't read three days earlier in *The New York Times*."

Two days after the Apollo shot, Vice President Agnew returned from his thirty-two-day around-the-world trip. It had not been a triumph. In Madrid, he attacked American black leaders, mentioning no names, as men producing nothing but complaints and recriminations, while for African leaders—"dedicated, enlightened, dynamic and extremely apt for the task that faces them"—he mentioned three names, Haile Selassie of Ethiopia, Joseph Mobutu of the Congo, and Jomo Kenyatta of Kenya. He did not mention that in Kenya, when a waiter spilled soup three places away from Agnew at a state dinner, Kenyatta leaped to his feet and beat the man to the floor with his golden-headed fly whisk.

ON AUGUST 4, the President called a no-cameras press conference in the Oval Office. Reporters asked questions about China, Vietnam, and continuing conflict in East Pakistan, but most of the time was taken up by a series of seven questions on the economy. His answers, taken together, seemed to soften considerably the all-out opposition to controls that he had asserted since his days at the Office of Price Administration in 1942. When, in August 1970, Congress had passed legislation giving the President authority to temporarily freeze prices, wages, and rents, as had been done in wartime, Nixon said he would never use that power.

This day, however, he was saying the same things he had always said, except for one new word, "permanent," saying: "Permanent wage and price controls in America would stifle the American economy, its dynamism, its productivity, and would be, I think, a mortal blow to the United States as a first-class economy. . . ." The President, it seems, was finally paying attention at home. In a *Harper's* article, published that week, former Nixon speechwriter Richard Whalen wrote: "So-called game plan economics has severely taxed the voters' patience by its s-l-o-w motion progress from intended recession to anticipated recovery. Unless the flush but frightened consumer begins to spend freely . . . he won't have much chance to be re-elected."

The next day, August 5, the Bureau of Labor Statistics reported that the wholesale price index had jumped 0.7 percent in July—the highest monthly increase since 1965. The bureau pegged unemployment at 5.5 percent, which, seasonally adjusted, was reported as a slight monthly increase. Then the Joint Economic Subcommittee on International Exchange and Payments issued a report stating that the dollar was overvalued in relation to foreign currencies: "A significant decrease in the exchange value of the dollar would stimulate exports, raise the price of imports, retard United States investment abroad and attract foreign investment in the stock and bond markets and American firms." The Treasury Department immediately attacked the report, stating that it was a misreading of economic data.

But that was a cover story. Treasury Secretary Connally had privately handed the President a plan he called "the big play." Nixon, in fact, had called the play—he liked to use football metaphors, saying he was the coach and Connally the quarterback—partly because he had been surprised when he had called in Republican congressional leaders to talk about China and all they had wanted to talk about were bad economic numbers. Then came bad poll numbers. The Harris poll was reporting a 73 percent negative on his handling of the economy. Gallup was reporting that a majority of Americans favored mandatory wage and price controls.

The problems of Coach Nixon and his flashy quarterback had been building for years, at home and abroad. The world had changed since 1944, when the United States and its World War II allies had created a new economic order of free trade and stable currencies based on the constant value of the dollar—backed up by tons of gold stored in vaults at Fort Knox, Kentucky. The gold there, valued at $35 an ounce, was worth more than $25 billion at the end of the war. Under the Bretton Woods Accords—named for a town in New Hampshire where the new order was created at a conference of finance ministers and bankers—governments, central banks, corporations, and individuals could exchange paper dollars for some of that gold at Fort Knox. Few did. The gold was there as symbolic proof of the backing of American wealth and constancy. The fixed price of gold meant rigid exchange rates for world currencies. The dollar was "good as gold"—even if only 25 percent of paper dollars were actually backed by gold bars. The idea was to prevent the kind of currency speculation, protectionism, and trade wars that preceded World War II.

That system had worked for a long time. World acceptance of United States domination of production and trade was a fact of life from 1944 until the 1960s. For the better part of the decade after World War II, Americans were living better than ever—better housed, clothed, and fed, with extra money for automobiles and even travel abroad—while Europeans and the Japanese were chilled and often hungry amid the ruins of their countries. Strains in the American order began to surface as West Europeans and Asians became capable once again of producing high-quality goods to challenge American models—with an advantage. Their labor costs were lower and the new and rebuilt factories in Japan and West Germany were more efficient than older American plants. So, a Japanese car, say a Toyota, could be sold for hundreds of dollars less than a Detroit-built Chevrolet. In 1966, the Japanese had sold sixty-six thousand cars in the United States; by the end of 1970, that number had reached seven hundred thousand. The same was true of textiles and shoes from all over the world. International trade was booming, but that meant job losses or lower job growth in Pittsburgh steel mills, Detroit auto plants, and New Hampshire shoe factories. And money that might have been invested in modernization at home was spilling into the ground of Vietnam.

So, by 1971, there was only $10.5 billion worth of gold in Fort Knox and foreign governments held $40 billion in dollar reserves. Foreign corporations, growing rich in the American market, and individuals held another $30 billion. By August, there was real fear of a run on the dollar—or on the gold that was the symbol of the American money machine. In one week, more than $5 billion in paper dollars were presented in banks in Japan, Great Britain, France, and Belgium for conversion into yen, pounds, and francs—and those foreign banks could, if they wished, present those paper dollars to the United States government and ask for $5 billion worth of gold.

What Connally was proposing privately to the President—in a plan drawn up by his undersecretary for international monetary policy, Paul Volcker—was a ninety-day across-the-board wage and price freeze, devaluation of the dollar by ending its convertibility into gold and thus ending rigid currency exchange rates, and a new 10 percent tax on all imports into the United States. "I am not sure this program will work, Mr. President," Connally said. "But I am sure that nothing less will work."

The idea was to wait a few weeks, anticipating that economic numbers would get worse, and so would public demands for action. One of the bonds between Connally and Nixon was a conviction that doing something, whether it worked or not, was almost always politically preferable to being accused of doing nothing. The President thought that September was the time to end gold conversion and January of 1972 might be the time to move on wages and prices.

MEANWHILE, Krogh, Young, Hunt, and Liddy were spending one day after another talking about Ellsberg, sifting through reports or rumors of group sex, mistresses, and drug use. On July 27, the FBI had reported to Krogh that Ellsberg's psychiatrist, Dr. Lewis Fielding, in Beverly Hills, California, had refused two requests for interviews about his patient.

Hunt and Liddy proposed breaking into the doctor's office to get Ellsberg's records, saying they had personally been involved in such "black-bag jobs" in the United States and, in Hunt's case, in foreign cities.

Krogh reported all that to Ehrlichman on August 5, saying that Hunt and Liddy had the contacts to put together a black-bag team. A day later, Ehrlichman passed on the President's response: "Tell Krogh he should do whatever he considers necessary to get to the bottom of the matter—to learn what Ellsberg's motives and potential further harmful action might be." Within days, Krogh and Young sent Ehrlichman a two-page memo, detailed and direct, updating the progress of investigations of Ellsberg and a dozen others, including his mother-in-law and prominent academics including Samuel Popkin of Harvard and Richard Falk of Princeton.

A second item read: "We have received the CIA preliminary psychological study . . . which I must say I am disappointed in and consider very superficial. . . . In this connection we would recommend that a covert operation be undertaken to examine all the medical files still held by Ellsberg's psychoanalyst covering the two-year period in which he was undergoing analysis."

The next line was an "Approve / Disapprove" box. Ehrlichman put "E" on the "Approve" line and wrote: "If done under your assurance that it is not traceable."

The final item in the Krogh memo read: "Howard Hunt has suggested, and we concur, that we have the FBI, through its London Legal Attache, request MI-5 to review their telephone taps on Soviet KGB personnel in England for the years 1952–53 (while Ellsberg was a student at Cambridge) to see if Ellsberg was overheard." Ehrlichman initialed "Approve."

WHILE SOME OF HIS MEN were planning a burglary on his verbal orders, the President and Kissinger had been working out the final wording of a secret letter to the Kremlin, trying to revive planning for a Moscow summit meeting. The letter was an ingenious self-invitation to a Moscow summit. Nixon and Kissinger had been told by the United States ambassador to the Soviet Union, Jacob Beam, that Soviet foreign minister Andrei Gromyko had hinted to him that Soviet leader Leonid Brezhnev was interested in becoming more involved in international affairs—a subject in which he had limited experience. The men of the Politburo had little confidence in Brezhnev's diplomatic skills—and tended to follow the lead of Gromyko and Premier Alexsey Kosygin. It was Kosygin who met with foreign leaders and traveled the world as head of state, even though he was outranked by Brezhnev, the general secretary of the Communist

Party. The secret of the secret letter, which listed "a number of ideas" for American-Soviet discussions "at the highest level," was that it was addressed not to Kosygin but to Brezhnev. The answer came back in five days, on August 10, rather than the usual weeks or months: Brezhnev would be happy to receive Nixon in Moscow in May or June of 1972. As usual, Nixon and Kissinger did not inform the State Department of the invitation and told Ambassador Dobrynin, who delivered the letters, to advise his superiors to ignore messages from Beam or Secretary of State Rogers.

On the day Brezhnev's letter arrived, the Dow-Jones stock index, the thermometer of confidence in the American economy, dropped to 839.50, down from the April 28 high of 950.80. A White House survey by pollster Albert Sindlinger, Jr., indicated that the index of consumer confidence had dropped to 55 percent, lower than during the 1957 recession, and the proportion of people who said they hoped Nixon would be reelected had dropped to 27 percent. On August 11, the British government delivered a polite letter to the Treasury Department asking for gold "cover" for $3 billion in paper dollars held by Her Majesty's Government. Volcker told Connally, who told Nixon that it was time to do something.

The next day, Thursday, August 12, the President gave Haldeman a list of thirteen men, headed by Connally, Burns, and Shultz, and told him to arrange transportation for all of them to Camp David by noon the next day.

Speechwriter Bill Safire was one. Haldeman's assistant, Larry Higby, called and told him to pack a bag and wait for a White House car to pick him up. He was not to tell his wife or secretary where he was going—which was easy because he didn't know. When the car came, Herbert Stein, a member of the Council of Economic Advisers, was sitting in the back. They headed for a helicopter pad along the Potomac.

"What's up?" Safire said.

"This could be the most important weekend in the history of economics since March 4, 1933," Stein answered.

That was the day Franklin Delano Roosevelt became president.

"We closing the banks?"

"Hardly," Stein said. "But I would not be surprised if the President were to close the gold window."

Safire had no idea what that meant, but wanted to hide his ignorance. He said: "How would you explain to a layman the significance of the gold window?"

"I wouldn't try," Stein said. "That's why you're along."

CHAPTER 22

August 15, 1971

THE PRESIDENT'S HELICOPTER arrived at Camp David just before
3 P.M. on Friday, August 13, and he went directly to Aspen Lodge. Haldeman was assigning cabins and beds for the ten men who had come in the
two helicopters: John Connally, George Shultz, Paul Volcker, Arthur
Burns, Paul McCracken, Herbert Stein, Pete Peterson, John Ehrlichman, Caspar Weinberger, and Bill Safire. Within fifteen minutes they
were seated in a circle in the living room of Aspen, with Connally on one
side of the President and Burns on the other. Nixon signed the Camp
David guest book and passed it to the others. He told them the world was
about to be made new: "Circumstances change. In this discussion, nobody is bound by past positions."

He turned first to Volcker. The Undersecretary of the Treasury,
the least known man there, was the one most responsible for the timing
of the secret meeting. On Thursday, at one of the intense end-of-the day
meetings that had been going on all week between the President, Connally, and Shultz, Volcker had convinced Connally and the President that
waiting until January, or even September, to deal with the gold problem
was too risky, because international money markets were restless. Safire
was about to learn about the gold window. Volcker was warning that
dozens of countries might follow Britain's example and be lined up Monday morning to claim their gold at Fort Knox.

Nixon, who seemed tense, began: "One of the reasons we are

holding this meeting at Camp David is for security. There are to be absolutely no calls made out of here. . . . Between now and Monday night, everyone here is to button his lip."

He talked for fifteen minutes and relaxed as he went along. "We are here to find solutions. We have to test ideas as to whether they will work. We have to test the cosmetic effect—to limit the consequences. It is easy to take spectacular action—and this will be the most significant economic action since World War II—the question is, how do you get out from under if it doesn't work? . . . My plan is to aim for 9 P.M. Monday night."

It was immediately obvious to everyone there that the President had already made up his mind. The decision had been made, on his yellow pads during his meetings with Connally. Shultz, now the director of the new Office of Management and Budget, had sat in on some of the sessions, and he generally opposed the idea of a grand new economic plan, arguing that the gradualism of Nixon's "Game Plan" was working. The plan was doing what it was supposed to do, gradually reducing inflation and then gradually reducing unemployment. But the politician who was president, and the politician who was secretary of the treasury, sensed that it was time to seize the initiative before foreigners or the American people did it for them, or to them. Nixon and Connally had created their rationale for bold action: The United States had, with great generosity, carried and nurtured the economies of its allies and trading partners, but now those partners were unfairly taking advantage of American benevolence, prospering under the American military and economic umbrella but conspiring to keep out American agricultural and industrial exports. Now, the United States must act in its own interests.

"We have to close the gold window," Connally began. It would be the end of the postwar era. The dollar would float like any other currency, its value going up and down based on how many marks or francs or pounds foreigners were willing to pay for dollars. "On the balance of payments, we should seriously consider an import tax in the range of 10 to 15 percent. . . . I strongly recommend the reinstatement of the investment tax credit. . . . I would suggest 8 to 10 percent. . . .

"The auto industry is under great pressure from foreign competition. For every 100,000 cars we don't sell, we lose 20,000 jobs. The difference here could amount to 300,000 jobs. There is no reason for excise taxes on automobiles. I recommend repeal, on the assurance the automakers will pass it on to the purchaser.

"The final step should be imposition of a wage and price freeze until January 1, 1972," Connally said, turning toward the President. "If you do this, the international financial people will realize you moved across the board strongly. This would be acting in consonance with the way people view you—great statesmanship and great courage. That's the right posture for you—a man ready to make far-reaching moves."

Then the President spoke, saying: "I would just like to add, first, with tax relief there would have to be budget cuts as well. Second, your wage-price restraint, as I understand it, would be one that would work for a brief period—maybe 90 days. You couldn't take it off without something to go into its place. . . . About closing the gold window: What effect it will have, we really don't know. . . ."

During a break, alone with Safire for a minute, Nixon said: "You know when all this was cooked up? Connally and me, we had it set up sixty days ago."

The speechwriter was as important as the economists, because the principal purpose of the session was to prepare the President for what he would tell the nation and the world. Nixon wanted to speak with one voice, his own; the advisers were supposed to do their talking now, in private. Most important, he wanted assurance that Burns, independent of the White House by statute, would stick with the party line. Making sure of that was a major goal of this secret weekend. The freeze was not a problem; Burns had been talking about the possibility of a freeze since early in the year—talk that had made Nixon angry. Now, the Fed chairman was still arguing against closing the gold window, mixing economic and political arguments.

"These major actions will electrify the world," Burns said. "The gold outflow will cease. . . . The risk is if you do it now, you will get the blame for the . . . devaluation of the dollar. I could write the editorial in *Pravda*: 'The Disintegration of Capitalism.' Never mind if it's right or wrong—consider how it will be exploited by the politicians. . . . Once the dollar floats, the basis for trade will change. . . . I would fear retaliation by other countries."

He turned to Connally and said: "How do you know the whole thing will not collapse on you two months before the election? This is a very uniquely powerful action."

Connally responded as a politician: "What's our immediate problem? We are meeting here because we are in trouble overseas. The British came in to ask us to cover $3 billion, all their dollar reserves. Anybody can topple us—anytime they want—we have left ourselves completely exposed."

"All the other countries know we have never acted against them," Burns said. "The good will—"

"We'll go broke getting their good will," Connally interrupted.

The President was calculating the words he would use and the reaction to them. He said: "The political side is different. . . . As far as people are concerned they will be generally alarmed by the closing of the window because of the way it will be covered by the media. You can be sure our political opponents—and most of the media—will be looking for items to frighten the hell out of people at a time we are trying to create confidence. People will applaud the wage-price stabilization, border tax and budget cuts. . . . The media will be vicious. On a thing like this— if I were on the other side I would do the same thing—I would kick our balls off. I can see it now: 'He's devalued the dollar. The dollar will be worth less.' "

He turned to Volcker for a minute and asked: "How much do you think your import tax would bring in?"

"A billion and a half to two billion."

"Be as honest as you can, but get the two billion."

Shultz was next. Nixon said: "Let's talk about the freeze. George?"

"First, an across-the-board freeze is best. Second, an atmosphere of crisis is necessary. Third, the life of the freeze must be short. Fourth, how do you stop it . . . ?" He answered his own last question himself, saying: "Don't worry about getting rid of it, labor will do that for you. . . . It will stop when labor blows it up with a big strike."

Then the President went back to the speech, telling Safire what he wanted to say: "I'm thinking of a speech of 10 minutes—concise, strong, confident. Not a lot of stuff about whining around that we are in a hell of a shape. . . . They will understand cutting the budget. I am cutting government employment—if I have to fire every Cabinet officer. The wage price thing. They will like it. Of course they'll scream like hell after they get it. . . . They will love that import tax—the country doesn't like foreigners. They will not understand closing the window. On gold flow and balance of payments, let experts talk to experts. . . . The question is, is the U.S. going to strive to be Number One economically? . . . We need action—inflation robs the working man. He's on a treadmill."

He said he wanted fifteen hundred words and wanted to tell Americans what he expected of them: "Labor, support the freeze. Businessmen, invest. Consumer, buy. All of us get off our butts. . . .

"I want this kept secret," he said. "The one thing that is sure to come on this is, why didn't we tell the press beforehand? Say, 'Why you dumb bastards, if we told you, you would have told the world and we would have lost all our gold.' "

At 7 P.M., the President broke up the meeting, dispatching the others into task forces on details and follow-through. He dined alone that night. The others ate together. During dinner, Volcker mentioned secrecy from an economist's perspective: "Fortunes could be made with this information."

"How? Exactly?" said Haldeman, getting a laugh.

"How much is your deficit, George?" Volcker asked Shultz.

"Twenty-three billion dollars."

"Give me a billion dollars and a free hand on Monday," Volcker said, "and I'll make it for you on the money market."

The President woke at 3:15 A.M. Saturday and began writing on the White House stationery at his bedside. He covered both sides of three sheets in an hour. At 4:30 A.M., he called Haldeman—waking him, of course—and read him the draft of a speech, saying that he wanted to broadcast it on Sunday night rather than Monday. Then he read his work into a bedside dictation machine, an IBM Executary, and walked out of Aspen Lodge an hour or so later—scaring the hell out of a Navy chief petty officer coming out of the presidential sauna.

"Good morning, Chief," said Nixon.

"Good morning, Ma'am," said the flustered sailor. "I mean, Sir!"

Nixon laughed and handed him four dictation belts and asked him to take them over to Rose Mary Woods in her cabin. She woke up at 6 A.M. and began typing—surprising Safire, who had been writing until 1 A.M. and was bringing over his draft. He heard the typing and said, "Is there another speechwriter up here?" She pointed over to Aspen, the President's lodge. Nixon had gone back to bed, leaving Safire to work up a polished draft. The President's dictation belt message to Safire began:

> Following is a rough draft of the Sunday night speech. I believe this is the best approach rather than start the gobbly-gook about crisis in international monetary affairs, the need for sacrifice, etc. . . . The text begins as follows: Good evening. I have addressed the nation a number of times on ending the war. Because of the progress we have made toward achieving that goal, this Sunday evening is an appropriate time for us to turn our attention to the challenges of peace. . . .
>
> Prosperity without war requires action on three fronts. More jobs for Americans; dropping the rise in the cost of living; protecting the value of our dollar against the international speculators who have launched a massive attack against it. . . .

Before he tried to go back to sleep, Nixon called Haldeman again, saying: "Be sure Bill understands that I have definite ideas. . . . Use gutsy rhetoric. Show the other people only the sections that concern them, don't circulate the drafts. I want it to be a surprise. I don't want this to be brittle and beautiful, but brutal and effective. Sunday, not Monday. Ten minutes."

He called Haldeman again at 8:40 A.M.: "This is going to put the Democrats in a hell of a spot." Then he began his usual Saturday morning phone list, using detailed scripts prepared by Haldeman's staff. The first one was to Senator Edward J. Gurney in Winter Lake, Florida, to congratulate him on the wedding of his daughter: "Sarah is 20 years old and will marry Michael (Mike) Stoner, 21, at 4 P.M. Saturday at the First Congregational Church. The couple have been dating for six years and Mike Stoner hails from nearby Maitland, Florida. . . . CAUTION: Gurney's wife has been mentally ill and is in an institution. Gurney's son committed suicide several years ago. The best time to call is 10:00 A.M. Saturday. . . . Gurney's home number is (305) 647-8013. The bride and the Senator will be there until the ceremony. . . . Talking Point: Sympathetic with problems of bride's father. Having gone through a recent wedding, you know how anxious he is for the event to be a success."

When he stepped outside after the calls, Nixon saw Shultz, who did not like one of the phrases in the first drafts of the President's speech. "Stop high prices," Shultz said, was wrong, because the best they could do was slow down the rate of increase. Safire changed the words to "Say no to higher prices."

"Is that okay, George?" Nixon asked.

"Well, I guess that's poetic license."

"George, you're getting to be a real politician," said the President.

He laughed again. It was a crisis now and he was happy. He sat by the pool alone with a yellow pad on Saturday afternoon playing with the text typed by Woods. He wanted to find a way to avoid the word "devaluation" in talking about the dollar. It was not the kind of word he liked to use. He wrestled with a few lines, then sent them to Safire:

> Let me lay to rest the bugaboo of devaluation. Will this action reduce the value of the dollar? The long-term purpose and the effect of this action will be to strengthen the $—not weaken it. Short term—$ will buy less. But the overwhelming majority who buy American products in America—your $ will be worth the same tomorrow as it is today.

When a president is happy, his men are, too. Safire, having the time of his life, thought it was obvious that even the grumpiest of the President's men were having the most fun they ever had—all in a good cause. Walking in the woods that evening, Burns said to the speechwriter:

"He's a President now. He has a noble motive in foreign affairs to reshape the world, or at least his motive is to earn the fame that comes from nobly reshaping the world. Who can say what his motive is? But it's moving him in the right direction."

On the economy, it was the opposite direction from the conservative, steady-as-you-go route the President had been traveling. In a long memo to the President on controls, written before the trip to Camp David, Stein had written: "Advantages: 1. This step will be recognized as action to check inflation and is unlikely to be outflanked by anyone asking for more. 2. It will probably slow the inflation rate down significantly for a time. . . . Disadvantages: It is a complete rejection of everything the Administration has said on the subject up to now. It fosters bad ideas about how an economy can be run and sets back progress towards better economic policy."

"We just have to demagogue it," the President said when he agreed to including a 10 percent cut in foreign aid. What he meant was that he was going to say that but not do it. At the last shared meal at Camp David, someone said, "After this, everybody here should get a Ph.D. in economics." One of the real economists cracked: "Yes, and everybody who already has one should turn theirs in."

The President dined alone again. But then he called Haldeman and Ehrlichman and Caspar Weinberger over to Aspen Lodge at 9 P.M. He was sitting in the lodge's small study with the lights off and a fire blazing, even though it was a hot August night. He rambled a bit, saying that he wanted to raise the spirit of the country as both Roosevelts had done. "It's important to try to be Number One," he said. "The Japs, Russians, Chinese and the Germans still have a sense of destiny and pride, a desire to give their best. . . . You must have a goal greater than self, either a nation or a person, or you can't be great. . . . The PR types have got to be sure the big point is not the actions, but the leadership in taking those actions."

After morning meetings on Sunday, Nixon sent his men back to Washington and stayed on alone at Camp David. "The political man"—as Nixon referred to himself during the long meeting of Friday the thirteenth—was worrying about the headlines he would make that night. He wrote them out. Were the newspapers going to say "Nixon Changes Mind" or "Nixon Acts Boldly"? He went back to Washington himself at 4 P.M., then went on the air, on all three television networks, at 9 P.M. from the Oval Office.

Nixon spoke for twenty minutes, beginning with words that defined his presidency in the way he wanted it to be remembered: "America has its best opportunity today to achieve two of its greatest ideals: to bring about a full generation of peace and to create a new era of prosperity. . . . Bold leadership ready to take bold action—it calls forth the greatness of a great people. . . ."

Then: "We must create more and better jobs; we must stop the rise in the cost of living; we must protect the dollar from the attacks of international money speculators." He listed ten initiatives:

• A one-year 10 percent investment credit would be made available for corporations building new plants or buying new equipment, and this would be followed by a permanent 5 percent credit;

• The 7 percent excise tax on new automobiles, which had been in effect for twenty-nine years, would be repealed;

• An additional fifty-dollar personal income tax exemption for all Americans scheduled for January 1, 1973, would be instituted instead on January 1, 1972, which meant a total exemption of one hundred dollars on that day;

• To offset those three tax reductions, the number of federal employees would be reduced by 5 percent and pay raises for all federal employees would be postponed;

• Foreign aid would be cut 10 percent;

• Welfare reform (the Family Assistance Plan) would be postponed for one year and revenue-sharing would be postponed three months;

• Prices and wages would be frozen for a period of ninety days;

• A Cost of Living Council would be appointed by executive order to create a price stability mechanism after those ninety days;

• The Secretary of Treasury would take whatever action was necessary to defend the dollar against speculators and suspend the convertibility of the dollar into gold;

• A temporary tax of 10 percent would be imposed on all imports into the United States.

It was dramatic stuff, probably overwhelming to surprised viewers who may have turned on their television sets to watch the popular cowboy show *Bonanza*—and there was indeed more than a bit of the demagoguery Nixon had said was necessary. He did use the line about laying to rest the bugaboo of devaluation, suggesting that there was something un-American about dealing with foreigners: "If you want to buy a foreign car or take a trip abroad, market conditions may cause your dollar to buy slightly less. But if you are among the overwhelming majority of Americans who buy American-made products in America, your dollar will be worth just as much tomorrow as it was today. . . . The American dollar must never again be a hostage in the hands of international speculators."

He ended with the spirit-lifting sermon he promised:

> Government with all its powers does not hold the key to the success of a people. That key, my fellow Americans, is in your hands. Every action I have taken tonight is designed to nurture and stimulate that competitive spirit to help us snap out of self-doubt, the self-disparagement that saps our energy and erodes our confidence in ourselves. . . . Whether the nation stays Number One depends on your competitive spirit, your sense of personal destiny, your pride in your country and yourself.

THE NEXT DAY'S HEADLINES said Nixon had acted boldly. These were the banners across the front pages of *The New York Times* over the next five days:

NIXON ORDERS 90-DAY WAGE-PRICE FREEZE
ASKS TAX CUTS, NEW JOBS IN BROAD PLAN
SEVERS LINK BETWEEN DOLLAR AND GOLD

CONGRESS LIKELY TO VOTE NIXON TAX CUTS
STOCK MARKET UP 32.93 IN RECORD TRADING
MOST WORLD CURRENCY DEALING IS HALTED

GOVERNMENT ASKS END OF STRIKES
DURING FREEZE ON PAY AND PRICES;
PRESIDENT CALLS FOR SACRIFICES

UNIONS REJECT NO-STRIKE APPEAL
PUBLIC EMPLOYEES' PAY IS FROZEN
EUROPE SPLIT IN MONETARY CRISIS

MEANY REFUSES TO BACK FREEZE;
ADMINISTRATION PLANNING MOVES
AFTER 90-DAY RESTRICTIONS EXPIRE

There were dozens of smaller reaction headlines in the *Times* each day the next week, most of them the ones Nixon wanted: "MANSFIELD PLEASED BY WAGE ACTION—McGOVERN CRITICAL," "RISE FOR DOW AVERAGE OF 30 KEY ISSUES LARGEST EVER . . . BONDS ALSO SOAR," "G.M. RESCINDS INCREASES IN PRICES OF ITS '72 CARS," "OBSERVERS SAY NIXON AIM IS 12 TO 15% DEVALUATION," "UNDERVALUED YEN CALLED MAIN TARGET OF SURCHARGE," "PRICE RISES SLACKING IN U.S.," "UNITED AUTO WORKERS, IN A SHIFT, PLEDGE TO ADAPT TO WAGE CONTROL."

"This makes Nixon's trip to China look like child's play," said the president of the Ford Motor Company, Lee Iacocca. Walter Heller, who had been President Kennedy's most influential economic adviser, had just five words: "No-no to go-go."

The Sindlinger poll reported that 75 percent of national respondents backed the plan. "In all the years I've been doing this," Alfred Sindlinger told *The Wall Street Journal,* "I've never seen anything this unanimous." Most newspaper editorials were pro-speech and pro-Nixon. "An act of courage and statesmanship unparalleled by any U.S. chief executive for at least a third of a century," said *The Philadelphia Inquirer.* "An activist flexing of muscles not seen since the early Roosevelt experiments," said the Baltimore *Sun.* In *The New York Times,* it was: "We applaud the scope and daring of his effort. . . ."

There were only a couple of sour notes. *The Christian Science Monitor,* in an editorial, asserted that the "New Economic Policy" favored business and the rich over the hopes of the poor, and the *Los Angeles Times* worried that the United States might be headed for a permanently regimented economy. George Meany, the AFL-CIO president, saw it as a rich man's plan, holding down wages but not corporate profits or the interest being paid to lenders and investors. The old man's anger might have threatened Nixon's dream of a new realigned majority party of ideological conservatives and working men, but, almost instantly, Nixon was again the favorite for 1972. The first Gallup poll after the economic policy speech showed Nixon 6 percentage points ahead of Muskie in a Presidential match-up, a 9-point gain for the President, who had fallen 3 points behind in June.

There was criticism from the economic right. One of the President's orders at Camp David had been for Shultz to brief Milton Friedman, his old colleague at the University of Chicago, telling him that

Nixon had to move on the temporary freeze before liberals in Congress mandated permanent wage-price regulation. Friedman was not impressed. On the same page of *Newsweek* where Paul Samuelson, among the best known of liberal economists, was generally praising Nixon for finally moving boldly, Friedman wrote: "Freezing individual prices and wages to halt inflation is like freezing the rudder of a boat and making it impossible to steer. . . . Sooner or later, and the sooner the better, it will end . . . in utter failure and the emergence into the open of the suppressed inflation."

Abroad, the reaction was chaos—and fear. The new import taxes and the de facto devaluation of the dollar, which meant little or nothing to most Americans, were expected to be a disaster for the countries that had prospered greatly on the jobs and profits generated by exports to the United States. In Germany, the moderate *Süddeutsche Zeitung* called it "A declaration of war in trade policy." The headline covering the front page of *France Soir* read: "The Money Crisis Risks the Breakdown of Europe." In England, the *Daily Telegraph* said it was "self-evidently protectionist and as such invites retaliation."

European stock markets crashed one after another. Most of the world's currency markets shut down. The dollar was simply no longer worth its official value, particularly against the Japanese yen and the West German mark. Nixon and Connally thought the yen—valued at 360 to the dollar on August 14—might rise as much as 25 percent against the dollar, making Japanese goods, particularly automobiles, that much more expensive in American showrooms. Economically, America's gain would be Japan's loss. Politically, Nixon's gain would be a loss for the leaders of all the other democracies.

"No. Not again!" said the Japanese prime minister, Eisaku Sato, when he was called by Secretary of State Rogers ten minutes before Nixon went on the air, which was seven minutes better than the three-minute notice Sato had received the month before, when Nixon announced he would be going to China. His government's foreign policy had been rocked by the China surprise; now it was his country's export-driven, oil-importing economy that would suffer. The leaders of OPEC, the Organization of Petroleum Exporting Countries, threatened to raise oil prices to make up for the inevitable decline in revenues and profits, because they had always insisted on doing business everywhere in the world only with dollars.

"Stunning" . . . "shocked" . . . "bombshell" were words that appeared in almost every press report. That was Nixon's way—"a swiftness and style that is virtually unmatched in modern American politics," said *Time*. The cover of *Newsweek,* under the headline "YOUR NEW DOLLAR," showed a one-dollar bill with an engraving of a smiling Nixon replacing George Washington. In *Time,* Hugh Sidey offered this analysis:

> Nixon clings to what is familiar until the last moment. Then, when the evidence overwhelms him or something happens in his gut, he decides to act, and nothing stands very long in his way. He abandons his philosophy, his promises, his speeches, his friends, his counselors. He marches out of one life into a new world without any apologies or looking back.

CHAPTER 23

September 8, 1971

On August 17, while the world figured out what to use for money, the President went to New York for a speech to the Knights of Columbus. He got a two-minute standing ovation when he endorsed a call by Terence Cardinal Cooke, the Catholic archbishop of New York, for federal aid to parochial schools. Then he headed for San Clemente by way of Springfield, Illinois, and Grand Teton National Park in Wyoming. In Springfield, where he signed legislation making Abraham Lincoln's home a national monument, Haldeman told him that Daniel Schorr of CBS News had ended a report on the New York speech by saying there were no White House plans to actually do anything to help Catholic schools. The implication was that Nixon was simply pandering to Catholics. "That's it!" Nixon said. He was still mad about a March 9 report in which Schorr had said that Nixon had private doubts on whether an ABM system would work—which he did. He told Haldeman to call the FBI, with a directive from the President: "Proceed with the full field background investigation of Mr. Daniel Louis Schorr." The next day, FBI agents around the country did twenty-five interviews on Schorr in less than six hours.

In California, the President's mood got even worse when he discovered that his beach had been fouled by an oil slick leaking from a Navy ship offshore. Attorney General Mitchell came in to talk about dinner the night before with Governor Ronald Reagan, saying that he had to spend most of the evening listening to complaints from the governor's wife, Nancy, about their seating and treatment at White House dinners. Nixon told Haldeman to invite them for dinner at his house. Then Kissinger came in with a more serious problem: the secret peace talks on Vietnam were going nowhere. He said the whole thing was heartbreaking, that perhaps they should wait for one more dry season and launch an all-out offensive to "break their backs." The President had another idea, a surprise: Tell the world in detail about the secret negotiations and try to force the communists to deal publicly—and blame the breakdown in the talks on Senate opponents of the war encouraging the North Vietnamese to fight on.

Dictating that into his tape recorder that night, Haldeman said: "This, of course, is the same line K has used for the past two years, over and over, and, I guess, what all of Johnson's advisers used with him to keep the thing escalating. I'm sure they really believed it at the time, but it's amazing how it sounds like a broken record."

A few days later, Kissinger was back, this time with another plan: he would fly secretly to Hanoi for peace negotiations. "Delusions of grandeur" was Nixon's comment to Haldeman.

Back in Washington after seventeen days away, the President was undecided about whether to attend the September 8 opening of the John F. Kennedy Center for the Performing Arts, a new marble box of concert halls and theaters on the Potomac. He had decided not to, but wavered when he received a handwritten note from Rose Kennedy—a letter he kept in his desk—saying: "Your presence will add a glowing tribute to my son, the late President, and will add dignity and lustre to this opening night. . . . Let us all show that our hearts as well as our minds are united. . . ." But, in the end, he could not bring himself to go; he announced that he would go the second night, after the Kennedys went home. On the morning after the inaugural performance—a new work, "Mass," by Leonard Bernstein—he called Haldeman for a report. After asking for more and more detail, he paused and made a joke: "If I'm assassinated, I want you to have them play 'Dante's Inferno' and have Lawrence Welk produce it."

On September 8, Ehrlichman came into the Oval Office. The tapes in the basement were rolling, recording every word. But Ehrlichman did not know that. The President asked what was happening with Bud Krogh and the "Plumbers."

"He's spending most of his time on the Ellsberg declassification," Ehrlichman began. "We had one little operation. It's been aborted out in Los Angeles, which, I think, is better that you don't know about. But we've got some dirty tricks under way. It may pay off. . . ."

He said they were having trouble getting CIA records on Kennedy's decisions or actions on Cuba and South Vietnam. Then the President switched the subject to getting the Internal Revenue Service to give them records on political opponents and stop investigations of their friends: "John, we have the power but are we using it to investigate contributors to Hubert Humphrey, contributors to Muskie, the Jews, you know, that are stealing every— You know, they have really tried to crucify Hobart Lewis, Robert Abplanalp, I mean, while we've been in office even. . . . And John Wayne, of course, and Paul Keyes. . . ." Lewis was the editor of *Reader's Digest.* "What the hell are we doing?

"Are we going after their tax returns?" Nixon continued. "Do you know what I mean? . . . Do you remember in 1962? Do you remember what they did to me in California? After those sons of bitches came out . . . I find—finally now they owe me more money. . . . And on the IRS, you could—are we looking into Muskie's return? . . . Hubert? Hubert's been in a lot of funny deals. . . ."

The little operation out in Los Angeles—designated in Ehrlichman memos as "Hunt/Liddy Special Project No. 1"—was breaking into the office of Daniel Ellsberg's psychiatrist, Dr. Fielding. The job had been done at midnight of September 3, the Friday night of Labor Day weekend. The operation was paid for by five thousand dollars in campaign funds provided by Colson on September 2. Three men went into the office, while Hunt watched Fielding's home and Liddy played the lookout on the street. The leader of the burglars was Bernard Barker, a Miami real estate agent, a Cuban who had worked for Hunt when he was a CIA officer. Barker recruited two other men, Felipe DeDiego and Eugenio Martinez, telling them: "We have to find some papers of a great traitor to the United States, who is a son-of-a-bitch. . . ." At 4 A.M. Pacific Time, Hunt telephoned Krogh at home to tell him the operation was a success, but they had found no file on Ellsberg. . . . Back in Washington on Tuesday, September 7, Hunt and Liddy reported to Bud Krogh and David Young in room 16 of the White House, showing them Polaroid photographs of the inside of Fielding's office—and asking for permission to break into Fielding's home to see if the files were hidden there. The next morning, at 10:45, the two young Plumbers reported to Ehrlichman, who seemed shocked by what he saw. "The thing should be terminated, discontinued, finalized, stopped . . . ," he said to Krogh. That was when he told the President there was a little operation.

Two days after that, Ehrlichman was back in the Oval Office, talking this time about breaking into the National Archives to photograph secret documents he believed had been deposited there by Morton Halperin, Leslie Gelb, and Paul Nitze, an adviser to Democratic presidents now working on the SALT talks. "There's a lot of hanky-panky with secret documents," he said. "Those three guys made a deposit into the National Archives under an agreement of a whole lot of papers. Now I'm going to steal those documents out of the Archives."

"You can do that . . . ," Nixon said.

"Yeah. And nobody can tell we've been in there . . . ," Ehrlichman continued, saying he could do it through Robert Kunzig, Nixon's administrator of the General Services Administration. "He can send the archivist out of town for a while and we can get in there and he will photograph and he'll reseal them."

Hour after hour over the next few days, Ehrlichman, Haldeman, Mitchell, Colson, and Kissinger were in and out of the Oval Office, talking about ways to use the Pentagon Papers. "I don't give a damn about the contents," the President told Mitchell. "I don't think people care. The main thing is to keep it stuck into the Democrats so that they squabble about it. Do you see what I mean? . . . Really to get our Democratic friends . . . fighting each other about it. It's their problem. It's not ours. . . . Goddamn, I want that thing inflamed."

He was raging again about the Internal Revenue Service. "Billy Graham tells me an astonishing thing," he told Haldeman on September 13. "The IRS is battering the shit out of him. Some son-of-a-bitch came to him and gave him a three-hour grilling. Connally took the name of the guy. . . . Now here's the point. Bob, please get me the names of the Jews, you know, the big Jewish contributors of the Democrats. . . . All right. Could we please investigate some of the cocksuckers? That's all." There was more of the same the next day: "You see, the IRS is full of Jews, Bob. . . . That's the reason they're after Graham. . . ."

Graham, in the office later to discuss holding his crusades in states critical to Nixon in 1972, had his own ideas about such things, as recorded by Haldeman in his diary: "There was considerable discussion of the terrible problem arising from the total Jewish domination of the media. . . . Graham has the strong feeling that the Bible says that there are satanic Jews and that's where our problem arises. . . ."

The President also kept coming back to ideas he had for 1972, beginning once again with finding proof that President Kennedy had ordered the assassination of Diem. Another was to persuade Eugene McCarthy to run again for president in 1972—the idea was to secretly pump $5 million of Republican money into a McCarthy campaign—as a way to split Democratic votes. Kissinger was his man there, coming in to say he was talking up the idea among antiwar Democratic contributors he knew. The President also wanted to split the Democrats by secretly financing a presidential campaign by a black Democrat. The figure used was again $5 million; the names mentioned were Carl Stokes, the mayor of Cleveland, New York Congresswoman Shirley Chisholm, and a Georgia state legislator, Julian Bond. Reading the news summary on September 28, Nixon circled the name "Rev. Jesse Jackson" and wrote: "What happened to the financing plan?"

Nixon himself brought up the killing of Diem in a press conference on September 16. Peter Lisagor of the Chicago *Daily News,* quoting Senator Henry Jackson, asked what "leverage" the United States had in elections to be held in South Vietnam. "If what the Senator is suggesting is that the United States should use its leverage now to overthrow Thieu, I would remind all concerned that the way we got into Vietnam was through overthrowing Diem and the complicity in the murder of Diem; and the way to get out of Vietnam, in my opinion, is not to overthrow Thieu with the inevitable consequence or the greatly increased danger, in my opinion, of that being followed by coup after coup. . . ."

The President thought he had raised the question and could sit back and let the press do the investigating. But nothing happened outside the White House. Inside, Hunt, on orders from Colson, had collected 240 cables between Washington and Saigon in October and November of 1963—Diem and his brother, Ngo Dinh Nhu, were killed by officers of their own army on November 1, 1963—but was unable to find one showing any kind of direct order from Kennedy. So, using a razor blade to cut out words, and some paste, then photocopying his handiwork, he fabricated a cable, dated October 29, 1963, to the American embassy in Saigon. The phony cable read: "At highest level meeting today, decision reluctantly made that neither you nor Harkin should intervene in behalf of Diem or Nhu in event they seek asylum."

ON SEPTEMBER 17, THE DAY after the press conference, the President received a note from Supreme Court Justice Hugo Black, who was gravely ill at Bethesda Naval Hospital. The eighty-six-year-old judge, who had served thirty-four years on the High Court, asked the President to announce his retirement. At the same time, Chief Justice Burger told Nixon that Justice John Marshall Harlan, who was seventy-two years old and suffering from bone cancer, also intended to retire. For the second time in just 27 months, the President had the power of choosing two new justices.

The next day, a Saturday, as he was boarding a helicopter to go to Camp David, Nixon pulled Haldeman aside and told him to schedule a breakfast with J. Edgar Hoover in the residence at 8:30 on Monday morning. "He's going to fire him, finally," Haldeman told Ehrlichman.

The idea of getting rid of Hoover was certainly fine with Ehrlichman, who had been pressing the President about the fact that the FBI director, first appointed by President Calvin Coolidge in 1924, was ignoring White House demands for a full field investigation of Ellsberg's background. Ehrlichman told Nixon that no more than two agents were assigned the case at any time, compared with the dozens who fanned out across the country asking questions about Dan Schorr. The in-house conspiracy theory for Hoover's inaction was that he was a friend of Ellsberg's father-in-law, a rich toy manufacturer named Louis Marx. Among those who believed that theory was Hoover's nominal superior, Attorney General Mitchell. The Justice Department's uneasy relationship with the FBI had reached a new low in mid-July when Mitchell's deputy, Robert Mardian, flew to San Clemente to report that at least four of Hoover's principal deputies were about to quit or be fired. One of them, William Sullivan, had told Mardian that Hoover was well aware of his enemies in the White House—and that the director was ready to use the transcripts of the 1969 taps on the seventeen reporters and Nixon assistants to keep his job. The President said he did not believe that, but he ordered Mardian back to Washington to try to collect all copies of the transcripts through Sullivan. From that date, July 12, 1971, all wiretapping reports were sent to Haldeman and Ehrlichman rather than to Nixon and Kissinger.

"It was a no-go," the President told Haldeman after his breakfast with Hoover on September 20.

"What happened?" asked Ehrlichman, who had prepared a talking paper for the President on why the resignation was necessary before the end of the year. One of Ehrlichman's arguments was that Nixon would then appoint the next director, a conservative in Hoover's tradition, rather than risk the appointment of a liberal by a new Democratic president.

"Don't ask," Haldeman answered. "He doesn't want to talk about it."

No wonder. The eggs-and-gossip session ended with the President's approving a Hoover plan to assign more FBI agents to United States embassies around the world as "legal attachés."

This time the President decided that his Attorney General, who had recommended Carswell and Haynsworth as Supreme Court nominees, would be only one part of the search operation for appointees to replace Black and Harlan. One of the advisers was his wife, Pat, who shocked him by publicly saying, during an aircraft-carrier launching in Newport News, Virginia, that she thought it was about time that a woman be appointed to the Court. More than a dozen names were under consideration, usually briefly, and Nixon did say he wanted women on the list, but the only one they came up with, Judge Mildred Lilley of Los Angeles, was too liberal for the President and got low ratings from the American Bar Association.

ON SEPTEMBER 21, the President finally managed to identify himself with auto racing. The circular driveway of the White House was lined with loud and shiny monsters and their drivers. The President wandered among them for ten minutes and then everyone was invited inside for an hour-long reception. A good time was had by all, as recorded by the star of the anecdotalist team, John Andrews:

> *Chicago Tribune* reporter Aldo Beckman . . . in jest, asked the elder Petty* how large a campaign contribution the racing organizations had promised for 1972 in return for the honor done them today. The poor man knit his brows seriously, paled a bit, then made a quick excuse and fled. . . . The receiving line queued up, the chief eavesdropper eased into his post behind the Chief Executive, and it was "Gentlemen, start your anecdotes." . . . The President took longer with these men, guest by rugged-faced guest, than I have ever seen him do. At his left stood the glad-handing racing impressario J. C. Agajanian. It is safe to guess that the Nixon back was slapped more times by the Agajanian right paw alone in that one hour, than by all the rest of the American people in all 32 months since the Inauguration.
>
> Nearly everybody coming through the line thanked the President lavishly for honoring racing this way. One of the warmest tributes came from Jackie Stewart, the Grand Prix ace. "Sir," he said in a Scots burr. . . . "You are the first head of state in any country to honor motor racing officially. It's a fine thing. We are tremendously grateful." . . . RN's feelings were probably summed up in this reply: "I like the people in it." (Then, with a quick punch to the fellow's chest . . .) "You got a lotta guts."

Haldeman, however, was not impressed. His style was demonstrated in a memo, stamped "HIGH PRIORITY," to Dwight Chapin, the organizer of the event: "Lest you think you have fulfilled your commitment with regard to a plan to identify the President with auto racing as a result of the event . . . let me assure you that is not the case. What you

---

* Retired stock car champion Lee Petty.

have given me so far is a brief celebrity stunt. Please try again and have the results in by Wednesday."

THE NEXT DAY the President met with Soviet foreign minister Andrei Gromyko. They exchanged diplomatic boilerplate for two hours and then the two of them and their interpreters went over to EOB 175. With Kissinger and Dobrynin waiting dutifully outside, Gromyko formally invited the President to meet Secretary Brezhnev in Moscow on May 22, 1972—a Moscow summit twelve weeks after Peking.

CHAPTER 24

October 21, 1971

JOHN ANDREWS was the designated anecdotalist standing behind President Nixon on September 30 at a White House reception for finance ministers and other officials in Washington for the annual meetings of the World Bank and the International Monetary Fund. He filed a report that included:

> One senses that he knows the political geography of the Planet Earth about as well as most Congressmen know their own districts. As the guests filed by, you got this kind of thing:
> Man from Argentina: RN sings a few bars of their national anthem for Connally's edification.
> Man from Liberia: "I was just writing your President a letter today. We were Vice Presidents together, you know."

For a change, though, the President was focused on domestic matters during the first couple of weeks of October: he was spending time on the Supreme Court nominations and preparing to announce "Phase II" of the New Economic Policy, the formation of a structure to deal with wage and price controls after the last day of the dramatic ninety-day price and wage freeze on November 13.

His first choice for the Supreme Court was a forty-seven-year-old congressman from Virginia, Richard H. Poff, the ranking Republican on the House Judiciary Committee. But Poff withdrew his name from consideration on October 2, after White House investigations came up with one thing after another that indicated a tough confirmation fight: Poff had voted against every civil rights bill introduced during his ten terms in the House, he had signed two antidesegregation manifestos, and he had trouble explaining how he had become rich on a congressman's salary.

Nixon reacted to that by saying he still wanted to make a southern statement, telling Haldeman he wanted to find someone obviously to the right of Poff. Maybe they should try Robert Byrd. "He's a real reactionary, the Democrats made him their whip," said Nixon, "and he was in the Ku Klux Klan when he was young." Send them a message.

The outline of Phase II, prepared by Herb Stein, was in shape by October 5 after hours of White House meetings between the President and most of the men who had been at Camp David in August. Stein's memos to the President, revised and refined over several weeks, ended with these recommendations: "The basic Phase II structure would be three elements: The Cost of Living Council, with an executive director, exercising supervision of the entire program on your behalf. . . . A Tripartite Pay Board (public, labor and management) . . . A Commission on Prices, Costs and Profits consisting of public members only."

The man who had the greatest influence on that structure was not in the room: George Meany. "A real patriot," the President had called him when unions were supporting the war in Vietnam and attacking antiwar demonstrators. But the campuses were calm now—"Youth Rebellion of Sixties Waning" was the front-page headline of a *New York Times* survey of students—and that calm reduced the class resentment of workingmen. Labor leaders, including Meany, were back to focusing on economic issues and protecting the jobs of their members. Among their differences with the President now was the "Philadelphia Plan," Nixon's symbolic reaching out to minority groups.

The plan, devised by Shultz, called for voluntary affirmative action on all federally assisted construction projects—integration "goals" rather than "quotas." In Philadelphia, the city where it began, the goal was to increase the number of blacks and other minorities in construction unions from 4 percent to 26 percent in four years. For Nixon, it was a way to deflect criticism on racial matters. To Meany, it was a scheme to divide the labor movement and take jobs away from his members. The two of them had also been dancing around controls for a year. The President had taken the lead, or stomped on Meany's toes, on August 15, using powers given him by congressional Democrats in the Economic Stabilization Act of 1971—the law Democrats had passed to embarrass Nixon. The Democrats thought they could take credit for trying to do something about inflation while Nixon continued to do nothing. But now the President had done something. So now Meany, enraged by controlled wages and a freeze on negotiated union contracts, was back in front of a House committee, saying, on October 4: "The Congress gave the President a blank check. . . . He has proved unworthy of that trust. . . . In view of the Administration's record of unkept promises, disastrous policies, sudden flip-flops and utterly lopsided programs, it is our considered contention that Congress must reassert control over the economy."

Outmaneuvered by the President, Congress was afraid to challenge the political popularity of the freeze. The consumer price index, which was rising at an annual rate of 4 percent before August 15, was now at 1.6 percent. Hourly wage rates, which had been increasing by 6.2 percent a year, were now running at 0.6 percent. Meany knew that Phase II could not survive the all-out opposition of organized labor. So did Nixon. "No program works without labor cooperation," the President told Haldeman.

ON OCTOBER 6, Nixon retreated to EOB 175 for a day of work on the Phase II announcement. But he lost the morning because he was so angry about an Immigration and Naturalization Service raid in Los Angeles. Agents had arrested thirty-six illegal aliens at Ramona, Inc., a Mexican food packaging company. The owner of the factory was Romana Acosta Banuelos, who was waiting to be confirmed as his nominee to be Treasurer of the United States. She said the raid was politics, although she had been raided six times over the past three years. The President blamed the newspaper that had fostered his early career as a Southern California politician, the *Los Angeles Times*.

The *Los Angeles Times*, a Republican newspaper for most of its history, had been changing under the leadership of a new generation of the Chandler family, the paper's owners. Otis Chandler, who in 1960 became publisher at the age of thirty, was turning the *Times* into a respected national paper, hiring outsiders from New York and Washington. The President called over Haldeman and began a tirade: "I want this whole goddamn bunch gone after. . . . I also want Otis Chandler's income tax. . . ."

Then Nixon called Mitchell, first telling him he wanted the Immigration and Naturalization Service district director in Los Angeles fired or transferred: "The fellow out there in the immigration service is a kike by the name of Rosenberg. He is out. He is to be out. . . ."

Then he continued: "I want you to direct the most trusted person you have in the Immigration Service to look <u>all</u> over the activities of the

Los Angeles Times. . . . Let me explain, because as a Californian, I know. Everybody in California hires them. . . . Otis Chandler—I want him checked with regard to his gardener. I understand he's a wetback. Is that clear?"

"Yes, sir," answered Mitchell. It was the first time the President's former law partner had been talked to that way.

"We're going after the Chandlers," Nixon went on, "every one, individually, collectively, their income tax. . . . Every one of those sons of bitches."

He turned back to Haldeman to talk about a pair of memos from Buchanan and Moynihan. Buchanan had sent Nixon an article titled "I.Q.," by Richard Herrnstein, from *The Atlantic Monthly,* saying in a cover memo: "Basically, it demonstrates that heredity, rather than environment, determines intelligence. . . . It is almost the iron law of intelligence that is being propounded here. . . . The importance of this article is difficult to overstate. . . . Every study we have shows blacks 15 I.Q. point below whites on average. . . . If there is no refutation, then it seems to me that a lot of what we are doing in terms of integration of blacks and whites—but, even more so, poor and well-to-do—is less likely to result in accommodation than it is in perpetual friction—as the incapable are placed consciously by government side-by-side with the capable."

Nixon sent the piece on to Moynihan with a brief query: "Pat, what are your comments?"

Late in September, Moynihan sent back eleven pages of comment, which Nixon read on October 7. "There was a time when such articles were written in Latin. It was better so," Moynihan began. He noted that increasing numbers of psychologists had come to think that heredity was more important than environment in determining intelligence and that the major races could be ranked, with Asians first, Caucasians second, and Africans third.

It gets close to thinking about the unthinkable. Frankly, I don't see how a society such as ours can live with this knowledge. . . . At a nastier level persons opposed to school integration can certainly find ammunition in this material. Doubtless someone will soon discover—what has been in the literature since 1915—that prisons are disproportionately filled with persons of low intelligence, and use this information for assorted ugly purposes.

It seems to me essential for you to proceed on the assumption that the scientists have not proved their case. . . . Herrnstein is probably right that the world's work is done by persons of talent, but the world is kept together by the decency of quite ordinary people. . . . Finally, may I plead that you say nothing about this subject, nor let anyone around you do so. . . . In the bowels of Christ I plead with you not to let the Vice President say anything.

Nixon said he agreed, telling Haldeman: "It's important for me to know these things and then do everything possible to deny them. No leader must say that, or say it regarding a Jew or a Catholic or anyone else, or else you'll encourage latent prejudice. It's clear that everybody is not equal, but we must ensure that anybody might go to the top." *

THE PRESIDENT went on national television that night to lay out Phase II, which had been revised to satisfy Meany. In addition to the Pay Board and the seven-member price commission, the President announced a new Interest and Dividends Commission, headed by Arthur Burns, to monitor the activities of investors, ready to take action against "windfall" profits. To that he added a good Republican defense of private enterprise and business: "Let us recognize an unassailable fact of economic life: All Americans will benefit from more profits. More profits fuel the expansion that generates more jobs. More profits mean more investments, which will make our goods more competitive in America and in the world. And more profits mean that there will be more tax revenues to pay for the programs that help people in need."

Although fines and sanctions and passing along corporate savings to consumers were mentioned, the President was deliberately vague about penalties and such. He gave no timetable, saying only, "When controls are no longer needed, we will get rid of them." In fact, he hoped for voluntary action, and much of the speech was praise and exhortation for the American people: "It is you who have answered the call to put the public interest ahead of the special interest. . . . Let us dedicate ourselves tonight . . . to join in a great common effort to stop inflation—and to create a new prosperity in a world of peace."

Meany did not think it was a common effort. "They double-crossed me" was his first reaction, though he managed to avoid using the phrase in public. What he said to reporters was: "I was misled by Secre-

---

* In 1982, during a two-hour conversation, Nixon told me that he thought "yellow" Asians were genetically superior to Caucasians, at least in intellect, and that blacks were markedly inferior to both Asians and Caucasians. He said, then, that he expected Asians to dominate the world by the middle of the twenty-first century. At home, he offered these thoughts: "What people resent is this business of some colleges pushing blacks too far for their own good, making them doctors and everything else. . . . The racism has receded, I think, but it's there and it always will be there. . . . A lot of people are just as racist now, but it's not fashionable anymore—and I think that's damned important. You can't talk about blacks like you once did."

tary Hodges"—meaning Secretary of Labor James D. Hodgson. The issue was whether the Cost of Living Council, chaired by the Secretary of the Treasury, would have veto power over the decisions of the fifteen-member Pay Board. Meany said labor would not consider the government's plans until after a special meeting of the AFL-CIO's executive board on October 12. That gave the President five days, and he used them to make the deal. On October 11, Hodgson and Shultz delivered a memo to Meany saying: "The Cost of Living Council will not approve, disapprove, or serve as an appeal level for decisions made by the Pay Board and Price Commission and it will not approve, revise, veto or revoke specific standards or criteria developed by the Pay Board and Price Commission." At the bottom was the President's handwriting: "O.K.—RN."

Nixon was relieved, and he scheduled a news conference in the White House press room at the same time as the AFL-CIO's closed meeting. Reporters crowded in, ready to poke and probe for details on the names and rules of Phase II, which was expected to begin in just a month, on November 15. One more time the President threw them off completely:

> Ladies and Gentlemen, I have an announcement which is embargoed till 12 noon Washington time and 7 o'clock Moscow time. . . . The leaders of the United States and the Soviet Union have agreed that a meeting between them would be desirable. . . . Such a meeting will take place in Moscow in the latter part of May 1972. President Nixon and Soviet leaders will review all major issues, with a view towards further improving their bilateral relations and enhancing the prospects of world peace.

He was back in the press room at 2:22 in the afternoon saying:

> I welcome the participation of organized labor in the work of the Pay Board and in helping make a success of the Nation's efforts at wage and price stabilization. Bringing the cost of living under control requires the public-spirited cooperation of all Americans. . . . Director Shultz will answer any technical questions you may have. . . . The question that inevitably arises after a discussion of this sort is, "Who won? Did labor win or did the administration win?" And the answer is, "The country won.

Actually Nixon won. Meany went along—and agreed to be a member of the Pay Board—because the nation was behind the President on controls.

• • •

"I DON'T THINK ANYBODY should have any delusions that our trying to get labor involved had anything to do with politics," the President said at the beginning of a Cabinet meeting later that afternoon. "Politically, having them as opponents would be helpful. Meany overplayed his hand, and that's why they came back. Next year they're going to be out to get us. . . . Our public posture should be that we welcome labor's acceptance of some responsibility." He also emphasized that whatever was said in public, for now the administration and organized labor were united on one big thing: unemployment. "I've seen lots of elections affected by unemployment, and none by inflation."

Then he moved on to the Moscow summit announcement, saying: "What does this have to do with China? They are separate. . . . It is very important to take that line. . . . We are on a very high wire. We must remember that we are ironically in a position where each rates the other as a greater enemy than the U.S. But the U.S.—to deal with either—must deal even-handedly. . . ."

Rogers, who had known nothing of the Nixon-Gromyko-Brezhnev game, then explained it, at great length, to his fellows at the table. When the Secretary of State finished, the President asked Kissinger, sitting along the wall with other staff, if he wanted to say anything. The national security adviser shook his head. He did not of course think the Soviet and China initiatives were separate. Nixon's China announcement had startled the Soviets, making it certain they would agree to a summit. They would have preferred that the Americans come to Moscow before going to Peking, but they were satisfied to have the Soviet meeting announced before any trip to China. "Triangular diplomacy" was a Kissinger phrase. Asked in private what that meant in the Soviet–China–United States game, he said: "Simple. We are always for the weaker of the other two."

Then Nixon called on Laird: "I understand the casualties are pretty low this week?"

"Seven," said the Defense Secretary. "They'll be announced Thursday."

"Remember," Nixon said, "when we first sat around this table, it was up to 350 a week."

Vietnam was sliding out of the national dialogue, with alternate flashing of bright and dark news. The campuses were generally quiet, though students at Kent State were petitioning for a new grand jury investigation of what happened there. "Never!" Nixon scrawled on his news summary. At the same time, crewmen aboard the aircraft carrier *Coral Sea* were circulating petitions against going on another tour of duty off Vietnam. More and more GIs were refusing orders to engage the enemy, and South Vietnamese veterans took fourteen American soldiers as hostages for eight hours after the GIs tried to drive a truck across a road filled with mourners at the funeral of an ARVN soldier killed in action. At Di Nam, a base near Saigon that Nixon had visited in 1969, guerrillas blew up five U.S. helicopters and escaped without a shot being fired. The Republican leader in the Senate, Hugh Scott, said during a press conference: "The sooner we get the hell out of there, the better. Period."

On October 14, someone—in the White House or from the American Bar Association's committee for evaluating nominees—leaked a list of six Supreme Court finalists, names designed to please Southerners and women: Senator Robert Byrd of West Virginia; Herschel Friday, the Arkansas attorney who represented Little Rock in its 1957 efforts to maintain segregated schools; two women judges, Mildred Lilley and Sylvia Bacon; and little-known judges from Mississippi and Florida. Photos of the six ran across the top of the front page of *The New York Times,* burying a story at the bottom of the page headlined: "Horrors of East Pakistan Turning Hope into Despair"—as many as nine million East Pakistanis were already refugees in India as the Pakistani army continued a brutal campaign to crush local opposition. The President ended the day with a reception for a group, organized by Colson, called Citizens for a New Prosperity. The anecdotalist for the event was Lee Huebner, who ended his report with: "There is the inevitable lady who smiles broadly when Hobart Lewis introduces her to the President and then blurts out: 'It's a President, Mr. Pleasure.' "

On the same day, Haldeman came out of the Oval Office and dictated an "Administratively Confidential—Time's Man of the Year" memo, which he sent to Ziegler: "About this time each year a faint-hearted effort is made to have President Nixon selected. This year—with the New American Revolution, the China Visit, and the economy moves—there should be a carefully planned, successful effort. . . . You should assume personal responsibility for this project and advise me, in writing, of your plans." A couple of days later, Haldeman dictated the thrust of a conversation with Nixon about China: "He wanted me to be sure to have Haig remind Henry that the P must see Chou En-lai and Mao alone—separately, without K—because he has done this with all other heads of state." On October 20, the Nobel Peace Prize winner was named, West German chancellor Willy Brandt, for "Ostpolitik," agreements he had initiated with East Germany and between the Soviet Union and allied occupying powers on access to Berlin. He was cited in words

Nixon thought should be his: "He stretched out his hand to reconciliation between countries that have long been enemies."

The next morning, Attorney General Mitchell came to the White House to tell the President that he had received a call the night before from Chief Justice Burger. The Chief Justice, reacting to the *Times* story and American Bar Association criticism of the list of six, said that he would resign if judges as undistinguished as the six named were actually appointed to the Supreme Court.

"Fuck him," Nixon said. "Let him resign."

"Fuck the ABA!" he said more than once. And that remark became public.

In the next issue of *The New Republic,* John Osborne wrote: "The story around Washington that the President said 'Fuck the ABA!' in a moment of extreme irritation with the American Bar Association and its judiciary committee of 12 eminent lawyers is correct. . . . Mr. Nixon often talks like that; the operative word is one of his favorites."

John Ehrlichman immediately dispatched a letter to the magazine's editors, writing: "The President's use of this obscenity in describing the ABA was supposed to have taken place during a meeting in the President's office on the morning of Friday, October 2. I happened to be present for that entire meeting. I would like to set the record straight: The President did not use the quoted obscenity at any time during that meeting. The simple fact is that in the many hours I have spent with the President I have never heard him use the word attributed to him in Mr. Osborne's piece."

Ehrlichman was a liar. He was also one of Osborne's best sources.

On October 21, the President spent the day in EOB 175, still working on the list of Supreme Court nominees. He planned to announce the names on television at 7:30 P.M. The night before, relying now on Ehrlichman instead of Mitchell, he had decided on two men who had not been publicly mentioned during the weeks of speculation: Lewis F. Powell Jr., a sixty-four-year-old Democrat who was a past president of the American Bar Association, and Senator Howard Baker, a forty-six-year-old Republican from Tennessee. Baker did not immediately accept the President's offer but said he would call with an answer before 9 A.M. He called at 9:30 and said yes. But Nixon had already changed his mind, choosing instead Assistant Attorney General William Rehnquist, forty-seven, the man he used to call "the clown" because of the way he dressed.

"Presidents come and go but the Supreme Court, through its decisions, goes on forever," he began in his speech that night. "They will make decisions which will affect your lives and the lives of your children for generations to come. . . ."

Despite the confusion of the past few weeks, Nixon laid out his thinking with precision—he had written the speech himself—saying he had searched for "the best lawyers . . . with a conservative judicial philosophy. . . . As a judicial conservative, I believe some Court decisions have gone too far in the past in weakening the peace forces as against the criminal forces in our society. . . . I believe the peace forces must not be denied the legal tools they need to protect the innocent. . . ."

When the cameras were turned off, he told Mitchell to end the agreement that allowed the American Bar Association to screen the qualifications of judges nominated by the president. He also gloated—"two hard-right conservatives," he called his appointees in private—that Rehnquist would not have had a chance of confirmation if he had not followed Haynsworth and Carswell.

A couple of hours later, Haldeman called to say, "A ten-strike, reaction is good."

"Well, probably so, except for my wife," Nixon answered. "Boy, is she mad."

CHAPTER 25

December 16, 1971

On October 25, the President's morning news summary reported that *Parade* magazine, the Sunday supplement to hundreds of newspapers, had done a flattering cover story on Henry Kissinger, writing of "brilliance, hard work, devotion to kids and enjoyment of starlets."

"Again this theme of K's power," Nixon wrote to Haldeman. "Not helpful." Then he added, "No K backgrounders for next three months."

On the other hand, the President was pleased with publicity about his new star, John Connally. In his diary, Haldeman included an odd note: "He's been thoroughly enjoying throughout the day the possibility of coming down with a cold. Since he's not been outside or anything where he would normally catch one, he's decided that there is something to the virus theory and he has caught Connally's virus, which seems to sort of please him. . . ."

The news summaries were also reporting more and more stories questioning the long reign of J. Edgar Hoover at the FBI. In the middle of that day, the President called in Ehrlichman for a long conversation about how to deal with the old man. Finally, Nixon said: "He has to realize he can't stay forever. . . . We may have on our hands here a man who will pull down the temple with him, including me. I don't think he would want to. I mean he considers himself a patriot, but he now sees himself, as McCarthy did, and perhaps Agnew now does, he sees himself as the issue, rather than the issue, which is the great weakness of any political man. . . ."

Then the subject turned, not for the first time, to Hoover's knowledge of White House wiretaps. Ehrlichman repeated that, for a time, wiretap orders and transcripts had been in the safe of William C. Sullivan, the associate director who now was at odds with Hoover. Nixon asked what kind of man Sullivan was, asking: "Will he rat on us?"

THAT NIGHT, in an unusual and ugly meeting of the United Nations General Assembly in New York, the People's Republic of China, the communist government of 750 million people, was admitted to the United Nations, ending twenty-two years of United States efforts to protect the seat of the Republic of China, Chiang Kai-shek's Nationalist government of 14 million people on the island of Taiwan. The American cause was not helped by photographs that day showing Kissinger in Peking with Chou En-lai, giving the impression, the correct one, that the United States wanted to have it both ways. But the Nationalists lost by a vote of 59 to 54, with 15 abstentions, on the long night's key question. Minutes later, the General Assembly voted 76 to 35, with 17 abstentions, to seat the People's Republic as the legitimate government of the country. There was something of an anti-American party in the General Assembly after the final vote was announced. Delegates on the winning side stood and cheered. The Tanzanians danced in the aisles; the Albanians shouted, "A great defeat for the Americans!"

Nixon had called Bush before the final vote and said, "Win it! Win it!" But by then the President's real concern was the reaction of conservatives in his own party. Just after midnight, the conservative he feared most, Governor Reagan of California, called the White House, getting John Mitchell at home, demanding that the United States announce that it would no longer abide by UN votes. Senator James Buckley issued a statement urging a major reduction in American UN funding and saying, "The action taken by the General Assembly tonight may well be recorded as the beginning of the end of the United Nations. . . ."

"We just have to ride this out," the President told Haldeman. The next time he talked to Kissinger he said: "We were going to lose the Taiwan vote anyway. . . . The problem is not Taiwan. The problem is the UN. The United States is getting kicked around by a bunch of goddamned Africans and cannibals and the rest." Reading coverage and analysis of the China vote, he marked one item and sent it along to Kissinger: "K—Very sophisticated piece." It was by Robert Elegant of the *Los Angeles Times* and the President's news summary described it this way: "He writes that the long arm of coincidence stretches only so far and it was hardly coincidence that had Kissinger in Peking for the UN vote. The Administration show for Taiwan was almost—though not quite—believable. . . . But then diplomacy is cynical."

Nixon's diplomacy was more often sophisticated. It was a high-wire act performed in secret, and this sometimes led to unforeseen consequences. The Republican leader in the Senate, Hugh Scott, took the President at his word and went before cameras to say: "I think we are going to wipe the smiles from the faces we saw on television during the United Nations voting." Then he led the Senate in voting 41 to 27 to eliminate all foreign aid—$3.3 billion—from the new federal budget.

The President's relationship with Congress was demonstrated by his surprise. In fact, he was as surprised as congressional leaders had been when he first said he was going to China. Now he reproached Scott and others, saying, "This is a highly irresponsible act which undoes 25 years of constructive bipartisan foreign policy and produces unacceptable risks to the national security of the United States." It took almost two weeks of private meetings and White House pleas and threats to persuade the Senate to restore $2.64 billion of the cuts. So, the Taiwan double-talk and double cross cost Nixon $700 million to play with, most of it in military aid to Korea, Cambodia, Israel, Greece, Spain, and Turkey.

But he was doing better with his latest Supreme Court nominees. "The appointments were a masterstroke," he boasted to Haldeman and Kissinger during an October 27 meeting.

"Rehnquist is pretty far right isn't he?" asked Kissinger.

"Oh, Christ," Haldeman said. "He's way to the right of Buchanan."

On November 9, *The Washington Post* published a story on the FBI's August investigation of Dan Schorr of CBS. Haldeman immediately concocted a cover story: the President would say at his next press conference that Schorr had been under consideration for a job as a government spokesman. Safire, delegated to prepare a draft answer for the next press conference, wrote: "The only objection to the FBI check seems to be that he was not asked beforehand if he were interested in the job. . . . Accordingly, I have ordered that whenever a member of the press"—Nixon scratched out the last five words and replaced them with "anybody"—"is being considered for a government job, he be informed beforehand why the customary FBI check is being made. . . ." But there was no Schorr question at the November 12 conference. So Ziegler had to release the answer later as a statement, hoping to deflect congressional rumblings of an investigation into the use of the FBI to intimidate reporters.

The news in the "news conference" (the phrase Nixon often used to avoid using the word "press") was an announcement that 45,000 more United States troops would be withdrawn from Vietnam by February 1, 1972, leaving a force of 139,000, about the number there at the end of 1965. The numbers had become the news in the war, especially weekly casualty figures. After the conference, the President noted an item in his news summary reporting that two United States helicopters had collided in Vietnam, killing four Americans, and sent a memo to Kissinger: "K—These are not to be included in battle casualties."

On the day of the news conference, Sigma Delta Chi, a journalism society holding its convention in Washington, asked its members, mostly newspaper editors, what they thought would be the principal issue of the 1972 presidential campaign. One hundred and seven of them answered "the economy," nine said "international affairs," one said "Vietnam." The President wrote on his news summary: "H+C+E—They must not be allowed to get away with this—International affairs is our issue; Economy is theirs regardless of what happens to it because Libs can always promise more."

For Nixon, the key to neutralizing *their* issue was reducing unemployment. There had been only two questions about the economy on November 12, but he used one of them to make the point that the number of jobs in the country increased by one million during the freeze. His concerns, though, were laid out in full in an angry letter—marked "Eyes Only"—to Arthur Burns, commenting on a piece in *The New York Times* by Leonard Silk, an economics reporter rarely sympathetic to the White House. The President wrote:

> As I read the story and absorbed it I could see clearly that he was gloating over the fact that our money supply had not been rising. . . . and then he proceeded to point out that one possible reason for this phenomenon was that I made the mistake of putting you in charge of the Committee on Interest Rates. . . . I would be less than honest with you if I were not to say that I have been flooded with calls from people in Wall Street. . . . Two of those who called pointed out that this is exactly what happened in 1959 and 1960 . . . helping to trigger the unemployment increase which was probably the decisive factor in our defeat in November of 1960. . . . I am not sending copies of this letter to anybody else. I think this has to be between me and you. But I do want you to know there is nothing I feel stronger about. . . . You owe it to yourself, as well as to our goal of getting the economy to move smartly up in the months ahead, to re-evaluate your decision with regard to holding the money supply down and take some action to move it up. . . .

Nixon had been shocked by Burns's independence as Fed chairman. In the summer, he had tried to bring his old friend into line by having Colson leak a story that Burns was seeking a $20,000 increase in his annual salary of $42,500 at the same time he promoted wage controls for others. In fact, Burns had privately told the President that *future* Fed chairmen should be paid on the same scale as the directors of European central banks. At that point, in August, Burns had stopped taking White House calls and told his friend Safire: "Bill, remind the people in the White House that there is such a thing as truth."

Meanwhile, Secretary Connally, who loved his cowboy image, was riding high around the world trying to barter trade concessions for the United States in return for dropping the border tax on imports from the New Economic Policy. He was not having much luck. The president of the New York Stock Exchange, Bernard J. Lasker, who was an important campaign contributor and fund-raiser, came to Washington to talk about a slow but steady decline in the market after the quick jump that followed the Camp David surprise. "We can't ride with the impasse Connally keeps projecting," Lasker said. "The longer it continues the worse off we'll be. . . ." International business was stalled—and was likely to stay that way until exchange rate questions were resolved. Kissinger did not know all that much about finance, but he was complaining that the deadlock was beginning to affect the dialogues of national security. The countries Connally was trying to push into trade concessions were the United States's most important allies, Great Britain, France, West Germany, and Japan. Finally the President told Connally it was time to come home—and to make a deal fixing exchange rates.

The speaker after Nixon at the journalists' convention was Secretary of State Rogers, whose answers produced this headline at the top of page one in *The New York Times*: "Rogers Expresses Fear of Full War in India, Pakistan."

Hundreds of thousands of East Pakistanis were reported dead; millions had fled to India as refugees. But that did not seem the issue to Nixon. He liked President Yahya Khan—and despised Prime Minister Indira Gandhi of India—and he was grateful to the Pakistanis for their help in the China initiative. And Yahya Khan, a stubborn man, believed it was only a matter of time before his army calmed and controlled the eastern wing of the country. Nixon's own stubbornness in choosing the likable military leader over the cold and calculating leader of the world's largest democracy was considered irrational in the State Department. Nixon, though, had already ignored an extraordinary April 7 cable from the twenty American professionals in the consulate in Dacca, who knew nothing of the China initiative at the time, that stated: "Our government has failed to denounce the suppression of democracy. We have chosen not to intervene, even morally, on the grounds that the Awami League conflict, in which unfortunately the overworked term genocide is applicable, is purely an internal matter. We, as professional public servants, express our dissent with current policy and fervently hope that our true and lasting interests here can be defined and our policies redirected."

The White House reaction was to call the consul, Archer Blood, to Washington for consultation, with no intention of ever letting him go back. He was immediately assigned to the personnel department. The signers were then picked off one by one, most of them taking early retirement.

The President saw the trouble on the Indian subcontinent as part of a worldwide struggle—more testing by the Soviets. Moscow was backing India, supplying its weapons, and China was more quietly supporting Pakistan. The United States continued to say almost nothing officially as the government of Pakistan slaughtered East Pakistanis and tried their elected leader, Sheikh Mujibur Rahman, in secret for treason. The sentence was death. The refugees kept coming—India said there were ten million and Pakistan said no, only three million—and some of them were going back as guerrillas, armed and trained by the Indians. Yahya Khan seemed oblivious to reality, apparently convinced that in a war both the Americans and the Chinese would come to his aid. Part of that was Kissinger's doing. When he came back from his secret trip to Peking in July he told Yahya that Chou En-lai had told him that the Chinese would intervene with men and arms if India moved against Pakistan. The actual wording by Chou was: "If India invaded Pakistan, China would not be an idle spectator but would support Pakistan." Kissinger had overinterpreted "support" and Khan had believed him. He believed the same about the United States. But most of the world, which included the Congress and people of the United States, was coming to see the Pakistanis as butchers and the Indians as potential liberators. So the President dispatched Kissinger to deliver a warning to India—a warning that dramatized White House contempt for Congress—which the country's ambassador, L. K. Jha, cabled to New Delhi quoting Kissinger as saying:

> You must realize that no matter how much you succeed in influencing important senators, you have to deal with this administration and that means the President. As for bringing about any change in the U.S. attitude, the President is angry with the Indian embassy's efforts with the Congress. The President does not feel that apart from the East Coast intellectuals, among whom I used to be counted at one time, there are many people in this country who are genuinely interested in or excited about the affairs of the

subcontinent. The Congressional leaders who support you do so because they want to use any excuse for attacking the President and not because they have any deep sympathies.

At the height of the troubles, India signed a twenty-year "Treaty of Peace, Friendship, and Cooperation" with the Soviet Union. That maneuver should have ended all hope that China would do anything that would give the Soviets a reason to escalate the Chinese-Soviet face-off along their own long border. Finally, there was the military balance: United States intelligence sources estimated that India had a three-to-one advantage in ground troops, a five-to-one advantage in combat aircraft, and a seven-to-one advantage in naval power.

When Kissinger was delegated to discuss those numbers with Yahya, the Pakistani leader told him that the true advantage was with the historical superiority of Muslim fighting men. Nixon was reduced to sending letters urging restraint. Even when he signed an order limiting the shipment of some spare parts and other military equipment to Pakistan, he wrote this below his signature: "To all hands. Don't squeeze Yahya at this time. RN." At the same time, Kissinger angrily told senior national security officials: "The President always says to tilt toward Pakistan, but every proposal I get is in the opposite direction. Sometimes I think I'm in a nuthouse."

Prime Minister Gandhi came to Washington in early November, meeting with the President for the better part of two days. Official notes of the meetings reported the President saying: "Absolutely nothing could be served by the disintegration of Pakistan. For India to initiate hostilities would be almost impossible to understand. . . . It would be impossible to calculate precisely the steps that other great powers might take." Mrs. Gandhi said: "India has never wished the destruction of Pakistan or its permanent crippling. Above all, India seeks the restoration of stability. We want to eliminate chaos at all costs."

Nixon thought Mrs. Gandhi was lying. "That bitch, that whore," he ranted in the Oval Office. The Indian leader had her own definitions: "Stability" was a weakened Pakistan. But Pakistan was weakening itself. And while the two leaders, and Kissinger, were in the Oval Office, more direct conversation was going on down the hall in the Cabinet Room, where Assistant Secretary of State Joseph Sisco, the one department official Kissinger respected, was meeting with India's foreign minister T. N. Kaul, along with U.S. ambassador Kenneth Keating and Hal Saunders of Kissinger's staff. Saunders's written report to Kissinger said: "Kaul . . . was tentative but negative, saying that India could not afford to take security risks until the political problem in East Pakistan was resolved."

He added that Kaul had said: "India has no territorial designs but if attacked . . . was determined that it would be a 'decisive war with decisive results.' . . . Kaul stressed that 'all' the refugees, irrespective of their religion, 'must' return."

For her part, Mrs. Gandhi privately portrayed Nixon as something of a puppet, saying: "It was not so much Mr. Nixon talking as Mr. Kissinger, because Mr. Nixon would talk for a few minutes and would then say, 'Isn't that right, Henry?' and from then on Henry would talk on for quite a while and then Nixon would say two words and then he would say, 'Wouldn't you say so, Henry?' "

Lies begat lies on all sides, though Yahya Khan's lies were really delusions. In fact, India was preparing to enter East Pakistan, and Yahya was considering plans to attack India from West Pakistan. It was a mad scheme, but one of his men, foreign secretary Sultan M. Khan, a career diplomat, reported the Pakistani leader's thinking this way: "The President said that the alternative was to lose East Pakistan through a process of attrition. India would then turn its full military might against West Pakistan. Military operations along West Pakistan's border would hold out the hope of (1) arousing the world to do something to halt the conflict, (2) relieving pressure on East Pakistan, and (3) making impressive gains across from West Pakistan"—perhaps taking back some or even all of Kashmir, a part of British India divided between and claimed by both countries. On November 14, India's defense minister, Jaglivan Ram, said Pakistan was planning preemptive bombing of Indian airfields in Kashmir, and his words were carried in *The Washington Post*.

On Monday, November 14, the national price freeze ended with inflation calculated at 1.9 percent, compared with 3.8 percent when it was initiated on August 15. Phase II of the New Economic Policy began with goals of holding price increases to an annual rate of 2.5 percent and wage increases to 5.5 percent. The difference in those figures was based on an estimated 3 percent increase in worker productivity. At the first Pay Board meeting, George Meany kept his overcoat on, claiming the room was chilly. At the second meeting, the board voted 10 to 5 to approve a 17.5 percent hourly pay increase negotiated by soft-coal miners in West Virginia. Then, when mine operators simultaneously applied to the Price Commission for a 17.5 percent increase in coal prices, the commission approved only half the increase, allowing a price rise of only 8 percent. Probably the most revealing statistic was the number of requests for rule clarifications received by the Price Commission during the first two weeks: four hundred thousand. *Business Week* quoted a Yale economist,

James Tobin, as saying: "The administration has undertaken an adventure in a controlled economy that is destined to diminish the rate of inflation from 4 percent plus to 3 percent minus a year. What are the great benefits of so modest a difference in the speed of inflation?"

Presumably Tobin, a liberal who had been an adviser to President Kennedy, knew the answer. The controls were enormously popular with the public and Nixon had seized the most important of campaign issues from the Democrats. The President was doing *something* about high prices. George Meany knew that, too. He did not like the President and he did not like wage controls, but he was serving, grouchily, on the Pay Board. Meany's way was to sulk and insult. He got his big chance to try to humiliate Nixon during the biennial meeting of the AFL-CIO in Bal Harbour, Florida, the third week in November.

The President wanted to make one more try to win over labor—or to exploit their political opposition—and he wanted to do it his way, with carefully rehearsed spontaneity. For more than a week he talked about playing, as he put it, "Daniel in the Lions' Den." He wanted a complete speech written—"Dull, routine stuff," he said—then he would throw away the text and say he wanted to speak from the heart on workingmen's devotion to the good of the country. Then he would say that what was good for America was his New Economic Policy.

On November 19 he went to Bal Harbour—and Meany played the grumpy lion. He removed the band from the hall so that there would be no "Hail to the Chief." The President was shown to a seat in the second row of executive council members arrayed behind Meany. Finally, the President was allowed to stand up. He waved his speech text, then put it aside, saying, "You like it straight from the shoulder. . . . I know from experience the past three years that when the chips are down organized labor is for America."

Nixon looked tired. He had been up most of the night, and the night before, working on his straight-from-the-shoulder remarks, then memorizing them. He concentrated on Vietnam and Cambodia. "Some wrote in those days that the President stood alone. But I was not alone. One hundred and fifty thousand American workers walked down Wall Street. . . ." When he switched to the price freeze near the end, he said, "It was a remarkable success." The audience groaned. "If you don't think so, go home and ask your wives, who go to the grocery." The audience laughed.

"The audience packed into the convention hall of the Americana Hotel," reported *The New York Times*, "reacted with polite hostility, punctuated occasionally by derisive laughter. As Mr. Nixon was shaking hands with some of the delegates after his speech, George Meany, the fed-eration's president, gaveled the convention to order. No sooner had Mr. Nixon left the hall than Mr. Meany announced, 'We will now proceed to Act II.' This touched off laughter, cheering, whistling and applause that far exceeded the minimal response to the President's 30-minute address."

The headline the next morning, a Saturday, in *The New York Times* was "PRESIDENT ASKS LABOR'S SUPPORT; RECEPTION IS COOL." The last three words upset Nixon. At 9 A.M., he was with Haldeman and Colson, saying, "Override 'Cool' and make this a 'Labor is rude to courageous President' story." He also wanted to get out the line that one of the pieces of AFL-CIO business taken care of that day was increasing Meany's salary from seventy thousand to ninety thousand dollars a year. He even personally wrote out lines for a speech to the Bal Harbour convention, telling his men to find someone to say his words of self-praise. "Let me tell you something about this man. As you know, I am a Democrat. . . . He is one of the most considerate, honest men I have ever had the privilege to know. . . . a fair man, a decent man. No one ever came into the Presidency owing organized labor less politically than he did. And no one in the Presidency has ever been more fair and more considerate than he has been. . . . I don't care what you say about me, but I care very much what you say about a man that I believe will go down in history as one of America's great Presidents."

He was getting ready to leave for Camp David when Haldeman came back into the Oval Office with good news: by 10 A.M., the White House had received almost five hundred telegrams about his cool and rude reception, and they were overwhelmingly favorable to him. Cheered up, the President gave Haldeman a quick three-point analysis of where they were: "First, we can't make peace with the labor unions; second, the Pay Board must be tough and not back down to them; and third, it'll be very hard to make the Hoffa move right now. . . ."

"The Hoffa move" was a pardon or executive clemency that would get James R. Hoffa, the former president of the International Brotherhood of Teamsters, out of the federal penitentiary in Lewisburg, Pennsylvania, where he had served four years of an eight-year sentence for fraud and attempted jury-tampering. Nixon, who had been supported by the Teamsters in the 1968 election, had been considering releasing Jimmy Hoffa in the annual Christmas package of 250 or so clemency releases, hoping holiday cheer would mellow criticism.

At Camp David, the President read the telegrams on the labor speech, getting into a better and better mood. He phoned Haldeman to read him some of the messages and heard that the press generally was attacking Meany as rude, a boor, an old man who did not know his place. The best headline was from *The Miami Herald:* "BIG LABOR BLOWS THE

GAME WITH AN INTENTIONAL FOUL." In *Life,* Hugh Sidey wrote: "In the White House the President's inner circle of advisers . . . were almost unanimous in opposing the trip. It is remarkable how little the men around Nixon understand him. The smell of crisis, the opportunity for political manipulation is always irresistible. Nixon went to Miami Beach, absorbed Meany's pathetic insults, clamped his jaw and said he would hold down inflation with or without labor's help."

Sidey asked for a long interview with the President in December, a tip-off that this year, finally, Nixon was to be *Time*'s "Man of the Year." Calling Haldeman from Camp David, Nixon also brought up a memo he had just read from Clark MacGregor, a former Minnesota congressman moved to the White House staff after losing a Senate race to Hubert Humphrey, on the possibility that Democrats in Congress were about to attach a rider to tax legislation that would mandate federal financing of presidential elections, providing $20.4 million each for the candidates of the two major parties. On Monday, he told MacGregor to fight the idea any way he could, calling it tax relief for the Democratic National Committee, which still had $9 million in debts from the 1968 campaign, while Republicans had more money than ever. Suddenly Kissinger burst in, saying that Pakistani radio was reporting a full-scale Indian invasion of East Pakistan. India was denying that and the CIA could not confirm it. Haldeman's last two notes for the day recorded: "By 9 o'clock tonight Henry still didn't have any confirmation. Our vast intelligence network doesn't seem to be able to tell us when a couple of major nations are at war, which is a little alarming. . . ." and "The President wants the White House Christmas parties all scheduled during the time he's gone, so he won't have to attend them."

It took days for the United States to learn details of the fighting along the border between East Pakistan and India. "Incursion in self-defense" was the language used by the Indians—sly wording that was not lost on Nixon. Indian troops—along with East Bengali guerrillas called the Mukti Bahini—had moved several miles into East Pakistan and occupied a number of villages for a day or two before withdrawing. In the Pakistani version, the Indian troops had been driven back in hard fighting. On November 29, in a post facto explanation, the Indians said that they had been called in to aid East Bengali guerrilla units under strong attack by Pakistani troops.

The President was not interested in those details or many others. He believed that Prime Minister Gandhi wanted a war and wanted to destroy all of Pakistan. He believed that the Soviet Union was encouraging India to destroy Pakistan and thus humiliate both the United States and China. He wanted all aid to India cut off. He wanted Kissinger to find ways to secretly aid Pakistan, and to stay in touch with China. Protect the China initiative.

On December 2, President Yahya Khan, who was slipping into long bouts of inaction, sent President Nixon a letter formally invoking article 1 of the 1959 aid treaty, which read: "In case of aggression against Pakistan, the Government of the United States of America, in accordance with the Constitution of the United States of America, will take such appropriate action, including the use of armed forces, as may be mutually agreed upon . . . in order to assist the Government of Pakistan at its request." Even though Pakistan was a member of the Southeast Asia Treaty Organization—SEATO was the NATO of Asia—the treaty words were essentially meaningless. In effect, only two secretive Americans, Nixon and Kissinger, felt true obligation toward Pakistan. Congress, the State Department, the press, and public opinion favored India. Long segments on the brutality of Pakistani soldiers were being shown each night on network news; Nixon's own news summaries called it "the horror show." In the Senate, Frank Church of Idaho was among many who rose to speak. He said: "I can't understand why in the face of the largest human migration in history, the suffering of so many people, the malnutrition, maiming, killing, there is not one word of official sympathy from Washington." As for State, Kissinger had been bouncing in and out of the Oval Office day after day complaining that Rogers had been telling reporters, on background, that the White House was trying to push him into an anti-India position—which was true. On cue, Kissinger told Haldeman he would resign if the Secretary of State undermined Pakistan, saying: "This is no idle threat."

There was better domestic news for the President that day. The Senate-House conference committee negotiating differences in tax bills passed by both houses pushed off the idea of public campaign financing, calling for reconsideration before the 1976 election. With that victory, a defensive one, the President took off for a weekend at Key Biscayne.

The next day, Friday, December 3, full-scale war broke out between India and Pakistan—not across the India–East Pakistan border, but a thousand miles away in Kashmir. Reports to the President were sketchy and contradictory at first, but it seemed that Pakistan had struck first, bombing airfields in northwestern India. "Suicidal," Kissinger told Nixon. In Islamabad, Yahya Khan called in the Chinese ambassador and then the American ambassador, Joseph Farland, and told them separately that India had commenced an air and land invasion of West Pakistan in Kashmir and east of Lahore—that was not true—and that Pakistan had responded with defensive measures against forward Indian airfields. He told the Chinese that he would have to withdraw Pakistani troops stationed near the Chinese border and suggested that the Chinese might consider engaging Indian forces in a disputed area called Ladakh. To Farland, an hour later, he said to tell Nixon that Pakistan would fight "to the bitter end" and asked for American military assistance.

Farland then told Foreign Secretary Sultan Khan that the first United States moves to aid Pakistan would be in the United Nations Security Council, but they would be vetoed by the Soviets. Then he said that he must return to the United States embassy. Asked why, Farland said that his air attache, a general named Charles Yaeger, called "Chuck," had told him that the Indian air force would respond to the raid by sending hundreds of planes to target Pakistani air bases and Pakistan would order all its planes into the air to engage the Indians and avoid being destroyed on the ground. Then, when the Pakistani planes had to land to refuel, the Indians would send a second wave of planes and destroy them. That is exactly what happened. By the next morning, airfields and oil and gas storage tanks across West Pakistan were in flames. The Indian army was advancing deeper into East Pakistan, passing by villagers along the roads, who were cheering: *"Joi Bangla!"*—"Victory for Bengal!" In Rawalpindi, Pakistan's military headquarters, Sultan Khan was sitting talking with President Yahya Khan. The President said he was counting on the United States to save Pakistan. The two men were sitting under sandbags in a pit just dug in the garden behind the President's house, his air-raid shelter. Someone came by to report that there was almost no gasoline left in the country for planes and tanks.

On December 3, the Washington Special Action Group (WSAG) was called together at 11 A.M. in the White House Situation Room. "I am getting hell every half hour from the President that we are not being tough enough on India," Kissinger began. "He just called me again. He does not believe we are carrying out his wishes. He wants to tilt in favor of Pakistan."

"What is happening in the West?" asked Sisco, one of the eleven men in the room. "Is a full-scale attack likely?"

Admiral Moorer answered: "The present pattern is puzzling in that the Paks have only struck at three small airfields, which did not house significant numbers of Indian combat aircraft. . . . The Pak attack is not credible. It has been made during late afternoon, which doesn't make sense. . . ."

"Is it possible that the Indians attacked first, and the Paks simply did what they could before dark in response?"

". . . Certainly possible," Moorer said.

After some talk of how to handle aid cut-offs, Kissinger closed by saying, "We have to take action. The President is blaming me, but you people are in the clear."

Sisco laughed. "That's ideal!"

Kissinger was not amused. He said: "We need to think about our treaty obligations. I remember a letter or memo interpreting our existing treaty with a special Indian tilt. When I visited Pakistan in 1962, I was briefed on a secret document or oral understanding about contingencies arising in other than a SEATO context. . . ." No one knew what he was talking about; there were no secret understandings.

The WSAG met the next day, Saturday. CIA director Helms reported that the agency did not yet know who started the action or why the Pakistanis had decided to bomb a few small airfields. There was, he continued, no declaration of war on either side—"No holds barred" were Mrs. Gandhi's words; Yahya said, "The final war with India"—but India was attacking East Pakistan on all sides and might occupy the country in just three or four days. Admiral Elmo Zumwalt said he thought Pakistan, with seventy thousand troops now in East Pakistan, might be able to hold out for a week or two. The official meeting minutes also recorded Kissinger's sarcasm about diplomatic and military people who seemed to be ignoring the President: "Dr. Kissinger said that whoever was putting out background information relative to the current situation is provoking the Presidential wrath. The President is under the 'illusion' that he is giving instructions; not that he is merely being kept apprised of affairs as they progress. Dr. Kissinger asked that this be kept in mind."

THE PRESIDENT stayed in Florida for most of Sunday, December 5, before returning to Washington late in the afternoon. He seemed strangely detached from the chaos in South Asia. In fact, Secretary of State Rogers was pleading with Haldeman to let him speak with the President by telephone before formulating an American position at a special session of the United Nations, and he finally sent a spokesman, identified in the press as "a senior State Department official," out to say on background: "The beginning of the crisis can fairly be said to be the use of force by Pakistan." But then he added: "We believe that since the beginning of the crisis Indian policy, in a systematic way, has led to the perpetuation of the crisis, a deepening of the crisis, and that India bears the major responsibility for the broader hostilities that have ensued."

In fact what the President wanted to talk about in calls to Haldeman and Ziegler that weekend was an NBC News special called "A Day in the Life of the President," scheduled to be filmed at the White House on Monday for broadcast two weeks later. He wanted a meeting set up to discuss Pakistan with Rogers, Kissinger, Connally, Moorer, Helms, and Laird. He also wanted "human interest-type phone calls," a visit from an old friend, and more of Mrs. Nixon and less of King Timahoe in the script.

The President's television day began at 7:45 A.M., with a breakfast meeting with congressional leaders. While the NBC crew was in the room, the President, Senators Mansfield and Scott, and the others talked about the death of Harriet McCormack, wife of the former Speaker of the House, John McCormack. As soon as the cameras and microphones were gone, questions began about Pakistan and India. The President said that information was coming out very slowly, but that it was obvious that India was the aggressor in both East and West Pakistan. Hale Boggs, the Democratic majority leader in the House, was the only one to bring up the way the Pakistani army had treated the Bengalis during more than six months of occupation. Mansfield said he thought the United States should leave this to the United Nations.

When the meeting broke up, NBC was invited back in to film a Kissinger briefing, which ended with a show call to George Bush, waiting by his phone at the United Nations in New York. "George," Nixon said. "Get the facts out with regard to what we have done, that we have worked for a political settlement, what we have done for the refugees and so forth and so on. If you see that some here in the Senate and House, for whatever reason, get out and misrepresent our opinions, I want you to hit it frontally, strongly and toughly; is that clear? Just take the gloves off and crack it, because you know exactly what we have done, O.K.?"

Actually Bush had no idea what "we" had done. Only Kissinger and Nixon knew. The television day continued with a staff meeting at 9:30. Shultz, who was there, pulled the President off camera to tell him that George Meany had suffered a heart attack and would be out of action for at least a couple of months. Then there was a Domestic Council meeting at 10:00 and, at 10:30, a ceremony accepting the credentials of five new ambassadors to the United States. One of them, Nawabzada Agha Mohammad Raza, happened to be from Pakistan, which gave Nixon the chance to say: "In recent months, your nation has been buffeted by natural and other catastrophes. We are happy that the United States has been able significantly to assist. . . . we have followed with sympathetic interest the efforts of the government and people of Pakistan. We have welcomed the efforts of President Yahya Khan to move to reduce tensions in the subcontinent."

Next, Nixon had a show economics meeting with Connally, Shultz, and Burns. His daughter Julie Eisenhower, as scripted, dropped in for ten minutes. Then someone realized that no "old friend dropping in" had been scheduled and Rose Mary Woods went down to the press room and found Willard Edwards of the *Chicago Tribune,* who had known

Nixon when he was in Congress, and the reporter came up and shook hands for the cameras. The President gave him cuff links and a tie clasp.

Off camera, at 11 A.M., WSAG, now eighteen "principals" and their assistants, began its third session on the war. It was 10 P.M. Monday in East Pakistan and India had already recognized Mujib's rebels as the government of a new country, Bangla Desh, "Bengal Nation." In New York, at the United Nations, Ambassador Bush, speaking for the United States, announced that the State Department was cutting off $87 million of nonmilitary aid to India, saying, "There's a quite clear aggressor. . . . it's India." A *Washington Post* editorial the next morning called those actions "Puzzling . . . punitive . . . laughable."

But there was no laughter in the White House, as both Nixon and Kissinger insisted that India was on the verge of attacking both East and West Pakistan—even though at the Monday meeting the army chief of staff, General William Westmoreland, had said that there was no real indication that the Indians intended to mount an invasion of West Pakistan. He estimated it would take at least a week to move an Indian division across the thousand miles from East to West Pakistan. To move all the Indian troops inside or around East Pakistan would take more than a month.

The minutes of the WSAG meeting continued:

> Dr. Kissinger asked what is to be done with Bangla Desh. Mr. Helms stated that for all practical purposes it is now an independent country. . . . Dr. Kissinger then asked whether we have the right to authorize Jordan or Saudi Arabia to transfer military equipment to Pakistan. . . . Van Hollen stated the United States cannot permit a third country to transfer arms which we have provided them when we, ourselves, do not authorize sale direct to the ultimate recipient. . . .* Dr. Kissinger said the President may want to honor those requests. . . . It is quite obvious that the President is not inclined to let the Paks be defeated.

The meeting broke up after two hours. The consensus, stated by Sisco, was: "From a political point of view our efforts would have to be directed at keeping the Indians from extinguishing West Pakistan." What Kissinger passed along to the President after that meeting included: "We don't really have any choice. We can't allow a friend of ours and China's to get screwed in a conflict with a friend of Russia's."

---

* Christopher Van Hollen was the senior South Asia analyst in the State Department.

At 1:30 P.M., for the NBC cameras, the President called together some of the WSAG members, along with Rogers and Connally, for a less than candid discussion of the same questions in EOB 175. The Secretary of State set the tone: "We can't be blamed for this—there have been many, many areas of the world we just can't be responsible for." The cameras also caught a Nixon smile when he got the word that the Senate had approved, by 89 to 1, the nomination of Lewis Powell to the Supreme Court and was beginning hearings on his second nominee, Assistant Attorney General William Rehnquist. Off camera, Kissinger went to Haldeman to say he was resigning—the reason, as far as Haldeman could tell, and as he told the President, was Kissinger's anger over how much time Rogers was getting on television. He said he wanted to announce his resignation in December, but then stay on through the China trip, scheduled for late February, and leave in June. Haldeman came out of the President's office, called Kissinger, and said Nixon wanted him to stay, but if he announced in December he should leave in December. No China.

On December 7, with Senators Edward Kennedy and Edmund Muskie leading a chorus of Democrats questioning the White House's two-man cold war with India, Kissinger was delegated to background the press. He began, "First of all, let us get a number of things straight. There have been some comments that the administration is anti-Indian. This is totally inaccurate."

By the end of that day, Indian forces occupied half of East Pakistan. The next morning, at the daily WSAG meeting, Kissinger brought up the Indian blockade of Pakistani ports, asking Undersecretary of State U. Alexis Johnson: "Can we allow a U.S. ally to go down completely while we participate in a blockade? Can we allow the Indians to scare us off, believing that if U.S. supplies are needed they will not be provided?"

Johnson answered that, legally, nations at war have the right to blockade. That set Kissinger off and he said once more: "We are not trying to be even-handed. . . . There can be no doubt what the President wants. The President does not want to be even-handed. The President believes that India is the attacker. We are trying to get across the idea that India has jeopardized relations with the United States. We cannot afford to ease India's state of mind."

The national security adviser was yelling his way through meetings—and Haldeman was telling the President about the tirades. This time he had a letter of resignation, too. "There's something wrong with Henry," Nixon said. "It's not just Pakistan. It's personal. He's tired." Haldeman thought a lot of it was that Kissinger knew that much of the Pakistan problem was his own fault, but he did not say that to Nixon. Instead, Kissinger's deputy, Colonel Haig, was brought in and he said that

Kissinger was exhausted and he was tired of fighting State day after day—particularly when State was basically right on India-Pakistan—but that no matter what threats he made he would not quit if it meant not getting to China with the President.

At the end of the day, after talking with Mitchell, the President told Haldeman he was going to pardon Jimmy Hoffa.

Whoever deserved blame for the United States's embarrassment in South Asia, the President and Kissinger still appeared to be of one mind. The news summary that day referred to a *Time* magazine quote: "Who attacked whom was still open to question. . . . But the U.S.'s blatant partiality toward Pakistan seemed both unreasonable and unwise." Nixon underlined the passage and scrawled, "K—This must be knocked down."

The next item summed up why Kissinger, if not Nixon, deserved blame: "*Newsweek* avoids saying who bore chief responsibility for provoking the conflict but 'It was clear that Yahya's bold gamble to cripple Indian air power with a single devastating Israeli-type blow had failed.' And India welcomed the opportunity to take off the gloves. It has successfully goaded Pakistan into starting an unwinnable war. The Indian goal of 25 years—dismembering Pakistan—is clearly in sight." Now, Nixon and Kissinger were united in believing, or saying, that the new Indian goal was eliminating all of Pakistan—and that the Soviet Union was pushing them in that direction, into invading West Pakistan.

Late on December 9, the Soviet minister of agriculture, Vladimir Matskevich, who was in the United States to meet with his new American counterpart, Secretary of Agriculture Earl Butz, was brought to the White House for a secret meeting. The President had a message for Brezhnev, an extraordinarily clear threat:

> What I want to suggest is that you ask whether India's gains— which are certain—are worth jeopardizing your relations with the United States. I don't say this in a threatening way. . . . The first requirement is a cease-fire. The second requirement is that India desist from attacks in West Pakistan. If India moves forces against West Pakistan, the United States cannot stand by. . . . If the Indians continue their military operations, we must inevitably look toward a confrontation between the Soviet Union and the United States.

Much different messages to China were delivered by Kissinger, who flew to New York the next day and met with the new Chinese ambassador to the United Nations, Huang Hua, at a CIA "safe" apartment in a building on the Upper East Side of Manhattan. It may not have been as safe or secret after Kissinger arrived in a limousine with Secret Service agents jumping out to block traffic on the streets while the national security adviser walked into the building.

First Kissinger handed the ambassador a "Top Secret / Sensitive" folder of United States intelligence and photos of Soviet installations and troop disposition along the Chinese-Soviet border, and said: "We have received a report that one of your personnel in a European country, in a conversation with another European, expressed uncertainty about the Soviet disposition on your borders and a desire for information about them. . . . We would be prepared at your request, and through whatever sources you wish, to give you whatever information we have about the disposition of Soviet forces"—from surveillance by spy satellites. "We read that you brought a master spy with you. . . . You don't need a master spy. We give you everything."

The surprised Chinese official thanked him profusely. Most of the conversation then was about the war in South Asia. Kissinger began:

> We have an intelligence report according to which Mrs. Gandhi told her cabinet that she wants to destroy the Pakistani army and air force and to annex Azad Kashmir,* and then to offer a cease-fire. This is what we believe must be prevented and this is why I have taken the liberty to ask for this meeting with the Ambassador. . . . We worked with a number of countries to provide aid to Pakistan. . . . We said that if they decide that their national security requires shipment of American arms to Pakistan, we are obliged to protest, but we will understand. We will not protest with great intensity. And we will make it up to them in next year's budget. . . . On this basis, four planes are leaving Jordan today and 22 over the weekend. Ammunition and other equipment is going from Iran. . . . Six planes from Turkey in the near future. This is very confidential obviously, and we are not eager for it to be known. At least not until Congress gets out of town. . . .

Back in Washington, the Senate, whose members were anxious to adjourn, approved the nomination of William Rehnquist to the Supreme Court by a 68-to-26 vote. In less than three years, Nixon had named four justices to the court. ABC News that night reported: "By naming four conservatives, Richard Nixon has determined the image and way of American institutions far beyond his own Presidency."

---

* Azad Kashmir is the Pakistani portion of the divided old Indian province of Kashmir.

The other big story was the naval movement Kissinger had talked about: a task force built around the aircraft carrier *Enterprise,* the most powerful ship in the world, with five thousand men and seventy-five combat aircraft, was heading from waters off Vietnam for a scheduled arrival in the Bay of Bengal just before noon on December 16. The official story was that the ships were needed to evacuate Americans in East Pakistan. Actually, though, there were only seventy-five men in the consulate in Dacca—their families had been sent home when troops from West Pakistan began terrorizing the city. The real mission was to show American resolve, to discourage Soviet moves, and, perhaps, to divert Indian ships and planes from the war. Notes of the WSAG meeting of December 8 recorded: "Dr. Kissinger stated that we may be in a situation where a country (India), equipped and supported by the Soviets, may be turning half of Pakistan into an impotent state and the other half into a vassal. . . ." The task force operation was code-named "Oh, Calcutta!" after a Broadway show that had created something of a sensation because it featured nudity.

On December 12, after a morning of listening to arguments between Rogers and Kissinger at Camp David, the President boarded *Air Force One* to fly to the Azores, the Portuguese islands in the Atlantic Ocean, for a meeting with President Pompidou of France to discuss the continuing differences between the United States and European countries over the value of currencies and the effect of taxes on trade. John Connally had been meeting in Rome with the Group of Ten—the industrialized nations of Europe and North America, along with Japan—and the Americans were finally retreating, offering to drop the import tax in return for exchange rates more favorable to United States trade. The biggest problem was the French, who wanted gold revalued. Stalemate again. So presidents Nixon and Pompidou had agreed to meet.

Nixon flew over with his dueling foreign policy advisers and the feuding continued. During a photo session starring the two leaders, Kissinger told Haldeman that he was not going into the meeting room. He planned to sit on a chair just outside the room ready for the dramatic moment when the President would call. "Don't push your luck, Henry," said Haldeman. He did, of course, and sat alone for two and a half hours, stewing. Then someone saw him there. It was Rogers, who had thought his rival was inside with the presidents. Kissinger took his frustration out on Haig, yelling at him to do something about that idiot George Bush. The President heard some of it and told Haldeman he was shocked.

Nixon and Pompidou talked money for two full days before agreeing to agree. Their final statement, read on December 14 in a sunny garden, began: "President Nixon and President Pompidou reached a broad area of agreement on measures necessary . . . to work toward a prompt realignment of exchange rates through a devaluation of the dollar and reevaluation of some other currencies. . . ." The actual numbers would be negotiated by a meeting of the Group of Ten in Washington. Nixon celebrated by staying up until 4:20 A.M. listening on Armed Forces Radio to a broadcast of the National Football League game between the Washington Redskins and the Los Angeles Rams. The American party flew back the next day. On *Air Force One*, Kissinger sat in the back for a time, briefing the five pool reporters allowed on board, who were expected to share their notes with the entire presidential press corps on landing. He was to be identified as "a high administration source." What he said produced this two-column headline on the front page of *The New York Times:* "NIXON MAY REVIEW TRIP UNLESS SOVIET CURBS INDIA." The story was big enough that *The Washington Post* decided to identify Kissinger as the source.

Within hours, on Nixon's instruction, Ron Ziegler called a press conference to say, "No U.S. official was suggesting or intending to suggest that the United States was considering canceling the United States–Soviet summit."

The plane landed at Andrews Air Force Base a little after four o'clock in the afternoon. By the time Nixon reached the White House, the annual presidential holiday reception for members of Congress was under way. He slipped into the building through the underground entrance from the Treasury building, to avoid the party, and went upstairs to watch a taped replay of the Redskins game in the solarium by himself. Across the world, in Dacca, MIG-21s of the Indian air force were bombing Government House, the residence of East Pakistan's governor, A. M. Malik, into a smoking ruin. In a bunker under the garden, Malik washed his feet, placed a handkerchief over his head, and prayed toward Mecca. Then, his hand shaking, Malik wrote out his resignation from office and handed it to a United Nations official named John Kelly. The city was surrounded by Indian troops. It was the eleventh day of the war in East Pakistan.

The next day, December 15, Nixon reported to the leaders of both parties and both houses of Congress on the meeting in the Azores, saying it was the best ever between presidents of France and the United States. "On the price front, our policy is succeeding," he said. "On the job front, we have a good chance to succeed, thanks to the tax bill just passed. . . . The reaction of the unsophisticated to devaluation is that prices will go up. For 95 percent of Americans who buy in America, it means no change in prices—and it means more jobs."

Nixon, Connally, and Kissinger then reported on the negotiations with the French and on the preliminary talks in Rome with other members of the Group of Ten. "We have broken the logjam," said the President. "A solution is now certain."

"Frankly, we used the Congress as a bargaining lever," he continued, saying that the price of gold was a serious and emotional issue to the French, but he had said the Congress would not approve any change until they knew the details of an international trade package. "I said, 'The Congress won't buy a pig in a poke.' "

"That was a hell of a translation problem," said Kissinger, who seemed to be coming out of his funk, even though he knew the President was mad as hell about the summit story.

"Each of the European countries hide behind their commitment to the Common Market," Connally added. "It is extremely difficult to get all your 'coons up one tree."

"That would be hard to translate too," said Nixon.

THE DIALOGUE WAS FUN, but the President wanted to talk economics and trade and more American jobs—and football—while Kissinger kept calling to talk about Pakistan, or Rogers, whom he was now blaming for public criticism of his own moves in South Asia. Finally, the President told Haldeman to stop the calls. He was going to Key Biscayne—and he wanted no calls there, either. He had had enough of his depressed national security adviser for a while.

Kissinger's despair was also getting tied up in yet another investigation of who leaked what. The Plumbers, David Young and Bud Krogh, were assigned to find the source of a Jack Anderson column on the Indo-Pakistani War. The seven hundred words included word-for-word material from the notes of the WSAG meeting of December 3, including Kissinger's words "I'm getting hell from the President. . . . He wants to tilt in favor of Pakistan."

ON DECEMBER 16, on a grassy field in Dacca called the Race Course, the Pakistani commander in East Pakistan, General A.A.K. Niazi, unconditionally surrendered his seventy thousand troops to the Indian commander, General Jagit Singh Aurora. India then declared a cease-fire in both the east and the west. Yahya Khan vowed to continue fighting in the west, where a tank battle was raging in a West Pakistani town called Shakagarth, but twenty-eight hours later, at 7:30 P.M. in Rawalpindi, he accepted a total cease-fire. The war was over.

That same day, Nixon received a letter from Prime Minister

Gandhi saying that the war could have been avoided if the United States had used its power and authority to foster or broker a political solution to the repression of East Pakistan. It was a blistering, contemptuous message meant for public consumption, released to the press as it was being delivered. She echoed the words of the American Declaration of Independence, saying: "All unprejudiced persons objectively surveying the grim events in Bangladesh since March 25 have recognized the revolt of 75 million people who were forced to the conclusion that neither their life, nor their liberty, to say nothing of the possibility of the pursuit of happiness, was available to them. . . . The fact of the matter is that the rulers of West Pakistan got away with the impression that they could do what they liked because no one, not even the United States, would choose to take a public position that while Pakistan's integrity was certainly sacrosanct, human rights, liberty were no less so. . . ."

Yahya Khan announced his resignation on December 18 and called on Deputy Prime Minister Zulfikar Ali Bhutto to form a new government of Pakistan—or what remained of it, the old West Pakistan. Bhutto, the leader of the Pakistan People's Party, which had won a majority of West Pakistan seats in the National Assembly elected in December 1970, was in the United States, where he had argued the Pakistani case at the United Nations until he walked out in tears on December 15, accusing the UN of "legalizing aggression." Bhutto, a graduate of the University of California at Berkeley, had a reputation for being anti-American, but he happened to be meeting with President Nixon on December 18, the day the news came.

The President apologized for having only a half hour free because the Group of Ten was meeting in Washington to determine specific currency exchange rates. Bhutto said he understood and added that he wanted to say that his attitude toward the United States had been greatly changed during the past months. He joked that he was willing to come back to manage Nixon's reelection campaign in 1972. The notes of their meeting included: "Mr. Bhutto stated that the real significance of recent events was the fact that the Soviet Union was able to neutralize Chinese flexibility and to vastly improve its influence in the area at the expense of Communist China. This would mean that Indian appetites for further aggression could be whetted. President Nixon replied that this was precisely his view."

Two hours later, the President went over to the Smithsonian Institution on the grassy mall between the Capitol and the Lincoln Memorial to announce that the Group of Ten had reached agreement: "It is my very great privilege to announce on behalf of the Finance Ministers and the other representatives of the ten nations involved, the conclusion of the

most significant monetary agreement in the history of the world. . . .
Now we have a new world, fortunately a much better world economically. . . ."

"I hope it lasts three months," said Paul Volcker under his breath.

The bottom line result of the negotiations, which had begun with
the President's announcement of a New Economic Policy in August, was
the elimination of the 10 percent surcharge on imported goods and an
8.57 percent devaluation of the United States dollar against other major
currencies. Paul McCracken, the chairman of the Council of Economic
Advisers, had estimated 350,000 new jobs in a memo to the White
House. Not good enough, Colson said. McCracken changed the estimate
to 500,000.

CHAPTER 26

January 2, 1972

AT 5 P.M. ON DECEMBER 21, the President returned to Washington after a meeting with British prime minister Edward Heath in Bermuda. John Ehrlichman asked to see Nixon on an urgent matter. His Plumbers, David Young and Bud Krogh, were certain they had found the source of the leaks of the minutes of WSAG Indo-Pakistan meetings to Jack Anderson.

Anderson had made a revealing mistake in listing the ships accompanying the carrier *Enterprise* on its trip from the China Sea to the Bay of Bengal. The columnist had listed three destroyers, the *Parsons*, the *Decatur*, and the *Tartar Sam*. But there was no Navy ship called *Tartar Sam*. Admiral Robert Welander, the Joint Chiefs of Staff liaison to the National Security Council, read the column in *The Washington Post* and immediately knew what had happened. He had written "Tartar SAM" on a memo to Kissinger about the naval task force, identifying not a ship but the type of surface-to-air missile on the destroyers. Only four men, including himself, had seen the memo. The others were Kissinger, Haig, and the man who had typed it, Yeoman Charles Radford. The Navy stenographer had personally handed the memo to Kissinger and Haig. Welander told Haig that he believed Radford must have leaked the minutes and added a possible motive: the young sailor had made many Indian friends during a year's service in the United States embassy in New Delhi.

Haig sent the admiral to Krogh and Young. Welander explained

"Tartar Sam," but he did not reveal that Radford's Pentagon assignment was to pass NSC documents through him to the Joint Chiefs. Welander had succeeded Admiral Rembrandt Robinson, the man who recruited Radford for the spying. Krogh and Young went to their boss, Ehrlichman, and he told them to interrogate Radford. That was done the next day, December 17, with Young and David Stewart of the Defense Investigation Service asking the questions. One of the first ones, always used by Stewart in leak-tracing, was: "Do you know Jack Anderson?"

"Yes sir, I do."

It turned out that Radford, a Mormon, had helped Anderson's parents find a Mormon service in New Delhi and had become a friend of the family. In fact, he had had dinner with Anderson four days before the columnist published the first WSAG minutes. But he denied passing any documents to the columnist then, or ever. When Stewart called him a traitor, Radford admitted he was passing documents—not to Anderson but to Admiral Moorer, the chairman of the Joint Chiefs of Staff. He broke down several times, crying, admitting that he had photocopied more than five thousand documents—taken from desks, burn bags, and even the briefcases used by Haig and Kissinger—including reports of Kissinger's conversations with Chou En-lai and notes of his secret meetings with the North Vietnamese in Paris. The young sailor said he was acting on orders, first from Robinson and then from Welander, but it also turned out that he despised Kissinger because of his arrogance and the way he treated his staff. Radford called Kissinger a tyrant. It also turned out that only a week before seeing Anderson, Radford's application for officer training had been rejected, even though it included recommendations from Welander and Haig.

Lie detector tests indicated that Radford was telling the truth about spying for the Pentagon and lying when he denied helping Anderson. Then Ehrlichman went to the President, who told him to question Welander himself. But Nixon showed no emotion at all, which surprised Ehrlichman. The President told him you always had to assume that the military served itself and was watching civilians.

The next day Ehrlichman questioned Admiral Welander for more than an hour, taping the session. The admiral talked easily, saying that he was only following orders and past procedure. He said the spying was necessary because Kissinger regularly withheld or distorted critical information the Pentagon needed. He confirmed but refused to sign a statement, prepared in advance by Ehrlichman, that read, in part: "Yeoman Charles Radford, while my aide in my capacity as Liaison Officer between the National Security Council and the Office of the Chairman of the Joint Chiefs of Staff, did obtain unauthorized copies of various documents and memoranda relating to, among other matters, memcons of private top-level meetings, internal White House political dealings, secret negotiations with foreign governments, contingency plans, political agreements, troop movements, telcons, secret channel papers and defense budget papers. . . . As I considered it part of my job to inform the Chairman of the Joint Chiefs, I either directly or indirectly passed those papers of particular interest on to him."

Ehrlichman, with Haldeman, told Kissinger on December 23. The national security adviser said he did not believe him. Ehrlichman played the Welander tape. Kissinger seemed calm, too, at first. But talking to Ehrlichman the next day, Christmas Eve, he realized that Nixon intended to cover up the spying. Nothing was to be made public and Admiral Moorer was to be routinely reappointed to another two-year term as chairman. He had been questioned by Attorney General Mitchell and had denied everything. He was obviously lying, but just as obviously the President did not want a confrontation with the military. When he heard from Ehrlichman that Moorer would be reappointed, Kissinger came roaring into Haldeman's office, out of control, yelling: "He won't fire Moorer! They can spy on him and spy on me and betray us and he won't fire them! . . . I assure you all this tolerance will lead to very serious consequences for this Administration."

Two hours later, Kissinger, who had not seen Nixon alone for two weeks, went, uninvited, to the President's EOB office and began a long, slow, monotone monologue: "I tell you, Mr. President, this is very serious. We cannot survive the kinds of internal weaknesses we are seeing." *

Nixon tried to joke about it, wishing Kissinger a merry Christmas. When Kissinger left, talking to himself as he went, the President called in Ehrlichman and told him to talk to Haig, to see if Haig could persuade Kissinger to see a psychiatrist. Thinking about Nixon's odd calm, Ehrlichman finally concluded that the President was not at all unhappy to let the chairman of the Joint Chiefs know he had something on him—"Moorer is our man now," Ehrlichman said later—and that he was consciously trying to separate Kissinger and Haig so that the ambitious general could keep an eye on the volatile professor. But when Ehrlichman approached Haig about watching Kissinger more closely, the general said: "The President needs Henry. You've got to realize the President isn't doing his homework these days. It's only Henry who pulls us through."

---

* When President Nixon essentially decided that there would be no White House investigation of Radford's spying, the sailor was assigned to a Naval Reserve Center in Salem, Oregon—near his family home. Ehrlichman, at Nixon's direction, ordered Krogh to go to the Justice Department for authorization to tap Radford's telephone in Oregon. He refused and was removed from the Plumbers assignment.

The President was still refusing to see Kissinger, telling Haldeman, "You handle him." The chief of staff dictated his thoughts about that during the last week of the year. He began by citing a conversation with a new Kissinger assistant, John Scali, a former ABC News diplomatic correspondent:

> I had a long talk with Scali. . . . the real problem is that he's convinced that Henry has practically taken leave of his senses— that he's lying to the press, lying to the Secretary and, worst of all, lying to the P, particularly on India-Pakistan. . . . The K-Rogers problem flared back up, as Rogers had a press conference and Henry called me tonight all hung up again, because he says Rogers has shot us down on two principal issues: first, saying there was no danger of cancellation of the Russian summit, which Henry was using as a threat; and second, saying there was no agreement to defend Pakistan, which the P had told Henry to get out that there was. . . . The P made the point to me that there's going to come a time when K's going to have to shape up and start worrying about the P, instead of worrying about himself. . . . Henry came over to talk to me. He says he's going through a period of very deep thinking and serious evaluation as to what his position is. He feels that the President has lost confidence in him and that he's being maneuvered by the P in the same way the P maneuvers Rogers and others, and this worries him. . . . He seemed very uptight. He admitted he was egotistical and nervous and all that, but also said that he was of great value to the P. . . . He tossed in this thing of his being essential to the China trip, and so on.

Kissinger's ideas, as recorded by Haldeman, included:

> Henry boiled it down to the point that he's got to have his demands met. First of all that Rogers has to understand that any attack on Kissinger by the State Department or any of its people is a direct attack on the President. Second, that all cables and communications out of State must be cleared at the White House first. Third, that there has to be no communication between State and the Soviets without prior knowledge of the White House and without a memcon afterwards summarizing everything that was discussed. . . .

• • •

As the President took off for holiday stays at both Key Biscayne and San Clemente, the White House pumped out year-end decisions and statements—and quieter political business. The Price Commission and Pay Board were announcing rollbacks, at least on high-visibility matters, ruling that the Postal Service could not raise the price of stamps, reducing a 12 percent raise for aerospace workers to 8 percent, and overruling a 34 percent rise in Blue Cross and Blue Shield rates for federal employees. Department stores and other retailers were ordered to publicly display the prices of items before the price freeze, so that customers could report increases to the Internal Revenue Service, which was supposed to be monitoring hundreds of thousands of small businesses and employers. The President approved a six-year $5.5 billion program to build reusable space shuttles to lift and place new space satellites. Jimmy Hoffa did not get a pardon, but he did get out of the federal penitentiary at Lewisburg; the President commuted his sentence with the proviso that he could not engage in union activity until March 1980, when his full thirteen-year sentence ended. There was also secret political business in progress, most of it directed at Senator Muskie, who was running ahead of the President in most polls. "Cool, strong and powerful," said Newsweek of the man from Maine. Spies were sending his daily schedules, along with some strategy memos and random thoughts, to the White House. The President was impressed enough to circulate material he was seeing with a note saying: "Haldeman's fellows have certainly got a source in the Muskie office. I'm sending you down a copy of a memo they stole."

That relative quiet was blasted on Christmas day, when more than two hundred United States planes based in South Vietnam, Thailand, and aboard aircraft carriers bombed North Vietnam in the largest single raid since President Johnson had halted daily bombing in November 1968. In Saigon, American reporters wrote that they believed that all combat-ready aircraft in the region were flying sorties in waves. The White House refused comment and the Defense Department issued a statement that said: "For a limited duration, protective air strikes against military targets in North Vietnam are being conducted by United States Air Force and United States Navy aircraft. The air strikes are in reaction to enemy activity which imperils the diminishing United States forces in South Vietnam."

By the fourth day of the bombing, December 28, there were some demonstrations around the country, most of them by Vietnam Veterans Against the War—a group of veterans occupied the Statue of Liberty for forty-eight hours, flying an upside-down American flag from the lady's crown—and most of them ineffectual. The movement had lost its momentum on the streets; Nixon had simply outmaneuvered and outwaited them. The opposition that concerned him now was in Congress, where antiwar legislators were coming closer to mobilizing the ultimate congressional power, cutting off funding.

In Key Biscayne, the President met for six hours with West German chancellor Willy Brandt. Those talks completed a cycle that had begun with the ten hours with Pompidou of France in the Azores and six hours over two days with Prime Minister Heath in Bermuda. Nixon had scheduled the meetings to talk about trade and currency, but spent most of the time assuring European allies that he would keep their interests in mind during the upcoming summits in China and the Soviet Union. The transcripts of those twenty-two hours of conversations provided a long record of the President's view of the world at the beginning of his reelection year.

"The U.S. in the long run cannot have a viable world without Europe," he had told Pompidou, as recorded by his note-taker, General Vernon Walters. "Europe cannot survive without the U.S. contribution to nuclear strength at this time. The Soviets know this and would like to divide the U.S. and Europe. The Soviets also know that at the heart of the European problem is the Germans. President Pompidou could not be more correct when he pointed out that Germany . . . is always potentially, despite its cultural and economic ties to the West, drawn towards the East. The East holds millions of Germans as hostages. This is why we must keep Germany economically, politically and militarily tightly within the European Community. Ostpolitik is a nice concept and can win a Nobel Prize. President Pompidou or himself in Brandt's place might do the same. But politically it was dangerous to risk old friends. . . ." Pompidou agreed, saying that Soviet-German relations would always be unpredictable because only the Soviets could give them what they wanted: reunification, the freedom of the seventeen million East Germans Nixon called "hostages."

On the President's mind in the conversations with both Pompidou and Brandt was their analyses of Soviet intentions and leaders. Nixon had never met General Secretary Brezhnev or Premier Kosygin. Pompidou, a European-style conservative, had conferred with each of them twice. Brandt, a Social Democrat, essentially a socialist, had done the same.

The French leader said the two Russians were quite different. Kosygin was dour and serious and had a great fear of Germany, perhaps because he was from Leningrad and had lived through the siege by Hitler's army. Brezhnev was from the Ukraine, from the south. He was a tough guy, but he was folksy, loved life, good food, good drink, and Western cars. He had a Rolls-Royce, a Citroën, a Mercedes, and a

Maserati—and talked about wanting an American car, too. He knew his people wanted consumer goods and, sooner or later, had to figure out a way to get them from Europe and America.

"Which do they fear more—China or the United States?" Nixon asked.

"They are obsessed with China," Pompidou said. "The dream of Yalta may not be over for the Soviets, they may still dream of sharing the world with the U.S. . . . China disturbs this idea and they don't like it. . . . They felt they could do nothing against China which was indestructible by its mass and in 20 to 50 years it will be so enormous that they will not be able to cope with it. Next they fear Germany. They feel Germany is capable of fomenting something. With the U.S. they feel complicity."

Nixon spoke of Germany and then of all Europe, saying: "It was no secret that the Germans felt that the U.S. could not be depended on. They felt that it was inevitable that the U.S. would withdraw from Europe except perhaps for a small force but the U.S. could not be counted upon to risk its survival to defend Europe in a nuclear war. . . . In the final analysis what determines U.S. and French policy is self-interest. . . . the U.S. and Western Europe, despite some differences of which they were aware, are inextricably tied together. In the long term it would be disastrous for the U.S. to leave Europe as a hostage to the USSR. . . . The U.S. in the long run cannot have a viable world without Europe."

And Pompidou responded that Europe was not viable without an engaged United States. He compared a Soviet attack to Pearl Harbor: "The hypothesis of a major conflict is it is not just a part of the U.S. fleet that might be destroyed but Western Europe, which would be lost to the Soviets. The U.S. would, of course, revenge them, but this would be small consolation to the Europeans in the cemetery."

Nixon agreed, but said: "Many Americans are naïve and softhearted. . . . Many intellectuals, the media and professors don't believe there is any threat from the Russians. What used to be called the cold war rhetoric is no longer saleable."

Pompidou asked Nixon why he thought that the Chinese and Soviets both seemed to be reaching out to the United States. Nixon said, "If there was not a strong Europe and if the Soviets did not have a threat in the East they would not be interested in talking to the U.S. . . . He did not believe Mao would be talking to the leader of the capitalists and courting the U.S. unless he was concerned by the Soviets and to a lesser extent by the Japanese. . . . The Chinese are far more exercised by the million Soviet troops along their borders than they are by our forces in Japan. . . . With regard to Vietnam it is our basic impression that the Chinese would like this to be settled, but they do not know how to go about it without moving Hanoi closer to Moscow and increasing their feeling of being encircled. . . ." Then the President said that "The attitude of the Chinese towards their neighbors can be summed up in this way—The Russians they hate and fear now. The Japanese they fear later but do not hate. For the Indians they feel contempt but they are there and backed by the USSR."

That thought led Nixon into one more defense of his decisions in the Indo-Pakistani War: "If in the last 72 hours we had pursued a policy of abstention, the objective consequence would have been a total Indian victory. Our strategy was to create enough pressure on India and the USSR so that they would not pursue the war to its ultimate consequences."

He repeated the line that Kissinger had been pushing in background briefings, saying, "The U.S. has treaty obligations to Pakistan as the Soviet Union had to India—"

This time, though, Kissinger jumped in to say: "We do not want to mislead President Pompidou. We did not have a final agreement." Americans, including those working in the White House, did not get the same correction.

With Heath, a fellow conservative, the President offered his view of the world at home: "The establishment has a guilt complex. They can't stand the fact that I, their political opponent, am rectifying their mistakes. In addition, the Establishment has this growing obsession with domestic problems. . . . They have never believed there was any real danger from the Left. They are turning inward. . . ."

Several times Nixon told Heath that he wanted Great Britain to take as much of a world role as it could afford; he was frustrated by the British withdrawal from the Persian Gulf, scheduled for the end of the year. "Britain is the only European country with a world view. Germany is a domestic mess; Italy seldom has a government. It is in the long-term interest of Europe—if it is to be a power center in the world—to have Britain in the Common Market. It will be a healthier world if Europe does develop a more cohesive line toward the rest of the world. The U.S. could play a short-range game of keeping everybody divided—but this won't do anybody any good."

Nixon said he was distressed by the British withdrawals from Asia, leaving the United States as the Westerners there: "The Japanese are all over Asia like a bunch of lice. Let's look at Japan and Germany—both have a sense of frustration and a memory of defeat. What must be done is to make sure we have a home for them. . . . Japan is today denied a nuclear capability; in terms of security, if our nuclear umbrella should become less credible, the effect on Japan would be a catastrophe. The biggest reason for our holding on in Vietnam is Japan. . . . We have to reassure the Asians that the Nixon Doctrine is not a way for us to get out of Asia at their expense but a way for us to stay in. . . . As for China, when we have two enemies, we want to tilt toward the weaker, not toward the stronger—though not in a way we can be caught at it."

On the Middle East, the President said: "The Soviets are putting in a large amount of equipment; this is affecting the balance though it has not yet overturned it. . . . You could say Israel was intransigent"—he said that Israelis were against American-Soviet negotiations—"maybe we should make a deal with the Soviets. If we could get the Soviets out without the Israelis' knowledge . . . To make it work, we need to keep the confidence of Mrs. Meir. We'll have to go forward, without fanfare, with Phantom deliveries."

The meetings with Chancellor Brandt began badly. Brandt thanked Nixon for American support of Ostpolitik—his reaching out to East Germany and other communist countries close to the German Federal Republic—but Nixon corrected him coolly, saying that his decision was not to support Brandt's initiative, only not to oppose it. Most of their time was spent on the President's questions about Brezhnev; and the West German leader, who had more experience with the Soviets than any reigning Western leader, went on at length, telling Nixon, according to minutes kept by Haig, that: "In August, 1970, Brezhnev appeared very unsure of himself, especially in the area of international affairs. . . . Brezhnev even resorted to reading from point papers that had been prepared for him. Conversely, during their meeting in September, Brezhnev was far more relaxed, far more at ease with the subject matter and obviously very confident that he was in charge. He had told Chancellor Brandt that he was completely responsible for Soviet relations with Western Europe and the United States while Kosygin was concentrating on India, Scandinavia and other less important areas. During this meeting Brezhnev asked Chancellor Brandt whether or not President Nixon was truly interested in peace. The Chancellor assured him that he was. 'There is now a genuine interest in Moscow in normalizing relations with Western Europe and the United States,' he said. 'The Soviets probably seek more economic and technical cooperation and are definitely interested in a reduction in armaments.' "

Nixon brought up the apparent improvement in relations between West Germany and the Soviet Union and asked Brandt why he thought that was happening. The principal reason, Brandt answered, was: "They hope at least temporarily to get acceptance of the status quo in Eastern Europe. The Soviets know that they cannot hold Eastern Europe forever, but they would like to prolong the process for as long as possible."

Nixon said it might also have to do with Soviet fear of China; perhaps the Russians were trying to calm their west flank so that they could concentrate on the Chinese problem on their eastern borders. Brandt nodded, then said, in Haig's account, that "Brezhnev mentioned the diversionist activities of the People's Republic. . . . These tactics, Brezhnev recounted with some emotion, were anti-Soviet. . . . The historical character of the Chinese people was strange and difficult for Western nations to understand. Brezhnev had told Chancellor Brandt that if one were to say to the Chinese that the wall is white, the Chinaman would reply that this is not so, it is in fact black. And this is the kind of logic that one is confronted with when dealing with the Chinese. . . . He referred to China as a nation of 800 million backward people who tilled the soil with their hands. . . . China had no automobiles and the upper class still rode bicycles. . . . In short, Brezhnev appeared to be adopting the tactic of belittling the Chinese because of a fundamental fear of China's power."

ON THE SECOND DAY OF 1972, the President sat down for a one-hour prime-time interview with White House correspondent Dan Rather of CBS News. The correspondent quoted Nixon's statement to *Time* in the magazine's "Man of the Year" issue: "The issue of Vietnam will not be an issue in the campaign as far as this administration is concerned, because we will have brought the American involvement to an end."

"May one properly assume," Rather continued, "that by Election Day there will be no Americans, land, sea or air . . . ?"

"Mr. Rather," Nixon began, "that depends on one circumstance, which is very much in my mind, and in the minds I know of all our listeners and viewers. That is the situation with our POWs. . . ."

The correspondent pushed the President on the bombing that began on Christmas and ended five days later, and the President repeated that it was being done only to protect American soldiers during their prolonged withdrawal.

Nixon liked a question about the possibility that George Wallace would run in Democratic presidential primaries rather than run as an independent in November, and answered with a hint of a smile: "That question should be directed to the Democratic candidate."

The interview produced two top-of-the-front-page stories in *The New York Times* of January 3:

PRESIDENT LINKS A PULLOUT TO RELEASE OF P.O.W.'S

NIXON INDICATES HE'LL RUN WITH AGNEW ON THE TICKET

To American conservatives, supporters of the war from the beginning, the headlines were linked. Nixon's war goals—or peace goals—had gone from victory to getting our prisoners back and the survival, probably temporary, of the South Vietnamese government of President Nguyen Van Thieu, who had been reelected in October in an election with no opponents. The conservatives knew their man. Whatever he said or argued, Nixon was commanding a slow retreat. He was more candid about that with Heath than with his fellow Republicans. The British prime minister had said: "We are moving more and more into a state of world affairs in which effective action is no longer possible. How much can you do?"

Nixon had answered: "Part of the reason for conducting our Vietnam withdrawal so slowly is to give some message that we are not prepared to pay *any* price for ending a war; we must now ask ourselves what we are willing to pay to avert war."

For months, the goal of Republican conservatives was the survival of Vice President Agnew, as rumors swirled about a Nixon-Connally ticket and ideas of a "New Party." Many on the right felt betrayed by Nixon, who was orchestrating a humiliating withdrawal from Vietnam, was reaching out to communist China, and had installed wage and price controls and advocated guaranteed incomes for poor people. A group of seventeen prominent eastern conservatives, led by William F. Buckley Jr., had announced "suspension" of support for the President. A conservative Ohio congressman, John M. Ashbrook, had announced his candidacy for the Republican presidential nomination.

On Agnew, though, the conservatives checked the President. Nixon told Rather: "My view is that one should not break up a winning combination. I believe that the Vice President has handled his difficult assignments with dignity, with courage. He has, at times, been a man of controversy, but when a man has done a good job in a position, when he has been part of a winning team, I believe that he should stay on the team."

In the *Time* "Man of the Year" interview, in the issue dated January 3, the President also spelled out his worldview, synthesizing some of what he had told European leaders:

> We must remember that the only time in the history of the world that we have had any extended periods of peace is when there has been a balance of power. It is when one nation becomes infinitely more powerful in relation to its potential competitor that the danger of war arises. . . . I think it will be a safer world and a better world if we have a strong, healthy United States, Eu-

rope, Soviet Union, China, Japan, each balancing the other, not playing one against the other, an even balance.

THE PRESIDENT FLEW to San Clemente on the morning of January 3 to plan his next surprise. He had decided to go on television to make public details of the two levels of negotiations going on in Paris; the idea was to show that the North Vietnamese had already rejected the peace schemes being advocated in Congress and by Democratic presidential candidates. He would announce new troop withdrawals on January 13—"That'll suck out the peaceniks," he said—and then go on television five days later to reveal the secrets of the negotiations.

That night, after dinner, he telephoned the coach of the Miami Dolphins, Don Shula, to talk football, especially the Super Bowl coming up between the Dolphins and the Dallas Cowboys. It was 10:30 P.M. in San Clemente, 1:30 A.M. in Miami. They talked about players and plays and strategies for a bit, and Shula told reporters about it the next day. He was impressed by how much Nixon knew about the game—and stories everywhere talked about America's First Fan.

On January 9, the First Fan hosted a private dinner for Cabinet members and senior staff, giving them a pep talk about peace and reelection, and ending: "The fourth quarter begins. The football analogy tells us that the fourth quarter determines the game. . . ."

CHAPTER 27

January 25, 1972

I N THE FIRST 1972 issue of *The New Republic*, John Osborne offered this assessment of President Nixon's first three years: "At the end of his first year Mr. Nixon seemed to me to have shown himself to be a better man than he had previously permitted himself to be and a better President than he appeared likely to be in his 1968 campaign. His second year inspired the conclusion that his wild swings from sober and often admirable proposals to raucous appeals to the basest instincts of the electorate made confidence in his fundamental integrity and good faith impossible. At the close of his third year and the beginning of the fourth, Mr. Nixon comes across to me as a President who, in defensive response to the negative view, has constructed a false image of himself and has persuaded himself that it is the true image. . . ."

The writer praised the President, faintly, for moving in the right directions on returning power to state and local governments, promoting national health care, making a commitment to consider environmental issues, recognizing the problems of the poor, and restraining inflation for a time.

"A conservative President," Osborne continued, "is accused by conservative supporters of cloaking liberal measures in conservative rhetoric and the accusation, allowing for some exaggeration of the liberal content, is so well founded that Mr. Nixon hardly bothers to deny its truth. . . . Mr. Nixon was believable when he said that he sees in himself a President who is in office at a point in time when it may be possible to do more than any President before him could do to promote a realistic and stable realignment of the world power structure."

The President's defensiveness was a personal thing, a measure of his extraordinary introversion. In fact, Richard Nixon was a man closed to critics but open to criticism—as long as it was private and only on paper. On most days, hundreds of pages of reporting, analysis, warnings, pleadings, and advice crossed his desk. He ignored or brushed aside a great deal of that, but dozens of memos and reports came back out of his office with scribbled notations. He could be flattered—and usually was by the few people he actually saw in person each day—but he was much more interested in what he considered to be tough-minded. On January 3, he pored over a memo from a new Colson assistant, Douglas Hallett, just a year out of Yale. Nixon had spotted Hallett when he was still in college and had written a piece praising Nixon for *The Wall Street Journal*.

Hallett focused on one of the President's most damaging tricks, big talk to gain small political advantage. "We have done almost everything imaginable to undermine our own credibility and consistency," wrote the new man. He cited "Go Forward Together," in 1969, "New Federalism," in 1970, and "New American Revolution," in 1971.

"What next?" Hallett wrote. "The Second Coming, perhaps."

The President's scribbled comment was: "Very perceptive. Absolutely correct. Too much rhetoric!"

"The welfare program is pronounced the greatest domestic program since the New Deal, but we expend far more effort trying to place Carswell on the Supreme Court," Hallett wrote. ". . . Trying to reassure the left, which cares everything about words, with substance; trying to reassure the right, which cares everything about substance, with words."

"H & E Note—A very legitimate criticism," Nixon wrote.

"Stop displaying the President as if he had a stick up his ass. Put him in gutsy, colorful, photographic situations with people."

"H—Good!"

"The hyper-individualistic—'We're Number 1'—frontier American philosophy is bankrupt and outdated. . . . Nixon comes across as: Man on the make; ashamed of and constantly running away from his past; unsure of his convictions; tactician instead of strategist; Grand Vizier of all Rotarians, substituting pomposity for eloquence. That is the public impression."

That was too much. "H—Wrong on this—Typical Ivy League" was the President's last comment.

The point about talking too big was also part of a memo the same day from Herbert Stein on the politics of the election-year economy: "In short, 1972 should be a year we can live with, if our own claims do not erect standards we are unlikely to meet. Employment will be up and unemployment down. Profits will be up, and probably the stock market also. After an awkward bulge in the December, January and February statistics, the inflation rate should moderate again. Anyway, no one has a more powerful anti-inflation program to propose than you have put in place. . . ." Still, to be sure, Stein added: "We should be looking for ways to pump up the economy more rapidly. . . . It would be desirable to get the needed additional stimulus from monetary policy. . . . When we talk about getting assistance from monetary policy for a more rapid rise of the economy we are talking about getting more than 6% monetary expansion. We should try to do that."

Nixon's one-word response to that was: "Vital."

Then he sat down and dictated another threatening letter to his old friend Arthur Burns: "You have given me absolute assurance that the money supply will move adequately to fuel an expanding economy in 1972. . . . We come down to the fundamental point that if the Fed is not able to move the money supply up vigorously and aggressively in the first quarter of this year, the Fed in general and you as its leader will inevitably get a major share of the blame. What could happen out of all this is that a major attack on the independence of the Fed will eventually develop. . . . You are really going to have to move. . . . all the fancy arguments as to who was at fault aren't going to make any difference at all if we fail."

Burns, who had been blaming timid and selfish bankers and businessmen for the fact that the economy was still stagnant, wrote at the bottom of the letter: "Never gave 'absolute assurance.' What nonsense! No answer is to be made to this letter. It's outrageous."

The Committee to Re-Elect the President had been in operation at 1701 Pennsylvania Avenue, a block from the White House, since March 1971. Fund-raising and polling had been the first orders of business. The first polls, by Robert Teeter, confirmed the decision to keep Nixon's name out of the committee title and out of the campaign slogan, which became "Now More Than Ever." Teeter's numbers indicated that voters found the President to be "informed . . . experienced . . . competent . . . safe . . . trained." Nixon was also seen as honest—a change from the past. But he did not score well in personal categories; he scored low and lower on "warm . . . open-minded . . . relaxed." Respondents thought he did not have a sense of humor. One Teeter recommendation was that the campaign ignore young voters, the eighteen-, nineteen-, and twenty-year-olds voting for the first time in a presidential election, saying it would be counterproductive to raise the numbers of young people who came out to vote. Nixon rejected that idea; he was afraid of stories saying he had written off youth.

CREEP, as the committee was inevitably called, was also moving ahead on so-called black advance—spying operations and schemes designed to disrupt Democratic campaigns. A retired Washington taxi driver was recruited to volunteer to drive Senator Edmund Muskie's car—the man was code-named "Sedan-Chair"—and then paid a thousand dollars a month by CREEP to report on what he heard and saw. It was his memos on Muskie's schedule that had impressed Nixon. Jack Caulfield, the retired New York detective in the basement of EOB, was put on the payroll, and so was G. Gordon Liddy, the former FBI agent, who became counsel to the committee. A friend of Caulfield's named James McCord, a former FBI man and a CIA agent, joined CREEP as a security coordinator; his specialty was physical security, protecting buildings against spies. Colson, still working out of the White House, reported to the President on January 12—referring to Action Memo P-1957—that he had placed a committee agent, John Venners, at a convention of an antiwar group, the National Youth Caucus. Colson said: "While we were unable to get on the program, Venners was successful in disrupting . . . by instigating a Black Caucus walk-out."

That same day, January 12, Governor George Wallace flew into Tallahassee, where he was going to address the Florida legislature the next day. In Washington, the Internal Revenue Service issued a short statement, but no press release, reporting that it was ending the eighteen-month-long corruption investigation of Alabama officials, the best known of them Gerald Wallace, the governor's brother. The next morning, as President Nixon was making a thirty-second appearance in the White House press room to announce that seventy thousand more American troops would be withdrawn from Vietnam before May 1, Governor Wallace told Floridians that he would enter the state's March 14 Democratic presidential primary—instead of running as a third-party candidate. In a state where he had carried three-quarters of sixty-seven counties in the three-way 1968 general election against Nixon and Humphrey, there was no way he could lose to Muskie, Humphrey, McGovern, Lindsay, and Senator Henry Jackson, and there was no way he was not going to damage the most moderate of those Democrats, Jackson, Muskie, and Humphrey.

Nixon was ecstatic, even as Wallace attacked him. "I make this prediction," said the Alabama governor. "If the people of Florida vote for me, Mr. Nixon in thirty or sixty days after this campaign is over will end busing himself. He's waiting to see if you're really opposed to this trifling with children. . . ." Wallace, as Nixon had said to Dan Rather, was now the Democrats' problem.

Writing from Alabama's capital, Montgomery, Evans and Novak said: "There is pervasive opinion here that a deal has been made between Wallace and the White House." Another columnist, Charles Bartlett of the *Chattanooga Times,* wrote that Wallace had said to a Republican friend, "Tell the President I'm going down to Florida and kick the hell out of those Democrats."

Back at the White House, where he was left to answer questions after the President's half-minute statement, Defense Secretary Laird told reporters: "This means our troop ceiling by May 1 will be down to 69,000. We no longer will have, with this announcement, any active U.S. military divisions in Vietnam. We will continue to use American air power to protect the remaining forces. The Vietnamization program has moved forward with sufficient vigor and progress so the South Vietnamese are in a position where they can provide for the security responsibilities in-country."

Alone at Camp David—partly to get away from Kissinger and his continuing threats to resign if he could not have his way with Rogers—the President decided to postpone his announcement of the details of secret negotiations with Vietnam, originally scheduled for January 18. He needed more time to get a better sense of how President Thieu might respond to hearing that he had been cut out of the real negotiations. The President delegated Haldeman to tell Rogers, who also did not know about the secret talks. Then Haldeman met with Kissinger, who was still arguing against blowing the private channel to the North Vietnamese. When Haldeman mentioned Rogers, Kissinger interrupted and went into a tirade for more than half an hour, finally saying, his voice shaking, "Tell me what your proposition is, and I'll do it. I'm not here to strike a treaty with the President." But each time Haldeman tried to tell him, Kissinger went off on another tirade, calling Rogers a "psychopath." He said he knew that the Secretary of State had gone to the publisher and the editor of *The Washington Post*—Katharine Graham and Ben Bradlee—and said that he, Rogers, not Kissinger, was responsible for the administration's foreign policy successes. Then Mitchell received a call from Nelson Rockefeller, who said Kissinger intended to resign before the end of the month.

"We may have to bite the bullet and get him out," Nixon told Haldeman. "If we don't, he'll be in the driver's seat during the campaign, and we've got to remember that he did leak things to us in '68, and we've got to assume he's capable of doing the same thing to our opponents in '72. . . . If we don't face up to it now he may go off cockeyed during the campaign as he did in '68."

In Congress, "withdrawal date" had become the rallying cry of most Democrats. Senators, particularly, were attacking the President almost daily for refusing to set a final deadline for the withdrawal of all American military personnel. Mansfield amendments in June and September specified that all American troops would leave in nine months and then six months, and the most recent House resolution saying the same thing had been defeated by only twenty-three votes. One of the party's candidates for president, Senator George McGovern, called Nixon a liar, saying: "It is simply not true—and the President knows it is not true—that our negotiators in Paris have ever discussed with the North Vietnamese the question of total withdrawal from Indochina in conjunction with the release of our prisoners."

"They're out on a limb there," said Nixon, as he talked about the speech with Haldeman. The idea was to try to saw it off by revealing the contents of the secret negotiations.

On Sunday, January 16, Bill Safire was in New Orleans watching the Miami Dolphins and Dallas Cowboys in the Super Bowl when the public address announcer called out his name and told him to call his office—which was, of course, the White House. Sixty million people watching television heard the announcement. When he got to a phone and called 202-456-1414, Larry Higby told him that the President was at Camp David and wanted him back as fast as he could get there. When Safire arrived at the White House, there was a memo from the President, marked, "TOP SECRET / SENSITIVE / EXCLUSIVELY EYES ONLY." It began: "After reading the proposed text of a Presidential TV speech on negotiation—which has been prepared by Henry's staff—I want you to read the memorandum that I am now dictating and then prepare the first draft of a television speech to be made on Tuesday, the 25th of January. . . . As you can tell from reading it, it has all the substance in it but there is too much turgid prose and too much complex discussion of eight points, seven points, nine points, etc., without getting to the heart of the matter—what we offered, what they turned down and what hopes are for a negotiated settlement now. . . ."

"There's good cops-and-robbers stuff here," the President told Safire, referring to Kissinger's secret comings and goings. He instructed him to change any "we" to "I" and to change mentions of "I asked Dr. Kissinger" to "I directed Dr. Kissinger."

Two days later, while he was going over a draft of the speech with Safire in EOB 175, the President began to talk again, repeating himself a couple of times, about Kissinger and Rogers. "I was reading about Disraeli and Melbourne last night. God, did they have fights in their cabinets. I'm sorry about how Henry and Bill go at each other—"

"Ego," Safire said.

"Ego is something we all have," Nixon said, "either you grow out of it or it takes you over. I've grown out of it. It's really a compensation for an inferiority complex. Henry has that, of course. Bill has it too. . . . I could always get along with anybody—Stassen, whoever, no matter what I thought of them. Not these two . . . You work your smooth way between them."

PRESIDENT NIXON went on national television at 8:30 P.M. on January 25. Early on, aiming at Democrats, specifically Democratic candidates for president, he said: "Some Americans, who believed what the North Vietnamese led them to believe, have charged that the United States has not pursued negotiations intensively. As the record I will now disclose will show, just the opposite is true." He revealed that Kissinger had made an even dozen secret trips to Paris, the first in August 1969, and in the course of secret negotiations had offered, in May 1971, a peace plan that linked American withdrawal to a cease-fire and the release of all American prisoners of war. That plan, he said, was rejected, and the North Vietnamese demanded that the United States "overthrow" the government of South Vietnam. The same thing happened, he continued, in August and September—again the deal-breaker was North Vietnamese insistence on the "overthrow" of the Thieu government.

Then the President revealed the offer secretly delivered to Paris by Kissinger on October 11. He described it this way: "Within six months of agreement, we shall withdraw all U.S. and allied forces from South Vietnam. We shall exchange all prisoners of war. There shall be a cease-fire through Indochina. There shall be a new presidential election in South Vietnam"—with Thieu, who would be a candidate, stepping down a month before the vote.

"That is where matters stand today," Nixon said. "The only reply to our plan has been an increase in troop infiltration from North Vietnam and Communist military offensives in Laos and Cambodia." He said the plan would be presented to the 142nd session of formal peace talks also taking place in Paris.

It was a startling night for most Americans—and a very political one, especially in Nixon's choice of words. "Overthrow" should have been "abandon"—the United States had financed Thieu's reelection in October—and "rejected" was used where "ignored" would have been more accurate. The resignation of Thieu one month before a new election was presented as the South Vietnamese leader's suggestion, when, in fact, the idea had been brought to him by Alexander Haig in an October visit to Saigon.

The North Vietnamese and the Vietcong representatives in Paris denounced the plan as an election-year trick. Antiwar members of Congress were less direct, playing for time to see what happened next. Senator J. William Fulbright, chairman of the Senate Foreign Relations Committee, said, "What looks generous to us may not look generous to North Vietnam. . . . We may have to do more to get a favorable response. . . ." Senator McGovern tried to claim victory, saying, "At the same time Mr. Nixon was bitterly opposed to the McGovern-Hatfield proposal to end the war, he was at the very same time offering it to the other side."

The press took its own tack. *The Wall Street Journal* and some conservative columnists declared that it was antiwar politicians who now had credibility problems. "WAR ISSUE IS DEFLATED" was the headline over William S. White's column in *The Washington Post*. But newspapers and television did something the President had never anticipated, focusing on the cops-and-robbers tales of Henry Kissinger, secret agent. A front-page *New York Times* headline was typical. Over a photograph of Kissinger leaving a Paris restaurant with a glamorous CBS News producer, Margaret Osmer, was: "A FEW CLUES FROM A SUPER SECRET AGENT."

Kissinger was on the covers of both *Time* and *Newsweek,* and was described as the most powerful professor to come to Washington since Woodrow Wilson. Then he was spread over six full pages of *Life,* under the headline "THE MOST IMPORTANT NO. 2 MAN IN HISTORY." In case anyone missed the point, an old Harvard colleague was quoted "not totally in jest" comparing the Kissinger-Nixon relationship to Aristotle and Philip of Macedonia.

Hugh Sidey gushed: "So deep had Nixon's trust of Kissinger grown, so thoroughly had Kissinger learned Nixon's mind . . . The girls Kissinger takes to Chasen's can't even imagine these endless, tedious hours of thinking, straining, groping for answers in a bewildering world."

Then there is a description of a morning meeting in the Cabinet Room: "In the hall, there is a quick, quiet tread. Henry Kissinger enters. . . . He is quickly at his place, across and to the left of the President's position, and he places the massive notebook before him. . . . Henry Kissinger dominates the room without doing anything. . . . His intellect fills the room. . . . Nixon opens the meeting. He states the problem and then he looks across the table to his left. 'Henry,' he says, 'Will you present the options for us.' . . . Kissinger is fanatical about being fair to every department, about presenting every dissent without distortion. . . . Rogers takes a furtive glance or two over the President's shoulder as if trying to get an idea what Kissinger will say next. There are no challenges from the audience, hostility having been overwhelmed by facts and intellect."

Life also pointed out that Kissinger, who had come to Washington seeing himself as a lone cowboy, now had 151 assistants of his own. One of the seven photographs of him at work was captioned: "Kissinger trades jokes with Secretary of State Rogers and presidential adviser Robert Haldeman."

Briefly after that, the spotlight of the press also discovered "Robert" Haldeman—his full name was Harry Robbins Haldeman—whose existence, to say nothing of his power, was still unknown to most Americans. The chief of staff without title—officially he was one of many called "Assistant to the President"—was sent out, with the President's permission and explicit coaching, to do a two-hour interview with Barbara Walters for use over three days on NBC's *Today* show. He said what Nixon told him to say: "You could say that his critics were unconsciously echoing the line the enemy wanted echoed. . . . Now, after this explanation—after the whole activity is on the record and is known, the only conclusion you can draw is that the critics now are consciously aiding and abetting the enemy of the United States." The words were a legal definition of treason.

The President himself responded with a short note to Haldeman and Colson, saying on January 28, 1972: "Within the next two weeks, it is vital to sustain a massive counterattack on the partisan critics of our peace proposal. Get a few very sharp lines and keep nailing them. . . . 'Playing politics with peace.' . . . 'Peace is too important for partisanship.' . . . 'They want to turn South Vietnam over to the Communists.' . . . In addition to these attack themes some strong positive lines should get out. I cannot emphasize too strongly, however, that the attack line will be more effective than the positive line. . . . We have often failed in the past in these PR efforts because we simply have not had colorful enough attack lines. . . ."

The President himself was attacked that night. He hosted a Medal of Freedom dinner for his friends, DeWitt and Lila Wallace of *Reader's Digest*. The entertainment was the mellow voices of the Ray Conniff Singers—mellow until one of the singers, a young woman named Carol Feraci, reached into the folds of her gown and pulled out a banner that read: "STOP THE KILLING!"

Across Seventeenth Street at CREEP headquarters, Jeb Magruder and his deputy, G. Gordon Liddy, were reevaluating the political intelligence operation Liddy had presented the day before to Magruder's boss, John Mitchell, who was still attorney general but was getting ready to move over as chairman of CREEP. Using flip charts mounted on easels, Liddy had laid out a $1 million scheme he called "Operation Gemstone." This was the answer to pressure from the President, transmitted through

Haldeman and Colson, to produce more and more intelligence on Democratic candidates and on the chairman of the Democratic National Committee, Larry O'Brien.

The flamboyant former FBI agent had a pointer in one hand. The other was bandaged because he had held it in a candle's flame to show the pain he was willing to endure in the name of will and loyalty. Gemstone concentrated on the Democratic and Republican national conventions. Liddy held the floor for more than half an hour, spelling out details of sub-operations called "Diamond," "Ruby," "Sapphire," and other gems:

> We need preventive action to break up demonstrations *before* they reach the television cameras. I can arrange for the services of highly trained squads, men who have worked successfully as street-fighting squads for the CIA. . . . Teams that are experienced in surgical relocation activities. In a word, General, they can kidnap a hostile leader with maximum secrecy and a minimum use of force. If, for instance, a prominent radical comes to our convention, these teams can drug him and take him across the border. . . . I have secured an option to lease a pleasure craft docked on the canal directly in front of the Fontainebleau Hotel. It is more than sixty feet long, with several staterooms, and expensively decorated in a Chinese motif. It can also be wired for both sight and sound. . . . We can, without much trouble, compromise these officials through the charms of some ladies I have arranged to have living on the boat. These are the finest call girls in the country. They are not dumb broads, but girls who can be trained and programmed. . . .

Mitchell, puffing his pipe, winked at White House counsel John Dean, who had once been his assistant, as Liddy talked of wiretaps and bugs and chase planes to intercept messages from the planes carrying Democratic candidates. Mitchell winked again, convincing Dean that he knew Gemstone was crazy. But the Attorney General did not shut it down. Instead he said, "Gordon, that's all very intriguing, but it's not quite what I had in mind."

Then Mitchell told the men from CREEP that the price was too high. He said come back with something cheaper—and more realistic. The same gang was back together in the Attorney General's office eight days later. This time the cost estimates were down to five hundred thousand dollars and most of the talk was of "surveillance" and "targets." The top priority, they concluded, was O'Brien; Liddy had plans for surveillance of both his convention office and his office at the Democratic

National Committee headquarters in the Watergate complex along the Potomac River. Mitchell suggested another target, Hank Greenspun, the publisher of the *Las Vegas Sun,* who, according to that morning's *New York Times,* had a file of Howard Hughes's political memos in his safe. The names of both O'Brien and Nixon were likely to be in those papers. The President's friend Rebozo had just gotten another fifty thousand dollars in cash from Hughes and, on the other side, O'Brien had been getting thirteen thousand dollars a month as a lobbyist for Hughes's companies.

Suddenly Dean said: "Excuse me for saying this. I don't think this kind of conversation should go on in the Attorney General's office."

In the Oval Office, the President was talking with an old Kennedy hand (and Nixon-hater), Richard Scammon, co-author of *The Real Majority.* They agreed on what Scammon had identified as the Social Issue—the political and cultural concerns of the middle class—and both talked about their respect for men in uniform, soldiers and police, and their disdain for intellectuals who wanted their battles fought by other people. The President was talking about an old California liberal named Spence who had once drawn him a diagram of how he thought American politics worked. Nixon drew two circles that overlapped a bit—he marked one "Republicans," the other "Democrats." Each circle had a sort of umbilical cord leading to two smaller circles, one on each side of the big ones. The smaller circles represented the hard core of the parties, the people who provided the support, the energy, the money and enthusiasm that fed the parties. The idea, Nixon said, was to move your big circle as far as you could toward the other big one—taking as many of the other guy's overlapping voters as possible without breaking the umbilical, because you could not win if you separated from your hard-core supporters.

Scammon loved it. Walking out of the office after forty-five minutes, he said to Chuck Colson: "By God, I have to admit, you may have finally gotten to me. I may find myself voting for Richard Nixon in November. Something I never thought I would do."

CHAPTER 28

February 22, 1972

T HE PRESIDENT BEGAN HIS JOURNEY to China on February 17, taking off by helicopter from the south lawn of the White House at 10:10 that morning. He said a few words to a crowd that included the leadership of both parties in Congress, and ended by quoting the words left by the first men on the moon: "We came in peace for all mankind."

He left on an ordinary Washington day. He had just accepted Attorney General John Mitchell's resignation to take over his reelection campaign and had nominated Assistant Attorney General Richard G. Kleindienst as Mitchell's successor. In a twenty-four-hour period, U.S. bombers dropped the greatest tonnage on South Vietnam of any day since June 1968, in an effort to disrupt North Vietnamese supply lines for an expected dry-season offensive. The House voted 234 to 127 to pass a $5.4 billion antipoverty bill greatly expanding expenditures for legal services for the poor and the Head Start early education program. The bill was sent to the Senate, and if it passed it would go to the White House, where Nixon had threatened to veto it. His bill, the Republican bill, which would have frozen antipoverty spending at current levels, had been defeated 206 to 159.

As usual Nixon had not made much time for those bills, instead spending most of his days prepping for the China trip. On one day, February 14, he had met with Senator James Buckley, the New York Conservative, who had just come back from a trip through East Asia, and with

André Malraux. When Nixon read in his news summary that Buckley, a great supporter of Chiang Kai-shek and Taiwan, wanted to see him, he scribbled: "NO . . . We can't have the nuts kick us and then use us."

But he did. Senator Buckley, whose brother William F. Buckley Jr. was organizing conservatives to "suspend support" of Nixon because of the China trip, came in with a long, businesslike memorandum of concerns. "A major fear is that the US will be willing to accept CHICOM assurances that it will 'renounce the use of force against Taiwan' in return for some US action which weakens the security tie with Taiwan. . . . There is great anxiety over the US making a secret deal with Peking . . . that the UN Command must be withdrawn from Korea."

Malraux was another matter. Kissinger, with perhaps a bit of spite for the Frenchman who had captivated another American president, John Kennedy, insisted that Malraux, now seventy, an old man with an astonishing facial tic, was out of date on China. But Nixon, too, was captured by Malraux's elegant prose and invited him for what turned out to be a long evening of flattery and vision at the White House.

"You are about to attempt one of the most important things of our century," Malraux had begun. "I think of the sixteenth-century explorers, who set out for a specific objective but often arrived at a totally different discovery. . . . You will be dealing with a colossus, but a colossus facing death. Mao's prime was fifty years ago. You will meet a man who has had a fantastic destiny and who believes that he is acting out the last act of his lifetime. You may think he is talking to you, but he will be in truth addressing Death. . . . It's worth the trip! You have the destiny of the world in your hands."

After dinner, Nixon and Malraux sat for a time by the fire in the family dining room upstairs in the White House. "Relations over the next twenty-five years between the U.S. and Japan and the U.S. and China will determine the fate of the Pacific," Nixon said. "Our withdrawal might create a vacuum that would be filled by another power, Japan or the Soviet Union." The President said that he read that Abraham Lincoln, on the night before his assassination, had told Cabinet members that he had had a dream of a voyage on strange seas and had seen the shore but could not identify anything on it: "He described the craft upon which he was sailing as bound for an uncertain shore beyond treacherous shoals."

"Perhaps I, too, am embarked on a strange voyage," Nixon said. "But my purpose is to try to manipulate the boat, avoid the reefs and arrive at my destination, which is better understanding of China."

"No one will know if you succeed for at least fifty years, Mr. President," Malraux said. "The Chinese are very patient."

Nixon was thrilled by the evening. As he walked Malraux to his car, the writer turned and said: "I am not de Gaulle, but I know what de Gaulle would say if he were here. He would say: 'All men who understand what you are embarking upon salute you!' "

Finally there were health considerations. Stephen Bull, Nixon's personal assistant, walked into the Oval Office a couple of days before takeoff and saw the President, who was not self-conscious with the few people he trusted, bending over his desk and being injected in a presidential buttock with gamma globulin to protect against hepatitis.

THE TAKEOFF of *Air Force One,* which Nixon named *Spirit of '76* before the trip, was televised live on all three networks. The plane headed across the United States to Honolulu where the entourage of three hundred Americans would stay for two nights and a day and then go on to Guam for a night. The route and timing had been laid out by White House physicians to minimize presidential jet lag. Nixon met with Haldeman, Kissinger, and Ziegler for three hours, going over details, including the list of just over one hundred reporters, news executives, and cameramen and other technicians who had been chosen by the White House for the trip. "Are there any non-Jews here?" Nixon asked as he read down the list.

Whatever their religion, there were only a few men on the list who had ever reported on China; many had never been to Asia. The press corps had been selected by the White House from two thousand applicants, and priority had been given to television people. Each of the three networks had four correspondents, including anchormen, and a total of twenty-five technicians. There were twenty-one newspaper reporters, most of them Washington bureau chiefs; six reporters and four photographers from the Associated Press and United Press International; six magazine writers; four radio broadcasters; three syndicated columnists; and one reporter from the Voice of America. Nixon and Kissinger had argued about choices for hours. The adviser wanted columnists—Kraft and Teddy White, an old China hand, were his favorites on the trip—but the President wanted the television people. His goal was to make the trip a pageant, a television spectacular live from the mysterious kingdom. The Chinese, using American plans, had built a broadcasting building and leased a Western Union worldwide transmission system. The great shots bouncing off new communications satellites would be of Nixon with Mao Tse-tung and Chou En-lai; of toasts and banquets; of Nixon in the old Forbidden City where the rulers of China, imperial and communist, had lived for centuries; of him and his wife on the Great Wall. But most of the words would be secret, perhaps forever.

For the first time as president, Nixon walked to the back of his
Boeing 707 and talked a bit with the seven pool correspondents and photographers on *Air Force One*. A full press plane, a Pan American Airways
charter, was ahead, scheduled to land first, as always, to witness presidential landings. He made small talk, as well as he could, beginning by
asking whether they knew how to use chopsticks. One reporter showed
him an elaborate China atlas with "Central Intelligence Agency" embossed on the cover. "Do you think they'll let us in with this?" he asked.

"This will probably show how much we don't know about
China," answered the President.

Nixon returned to his three "rooms" up front and studied again a
four-foot-high pile of "Eyes Only" briefings from Kissinger. The national
security adviser himself had written five hundred pages on his talks with
Chou En-lai, and had briefed the President for more than forty hours.
There were supposed to be no surprises when Nixon and Chou sat down
together in closed sessions. After one of the early briefings, in a memo to
himself, Nixon had begun: "Risks for them—1. U.S. is the devil. . . ."

In a memo written on February 5, Kissinger said:

> These people are both fanatic and pragmatic. They are tough
> ideologues who totally disagree with us on where the world is
> going, or should be going. At the same time, they are hard realists
> who calculate they need us because of a threatening Soviet Union,
> a resurgent Japan, and a potentially independent Taiwan. . . .
> When one refers to the Chinese one is in effect discussing Mao
> and Chou. . . . They have been surmounting towering internal
> and external obstacles for some fifty years. They take a long view.
> They see history on their side. . . .
> They will be seeking an answer to their decisive question—
> "Does this American leader know where he's going?" Indeed,
> Chou told me the Chinese really turned on the Russians after
> Khrushchev stopped off in Peking. . . . His performance at that
> time convinced the Chinese that he was a bully who did not know
> where he was headed over the longer term. . . . What they need to
> be clear about is whether you know your own objectives, under-
> stand theirs, and are serious about both.

Kissinger presented seventy-four-year-old Chou as "the tactician,
the administrator, the negotiator, the master of details and thrust and
parry—he is clearly running China." He had not met Mao but reported
that others saw him as "the philosopher, the poet, the grand strategist,
the inspirer, the romantic." Nixon memorized it all, hundreds of pages of

talking points. After talking to Kissinger for hours on February 18, he made these notes on his yellow pad:

> What they want: 1. Build up their world credentials . . .
> 2. Taiwan . . . 3. Get U.S. out of Asia.

> What we want: 1. Indo-China (?) . . . 2. Communication—To restrain Chinese expansion in Asia . . . 3. In Future—Reduce threat of confrontation by China Super Power.

> What we both want: 1. Reduce danger of confrontation & conflict . . . 2. A more stable Asia . . . 3. A restraint on U.S.S.R.

That day, sitting alone with his yellow pads, the President memorized part of a poem Mao had written in 1959 after returning to his home village after thirty-two years of making revolution:

> *It is the bitter sacrifice*
> *that strengthens our firm resolve*
> *and which gives us the courage*
> *to dare to change heaven and skies*
> *To change the sun—and to make a new world.*

A page later, he rejected one bit of Kissinger's advice—"We can agree to more than we say"—writing: "1. Too dangerous, 2. Sounds Tricky."

In Hawaii, a new Kissinger memo advised the President:

> The crucial factor will be the Chinese judgment of our seriousness and reliability; this litmus test will determine their future policy. If we fail it . . . they could easily resort to the tempting levers of public opinion. They could then deal with us like the North Vietnamese do—inviting in opposition politicians, dealing with unfriendly private groups, appealing to hostile journalists, lambasting us in the United Nations. . . . We can be certain that they would be especially skillful at this game; we would pay a double price at home and abroad for our alleged naivete at trying to deal with these people in the first place.

After the stop on Guam and a landing in Shanghai to board Chinese navigators, *Air Force One* headed toward Peking's Capital Airport. Sitting alone now, looking out, Nixon thought the villages looked like pictures from the Middle Ages. The plane landed at 11:32 A.M., Monday,

February 21. In Washington, it was thirteen hours earlier, 8:32 P.M., Sunday, February 20. The tarmac was gray and windy and cold, 34 degrees; the buildings were quiet. "That is affirmative—no crowd," a Secret Service man on the ground had radioed Haldeman as the plane began its final approach. There seemed to be no one there, except for Chou En-lai, two dozen officials and some of their assistants, a 350-man honor guard, and an army band that played the national anthems. When the music stopped, Hugh Sidey, standing thirty yards from the plane, could hear Nixon complaining about his inner clock. He had received the minimum greeting for a visiting head of state, correct and cool. The only thing that seemed different from Kissinger's secret trips was a single American flag on a terminal building. The largest billboard Nixon saw, in English, read: "PEOPLE OF OPPRESSED NATIONS THE WORLD OVER—UNITE!"

But American network cameras were there and the President played out the scene as he had rehearsed it over and over again. He stepped out of the plane alone; then, a few beats later, his wife, Pat, emerged to follow him down the stairs. Haldeman's men blocked everyone else, pushing back Kissinger and Rogers, until the President reached out, in a move slightly exaggerated, for a handshake with Chou. It was no ordinary handshake. The Premier had often mentioned to Kissinger the day in 1954, in Geneva, during the conferences that ended the French war in Indochina, when Secretary of State John Foster Dulles had refused to shake his hand.

The streets were almost empty as the official party, in a line of old Russian Zil limousines, was driven fifteen miles into the city. On each block there might be one person on a bicycle and a family walking along, but none looked up and some of the Americans guessed, correctly, that they were props, actors. The real pedestrians and cyclists were being held behind barricades a block away from the motorcade route. In a limousine with curtained windows, Chou thanked Nixon: "Your handshake came over the vastest ocean in the world—twenty-five years of no communication." In the city, the paved plain of Tiananmen Square, where more than five hundred thousand people had turned out to cheer the Emperor of Ethiopia and the President of Romania, was deserted this time. The Americans were nervous. Nixon worried about what it all looked like on television at home.

The Nixons were shown to a government guest house, called Taio Yu Tai, "the Fishing Ledge." The quaintness of the name hid the fact that this was the house where Chiang Ch'ing, Mao's wife, and the other members of the "Gang of Four" had planned the "Great Proletarian Cultural Revolution" to wipe out the Chairman's opposition and most of his possible successors, along with hundreds and hundreds of thousands of other Chinese whose great sin was usually that they were not young and had some education. Chou himself had barely survived the purge.

The Premier, whom Nixon called "Prime Minister," and his wife, who had been waiting at the guest house, sipped tea with the Nixons. After a few minutes, Chou rose, saying he was sure the Nixons wanted to rest before the evening's official banquet. American cameras and reporters were outside, waiting for the President's departure for a procedural meeting with Chou at 4:30. Nixon was enormously impressed with Chou, as Kissinger had been in June. Chou was a graduate of Nankai University, an American missionary school in Tientsin, where a motto, which could have been Nixon's own, hung on the walls:

> *Face clean, hair cut, clothes neat, buttoned tight,*
> *Posture straight, shoulders square, chest out, back straight,*
> *Beware of arrogance, hot temper and idleness—*
> *In all show amiability, composure and dignity.*

At 2:30, as Nixon was getting ready to take a shower upstairs, Kissinger hurried into the house, saying that Chairman Mao wanted to see the President. Nixon waited five minutes before coming down to ride to Mao's house in a corner of the old Forbidden City of the emperors with Chou, Kissinger, and Winston Lord, the American note-taker. The President said that he did not want Rogers or any State Department personnel to know where he was—he did not want to take the chance they would know or leak his new secrets—which meant that the Americans accepted Chinese interpreters that day and at most other meetings.

As they were being driven to Mao's house, a barber was shaving the Chairman and cutting his hair. Mao had left the house only once in five months. He was semiconscious much of that time, suffering from a variety of diseases, including heart trouble, pneumonia, and Parkinson's disease. This day, however, he was restless after lunch and did not want to take his usual nap. His mind was clear and he wanted to see the President of the United States. Aides rushed about, dressing him, removing the medical bed and equipment from his study. Nixon and Kissinger knew nothing of this, but in the months of negotiations leading to this day, Kissinger had promised that the Americans would not reveal China's greatest secret, the state of Mao's health. Until this summons, Chou had not known whether the Chairman would actually meet the Americans.

In his own diary, Nixon carefully described the scene: "We were escorted into a room that was not elaborate, filled with books and papers. Several of the books were open to various pages on the coffee table next to where he was sitting. His girl secretary helped him to his feet.

When I shook his hand, he said, 'I can't talk very well.' . . . He reached out his hand, and I reached out mine, he held it for about a minute."

Chinese photographers came in as the Americans sat down in a semicircle of big brown stuffed chairs. There was some small talk as the photographers did their work. Kissinger said he assigned Mao's writings to his students at Harvard. The chairman, who was seventy-eight years old, smiled at that, but had obvious trouble answering. A series of strokes had taken their toll. He had to gather himself before each sentence. Finally, with a burst of air, he said, "Those writings of mine are nothing. . . ."

"The Chairman's writings moved a nation and have changed the world," Nixon said.

"I haven't been able to change it," Mao said. "I've only been able to change a few places in the vicinity of Peking." Then he said, "Our common friend Generalissimo Chiang Kai-shek doesn't approve of all this. He calls us Communist bandits. . . ."

"What does the chairman call Chiang Kai-shek?" Nixon asked.

". . . We abuse each other," Mao answered, adding that he knew Chiang a lot longer than Nixon did.

"We two must not monopolize the whole show," Mao said, continuing the polite opening. "It won't do if we don't let Dr. Kissinger have a say. You have been made famous by your trips to China."

"It was the President who set the direction and worked out the plan," said Kissinger.

"He is a very wise assistant to say it that way," Nixon said with a smile, winning a hearty laugh from the Chinese leaders.

As slow as he was physically, Mao was obviously well briefed. He knew that Nixon had told a Chinese official who had been aboard *Air Force One* from Shanghai to Peking that he thought of Mao as a man with whom one could discuss philosophy. And the Chinese leader used that line to turn the conversation in a more serious direction, saying that indeed his role was to discuss philosophical questions: "That is to say that I voted for you during your election. . . ."

". . . The lesser of two evils," said Nixon.

"I like rightists," Mao continued. "People say that you are rightists, that the Republican Party is to the right. . . . I am comparatively happy when these people on the right come into power."

"I think the important thing to note is that in America, at least at this time, those on the right can do what those on the left talk about," Nixon responded.

"There is another point, Mr. President," Kissinger interjected, courting both men. "Those on the left are pro-Soviet and would not encourage a move toward the People's Republic, and in fact criticize you on these grounds."

"Exactly that," Mao said, the words exploding with a breath. "Some are opposing you. In our country also there is a reactionary group that is opposed to our contact with you. The result was that they got on an airplane and fled abroad."

"Maybe you know this," said Chou, who was deferential throughout. The Americans knew only that Mao was speaking of the overthrow of Lin Piao, the defense minister who had been considered his likely successor until he disappeared in September 1971. "The Soviet Union, they finally went to dig out the corpses . . . ," Mao said in another burst.

"In Outer Mongolia," Chou added.

The world did not know yet, but Lin Piao and his family had died in a plane crash in Outer Mongolia on September 12, 1971, apparently while trying to flee to the Soviet Union after a failed military coup against Mao.

Nixon began to explain his actions during the Indo-Pakistani War, but Mao cut him off, asking whether he intended to discuss their philosophic differences.

"The Chairman can be sure," Nixon said, "that whatever we discuss, nothing goes beyond this room." He added that he did want to talk about India and Japan, but he would do that with Chou.

"Good," Mao said. "All those troublesome problems I don't want to get into very much."

He did add, though, that President Yahya Khan had urged the Chinese to meet with Nixon. "He said," Mao continued, "it should be compared whether President Johnson or President Nixon would be better. . . . Yahya said the two men cannot be compared. He said that one was like a gangster—he meant Johnson. I don't know how he got that impression. We on our side were not happy with that President either. We were not happy with your former Presidents from Truman through Johnson."

Mao was tiring. Chou was looking at his watch. So Nixon went to his main point: "What brings us together is a recognition on our part that what is important is not a nation's internal political philosophy. What is important is its policy toward the rest of the world and toward us. . . . Also—maybe you don't believe this but I do—neither China nor the United States, both great nations, wants to dominate the world. . . . We can find common ground, despite our differences, to build a world structure in which we both can be safe to develop in our own ways on our own roads. That cannot be said about some other nations in the world."

"Neither do we threaten Japan or South Korea," Mao said. Then he added: "Do you think we have covered enough today?"

"Yes," Nixon said. "Mr. Chairman, we know that you and the Prime Minister have taken great risks in inviting us here. For us also it was a difficult decision. But having read some of the Chairman's statements, I know he is one who sees when an opportunity comes, that you must seize the hour, seize the day"—words from a poem by Mao. "You do not know me. Since you do not know me, you shouldn't trust me. You will find I never say something I cannot do. And I will always do more than I can say. . . . The Chairman's life is well known to all of us. He came from a very poor family to the top of the most populous nation in the world, a great nation. My background is not so well known. I also came from a very poor family, and to the top of a very great nation. History has brought us together. . . . The question is whether we, with different philosophies, can make a breakthrough that will serve not just China and America, but the whole world in the years ahead. And that is why we are here."

Mao answered, "Your book, *The Six Crises,* is not a bad book. . . . I don't know much about the United States. I must ask you to send some teachers here, mainly teachers of history and geography."

The meeting was winding down and Nixon said the Chairman looked well. "Appearances are deceiving," Mao said.

There was one last piece of business concerning the session. The President's men asked the Chinese photographers to cut Winston Lord out of their pictures before they were given to the press. That way they could tell the State Department that the Chinese had insisted that only the President and Kissinger come to Mao's house.

EVERYTHING WAS DIFFERENT after the meeting. The coolness of the airport and the ride turned into the smiles of a sunny winter. Back in his guest house, an almost giddy Nixon rushed off for his first plenary session with Chou. A line of ten Americans, now including Rogers and his men, faced a line of nineteen Chinese across a long table in an elaborate meeting room of the Great Hall of the People. The meeting was about procedure and the details of preparing a final communiqué, but Nixon and Chou began talking about the famous non-handshake of 1954. "We will shake hands," said Nixon, standing and reaching across the table. Chou, too, stood and took his hand again. Nixon had memorized so much and was so excited that he was speaking in something like Chinese slogans: "The whole world is watching. . . . We have broken out of the old pattern. As the Prime Minister has said in a meeting with Dr.

Kissinger, the helmsman must ride with the waves or he will be submerged with the tide."

The first order of business, initiated by Chou, was what to do about the American press. "They wanted me to receive them," said the Premier. "It is not very easy for me to answer their questions in the middle. Nor am I very adept at briefing conferences like Mr. Kissinger. Because I might tell the truth about what went on. . . ."

Then it was time for the welcoming banquet in the Great Hall itself. Chou toasted the President: "The gates to friendly contact have finally been opened. . . . Differences should not hinder China and the United States from establishing normal state relations on the basis of the five principles of mutual respect for sovereignty and territorial integrity; mutual non-aggression; non-interference in each other's internal affairs; equality and mutual benefit, and peaceful coexistence. . . ." Then the Premier, a graceful man who spoke English, circled the room, toasting each of the Americans, with a slight bow and a sip of mao-tai, the Chinese sorghum brandy, bottled liquid fire.

President Nixon had memorized his toast, and that had caused a strange scene in the American party between Dwight Chapin, the White House advance chief, and Charles Freeman Jr., a State Department interpreter. Chapin assigned Freeman to do the translation at the dinner and Freeman asked for the text. Chapin said the President would speak extemporaneously. But Freeman knew that was not true, he had worked on a draft of the remarks—and he knew the President was going to quote Mao's poetry. Chapin again refused to give him the text and Freeman said, "If you think I'm going to get up and ad lib Chairman Mao back into Chinese, you're out of your mind."

"This is an order from the President," Chapin said, but Freeman refused again. So a Chinese translator, with the text, was doing the translation as Nixon spoke: "At this very moment, through the wonder of telecommunications, more people are seeing and hearing what we say than on any other occasion in the history of the world. Yet, what we say here will not be long remembered. What we do here can change the world. . . . Chairman Mao has written: 'So many deeds cry out to be done, and always urgently. The world rolls on. Time passes. Ten thousand years are too long. Seize the day, seize the hour.' This is the hour. This is the day for our two peoples to rise to the heights of greatness which can build a new and better world." Then he circled the room as Chou had, clinking glasses, sipping and bowing with each of the seventy Chinese guests as an orchestra played "America the Beautiful."

Back in his guest house, a tired but happy President heard reports of television and newspaper play back home. Television was indeed showing and speaking wonder—the banquet was televised live by all three networks for four hours—with almost no talk of politics or policy.

Chinese television ran ten minutes of the Mao-Nixon meeting, without sound. By mid-afternoon, *Jenmin Jih Pao,* "The People's Daily," with two of its six pages crammed with photos of the leaders, was sold out for the first time in memory. The first crowds the Americans saw were people gathering around billboards that displayed the pages of the paper.

THE NEXT DAY, Tuesday, February 22, there were only ten people in the room when Nixon and Chou sat down to discuss the content of the joint communiqué the governments would issue at the end of the President's visit. Chou, the host, asked the President whether he wished to begin with a discussion of the Taiwan issue and then move on to a general discussion of world affairs, or begin with the world and move on to Taiwan.

"Taiwan," Nixon answered. But first he wanted to talk again about secrecy. He said that the only Americans who would see the transcript of the negotiating sessions were the three men at the table with him—Kissinger, Lord, and John Holdridge, the China expert on the National Security Council—and General Haig, who was back in Washington. He said he would show excerpts where necessary to Rogers and to the State Department's East Asia expert, Marshall Green. Chou, who had heard the same thing from Kissinger, said nothing. Nixon added: "Our State Department leaks like a sieve. Also, within our bureaucracy there is a great opposition to many of the positions I have taken, for example, our positions with respect to India and Pakistan."

The President then spoke for more than an hour and a half. The script had been worked out in days and nights of conversation between Kissinger and Chou, but it was still an extraordinary performance. The President was direct and more candid than he ever was with his own staff and Cabinet. He went right to the main points—and China's main point was acknowledgment that Taiwan was theirs, perhaps not tomorrow or even in twenty years, but part of China forever. Nixon spoke firmly and easily, revealing decisions he had made without telling his own assistants or the American people, contradicting policy, public rhetoric, and commitments—and, as far as anyone knew, his own convictions. He began:

> Principle one, there is one China, and Taiwan is part of China. There will be no more statements made—if I can control our bureaucracy—to the effect that the status of Taiwan is undetermined.

Second, we have not and will not support any Taiwan independence movement.

Third, we will, to the extent we are able, use our influence to discourage Japan from moving into Taiwan as our presence becomes less. . . .

The fourth point is that we will support any peaceful resolution of the Taiwan issue that can be worked out. And related to that point, we will not support any military attempts by the Government of Taiwan to resort to a military return to the mainland. Finally, we seek the normalization of relations with the People's Republic. . . . I would add that, as Dr. Kissinger has pointed out, two-thirds of our present forces on Taiwan are related to our forces in Southeast Asia. These forces, regardless of what we do here, will be removed as the situation in Southeast Asia is resolved. I have made that decision. And the reduction of the remaining military presence in Taiwan will go forward as progress is made on the peaceful resolution of the problem.

The problem here, Mr. Prime Minister, is not in what we are going to do, the problem is in what we are going to say about it.

After meeting China's condition in the first minutes, Nixon spoke of what he saw as his problems and his opposition at home: "In complete candor, the left wants this trip to fail, not because of Taiwan but because of the Soviet Union. And the right, for deeply principled ideological reasons, believes that no concessions at all should be made regarding Taiwan." He also mentioned pro-India Americans, who he said opposed U.S.–China détente.

Kissinger spoke for the first time: "You forgot the pro-Japanese—"

"The unholy alliance of the far right, the pro-Soviet left, and pro-Indian left . . . ," Nixon said, and added, "those who are pro-Japan." Then he said: "What we are trying to find is language which will not give this strong coalition. . . . the opportunity to gang up and say in effect that the American President went to Peking and sold Taiwan down the river. . . . Our problem is to be clever enough to find language which will meet your need yet does not stir up the animals. . . ."

To Nixon, calming the animals—to win time and options for secret maneuver—was central to leadership. He shifted next to one of his principal arguments in Peking: what the Chinese said in public was their business, but he wanted to persuade them that it was in their interest not to try to push the United States out of Asia. The President argued that the real threats to China were the Soviet Union, Japanese rearmament, and development of nuclear weapons. He knew, from Kissinger's memos, that one of Chou's first questions to the Americans had been, "Can you control the wild horse of Japan?"

"Don't say, 'We oppose rearmament of Japan,' " Kissinger had told Nixon in briefing memos. "Say 'We oppose a nuclear Japan.' "

The President went on, essentially proposing an American-Chinese alliance, an understanding hidden behind clouds of old rhetoric. "I am in disagreement with the Prime Minister's analysis of what America's role in the world should be," he began, referring again to the transcripts of Kissinger's conversations with Chou. "Publicly I think that the Prime Minister and Chairman Mao have to take the position that the United States is a great capitalist, imperialist power reaching out its hands and it should go home from Asia, home from Europe, and let the democratic forces and liberation forces develop in their own way. . . ." But, he continued, "I believe that the interests of China as well as the interests of the U.S. urgently require that the U.S., with certain exceptions which we can discuss later, should maintain a military presence in Europe, in Japan, and of course our naval forces in the Pacific. . . .

"Each of us had to put the survival of his nation first, and if the U.S. were to reduce its military strength, and if the U.S. were to withdraw from the areas I have described in the world, the dangers to the U.S. would be great—and the dangers to China would be greater.

"I do not impute any motives of the present leaders of the Soviet Union. I have to respect what they say, but I must make policy based on what they do. And in terms of the nuclear balance, the Soviet Union has been moving ahead at a very alarming rate over the past four years. . . . With respect to China, the Soviet Union has more forces on the Sino-Soviet border than it has arrayed against the Western Alliance. . . . I think that the Prime Minister in terms of his philosophy has taken exactly the correct position with respect to Japan, for example the U.S. should withdraw its troops, the treaty between the U.S. and Japan should be abrogated, and Japan should be left to become a neutral country that is unarmed. I think that the Prime Minister has to continue to say that. . . . The U.S. can get out of Japanese waters, but others will fish there. And both China and the U.S. have had very difficult experiences with Japanese militarism. . . . The Japanese, with their enormously productive economy, their great natural drive and their memories of the war they lost, could well turn toward building their own defense in the event that the U.S. guarantee were removed. . . . It also has the option of moving toward the Soviet Union. . . .

"I realize that I sound . . . like an old cold warrior," Nixon said, and Chou laughed. "But it is the world as I see it. . . . I believe that our interests are in common in the respects I have mentioned. . . .

"I will just close by saying after this analysis I would not want to leave the impression that the U.S. is not going to try to go to the source of the trouble, the Soviet Union, and try to make any agreements that will reduce the common danger. . . . We are going to try, for example, to get an arms limitation agreement and also make progress on the Middle East. . . ."

Finally, Nixon pledged to keep the Chinese, through Kissinger, fully informed on all contacts with the Soviets. And more. The President suggested that secret military and intelligence cooperation between China and the United States could be arranged.

Kissinger interrupted: "We have."

"O.K.," Nixon said.

"Thank you," Chou said, in English. "Shall we recess for ten minutes?"

WHEN THEY CAME BACK, the Premier offered his own tour of post–World War II politics and history, beginning: "The U.S. forces left China, the Soviet forces, too, left China, and the Chinese people themselves filled up the vacuum. . . . The situation in China today is what it was like two hundred years ago when the British colonial forces were driven out of America, and the American people themselves filled up the vacuum."

The villain of Chou's piece was President Harry Truman. "History twists and turns. . . . Why did we send the Chinese people's volunteers during the Korean War? Because Truman compelled us. He sent the Seventh Fleet into the Taiwan Straits so that it wasn't possible for us to regain Taiwan. What was more, his troops pressed straight toward the boundary of the Yalu River. . . . We could not stand idly by. We had to show that what we say counts. We couldn't be sure, though, that we would win, because the Soviets were not willing to send forces. . . .

"Now the Taiwan question can be discussed rather easily," Chou continued, and said he was taking the President at his word. "We have already waited over twenty years—I am very frank here—and we can wait a few more years. . . . We can tell Mr. President in advance, and also Japan, that when Taiwan returns to the Motherland, we will not establish any nuclear bases there. . . .

"The most pressing question now is Indochina. The Democratic Party tried to put you on the spot on this question by alleging that you came to China to settle Vietnam. Of course this is not possible. We are not in a position to settle it in talks. . . . Our position is that so long as you are continuing your Vietnamization, Laoization and Cambodianization policy, and they continue fighting, we can do nothing but continue to support them. . . . You went there by accident. Why not give this up? . . . Be bold."

Nixon knew in advance what that answer would be, both from the transcripts of Kissinger's talks with Chou and a failed attempt—on February 6 in Paris—to persuade the Chinese to arrange a meeting in China between the President and Le Duc Tho or another North Vietnamese negotiator. Now, at the first mention of the war, Nixon seemed to resent Chou's cavalier advice and said only: "We are not going to walk out of there without an agreement. . . . The U.S. would then be a nation which would, in my opinion, deserve nothing but contempt before the people and nations of the world, whatever their philosophies."

Chou spent most of his time talking about the power of the United States and the Soviet Union and the arms race between the two superpowers: "What we are concerned about is that you two big powers spend so much money on arms expansion. What does this mean for the future of the world? . . . The worst possibility is the eventuality that you would all attack China—the Soviet Union comes from the north, the Japanese and the U.S. from the east, and India into China's Tibet. Under these circumstances, of course, our people would have to make terrific sacrifices."

"I understand," Nixon said. "I would say that a strong China is in the interests of world peace at this point. I don't mean to suggest that China should change its policy and become a superpower. But a strong China can help provide the balance of power in this key part of the world—that is desperately needed. Then, too, I have a selfish reason—if China could become a second superpower, the U.S. could reduce its own armaments."

Chou laughed and had the session's last words: "You have too much confidence in us. . . . We don't want to spend too much money. We don't wish to expand."

That night the Nixons were an audience for an extraordinary piece of political theater, a spectacular performance of Chinese propaganda ballet. Sidey described it in a cable to *Time:* "The President and Mrs. Nixon sat there with Mao's wife, Chiang Ch'ing, cosily wedged between them, a bottle of fizzy orange drink and tea on the table in front, while on the stage 'The Red Detachment of Women' unfolded in vivid song, dance and meaning. Despotic Landlord beat a peasant girl who ran off and joined the Communists. Together they launched their war of liberation, winning victory after victory, coming back to kill Despotic Landlord—finally marching into the red sun, swords flashing, machine guns chattering, grenades exploding. . . ."

The President woke the next morning at 6 A.M. and filled a page of notes that ended: "Your people expect action on Taiwan. Our people expect action on Vietnam. Neither can act immediately. But both are inevitable. Let us not embarrass each other."

THE SECOND DAY of the Nixon-Chou conversations began the next afternoon. But it was soon obvious that work at the top had already been done, and that what was left was the wording of the communiqué being negotiated on the American side by Kissinger. Both Nixon and Chou wandered into conversations and old war stories, drifting musings about how much both men liked Yahya Khan, but how bad a leader he was. In passing, the Chinese premier echoed Brezhnev's reading of China, saying of the Soviets, "They just don't listen to reason." Nixon asked him when Marshal Chen Yi, the Chinese military leader, had died. "Just recently. . . . He had cancer of the stomach," Chou answered. Then he asked, quite innocently, "Do you have a way of curing cancer?"

Nixon told a story he said he had never told before—about Syngman Rhee, the former president of South Korea. "In 1953, my first trip around the world as Vice President, President Eisenhower gave me a long oral message for Rhee. Rhee was thinking about going north—invading North Korea—and I had the unpleasant duty to tell him that he couldn't go, and that if he did we wouldn't support him. Rhee cried when I told him."

Chou won the never-been-told-before contest with a story about the Chen Pao incident. Chen Pao was an island in the Ussuri River, the northeastern boundary between China and the Soviet Union, where troops of the two countries fought each other in 1969. "Kosygin called us. He asked the operator to find Chairman Mao. Without orders, the operator answered him: 'You are a revisionist, therefore I will not connect you.' Then Kosygin said, 'If you will not try to reach the Chairman, will you please find the Prime Minister?' The telephone operator gave him the same answer again."

The President also went off on a tangent to praise Kissinger—perhaps because Kissinger and Rogers were squabbling again and each had come to Nixon's guest house that morning to complain about the other—with just a bit of an I'm-still-the-boss barb at the end, saying: "He takes the long view, which is something I try to do also. . . . The Prime Minister can be sure that if we survive the next political battle, as we hope and expect to do, I will still have Dr. Kissinger with me. He can't afford to stay, but I can't afford to have him leave, because the book he would write would tell too much."

"I will not leave as long as the President thinks I can be of service," Kissinger dutifully said. "I will not write a book in any event."

Later, Chou said that Rogers had gone to the Chinese foreign minister to ask to be included in the negotiating sessions on the communiqué being prepared by Kissinger and China's deputy foreign minister, Ch'iao Kuan-hua.

"There is a misunderstanding. . . . I have delegated Dr. Kissinger. . . . That is the way we would like to have it done."

As the afternoon wore on, Nixon, the host for this section, said it was getting late but he had one more question for Chou, and asked for his evaluations of Soviet leaders. The Premier covered that in a couple of sentences, describing Brezhnev as stronger, more ambitious, more emotional, and Kosygin as more the technocrat, short-sighted. Then he offered his impressions of Soviet directions: "The policy of the Soviet Union, although they don't admit it themselves, is actually a policy of expansion. . . . We have called them 'socialist imperialists.' They don't like the name because it is taken from Lenin. . . . Lenin talked about people who were socialist in words but imperialist in deeds. We began to give them this name when they invaded Czechoslovakia. . . . Just by coincidence the Romanian national day occurred at that time. On that day I personally went to the Romanian embassy and in front of the Soviet ambassador gave them that title. Since then they have hated us to the very core. . . ."

"Do they fear that you threaten their leadership of the so-called socialist camp?" Nixon asked.

"We don't even recognize them as belonging to the socialist camp. . . . The socialist camp no longer exists because there are many different ideas."

THAT NIGHT, after an Americans-only dinner in the guesthouse—steak and potatoes and ice cream—the President and his party moved over the Capital Gymnasium to join eighteen thousand spectators at a Chinese sports exhibition featuring gymnastics, badminton, and Ping-Pong. Haldeman recorded the evening with what may have been the envy of an old advance man. "The impression from the gym show was one of total control, the hall was packed, every seat was filled. They were filled by sections, with the big section filled with an army group in green uniforms, another section for an army group with blue uniforms, other sections for people in civilian clothes, a section for athletes in red sweat-suits, another for athletes in blue sweat-suits, etc. Also, they had a lighting system that enabled them to turn on sections of overhead lights for the television cameras, and as each section was lighted from time to time, the people in it would all start cheering for the camera. The regimentation is enormous. The athletes themselves march in with a big strut and swinging arms, stand at attention and face the Premier before they start their particular event. The level of control is almost total. . . ."

THE PRESIDENT WAS TIRING and American reporters were frustrated. Sidey was reporting back that he had no idea what was going on. The only words American correspondents had been allowed to hear were the toasts by Chou and Nixon the night before. Sidey wrote: "Nixon and Chou collaborated in engaging in the deepest secret diplomacy since World War II. . . . My great fear is that the Nixon administration will pick up some pointers from Mao's regime. A remote Nixon has gone completely beyond reach here. They say he had a meeting with Mao, but we only have a few photos and the word of Ron Ziegler. . . . It is tiring, constant. Not only are we trying to find out what Nixon is really doing, which is impossible, but we are trying to find out about Peking and China. . . . There are few taxis and the official cars are in constant use. We are at the mercy of our hosts, which is certainly the way they wanted it."

"Nothing was disclosed about the direction of conversation," began Max Frankel in the second paragraph of the lead story of the next day's *New York Times.* One of the few correspondents there with extensive experience in Asia, R. H. Shackford of Scripps Howard wrote: "The business sessions were conducted in total secrecy. No information—not even the subjects being discussed—was announced or 'leaked' to the press. . . . The minutes of the meetings between the Americans and the Chinese officials at various levels are the most important top secret documents in existence today." Joseph Kraft found himself sitting next to a high official of the Chinese press office and seized the moment to ask him what happened to Lin Piao. The man answered: "Eat your lunch!"

In *The New Republic,* John Osborne talked about extracting details from Ron Ziegler and other members of the entourage, writing finally, and incorrectly: "Often reported in recent years to be dead or incapacitated, Mao appeared to Nixon and Kissinger during their hour with him to be in excellent health, alert and in total command. . . . Nothing whatever about the substance of the talk with Mao was divulged. The only fact that emerged, other than the Chairman's appearance of bouncy health, was that Premier Chou played the part of a humble follower and subordinate when he was in Mao's presence."

But the pictures were great. On Thursday, February 24, a bright, sunny, 20-degrees day, the Nixons became guided tourists. They were driven forty miles from Peking to see the tombs of Ming dynasty emperors, guarded by miles of statues of fierce-looking fantasy animals, and then to the Great Wall of China. They were trailed everywhere by millions of dollars' worth of television talent—Walter Cronkite, Eric Sevareid, Barbara Walters, and Harry Reasoner. Semidesperate American print reporters got their first exclusives by figuring out that the families and children posing for pictures with the President—along with everyone else at the tombs—were props bused in by local revolutionary committees. At the Wall, reporters had a brief chance to question Nixon and were rewarded by a quote heard round the world: "I think you would have to conclude that this is a great wall. . . ." After that, some of the most celebrated byliners in the country—including Teddy White, Bill Buckley, and James Michener—decided they might do better with Mrs. Nixon, who was being guided through schools, hospitals, and factories. They were rewarded at a glasswork factory when Mrs. Nixon, watching artisans making glass flowers, asked: "Do they use their own judgment on what they mix together? Can they just take a little bit of this and a little bit of this?" The answer from the chairman of the glassworks revolutionary committee was, "No, they have a certain design."

THE THIRD SESSION of the Chou talks began after the tour. This time the principals began going line by line and word by word through the communiqué being put together by Kissinger and Ch'iao Kuan-hua, who were working together far into the nights.

Nixon laid out his problem first: "My goal is normalization with the People's Republic. I realize that solving the Taiwan problem is indispensable to achieving that goal but . . . I must be able to go back to Washington and say that no secret deals have been made. . . . So, what I must do is have what we would call 'running room,' which the communiqué language I hope will provide. . . .

"If someone asks me when I return, do you have a deal with the Prime Minister that you are going to withdraw all American forces from Taiwan, I will say 'No.' . . . I can do it gradually but inevitably. But if I were to announce it now . . . it would raise the issue at the wrong time."

Chou agreed to no time limit. Then he added: "While your forces are still on Taiwan—you will discourage the Japanese from coming in?"

"I will go further," Nixon said. "We will try to keep Japanese forces from coming into Taiwan *after* our forces leave."

"You would not support or allow a Taiwan Independence Movement, nor encourage it, either in the U.S. or Taiwan?"

Kissinger interrupted Chou to say: " 'Allow' is beyond our capability."

"Discourage?" Chou asked.

"Discourage," Nixon said.

As to Vietnam, the President said he was sure the Chinese understood that many Americans thought that what he and Chou were doing at this very moment was negotiating the end of the war. "Of course," he continued, "what the Prime Minister is telling us is that he cannot help us in Vietnam. . . . Obviously what will be said, even with a skillful communiqué, is what the People's Republic wanted from us was movement on Taiwan and he got it; and what we wanted was help on Vietnam, and we got nothing."

Chou repeated what he had said before: the way to solve your Vietnam problem is to get out. They switched to Cambodia. "We have never meddled in their affairs," Chou said. "As I see it, Prince Sihanouk is quite an intelligent man. . . . He is neither a communist nor a socialist nor a Marxist, but a patriot. . . ."

"No one believes this," Nixon said, "but it was not our policy that deposed him in Cambodia."

Chou laughed, then said: "We had a dispute about that with Dr. Kissinger."

The Premier then asked the President about the Middle East, saying that Kissinger had avoided discussing it by saying he was Jewish, so his opinions were suspect. Nixon, indeed the old Cold Warrior, laid down his line: "The Soviet Union is playing for much bigger stakes. It is playing for a dominant role in the Mediterranean. It is playing for the gateway to Africa. . . . Israel is only a pawn, a pretext as far as the Soviets are concerned. . . . My concern"—he looked toward Kissinger—"incidentally it is his, too, he says he is Jewish, but he is an American first. Our concern is much bigger than Israel. We believe the Soviet Union is moving. . . . It must be resisted. . . ."

THE NEXT MORNING, Nixon called in Kissinger to talk again about the communiqué's language on Taiwan. Kissinger said that he and Ch'iao had been at it all night and might be again. "You two are young, you don't need sleep . . . ," Nixon said. "I've had a tough time sleeping here." He looked weary. He wanted to know whether they could cut out the toasts and glass-clinking at the banquet coming up. "We have to do it their way," Kissinger said.

The next Nixon-Chou meeting to go over the language again had been scheduled for 3 P.M., but it was postponed every fifteen minutes to wait for Kissinger and Ch'iao to come up with the language of the Taiwan paragraph. Finally, at 5:45 P.M., Chou and Nixon sat down again, without agreement. The Premier suggested they meet again at the airport before Nixon and most of the American party flew off to the lake resort city of Hangchow, south of Peking.

"You can say more," Chou said.

"No," Nixon said. "I'm through talking."

Chou was not. He wanted to talk about the President's scheduled summit meeting in Moscow in May. Tension between China and the Soviet Union, he said, had reached the point that the Chinese were requiring families to dig underground shelters and the government was linking them together in a network to survive Soviet bombing. The Premier said that if the Soviet Union asked what had happened during these Peking meetings, he would suggest that the United States emphasize that neither the Americans nor the Chinese were seeking hegemony in the Pacific, and that the Chinese would never deliberately provoke the Soviets along their borders and wanted both sides to disengage in the disputed border areas.

"We find it very difficult to understand them," Chou said. "It is truly a kind of pathology."

He had another question: "Why is it not possible for Israel to return to the Arab nations the lands that it occupies? Wouldn't that be beneficial to the relaxing of tensions?"

"Israel feels that it cannot return territory unless there is a better balance," the President replied, "so that it is better able to defend itself against an attack. . . . But the subject of returning territory is one we are constantly discussing. . . ."

Back at the guest house, Haldeman told Nixon that Rogers was complaining more and more about being cut out of meetings. Suddenly, unannounced, Rogers was at the door, asking when he would get to see Mao. The President nodded to Kissinger, who said there wasn't going to be another meeting because Mao was too ill. "Wrong!" Haldeman told him later. "We're not supposed to say anything about that."

Kissinger left to resume work on the communiqué—and a half hour later rushed back in. He was elated, saying they had worked out words that both sides could accept. "It's a victory," he said. Nixon agreed. The Chinese concession was to allow some fudging of the American commitment to "withdraw" from Taiwan, allowing that word to be softened with the phrases "progressively reduce" and "as the tension in the area diminishes."

After the night's banquet, the President came back to the guest house, worrying that his secretary of state would inadvertently disclose the truth about Mao's health. He sent Haldeman over to tell Rogers not to say anything about Mao to anyone. Ziegler came in to report that he had told the American press contingent that "basic agreement" had been reached on the final communiqué. The day's New York Times led with the story citing Ziegler, then adding, "He gave no details on the nature of the agreements reached or the subjects that the communiqué would cover."

THE PRESIDENT and Chou rode out to the airport together, talking about the impact of adversity on character, a subject on which Nixon considered himself an expert. He said he had learned more from his defeats than from his victories, and that what he wanted from life was to win one more than he lost.

There were twenty-three people at the morning meeting at the airport—including Rogers. There was no real business as everyone complimented everyone else for a while. Then Chou said he wanted to make a confession of error: "I have found a shortcoming your press pointed out to us. . . . Some people got some young children there to prettify the tombs, and it was putting up a false appearance. Your press correspondents have pointed this out, and we admit that this was wrong. We do not want to cover up the mistake. . . . We have criticized those who did this."

It was teatime again and Nixon and Chou sat together in big armchairs at the airport. This was Saturday, February 26. The President had spent more than forty hours with Chou and suddenly had enough of his company. They were sitting next to each other as the Premier pointed out one picture after another on the walls, explaining each one. Nixon's face got blanker and blanker. He tried a smile but it fell instantly. He glared at Chou for an instant, then said, "What the hell are you talking about!"

On the plane to Hangchow, a noisy Russian-made turboprop, the President walked out of the private compartment he shared with Chou in the rear of the plane, cleared out some of his surprised staff, and sat down next to Haldeman for most of the two-hour flight. In Hangchow ("West Lake" in English), a charming place of small islands and stone bridges and pagodas, it was Chou who disappeared. When the motorcade from the airport—a new terminal had been built there in forty days for Nixon's arrival—reached the lake, the Premier was not there. It took a while to find him; he was walking alone in a small woods near the lake. Then they were all off to see such delights as the Island of Three Towers Reflecting the Moon.

It was on to Shanghai the next morning, after the President took an hour to go over news reports from home with Ziegler and Haldeman. The oddest item was a story from Manchester, New Hampshire, where some papers were reporting that Senator Muskie, the Democratic front-runner, had broken into tears as he spoke angrily to a small crowd in front of the offices of the Manchester *Union Leader*. The paper had been attacking him regularly and had just published an anonymous letter in which the writer accused the candidate of making fun of "Canucks," French Canadians living in New England, and portrayed his wife as a hard-cursing drinker. Nixon was intrigued, but even back at the White House his men were confused about what had actually happened. Upon landing in Shanghai, the Americans were driven to the city's Industrial Exhibition. The President looked as if he could sleep on his feet. "Machinery has always impressed me," he said. "But I know nothing about it. All I can do is change the tire on a car."

When he got to the Ching Kiang Guest House, Kissinger was there with a report on the final version of the communiqué, including some changes asked for by Rogers after he had finally seen the document. The communiqué text mentioned United States treaty commitments to the defense of Japan and Korea, but made no mention of similar treaties with Taiwan. Rogers's men won the day on that by pointing out a bit of history: in early 1950, Secretary of State Dean Acheson had not mentioned South Korea in a list of American defense commitments, and that was considered a factor in North Korea's decision to invade South Korea a few months later. Nixon sent Kissinger back to Ch'iao and, pushed now by deadline problems, they removed mentions of the Japanese and Korean treaties. Nixon preferred unease in Tokyo and Seoul, which could be soothed by private commitments, to questions from Democrats and reporters about why only the Taiwan treaties were being ignored. Then Rogers came back again with more problems. "Tell him I'm asleep or something," Nixon told Haldeman. "Tell him anything. I don't want to see him."

But he came downstairs, listened to Rogers's new reservations, and rebutted them one by one. That done, he said, quite coldly: "Now, I expect the State Department to stay behind this 100 percent." He was asleep, taking a three-hour nap, when the text of the Shanghai Communiqué was released.

"WE HAVE BEEN here a week," the President said in his toast at the Shanghai banquet. "This was the week that changed the world. . . . The joint communiqué which we have issued today will make headlines around the world tomorrow."

It did, of course. The headline across eight columns in *The New York Times* was:

NIXON AND CHOU AGREE TO RENEW CONTACTS
U.S. TO WITHDRAW GRADUALLY FROM TAIWAN

One of the headlines below that was: "TAIPEI IS BITTER."

The communiqué itself was less than two thousand words, most of them restatements of familiar arguments and positions.

> The U.S. side stated: . . . The United States supports individual freedom and social progress for all the peoples of the world, free of outside pressure or intervention. . . . The United States places the highest value on its friendly relations with Japan. . . .
>
> The Chinese side stated: Wherever there is oppression, there is resistance. Countries want independence, nations want liberation, the people want revolution. . . . The Chinese side expressed its firm support to the peoples of Vietnam, Laos and Cambodia. . . .

Both sides signed on to: "Progress toward the normalization of relations between China and the United States is in the interest of all countries. . . ." They both also agreed on a sentence designed to be a warning to the Soviet Union: "The two sides stated that . . . neither should seek hegemony in the Asia-Pacific region and each is opposed to efforts by any other country or groups of countries to establish such hegemony."

And finally:

> The Chinese side reaffirmed its position: Taiwan is a province of China. . . . the liberation of Taiwan is China's internal affair in which no other country has the right to interfere; and all U.S. forces and military installations must be withdrawn. . . .
>
> The U.S. side declared: The United States acknowledges that all Chinese on either side of the Taiwan Strait maintain there is but one China and that Taiwan is a part of China. . . . It reaffirms its interest in a peaceful settlement of the Taiwan question by the Chinese themselves. With this prospect in mind, it affirms the ultimate objective of the withdrawal of all U.S. forces and military installations from Taiwan. . . .

Now, the President could not get to sleep, he was too keyed up. He had also drunk more than a few mao-tais from lunch through his last banquet. At that dinner, he gave his first extemporaneous toast—and he got carried away, appointing the United States as guardian of China and policeman of the world, saying: "This great city, over the past, has on many occasions been the victim of foreign aggression and foreign occupation. And we join the Chinese people, we the American people, in our dedication to this principle: that never again shall foreign domination, foreign occupation, be visited on this city or any part of China, or any independent country in the world."

He told Haldeman to call Kissinger and then he ordered several more rounds of the Chinese firewater. He was still talking at 2 A.M., with Kissinger seated on the couch, his head rolling in fatigue. When Haldeman, who did not drink, offered the opinion that they all needed some sleep, Nixon said: "If Chou can stay up all night, so can I."

Political time was the subject of the final conversation between Nixon and Chou, with the Premier saying it was odd that he was the older of them but Nixon had less time to implement the changes the communiqué listed—ten months or four years and ten months, depending on the coming election. (In his notes, Nixon checked that point, writing: "Age: My life is ten months or five years—Then done—I have little time.") The leaders agreed that there would be many times when their governments would be on opposite sides of issues and local disputes. Then Nixon said, "Maybe we can avoid personal references—"

"Also adjectives," said Kissinger.

Chou said the President was free to announce that the leaders of the Senate, Democrat Mike Mansfield and Republican Hugh Scott, would be invited to Peking. Nixon, who had suggested the invitation, responded, "Remember what I said, that Mansfield of the other party keeps secrets better than Scott of my own party."

Then Chou said he wanted to make a point: "We are extremely sad that North Vietnam has been bombed in the period just before and during your visit here. . . ."

"A point of honor," Kissinger said. "I don't believe that we have bombed in North Vietnam while we are here."

"In the DMZ, the line along the DMZ, on both sides," Chou said.

"Not while we are here," Kissinger repeated.

"Yes."

"We will check it."

"It has already reached Quang Nhin."

"We will check. There was an order not to do it."

"You can find out on your return to the United States."

On the ride to the airport, the Shanghai chairman, Chang Ch'un-chi'iao, sat next to the President. He pointed out the window at a large children's park and said: "Twenty-five years ago—before the liberation— that was a golf course. There was a sign on it: 'No Chinese allowed.' "

CHAPTER 29

April 7, 1972

PRESIDENT NIXON returned to Andrews Air Force Base at 9:30 on the night of February 28, and at 10 the next morning he began three hours of separate briefings with congressional leaders and then with his Cabinet. He described his meetings with Chou and Mao—saying the Chairman was quick and alert—and then summarized what happened in only a few words: "The most fundamental point is the new relationship between two powers—the most populous, and the most powerful—in which we say to each other that we support the proposition of peaceful settlement of international disputes and with each other. The simple thing that brought us together was a common interest. . . . we both want to build a structure of peace in the Pacific and in the World. . . . There will continue to be differences—the question is whether we're going to live with them or die for them."

He was more relaxed, naturally, with his own people, saying, "I ought to tell you—Bill and Henry and I ought to be sleeping at this hour—so if we are inarticulate, it's because we're asleep."

Kissinger didn't miss a beat, saying: "I can talk inarticulately even when I'm awake."

In the meeting with twenty Senate and House leaders of both parties, the President was pushed a little harder on exactly what the United States was going to do about Taiwan, but in his answers he stuck to the language of the communiqué. At one point, almost in passing, he said something that made it clear he understood and believed what Chou had said about President Truman and past American mistakes. According to the official notes: "The President pointed out that had this meeting occurred 25 years ago, Korea might have been avoided."

At the meeting with congressional leaders, Senator Fulbright asked three questions about the Chinese and the war in Vietnam, but the President deflected them. As the meeting broke up, he blocked the senator at the door and urged him not to bring up those questions in public, particularly those about American prisoners of war. "The string could break," said the President, a little mysteriously. He pointed a finger at Fulbright and said, "O.K., Bill? Agreed?"

Fulbright nodded. Then the President took off for Key Biscayne for a couple of days of rest in the sun, which was interrupted only by calls about Pat Buchanan, who wanted to resign because he did not agree with the Shanghai Communiqué. He thought his president had sold out to the communists in China—a theme that dominated conservative journalism and comment as soon as the trip ended. In the *National Review,* William F. Buckley wrote under the headline "Veni, Vidi, Victus"—we came, we saw, we were conquered.

That first day back in Washington was a bad-news day for the President. After their meeting with Nixon at the White House, the two Senate leaders, Scott and Mansfield, went back up to Capitol Hill and business as usual. The two of them had been working together to defeat an antibusing bill supported by the President. The key wording of the bill, introduced by Senator Robert P. Griffin of Michigan, was: "No court shall have jurisdiction to make any decision, enter any judgment or issue any order the effect of which would be to require that pupils be transported to or from school on the basis of their race, color, religion or national origin."

That was defeated by a 50-to-47 vote. Instead, the Senate passed a Mansfield-Scott compromise that would bar federal funding of busing, unless the busing was requested by local authorities, and would also delay court orders mandating school busing across school district lines. The second provision was considered a moderate response to a political firestorm that exploded after a federal district court judge not only ordered desegregation of the schools of Richmond, Virginia, but specified how that should be done, calling for busing some of the city's black students—70 percent of the city's enrollment—to 90-percent-white schools in the suburbs of Chesterfield and Henrico Counties. Suddenly the political attention of the country focused on Florida, where a presidential primary was scheduled for March 14. On the Democratic side, George Wallace had separated himself from the field—Edmund Muskie, Hubert

Humphrey, George McGovern, and seven other more liberal Democrats—by pounding away at racial themes, saying: "A victory for George Wallace is going to result in taking the batteries out of the buses that transport the little children throughout the state of Florida. . . . They get on the bus dark in the morning, get off dark in the afternoon, and all because of some social schemer in Washington." There was also a referendum on the ballot calling for an amendment to the United States Constitution granting every child the right to attend the public school nearest to home.

The Senate busing vote led in most papers the next morning. On the front page of *The New York Times,* a smaller headline below that read: "ALLEGED MEMO TIES I.T.T. TRUST ACTION TO G.O.P. FUNDING." It was another Jack Anderson special. The columnist had gotten his hands on a June 25, 1971, memo signed by a lobbyist for International Telephone and Telegraph Corporation that seemed to indicate that the company's antitrust settlement with the Justice Department was part of a deal in which ITT was going to put up four hundred thousand dollars to pay part of the costs of the 1972 Republican National Convention. The memo, signed by lobbyist Dita Beard, named names—and one of them was Richard Nixon. Another was Richard Kleindienst, who was awaiting confirmation as attorney general.

A week later, on March 7, the people of New Hampshire cast the first presidential votes of the year and the President won more than 70 percent of the Republican primary vote against Congressmen Paul McCloskey of California on the left and John Ashbrook of Ohio on the right. On the Democratic side, Muskie won with 48 percent and McGovern was second with 37 percent, far higher than polls had predicted. Wallace was waiting for them now in the Florida vote on March 14. But the campaigns had to share front pages and nightly newscasts with the ITT story, which was turning into a soap opera. Dita Beard, called to testify by a Senate committee, had disappeared—and then was found in a Denver hospital.

On March 14, George Wallace won big in the Florida Democratic primary, taking 42 percent of the vote and seventy-five convention delegates against ten opponents. Muskie, supposed to be the front-runner, got 14 percent. McGovern, who did not campaign in the state, won just 5 percent. The only thing that got more votes than the Alabama governor's total of 516,103 was the antibusing amendment referendum, which carried with more than 1,096,000, to 384,000 against. Nixon won 357,143 votes, 87 percent of the Republican vote against Ashbrook and McCloskey, who had already withdrawn.

That same day, the President called Bill Safire to Camp David to work on an antibusing speech. He was searching for a legal equivalent of taking the batteries out of school buses. "I don't want a Wallace-type speech," Nixon told him. "Start off by saying my position on busing is well known—I've always been against it. On segregation, I've always been against that, too. Now the question is, how can we deal with segregation in a way that does not result in busing? Here's the kind of thing I want to say to make it understandable. For example, when an eight-year-old child is within five minutes of a school, and could walk to school, but because of a court order to bus for racial balance he has an extra hour's ride. . . . This has got to stop."

On Safire's first draft, the President wrote: "Make it more vivid. . . . make a stronger attack on lower courts' chaos. . . ." Then, at the bottom, he added: "1. Purpose of desegregation is better education. . . . 2. Busing as means for education brings inferior education. . . . 3. Therefore desegregation sans busing."

On March 16, the President spoke many of the same words on national television, calling for an immediate halt, a moratorium, on all new busing orders by federal courts. Then he said he would propose an Equal Education Opportunities Act, which would mandate that $2.5 billion in federal education aid to states be spent in areas, usually urban slums, of greatest educational need—the money was the same $1.5 billion he had proposed to aid desegregation the year before plus the shifting of $1 billion already appropriated for troubled local schools. The actual legislation he sent to Congress the next morning was more sweeping than the speech: now he asked for a permanent halt, in effect a law limiting court jurisdiction over school integration. Whatever he said about his own concerns, he was dumping the problem once again—onto the Congress, as he had dumped it onto the courts two years before.

As the President prepared to speak, a man wearing a red wig and identifying himself as "Edward J. Hamilton" was talking his way into Dita Beard's room at the Rocky Mountain Osteopathic Hospital. The daughter of the ITT lobbyist asked "Mr. Hamilton" whom he represented. The answer was: "High Washington levels who are interested in your mother's welfare."

"Mr. Hamilton" was E. Howard Hunt. He had been sent to Denver by Chuck Colson. His job was to get Mrs. Beard to say the memo on front pages across the country was a forgery, and he accomplished that mission. Twenty-four hours later, on the afternoon of March 17, Beard's lawyer in Denver and Senate Republican leader Hugh Scott in Washington simultaneously released a statement from her saying the memo was "a hoax . . . a forgery . . . a cruel fraud."

The President was asked about the Beard affair during his March

24 press conference. Nixon took the offensive, saying the opposite of what he had been saying in private, praising Assistant Attorney General McLaren and the Antitrust Division: "We moved on I.T.T. We are proud of that record. . . ."

Most of the press conference focused on the story of the day: George Meany and two other labor members had resigned from the Pay Board, claiming that Phase II of the administration's wage and price controls was holding down wages—to 5.5 percent on an annual basis—while allowing prices and profits to rise higher and higher. The President went on the offensive again, saying that the problem was food prices, which were exempt from controls, and the villains were "the middlemen"—that is, processing companies, truckers, and retailers, who generally accounted for two-thirds of supermarket prices. He had an example ready, from John Connally, saying farmers were getting thirty cents a dozen for eggs, but at the Hotel Pierre in New York, one of the most expensive eating places in the country, two eggs were five dollars, which added up to thirty dollars a dozen.

When an ITT question turned to campaign finance, the President said: "Nobody gets anything back as far as general contributions are concerned in this administration. . . . As far as such contributions are concerned, they should always, of course, comply with the law."

But there was no law. The Corrupt Practices Act of 1925 was to be replaced by the Federal Election Campaign Act of 1972, a compromise bill that passed both houses of Congress by huge margins and was signed into law by the President on February 7. (Nixon, as he had done on many other domestic bills, figured if you can't beat it with a veto, then sign it and take the credit.) The new law would not take effect until April 7—sixty days after the President signed it on February 7. Led by Senator McGovern, the Democratic candidates for president declared that they would voluntarily release the names of contributors and list contribution amounts. The President and CREEP said nothing. Herb Kalmbach, the President's lawyer in California, delivered the cash he had been secretly collecting—"Anybody who wants to be an ambassador must give at least $250,000," was one of Nixon's orders—to Hugh Sloan, the treasurer of CREEP's finance committee. The total was $915,037.68—$233,800 of it in $100 bills.

In those sixty days, the President and his committee collected more than $20 million—almost $2 million of it in cash—with no requirement or intention to name names and amounts. Sloan handled $6 million in just two days, April 5 and 6. He had so much cash on hand that he asked G. Gordon Liddy, who had the title of counsel to CREEP's finance committee, to walk with him to the bank to deposit some of the money stacked on his desk and stuffed into desk drawers and safes. "Wait a minute," Liddy said, and went to his office and came back with a pistol.

The contributors, secret at the time, included several executives and companies in trouble with the Justice Department or the Internal Revenue Service, or seeking government contracts. Some were Democrats giving to their party openly and to the Republicans secretly. Some just liked Nixon or his politics. The money came in wire transfers, corporate checks, personal checks, third-party checks—and cash. Much of it was "laundered"—passed through banks in Mexico and Venezuela to hide the names of the donors. Liddy moved at least $114,000 through the accounts of Bernard Barker, the Cuban-American real estate man who had been part of the plumbers' Los Angeles burglary team—Republic National Bank of Miami and then Barker withdrew the money by writing checks to Banco Internacional in Mexico City. Moving the money around also gave Liddy the chance to check out targets of opportunity at the Democratic National Convention, scheduled for August in Miami Beach, sending back reports and taped transcripts of his conversations to Attorney General Mitchell.*

Sloan had more than a million dollars in cash in his office safe and he handed it out pretty much on demand—$350,000 to a Haldeman assistant, $250,000 to Kalmbach, $199,000 to Liddy. More cash was kept in safe deposit boxes in New York, in Washington, in Los Angeles, in Miami. The committee was able to move some of the money by prepaying for campaign services and buying television and radio commercial time for later use. E. Howard Hunt and other operatives carried cash to dozens of young men and women recruited to spy on Democratic campaigns and report back to CREEP.

The Anderson columns on ITT brought the company's 1970 anti-Allende operations in Chile back into the news. The Chile columns triggered an immediate denial from the State Department and then the White House. After Ziegler passed along the denials to the press on the day of his press conference, the President called to ask him how it went. The press secretary said that there was a problem denying everything because

---

* The names and amounts of contributions to CREEP in the period before April 7, 1972, became public in September of 1973 because of lawsuits filed by Common Cause. The best-known names were: W. Clement Stone of Combined Insurance Co., who contributed at least $2 million; Richard Mellon Scaife, $1 million; Arthur K. Watson of IBM, $300,000; Walter Annenberg, $250,000; Robert Vesco of International Controls Corporation, the target of Federal fraud investigations, $200,000; Armand Hammer of Occidental Petroleum, Dwayne Andreas of Archer Daniels Midland, Robert Allen of Gulf Resources and Chemical Corporation, William Liedtke of Pennzoil, George Spater of American Airlines, George Steinbrenner of American Shipbuilding, and H. Ross Perot of Electronic Data Systems Inc.

of Edward Korry, the United States ambassador in Chile at the time. "Why?" Nixon asked.

"Well," Ziegler answered, "Korry said that he had received instructions to do anything short of a Dominican-type...." "Dominican-type" meant assassination, referring to the 1961 killing of Rafael Trujillo, the dictator who ruled the Dominican Republic for more than thirty years.

Nixon had his own take on Korry, telling Ziegler: "Well, he was—he was instructed to. But he just failed, the son of a bitch. That was his main problem. He should have kept Allende from getting in."

Scandal was beginning to attach to the White House. On his news summary, the President underlined a Sidey report questioning how Kalmbach, a middling local lawyer, was suddenly representing many of the most important companies in the country, including United Airlines, Marriott Hotels, Travelers Insurance, and Music Corporation of America. An analysis by Edwin Roberts of *The National Observer,* usually friendly to the administration, said: "Even if there was no explicit wrongdoing, as appears to be the case, we are left with a strong odor of corporate and administration contempt for the public's intelligence. . . . the aroma is there and in this election year it is peeling the paint off the GOP's house."

Nixon was mad as hell, asking Haldeman why he could not find someone to rifle Anderson's files—the way the columnist seemed to be doing with ITT and the government. His anger at the press boiled over again when he saw that John Osborne of *The New Republic* had written that he was surprised that no one at the White House, Nixon included, was bright enough to foresee what would happen, sooner or later, when the ITT machinations became public. Nixon dictated a rambling "Eyes Only" memo to Haldeman and Ziegler:

> What we have to realize is the cold fact that both Sidey and Osborne are totally against us. They are not honest reporters. They are out to defeat us. . . . Both have spoken in the most vicious derogatory terms of RN in the place where you really find out what the people think—the Georgetown cocktail parties. The evidence on this is absolutely conclusive. You do not need to ask me where I got it . . .

CHAPTER 30

May 1, 1972

THE COMMUNISTS' SPRING OFFENSIVE began later than usual in 1972. On March 30, with only six weeks to go before the traditional start of the summer monsoon season, more than fifteen thousand North Vietnamese regulars crossed the DMZ into Quang Tri Province.

The South Vietnamese, the Americans, and the South Koreans (there were almost forty thousand South Korean troops in the province) were surprised, not by the attack—that happened every spring—but by the fact that the North Vietnamese came as an army, not as guerrillas. They were in the open, using hundreds of new Soviet T-54 tanks, rolling toward the Quang Tri City, with a population of thirty-five thousand, which had been defended by a United States infantry division until the division was withdrawn in August 1971, and then south to Hue and possibly Da Nang.

It was a cloudy day, already raining, so the South Vietnamese could not fly air support for their troops on the ground and high-flying American B-52s could only bomb blind through the cover. The Koreans, usually the bravest of soldiers, did not want to fight. What was the point? The Americans were already going home—only eighty-five thousand or so United States troops remained in the south, and there were no large American combat units left in the country. By Easter Sunday, April 2, the North Vietnamese had taken half the province.

At the same time, a larger force of North Vietnamese, attacking South Vietnam from Laos and Cambodia, was moving east toward Kontum in the Central Highlands, and Vietcong units were moving on old U.S. fire bases in the Mekong Delta near Saigon.

The President was frantic, insisting the weather was good enough to fly and accusing the Joint Chiefs of using the clouds as an excuse. On April 4, he told Haldeman: "The bastards have never been bombed like they're going to be bombed this time. . . . The Air Force isn't worth a shit. . . . they won't fly."

The Army of Vietnam, the South Vietnamese army, replacing the Americans, often fought bravely, sometimes well, but tens of thousands ran for their lives, joining civilian refugees fleeing toward the south.

The President's moods were being whipsawed by events. Kissinger was talking of defeat. "Defeat is not an option," Nixon answered. "I don't give a damn about domestic reaction. . . . sitting in this office wouldn't be worth it. The foreign policy of the United States will have been destroyed, and the Soviets will have established that they can accomplish what they are after by using the force of arms in third countries."

Alone, the President was in despair, writing in his diary: "It is ironic that having come this far, our fate is really in the hands of the South Vietnamese. If we fail it will be because the American way simply isn't as effective as the Communist way in supporting countries abroad. I have a feeling that this may be the case. We give them the most modern arms, we emphasize the material to the exclusion of the spiritual and the Spartan life, and it may be that we soften them up rather than harden them for the battle. . . ."

On April 6, the weather began to clear and hundreds of United States planes, both Air Force and Navy fighter-bombers, were in the air. They were targeting North Vietnamese surface-to-air missile installations along the DMZ, and concentrations of North Vietnamese troops farther south, many of them set up in artillery bases built by Americans and lost or abandoned by South Vietnamese troops. Within sixty miles of Saigon, twenty thousand Vietcong and North Vietnamese troops had cut off one of the main roads to the capital and were surrounding a provincial capital, An Loc.

IN WASHINGTON, the talk of the day was not of the war but of one of its earliest and most consistent critics, George McGovern, who had defeated Humphrey and Wallace in the Wisconsin Democratic primary election. Muskie, the man Nixon had feared most, finished fourth. Suddenly, it seemed possible to Nixon that his opponent was going to be a man he considered unelectable. Whatever his virtues, McGovern was a modern prairie populist, a man Nixon believed was simply outside the political mainstream of the nation, a Barry Goldwater of the left.

"McGovern's the One," wrote Buchanan in a memo to the President. "RN swamps him in the polls—and people do not yet know what a wildman he is." Nixon agreed, but it bothered him that McGovern had been endorsed by eighty-three National Football League players, including fifteen Washington Redskins. Reading that in his news summary, the President wrote: "Blacks?"

In the week after the Wisconsin primary, in which he received 97 percent of the Republican vote, Nixon dictated a series of political memos, including one on April 11 that laid out his issue priorities:

1. Peace and foreign policy generally still have to be at the top of the list. Temporarily, the emphasis will not be on the generation of peace—that will come back when we go to Moscow. . . .

2. Cost of living with particular emphasis on the cost of food.

3. Crime with particular emphasis on drugs.

4. Property tax—of course, in those areas where people are interested hit hard on tax relief for non-public schools.

5. Jobs.

6. Busing . . .

7. "For all the people"—answer the charges that we are solely interested in big business, etc. This will require some real PR effort.

8. Reform . . . We have an excellent program of reform—welfare, revenue sharing, reorganization, health, environment, etc. . . .

The list was not exactly what it seemed. The President was spending as much time as possible on foreign affairs, buying that time by periodically proposing domestic "reforms"—the Family Assistance Plan, a national value-added tax to reduce local property taxes, and a national health care program. But, except for revenue-sharing, the administration's interest in domestic change usually lasted only as long as the headlines. In fact, that was the whole idea. The President called in Haldeman to say: "Ehrlichman has got to understand that all that matters is the story. . . . Spell it out very clear that I expect him to drop the substantive activity and move to the more important thing of what word we get out."

Nixon then expanded that order, spelling out his priorities, even his view of the presidency, writing to Ehrlichman:

I want you to concentrate on selling our domestic programs and answering attacks on them, rather than developing those programs. . . . Substance in the case of foreign policy is infinitely more important than substance is in the case of domestic policy. . . . In other words, while selling foreign policy is important, substance is indispensable. The classic example, of course, is Chamberlain coming back from Munich receiving an 85% approval in the British Gallup poll because he had brought "peace in our time." Within a year the fact that he had made such a grievous error on substance resulted also in his losing his public support. . . . Mistakes in domestic policy can be rectified. Very seldom is that the case where a major foreign policy mistake is made.*

Through the week, the President ordered more bombers to air bases in Guam and Thailand and in and near South Vietnam and more naval presence off the country's coasts. By April 12, the United States had increased the number of combat-ready B-52s from 45 to 130. The number of ships offshore went from twenty to forty, including two new aircraft carriers; the number of combat-ready Navy fighter-bombers went from 150 to 275. Land-based attack planes were increased from 445 to 705. On the other side, the number of North Vietnamese regulars in the south had been increased by about 150,000, and they were equipped with more modern Soviet-built weapons than ever before. The lines were drawn.

In an April 12 briefing of Republican congressional leaders, the President and Kissinger defined North Vietnamese war aims this way: "What the enemy desires is a 'Government of National Concord.' What the enemy wants is for us to do something for them they cannot do for themselves. What the enemy seeks is to inflict such a defeat on the ARVN that the GVN collapses. And create so much turmoil in this country that we will collapse. Then they will go into negotiations. They answered our proposals with a buildup; our overtures with an invasion. They attacked because they no longer believed time was on their side."

Ironically, despite huge deliveries of new Soviet weaponry to the North Vietnamese, relations between the United States and the Soviet Union seemed to be better than ever. Secretary of Agriculture Earl Butz was in Moscow negotiating deals for $200 million of Soviet purchases of American grain. Meanwhile, Kissinger was preparing for a secret trip to plan Nixon's summit trip in May.

The United States struck on April 16, bombing North Vietnam heavily and systematically for the first time since the spring of 1968.

---

* Nixon, like many politicians of his time, was obsessed with the symbolism of Chamberlain and Munich. When he was vice president, according to President Eisenhower's secretary, Ann Whitman, he prohibited staff members from carrying umbrellas when they met him at airports because he was afraid photographs might evoke the famous photo of Chamberlain carrying a rolled umbrella when he returned from meeting Hitler in September of 1938.

Waves of B-52s bombed the port city of Haiphong, while Navy F-4 fighter-bombers bombed and strafed Hanoi. The principal targets were docks, warehouses, and oil depots—shipping points for the spring offensive—and four Soviet ships in Haiphong harbor were among those hit. Three days later Kissinger left for Moscow, secretly, with orders from the President to discuss Vietnam first—the Soviet military shipments to North Vietnam—before talking about arms control or any other issues.

"WELL, WE REALLY LEFT THEM our calling card this weekend," the President said to Haldeman at Camp David that Sunday. They were there, along with Haig and Rebozo, in the mountains for three cloudy, rainy days to provide cover for the secret Moscow trip. The official story was that Kissinger was with them. Nixon talked that weekend about reorganizing the administration after the election, telling Haldeman he wanted to ask the entire Cabinet to resign, then keep a few of them and choose a new group of totally loyal and selfless younger men to serve during a second term. "We'll build a new establishment," the President said—that would be his great goal after 1972.

Kissinger had left for Moscow in the early morning hours of Thursday, April 20, after staying until midnight at a dinner party in Georgetown. At Andrews Air Force Base, he met an unusual traveling companion, Soviet ambassador Dobrynin. The Soviets had been urging Kissinger to come to make arrangements for the Nixon-Brezhnev summit in May. They seemed to want exactly the same attention that the Chinese had gotten before the President went to Peking. For two weeks, Nixon had refused to let Kissinger go, finally giving him permission with orders to come back home if the Soviets would not agree to restrain the North Vietnamese.

There was great and growing tension between the President and his adviser. Kissinger was determined to duplicate the China success, which he saw as his own, but the President was worried that the Soviets were setting him up. If the May summit was going to be canceled over Vietnam, he wanted to do the canceling rather than give Brezhnev that chance. That mistrust produced days of tense overlapping cables to and from Camp David, with Haig acting as the buffer between Nixon and Kissinger, whose first communication included: "Brezhnev wants a summit at almost any cost. He has told me in effect that he would not cancel it under any circumstances. He swears he knew nothing of Hanoi's offensive."

Haig transmitted a Nixon message that he would give up the summit rather than back down in Vietnam; then the general added: "You should be aware that the President has received results of a Sindlinger Poll which indicates his popularity has risen sharply since the escalation of fighting in Vietnam."

The next cable to Kissinger from Haig read: "President is also increasingly restless at Camp David and has asked me to advise you that you must be at Camp David not later than 6:00 P.M. Washington time Monday evening. . . . As I completed this message, the President just called again and added that he views Soviet positions on South Vietnam as frenzied and frivolous and, therefore, is determined to go forward with additional strikes on Hanoi and Haiphong. . . ."

Kissinger answered: "I am reading your messages with increasing astonishment. I cannot share the theory on which Washington operates. I do not believe that Moscow is in direct collusion with Hanoi. . . . Please keep everybody calm. We are approaching the successful culmination of our policies. . . ."

Kissinger talked his long distance way into staying another day, then defied Nixon's orders by moving on to arms control discussions, quickly discovering that Brezhnev was willing to move significantly toward American positions. With Gromyko negotiating for the Soviets, both sides agreed that the deadlocked question of ABM deployment might be resolved by allowing each side two antiballistic missile sites, one near each capital city and one to protect existing offensive missile sites. In addition, the Soviets were willing to negotiate a cap on submarine-fired missiles and agree to limit offensive missile deployment for five years. Triumphantly, Kissinger cabled: "You will be able to sign the most important arms control agreement ever concluded. . . ." Nixon, who had never been particularly interested in the details of arms control, cabled back that such triumphs only scored points with "a few sophisticates." He added insult: "Rebozo joins us in sending our regards."

Kissinger figured the President was drinking too much, not so unusual when Rebozo was around. He had other suspicions, too, that Haig was making good use of his time with the boss. In fact, he was. Haig made it clear he agreed with the President, not Kissinger, about sustained bombing in North Vietnam. In his diary, Nixon wrote, "Haig emphasized that even more important than how Vietnam comes out is for us to handle these matters in a way that I can survive in office."

Kissinger arrived at Camp David on April 25. The meeting with Nixon was tense at first, but soon enough the two of them were walking the grounds with their heads together, nodding, even laughing.

Nixon decided to go on television two days later. "The communists have failed in their efforts to win over the people of South Vietnam, politically," he said. "And General Abrams believes that they will fail in their efforts to conquer South Vietnam militarily. . . . Some battles will be lost, he says, others will be won by the South Vietnamese. But his conclusion is that if we continue to provide air and sea support, the enemy will fail in its desperate attempt. . . . Consequently, I am announcing tonight that over the next two months 20,000 more Americans will be brought home from Vietnam. . . ."

Quang Tri City fell to the North Vietnamese on May 1. Communist troops were within fifteen miles of Hue, and South Vietnamese deserters were looting and burning as more than 150,000 refugees fled the ancient capital of all Vietnam. An Loc and Kontum, under siege, were ruins created by North Vietnamese artillery and American bombing. The President and Kissinger were meeting just before Kissinger was to leave for Paris, secretly once again, for a meeting with Le Duc Tho, when news of the fall of Quang Tri came in a cable from General Abrams in Saigon.

"What else does he say?" Nixon asked.

Kissinger hesitated before responding: "He feels that he has to report that it is quite possible that the South Vietnamese have lost their will to fight."

Nixon took the cable and read it himself, then said: "Whatever happens, this doesn't change my feelings about the negotiations. I don't want you to give the North Vietnamese a thing. They'll be riding high because of all this, so you'll have to bring them down by your manner. No nonsense. No niceness. No accommodations. And we'll just have to let our Soviet friends know that I'm willing to give up the summit if this is the price they have in mind to make us pay for it. . . ." He paused again, and then said for the first time that it was possible the United States would be defeated in Vietnam.

In a last memo before Kissinger left for Paris, the President wrote: "Forget the domestic reaction. Now is the best time to hit them. We have crossed the Rubicon and we must win—if possible, tip the balance in favor of the South Vietnamese for battles to come when we no longer will be able to help this with major air strikes. . . . The President has had enough and now you have only one message to give them—Settle or else!"

THAT SAME DAY, Nixon wrote to Haldeman about the press, saying: "We need the kind of attack which will get to their vulnerable spot—their total support of ultra-liberal causes. . . . The handling of the war news over the past four weeks is just a little taste of what is to follow between now and election as far as the press is concerned. Naturally the press has a vested interest in seeing the United States lose the war and they are doing their desperate best to report all the bad news and to downplay the good news. As far as the election is concerned, they will be absolutely vicious and violent on this score. . . . I cannot emphasize too strongly my feeling that much more than any single issue that we are going to emphasize, the discrediting of the press must be our major objective over the next few months."

Later that day, the Pulitzer Prizes for 1971 were announced. The biggest winners were *The New York Times* for its publication of the Pentagon Papers and Jack Anderson for his columns on the President's tilt toward Pakistan during the Indo-Pakistani War.

At 9:15 on the morning of May 2 in Washington, as Kissinger was meeting with Le Duc Tho in Paris, Haldeman received a telephone call from Kleindienst, still the acting attorney general. He walked into the Oval Office to tell the President that J. Edgar Hoover, the director of the FBI for forty-eight years, had died in his sleep at the age of seventy-seven. A problem solved. Nixon decided immediately that the body should lie in state in the Capitol Rotunda. Hoover would be the twenty-first American to be so honored.

The President was discussing the appointment of a successor when he received a cable from Kissinger. He was on his way back home. The talk with Le Duc Tho had been nothing more than a trading of insults. By 6 P.M., Kissinger was at Andrews Air Force Base. A helicopter took him to the dock where Nixon waited on board the *Sequoia*. Kissinger was discouraged, but he still argued against canceling the Moscow summit. Nixon disagreed, repeating something Connally had told him the day before: "Whatever else happens, we cannot lose this war. The summit isn't worth a damn if the price for it is losing in Vietnam. My instinct tells me that the country can take losing the summit, but it can't take losing the war."

Nixon then told Haldeman he wanted an overnight national poll with just one question: How would the public react if he canceled the Brezhnev meetings? Then he asked for contingency plans for intensified bombing of Hanoi—it was code-named "Linebacker"—and mining of the harbor at Haiphong, where Soviet ships were bringing in cargoes of weaponry.

The poll requested by the President showed that most Americans, 60 percent or more, believed that he should go to Moscow, no matter what was happening in Vietnam. For the next few days, in EOB 175 and at Camp David, Nixon had meeting after meeting to discuss his options in Vietnam. On the afternoon of Friday, May 5, he traveled up to Camp David. That same day, James McCord, the security director of the Committee to Re-Elect the President, was renting room 419 at the Howard Johnson Motor Inn, a room with a view of the offices of the Democratic

National Committee headquarters in the Watergate office building. The President was with his daughter Julie, and he told her he had decided to launch more massive bombing. There were already a thousand U.S. combat aircraft available for the strikes and to blockade the harbor at Haiphong with mines dropped from the sky. The "execute" order had to be given at 2 P.M. on Monday, allowing the military just enough time to begin the campaign as he spoke to the nation at 9 P.M.

To Nixon's surprise, as recorded in his diary that night, Julie argued with him. "She also was aware of the fact that many had become so disillusioned with the war that we might not have enough public support for it. I mentioned the fact that if we did not do this the United States would cease to be a respected great power. She rejoined with the observation that there were many who felt that the United States should not be a great power. This, of course, is the kind of poison that is fed into so many of the younger generation by their professors. . . ."

The last Nixon-Kissinger meeting in the hideaway office was on Monday, May 8. The President broke it up saying, "Well, it's 2 o'clock, the time's up. We go." Kissinger kept arguing. "Nope, the decision is made," Nixon said. "No further discussion."

At 6 P.M. Nixon ate his usual pre-speech dinner, a small bowl of wheat germ. He fiddled with the speech for more than an hour, then he jogged in place for ten minutes and took a cold shower. He walked over to the Cabinet Room at 8 P.M. to tell congressional leaders what he was about to tell the world.

He began with Kissinger's cold meeting with Le Duc Tho. Then he said: "We have to do something to deny the weapons of war to those who would use them for aggression. That is why all harbors will be mined. All countries who have ships in them have been informed. Our military forces will have instructions to cut off supplies to the enemy in every way. Our air strikes in North Vietnam will be directed primarily to the three railroads that lead to South Vietnam. We have made a new offer on the peace side. I am indicating that we will continue this interdiction by sea and rail until the enemy releases our POWs and agrees to a cease-fire. Then all Americans will be out by four months."

When the questioning began—Senator Fulbright and a couple of others were hostile—Nixon said: "They spit in our eye in Paris. We have brought home half a million men and they spit in our eye. What else can we do? . . . It was a very difficult decision for me to make. If you can give me your support, I would appreciate it. If you cannot, I will understand."

The speech itself at 9 P.M. on national television was familiar in many ways—the history of escalation under Kennedy and Johnson, and of offers spurned in Paris. The key paragraph read: "All entrances to

North Vietnamese ports will be mined to prevent access to these ports and North Vietnamese naval operations from these ports. . . . Rail and all other communications will be cut off to the maximum extent possible. Air and naval strikes against military targets in North Vietnam will continue."

There was also significant change in United States policy buried in the President's text: "These actions I have ordered will cease when the following conditions are met. First, all American prisoners of war must be returned. Second, there must be an internationally supervised cease-fire throughout Indochina. . . ." The President had dropped, without mention, any requirement that North Vietnamese troops withdraw from South Vietnam. To President Thieu, reading the text and a letter from Nixon after the speech, this was the beginning of the betrayal he believed was coming sooner or later.

As the President spoke, more than two hundred United States Navy planes began dropping the mines across the entrance to the harbor of Haiphong and of six smaller North Vietnamese ports. The mines were set to be activated in fifty-seven hours to allow foreign ships, mainly Soviet cargo vessels, to leave those ports. In the early hours of the morning after the speech, Tuesday, May 9, in Washington, the President dictated a memo to Kissinger:

> I cannot emphasize too strongly that I have determined that we should go for broke. . . . I am totally unsatisfied at this time at the plans the military have suggested as far as air activities are concerned. . . . Now that I have made this tough watershed decision I intend to stop at nothing to bring the enemy to his knees. . . . Needless to say, indiscriminate bombing of civilian areas is not what I have in mind. On the other hand, if the target is important enough, I will approve a plan that goes after it even if there is a risk of some civilian casualties. We have the power. The only question is whether we have the will to use that power. What distinguishes me from Johnson is that I have the will in spades. If we now fail it will be because the bureaucrats and the bureaucracy and particularly those in the Defense Department, who will of course be vigorously assisted by their allies in State, will find ways to erode the strong decisive action I have indicated we are going to take. . . .

A few days later Nixon sent a memo on military strategy to both Kissinger and Haig. Citing Generals George Patton and Douglas MacArthur, along with Winston Churchill, Nixon talked about massing tanks for a surprise offensive into North Vietnam:

Our military leadership has been a sad chapter in the military history of this country. . . . During the past three and a half years when we have begged them to come up with new initiatives they have dragged their feet or even openly blocked them. . . . In the first four weeks of the enemy offensive, they made enormously effective use of tanks primarily because they used surprise and mass numbers. Using big headlights on tanks and using them at night is an idea which, of course, would never have occurred to any of our group of timid tank commanders. . . . The purpose of this memorandum is not to order a tank attack. . . . My purpose is to try to get the military off their duffs and come up with some new ideas like the landing of helicopter troops behind the North Vietnamese lines.

More than three-quarters of the American people backed the President on the speech, at least according to White House polls that night. Antiwar organizers tried to crank up their machinery one more time. So did the White House, dispatching counsel John Dean to the bomb shelter to monitor expected weekend trouble in the streets and on the campuses. His memo to the President on Monday, May 15, read:

Protest activity this past weekend fell dramatically short of what had been promised by many antiwar activists. . . . Numerous regional demonstrations, largely sponsored by the National Peace Action Coalition, were held across the country on Saturday, but none drew more than several thousand participants. . . . Listed below are the demonstrations. . . .

WASHINGTON, D.C.—Between 10 and 11:00 A.M., a crowd of 500–700 persons assembled at the Ellipse for a march to the Capitol. . . . By the time the group reached the Capitol, the crowd had reached a peak of 1,000–1,200. . . . NEW YORK CITY, NY— Approximately 2–3,000 demonstrators attended a rally in Central Park. No incidents or arrests occurred. . . . CHICAGO, ILL.— Approximately 2,900 demonstrators rallied in Grant Park. . . . DENVER, COLORADO—Approximately 2,000 persons attended a rally. . . . SAN FRANCISCO, CALIF.—Near the Embarcadero about 1,200 persons assembled. . . . ST. PAUL, MINN.—Approximately 5,000 individuals, primarily consisting of students from the University of Minnesota . . . SANTA BARBARA, CALIF.—About 1,000 students picketed Government buildings and Republican Headquarters. . . . DEL MAR, CALIF.—Approximately 300 protesters interfered with railroad operations. Police arrested 35 persons. . . . KEY BISCAYNE, FLA.—Six boats with approximately 40 demonstrators attempted a "Blockade for Peace." The boats approached within 2½ miles of the President's Key Biscayne residence and floated balloons to represent the mining in North Vietnam harbors. A counter-demonstration in support of the President was held by Cubans in another boat who pelted the protestors with eggs. . . . BOSTON, MASS.—Approximately 1,500 demonstrators at the Boston Common . . . ALBUQUERQUE, NEW MEXICO—On the University of New Mexico campus approximately 1,000 persons held a peaceful march and rally. . . . PORTLAND, OREGON—Approximately 300 demonstrators assembled and held a peaceful rally. . . .

The movement was parodying itself. But then so was the White House. Annoyed by a Haldeman memo demanding written reports on any contact with demonstrators, Colson replied: "This is to advise you that I am planning tomorrow night to drive my Pontiac Station Wagon up onto the curb of Pennsylvania Avenue in front of the White House and run over all of the hippies who are lying there. My plan is to do this while they are asleep sometime between 2 and 3 A.M. Would you please let me know what coordination you would like to arrange?"

The active opposition was no longer numerous or young. Opposition was elite now; much of the American establishment Nixon hated was organized against him. He was being attacked in newspaper editorials and speeches by Democratic members of Congress. *The New York Times* wanted a cutoff of funding for the war, "to save the President from himself and the nation from disaster." *The Washington Post* said: "The only relief from this grim scene is that Mr. Nixon is coming to the end of a term and the American people will shortly have the opportunity to render a direct judgment on his policy."

A caucus of Democratic members of the Senate voted 29 to 14 to condemn the escalation. Senator McGovern said: "The President must not have a free hand in Indo-China anymore. . . . The political regime in Saigon is not worth the loss of one more American life."

Those voices also had another gripe with Nixon: he had blown the Moscow summit. Or so they thought. But they got it wrong. To the Soviet Union, worried about China and needing Western grain and consumer goods, the summit was more important than Indochina. Dobrynin suggested to Kissinger that the President invite in the Soviet trade minister, Nikolai Patolichev, while he was in Washington, which Nixon did on November 11. The minister was in the Oval Office for more than an hour. Vietnam was never mentioned. Reporters gathered outside the

White House, ready to record a summit cancellation. Patolichev walked up to the microphones with a smile. The first question was whether the summit was still on. "I don't know why you asked this question," he said. "Have you any doubts? . . . We never had any doubts."

By that weekend, Kissinger and Dobrynin were negotiating over an exchange of gifts between the two leaders. Dobrynin said the Soviets thought the President might want a hydrofoil to use in Biscayne Bay. And Brezhnev? "A Cadillac," said the ambassador.

CHAPTER 31

May 15, 1972

T HE PRESIDENT MET with John Connally four times on May 15. The Treasury Secretary was seeing the President regularly, discussing the political side of the bombing and mining in North Vietnam—and discussing the details of his own resignation the next day to return to Texas and begin organizing a "Democrats for Nixon" committee for the coming campaign. After Connally left one meeting a little after 4 P.M., the President sat down with Donald Kendall of PepsiCo, who was setting up "Business for the President" committees around the country. Haldeman came in at about five o'clock. He beckoned the President out of the office, away from Kendall, and said quietly, "We just got word over the Secret Service wire that George Wallace was shot at a rally in Maryland."

Nixon seemed annoyed by the interruption. It took him a moment. Finally he asked, "Is he killed?"

"No," Haldeman said. He added that apparently a lone gunman, a white man, had shot the governor after a campaign speech at a shopping center in Laurel, Maryland, just fifteen miles from the White House.

"Okay," Nixon said, and went back in to talk with Kendall. After the meeting he dictated a memo: "I was distressed to learn from Don Kendall that in his trying to get Business Chairmen for us in the various States, he had struck out in city after city. . . . The business elite, if anything, has less guts than the labor elite or the farm elite. . . . I told Don that we have to realize that the old establishment just like the old establishment in the university community and in the media simply weren't going to be with us and that we had to build a new establishment."

An hour later, after some discussions with Kissinger and others on the Soviet summit, the President called in Haldeman and Colson to find out what had happened in Laurel. They did not know much and Nixon was angry—at them, but more so at the FBI and the Secret Service. Haldeman said they were pushing Kleindienst and L. Patrick Gray, a loyalist who had been moved from associate attorney general to acting director of the FBI. "Do they understand," asked Nixon, "that the question here was not on the legalities or specifics. Don't worry about doing it all by the book, the problem is who wins the public opinion. It's all PR. . . . What matters for the next 24 to 48 hours is trying to get the right posture set before the press immediately leaps on exactly the wrong thing and starts making a big point of how the guy is a right-wing radical. . . ."

The guy was named Arthur Bremer. He was twenty-one years old, from Milwaukee, where he had worked as a volunteer at Wallace headquarters before the Wisconsin primary. Then, in a 1967 blue Rambler he had bought for seven hundred dollars, Bremer had followed the Wallace campaign as the governor went from rally to rally in Michigan and Maryland. Polls showed Wallace ahead in both of those states—and the prospect of a Michigan win, his first in the North, was expected to make him a true national candidate for the first time. Bremer caught up with him on the day before the two primaries. "Hey, George," he yelled as the governor worked a rope line. When Wallace reached him, Bremer lifted a snub-nosed .38-caliber revolver and fired five shots from less than three feet away, hitting the governor in the forearm, the abdomen, and chest. Bremer was wrestled to the ground. The only thing he said in the hours after the shooting was, "Do you think they'll buy my book?" The governor was rushed to Holy Cross Hospital in Silver Spring. After five hours of emergency surgery, doctors announced that his condition was "serious," but that they expected a full recovery. Then they said both his legs were paralyzed. The last bullet had lodged in his spine.

FBI agents in Milwaukee were dispatched to the address on Bremer's driver's license, but they had no search warrant and waited outside the apartment building at 2433 West Michigan Street. At the same time, the Secret Service had sent local agents to the building, and they persuaded the building manager to let them into the two-room apartment. They sat down and began going through piles of paper—overdue bills, a suicide note, pornography, a gun magazine, pamphlets from the American Civil Liberties Union and the Black Panthers, and a calendar of presidential primaries. The waiting FBI agents standing downstairs heard the noise upstairs and they confronted the Secret Service men. They began shouting at each other.

Beginning at 7:30 P.M., Colson, and sometimes the President himself, began a series of calls to Mark Felt, the assistant director of the FBI, and to Gray, asking who Bremer was, whose side he was on. The President said again that if Bremer was a right-winger it could cost him the election. "It's all PR now . . . ," he repeated to Haldeman. "The story regarding the guy and so on." EOB 175 was operating as a kind of war room. Nixon said that the greatest thing would be finding McGovern literature in the apartment. At 9:30, he telephoned Colson, asking the question he had been asking for hours: "Is he a left-winger or a right-winger?"

"Well, he's going to be a left-winger by the time we get through, I think," Colson said.

"Good," the President said. "Keep at that."

"Yeah," Colson continued. "I just wish that, God, that I'd thought sooner about planting literature out there."

The FBI agents in Milwaukee still had not entered the apartment. Colson telephoned Howard Hunt and told him to take the first plane out there—he repeated the President's words about McGovern literature—and get inside the apartment. Hunt was packing disguises for the trip when Colson and the President were informed that while the FBI and Secret Service were arguing downstairs, reporters and photographers had found the building superintendent, who let them look over the place and take pictures. Colson called some Washington reporters he knew and told them Bremer was a dues-paying member of the Young Democrats of Milwaukee—a lie that got into several newspapers. In Laurel, meanwhile, the FBI was trying to decipher an incoherent 137-page diary they found in Bremer's car.

"Hey world! Come here! I wanna talk to ya! . . . Now, I start my diary of my personal plan to kill by pistol either Richard Nixon or George Wallace," the diary began. It revealed that what Bremer wanted was to be famous, respected. On April 14, in Ottawa, Canada, during a brief Nixon visit, he had stalked the President, hoping to kill him, but changed his mind because presidential security was too tight. Then, roaming the country in the Rambler, he set his sights on an easier target, Wallace.

Wallace was still in serious condition at Holy Cross the next evening, as election returns came in from Michigan and Maryland. He won both states, getting 51 percent of the Michigan vote, with McGovern at 26 percent and Humphrey trailing with 17 percent. In Maryland, Wallace won another majority in a ten-candidate field, with Humphrey second and McGovern third. Exit polling indicated that a sympathy vote for the wounded governor was not significant; it was obvious that voters wanted to send a message about busing and other issues. The Democratic race was down to the three, with Wallace's second wife, Cornelia, and his staff delivering optimistic reports on his condition. But Nixon, who had sent one of his physicians, Dr. William Lukash, to Wallace's room, knew the governor had almost no chance of ever being able to walk again.

In eight primaries so far, the Alabama governor had rolled up more votes than any of his Democratic rivals, 3,334,914 to 2,606,186 for Humphrey and 2,183,533 for McGovern. But McGovern, who had chaired a party commission that had changed and greatly complicated the rules for winning and allocating convention delegates by race and gender, was far ahead in that count: the most liberal of the candidates, he had won 560 delegates of the 1,509 needed for nomination at the Democratic National Convention in Miami Beach. Wallace had 324 and Humphrey 311. "Fantastic!" Nixon said. Wallace had indeed shattered the Democrats. McGovern, said Nixon once more, was unelectable and Humphrey was damaged goods. And Wallace had demonstrated the power of busing as a national issue.

The President spent most of the day with Connally. The Treasury Secretary's resignation was announced—he had agreed to stay one year and had served seventeen months—and the two lavished praise on each other at a press conference and in meetings with the Cabinet and congressional leaders. The new secretary would be George Shultz, and his position as director of the new OMB would be taken by his deputy, Caspar Weinberger. As the day was ending, the President walked back to the Treasury building with Connally, both waving to tourists on the other side of the iron fence around the White House grounds. As they reached the Treasury building, Nixon went over to the crowd and began shaking hands. The Secret Service didn't like that, but he said it was important after the Wallace shooting to demonstrate that the President was not afraid of the American people.

In a memo to Kissinger, Nixon laid out plans for a world tour during the Treasury Secretary's last days in office: "The Connally trip is vitally important, not only from the standpoint of our personal relationship, but also in terms, I believe, of the good it can do in the foreign policy area. What I have in mind is that he should go first-class with a Presidential-type aircraft to four countries in Latin America—Peru, Brazil, Argentina and Colombia. After that I think it might be well for him to go to Australia and New Zealand. . . ."

Then Nixon helicoptered to Camp David to study for the Soviet summit. The news of the day was not bad. The consumer price index was only up 0.2 percent for April as food prices dropped by that same percentage. In Vietnam the communist drives on Kontum and An Loc had been stalled; the cities were surrounded but South Vietnamese units were standing and fighting on the ground, particularly at An Loc, and the Americans were using helicopter gunships to try to drive enemy troops into more open areas where they were vulnerable to prearranged B-52 bombing. But Nixon was not impressed, rocketing one military memo after another to Kissinger or Haig:

> I am thoroughly disgusted with the consistent failure to carry out orders that I have given over the past three and a half years, and particularly in the past critical eight weeks, with regard to Vietnam. I refer specifically to the fact that I have ordered, on occasion after occasion, an increase in the quantity and quality of weapons made available to the South Vietnamese. All that we have gotten from the Pentagon is the runaround and a sometimes deliberate sabotage of the orders that I have given. . . . They are supposed to take orders from the Commander-in-Chief. The trouble is that we left too many of the McNamara people in high places and they are constantly sabotaging everything we are trying to do.

> Finally, I have told Henry today that I wanted more B-52s sent to Vietnam. . . . I want you to convey directly to the Air Force that I am thoroughly disgusted with their performance in North Vietnam. Their refusal to fly unless the ceiling is 4000 feet or more is without doubt one of the most pusillanimous attitudes we have ever had in the whole fine history of the U.S. military. . . . I blame the commanders who, because they have been playing "how not to lose" so long, now can't bring themselves to start playing "how to win." Under the circumstances, I have decided to take command of all strikes in North Vietnam in the Hanoi-Haiphong area out from under any Air Force jurisdiction whatever. The orders will be given directly from a Naval commander whom I will select. . . . I want you to convey my utter disgust to Moorer which he in turn can pass on to the Chiefs and also convey it to General Abrams and Ambassador Bunker in the field. It is time for these people either to shape up or get out.

He had offered a similar opinion of the CIA the day before: "The problem is the CIA is a muscle-bound bureaucracy, which has completely paralyzed its brain. . . . I want a study made immediately as to how many people in CIA could be removed by Presidential action. . . ." That got him thinking about elite colleges again and he added, "I want you to quit recruiting from any of the Ivy League schools or any other universities where either the university president or the university faculties have taken action condemning our efforts to bring the war in Vietnam to an end."

On the morning of May 19, Nixon had gone with Dr. Lukash to Holy Cross Hospital to see Wallace. He spent twenty minutes with the governor and his wife, who noticed that the President was wearing television makeup. He noticed her, too, writing in his diary that night: "I was again impressed about the attractiveness of Mrs. Wallace. She has great verve. . . . He is, though a demagogue, somewhat sentimental in terms of his strong patriotism, like most Southerners. . . ." As Nixon was leaving, Wallace saluted him weakly and the President saluted back.

In the afternoon, the President, who was scheduled to leave the next morning for Salzburg, Austria, where he would stay overnight before flying on to Moscow, held a long briefing for congressional leaders, telling them that there had been great progress on the arms negotiations in Helsinki. "We hope to negotiate an ABM treaty and simultaneously freeze offensive weapons," he said. "That is our goal."

Reporting on his own negotiations in Moscow, Kissinger added: "It is not inconceivable that the Soviet leadership is interested in a period of détente for the purpose of softening up the United States and then pushing us out of Europe. But whatever their motive, we should not be afraid. Our strategy will be to create vested interests for peace within the Soviet structure which would help encourage restraint on their actions."

Then the President said: "The Soviets have now achieved nuclear parity. We have MIRV, but they have more missiles. If either President Eisenhower or President Kennedy had gone to Moscow they both would have gone in a position where they were looking down the throat of the Soviets. But the situation has now changed."

Nixon said that Brezhnev had told Kissinger a story, and then he repeated the story. He said it showed there might be a new relationship developing between the two superpowers:

> The story is this: A city merchant in Russia was walking in the country when he saw two signs on the road at a fork, both of which were the path to the village he wanted to visit. He saw a woodsman standing nearby and asked how long it would take for him to reach the village. The woodsman said nothing. . . . As he walked off, the woodsman yelled, "Fifteen minutes." The merchant stopped and asked why he hadn't told him when he asked.

The woodsman answered that he had to see how long the merchant's steps were.

Before the President left on May 20, he pumped out a small storm of memos on matters small and great:

> The situation in Canada was intolerable. The jump seats were constructed in such a way that they bent completely back on both Pat and me so that in her case she had to put her legs over on the other side and I, of course, was totally uncomfortable all the way. . . . I do not want to have in the Soviet Union two interpreters if that is going to mean crowding the car. What we have to realize is that room must be left for me to sit comfortably in the car without some interpreter or some Secret Service man sitting in my lap.

> While we are in Moscow it is vitally important that our bombing activity continue, at least at its present level and if possible above the present level. . . . so that there can be no charge at home that we have let up on our strikes, and also so that the enemy will not get any impression that because of our Moscow trip we let up on our strikes. . . . There should be a minimum of 1200 air sorties a day. . . . Concentrate on those targets which will have major impact on civilian morale. . . .

> We face a critical problem in terms of avoiding a massive right-wing revolt on the SALT agreement. All of us who have worked on this problem know that the deal we are making is in our best interest, but for a very practical reason that the right-wing will never understand—that we simply can't get from the Congress the additional funds needed to continue the arms race with the Soviet in either the defensive or offensive missile category.

THE PRESIDENT, his wife, and his party took off from Andrews Air Force Base shortly after nine o'clock on the morning of May 20. Spirits were high on the *Spirit of '76*. But on the ground, *Life* magazine raised some obvious questions about the trip and American foreign policy in general in a full-page editorial:

> Something is now terribly askew in the conduct of our foreign affairs. . . . This is an appropriate time to ask where does democ-

racy fit in the waging of an undeclared war. Is its proper role only to go along with what a President decides, assenting to actions already in progress before we are told of them? . . . To receive without debate his extensions of the field of battle and otherwise to sit loyally mute? . . . Too much turns on one man's introspective responses—a man who seems incapable of seeking wide counsel even inside his own administration.

CHAPTER 32

June 17, 1972

T HIS HAS GOT TO BE one of the great diplomatic coups of all times!"
Kissinger said, coming into the President's cabin on *Air Force One*. The
Americans were bombing North Vietnam, they had sunk a Soviet merchant ship and killed two Russian sailors, and still they were on their way
to Moscow. "Three weeks ago everyone predicted it would be called off,
and today we're on our way."

The President was excited, too, although he did remember that
Kissinger was among the principal doubters. Now it was another Nixon
first. He was going to be the first president ever to visit Moscow. It was
clear by now that as much as Nixon wanted a summit, Brezhnev needed
one. The Soviet leader wanted to remind the world that his country, not
China, was the "other" superpower—even if its treasure was being
drained by the arms race against the more productive economies of the
United States and its allies. "Détente" was the word of the day in newspapers around the world.

But whatever the costs at home, the Soviets had greatly upgraded
their missilery in the years since their humiliation during the 1962 Cuban
missile crisis. They were continuing to develop and build giant strategic
missiles capable of reaching all of the United States. They had at least
1,500 intercontinental rockets and were producing 250 more each year.
They had installed a rudimentary antimissile system around Moscow.
The United States had 1,054 ICBMs and was not producing new ones.

Numbers, however, did not tell the whole story. Both sides had more than enough missiles to level the other. And the Americans had a much more potent bomber fleet and had sophisticated missile-carrying submarines in all the world's oceans. American guidance systems were significantly better and the military was ready to begin installing MIRVs, multiple-reentry systems that would make each Minuteman missile capable of firing eight nuclear warheads instead of one. Then there was Nixon's ABM, Safeguard.

Safeguard existed only on paper and many of the paper numbers did not add up. But the President was not greatly interested in those numbers. His arms control strategy was to trade off the paper ABM for a cap on Soviet production of new and larger missiles and nuclear missile-firing submarines. "Bullshit!" was his response to Gerard Smith, chief negotiator for the United States, when Smith began quoting strings of numbers in one of their few meetings. The President was not going to the Kremlin to argue; he was going there to sign the papers. The numbers had been argued and calibrated for two years by Smith and his men, but now Smith was in Helsinki and the final negotiations had been taken over by Kissinger, who was no numbers man either. The White House had quickly, and secretly, slapped together two SALT treaties and seven other agreements, which included environmental cooperation; trade, scientific, and medical exchanges; a maritime protocol; and a joint space project that would climax with an attempt to link a United States Apollo capsule with a Soviet Soyuz capsule in three years. Finally there was to be a joint "Declaration of Principles" intended to be a working guide to détente.

The President arrived in Moscow at 4 P.M. on Monday, May 22. A fifty-car motorcade of Soviet Zil limousines modeled on Packards of the late 1950s raced toward the Kremlin on deserted boulevards. The side streets were blockaded by buses, but the President did see crowds of Russians being held back behind the buses. A few minutes after the Nixons reached their rooms, an entire floor of the Kremlin's Grand Palace, Kissinger came in to say that Leonid Brezhnev was waiting for the President. The two leaders had tea and talked for two hours, with Nixon thinking that Brezhnev, who was obviously no numbers man either, reminded him of American labor leaders. Brezhnev had begun by complaining about United States actions in Vietnam, but quickly changed the subject to the Soviet-American alliance of World War II, and the fact that Franklin D. Roosevelt was still a hero in the Soviet Union. Nixon spoke of Roosevelt, Churchill, and Stalin and said: "That is the kind of relationship that I should like to establish with the General Secretary. . . ."

"I am perfectly ready on my side," said Brezhnev.

The Soviet leader did most of the talking over two and a half more hours that day, telling stories, laughing at them, and making it clear that he wanted a deal. He challenged Nixon on only a few details. One was the limit on new submarine development. The United States had shut down production of Polaris-class submarines after almost twenty years and already begun the long process of developing a new-generation super-submarine, but still wanted to limit Soviet production of smaller ones.

"You are going to build new submarines," Brezhnev said, slapping the table. "How am I going to answer my people who say that all this agreement does is to hold us still while you are putting new weapons into production?"

The President countered that the Soviet Union was building nine new subs each year, while the United States was still debating upgrading. "Look, you and I know it is the first submarine that counts, because after that you can build as many as your productive capacity permits."

Brezhnev let it go. After all, the framework of the ABM and SALT treaties had been hammered out over more than two years of work in Helsinki and Vienna. Then the final shape had been decided in secret—secret from Smith, from Laird, and from Rogers—in the Kissinger-Dobrynin back channel.

As the two men wound down their first conversations, Nixon asked for a favor: Could Brezhnev mention the idea of the joint declaration of principles as his idea when Secretary Rogers joined the talks? Neither Nixon nor Kissinger had told Rogers about the declaration, so they wanted it to seem a Russian surprise. And the Secretary of State was already upset because Nixon and Kissinger were staying inside the Kremlin while he was assigned a suite outside the walls in the new Rossiya Hotel. "He might as well be in Siberia," said Kissinger, who had made the arrangements himself.

Nixon had trouble sleeping that night after the toasts and drinking of a grand welcoming banquet. At 4:30 in the morning, in the gray brightness of the northern latitudes, he was walking around the streets of the Kremlin alone—except for security men in every doorway and window—asking stiff Soviet guards how old they were. Then he went back to his room for a couple of hours of sleep before his first official meeting, on Tuesday, with a full array of leaders and staff facing each other across a long table in St. Catherine's Hall in the Kremlin. Nixon sat in the middle facing Brezhnev, flanked by Rogers and Kissinger. The national security adviser was content, sure that his president would say nothing of significance with State Department people in the hall. Nixon began: "I know that my reputation is one of being a very hard-line, cold-war-oriented anti-communist—"

"I had heard this sometime back," interjected Premier Aleksey

Kosygin, a man never known for wit before. His bona fides acknowledged, the President listened as Brezhnev suggested signing ceremonies each afternoon at five o'clock. Nixon agreed, and then turned to a discussion of European security issues. He suggested that Rogers and Gromyko concentrate on European matters, thus leaving everything else to Kissinger. Brezhnev, knowing now what was going on with the Americans, agreed, saying that perhaps Gromyko could also work with Kissinger on the SALT treaty—and on a closing declaration of principles. Everyone nodded, as if they had never heard of that before.

"You obviously cooked up this deal," Rogers said angrily to Kissinger when the meeting broke up after two hours. Then he complained to the President, who was the actual deal cooker, saying, "I might as well go home."

The first agreements—on the environment and public health issues—were signed that afternoon, and Kissinger followed the President back to his rooms to complain about Rogers. Nixon finally got away from the two of them when Haldeman came in with the news that George McGovern had won the Oregon Democratic primary, getting 49 percent of the vote to 20 percent for Wallace and 13 percent for Humphrey.

From the perspective of Moscow, the President saw that his real political problems were on the right. *The New York Times* of May 24 reported that the United States was prepared formally and legally to accept the Soviet superiority in ICBMs, and that conservative members of Congress and the Joint Chiefs of Staff were grumbling, still mostly in private. One who spoke out was Congressman John Ashbrook, who accused Nixon of being on the verge of "dooming the United States to nuclear inferiority."

Then Nixon was "kidnapped"—that was the word Kissinger used. After the signing of the environmental and health agreements, as Nixon prepared to go back to his rooms before being driven to a government dacha on the Moscow River for a small dinner, Brezhnev took his arm and said, "Why don't we go to the country right now?" In a moment, Nixon was on a small elevator. The President's military aide, Marine Lieutenant Colonel Jack Brennan, reported:

> The rest of us, including other top Soviet officials, ran like hell down three flights of stairs. Amazingly enough, at the bottom of the stairs, a motorcade was formed by the Soviets, of course. The drive took thirty-five minutes. . . . an atmosphere like that of Camp David. Very tall Pine trees—very rustic and relaxing atmosphere. The Dacha itself overlooks the Moscow River, probably 75 feet above the River. . . . Periodically, we would see rather

nice homes, obviously summer homes of other prominent Muscovites. . . . Several people along the banks were fishing and some children were swimming in the nude.

A report by the Secret Service agent in charge, William Duncan, continued less casually:

It is my opinion that this trip started from the Kremlin with the intent of the Soviets. . . . The party proceeded north on the Moscow River for 20 minutes at 90 kilometers an hour. The River was smooth as glass. We met a police boat which was towing another boat and the driver of Searchlight's hydrofoil had to display a flag and wave the boat over to the side. We passed one young man who was standing by a small fire apparently preparing to camp. The party passed a man in civilian clothes who was fishing. The fisherman apparently recognized one of the officials in the boat; he laid down his fishing rod, stood up, assumed attention, and saluted. . . .

In the boat and then back in the dacha for another three hours, Brezhnev, Kosygin, and Soviet president Nikolai Podgorny worked Nixon over. The subject was Vietnam, and the Soviet leaders took turns describing American tactics as "Nazi-like" and calling President Thieu "your mercenary president so-called." Nixon mostly listened, but he did get in a couple of shots. When Kosygin added, "Someone you call president who was not chosen by anyone," Nixon responded, "Who chose the President of North Vietnam?"

It was one of only two remarks Nixon made during the tirade. Then, as quickly as they began, the lectures were over. Kissinger, who got there by jumping into a car with Secret Service agents, was convinced it was an act. The Soviets wanted to create a transcript to show North Vietnamese leaders. The group adjourned for dinner and cognac toasts upstairs, joking and shouting the night away.

BACK AT THE KREMLIN at 1 A.M., the President was lying naked on a table, getting a massage from his chiropractor, Dr. Niland, when Kissinger arrived to say that his SALT negotiations with Gromyko were deadlocked, primarily because the Soviet professionals did not seem bound by the concessions Brezhnev had casually made in his sessions with Nixon. (The American professionals were still far away in Helsinki, convinced they were being kept away so Kissinger could claim all the credit.)

Nixon turned the conversation toward home. He was focused on the growing conservative and military opposition to treaty terms being reported to him from Washington after the story in *The New York Times*. Two important conservative senators, Republican Barry M. Goldwater of Arizona and Democrat Henry Jackson, were threatening, in private, to attack the negotiations. Kissinger said if names like that got into the press the results would be devastating. Nixon did not need reminding and he lifted his head and sort of growled: "The hell with the political consequences. We are going to make an agreement on our terms regardless of the political consequences. . . ."

Nixon stayed on the massage table and Kissinger went back to the negotiating table, where Gromyko and he worked until 3 A.M. It was obvious that the Soviet decisions would be made by the Politburo, which was meeting in secret later in the day. The decision came at 11:15 A.M., Friday, May 26. The Soviets accepted almost every American condition. The signing was scheduled for that night at Spaso House, the residence of the American ambassador. Only then were Gerard Smith and the other official SALT negotiators called from Helsinki. They arrived at the Kremlin an hour before the 11 P.M. signing—and then could not find cars to get them to Spaso House. Smith was almost incoherent with rage, complaining that there had been no expert analysis of the terms, no National Security Council discussion. He said that at least Brezhnev and Gromyko had to consult with the Politburo—on the American side, Nixon and Kissinger talked only to each other.

Kissinger and Smith presided over a press briefing before the signing, but it was halted after they began to contradict each other, arguing over what was in the treaty. Now Kissinger was pacing Kremlin halls, cursing Smith and Rogers. Haldeman walked with him, trying to calm him down enough to speak to the President. When Nixon, who did not know what was happening, summoned Kissinger, Haldeman went instead, but after a couple minutes Kissinger appeared, still livid, and began ranting at the President.

Nixon told Haldeman to call Rogers and tell him that he was not to speak to the press without his express permission. "If he doesn't like it, fire him," he said.

"What good will that accomplish?"

"I guess you're right," the President said. "Forget it."

He paced for a couple of minutes, sort of talking to himself, then grabbed a phone and asked for Rogers. When the Secretary of State came on, Nixon hung up without saying a word.

In Washington, it was just past six o'clock on Friday evening. Howard Hunt, officially a member of the White House staff, and G. Gordon Liddy, counsel to the finance chairman of the Committee to Re-Elect the President, were hosting a pre-burglary banquet in the Continental Room of the Watergate Hotel. Their guests were James McCord, the committee's security coordinator, and six Miami men, led by Bernard Barker, Hunt's old friend from Bay of Pigs days. McCord had been given sixty-five thousand dollars in cash by Liddy to buy surveillance equipment. Pretending to be looking for someone, he had been spending time around the offices of the Democratic National Committee on the sixth floor of the Watergate office complex, which was next to the hotel—and was also connected to the apartment buildings where Mitchell, Maurice Stans, and Robert Dole all lived. The men in the Continental Room finished their dessert, brandy, and cigars by 10 P.M. and six of them left. Hunt and Virgilio Gonzalez remained, hiding in a closet. At midnight, Hunt and Gonzalez snuck out of the room and tried to pick the lock of a door leading to the office building, where they intended to break into DNC headquarters. They couldn't do it. Meanwhile, Liddy, McCord, three of the Cubans, and a former FBI man named Alfred Baldwin were in a car outside their target, McGovern for President headquarters a couple of miles away on Capitol Hill. They were waiting for a volunteer to close down those offices, but the man never came out. At 5 A.M., they quit. "Abort the mission," was Liddy's order. Hunt and Gonzalez were back in the Continental Room closet waiting for daylight to leave the hotel.

NIXON AND BREZHNEV signed the final summit agreements on Soviet television in front of dozens of officials of both governments. The President snuck his own silver Parker ballpoint out of his pocket when he signed; he wanted to give the pen to Kissinger. He also looked toward one column near the corner of the hall. His wife, the only woman in the room, was standing behind it, a witness unseen. The papers were, in effect, one treaty and an executive agreement. The treaty involved only ABMs, limiting each side to two hundred antiballistic missiles at two sites, one outside the country's capital and one guarding ICBMs, offensive intercontinental ballistic missiles, in silos. The agreement limited the number of land- and sea-based missiles on each side to those already deployed or in production. The treaty, which included a clause committing the countries to refrain from beginning to build new ABM systems, would require confirmation by the United States Senate.

The next morning, Nixon flew to Leningrad, leaving Kissinger in Moscow to negotiate the wording of the summit's "Declaration of Basic Principles." It was a strange day of sight-seeing for the President, with soldiers standing in every doorway, preventing people from coming into

the streets when he was near. He was guided to the Tomb of the Unknown Soldier, past long grassy hillocks, the mass graves of the hundreds
of thousands of the city's people who died during the Nazi siege in World
War II. At Piskaryev Cemetery Nixon was obviously moved as a young
woman read excerpts from the diary of a twelve-year-old named Tanya.
The last line was: "All are dead. Only Tanya is alive."

"Tanya died too," said the guide, breaking into tears. Nixon
made the story the centerpiece of his twenty-minute speech on Soviet television the next night, after the signing of the communiqué that afternoon.
The final statement was essentially a hopeful pledge of détente, the key
paragraph reading:

> Guided by their obligations under the Charter of the United
> Nations . . . The USA and USSR attach major importance to pre-
> venting the development of situations capable of causing a dan-
> gerous exacerbation of their relations. Therefore, they will do
> their utmost to avoid military confrontations and to prevent the
> outbreak of nuclear war. They will always exercise restraint in
> their mutual relations, and will be prepared to negotiate and set-
> tle differences by peaceful means.

On May 28, the night the President was on Soviet television,
Hunt and Liddy's men finally got inside Democratic headquarters. Hunt
had sent Gonzalez back to Miami for more tools, and he had come back
with a clinking bagful of picks and pries. They got in at just about midnight, after taping open the locks on the doors between the sub-basement
garage and the sixth floor. "The horse is in the house," Gonzalez told
Hunt on a walkie-talkie. Hunt called McCord, who was across Virginia
Avenue at a room in the Howard Johnson's Motor Inn. At 1:30 A.M.,
McCord crossed the street, went upstairs, and installed bugs in the telephones of Larry O'Brien's secretary and a deputy named Spencer Oliver.
Barker searched through filing cabinets, pulling out documents, which
were then photographed by one of the Cubans, Eugenio Martinez. In
room 723 of the motor inn, Liddy and Hunt embraced and cheered.
When Barker came back, Liddy slapped him on the back and said,
"Good job, Macho!"

During a final four-hand clasp with Brezhnev, the President said:
"You have my commitment that privately or publicly I will take no steps
directed against the interests of the Soviet Union. But you should rely on
what I say in private channel, not on what anyone else tells you. There
are not only certain forces in the world, but also representatives of the
press who are not interested in better relations between us."

Then the President left for the airport and a trip to Kiev on a Soviet Ilyushin-62. One of the plane's four engines failed on takeoff and the plane taxied back to the terminal. As the presidential party prepared to switch to another plane, Kosygin and Podgorny came aboard and asked the President how he wished the pilot to be punished. Nixon did not think they were kidding. He said, "He should not be punished, he should be promoted because he was smart enough to think first about our safety."

After Kiev, the President flew on to Teheran for a brief appearance with the Shah of Iran and then to Warsaw, where enthusiastic crowds chanted "Neek-son! Neek-son!" At a state banquet, someone told him proudly that one of the clarinet players in the orchestra, a young woman, was an American, a Peace Corps volunteer. "Find out what she's doing there," he told Haldeman. "What a waste of money!" That started him off on how much the trip cost. "Too much staff," said Nixon. "When you have too many spear-carriers along, you find that every time you turn around, they're sticking you in the ass with a spear."

Watching the President from a distance, Kissinger and Safire talked about the week. "Not bad for a couple of Jewish boys, huh?" said the national security adviser. "Been one hell of a week, Henry," the speechwriter answered. "What does the President do for an encore?"

"Make peace in Vietnam," said Kissinger.

"THE COVERAGE has been incredible," Nixon heard from Colson in a May 31 memo. "The President is riding a wave of support that is stronger than anything I have ever seen. . . . Our task, however, is not to achieve great public support for SALT, but rather to strengthen the President's personal image as one of the great world leaders of this century."

The coverage was not only incredible, some of it was incredulous. John Osborne of *The New Republic,* seeing an American flag flying above the Kremlin's Grand Palace, filed a report from Moscow that included this paragraph: "Results aside, the fact that dominates the occasion is that Richard Nixon is here, buddying up with the leaders of the world's greatest Communist power. . . . The observer must pause at times and succumb to the wonder that this man, this seeming model of mediocrity, should be the first President of the United States to do what he has done this year, within four months, in Peking and now in Moscow. . . . The Soviet hierarchy is glad that the President is here and all of us should be too."

After landing at Andrews Air Force Base on June 1, the President went directly to the Capitol to deliver a nationally televised report to a joint session of Congress. He laid out a straightforward list of the agreements in Moscow and, referring to his China trip, said: "This one series of meetings has not rendered an imperfect world suddenly perfect. There still are deep philosophical differences; there are still parts of the world where age-old hatreds persist. The threat of war has not been eliminated—it has been reduced."

At ten o'clock the next morning, Nixon invited congressional leaders of both parties into the East Room of the White House for a secret briefing on the summit. Nixon and Kissinger were both tired men, exhausted, really, but the talk and questions went on for two hours and each of them talked at length, giving rather clear portraits of different, if complementary, worldviews.

"We were not present at the creation, and therefore we have to deal with the facts as they are," Nixon began. His great intellectual strength was connecting the dots, seeing the world whole and from different angles, and he tried to describe the world as it might look to Brezhnev. He said that any Soviet leader would seek effective military parity with the United States, but know that even with a greater population, his country, economically, could not produce half what the Americans were producing. He also would see a potential rival, a potential third superpower, China, with eight hundred million people on one border, and restless neighbors on the other side—Poland, Czechoslovakia, Hungary, Romania—wanting cultural ties and economic links to the Western powers. "Soviet leaders," he continued, "naturally will conclude that their interests would be served by a better relationship with the United States. . . .

"They know that the United States with its enormous economic power is not going to allow the Soviet Union to get into a position where it is looking down our throats. . . . They have to make a command decision. Do they want to continue a race which will mean more and more of their production will continue to go into military production when they so desperately need more consumer goods? Do they want to continue a race that they are not going to be able to win, regardless of what happens? Do they want to continue a race which does run the risk of war in the future? Because as the race continues . . . who knows whether we will always have rational men in positions of power in the major countries of the world. . . .

"So the Soviet leaders, it seems to me, . . . conclude that while they are still opposed to us ideologically, while they still, and I will use the term 'want to win,' they want Communism to win in the world, they, however, are pragmatic enough to realize that a nuclear arms race is not to their advantage. They made these agreements for their reasons, and we made them for ours."

Then he said the imbalances favoring the United States did not guarantee victory in the end: "Don't underestimate what a system that is totalitarian in character can do with the kind of fanatical leadership you have in the People's Republic of China and the Soviet Union. They can be a very formidable opponent. Leaving out the systems, just erase Communism from the top, and call it a fascist dictatorship, call it any kind of a system. . . . The Russian people are a formidable people. . . . Never assume because our system is best for us, because in any kind of a race we will win economically, because we unleash the great powers of freedom, that it is inevitable that in any contest we will eventually come out ahead. . . .

"What do we do about all of this? . . . The reason that I reached the conclusion that the United States should make the move that it has, has nothing to do with a change of philosophy, a change in ideology. What it has to do with is with the survival of the United States and with the chance of the survival of civilization, if I can put it in a melodramatic way."

Kissinger was more tactical as he offered a theory of Soviet moves since Nixon took office in 1969: "The first year they tried to get into generalities as they always like to. The second year they tried what we call a differential détente, which is to say they tried to get good relations with Europe and a posture of hostility toward the United States. That was the summer in which we had the nuclear submarine base in Cuba, we had the missile crisis in the Middle East, and we had harassment on the autobahn toward Berlin, all of them happening in the same three months' period, and all of them really based on the proposition that the United States could be divided from its European allies, and could be isolated by a policy of relaxation towards Europe, and a policy of tension toward the United States. . . . These policies failed because the President stood firm in each of these areas. . . ."

Kissinger tended to exaggerate immediate threats, and he rewrote history where it suited his purposes, tracing the arms control agreements to the 1970 crisis in Jordan: "They found themselves in the Middle East at the very edge of a precipice, in which they had to look down the threat of nuclear war on the basis of actions of governments they had absolutely no possibility of controlling. They had no way of knowing what the Syrian tanks were going to do, and the luckiest thing that ever happened to the Soviet Union was the incompetence of its Syrian ally. What would have happened if their Syrian allies had been a little more competent, and the Israelis then had struck? . . . a sequence of events that could not be controlled from Moscow, and could not be controlled from Washington . . . It is our judgment, it is this realization that brought the Soviet leaders, against their instincts, against their philosophy, and maybe even against their preferences, to working on a détente with the United States. . . ."

The Kissinger argument was that both sides now realized that old military strategies based on gaining small advantages were useless because with nuclear weapons no country had a realistic possibility of gaining enough advantage to expect to win a war without being destroyed itself. He went on: "If you analyze it carefully, you have to say the offensive part of the agreement is to the disadvantage of the Soviet Union so much that you wonder they signed it. . . . If they wanted to, they could produce, as all of you who are on the Armed Services Committees know, eight or nine submarines a year, and we could produce none. But why did the Soviet Union sign an agreement which stopped an ongoing production line for them? . . . What can you do with these weapons unless you can get an overwhelming superiority that no opponent will permit?"

The President cut in to say: "Frankly, if either side determines it doesn't like the deal, we can have a pretty good war with the weapons that are not frozen, so what we really come down to is that we have started a process not only for the limitation of arms, but we have started a process in many other fields. . . . We haven't mentioned Vietnam, and it is best that we not talk about it this morning. It was discussed at length. What will happen will happen. . . .

"So what we are asking you to join us in, basically, is a great venture. . . . In the nuclear age, there is no alternative for responsible leaders of countries, whatever their philosophies, than to sit down and work out and start on the long road of controlling the arms race. . . . As you examine the agreements, put yourself in the position that they were in and we were in, and what would you do? Would you do this, or nothing? . . . If we can learn to live together on these issues and work together and negotiate on these and all of the others, we may change the world for a while. . . . I wouldn't say that publicly, but that is what I really think."

Nixon left immediately for Key Biscayne. He was exhausted. He told Haldeman he was too tired to make decisions, that if anything came up on domestic issues, Ehrlichman should handle them. He returned to Washington four days later, on June 6, but stayed only for the day, dictating a flurry of memos before going on to Camp David.

To Mitchell, Nixon wrote of the coming campaign, targeting well-known symbols of youth, disorder, and the left: "One of the factors that brought Goldwater down to such a shattering defeat in 1964 was the success of the media in tying him to ultra-right-wing supporters like H. L. Hunt, the John Birch society, etc. . . . The fact that Abbie Hoffman, Jerry Rubin, Angela Davis, among others, support McGovern, should be widely publicized and used at every point. Keep calling on him to repudiate them daily. . . ."

In a memo to Kissinger, the subject was the stalling of the North Vietnamese offensive: "I think the tactics of our left-wing friends on Southeast Asia are becoming rather clear in the last few days. They are petrified at the thought that our diplomatic and military initiatives may succeed. Consequently, they have made a decision at the highest level to attempt to destroy American confidence in the South Vietnamese and Cambodians through articles by left-wing reporters. The *Times* had one story on South Vietnam's 'recession' and there is a story again today on Cambodia's political problems. Along the same lines, it is no accident that after Tony Lewis wrote those shocking Communist-line pieces from Hanoi for the *Times,* Selig Harrison of *The Washington Post* now is on the scene in Hanoi writing about how nice the little 12-year-old boys and girls are. . . . We must continue to try to discredit people like Harrison and Tony Lewis who obviously would never be let into Hanoi unless they had a prior commitment to write the Communist party line. . . ."

On June 10, the results of the California Democratic primary, in which McGovern defeated Humphrey, prompted a memo to the President from Buchanan. The speechwriter cited poll results showing Nixon leading McGovern 43 percent to 30 percent with George Wallace running as an independent, and 53 percent to 34 percent without a Wallace candidacy. Nixon answered the same day:

The Eastern Establishment media finally has a candidate who almost totally shares their views. *The New York Times, The Washington Post, Time, Newsweek* and the three television networks . . . their editorial bias comes down on the side of amnesty, pot, abortion, confiscation of wealth (unless it is theirs), massive increases in welfare, unilateral disarmament, reduction of their defenses, and surrender in Vietnam. . . . The working press, because they really believe in their hearts exactly what McGovern believes in, are frantically doing everything they can to clean him up and make him a respectable candidate. . . . Here we see the fundamental difference between the right wing extremists and the left wing extremists. The right wingers would rather lose than give up any one iota as far as principle is concerned. The left wing's primary motivation is power. They are always willing to compromise their principles in order to get power. . . .

Nixon did not compromise his attitudes in a private meeting the next day with Republican congressional leaders. Talking of "jackass amendments" to end the war in Vietnam and McGovern's calls to cut defense spending, he compared them with aid-to-Israel amendments that passed by large margins and no debate. "If you cut the defense budget, you cut American credibility," he said. "The moment U.S. credibility collapses, the Jews can check out of Israel and go back to Germany."

Later that day, June 13, talking to Colson, the President said he wanted around-the-clock surveillance of McGovern until the election. "You never know what you're going to find," he said. "Find a good young reporter and say he's going to do a book. And he just goes over there with his press pass. He doesn't open his mouth, but he just covers the sonofabitch like a blanket."

Then the President left for Florida for a long weekend. He was on Walker's Cay in the Bahamas, 150 miles from Key Biscayne, at the house of his friend Robert Abplanalp, who owned the little island. He did not return to his own house until Sunday morning, June 18. He called Billy Graham to talk about George Wallace, and the preacher said he was willing to try to persuade the Alabama governor not to run as an independent after the Democratic National Convention. Then George Shultz called, telling Haldeman that George Meany of the AFL-CIO had invited him to play golf and had told him on the green that he would not support McGovern if he won the Democratic nomination.

The President, who had not seen Haldeman on Key Biscayne, met him for the flight back to Washington Monday evening. "On the way back," he wrote in his diary that night, "I got the disturbing news from Bob Haldeman that the break-in of the Democratic National Committee involved someone on the payroll of the Committee to Re-Elect the President. . . ."

In his diary, Nixon did not indicate that he knew anything about the burglary and arrests three days before.

The law—three Washington policemen—had caught up with Liddy and Hunt's burglars in the early hours of Saturday morning, June 17. On June 14, Liddy had told Hunt they had to go back into O'Brien's office because one bug installed by McCord on May 27 was not working. And most of what they were getting from the other bug, and passing along to Jeb Magruder, the deputy chairman of CREEP, was secretaries and clerks gossiping about dates and friends. Hunt brought back Barker, Martinez, Gonzalez, and Frank Sturgis, an American who had grown up in pre-Castro Cuba. After a lobster dinner at the Watergate Hotel, McCord volunteered to tape the locks of the doors this time. He did it wrong, putting the tape horizontally across the locks so that it was visible when the door was closed. The burglary team then waited for hours for the last volunteer to leave the DNC at about 1 A.M. At almost the same time a building guard named Frank Wills spotted the tape on a basement door and pulled it off.

Gonzalez picked the basement lock and the burglars broke into the offices by taking a back door off its hinges. At 1:50 A.M., Wills spotted new tape on the basement door and called the police. A squad of three plainclothes officers just off duty were having a drink in Georgetown, only a couple of minutes away from the Watergate, heard the call, and volunteered to answer it. Hunt's lookout, Alfred Baldwin, standing at the window on the seventh floor of the Howard Johnson Motor Inn, saw them arrive in an unmarked car but did not realize they were police. Then he saw the eighth-floor lights go on and he saw that they had flashlights and drawn guns. He used his walkie-talkie to call Hunt in room 214 at the Watergate Hotel. Hunt tried to call Barker on the sixth floor, but the Cuban had turned off his walkie-talkie because its static was so loud. Working their way down, the police spotted tape on the doorway to the sixth floor. Moving from room to room, guns still drawn, shouting "Police! Come out!" the plainclothesmen, looking more like hippies than cops, found McCord and the Cubans, all in business suits, with their hands up. They were wearing blue surgical gloves.

Barker turned his walkie-talkie on and whispered, "They've got us." Hunt and Liddy threw the electronic equipment in room 214 into two suitcases and walked out of the hotel to their cars on the street. They left behind thirty-two consecutively numbered new $100 bills, two address books with Howard Hunt's name and White House telephone number in them, and a $6.36 check from Hunt to his country club. The police found it all the next day.

CHAPTER 33

June 23, 1972

THE FIVE MEN ARRESTED at the Watergate in the pre-dawn on Saturday were not allowed to make any telephone calls. But telephone calls between the CIA, the White House, CREEP, and Haldeman in Key Biscayne had begun sometime shortly after 5 A.M. When the men appeared in court at 3:30 P.M. for a preliminary hearing, lawyers had already been to police headquarters and were in court waiting to represent them. When the arrested men were asked their occupations, only one of them spoke up, saying, "Anticommunist." The others nodded, but then James McCord stepped up to the bench and said quietly: "Security consultant, retired from government service."

Asked which part of the government, he said: "Central Intelligence Agency."

At CREEP, G. Gordon Liddy was shredding his files. Howard Hunt was doing the same. Chuck Colson ordered an assistant to destroy White House phone directories that listed Hunt. Jeb Magruder, the deputy director of the reelection committee, was burning his copies of Gemstone files in a fireplace at home—after he had talked to his boss, John Mitchell, who was in California for fund-raising events. At noon Saturday, Liddy had burst into the dining room of Burning Tree Country Club in Bethesda, Maryland, found Attorney General Richard Kleindienst, and said Mitchell wanted the five men released from jail. Kliendienst did not believe him and did not have the power to do it anyway.

On Sunday morning, the Associated Press moved a story saying that the phone directory at CREEP listed a James McCord. Mitchell issued a statement that McCord was not operating under committee orders, then flew back to Washington on Monday, leaving his wife at the Newporter Inn in Newport Beach. An hour after the President reached the White House Monday night, Tuesday's edition of *The Washington Post* came out with a front-page headline saying: "WHITE HOUSE CONSULTANT LINKED TO BUGGING SUSPECTS."

The *Post* had found Howard Hunt. The police had told the newspaper's Eugene Bachinski, a regular at headquarters, about Hunt's country club check, adding that his name was in the address books of the men from Miami. He passed it along to the young reporter writing Tuesday's story, Bob Woodward. Because it was a local burglary on a weekend, the paper had assigned the story to two junior reporters, Woodward, who was twenty-nine and had been with the paper for only nine months, and twenty-eight-year-old Carl Bernstein. Woodward, the lowest-paid reporter on the staff, had called the White House and asked for Hunt, and was told he worked in Colson's office. After the story appeared, White House counsel John Dean and an assistant went through the contents of Hunt's office safe and found a .25-caliber Colt revolver with live ammunition. Dean's reaction was simple: "Holy shit!"

McCord's attaché case was in there, too, filled with electronic gear and a tear-gas canister. There were CIA psychological profiles of Daniel Ellsberg, stacks of pages from the Pentagon Papers, memos to and from Colson, and two diplomatic cables Hunt had fabricated to make it appear that President Kennedy had directly ordered the assassination of South Vietnamese President Diem in November 1963. Referring to Diem and his brother, Ngo Dinh Nhu, a pasted-up phony message read: "We believe the future success of Vietnam efforts depends upon replacement Nhu and Diem. . . . Leaders of successful coup deserve clean slate. . . . by making sure neither brother survives. All of us here realize this instruction places you in uncomfortable and distasteful position."

Dean reported to Ehrlichman on the contents of the safe and asked what to do with them. "Deep six them," was the answer. When he asked what that meant, Ehrlichman answered: "When you cross over the bridge on the way home, just toss the briefcase into the river."

The Watergate story got three or four minutes on all the nightly news programs, correspondents quoting a Ron Ziegler comment, "It's a third-rate burglary. . . . nothing the President would be involved with, obviously." The President himself had two comments on that, writing on his news summary: "He understated. Attempt at burglary . . . Haven't there been some other break-ins in political and government offices?

Where were the cries of anguish when the *Times* and Anderson got prizes for publishing stolen top secret government documents?"

"Exotic" was the word John Chancellor of NBC News used to describe the burglary report. He smiled. So did most political reporters. They were concentrating on the McGovern campaign, mocking the senator's chances of defeating Nixon in November. On ABC News, Hubert Humphrey said a McGovern race would lead to an astonishing defection of moderate Democrats to Republican candidates in congressional races. In *The National Observer,* Ben Wattenberg described McGovern as "essentially a fourth-party candidate." *Time* devoted five pages to McGovern's campaign proposals and offered a vision of society as it might be conjured up by both McGovern's most severe critics and his most devoted followers: "The neighborhood draft dodger has triumphantly returned home to take one of the new jobs at Freedom Fleet, a bus company shuttling ghetto children to racially balanced schools in the suburbs. After work, the ex-expatriate picks up his date at the corner abortion parlor, stops next door at Pot City for some Acapulco gold, and then trips off to Timothy Leary's Dizzyland, a new chain of rock-'n'-roll-your-own nightclubs springing up in abandoned American Legion halls."

On Tuesday, June 20, Watergate was the subject of an unusual 8 A.M. meeting between Mitchell, Haldeman, and Ehrlichman. The campaign chief asserted that their job was to protect the President at any cost, saying that their first objective must be to stop investigations as soon as possible because, sooner or later, they would lead to other operations. "Horrors" was the word Mitchell used. The horrors list began with wiretaps and included the Ellsberg break-in, the ITT manipulations, nine months of around-the-clock surveillance of Senator Edward Kennedy, a political sabotage squad put together by a friend of Dwight Chapin's named Donald Segretti to disrupt Democratic events, Hunt's phony cables, and possible break-ins at embassies, particularly one at the Chilean embassy on May 13.

At 10:30 A.M., the President began a series of one-on-one meetings, calling Ehrlichman first and spending an hour with him, and then calling in Haldeman. Nixon told his chief of staff that it was essential to restrain FBI investigations. Taking notes, as always, Haldeman wrote: "What is our counter-attack? PR offensive to top this—hit the opposition with their activities." Part of the idea was to dismiss the break-in as some kind of prank.

Haldeman got the impression that the President thought Colson had ordered the burglary—"Don't let Colson give me any details." Outside the Oval Office, most of the staff, beginning with Ziegler, were shocked and confused, but they were whispering Colson's name. After all, Hunt was Colson's man.*

At 4:30 P.M., Nixon called Haldeman over to EOB 175. The chief of staff told him that the Democratic National Committee had announced it would file a civil suit against CREEP for $1 million in damages, claiming the break-in was an invasion of privacy and a civil rights violation. It was a clever way to get depositions from Nixon's men, beginning with Mitchell.

"I don't know what the law is," Nixon said. "I mean, I don't know how long it takes."

"Dean said you could stall it for a couple of months, probably down to the election. . . ."

"It's fortunately, it's fortunately a bizarre story," said the President.

Haldeman talked about the burglars: "McCord, I guess, will say that he was working with the Cubans, who wanted to put this in for their own political reasons. . . . Hunt disappeared or is in the process of disappearing. He can undisappear if we want him to."

"Yes," said Nixon. "Now of course they're trying to tie these guys to Colson and the White House. . . . It's strange—if Colson doesn't run out, it doesn't go anywhere. . . ."

"You don't know what he did?" Nixon said a couple of minutes later.

"I think we all knew that there were some . . ."

" Intelligence," Nixon finished the sentence.

". . . some activities, and we were getting reports, or some input anyway. But I don't think—I don't think Chuck knew specifically that this was under way. He seems to take all the blame himself."

"Did he?" said Nixon. "Good."

Then he added: "This Oval Office business"—the tapes—"complicates things all over."

"I haven't listened to the tapes," Haldeman said.

"They're kept for future purposes," Nixon said.

"Super-secure," Haldeman replied. "There are only three people that know."

"Well," Nixon said later. "Does Hunt work for us or what?"

"I don't know," Haldeman said. "I haven't gotten an answer to . . .—apparently McCord had Hunt working with him, or Hunt had

---

* The morning meeting with Haldeman on June 20, 1972, was recorded by the White House taping system. Eighteen and a half minutes of that tape were erased sometime before the tapes were delivered to congressional investigators in 1974.

McCord working with him, and with these Cubans. They're all tied to-gether. . . ."

"How does the press know about this?" Nixon asked.

"They don't," Haldeman answered. "Oh, they know Hunt's in-volved because they found his name in the address book of two of the Cubans. . . ."

After more than an hour, Nixon closed down the conversation: "My God, the committee isn't worth bugging, in my opinion. That's my public line."

The President called Haldeman at home that night, saying that perhaps Watergate could be turned to advantage, that the Cuban connec-tion could be used to remind people of President Kennedy's blunders at the Bay of Pigs. Then he added: "Those people who got caught are going to need money. I've been thinking about how to do it."

It began all over again the next day, June 21, with the micro-phones in the President's desk and in the fireplace near the couch and chairs used as a seating area in the Oval Office area picking up most every word. "What's the dope on the Watergate incident? Anything break on that?" the President began at 9:30 A.M.

"There's nothing new," Haldeman answered. "The whole ques-tion now is, Mitchell's concern is the FBI, the question of how far they're going in the process. . . . Mitchell laid out a scenario. . . . which would involve this guy Liddy at the committee confessing and taking, moving the thing up to that level, saying: 'Yeah, I did it, I did it; I hired these guys, sent them over there, because I thought it would be a good move and build me up in the operation. . . . ' "

"You mean you'd have Liddy confess and say he did it unautho-rized?" Nixon said.

That was the idea. They went back and forth on that until the President said: "The reaction is going to be primarily Washington and not the country, because I think the country doesn't give much of a shit about it other than the ones we've already bugged. . . . Everybody around here is all mortified by it. It's a horrible thing to rebut. . . . Most people around the country think that this is routine, that everybody's trying to bug everybody else, it's politics." That gave him an idea. He said whenever there was a leak about Republican plans, the campaign should say that proves McGovern was bugging them—and maybe they should plant a bug on themselves and say McGovern did it. "That's my view. . . . I don't think they're going to see a great uproar in the country about the Republican committee trying to bug the Democratic head-quarters."

"Then," Haldeman replied, "it seems to me that argues for following the Liddy scenario, saying: Sure, some little lawyer who was trying to make a name for himself did a stupid thing."

"Is Liddy willing?"

"He says he is. Apparently he is a little bit nuts. . . . apparently he's sort of a Tom Huston type guy. . . . He sort of likes the dramatic. He's said, 'If you want to put me before a firing squad and shoot me, that's fine. I'd kind of like to be like Nathan Hale.' "

Later that day, at 4 P.M., the President worked on another cover story idea with Colson: they could say that the whole thing was a CIA operation. That, after all, was the way the White House had ended the investigation of the Green Berets charged with assassination in Vietnam in August 1969.

"I think that we could develop a theory as to the CIA if we wanted to," Colson said. "We know that Hunt has all these ties with these people."

"He worked with them," Nixon said.

"Oh, he was their boss, and they were all CIA," Colson said. "You take the cash, you go down to Latin America. . . . We're in great shape with the Cubans, and they're proud of it. There's a lot of muscle in that gang."

They talked for more than an hour, until the President said, "Don't let the bastards get you down, Chuck."

By the next morning, Haldeman was in a pretty good mood when he came into the Oval Office. He told the President that the FBI had not been able to trace the $100 bills found at the Watergate and in the pockets of the burglars. Investigators knew the money came from the Republic National Bank in Miami, but the bank had no records of origin.

Haldeman was also working on one more diversion. He told the President: "We've got another thing going which has taken hold a little bit, which is we've started moving on the Hill, letting it come out from there, which is that this whole thing is a Jack Anderson thing, that Jack Anderson did it. . . . We started a rumor yesterday morning and it's starting to come back already—"

"What?" Nixon interrupted.

"That Jack Anderson was bugging the Democratic offices. . . . The great thing about this is that it is so totally fucked up and so badly done that nobody believes—"

"That we could have done it," Nixon completed the sentence. "Well, it sounds like a comic opera, really."

"It would make a funny goddamn movie."

The President began to laugh, then said, "I mean, here's these Cubans with their accents—"

"Wearing these rubber gloves," Haldeman picked up, "standing there in their expensive, well-made business suits, wearing rubber gloves, and put their hands up and shouting 'Don't shoot' when the police come in. . . ."

Then, serious, Haldeman said, "Also, they have no case on Hunt."

"Why?" Nixon asked.

"They can't put him into the scene at all."

"We know where he was, though."

"But they don't. The FBI doesn't."

"That's right," Nixon agreed.

Haldeman went on: "The thing we forget is that we know too much and therefore read too much into what we see that other people can't read into. I mean, what seems obvious to us because of what we know is not obvious to other people."

Other people heard the President on Watergate the next day, during an afternoon press conference in the Oval Office, his first in more than three months. He brushed off the only question on the matter by saying he was waiting for word from the FBI and Washington police, adding: "This kind of activity, as Mr. Ziegler has indicated, has no place whatever in our electoral process, or in our governmental process. And, as Mr. Ziegler has stated, the White House has had no involvement whatever in this particular incident."

Newspapers and television focused on other news the next morning, June 23. The President said he might order new price controls because of rising food prices, but expressed satisfaction that the rate of inflation had been reduced from 6 percent to about 3 percent in the ten months since he ordered wage and price controls; the Supreme Court had, for the first time since 1954, decided a school desegregation case by other than a unanimous vote, ruling 5–4 that a predominantly white town in Virginia could not withdraw from a heavily black county school system; and the Court, in another 5–4 vote, declared capital punishment to be a violation of the Constitution's ban on "cruel and unusual punishment." In both cases, the four Nixon appointees were in the minority. On Watergate, *The New York Times,* NBC News, and ABC News speculated that the burglary was the work of right-wing Cubans trying to find out whether McGovern and the Democrats were planning to reestablish diplomatic relations with the Castro government.

Two news summary items caught the President's eye that morning. The first was an ABC News report that a South Vietnamese relief column had once more failed to break the siege of An Loc. Nixon, who had seen intelligence reports complaining that South Vietnamese pilots were refusing to fly ground cover near An Loc, scribbled a note to Haig: "Al, wire Abrams—this is becoming an issue—even a joke by critics of ARVN. Unless there's a strong military reason, have Abrams tell Thieu to get off his tail and push this outfit in there."

The second item was a story by Helen Thomas about a telephone call she had received from Martha Mitchell. Mrs. Mitchell said she was being held prisoner in a cottage at the Newporter Inn, where her husband had left her when he rushed back to Washington. She told Thomas she had been prevented from using the telephone after she became agitated by the arrest of McCord at the Watergate—she knew him because he would periodically sweep her home for telephone bugs. She was able to dial Thomas, she said, while pretending to be asleep. Then she said: "That's it. I've given John an ultimatum. I'm going to leave him unless he gets out of the campaign. I'm sick and tired of politics. Politics is a dirty business." Suddenly her voice changed—she was screaming, "You just get away—get away!"—and the line went dead.

"Poor John!" the President wrote. Then he read Mitchell's comment when Thomas called him in Washington: "She's great. That little sweetheart. I love her so much. She gets a little upset about politics, but she loves me and I love her and that's what counts."

"Good answer by John," Nixon wrote.

Haldeman came into the office, just after 10 A.M. Bad news. The FBI investigators had been able to use the thirty-two $100 bills found at the Howard Johnson Motor Inn on June 17 to trace the $114,000 Liddy had sent to Barker. They had already come up with the name of Kenneth Dahlberg, a Republican fund-raiser who had received $25,000 from Dwayne Andreas, a Hubert Humphrey friend covering his political bets by secretly giving money to Nixon.

The President decided that the time had come to push the CIA to block the FBI. Haldeman told him that Pat Gray, the acting director of the FBI, simply did not know enough about how the bureau worked to shut his men down. "Mitchell came up with the plan yesterday," Haldeman said, "and John Dean analyzed it very carefully last night and concludes—concurs—now with Mitchell's recommendation that the only way to solve this is for us to have Walters"—General Vernon Walters, now deputy CIA director—"call Pat Gray and just say, 'Stay the hell out of this. . . . this is business here, we don't want you to go any further on it.' "

"All right. Fine," Nixon said after listening awhile. "I mean you just—well, we protected Helms from one hell of a lot of things. . . . This involves these Cubans, Hunt, and a lot of hanky-panky that we have nothing to do with ourselves. What the hell, did Mitchell know about this thing to any much of a degree?"

"I think so," Haldeman answered. "I don't think he knew the details, but I think he knew."

"Well, who was the asshole who did? Liddy? . . . Isn't that the problem?"

"No," Haldeman said, "but he was under pressure, apparently, to get more information, and as he got more pressure, he pushed the people harder to move—"

"Pressure from Mitchell?"

"Apparently . . ."

After a couple of more minutes, the President said, ". . . I'm not going to get that involved. . . ."

"No, sir. We don't want you to."

"You call them in. Good. Good deal. Play it tough. That's the way they play it and that's the way we are going to play it," the President said. "When you get these people . . . say: 'Look, the problem is that this will open the whole, the whole Bay of Pigs thing, and the President just feels that'—without going into the details—don't, don't lie to them to the extent to say there is no involvement, but just say this is sort of a comedy of errors, bizarre, without getting into it. . . . that they should call the FBI in and say that we wish for the country, 'don't go any further into this case,' period. . . ."

Haldeman came back to the President that afternoon to say that he had called Walters and asked him and CIA Director Richard Helms to come to the White House. He told Nixon: "Well, it's no problem. Had the . . . two of them in. . . . I didn't mention Hunt at the opening. I just said that, that, uh, this thing which we give direction to, we're gonna create some very major potential problems because they were exploring leads that led back into—to, uh, areas that will be harmful to the CIA, harmful to the government. . . . Gray had called Helms, which we knew, and said, 'I think we've run right into the middle of a CIA covert operation.' "

"Gray said that?"

"Yeah, and Helms said 'Nothing, nothing we've got at this point.' " *

But, Haldeman reported, Helms had relented, saying he would try to be helpful, saying, "We'll handle anything, we'll do anything you want." But the CIA director, a veteran of bureaucratic scheming, added that he wanted to know the reason. In writing. Walters had said then that he would call Gray.

---

* The three June 23, 1972, tapes were made public on August 5,1974—and became known as the "smoking gun" tapes because they depicted the President ordering a cover-up.

The White House effort to use the CIA to block the FBI failed within a day or two, because the Justice Department investigation was being driven not by Gray or his men but by a local prosecutor, Earl Silbert, principal assistant to the United States attorney for the District of Columbia, who was calling witnesses before a D.C. grand jury. So, on June 26, Haldeman and Nixon talked about the possibility of having John Mitchell resign as chairman of the reelection committee and take the blame for the burglary, explaining that he was distracted by personal problems. The personal problem, of course, was his wife, living now at the Westchester Country Club near New York City, but still making telephone calls, claiming that she had been drugged and taken across the country by force.

"It's getting pretty big, the story; don't you agree?" Nixon said.

"Yeah," Haldeman answered. "If they run this stuff about throwing her on the bed and sticking a needle in her behind and that kind of stuff. . . . You could use this as a basis for Mitchell pulling out. . . . The only way you can do that is to hang him on it, say: 'Well, yeah, he did it, and that's why we have to get rid of him.' "

"I can't do that. I won't do that to him," Nixon said. "I'd rather, shit, lose the election. I really would."

Then they talked about what else might come up as the Washington grand jury called witnesses. "Apparently," Haldeman said, "with our limited resources in that area, they used the same people for a wide range of things. So you've got them all—you've got cross-ties in your leading people and all that. If these guys were only on this thing, you could cut them loose and sink them without a trace."

"You mean they've been on ITT?" Nixon asked.

"And other stuff."

"Black holes?"

Haldeman took that to mean black-bag jobs and answered, "Apparently a lot of stuff. There's stuff I don't know anything about."

That night the President dictated a diary note that began with Watergate but ended with a note he had received from Kissinger concerning *The Washington Post* and its publisher: "Henry told me of an interesting conversation he had with Stewart Alsop. Stewart, apparently, is still critically ill and had been out to dinner with Kay Graham. He had been arguing emphatically with regard to the necessity to support RN because of what he had accomplished in foreign policy, and also the danger of having McGovern in the Presidency. He said that Kay Graham finally blew up and said, 'I hate him and I'm going to do everything I can to beat him.' "

· · ·

BY JUNE 28, the President had decided that Mitchell, who was in New York with his wife, had to go. Haldeman and he spent more than two hours discussing how to handle the CREEP resignation.

"Go back to Mitchell," Nixon said. "I think, as I understand it—and I don't want to know because I've got to answer at a press conference. But as I understand it, John did not know specifically about this caper. . . . I mean, if down the line, Cubans and others before us, working for some asshole, and they do something stupid, we can't be responsible for that. . . . It's a beautiful opportunity. He'll gain great sympathy. The Martha fans will think: Isn't that a wonderful thing, that the man has given up—you know, it's kind of like the Duke of Windsor giving up the throne for the woman he loves, this sort of stuff. I mean, it has a little of that flavor to this. The poor woman hasn't been well and all and he's going to be by her side, and all of that."

Later that day, Haldeman called in John Dean, who was delegated to find a way to get money to buy the silence of the five burglars as well as Hunt and Liddy. Dean called Herb Kalmbach in Newport Beach. Kalmbach had control over the campaign cash in California safe deposit boxes. Dean told him to take the overnight flight from Los Angeles to Washington.

The President went to Camp David that night to prepare for a press conference on June 29, his first live televised conference in more than thirteen months. He returned in mid-afternoon and called Haldeman to ask about his meeting with Mitchell. They met in EOB 175 and Haldeman said Mitchell wanted to leave. He told Nixon of his friend's anguish, saying that the stories about Newport Beach were true: Martha Mitchell had trashed a hotel room and a doctor had thrown her on the bed and injected a sedative. "He's afraid she'll jump off the balcony at the Watergate," Haldeman concluded. "So he's got to quit."

As Nixon and Haldeman talked, Dean walked out of the White House to meet Kalmbach in Lafayette Park across Pennsylvania Avenue. He told the President's personal attorney that his job was to secretly raise the money for the Watergate defendants and Hunt and Liddy and work out plans for Tony Ulasewicz, the former New York cop, to deliver the cash—all in secret. After Kalmbach checked in at the Statler Hilton, Maurice Stans came over from CREEP to give him a briefcase containing 751 $100 bills.

There were twenty-two questions at the press conference that night and none involved Watergate or investigations. The principal news break was the President's announcement that United States negotiators would return to the Vietnam peace talks in Paris on July 13, during the Democratic National Convention.

The next day Nixon had lunch with Mitchell and Haldeman, in EOB 175. The President had his usual cottage cheese as the others ate crab soufflé. He noticed that his friend's hands were shaking so badly that he could barely hold a spoon. Mitchell said he had to return to New York. That night Nixon wrote in his diary: "Without Martha, I'm sure that the Watergate thing would never have happened."

Late that afternoon, the President invited Clark MacGregor in and asked him to take over the reelection committee. Nixon talked with him and Haldeman for another hour and a half, ready to assure him that the CREEP problems were over. But MacGregor interrupted, saying: "I don't need to know anything about the past, but I need to, I guess, to know something about the future. I have said to people absolutely flat out, I've talked to congressmen and senators, the Committee to Re-Elect the President and the White House had absolutely nothing to do with this incident."

"That's the line you should take," Nixon said. "I know the White House had nothing to do with it. . . ."

Haldeman acted as something of a straight man as the President reassured MacGregor. At one point, he brought up Liddy's name, but the President acted as if he never heard it before and then said: "To me, it's such a crude goddamn thing. You almost think it's a bunch of double agents. . . . almost like a fix."

As soon as MacGregor left the office, Haldeman turned to Nixon and said, "I told him about the Liddy thing because he's going to find it out right away anyway."

Liddy, whose name was not yet public, had been fired two days before by his supposed boss, Maurice Stans, but he was still refusing to cooperate with FBI investigators. He was willing to say that he had been ordered to return the Barker money—the twenty-five thousand dollars from Dahlberg and eighty-nine thousand dollars from a company called Gulf Resources and Chemical, Inc., which had ended up in the hands of a Mexican lawyer named Manuel Ogarrio—as illegal donations because they had arrived after the April 7 deadline, but had decided on his own to use it for covert operations.

"A true believer . . . ," the President said. "We'll take care of him. Well, it's good to have some people like that."

"If he gets hung on it," Haldeman said, "then we'll wait a discreet interval and pardon him."

"You don't want to pardon him now," Nixon said.

"After the election," Haldeman said. As the conversation was ending, Nixon brought up the name of Bobby Baker, a Lyndon Johnson assistant who had gone to prison. Haldeman said that hurt Johnson's image, but Nixon cut him off: "Bullshit. How could he be hurt when he won 61 to 39?"

That night, alone with history, the President wrote in his diary: ". . . I am satisfied that nobody in the White House had any knowledge or approved any such activity, and that Mitchell was not aware of it as well."

ON SATURDAY, the President took off for San Clemente, talking campaign politics on the plane, saying he wanted to ignore the Democratic National Convention, scheduled to begin in Miami Beach on July 10. "Let McGovern sink himself. . . . No truth squads or any of that," he told his speechwriters. His last official act before leaving town for two weeks was signing a debt-ceiling bill with a provision increasing Social Security benefits by 20 percent—and indexing benefits to keep pace with future inflation. He had opposed the increase as inflationary, but when it passed by overwhelming margins in both the House and the Senate he knew he could have it both ways, fighting inflation with his words, but delighting twenty-eight million voters who would get their increased pension checks a month before the election, while the payroll tax to pay for it all would not take effect until 1973.

The President could barely stay awake late enough to watch McGovern's acceptance speech at the Democratic National Convention. The night of July 13 dragged on and on as delegates on the floor nominated thirty-nine candidates for vice president, including Martha Mitchell and Mao Tse-tung. It was almost midnight on the Pacific Coast, 3 A.M. July 14 on the East Coast, when the nominee finally got to speak. Nixon was watching with his wife. John Connally, who was staying at Casa Pacifica, had given up and gone to bed, like most other Americans. The Nixons watched the Democrats explode on national television. Mayor Richard Daley of Chicago, chairman of the Illinois delegation, was among the delegates whose seats were taken away by the credentials committee interpreting new racial and gender balancing guidelines written by the reform commission headed by McGovern himself. In Daley's place, Reverend Jesse Jackson, a young Chicago civil rights activist wearing a dashiki, sat holding the state's standard, or occasionally jumping up to pump it into the air and chant, "Freedom Now! Freedom Now!" One after another, the best-known men in the party, beginning with Edward Kennedy and Edmund Muskie, rejected McGovern's invitation to run for vice president. After considering twenty-four possible running mates on the day of the vice presidential balloting, McGovern settled on a freshman senator, Thomas F. Eagleton of Missouri.

On the morning after the convention, McGovern proudly announced the replacement of Larry O'Brien as chairman of the Democratic National Committee with the first woman to hold a national chairmanship, Jean Miles Westwood of Utah. At the same time, President Nixon and John Connally appeared together on television from San Clemente to announce that the former Democratic governor of Texas would head "Democrats for Nixon." It was a consolation prize, really, because the President still wanted to dump Vice President Agnew, but he had concluded that he could not do that without exploding his own party.

Back in Washington, on July 19, the President sent a memo to Connally about a conversation with George Smathers, a former Democratic senator from Florida:

> I talked to Smathers on the phone last night and he said that he would be ready to join you and the Democrats for Nixon organization just as soon as a primary involving his son, Bruce, who is running for the state legislature as a Democrat, gets the nomination as he hopes in the Jacksonville area. . . . He said that he had already talked to Senators Warren Magnuson, Russell Long, Bob Byrd, Jennings Randolph, Herman Talmadge, and Joe Montoya. He said that all of them were very unhappy about the McGovern nomination and were trying to figure out ways that they could avoid endorsing him. . . .

The next memo to Connally read:

> Right after our conversation today I called President Johnson and reached him at the ranch. . . . I told him that I knew and respected his position with regard to supporting the nominees of his Party as a former President but that I would greatly appreciate it if when individuals who were in his Administration or who were supporters of his asked him about joining you in Democrats for Nixon that he might take the position of neutrality. . . . He then went on to say that he had agreed with most of the positions that I had taken during my tenure in office and that he found himself in sharp disagreement with the nominees of his Party and would therefore not discourage any of his friends who wanted to join you. . . . He said, as a matter of fact, he had a very difficult problem with his own family, particularly his two daughters and sons-in-law, all of whom had expressed a desire to oppose McGovern. . . .

CHAPTER 34

August 22, 1972

O<small>N</small> J<small>ULY</small> 18, the day the President left San Clemente for the trip back to Washington, he and most of the rest of the world were stunned by news from Cairo. President Anwar Sadat of Egypt—a man Kissinger had privately predicted would last only weeks in office after the death of President Nasser in September 1970—had ordered Soviet military advisers and technicians to get out of his country immediately. But it was not Kissinger or Rogers, who had been handling the Middle East portfolio, that the President called in when he came into the Oval Office the next day. He wanted to talk to John Ehrlichman.

"Give me an update on Watergate, where it now stands," he said. "What's the next move?"

"Magruder is probably going to have to take the slide."

"How does he slide?"

"Well, he'll just have to take whatever lumps come, have to take responsibility for the thing. They're not going to be able to contrive a story that indicates that he didn't know what was going on." Ehrlichman continued: "I think that's what Dean's working on this morning."

"Did he know?" Nixon asked.

"Oh, yes. Oh Lord, yes. He's in it with both feet."

"He can't contrive a story, then," said Nixon, who began reminiscing about scandals past, focusing, as always, on his pursuit of Alger Hiss's links to communist espionage: "If you cover up you're going to get caught. And if you lie, you're going to be guilty of perjury."

"It's a hell of a goddamned thing," the President went on. "I hate to see it, but let me say we'll take care of Magruder immediately afterwards. . . ."

Ehrlichman said the problem was that they were not sure how to limit Magruder's testimony once investigators began questioning his story.

"The main thing is whether he is the one where it stops," Nixon said. "Or whether he goes to Mitchell or Haldeman."

They talked on for an hour, contriving scenarios to contain the two investigations, the criminal grand jury hearings and the Democrats' civil suit. Ehrlichman told Nixon that the Democrats had hired one of Washington's most feared lawyers, Edward Bennett Williams, for the civil suit. He imitated how Williams might cross-examine Magruder, deepening his voice to say: "But even notwithstanding that, Mr. Magruder, when such and such a matter came up, you didn't decide that yourself, you checked with Mr. Mitchell?"

"I must say," Nixon remarked after a while, "I can't see how Magruder could stand firm on Mitchell. He may not be tough enough."

The next day, July 20, Nixon asked Haldeman exactly how the Watergate investigations were being handled in the White House.

"Dean is watching it on almost a full-time basis and reporting to me and Ehrlichman on a continuing basis," Haldeman answered. "There's no one else in the White House that has any knowledge of what's going on there at all. . . . There's no need for anybody to know. There's nothing they can do about it."

"That's right," Nixon said, and he laughed. "It's enough for just a few of us that know to worry about it."

"Actually," said Haldeman, "There's nothing any of us can do, either."

"I had a strange dream last night," the President said without elaborating. "It's going to be a nasty issue for a few days. I can't believe that—we're whistling in the dark, but I can't believe that they can tie this thing to me. What's your feeling?"

"It'll be messy . . . ," Haldeman said.

IN PUBLIC, nothing seemed neater than the President's path to reelection. During the three weeks Nixon had been in California, there had been only one Watergate story each in *Time* and *Newsweek,* and just three short stories on court proceedings in *The Washington Post*. The President's approval rating was over 60 percent in most polls, he was leading McGovern by 14 percentage points in the Gallup poll, and the executive council of Meany's AFL-CIO had voted 27 to 3 to remain neutral in the election, the first time ever the council had not endorsed a Democratic candidate for president. Monthly economic statistics that were released showed that the gross national product was growing at an annual rate of 8.9 percent and the rate of inflation was dropping in most parts of the country.

The only potential problem on the election horizon still seemed to be George Wallace, who had spoken at the Democratic convention—dramatically rolling up a ramp to the stage in his wheelchair—but still had not publicly ruled out a third-party candidacy. John Connally and Billy Graham were meeting with Wallace to assure him that he would have whatever he wanted or needed as long as Nixon was in office. "Find out what he wants," the President had told Connally. The Texan came back and said, "He wants respect. . . . and he's a very sick man."

"We might well say that this was the day the election was won," said Connally, telling Nixon that Wallace was in no shape to take the nomination of the American Independent Party, which he had formed in 1968, and without Wallace in the race there was no way McGovern could win. It would, however, cost a little money. Nixon agreed to pay Wallace's campaign staff for the rest of the year.

The only thing that did not seem to be breaking the President's way involved his vice president. On July 22, Nixon announced officially that Agnew was his choice. But he continued to tell Haldeman and others that he had a plan to persuade Agnew to resign during a second term. Hours after the announcement, Nixon saw the text of a speech the Vice President planned to give the next day in Oregon attacking the press. "No, no, no," Nixon said in frustration, laying down the rules for the rest of the year: no attacks on the press, or on Democrats, either. He ordered his men not to use the word "Democrats" negatively, that all campaign attacks were to be on "McGovernites."

He ended a long memo on campaign press strategy: "As long as we appear to have a rather substantial lead in the polls, the Sideys and even the Chancellors will suck around. . . . Play them as suckers, not as friends."

At night, the President continued to dictate political memos, writing little scripts for his people, including his daughters, Tricia and Julie, who received this one on July 24 "FROM THE PRESIDENT: . . . On a personal side, you might mention some of our Christmas parties where I played the piano for group singing, etc., always by ear. . . . You can say that these kinds of events are not publicly known but they have been part of the Nixon story that is to you most heartwarming. And also point out that when you had your birthday parties, etc., that from time to time I played a birthday song for you."

By then Nixon was relatively confident that Watergate was under control. Certainly, he told Haldeman on July 25, court delays, confusion, and White House stonewalling—Dean seemed to be in control and nobody was talking—meant that there were going to be no trials before the election. "They're going to keep, keep, keep investigating," he said. "Let it go." The two of them were even getting some laughs out of it.

"What Hunt is doing is using all of the goddamn permissive crap that the previous Supreme Court has given us for his purposes," Nixon said.

"The same way that murderers and rapists get off," Haldeman said.

"The murderers and rapists have gotten off because of publicity, publicity, too much publicity," Nixon said. "I never agreed with it, but now that the court has spoken that's the law of the land. And if it's good for a murderer, it's good for a wiretapper. . . ."

They couldn't stop laughing at that one.

LATER THAT AFTERNOON, while the President was meeting with Haig, Haldeman walked in holding an Associated Press bulletin that reported an extraordinary press conference in South Dakota. The Democratic candidate for vice president, Senator Eagleton, knowing that newspaper reporters were checking his health records after receiving anonymous calls about nervous breakdowns, had announced that he had been hospitalized three times between 1960 and 1966 for "nervous exhaustion" and "depression"—and twice had undergone electroshock therapy. Standing at his side, McGovern acknowledged that he had not known about any of this—Eagleton had lied when McGovern's men questioned him about skeletons in closets—but that he still would have chosen the Missouri senator if he had known. Then Connally called to say: "My God . . . They nominated a crazy man."

The President held a press conference on July 27. He was asked five questions about the vice presidency—both Eagleton and Agnew—and five about Vietnam. There were no Watergate questions.

The subject did not come up the next day, either, when Nixon, the target of union hatred for more than twenty years, spent the afternoon golfing with George Meany, who began by saying on the first hole, "Eagleton should have told McGovern but now McGovern has handled it like a fool. . . ." On the eighteenth hole, the labor leader said, "I want you to know now that I am not going to vote for you, and I am not going to vote for McGovern." But he said his wife and two of his daughters would vote for Nixon. "Just so you don't get a swelled head about my wife voting for you," he added, "I want to tell you why—she don't like McGovern."

The President had a romantic view of the old man. They hated the same people, though Nixon had to be more careful about showing that in public. In his diary, he wrote: "The American leader class has really had it in terms of their ability to lead. It's really sickening to have to receive them at the White House as I often do and to hear them whine and whimper and that's one of the reasons why I enjoy very much more receiving labor leaders and people from middle America who still have character and guts and a bit of patriotism. . . . Frankly, I have more in common with them from a personal standpoint than does McGovern or the intellectuals generally. They like labor as a mass. I like them individually. . . ."

A couple of days later he expressed himself about Meany's adversaries, businessmen, after reading a memo from Donald Rumsfeld, the director of the Price Commission, saying automobile manufacturers wanted to raise the prices of their 1973 models from eighty-one dollars to ninety-one dollars. Rumsfeld wanted the President's backing to cut the rise in half. Nixon's scrawled comment read: "I won't ask these people for anything—they should be sensible enough to hold off on something like this until after November. If their selfishness prevails over their good sense, they can go to hell—and that is exactly where McGovern would send them. . . . Remind me of how they respond to your request—after November 7th."

On July 31, after a week of tortured days for Democrats, McGovern asked Eagleton to resign from the ticket. The eight-column banner headline in *The Washington Post* of August 1 buried the first significant scoop by Woodward and Bernstein. Prosecutors in Miami had showed Bernstein the $25,000 check signed by Dahlberg, and Woodward had found the man in Minneapolis. Dahlberg said he had turned the check over to CREEP, but no one asked him whose money it was.

The press was chasing McGovern, not CREEP. The Democratic nominee went looking again for someone willing to run with him. Kennedy said no. Senator Abraham Ribicoff of Connecticut said no. Humphrey. Muskie. Governor Reubin Askew of Florida. All no. On August 5, Sargent Shriver said yes. The former director of both the Peace Corps and the Office of Economic Opportunity—and Ted Kennedy's brother-in-law—was formally selected at a meeting of the Democratic National Committee on August 9. Nixon was enjoying himself. He was spending only an hour or two a day on Watergate, usually in briefings by Haldeman and Ehrlichman, who was getting most of his information from John Dean. The counsel reported that there would be seven indictments by the Washington grand jury in mid-September, the five burglars, Hunt, and Liddy. Haldeman passed that on to the President this way: "Everybody's satisfied. They're all out of jail, they've all been taken care of. We've done a lot of discreet checking to be sure there's no discontent in the ranks, and there isn't any."

"Hunt's happy," Haldeman said, in answer to Nixon's first question.

"At considerable cost, I guess?" said Nixon

"Yes."

"It's worth it."

"It's very expensive. It's a costly—"

The President cut him off, saying: "That's what the money is for. ... They have to be paid. That's all there is to that. They have to be paid."

Nixon was talking now of using the government to destroy McGovern and his people, as he believed Democratic administrations had done to him in the past, particularly when his income taxes were audited after his book *Six Crises* became a best-seller. "John," he said to Ehrlichman, "the point is, as I told you, in 1961, the first year I ever made any money, when I wrote the damn book, those sons of bitches came up and they went after it: How much did you pay for your house, and all the rest. It was horrible. . . ."

He wanted to know what was being done to others now: "What in the name of God are we doing on this one? What are we doing about the financial contributors? Now, those lists there . . . Are we looking over the financial contributors to the Democratic National Committee? Are we running their income tax returns? Is the Justice Department checking to see whether or not there are any antitrust suits? . . . We have all this power and we aren't using it. Now, what the Christ is the matter? In other words, I'm just thinking about, for example, if there's information on Larry O'Brien. What is being done? Who is doing this full-time? What in the name of God are we doing?"

"The short answer to your question is nothing" said Ehrlichman, who had just come back from the Defense Department, where he had collected McGovern's military records to see whether there was any dirt there. Before that he had been at Treasury trying to get the tax records of McGovern's largest contributor, a Virgin Islands businessman named Henry Kimmelman. There was a memo on the President's desk from Pat Buchanan saying that an informant reported that Kimmelman had sat next to Pat Moynihan on a Washington to New York Eastern Airlines shuttle flight. Nixon wanted to know what they talked about.

Mention of Kimmelman also prompted Nixon to say: "Scare the shit out of them. Scare the shit out of them. Now, there are some Jews with the Mafia that are involved in this all, too."

George Shultz, the new secretary of the treasury, was one of the problems on getting tax returns. "Everybody thinks George is an honest, decent man . . . ," said Nixon. He did not mean it as a compliment. "George has got a fantasy. . . . What's he trying to do, say that you can't play politics with IRS? . . . Just tell George he should do it."

"I will," Ehrlichman said. Three days later he had Kimmelman's tax returns.

In mid-August, the President retired to Camp David. He was isolating himself again, telling Haldeman that he would not be reading the news summary for a week or so, but wanted a call with a verbal summary of the summary each day at 5 P.M. That was break time in the writing of his acceptance speech for the Republican National Convention. During one of the 5 P.M. calls, Haldeman told Nixon that Larry O'Brien's tax returns were being audited and that the former DNC chairman, who had agreed to manage the stumbling McGovern campaign, had asked for a postponement on the tax proceeding until after the election in November. "So," Haldeman said, "we've got his files and now we can do some exploring."

"That's a lot of nerve," said Nixon, "to say put it off until after the election."

ON THE DAY the President began writing, August 13, 1,053 men of the Third Battalion, twenty-first Infantry, stationed near Da Nang, gave up their positions to South Vietnamese troops and headed for home—and thirteen separate missions dropped three thousand tons of bombs on North Vietnamese roads and supply lines. "Vietnamization," for the Americans, meant replacing manpower with airpower, and it had produced a stalemate, stalling the offensive from the north that had begun on March 30. Kissinger was in Paris, meeting once more with North Vietnamese negotiators to discuss not the war but, indirectly, the Nixon-McGovern contest. The secret words were transcended by a political reality: the communists might get a better deal if McGovern were elected on November 7, but McGovern had little chance of winning. And Nixon was determined to bomb the North Vietnamese into negotiating a cease-fire. Kissinger's message was that they could get a better deal before election day. The United States threat was more than continued bombing, it was intensified bombing between Nixon's reelection and the convening of a new Congress in January 1973, one that might refuse to appropriate more money for more bombing. The President had to deal before the end of the year and the North Vietnamese had to decide how much more they could take.

Part of the political reality was that there was really not much chance that the makeup of Congress was going to change, even if Nixon defeated McGovern in a landslide—because the President had no intention of sharing his popularity, or McGovern's unpopularity. In a memo to Haldeman, he wrote: "We have to remember that Connally's organization and our major labor supporters are supporting only the President for re-election and are making a great point of the fact that they are supporting Democratic candidates for the House and Senate. . . . Anything we do in behalf of House and Senate candidates must be <u>very low profile</u> . . . go very light on any linkage between the Presidential campaign and the campaigns for the House and Senate. . . ." He cited Harris polls at the end of the memo, saying he wanted the campaign to emphasize hard line policies on Vietnam.

The bombing was the hard-line policy. In negotiations, the American line had softened significantly over the years. There were only two principal issues to negotiate since Nixon and Kissinger had accepted the idea of a cease-fire in place, which would leave North Vietnamese troops in South Vietnam. What was left now was the American demand for the return of all prisoners, and the North Vietnamese demand that the Thieu government in Saigon be removed, to affirm their political victory. With Nixon's reelection all but certain, this time it was the North Vietnamese and not the Americans who compromised, indicating they would consider some sort of coalition government in Saigon. The next day, August 15, Kissinger flew to Saigon, thinking that the end of the fighting might be near. In an "Exclusively Eyes-Only" cable to the President he wrote:

> We have gotten closer to a negotiated settlement than ever before. . . . We still have a chance to make an honorable peace. . . . The North Vietnamese will be watching the polls in our country and the developments in South Vietnam and deciding whether to compromise before November. They have an agonizing choice. They can make a deal with an Administration that will give them a fair chance to jockey for power in the South, but refuses to guarantee their victory. Or they can hold out, knowing that this course almost certainly means they will face the same administration with a fresh four-year mandate. . . .

The President was not that impressed. In the margins of that cable, he wrote Haig: "Which means we have no progress in 15 meetings. . . . No progress was made and none can be expected."

Also, Thieu's reaction was not what Kissinger had expected. The South Vietnamese leader had always agreed to American initiatives, but in hindsight Kissinger realized that was because he always knew Hanoi would reject them. Now Thieu seemed to be stalling, as if he preferred military combat, particularly with American help, to political struggle. He tried to put down his marker with a speech criticizing the peace process: "There is only one way to force the Communists to negotiate and that consists of the total destruction of their economic and war potential." Thieu wanted six to seven months more of intensive bombing.

On August 16, McGovern declined Nixon's offers of foreign policy briefings by Kissinger, saying he could learn more by reading the newspapers. The Democratic nominee was already on record as saying that he would withdraw all United States troops from Vietnam whether or not the North Vietnamese released American prisoners, saying he expected they would do that. Then, on August 19, McGovern said that if he won the presidency, he assumed that Thieu and his "cohorts" would flee their country. Asked about Nixon and Watergate, McGovern answered: "It's the kind of thing you expect under a person like Hitler."

On August 22, the Republican National Convention renominated Nixon by a vote of 1,327 to 1. The President's acceptance speech the next night—which he began just before 10:30 P.M. Eastern Standard Time—was watched in more than twenty million American homes, compared with the three million or so for McGovern's early-morning speech five weeks before. The Gallup poll completed August 30 reported: Nixon, 64 percent; McGovern, 30 percent; Undecided, 6 percent.

After the convention, Senator Eagleton called the White House, talking to Pat Buchanan, to thank the President for a sympathetic note Nixon had sent to his thirteen-year-old son, Terry. The President had written in longhand: "Winston Churchill once pointed out that 'Politics is even more difficult than war. Because in politics you die many times; in war you die only once.' . . . What matters is not that your father fought a terribly difficult battle and lost. What matters is that in fighting the battle he won the admiration of foes and friends alike because of the courage, poise and just plain guts he showed against overwhelming odds."

As for McGovern, Nixon had these words in a meeting about the campaign after the conventions: "When you've got a fellow, you've got a fellow who is under attack like this, who has fallen on his ass a few times, what you do is to kick him again. I mean, you have to keep whacking, whacking, and whacking."

CHAPTER 35

November 7, 1972

T
HIS IS MY LAST CAMPAIGN," the President told everyone he saw after the conventions. But there was no point in campaigning. George McGovern was destroying himself. The bottom line, according to polls, was that even people who agreed with the Democrat on specific issues questioned his qualifications—and even his patriotism. The economy was relatively good, the numbers were a lot better than they had been before Nixon was elected in 1968. There was stalemate on the ground in Vietnam. If the North Vietnamese had ever really thought their spring offensive might lead them right into Saigon and victory, then they had failed. United States bombers flew every day, blasting the North again and again and again, with minimal risk to American men. The biggest news in the world was the murder of nine Israeli athletes by an Arab commando squad at the Olympic Games in Munich.

And campaign money was rolling in so fast there was hardly time to count it and tell the President. On September 13, he read stories in *The New York Times* and *The Washington Post* about six-figure donations from a Texas oilman and developer named W. T. Duncan and from Mr. and Mrs. Ray Kroc, the owners of the McDonald's hamburger chain, and he told Haldeman: "I noticed the story in the *Post* this morning talking about three big Nixon contributors, none of whom I knew."

One rule of the non-campaign was that the President would do no one-on-one interviews until after the election. He made two exceptions, both embargoed until after election day. One was with Garnett D. Horner of the *Washington Star,* a reporter he had known since the 1950s. The other was with Theodore H. White, author of the *Making of the President* books, which White had begun with the Nixon-Kennedy race of 1960. White's pitch this time, in a letter to Nixon, one he kept in his desk, was hard to resist: "The story, as I see it, is fascinating. . . . Sometime in Richard Nixon's first administration we reached the end of the post-war world and began to approach a new world whose name and dimensions I cannot yet describe. And it is even more difficult to describe the planning and actions of a President, faced with a hostile majority in Congress and buffeted by the press, who could so deftly maneuver America to the confrontation with new realities. . . ."

Nixon told White that he planned to make no campaign appearances until the last three weeks of the campaign: "I'm not going into the states for the purpose of supporting Senate or House candidates, the way FDR did, or the way I did in 1970. . . . Part of our problem is that we have a lot of lousy candidates. The good ones will go up with me, the bad ones will go down."

Then, as if he were talking to himself, the President began a long monologue on his presidency. He spoke of his foreign policy triumphs, particularly China, then focused in on the changes at home in four years. Nixon, with his lack of interest in the specifics of legislation, presented himself, domestically, as essentially a candidate of order:

"We came in with 43 percent of the vote, with the establishment giving us nothing but a kick in the butt, and the press kicking the bejeezus out of us, the intellectuals against us. . . . Those four years weren't an easy period. When I came in, LBJ couldn't even leave the White House— he was right, he shouldn't have subjected himself to violence. But I can travel in all fifty states now. We started with the country in a hell of a shape. You've forgotten the days when 200,000 people marched on the White House. We've been fighting uphill on foreign policy. But domestic policy! It's been uphill all the way; we didn't have a mandate; we didn't have the Congress. Now we've got an opportunity we couldn't even dream of four years ago, but I don't see it as a revolutionary hundred days. We've go to look over our institutions and return them to old values. . . ."

Watergate did not come up in the interview. The most important new thing the public had learned was that investigators for the General Accounting Office, monitoring compliance of new campaign funding laws, had finally discovered that the twenty-five thousand dollars that ended up in Barker's Miami account had come not from a Republican but from a Humphrey man. That information was passed along to the

Justice Department, which the President and his men knew was already preparing to wrap up its investigation after the indictment of the five burglars plus Hunt and Liddy.

Nixon was confident enough now to talk about perhaps creating a "Warren Commission," chaired by retired Chief Justice Earl Warren, to investigate the investigation—to give the public confidence that the Justice Department's efforts had been exhaustive. He even brought in his old rival, Governor Nelson Rockefeller.

"Nelson, let me fill you in," he said on September 14. "You should know these things. This record, this distressing Watergate thing, as you probably know, as you have been told today, is one of those goddamned things that a bunch of kids—"

"Maybe, I'm better off not to know, Mr. President," said the governor, determined to proclaim ignorance when reporters asked. In fact, Rockefeller knew a great deal about what was happening in the White House. Kissinger briefed him regularly and vividly. The governor had his own theory about such doings: he thought the President was nuts. Rockefeller had been telling friends, seriously, for a couple of years about odd and dangerous behavior in the Oval Office. "People don't understand the strain Nixon is under," he would say. "The man is being pushed too far, beyond his capacity." But to Nixon face to face that day the governor said only that he thought the public was cynical about the story: "They know it's going on all the time."

In his diary, Nixon dictated: "I had a rather curious dream of speaking in some sort of a rally and going on a bit too long and Rockefeller standing up in the middle and taking over the microphone on an applause line. . . . It is a subconscious reaction. It is interesting."

On September 15, the federal grand jury announced the seven indictments for wiretapping and stealing documents. A Justice Department statement read: "We have absolutely no evidence that any others should be charged."

The President greatly enjoyed the coverage, particularly the fact that the burglars were telling reporters that they would never inform on superiors, and then would switch to little speeches of militant anticommunism. "Is the line pretty well set now on, when asked about the Watergate, as to what everybody says and does, to stonewall?" he asked Haldeman. "These Cubans. I saw that news summary and I thought I'd die. It's so funny."

"They sound very believable, the Cubans, don't they?" he continued.

"Totally believable," Haldeman answered. "I think they really believe it. I mean, that was their motivation. . . . They're afraid of

McGovern. They're afraid he'll sell out to the communists, which he will."

When John Dean came in later, the President greeted him by saying, "Well, you had quite a day today, didn't you? You got Watergate on the way, huh?"

"I think we can say 'well' at this point," Dean said. "The press is playing it just as we expect. . . . I think that I can say that fifty-four days from now"—the time until Election Day—"that not a thing will come crashing down to our surprise."

"I want the most comprehensive notes on all those that tried to do us in," the President told Dean. "They are asking for it and they are going to get it. . . . We have not used the power in the first four years, as you know. . . . but things are going to change now."

"That's an exciting prospect," Dean said.

In South Vietnam that day, Thieu's marines recaptured Quang Tri City—or what was left of it. What had been a city of thirty-five thousand was obliterated after four months of communist occupation and heavy American bombing. Kissinger was in Paris for another secret meeting with Le Duc Tho and the North Vietnamese negotiators. He returned to Washington the next day to report to the President and then to the public in a news conference. But the reports were quite different. The public report, as recorded by *The New York Times*:

KISSINGER HINTS
LITTLE PROGRESS
AT PARIS SESSION

What Kissinger told Nixon was that he was certain the North Vietnamese were anxious to settle because they thought they could get a better deal now than they could after the President was reelected. Haldeman recorded Kissinger's account, beginning with Le Duc Tho saying, "Do you really want to bring this to an end now?"

"Yes," Kissinger said.

"Okay," said the chief Vietnamese negotiator, coming around the table to shake hands. "Should we do it by October 15?"

"That would be fine."

It was not so fine with President Nixon, nor with President Thieu of South Vietnam. After a meeting with Nixon, Alexander Haig had cabled Kissinger the day before the September 15 meeting: "The President stated that the NSC"—meaning Kissinger—"does not seem to understand that the American people are no longer interested in a solution based on compromise, favor continued bombing and want to see the

United States prevail after all these years. . . . I emphasize to you his wish that the record you establish tomorrow in your discussions be a tough one which in a public sense would appeal to the Hawk and not the Dove. . . ."

Nixon was reading polls—voters favored continued heavy bombing by 55 percent to 32, according to Harris—and the President seemed tempted more than a little by the idea of waiting until after the election and then, mandate in hand, bombarding the North Vietnamese until they settled for tougher terms. Thieu was worried that Kissinger was secretly bargaining away South Vietnamese objections to coalition government in the south after the shooting stopped, as the Americans had bargained away provisions the year before that no North Vietnamese troops would remain in the south after a cease-fire. Thieu had asked Kissinger in August whether the United States would trade leaving North Vietnamese troops in the south for the release of American prisoners of war. Kissinger said he doubted the North Vietnamese would do that. But finally he said yes.

Now Thieu's last stand was demanding assurance that the United States would continue to oppose any kind of commission that would give North Vietnam a share of governing power in South Vietnam. In fact, Kissinger had already moved in that direction in Paris, proposing a "Committee of National Reconciliation," with representation from Saigon, Hanoi, and the Vietcong, that would oversee elections in which the communists could participate. The North Vietnamese concession, which led to the Kissinger–Le Duc Tho handshake, was finally giving up on their demand that the United States remove Thieu from office. Now Kissinger's idea was that Thieu and his government would be left with a fighting chance and American equipment. But Thieu sensed that Kissinger, and perhaps Nixon, too, now saw the Saigon government as the last obstacle to peace or at least to a cease-fire. And he was right, at least about Kissinger, who now used the same word to describe the two Vietnamese, Le Duc Tho, the enemy, and Thieu, the ally: "Insolent."

On September 26 and 27, Kissinger and Le Duc Tho met outside Paris in the village of Gif-sur-Yvette and quickly reached substantial agreement on a settlement of military issues, including a cease-fire and release of prisoners. After talking to Kissinger, Nixon dispatched Haig to Saigon to try to persuade Thieu to accept a political settlement, which would not force him to resign but would create the Committee of National Reconciliation. That mission failed. Thieu was in tears. He objected to almost every provision of the Kissinger–Le Duc Tho agreements, telling Haig that if the Americans went forward, "We shall be obliged to clarify and defend publicly our views on this subject."

The President answered Thieu in a personal letter, delivered by Ambassador Ellsworth Bunker, making both promises and threats:

> There is no doubt that there are serious disagreements between us, but it should be clearly understood that these disagreements are tactical in character and involve no basic difference as to the objectives we both seek—the preservation of a non-communist structure in South Viet-Nam. . . . I give you my firm assurance that there will be no settlement arrived at, the provisions of which have not been discussed personally with you well beforehand. This applies specifically to the next round of talks in Paris. In these talks, Dr. Kissinger will explore what concrete security guarantees the other side is willing to give us as the basis for further discussions on the political point which might be undertaken following consultations with you. In this context I would urge you to take every measure to avoid the development of an atmosphere which could lead to events similar to those which we abhorred in 1963. . . .

What happened in 1963—on November 2, 1963—was the assassination of South Vietnamese president Ngo Dinh Diem by his own officers during a military coup approved by President John F. Kennedy. General Nguyen Van Thieu had been one of the South Vietnamese officers the Americans encouraged to overthrow Diem—an event that triggered a series of coups and counter-coups that eventually led to Thieu's ascension to power in 1967.

The mood at Gif-sur-Yvette was different when Kissinger returned there on October 8. The American began the session by remarking about passing a racetrack on the way out from Paris, then went on to say that he had heard that on one French track the crowd lost sight of the race for a few moments when the horses were hidden by a stand of trees. "You can't see them," he said, "and I'm told that's where the jockeys decide who will win."

"Are we making a race to peace or to war?" Le Duc Tho responded.

"To peace," Kissinger said. "And we're behind the trees!"

Late that afternoon, Le Duc Tho said it would take many weeks to negotiate all the details that had piled up during years of talks. He suggested that the United States and North Vietnam could sign an agreement on the specific military issues between them—withdrawal schedules, prisoners, resupply of troops and allies—and consider only main principles on the political issues between the two Vietnams. Then he handed

Kissinger a draft agreement, saying, with only some exaggeration, that it really was a restatement of American positions over the past four years. There was no mention of ousting the Thieu government as a prerequisite for a cease-fire. The minute they were outside alone, Kissinger and his personal assistant, Winston Lord, shook hands and whispered, "We've done it."

That night Kissinger cabled Haldeman: "Tell the President that there has been some definite progress at today's first session and that he can harbor some confidence the outcome will be positive. . . ."

He cabled Ambassador Bunker in Saigon at the same time: "The other side may surface a cease-fire proposal during these meetings. . . . essential that Thieu instruct his commanders to move promptly and seize the maximum amount of critical territory."

Nixon did not respond to the cable from Paris. And he had no one to talk to about the war. Only a few men in the White House—Kissinger, Haig, and National Security Council staffers—had knowledge of what was actually happening in Paris, in Saigon, and in Hanoi. All those men were in Gif-sur-Yvette. The President had long since cut himself off from established experts in the departments of State and Defense and he was alone. By choice. But he was often diplomatically blind. Haig was becoming the man the President trusted most on foreign policy. The ambitious young general had become the most important double agent in a White House filled with them—and Kissinger had brought him to France to keep an eye on him.

Kissinger knew that Haig sided with the President in thinking that a more orderly and more favorable Vietnam settlement could be negotiated after the election, and that such an agreement before the election might further alienate Republican conservatives who were still in ideological shock over the trips to Peking and Moscow. But there was something else Kissinger knew: The agreement he was negotiating—alone, for all practical purposes—would have a life of its own. The President would not have control of the situation once the North Vietnamese had the option of releasing the agreements made at Gif-sur-Yvette.

The next night's cable from Kissinger dramatized the President's isolation. Kissinger wrote only: "The negotiations during this round have been so complex and sensitive that we have been unable to report their content in detail. . . . We know exactly what we are doing, and just as we have not let you down in the past, we will not do so now. Pending our return and my direct report to you it is imperative that nothing be said in reply to McGovern or in any other context bearing on the current talks."

Then he added a postscript for Haldeman, who saw those messages first, a plea for the chief of staff to keep the President calm: "Please hold everything steady there. I recognize the uncertainties there but excessive nervousness can only jeopardize the outcome here."

The next day, October 10, the Kissinger cable said: "We have decided to stay one more day in expectation that we may score a major breakthrough."

Again there was no response from the President.

That night Senator McGovern made his principal campaign speech on national television, buying a half hour of prime time on CBS to reach an estimated twenty million Americans. On Inauguration Day, he said, he would halt the bombing of North Vietnam and withdraw all military and political support from South Vietnam. Press reaction was not encouraging. James Reston of *The New York Times* wrote: "He went so far in meeting Hanoi's war aims that he may actually have lost more support by his TV speech than he gained." Columnist Joseph Kraft added: "Apparently without knowing it, he is prepared to accept worse terms than the other side is offering."

Also on October 10, the *Washington Post* team of Woodward and Bernstein came up with their first big page-one story since the indictments of the Watergate burglars. They had discovered Donald Segretti and they reported that the young lawyer from Los Angeles had been in charge of recruiting fifty young operatives who went around the country trying to disrupt the lives and campaigns of Democrats. His "pranksters," as he called them, were paid from the funds held by Kalmbach. They waved embarrassing signs—one was, "If you like Hitler, you'll just love Wallace. VOTE FOR MUSKIE"—distributed bogus leaflets and schedules, called reporters with fabricated rumors, and cranked out phony letters about sex and such under phony Democratic Party letterheads, throwing lies to the winds to see what happened. Their most famous trick was hiring a plane to fly over Miami Beach during the Democratic National Convention trailing a banner that read "PEACE POT PROMISCUITY—VOTE MCGOVERN."

"Segretti, just so you know, is incommunicado," Haldeman told the President after the story appeared. "But he calls John Dean from a public phone and calls on a line that's not traceable every day around noon. He'll do anything. I'm told he was supposedly the ideal guy for this kind of thing. He's a guy that loves this sort of college prank politics. Chapin had known him in campus politics at SC"—the appointments secretary and Segretti were friends at the University of Southern California—". . . They recruited him."

Nixon had an idea: Segretti should sue the *Post.* "I know he'll lose it, but good God, in the public mind it creates an impression that they lied . . . ," said the President. "Right, Bob? You see the point? Sue the sons of bitches."

John Connally called to say the White House should not deny the story: "I'd have Clark MacGregor or Bob Dole say, sure, what the fuck's wrong with this? Sure, Segretti, we hired him. You bet we hired him, and we hired him to go and case the rallies of all these people—"

"See how they operate," Nixon interrupted. Then he began talking about how ordinary he thought dirty politics were. "Edgar Hoover told Mitchell that our plane was bugged for the last two weeks of the campaign. Johnson had it bugged. He ordered it bugged. And so was Humphrey's, I think. I'm not sure about Humphrey's. I know about ours. But the reason he says he had it bugged is because he had his Vietnam plans in there and he had to have information as to what we were going to say about Vietnam. . . . Johnson knew every conversation. And you know where it was bugged? In my compartment. So every conversation I had, for two weeks Johnson had it."

"They asked me at the press conference this morning if this went on during the Johnson administration," Connally replied. "I said, 'I don't know; I wasn't part of the Johnson administration; I was in Texas, being Governor of Texas.' But I said, 'I would not want to give that or any other administration in my lifetime any seal of purity.' "

Later, Haldeman came in to tell Nixon that his men had discovered that most of the Watergate leaks were coming from the FBI. "It's pretty high up," he said, and named the deputy director. "Mark Felt."

"Now why the hell would he do that?" the President asked.

"You can't say anything about this, because it will screw up our source. . . . Mitchell is the only one that knows this and he feels very strongly that we better not do anything because . . . if we move on him, he'll go out and unload everything. He knows everything that's to be known in the FBI. He has access to absolutely everything."

"What would you do with Felt?" Nixon said.

"Well, I asked Dean. . . . He says you can't prosecute him, that he hasn't committed any crime. Dean's concerned if you let him know now he'll go out and go on network television. . . . I think he wants to be in the top spot."

"That's a hell of a way for him to get to the top," Nixon said. ". . . Is he a Catholic?"

"Jewish," Haldeman answered.

"Christ," said the President. "Put a Jew in there? . . . What's the conveyor belt for Felt?"

"The *Post*."

"It could be the Jewish thing," said Nixon. "I don't know. It's always a possibility."

• • •

ON OCTOBER 11, the fourth day of long meetings between Kissinger and Le Duc Tho, the negotiators concluded a working draft of the new communist proposals. Kissinger cabled home with a new level of condescension: "Have just completed extremely long session here. It is essential that I have ample time with the President tomorrow for thorough review of situation since careful game plan is now required."

Kissinger prevailed. He arrived back in Washington just before 6 P.M. on October 12 and, with Haig, went directly to EOB 175, where the President was talking to Colson. Kissinger thought Colson was nothing but a political thug and would not speak until he left. When the door closed, Kissinger said: "Well, Mr. President, it looks like we've got three out of three!"—the opening to China, the beginning of détente with the Soviets, and peace in Vietnam.

Kissinger pulled out his red "Eyes Only" file and began by telling the President that the deal was far better than they ever expected. Nixon seemed noncommittal as he heard the proposals for the first time: a cease-fire in place followed in sixty days by a complete withdrawal of United States troops and exchange of prisoners of war; closing of border sanctuaries in Laos and Cambodia; and a "National Council of Reconciliation and Concord," with representation from the government in Saigon, the Vietcong, and neutrals, which would formulate the future of the country by unanimous consent—meaning Thieu had a veto. There would also be unspecified American aid to rebuild the country, which Nixon believed would give the United States future leverage in Vietnamese affairs.

The President's anger faded as he listened. This was peace with honor, he thought, though several times he interrupted to say there were going to be problems with Thieu. He also expected that North Vietnam would violate the accords from day one. But that was no longer the point. Getting out without disaster or more humiliation was the point. He ordered up steaks from the White House mess, then called his valet, Manolo Sanchez, and told him to bring over the best wine in the house, a 1957 Lafite-Rothschild—this time with no napkin hiding the label.

The next morning, Nixon ordered a reduction of bombing of North Vietnam, down to two hundred sorties a day—since May 8 the Americans had dropped 150,000 tons of bombs on North Vietnam—and sent a message to Paris, where Winston Lord had stayed to work on the writing of the settlement: "The President accepts the basic draft of 'An Agreement on Ending The War and Restoring Peace in Vietnam' except for some technical issues to be discussed between Minister Xuan Thuy and Dr. Kissinger on October 17. . . ."

Nixon worked out a peace schedule. Kissinger would go to

Saigon and then Hanoi, and on October 26, Nixon in Washington and Pham Van Dong in Hanoi would announce the end of the American war. The peace agreement would then be signed in Paris on October 31 by the United States and North Vietnam and by the South Vietnamese government and the National Liberation Front (the Vietcong).

After the Paris session on October 17, Kissinger flew to Saigon for three days of meetings with Thieu. By now, the world press knew something was happening. *The New York Times* lead headline of October 18, with a Washington dateline, was:

KISSINGER FLYING
TO SOUTH VIETNAM
AFTER PARIS TALKS

Washington Signs Indicate
Cease-Fire Negotiations
Are at Critical Point

Kissinger arrived at the Presidential Palace in Saigon at the designated hour, 10 A.M., on October 19. He was kept waiting for fifteen minutes, seething, as reporters from around the world watched. In Thieu's office, he presented the President of the Republic of Vietnam with a letter from the President of the United States:

> As you know, throughout the four years of my Administration the United States has stood firmly behind your Government and its people in our support for their valiant struggle to resist aggression and preserve their right to determine their own political future. . . .
>
> Until very recently the North Vietnamese negotiators have held firmly to their long established position that any settlement would have to include your resignation and the dismantlement of the Government of the Republic of Vietnam and its institutions. . . . It now seems, however, that the combination of the perseverance and heroism of your Government and its fighting forces, the measures taken by the United States on the 8th of May, 1972, and our firmness at the conference table have caused a fundamental shift in Hanoi. . . . We and Hanoi's negotiators have reached essential agreement on a text which provides for a cessation of hostilities. . . .

The most important sentences read:

I do, however, want you to know that I believe we have no reasonable alternative but to accept this agreement. It represents major movement by the other side, and it is my firm conviction that its implementation will leave you and your people with the ability to defend yourselves and decide the political destiny of South Vietnam."

In longhand, under his signature, Nixon added: "Dr. Kissinger's comments have my total backing."

Kissinger spent thirty minutes explaining the agreement and only then handed the text, in English, to President Thieu. Alone with his own people, Thieu said, in Vietnamese, "I wanted to punch him in the mouth." He considered the agreement a betrayal, a document of surrender. The Vietnamese asked for a copy of the agreement in their own language, and it was delivered by the Americans that evening. Thieu did not tell the Americans that he already knew the essentials of the agreement. Two days before, he had read a ten-page summary of the final document and plan for post-cease-fire action captured in a Vietcong bunker south of Da Nang. The local political commissar in a remote village knew the details before the President of South Vietnam. The "General Instructions for a Cease-Fire," included a critical fact that Kissinger had still not admitted to Thieu: there was no mention of withdrawal by the 140,000 North Vietnamese troops in South Vietnam. In fact, much of the captured document was detailed plans to seize more territory before the cease-fire went into effect.

The next day's meeting was scheduled for 9 A.M. The Americans were told to stand by, which they did for five hours. At 2 P.M., Thieu began: "We have made a cursory analysis and we would like to ask for a few points of clarification and then have more time to study the text in English and Vietnamese. . . . By the way, what are these *three* 'Indochinese states' that are referred to?"

The phrase meant Laos, Cambodia, and a single Vietnam—it appeared three times in the English text—although the war had been fought to preserve two Vietnams.

"Ah," said Kissinger. "That must be a typographical error."

The American could not, of course, understand the Vietnamese text—North Vietnamese interpreters and translators were used at Gif-sur-Yvette. But the South Vietnamese were shaken by what they read in their own language. In Vietnamese, they said, what Kissinger said meant "committee" or "council" actually meant "government structure," the Americans were called "pirates," and the South Vietnamese were called "vassals." The situation, at least from the perspective of Thieu's palace, got even worse that day when the allies saw the text of an interview with Pham Van Dong in Hanoi. Dong had invited an American journalist, Arnaud de Borchgrave of *Newsweek,* then told him that after the Americans left there would be two administrations and two armies in the south.

Thieu read the situation the same way. He told Kissinger a story about a man catching a thief in his bedroom. He calls the police and they come, but they cannot get the thief out of the house. The police chief puts his gun back in its holster and says, "He's not such a bad guy. Why don't you try to learn to live with him? After a while he may get homesick and go back to his own family." Or, Thieu said, "He might rape your wife."

In Washington, the President was talking to Haig and General William Westmoreland, who were both telling him that Thieu was going to reject the Paris agreements. On October 20, according to Haig's meeting notes, Westmoreland said: "Any inference that this was an imposed settlement could prove fatal to Thieu's own political base. . . ." In fact, the leader described by Westmoreland might have sounded familiar to Nixon: "An extremely suspicious man who was devious, capable of sharp turns, and had a conspiratorial outlook that had enabled him to survive through many difficult years. It was essential that the United States work patiently with Thieu and recognize the difficulty that relinquishment of his territory would pose. . . . the plan was not adequate to the realities of the situation."

"President Nixon emphasized that he had no intention of being stampeded," Haig wrote. The President cabled Kissinger: "We must have Thieu as a willing partner in making any agreement. It cannot be a shotgun marriage."

But the President did not know the tenor and tension of the Kissinger-Thieu sessions. American and communist sources in Vietnam were continuing to hint that the war was in its final days. By October 21, after Kissinger had met with Thieu for more than eight hours over two days, a French newspaper, *France Soir,* reported rumors that a cease-fire would be announced within ten days. The *New York Times* report of that paragraph of news created "a peace rally" on Wall Street, with the Dow-Jones industrial average jumping 10.09 points to close at 942.81.

By the next day, October 22, dozens of news outlets around the world were printing and broadcasting reports from Hanoi that a cease-fire was imminent. Most of those stories got the details wrong, usually saying that the settlement involved a withdrawal of North Vietnamese troops from South Vietnam and a new coalition government in Saigon. The President, who was at Camp David, telephoned Haldeman to order a quick poll on whether voters expected a settlement before election day—and what they wanted in a settlement. Then he went back to watching the seventh game of the World Series between the Oakland Athletics and the Cincinnati Reds on television, as he read the memos of the day. One was an endorsement report from Herb Klein: 213 newspapers so far had published editorials supporting Nixon's reelection, to 12 for McGovern—one of the 12 was *The New York Times*.

From Saigon, Kissinger fought back against Haig and Westmoreland, sending cables to the President: "We have obtained concessions that nobody thought were possible last month, or for that matter last week. . . . Washington must understand that this is not a Sunday school picnic. We are dealing with fanatics who have been fighting for twenty-five years. . . . We cannot be sure how long they will be willing to settle on the terms that are now within our grasp."

Now the President had his shotgun in hand. Kissinger arranged for a telegram to be delivered to the palace while he was meeting with Thieu that day. "Mr. President," Kissinger said, "may I read you the telegram from President Nixon?"

Thieu nodded and Kissinger began to read: "Were you to find the agreement to be unacceptable at this point and the other side were to reveal the extraordinary limits to which it has gone in meeting demands put upon them, it is my judgment that your decision would have the most serious effects upon my ability to continue to provide support for you and for the government of South Vietnam."

Thieu was alone, but he was not yielding. He told Bunker and Kissinger: "I do not appreciate the fact that your people are going around town telling everybody that I signed. I have not signed anything. I do not object to peace, but I have not gotten any satisfactory answers from you and I am not going to sign."

Kissinger replied: "We have fought for four years, have mortgaged our whole foreign policy to the defense of one country. . . . You're the last obstacle to peace." Kissinger seemed to be in a rage. "If you do not sign, we're going to go on our own."

Kissinger threatened: "I'm not going to come back to South Vietnam." Thieu, relatively fluent in English, countered: "Why? Are you rushing to get the Nobel Prize?"

"Is that your final position, not to sign, Mr. President?" Bunker asked.

"Yes, that is my final position. I will not sign and I would like you to convey my position to Mr. Nixon. Please go back to Washington and tell President Nixon I need answers."

What Kissinger told Nixon, in two cables that night, was: "Thieu has just rejected the entire plan or any modification of it. He insists that any settlement must contain absolute guarantees of the DMZ, total withdrawal of all North Vietnamese forces, and total self-determination of South Vietnam. . . . It is hard to exaggerate the toughness of Thieu's position. . . . His demands verge on insanity."

Kissinger was scheduled to leave the next day, October 23, but he asked Thieu for another meeting in the morning.

"What for?" Thieu asked.

"The press still thinks we have a solution at hand, so let us have a short meeting and make sure that the consultation between allies is taking place."

"Well, if that is of some help to you, fine, we'll have a short meeting tomorrow, five minutes," said Thieu. In those minutes Kissinger said: "If we continue our confrontation, you will win victories, but we will both lose in the end. It is a fact that in the United States all the press, the media, and the intellectuals have a vested interest in our defeat. If I have seemed impatient in the last days it is because I saw opportunity slipping away. This is why I leave with such a sense of tragedy."

Before he left Saigon, Kissinger sent a message, routed through Washington and Paris, to Pham Van Dong in Hanoi: "Unfortunately the difficulties in Saigon have proved somewhat more complex than originally anticipated. Some of them concern matters which the U.S. side is honor-bound to put before the Democratic Republic of Vietnam." He signed the message "President Nixon." In fact, the President never saw it. He was campaigning with Governor Rockefeller in New York. The message also said that the President was calling Kissinger home from Saigon for consultations and asked for another meeting in France to discuss changing the agreement. A second message, again signed in Nixon's name, offered to suspend bombing of the North if there was a final meeting. The answer from the North Vietnamese was no; their cables said they expected Kissinger in Hanoi on schedule.

As Kissinger arrived at Tan Son Nhut Airport outside Saigon for the journey home, he saw reporters and photographers being kept behind a barrier and walked over to them before boarding his plane. "Was it a productive trip?" one asked.

"Yes," Kissinger replied. "It always is when I come here."

ON OCTOBER 24, the day after Kissinger returned to Washington, President Thieu went on television and radio and spoke for two hours, saying that he believed a cease-fire was near. He did not disclose the terms of the Gif-sur-Yvette agreement, saying only that his government would never accept a plan that left North Vietnamese troops below the DMZ. That was the lead story of the next day's *New York Times* under a four-column headline:

THIEU ASSAILS PEACE-PLAN TERMS,
ASKS GUARANTEE, HANOI PULLOUT
U.S. LIMITS NORTH VIETNAM RAIDS

The *Washington Post* headline that morning on the top of page one was:

Testimony Ties
Top Nixon Aide
To Secret Fund

The story, by Woodward and Bernstein, reported that Hugh Sloan, CREEP's treasurer, had told the District of Columbia grand jury that Haldeman controlled a secret White House fund of more than seven hundred thousand dollars in cash, which was being used to pay the bills for Liddy, Hunt, and their burglars. The story was wrong. Haldeman did control most everything in the White House, using the President's name just as Kissinger was doing in Paris and Saigon, but Sloan had never mentioned the chief of staff in his testimony. Nixon, talking with Colson in EOB 175, said the *Post*'s mistake might give his men a chance to retaliate, perhaps by moving to deny license renewals for television stations owned by the newspaper. "We're going to screw them. . . . They don't really realize how rough I can play. I've been such a nice guy around here a lot of times. . . . But when I start, I will kill them. They should give some thought to taking on the guy that went into Cambodia and Laos, ran the Cambodian bombing campaign. What the hell do they think they're doing in there?"

The next day *The New York Times,* still downplaying Watergate, had four Vietnam stories arrayed under a five-column headline:

U.S. IS SAID TO AGREE WITH HANOI
ON FRAMEWORK OF A CEASE-FIRE;
EXPECTS SAIGON TO ACCEPT SOON

The lead story by Flora Lewis, attributed to French sources and readings of the agreement in three languages—Vietnamese, French, and English—on Radio Hanoi, brought the public up to date on what Kissinger had been doing behind closed doors the past few weeks. The point of the broadcasts was to demand that the settlement be signed, as scheduled, on October 31. The President and his national security adviser met in the Oval Office at 7 A.M. and Nixon decided to break his own "Kissinger rule"—the rule that prohibited Kissinger from going on television because of his German accent. Three hours later, at 10 A.M. on October 26, the national security adviser held his first televised news conference.

"We have now heard from both Vietnams," Kissinger began, "and it is obvious that a war that has been raging for ten years is drawing to a conclusion. . . . We believe that peace is at hand."

The first question was why the administration could not have made this deal in 1969. Kissinger answered, "There was no possibility of achieving this agreement four years ago because the other side consistently refused to discuss the separation of the political and military issues, because it always insisted that it had to settle the political issues with us, and that we had to predetermine the future of South Vietnam in a negotiation with North Vietnam."

"PEACE IS AT HAND," was instant shorthand, heard 'round the country. James Reston praised Kissinger in a column titled "The End of the Tunnel." The headline on *Newsweek*'s cover was "Good-Bye Vietnam" and a story inside carried the headline "How Kissinger Did It." Within days, though, Senator McGovern was calling the whole thing a fraud, "a cruel political deception." On November 4, the Democratic presidential candidate added: "There has been no 'major breakthrough' for peace as Mr. Nixon also pretended. . . . Instead there has been a fatal breakdown on the central issues and now this chance for an agreement is gone." The next day he said: "I'm going to give you one more warning. If Mr. Nixon is elected on Tuesday, we may very well have four more years of war in Southeast Asia. . . . He's going to stay there. He's going to keep our troops there. He's going to keep the bombers flying. He's going to confine the prisoners to their cells in Hanoi for whatever time it takes for him to keep his friend General Thieu in office."

Nixon ignored him. He was giving what amounted to a victory speech to his Cabinet and staff on October 29, coming back from his last day of campaigning, talking about seeing a family hold up a sign the day before in Ohio: "NO AMNESTY. WE LOST OUR SON IN VIETNAM." He had stopped the motorcade to talk to them, getting more sentimental as he talked about the man's calloused hands and his wife's red hands. "She couldn't have all those fancy things that you read about in *Vogue* and the rest as to how to make your hands pretty and lovely. . . . My mother's hands were not pretty, but I always thought they were beautiful because I knew how much she did and how hard she worked." He got back on track then and ended: "In these next four years, we are going to try to make it the best four years in American history."

Canceling a weekend of campaign work, the President flew to San

Clemente on November 4; he would cast his own vote there. On Tuesday, November 7, he voted, clumsily dropping his ballot inside the booth, then bending down under the voting machine curtain to retrieve it. A dozen photographers, there for the ritual, flashed away as Ron Ziegler cried: "Stop that! Stop that! No pictures!" Then the President flew back to Washington, spending some time on the plane with Haldeman, who said that perhaps he and Ehrlichman should resign and Kissinger should, too, when Vietnam was settled. That way he could have a new start for his second term, putting Watergate, Vietnam, and charges of isolation behind him. The President said no to that. But he told Haldeman to collect resignations from all Cabinet members and staff, because he intended to get rid of many of them. That was how he would start anew.

Nixon arrived at the White House at 6 P.M., cheered by staff members on the lawn as his helicopter landed. He ate dinner with his wife and his daughters and their husbands, then went alone to the Lincoln sitting room to wait for results. He put the sound track from "Victory at Sea," a documentary film series about World War II, onto a record player and turned the volume up.

President Nixon carried forty-nine of the fifty states, winning 60.7 percent of the popular vote—47,169,841 votes to 29,172,767 for McGovern. The margin was the greatest in American history. He swept the South, winning 79 percent of the vote in Mississippi; he became the first Republican ever to win a majority of Catholic voters; he won half the youth vote. He won more than 35 percent of Democratic voters, even as Republicans lost two seats in the Senate, increasing the Democratic margin to 57 to 43. His party gained twelve House seats, reducing the Democratic margin there to 243 to 192. Nixon stayed up until 4 A.M., watching returns, feeling the strange melancholy he always did in victory.

He was in the office early the next morning, November 8. The news summary on his desk began with a quote from John Chancellor, the *NBC Nightly News* anchorman: "This is the most spectacular landslide election in the history of United States politics." The summary continued with five pages of similar copy, with newspapers and television across the country praising the man and his record. At the bottom of the last page, the President, alone in his office, wrote:

> The opposition line will be:
>
> 1. McG's mistakes lost it and not his views and not RN's strength,
>
> 2. The low vote proves no one liked either candidate,
>
> 3. RN let down his party.

At eleven o'clock that morning, Nixon met with his staff in the Roosevelt Room. To many in the room he seemed oddly cool and quietly angry as he thanked them all for their loyalty, then said something few of them understood. He said he had been reading Robert Blake's *Disraeli* and was struck by his description a century ago of William Gladstone's ministers as "exhausted volcanoes"—then mumbled something about embers that once shot sparks into the sky.

"I believe men exhaust themselves in government without realizing it," the President said. "You are my first team, but today we start fresh for the next four years. We need new blood, fresh ideas. Change is important. . . . Bob, you take over."

Nixon left then, turning the meeting over to Haldeman. The men and women of the White House stood to applaud his exit, then sat down. The chief explained what Nixon's words meant: a reorganization of the administration. He told them that they were expected to deliver letters of resignation before the end of the day, then he passed out photocopied forms requiring them to list all official documents in their possession. "These must be in by November 10," he said, "This should accompany your pro forma letter of resignation to be effective at the pleasure of the President." They were stunned. Speechless. Were they being fired? Haldeman said they would know within a month whether or not they could remain. At noon, the same drama was played out with the entire Cabinet, with Haldeman again passing out the forms.

Back in the Oval Office, Nixon told Haldeman that he should expect criticism from Republicans around the country complaining that so many senators and congressmen ran far behind the President because that President had done so little for local parties and candidates. "Cut that off," Nixon said. "Make sure that we start pissing on the party before they begin pissing on me. Blame bad candidates and sloppy organization."

At 4 P.M., after less than a day in Washington, the President took off for Key Biscayne.

CHAPTER 36

December 19, 1972

On the victory flight to Florida, Nixon told Haldeman that he had heard that eighty of eighty-nine members of the White House press corps had voted for McGovern. Wherever he got that number, what he wanted now was to get out the story he said was being suppressed: that this was the dirtiest campaign in history—by McGovern.

"Freeze them," he said, dictating lists of offenses by *Time* and *Newsweek, The New York Times* and *The Washington Post,* and CBS News. Jack Anderson, too, who was running columns about how much government money had been spent on Nixon's San Clemente property. Then Nixon had a brainstorm, telling Haldeman to have Ehrlichman make arrangements to give the house and grounds to the government: "Do it quick! Rub their noses in it!"

"That's crazy," Ehrlichman said later. "That house is the only major asset he has."

As the President flew south, the *Washington Star* came out with the Garnett Horner interview, recorded on November 5, quoting Nixon as saying his reelection marked the end of the whole area of permissiveness: "We have passed through a very great spiritual crisis in this country. Vietnam was only part of the problem and in many cases was only an excuse rather than a reason. . . . The average American is just like the child in the family. You give him some responsibility and he is going to amount to something.... . Pamper him and cater to him too much, you are going to make him soft, spoiled and eventually a very weak individual."

On November 12, the President flew to Washington, stayed a day, and then retreated to Camp David—his 117th visit since he took office. He intended to stay there for as long as it took to make a revolution. Congress and the public had ignored the New American Revolution he had declared in his 1971 State of the Union address—except for revenue sharing. Now, he wanted to try the same thing again with executive orders, budget manipulation, and personnel purges. He wanted to seize control of the government he believed was filled with time-serving incompetents and secret enemies. He was convinced that his orders were being ignored or subverted by bureaucrats in the State and Defense Departments, by Justice Department lawyers, by appointees at HEW, by the FBI and the IRS, by liberal numbers collectors in the Bureau of Labor Statistics.

He intended to reorganize and reduce the size of the executive branch of the government and bring it under his own direct control. That was the point of demanding letters of resignation on the day after the election. He intended to personally choose general counsels, public affairs directors and spokesmen, personnel directors, legislative liaisons, and the chief administrative executives of every agency.

The reorganization plan went back to April 24, when Nixon ordered Haldeman to distribute an action memo to a few staffers: "We should start immediate contingency planning for post-November staffing on the basis of resignations of all present holders of Cabinet and top agency posts. For restaffing, we should start on the basis of bringing in people of total loyalty. . . . we should look for people with complete selflessness who don't need to be babied. . . . The point here will be to develop the building of the new establishment." Then in September he had told Haldeman and Enrlichman: "You've got to do it fast. . . . after the first of the year it's too late. You've got to do it right after the election. You've got one week, and that's the time to get all those resignations in and say, 'Look you're out, you're out, you're finished, you're done, done, finished.' Knock them the hell out of there."

During the campaign, Ehrlichman and Roy Ash of Litton Industries had updated the forgotten 1971 paper reorganization of the executive branch. Under the plan, four Cabinet departments would continue to function separately: State, Defense, Justice, and the Treasury. But other departments would be merged into four "Super-Cabinet" positions—Economic Affairs, Human Resources, Natural Resources, and Community Development—whose secretaries would be counselors to the President working out of the White House, supervising new mixes of departments, agencies, commissions, and boards.

Ehrlichman, Haldeman, and two of Haldeman's assistants, Larry Higby and Todd Hullen, joined the President at Camp David. They were told that they would be there for several weeks. Their mission was to take the executive branch apart and put it back together as an extension of one man, Richard Nixon. "After Christmas, it will be too late," the President told them, then added: "No Harvard men, look for men who went to Villanova. . . . I want four Catholics in the Cabinet."

The President moved into Aspen Lodge without fanfare. Most people in the White House had no idea how long he intended to stay there. He just did not come back. The Watergate account was delegated to John Dean. As for Vietnam, Haig had been dispatched to Saigon on the day after the election with a harsh letter from Nixon to Thieu, which read in part:

> Your continuing distortions of the agreement and attacks upon it were unfair and self-defeating. They have been disconcerting and highly embarrassing to me. . . . We are at the point where I need to know unambiguously whether you will join us in the effort General Haig is going to outline or whether we must contemplate alternative courses of action which I believe would be detrimental to the interest of both of our countries. . . . Our alliance and its achievements have been based on mutual trust. If you will give me continued trust, together we shall succeed.

The words were Kissinger's. Nixon thought it was too egocentric, but he let it be sent, telling Ehrlichman something Eisenhower had once told him: "A true executive can sign a poor letter without changing it."

Haig and Kissinger were summoned to Camp David on the afternoon of November 13. Haig reported: "We are now dealing with a razor's edge situation. . . ." He repeated something Thieu had told him: "You, General Haig, are a general. I am a general. Have you ever seen any peace accord in the history of the world in which the invaders had been permitted to stay in the territories they had invaded? Would you permit Russian troops to stay in the United States and say that you had reached a peace accord with Russia?"

Nixon's response, put together that day, was conciliatory: "You have my absolute assurance that if Hanoi fails to abide by the terms of this agreement it is my intention to take swift and severe retaliatory action."

There was a certain desperation on both sides of that exchange. Thieu, who disliked and distrusted Kissinger, was trying to deal one on one with Nixon. And Nixon had every reason to believe that funding for the war could be cut off anytime after the new Congress convened on January 3. No matter what the South Vietnamese president did or said, the American president had made up his mind to send Kissinger back to Paris and to go ahead with the settlement before the end of the year. After just thirty-five minutes, Nixon dismissed Kissinger and Haig, then resumed his reorganization talks with Haldeman and Ehrlichman.

The living room of Aspen Lodge became the White House in voluntary exile. An around-the-clock routine quickly developed. The President would sit for hours with Haldeman, or Haldeman and Ehrlichman, tossing around names, deciding who was in and who was out. Then Haldeman or one of his aides would order Cabinet members or staffers to come up one at a time, some to be fired, some to be promoted, many to be shifted around according to notes and little charts on yellow pads. When each man arrived, Haldeman or Ehrlichman told him what the President wanted; then he would be taken to Aspen Lodge.

It was a cool business in the Haldeman manner. Those asked to stay were required to check off and sign a five-page, fifteen-item list, which included these items:

> The essence of the new organization is the concept that Secretaries and Counselors to the President are the President's men and not the creatures of their departments. . . . not the Department's advocate to the President.

> No policy-making power resides in any Policy Council, Policy Group, Assistant to the President, Counselor to the President, or Cabinet Secretary, except as expressly delegated by the President.

> A Cabinet Secretary should not be encouraged to anticipate either free access or frequent consultation with the President. . . . Cabinet meetings will be rare. . . .

> Control over selection of personnel will be retained by the President and delegated from time to time to his assistants. . . .

> The Secretary agrees to submit to the appropriate Counselor all Congressional testimony and public statements for clearance. . . . Cabinet Secretaries and agency heads will be held accountable for unauthorized disclosure of information and documents.

Ehrlichman and Haldeman were most faithful scribes, filling hundreds of pages as the meetings in Aspen Lodge went on day after day behind the chain-link fences and spotlights on the perimeter of the two-hundred-acre mountain retreat. Their notes quoting the President and recording his orders included: "Not brains, we want loyalty"; "Foreign Service appointments—based first on loyalty then competence"; "Get good hacks in the departments as Secretaries under this system"; "Fewer people talk to the President—cut the staff"; "Eliminate the politicians, except George Bush. He'd do anything for the cause"; "Do quotas—balance—Too many Jews. Tell Richardson this in spades"; "Italian, Mexican—couldn't find any. Plenty of blacks—must keep some incompetent blacks"; "Publicize Ash and Shultz as Catholic"; "Genius needs to be recognized—e.g. HAK. Henry is a rag merchant, starts at 50 percent to get 25 percent. That's why he's so good with the Russians."

The retreat was not exactly a pleasant few weeks in the mountains. Haldeman was running Camp David in his own image. In late November, Pat Nixon and her daughter, Julie Eisenhower, were there for a couple of days. They walked in on the President and said they wanted to show him something. The three of them went to the dining lodge and they showed him the main dining room, which was empty. Then they took him to a small room with four tables, filled with drivers, helicopter pilots, cooks, doctors, and other support staff. Haldeman had made the main room off-limits to everyone except himself, Ehrlichman, and their assistants, so that no one could hear their conversations.

KISSINGER WAS IN PARIS AGAIN, driving out each day to meet with Le Duc Tho for long sessions at Gif-sur-Yvette. He had begun by handing the North Vietnamese a list of sixty-nine changes demanded by Thieu in the October 8 settlement. Since then the press of the world had discovered the house and it was ringed with ladders and scaffolds to take photos over the walls. The press had also discovered more about Kissinger, who had long since progressed from secrecy to celebrity. On the day he began the newest round of meetings with Le Duc Tho, November 20, *The New Republic* published an interview Kissinger had done on November 2 with Italian journalist Oriana Fallaci. The article's most memorable quote captured Kissinger's ego, America's imagination, and Nixon's fury. "I've always acted alone," he told Fallaci. "Americans admire that enormously. Americans admire the cowboy leading the caravan alone astride his horse, the cowboy entering the village or city alone on his horse. . . . This romantic, surprising character suits me, because being alone has always been part of my style."

At Camp David, the President delegated Haldeman to talk to Haig about whether it was time for Henry to go. Haldeman reported back: "Al said he understood perfectly, he was very concerned. Henry, in his view, is completely paranoid—is on an up-and-down cycle all the time, and he has bottomed out on his down cycle now and is coming up, but was in absolutely terrible shape in Paris. . . . he was in even worse shape in Saigon before that. And basically the screw-up was Henry's fault, in that he committed to final negotiation and settlement before he really should have, which really screwed things up with the North Vietnamese and the South Vietnamese. Al feels that Henry needs a very good, long vacation, and that we should be sure he gets it."

Talking about it with Haldeman and Ehrlichman after dinner together in Aspen Lodge, the President went over the number of times Kissinger had urged him to go on television and attack North Vietnamese negotiating tactics; then he looked into the fire and said: "There is no point in going on television to ask the American people to support more of the same in Vietnam. We can't rally them to support us when it's nothing new. Henry doesn't seem to understand that. Or does he? Maybe he just wants people to associate me with the failure."

Then the President told Haldeman that he should let Kissinger know that there was a complete taped record of their conversations, and that Nixon could protect himself against Kissinger's boasting and distortion. He changed his mind on that one within minutes, but did order Haldeman to send a curt "Eyes Only" back-channel cable to Paris on November 22: "The President is very disappointed in the lack of progress. . . . unless the other side shows the same willingness to be reasonable that we are showing, I am directing you to discontinue the talks and shall then have to resume military activity. . . . You should inform them they will find now, with the election behind us, he will take whatever action he considers necessary to protect the United States' interest."

Then the President called Haldeman back to add a softer line at the end: "Not a directive—for possible use with the North Vietnamese." Kissinger kept talking. And the next day, November 23, Nixon sent another cable to Paris: "We are in a public relations corner . . . ," meaning that Kissinger's "peace at hand" line left the American people believing the war was essentially over. Still, Nixon added that he was ready to begin even more massive bombings—there had been twelve B-52 runs over North Vietnam that day—if the talks broke off.

On November 24, the President, still at Camp David, sent a longer cable to Kissinger, with instructions to pass it on to Thieu. He said that he had consulted with senators who had consistently supported the war, both Republicans and Democrats, who said that they were prepared to end all military and economic aid to South Vietnam if the Saigon government was the last roadblock to peace. The message continued: "My evaluation is that the date of the cut-off would be February 1. . . . You must tell Thieu that I feel we have now reached the crossroads. . . . Either he trusts me and signs what I have determined is the best agreement we can get or we have to go it alone and end our own involvement in the war on the best terms we can get."

WITH THE THREAT MADE CLEAR, Nixon took off with his wife and daughters for a weekend of shopping in New York, returning to Camp David on Sunday.

On Monday afternoon, November 27, the President called together the reporters who had been camping out around the gates. They met in the helicopter hanger and the President spent twenty minutes telling them something about what he had been doing and why he chose to do it away from Washington: "I find that up here on top of a mountain it is easier for me to get on top of the job, to think in a more relaxed way at times. . . . My study of elections in this country, and of second terms particularly, is that second terms almost inevitably are downhill. . . . What I am trying to do is change that historical pattern. The only way that historical pattern can be changed is to change not only some of the players but also some of the plays. . . ."

The first changes he announced were no change. He knocked down the rumor that he was about to appoint John Connally as secretary of state. He did not announce the reason: the Texan wanted a year to make money. He had told the President he thought he could make $10 million or more in land deals back home. And Nixon did not say that Secretary of State Rogers was scheduled to leave on June 1. The first changes he announced were the resignations of Melvin Laird as secretary of defense and George Romney at HUD. He had offered Laird's job to Rockefeller, but the governor said he was interested only in being secretary of state. Kissinger was opposed to that idea. Then Nixon said he would be staying at Camp David for another two weeks to work on budget matters and sub-Cabinet appointments.

Announcements, great and small, began the next day and continued for more than three weeks—one, two, or three a day. Elliot Richardson moved from HEW to Defense. Caspar Weinberger took over HEW and was replaced by Roy Ash as director of OMB. Peter Brennan, the President's favorite hard-hat guy, was the new secretary of labor. Nixon brought in loyalists, Kenneth Rush and William Casey, as deputy secretary of state and undersecretary for economic affairs. Treasury Secretary Shultz kept his job and was, in addition, named an assistant to the President, with oversight of the Commerce, Labor, Transportation, and Agriculture Departments. Undersecretary of Commerce James Lynn was named HUD secretary. John Volpe was pushed out as secretary of transportation. Pete Peterson was out as secretary of commerce, replaced by Frederick B. Dent, a South Carolina textiles executive. William E. Simon, a New York bond trader, was named deputy secretary of the treasury. The entire second level of the Justice Department was removed and so was most of that tier in HEW—anyone touched by busing disputes was gone. Robert Bork was named solicitor general. Bud Krogh was named undersecretary of transportation. Anne Armstrong, the cochairman of the Republican National Committee, was named counselor to the President with Cabinet rank, which made her the first woman in the Cabinet since 1955. Bob Finch, Chuck Colson, Harry Dent, and Donald Rumsfeld were leaving the White House. CIA Director Richard Helms was named ambassador to Iran, and was replaced by James Schlesinger, who had been chairman of the Atomic Energy Commission. George Bush was named to replace Dole as chairman of the Republican National Committee. John Scali was named to replace Bush at the United Nations, with the condition that he emphasize his Italian and Catholic roots and regularly attend Mass in New York.

By the time the President came down from the mountain, he had accepted fifty-seven resignations and retirements. He had made thirty new appointments, many of them younger men, such as Krogh, inserted into departments as the President's watchdogs.

ON DECEMBER 4, Kissinger and Haig had returned to Paris. The communist negotiators rejected each of the sixty-nine points submitted by President Thieu, leaving Kissinger in a quandary. Haldeman paraphrased it after listening in on a Nixon-Kissinger telephone conversation: "Henry is concerned because he will have to convince the North Vietnamese that if we don't get an agreement we're going to stay in, and he has to convince the South Vietnamese that if we don't get an agreement we're going to get out."

The reason that the President and his national security adviser were conferring by telephone had less to do with the fact that Nixon was still at Camp David than with the personal tension and distrust between them as peace seemed further from hand than it had in late October. The Americans were bombing. The South Vietnamese were refusing to give in. The North Vietnamese seemed to be stalling. By the afternoon of December 6, Kissinger cabled home that the talks were almost certain to fail. Nixon told Haldeman, "The real problem at this point is that we have a weak link as a negotiator."

Kissinger telephoned Camp David the next day. Nixon told Haldeman to talk to him and went out for a swim in his steamy heated pool. Later he said he thought Kissinger had a suicidal complex and told Haldeman to prepare an extensive memorandum for the files on Kissinger's mental processes. Back in Washington, where subordinates were handling most matters other than Vietnam and reorganization, Shultz announced that the President intended to ask Congress to extend wage and price control regulations beyond their April 30, 1973, deadline.

Two days later, Nixon wrote in his diary: "What happened here is that Henry went back to Paris firmly convinced that he would quickly, within a matter of two days, reach agreement. . . . The North Vietnamese surprised him by slapping him in the face with a wet fish. The North wants to humiliate the South. The South wants to drive the North out of South Vietnam. . . . and get us to stick with them until this goal is accomplished. . . . Expectations have been built so high now that our failing to bring the war to an end would have a terribly depressing effect on this country, and no television speech is going to rally the people."

In other words, he was saying, my national security adviser screwed up by telling the people that peace was at hand when it wasn't.

In Washington, an airplane crash put Watergate back on page one. Forty-six people died in the crash of United Airlines flight 553 from Washington to Chicago. One of them was Dorothy Hunt, E. Howard Hunt's wife. Police found one hundred new $100 bills in her purse. On Monday morning, December 11, the day Nixon returned to the White House, Haldeman and Ehrlichman told the President that Mrs. Hunt had distributed more than two hundred thousand dollars of CREEP and White House cash to her husband and the Watergate burglars. The cash was passed to her by Anthony Ulasewicz, who would drive from the White House to National Airport and drop the money in rented lockers.

"Do they have any reading yet on the traceability of the ten-thousand-dollar bag?" Nixon asked. Haldeman said John Dean had spent the weekend working on that, and so far, apparently, no one was checking the serial numbers of the bills. Nixon changed the subject, saying that he had to hold a press conference soon, but to do that he needed some kind of formal statement from Dean or investigators that no one currently employed in the White House was involved in Watergate or Segretti's campaign sabotage—something he could use to cut off questioning. "Basically," he said, sounding like his own defense lawyer, "basically, the point is I didn't take over the campaign, as you may recall, until after the convention. . . . Let's face it, we all know who the hell should have handled this, goddamn it, it was Mitchell, and he wasn't handling it. . . ."

"There are no good choices if you start down that road," Ehrlichman said. ". . . Because that opens the doors, doors, doors, doors, and doors."

"If you start down that road . . . ," Nixon agreed. "Somebody did it. . . . Magruder, Mitchell or higher—someone gave the orders."

Kissinger returned to Washington on December 13. "There is every appearance that the final stage has been reached," said John Chancellor at the top of *The NBC Nightly News,* and that was pretty much what Americans were hearing and reading about Vietnam. In fact, Kissinger had come back to report failure. His words to the President included these on the North Vietnamese: "They're just a bunch of shits. Tawdry, filthy shits. They make the Russians look good, compared to the way the Russians make the Chinese look good when it comes to negotiating in a responsible decent way!"

The only optimistic news was that, formally, the Paris talks were continuing and Kissinger and Le Duc Tho were scheduled to meet again on January 8.

After seeing Kissinger, the President sat for a while in the Oval Office with Haldeman and Ehrlichman, as he often did at the end of the day, and the subject turned to Watergate. They were worried about Pat Gray, the acting FBI director, who was a Mitchell loyalist, and who seemed to believe that the White House was covering up, maybe at Mitchell's expense. "Gray had the idea," Nixon said, "that the White House staff was really involved in this goddamned thing and that the White House staff was trying to keep him from getting at it. . . . Maybe he thinks the White House ordered the whole goddamn thing. . . ."

The next morning Kissinger asked Haldeman for advice on his deteriorating relationship with the President. The chief of staff suggested that he stop speaking and leaking to the press, citing an Osborne column in the current *New Republic* discussing where Kissinger ended and Nixon began. Kissinger said he never saw Osborne. Haldeman pulled out the magazine and began to read direct quotes attributed to Kissinger, who then said, "Well, he called me. . . . on the telephone."

That day, December 14, the President ordered the Joint Chiefs of Staff to reseed the mines in Haiphong harbor and to initiate massive bombing of Hanoi and Haiphong. When the chairman, Admiral Moorer, began questioning him, the President cut him off, saying: "I don't want any more of this crap about the fact that we couldn't hit this target or that one. This is your chance to use military power effectively to win this war, and if you don't, I'll consider you responsible."

Haldeman noticed that Nixon was limping after the Chiefs left the office. It turned out he had cracked his foot against the edge of the pool at Camp David and it had been hurting for a few days. "You should see a doctor," Haldeman said, not for the first time in his years around Nixon. It was a suggestion the President regularly ignored, even when it came from a Christian Scientist. Haldeman did not believe in doctors. Nixon did not like them or he thought seeing them was a sign of weakness. When his chief of staff said the foot might be broken, the boss said that it only hurt when he walked and, anyway, a shoe was as good as a splint.

THE FIRST WAVE of B-52s, 129 of them, along with hundreds of F-111s and A-6 fighter-bombers, began bombing in the early morning hours of December 18. The operation was code-named Linebacker II. Three bombers were shot down by a new, sophisticated ground-to-air missile defense system around Hanoi—a surprise to the Americans—which the White House believed to be manned by Soviet gunners.

Neither the President nor anyone else announced the new levels of bombing until reports came in the next day from Hanoi. Then Ziegler was told to respond to questions by saying that the bombing and mining would continue until the North Vietnamese met minimum American demands for a cease-fire and the release of prisoners of war. While the press secretary was being briefed in the Oval Office on what not to say, he brought up a sore subject: *Time* was naming the President and Kissinger as joint "Men of the Year." Nixon told him to order Kissinger not to speak with anyone from the magazine, and then to see if there was a way White House telephone operators could block all press calls to and from Kissinger's office.

As the bombing hit places never attacked before—the targets were said to be airfields, power plants, rail yards, and communication centers—Haig took off for Saigon, with a blunt message from Nixon to Thieu:

> I have asked General Haig to obtain your answer to this absolutely final offer on my part for us to work together in seeking a settlement along the lines I have approved or to go our separate ways. . . . You must decide now whether you desire to continue our alliance or whether you want me to seek a settlement with the enemy which serves U.S. interests alone.

When Haig finished reading the message, he said in a loud voice, as he had been instructed to by the President: "Under no circumstances will President Nixon accept a veto from Saigon in regard to a peace settlement."

After many questions, Thieu looked at Haig for several moments, then said: "It is very clear to me that there will be no peace as a result of this agreement. . . . After the cease-fire, the enemy will spread out his troops, join the Viet Cong, and use kidnapping and murder with knives and bayonets. Then, after U.S. troops have been withdrawn, they will take up their guns again and resort to guerrilla warfare, but always at a level that does not justify U.S. retaliation."

In Hanoi, French and Swedish journalists reported that residential neighborhoods had been reduced to rubble, and the North Vietnamese government issued a statement saying the Americans were "insane." In Washington, after reading Haig's report of his meeting with Thieu, Kissinger said the South Vietnamese were "maniacs." The press was using the words "Christmas Bombing." "A Stone Age tactic," said Senator Mike Mansfield. Senator William Saxbe, a Republican, said, "President Nixon seems to have lost his senses on this issue." In *The New York Times,* Reston called the action "War by tantrum."

On December 20, the President went to Bethesda Naval Hospital for his annual physical examination, and was told that he did have a splinter fracture in his foot. Then he headed for Key Biscayne with Pat for Christmas. Julie and Tricia were with their husbands in Europe. Nixon woke at 4 A.M. on Christmas Eve and dictated:

> I must get away from the thought of considering the office at any time a burden. I actually do not consider it a burden, an agony etc. . . . It is God's great gift to me to have the opportunity to exert leadership, not only for America, but on the world scene. From this day forward I am going to look upon it that way and rise to the challenge with as much excitement, energy, enthusiasm and, wherever possible, real joy that I can muster."

A couple of days later he dictated a memo about using his time, saying he wanted to make only a half-dozen phone calls each day. "One point I have already made is that we are going to knock off calls on birthdays. . . . the same will, incidentally, hold true of letters to people on their birthdays."

He ordered a thirty-six-hour bombing pause for the holiday, writing to himself: "No planes flew. No bombs were dropped. For a day we were at peace."

So far, B-52s had flown more than twelve hundred strikes in a six-thousand-square-mile triangle encompassing Hanoi, Haiphong, and the port of Thanh Hoa—and there were more credible reports of damage in residential neighborhoods. The embassies of India, Cuba, and Egypt suffered damage. Fifteen bombers were shot down and ninety-five crewmen were killed or captured. On the day after Christmas, the bombing resumed, with 116 B-52s in the air. On December 28, the North Vietnamese confirmed that their delegates would be in Paris to continue the prebombing schedule of technical talks on January 2 and a new session of negotiations on January 8. On the afternoon of December 29, just before he left with his wife for Camp David, the President called Colson, the only senior aide around on the day before the New Year weekend, and said: "I have something to tell you, but not another person in this building can know. The North Vietnamese have agreed to go back to the negotiating table on our terms. They can't take the bombing anymore."

That evening, the President ordered a halt in the bombing of Hanoi and Haiphong, though planes continued to bomb other parts of Vietnam.

Colson walked the President and his wife to *Marine One*, the helicopter waiting to take them to Camp David for a day and a half before Mrs. Nixon had to take off for California to preside over Rose Bowl festivities in Pasadena. The President was alone on New Year's Eve, the last day of his year of triumph. He gave most of the White House's domestic staff the night off. Manolo Sanchez cooked him some bacon and eggs for dinner.

CHAPTER 37

January 23, 1973

THE PRESIDENT was in the Oval Office at 9:30 A.M. on the first day of 1973. He called in Colson ten minutes later—Haldeman and Ehrlichman were taking a couple of days off—and told him that he wanted the Secret Service to begin logging all calls to and from Kissinger. What had set him off was James Reston's column that morning, which seemed to say that the national security adviser had been against the Christmas bombing. The man from the *Times* hummed a familiar tune with these words: "Kissinger is too much a scholar, with too good a sense of humor and history, to put his own thoughts ahead of the President's."

Kissinger was resting for a couple of days in Palm Springs, California, and was indeed spending a lot of time on the phone. Colson bustled in with the news that the logs showed he had talked for hours with columnist Joseph Kraft. Nixon told Colson to call Kissinger and confront him with that. Kissinger, who knew nothing of the logs, told Colson: "I wouldn't talk to that son-of-a-bitch."

"He had just hung up from talking to him and then he said he didn't," Colson told the President.

On the afternoon of January 2, the President and Colson talked about Watergate. "Let's face it," Nixon said. "The main thing that was unfortunate from the standpoint of the presidency on Watergate was the Segretti business, and Haldeman slipped a bit . . . he shouldn't have had, say, Chapin, working on the damn thing. My point is that's too goddamn close. . . . That kind of operation should be on the outside."

"Three steps removed," Colson said.

"We had a White House man, a White House man, directly involved in a political operation, Chuck. You get the point?"

Colson was a White House man, too, and he began covering himself: "I did a hell of a lot of things on the outside—and you never read about it. The things you read about were the things I didn't do. Watergate and Segretti. I had nothing to do with it. . . ."

"Particularly with Segretti and the committee," said Nixon, who was doing the same thing. "It was a mistake to have it financed out of . . . Kalmbach. It was very close to me."

"Which was unnecessary," said Colson. "I did things out of Boston, we did some blackmail and you say, my God. I'll go to my grave before I ever disclose it, but we did a hell of a lot of things and never got caught. . . ."

"Our Democratic friends did a hell of a lot of things, too, and never got caught," Nixon continued. "Because they're used to it. But our people were too goddamn naive, in my opinion, amateurish."

Haldeman was back the next day, doing the same thing Colson was, pointing the other way. And it was Colson he pointed at, saying, "Even though Colson's going to be missed, there was more to his involvement in some of this stuff than I realized."

"Which part?" Nixon asked.

"Watergate."

"Colson? Does he know?"

"I think he knows."

"Does he know you know?"

"I don't think he knows I know."

"What do you mean, through Hunt or what?" Nixon asked.

"Yes, through Hunt and Liddy. And if Liddy decides to pull the cord, Colson could be in some real soup. Liddy can do it under oath and then Colson is in a position of having perjured himself. See, Colson and Mitchell have both perjured themselves under oath already. . . ."

"You mean Colson was aware of the Watergate bugging? That's hard for me to believe."

"Not only was aware of it," Haldeman said, "but was pushing very hard for results. . . ."

"Does Mitchell know that Colson was involved, and does Colson know that Mitchell was involved?" Nixon asked.

"I think the answer is yes to both of those."

The President and his men were spending more time talking about Watergate than they had since the summer. The trials of the burglars were scheduled to begin on January 11, before John J. Sirica, the sixty-nine-year-old chief judge of the United States District Court. The White House problem now was E. Howard Hunt, who wanted a promise of executive clemency if he pleaded guilty along with his four Miami friends. He was pressing Colson, who brought the problem to Ehrlichman and Dean. By January 8, Nixon was drawn into it, telling Colson: "Hunt's is a simple case. I mean, after all, the man's wife is dead, was killed; he's got one child that has—"

"Brain damage from an automobile accident," Colson said.

"We'll build that son-of-a-bitch up like nobody's business. We'll have Buckley"—William F. Buckley was the godfather of three of Hunt's children—"write a column and say, you know, that he, he should have clemency, if you have given eighteen years of service. . . ."

JANUARY 9 was the President's sixtieth birthday, and he marked it by filling two pages of a legal pad with thoughts for an interview he had granted to the Associated Press for later that day: "Live every day as if last. . . . Think young—staff youngest. . . . No one is finished until—he quits."

At noon, Haldeman came into the Oval Office with an "Eyes Only" cable from Kissinger in Paris. Nixon put on his reading glasses, something he did only with people he trusted, and read: "We celebrated the President's birthday today by making a major breakthrough in the negotiations. In sum, we settled all the outstanding questions in the text of the agreement, made major progress on the method of signing the agreement. . . ." But he warned, too: "The Vietnamese have broken our hearts several times before. . . . I cannot overemphasize the absolute necessity that this information be confined to the President alone. There must not be the slightest hint of the present status to the bureaucracy, Cabinet members, the Congress, or anyone else. If a wave of euphoria begins in Washington, the North Vietnamese are apt to revert to their natural beastliness, and the South Vietnamese will do their best to sabotage our progress."

The President looked up and said, "Henry's probably overoptimistic again." But, then he said to respond, "It's the best birthday present I've gotten in sixty years."

IN THE EARLY MORNING HOURS of January 11, the day the Watergate trial was to begin, the President sat with his yellow pad, writing across the top of the page: "Goals for 2d Term." He had three subheads: "Substance," "Political," and "Personal." Under the first, he wrote: "Russia—SALT; China—Exchanges; Mideast—Settlement; Europe—Community; Latin

America—Trade; Defense and Intelligence—Cut duplication, Improve hardware, Restore respect; International Monetary and Trade; Crime; Education; Health; Land Use; Race; Labor-Management; Prices & Wages; Cut size of govt.—Make efficient; Reform; Growth."

Under "Political" he wrote: "Strengthen Party; Better candidates for '74; RN campaign in '74? New Majority; New Establishment; Press; Intellectuals; Business; Social; Arts."

And under "Personal" he wrote: "Restore respect for office; New idealism—respect for flag, country; Compassion—understanding."

Later in the day, he received an offer of help in winning a settlement in the Middle East. Vice President Agnew, whose principal responsibility, intergovernmental relations, had been given to Ehrlichman in the Camp David reorganization, asked to see Nixon. He said he had an idea to help divert the bad press the President was getting on Vietnam. He obviously had no idea the President was anticipating some very good press. Agnew said he wanted to go to Egypt and see President Anwar Sadat to craft a peace plan. Nixon was so astonished that he could not speak at first.

"No," he said when he got his voice back, then softened the answer by saying that the risk of failure was too high to send someone of such high office. Later, he told Haldeman and Ehrlichman that they had to work out a strategy to make sure that the Vice President would not be seen as his successor. "Rockefeller and Connally," said Nixon, "are the only ones who could handle the job."

That afternoon, Howard Hunt offered to plead guilty to six Watergate charges against him—conspiracy, second-degree burglary, and wiretapping among them. Then Judge Siricia began asking him questions about authorization from higher-ups. "To my knowledge, there was none," Hunt answered. Outside the Federal Courthouse on Pennsylvania Avenue, he told reporters: "Anything I may have done I believed to be in the best interests of my country."

That was the next morning's second story. The President had announced Phase III, which was essentially "phaseout," of his New Economic Policy, prompting an eight-column headline in *The New York Times*:

MANDATORY WAGE-PRICE CONTROLS ENDED
EXCEPT IN FOOD, HEALTH, BUILDING FIELDS;
NIXON CALLS FOR VOLUNTARY COMPLIANCE

The President declared victory, saying that the inflation rate had been halved during the seventeen months of mandatory controls and announcing that he was dismantling the Pay Board and the Price Commission. Then he headed for Key Biscayne.

THE OFFICIAL STORY, handed out by Ron Ziegler, was that Nixon needed time alone to work on his second Inaugural address. In fact, he was going to meet Kissinger to work out the details of announcing the end of the American war in Vietnam, in a setting where there was less chance of the story leaking. He told Haldeman to keep the national security adviser in his sight all week, suggesting that Kissinger's friend, Nancy Maginnes, be brought to Florida to keep him company and away from phones and columnists. So far the press had no clue that peace was closer to hand. On Saturday, January 13, *The New York Times,* reporting on Kissinger's twenty-seven hours of meetings with Le Duc Tho, said he was expected to stay in Paris until at least mid-week. Actually, he was flying to Florida by way of Andrews Air Force Base. When Kissinger's plane landed at Andrews Air Force Base to pick up Haig and then proceed to Florida, the pilot was ordered to taxi to a far corner of the airport, out of sight of reporters waiting in the small terminal there.

The President and his national security adviser got together after 1 A.M. on January 14 and talked for more than an hour. When they finally stood up, Nixon walked Kissinger to his car, something he had never done before. He walked back inside his house and dictated to his diary: "I told him the country was indebted to him for what he had done. It is not really a comfortable feeling for me to praise people so openly. . . . He, in turn, responded that without my having the, as he put it, courage to make the difficult decision of December 18, we would not be where we are today."

General Haig, whom the President had just made vice chief of staff of the Army, jumping him over 243 more senior generals, was dispatched to Saigon later that day to deliver another letter from Nixon to Thieu, which read in part: "I have irrevocably decided to proceed to initial the Agreement on January 23, 1973, and to sign it on January 27, 1973, in Paris. I will do so, if necessary, alone. In that case I shall have to explain publicly that your government obstructs peace. The result will be an inevitable and immediate termination of U.S. economic and military assistance."

But if Thieu accepted the agreement, the President continued: "At the time of signing the agreement I will make emphatically clear that the United States recognizes your government as the only legal government of South Vietnam; that we do not recognize the right of any foreign troops to be present on South Vietnamese territory; that we will react strongly in the event the agreement is violated. . . ."

On Tuesday, January 16, in Key Biscayne, the President and Kissinger conferred for more than six hours and then Ziegler announced: "Because of the progress made in negotiations between Dr. Kissinger and special adviser Le Duc Tho, President Nixon has directed that the bombing, shelling, and any further mining of North Vietnam be suspended." Two lines of the Nixon presidency intersected high on the front pages of newspapers across the country the next day. *The New York Times* handled the stories this way:

PRESIDENT HALTS ALL BOMBING,
MINING AND SHELLING OF NORTH;
POINTS TO "PROGRESS" IN TALKS

4 MORE ADMIT
GUILT AS SPIES
IN WATERGATE

On the first day of the trial before Judge Sirica, the four men from Miami, led by Bernard Barker, had pleaded guilty to seven charges of second-degree burglary and wiretapping. The judge questioned the four about whether they knew if White House officials ordered the break-in and each answered no. He asked each if he knew the source of the money for his legal expenses and living costs—hundreds of thousands of dollars—and again each said no.

"Well," Sirica said, "I'm sorry, but I don't believe you."

Two defendants, Liddy and McCord, pleaded "not guilty." The trial continued, and so did efforts to guarantee the silence of the two men. Liddy seemed determined to play out his lonely role of martyr in the cause of liberty, vowing to go to prison rather than betray his employers. McCord, though, was a different story. Referring to nineteen years of service at the Central Intelligence Agency, he had written six anonymous letters—two of them to Richard Helms, four to an old friend named Paul Gaynor at the CIA, warning that the White House intended to blame the agency for the crimes of Watergate. His seventh unsigned letter, mailed late in December, was to his friend Jack Caulfield, the New York cop who had hired him a year before, and who was now on the payroll of the Internal Revenue Service: "If Helms goes and the Watergate operation is laid at CIA's feet, where it does not belong, every tree in the forest will fall. . . . Just pass the message that if they want it to blow, they are on exactly the right course."

That message did get through—Caulfield knew it had to be from McCord—first to Dean and then to Mitchell. On January 5 and again on

January 12, Caulfield had met with McCord, saying he represented "the highest level of the White House," promising his old friend that if he pleaded guilty his family would be taken care of and he, like Hunt, would receive executive clemency after a few months in prison.

On January 17, with the President still in Key Biscayne waiting for Haig's return from Saigon, the Watergate trial went into secret session to take testimony on McCord's wiretapping operations.

On that day, too, and the next, Thieu and Nixon exchanged new letters, but their content was the same: the South Vietnamese president said he would not sign the agreement and the American president said that if he did not, United States aid to South Vietnam would be ended. Nixon also tried to increase the pressure on Thieu by asking two of South Vietnam's most assertive advocates in the Senate—John Stennis of Mississippi and Barry Goldwater of Arizona—to send statements to Saigon repeating the aid message. Then, at noon on January 18, as the President worked on his Inaugural address, Ziegler announced that Kissinger and Le Duc Tho would meet in Paris on January 23 to complete the final wording of the text of an agreement to end the United States' longest war. The same announcement was made at the same hour in Hanoi.

In Saigon, President Thieu was telling his Cabinet: "The United States leaves us without any alternative except that if we sign, aid will continue and there is a pledge of retaliation if the agreements are violated. Otherwise they will leave us alone. Kissinger treats both Vietnams as adversaries. . . . The Americans let the war become their war; when they liked the war, they carried it forward. When they want to stop it, they impose on both sides to stop it. When the Americans wanted to enter, we had no choice, and now when they are ready to leave we have no choice. . . . If Kissinger had the power to bomb the Independence Palace to force me to sign the agreement, he would not hesitate to do so."

On the morning of January 20, the President, back in Washington, was up early, running five hundred steps in place, walking over to the Lincoln sitting room to say a prayer, and then preparing to ride to the Capitol to take the oath for his second term. The day's *Washington Post* ran a twenty-two-page section on his first term, "The Nixon Years." The word "Watergate" did not appear in those pages.

Before he left the White House, the President received a cable from Saigon reporting that President Thieu was sending his foreign minister to Paris to participate in the completion of the agreement text. The South Vietnamese leader had excused himself from a reception after his daughter's wedding to meet with Ambassador Ellsworth Bunker for a half hour. Later that night Thieu had told an aide: "The Americans really left me no choice—either sign or they will cut off aid. On the other hand we have obtained an absolute guarantee from Nixon to defend the country. I am going to agree to sign and hold him to his word."

"Can you really trust Nixon?" asked the aide, Hoang Duc Nha.

"He is a man of honor. I am going to trust him," Thieu responded.

NIXON'S SECOND INAUGURAL ADDRESS was short, only 1,855 words. He concluded by saying: "Let us again learn to debate our differences with civility and decency, and let each of us reach out for that precious quality government cannot provide—a new level of respect for the rights of one another. . . . We shall answer to God, to history, and to our conscience for the way in which we use these years. . . ."

Two days later, Lyndon Baines Johnson, the thirty-sixth president, died in Texas. That was the lead headline in almost every newspaper in the country. But there was another story that day, one that prompted *Newsweek* to report: "The end of a war and the death of a President got bigger headlines. But, in a quiet way, a third event last week may have as lasting an influence on American life: for all practical purposes the U.S. Supreme Court legalized abortion, saying that the termination of an unwanted pregnancy is up to a woman and her doctor. In one of the boldest and most sweeping decisions of the Nixon years, the court ruled 7 to 2 that the criminal abortion laws of almost every state violate a constitutional 'right of privacy' and must therefore be struck down." The case, *Roe v. Wade,* was filed in the name of a Dallas waitress barred by Texas law from terminating her pregnancy, and three of the four justices Nixon had appointed voted with the majority. The President did not comment directly on the decision. The White House press office handed out an old statement in which he had called abortion an unacceptable form of population control. The majority opinion was written by Justice Blackmun, who used the conservative argument that government should impinge as little as possible on the lives of citizens.

TESTIMONY in the Watergate trial resumed the next day, January 23. Hugh Sloan, the young White House aide who had come into the Oval Office with his new bride for the President's blessing in January 1971, was called as a witness in the trial of Liddy and McCord. Judge Sirica became impatient with the questioning by the prosecutors; he excused the jury and began his own interrogation. In answer to a question about higher-ups, Sloan said that he had disbursed $199,000 to Liddy for campaign intelligence operations—and that the transaction had been approved by both Attorney General Mitchell and Maurice Stans, the finance chairman of CREEP.

At 10 P.M. that night, the President went on all three networks. He read a ten-minute statement that began: "I have asked for this radio and television time tonight for the purpose of announcing that we today have concluded an agreement to end the war and bring peace with honor in Vietnam and Southeast Asia." He said that Henry Kissinger and Le Duc Tho had initialed "The Agreement on Ending the War and Restoring Peace in Vietnam" that day in Paris. Then he announced that a cease-fire would go into effect at 7 P.M. Washington time on January 27, that within sixty days, the 23,700 United States military personnel still in South Vietnam would be withdrawn and all American prisoners of war would be released.

In eleven years, more than 8.7 million Americans had gone there and 58,151 of them had died there, along with more than 2.1 million Vietnamese, civilian and military, on both sides. The United States had provided South Vietnam with $138 billion in military aid and $8.5 billion in other economic aid. The last of the nine "chapters" of the agreement stipulated that the United States would contribute further economic aid to the reconstruction of both South Vietnam and North Vietnam. All this, the President said, had been crafted in close consultation with President Thieu—which of course was not true.

Nixon went back upstairs to the residence. His wife hugged him. He spoke for a bit with his daughters and Tricia's husband, Edward Cox. Then he went into the Lincoln sitting room, turned on some music, and sat alone staring into the fire. At midnight, he called Kissinger, who was back and in his office. "He was talking to me," Kissinger said the next morning, "but he was really addressing himself."

A man alone. The President's odd style, at least what the public knew of it, had been a subject of conversation, at least among those who talk and write of such things. During the campaign, in one of its last issues, *Life* magazine had published an editorial saying: "The Nixon administration had remained a small junta, suspicious of the bureaucrats it presides over, ill at ease with Congress, distrustful of those it can't control, at once defensive and sometimes outright arrogant in behavior. It is unnecessarily inhospitable to people whose ideas might occasionally help it. The junta's deep sense of being surrounded by enemies has permeated the Washington atmosphere. . . ."

The great victory obviously did not change the fact that the Nixon administration seemed to be imploding on the man at the center. "Nixon: The Cocoon of Power" was the subject of a pre-Inaugural essay by Mel Elfin, the Washington bureau chief of *Newsweek*. He wrote that when Ziegler announced that the President would not deliver his 1973 State of the Union address—it would be sent as a letter—a reporter asked, only half facetiously: "Does the President still plan to deliver the Inaugural Address orally?" Then he wrote: "Washington has been mystified—and troubled—by Richard Nixon's behavior since his re-election. The President's imperious attitude toward the Congress, his remoteness from the press and his aloofness from the capital city in which he is supposed to be the leading resident all seem more appropriate to the royal court at Versailles than to the White House. . . . In December he ordered the most massive air raids in history without a word of explanation to anyone."

What his critics saw as strangeness, the President saw as strength. "The basic line here is the character: the lonely man in the White House," Nixon told Haldeman. "Tell Kissinger he's got to get across the lonely and heroic courage of the President." Hour after hour and day after day at the end of January, he sat with Haldeman and he dictated his frustration with Kissinger's grabbing so much credit for peace—or being given all the credit by a press and establishment determined to cut down any credit for Nixon. Haldeman took it all down: "The President alone held on and pulled it out. . . . with little support from government, active opposition from the Senate and some House members, overwhelming opposition from the media and opinion leaders, including religious, education and business. Henry should realize that the way to show that he and the President don't differ is for him to sell what the President did in his appearances, especially to sell the hell out of the bombing. . . . The missing link now is the 'Profile in Courage.' We've analyzed the editorials and it's not coming through. . . . Henry has to build the President. . . . The media is trying to build the Kissinger role and downgrade the President's role, making the point that the agreement was done by Kissinger over the President's dead body."

Reading a transcript of Kissinger's briefing to Congress on January 26, Nixon counted only three references to himself. He compared it to a briefing when settlement seemed impossible and found fourteen references. He also wanted Kissinger to use the phrase "Peace with Honor" and call the other side "the Communists," but Kissinger never did. Nixon told Colson that he wanted him to organize a campaign to send letters to Kissinger demanding that he should be supporting the President, not taking all the credit himself.

Still, Nixon was not willing to confront Kissinger directly. Each day he sent Haldeman around to read Kissinger lists of public relations points, always beginning with "lonely courage" lines. And he was finding new ways to cut off personal contact—in a big way with the reorganization and in smaller matters of protocol. Among the first orders he gave in the second term was the elimination of birthday calls to senators and such; telegrams would do. He also decreed an end to receiving credentials from ambassadors; the Vice President or the Secretary of State could do that. That one was quickly withdrawn when John Dean told him the ambassadorial duty was mandated in the Constitution.

But, whether they liked it or not in Georgetown, Manhattan, or Cambridge, the Gallup poll of January 24 equalled the highest Gallup reading of his tenure: 68 percent of respondents in the national survey approved of the job he was doing. On the question of whether there was "peace with honor," 58 percent said yes, 29 percent said no—although only 35 percent of respondents said they believed the agreement was likely to survive. (When Ehrlichman asked Kissinger how long South Vietnam would last, the national security adviser answered: "I think that if they're lucky they can hold out for a year and a half.")

At the second Cabinet meeting of the second term, the President passed out leather-bound calendars covering the four years from January 20, 1973, to January 20, 1977. Each page listed the number of days left in the Nixon administration, beginning with 1,461. "Let us live them to the hilt," he said. "They can stand out as great days for America and great moments in the history of mankind."

In his Inaugural address, Nixon had played with a phrase used famously by President Kennedy, "Ask not what your country can do for you, ask what you can do for your country," and had come up with a Republican version: "Let each of us ask not what government can do for me, but what I can do for myself." It was a good prelude to the $268.7 billion budget he delivered to Congress on January 27. *Time* heralded it as "A Call to Counter-Revolution." What it countered was the trend toward bigger and more socially conscious government that began with Franklin Roosevelt's New Deal in the 1930s and continued through Johnson's Great Society. The document, prepared by Caspar Weinberger and Roy Ash of the new OMB, proposed no new programs and eliminated or cut one hundred existing federal programs, including ones benefiting the unemployed, farmers, students, veterans, small businessmen, the mentally ill, and people living in federal housing.

The major symbolic moves were proposals to break up the Office of Economic Opportunity and to phase out urban renewal and Model Cities programs—and to finally abandon Nixon's own Family Assistance Plan. Part of the philosophy of the budget was to eliminate specific program grants for such things as vocational education and slum clearance, giving states instead block grants, under the name Special Revenue Sharing, to use at state and local discretion. Nixon also made clear his intention of not spending money appropriated by Congress for programs he considered unnecessary. There was a name for that, too, "impoundment." Congressional estimates indicated the President was refusing to spend at least $12.2 billion already appropriated.

THE WATERGATE TRIAL ENDED on January 30. In his summation, the prosecutor, Earl Silbert, called Liddy "the leader of the conspiracy, the money man, the boss"—which was the story as concocted in the White House. The jury was out for just ninety minutes and it came back with guilty verdicts for both Liddy and McCord on counts of conspiracy, burglary, and illegal wiretapping. By order of Judge Sirica, both men were immediately jailed while he considered bail. McCord was facing a maximum of forty-five years in prison. Liddy, facing a possible thirty-five years, snapped military salutes to friends as he was led from the courtroom. Judge Sirica was an angry man who sensed he had been lied to. When it was over he said: "I am still not satisfied that the pertinent facts have been produced before an American jury." He added that he hoped the Senate would go ahead with a Watergate investigation.

The next day the President held his first news conference in almost four months. The only Watergate question, which Nixon easily deflected, focused on whether he would claim "executive privilege" if members of the White House staff were called before a Senate committee. Most of the questions were about Vietnam and impoundment, and there was more than a little edge to his answers. The first concerned "healing the wounds of the war"—and amnesty for draft resisters. Nixon answered:

> Well, it takes two to heal wounds. . . . We think we have taken a big step toward ending a long and difficult war which was not begun while we were here. . . . as far as this Administration is concerned, we have done the very best that we can against very great obstacles, and we finally have achieved a peace with honor. I know it gags some of you to write that phrase, but it is true, and most Americans realize it is true. . . .
>
> As far as amnesty is concerned . . . Certainly I have sympathy for any individual who has made a mistake. We have all made mistakes. But also, it is a rule of life, we all have to pay for our mistakes. The war is over. Many Americans paid a very high price to serve their country, some with their lives, some as prisoners of war for as long as six to seven years, and of course, two million gave two to three years out of their lives, serving in a country far

away in a war that they realize had very little support among the so-called better people—the media, intellectual circles and the rest. . . . Amnesty means forgiveness. . . . Those who served paid their price. Those who deserted must pay their price. . . . The price is a criminal penalty for disobeying the laws of the United States. If they want to return to the United States they must pay the penalty.

The President was just as testy when asked about impoundment: "This Congress has not been responsible on money. . . . Now the point is, the Congress has to decide, does it want to raise taxes in order to spend more or does it want to cut, as the President is trying to cut? The difficulty, of course—and I have been a Member of Congress—is that the Congress represents special interests."

NIXON TURNED BACK to Watergate on February 3, focusing on the trial and Judge Sirica, asking Colson: "What the hell is the strategy going to be here now? . . . His goddamn conduct is shocking. As a judge." He wondered whether Sirica might be looking for a Supreme Court appointment if the Democrats took power.

"No. No," Colson said. "Sirica is a tough, hard-boiled, law-and-order judge. . . . He is a Republican. I know him pretty well. I have been with him at various events—social events. Very decent guy, dedicated to you and to Eisenhower. . . . The only thing I can figure is that he—this case just got under his craw for some reason, and he is a hot-headed Italian, and he blew on it."

Nixon was not satisfied with that, wanting to know why Sirica was pushing for a Senate investigation, adding: "Thank God it's Ervin." It seemed that if the Senate decided to hold hearings, the job would be turned over to seventy-six-year-old Senator Sam Ervin, a North Carolina Democrat, who was seen as an expert on the Constitution, the kind of strict constructionist conservative that the President saw as part of his New Majority.

"At least, he is now going to be hoisted on his own petard, because he is the great constitutionalist, and talk about hearsay and all the rest," Nixon said. "If I were on the Committee, I'd tear the hell out of him. . . ."

He continued: "We can't let Mitchell get involved. We have to protect him. Of course, we have also got to be sure that Haldeman's not involved, we've got to be sure they don't piss around on you, or Ehrlichman, anybody. But the point is that . . . I don't think the country is all that stirred up. . . ."

"The country is bored with it," Colson said. "We get less than one percent whoever mentions Watergate. It's a Washington issue. It's a way to get at us. It's the way Democrats think they can use it to embarrass us, and keep us on the defensive, and keep us worried, and keep us from doing other things."

It was true that a month before the election, national polls indicated that more than half the people in the country had never heard of Watergate. With the exception of *The Washington Post,* most of the press had ignored the story during the campaign, focusing instead on the blunders of the McGovern campaign. The *Post* team of Woodward and Bernstein had annoyed the President greatly with stories on the Dahlberg check, secret funds, and the Segretti operation, but basically the White House cover-up was working. Kraft, the wiretapped columnist, spoke for a lot of the established press when he wrote: "President Nixon and John Mitchell could not have been involved in Watergate because they are too honorable and high-minded, too sensitive to the requirements of decency, fair play, and law." It was only on January 14, ten weeks after the election, that Seymour Hersh, now working for *The New York Times,* reported on the use of secret campaign cash to support the Miami burglars.

On the same day the President talked about Sirica, he spent more than an hour with a friendly pollster, Albert Sindlinger, to discuss the demographics of his great victory. The notes of the meeting read: "Sindlinger indicated that the primary reason for the huge mandate the President received and the reason that 19.5 million Democrats voted for him was because of the President's stand on two issues: 1) Vietnam; 2) Wage and Price Controls." But the war was over and controls were being phased out. "Sindlinger recommended that the President continue his strong stand on law and order, continue his strong stand on cutting the budget, and to push in some way to solve the inflation and food prices problem."

After Sindlinger left, the President met for ten minutes with the widow and five children of Lieutenant Colonel William Nolde, who had been the last American to die in South Vietnam before the cease-fire. He was killed in a rocket attack on An Loc on January 27. Nixon was surprised when he saw Nolde's seventeen-year-old son, who had long hair and a ragged beard, but the boy told the President that he was proud his father died for peace. His sixteen-year-old sister, a perfect blond teenager, asked, "Can I kiss you, Mr. President?"

That same day, *The New York Times* announced that the paper was hiring one of the President's men, Bill Safire, as a columnist—as politically influential a position as any in journalism. But when the paper's president and publisher, Arthur O. Sulzberger, said he had been looking for a conservative voice for some time, Nixon's reaction was a sarcastic comment scrawled on his news summary that day: "H & Buchanan—

Safire a conservative!? Be sure to inform *Human Events!*" Another item he saw, from *The Christian Science Monitor,* that said the White House had scheduled headline-making announcements to push out news from the Watergate trial, triggered more sarcasm: "Z—like ending the war? We really are geniuses!"

On February 7, the Senate voted 77 to 0 to create the Senate Select Committee on Presidential Campaign Activities, with Ervin as chairman and a budget of five hundred thousand dollars. It was to include three other Democrats and three Republicans. "I don't see how the Senate can destroy us," Nixon said that day. "The problem with all this is that it is going to be a television story. But, on the other side of the coin, it may wear out the story after a certain length of time." Haldeman picked up on that: "You hear the same old crap over and over, and I just can't imagine that the people really get very interested."

On Thursday, February 8, the President flew to San Clemente, planning to stay there for ten days or so. He had begun the day with a long Cabinet breakfast, talking for more than an hour, mostly about impoundment and the federal budget he was submitting to Congress. Switching to foreign affairs, he began talking about meeting Mrs. Nolde. "She carried herself like a queen. Then the kids came by—the seventeen-year-old boy with a red, scraggly beard—if he had not been a member of the Nolde family, I don't know if the Secret Service would have let him in, but he was a great kid. Really proud of his Dad. . . . Then the sixteen-year-old daughter came through. You might expect her to be crying, but she was not crying. She said to me . . ."

Haldeman, buried in his legal pad, suddenly realized the room was still. He looked up and the President was just standing there, trying to speak. He couldn't. After fifteen seconds or so, he said, "Well, anyway . . ." And he stopped again. Finally he whispered, "I guess that's what it's all about." He turned and walked out of the State Dining Room.

On the flight west, Nixon talked about stories reporting that he has been nominated for a Nobel Peace Prize, but he wanted that nomination withdrawn. There was just too much political risk of the story becoming "Nixon Loses Peace Prize." Publicly, he would take the position that no leader should receive awards for just doing his job—and peace was part of his job.

Then he called in Haldeman to talk about his schedule. He said he wanted more time alone and dictated new rules: all trips should begin in Florida or California, rather than Washington, so that he would never have to invite members of Congress to travel on *Air Force One;* Aspen

Lodge at Camp David should be closed to everyone but himself; no more Camp David visits for foreign leaders; no more state arrival ceremonies; no more embassy lunches; no more meetings in New York; Thursdays free in case he wanted to do a press conference; no more Friday afternoon meetings.

ON THE MORNING of February 12, the President took a telephone call from Clark Air Force Base in Manila. The voice on the other end said, "This is Colonel Risner, sir, reporting for duty."

Robinson Risner, United States Air Force, a prisoner of war for more than seven years, kept in solitary confinement for four of those years, was in the first group of prisoners released in Hanoi and from prison camps in Vietcong-controlled areas of South Vietnam. He was the ranking officer of the first group of 142 men brought home by three Air Force transports. The first man off the first plane to land, Navy Captain Jeremiah Denton, said: "We are honored to have the opportunity to serve our country under difficult circumstances. We are profoundly grateful to our Commander-in-Chief, and to our nation for this day. God Bless America."

It was a tremendously moving time, with television bringing the country together to honor the few men who were hailed as heroes when they returned from Vietnam. Most of the other veterans, the millions of them, had come back into the turmoil and hatreds that divided the country during the war; some were shunned, some were vilified, called "baby-killers." But the POWs, most of them pilots and airmen, were welcomed with honor. The President had asked Lady Bird Johnson if the flags of the country, at half-mast for thirty days to honor her husband, could be raised high for these men—and they were. No one had known what these warriors, many of them career military, would look like and how they would act when they touched down in an America different from the one they remembered. The answer came at Clark. They were healthier than expected, they kissed the ground and blessed America. They thanked the President. An Air Force colonel, James Kasler, said: "President Nixon has brought us home with honor. God bless those Americans who supported our President through this long ordeal." Air Force Captain David Gray Jr. said: "A loving President preserved my honor. . . . Thank you, Heavenly Father. Thank you, President Nixon. . . . Thank you, America."

"A Celebration of Men Redeemed," was the headline across the cover of *Time* magazine. Television cameras were everywhere, at Clark and with the mothers, the fathers, the wives, and the children of the men as the first phone calls home were made. Then there was film of women and children breaking away from military escorts and racing across tarmacs to touch their sons, their husbands, their fathers. At first, the show was tightly controlled. In Hanoi, Saigon, and Manila, the press was barred and the first film shown on network news was taken by Air Force cameramen. The President was thrilled by it all—he ordered that orchid corsages be sent to POW wives, paying for them himself—and he decided to leave California to get back to Washington and be the man in the middle of what *The New York Times* called "Happy Hubbub"—television and newspapers were running stories on how much ice cream and coffee each man was consuming. The longest-serving prisoner, Lieutenant Commander Everett Alvarez, a Navy pilot, asked what was the most surprising thing he saw after eight years in prison, answered: "Mini-skirts." This was what America wanted.

What America did not seem to want was the aid Nixon had pledged to Vietnam, both South and North, in the peace agreement. When some of the POWS began to talk about beatings and torture, one man saying he had been shackled for five years, the President wrote on his news summary: "K—This kind of story will make our aid program harder to get." On a news summary report that Barry Goldwater was leading Senate conservatives in opposition, and even J. William Fulbright said aid should not be considered until after impounded domestic funding was released by the President, Nixon wrote: "K—Note our problem." *Newsweek*'s headline on the issue was, "Nixon's Touchy IOU to Hanoi." The magazine quoted a Republican leader in the Senate as saying privately: "It just won't wash. How can a senator support cuts in hospital, flood and education spending at home and then vote money for the same thing in Hanoi?" On the record, Senator Herman Talmadge of Georgia said, "I wouldn't give them so much as one cancelled postage stamp."

On his first day back in Washington, February 13, the President met for forty minutes with John Scali, who was preparing to take over as United States ambassador to the United Nations. The note-taker, General Brent Scowcroft, a Kissinger assistant, recorded: "The President told Scali that with regard to the Middle East we were following two approaches—an open approach by Secretary Rogers and another through our private contacts with the Soviet Union, the Egyptians and the Israelis. He, Scali, must know nothing officially of any one of these private approaches. . . . he should keep totally to the public line. . . ."

Then Nixon added: "We do not intend to lecture countries on their internal structure, either in cases like the Philippines at present, or that of the Communist countries. Our concern is for foreign policy behavior and we will aid dictatorships if it is in our interest to do so. Our opposition to Cuba, the USSR and PRC has been based on their external policy of aggression and subversion. When they modify those policies, we will modify our policy toward them."

On February 22, Senator Howard Baker of Tennessee, just named the ranking Republican of Ervin's Watergate committee, came to the White House to talk with Nixon, saying first, "Nobody knows I'm here."

"The press is really after bigger fish," Nixon said. "I'm not excited about this. . . . I know you'll do a good job. The main thing is to have no damn cover-up. That's the worst thing that can happen. . . . But also if it gets rough, you may have to at a certain time turn and get away from this. . . ."

Four days later, on February 27, the President met with John Dean for the first time since September 15. The subject was Watergate and they talked for twenty-five minutes. The next day they met for more than an hour. Nixon offered Dean coffee, which the young lawyer never drank. But he said yes, because that was what ambitious young men said to presidents. As they wound down the next day, the President told Dean to go to Kleindienst and Baker, to find ways to contain the Ervin hearings, saying: "We have to work together on this thing. . . . Let's remember this was not done by the White House. This was done by the Committee to Re-Elect, and Mitchell was the chairman. . . . And Kleindienst owes Mitchell everything. . . . Baker's got to realize this, and if he lets things get out of hand he is going to potentially ruin John Mitchell. . . . There is no question what they're after. They would like to get Haldeman or Colson, Ehrlichman."

"Or possibly Dean . . . ," said the counsel.

THE PRESIDENT held a press conference on March 2. Most of the early questions focused on the American endgame in Vietnam, with Peter Lisagor of the Chicago *Daily News* asking the first question: "Mr. President, could I ask you whether aid to North Vietnam was a condition of the cease-fire agreement?"

"No, it was not," Nixon answered. "The provision for assistance to Vietnam on the economic side is one that we believe is in the interest of creating lasting peace. . . . We, of course, will have to have Congressional support." Which, of course, was going to be tough to get—but, he added, public opinion had also been against aid for the rebuilding of Germany and Japan after World War II. The idea, he said, was to give the North Vietnamese a stake in peace rather than in continuing war.

"Mr. President," he was asked later, "Now that the Watergate case is over, the trial is over, could you give us your view on the verdict and what implications you see in the verdict on public confidence in the political system?"

"No," he answered. "It would not be proper for me to comment on the case when it not only is not over, but particularly when it is also on appeal. I will simply say with regard to the Watergate case what I have said previously, that the investigation conducted by Mr. Dean, the White House Counsel, in which, incidentally, he had access to the FBI records on this particular matter because I directed him to conduct this investigation, indicates that no one on the White House Staff, at the time he conducted the investigation—that was last July and August—was involved or had knowledge of the Watergate matter."

The next question came from Clark Mollenhoff, who had left his White House job to go back to his paper, *The Des Moines Register.* He referred to the ongoing confirmation hearings for L. Patrick Gray for director of the FBI: "Mr. President, yesterday at the Gray hearings, Senator Tunney suggested he might ask the committee to ask for John Dean to appear before that hearing to talk about the Watergate case and the FBI–White House relationship. Would you object to that?"

"Of course," Nixon said. "It is executive privilege. . . . No President could ever agree to allow the Counsel to the President to go down and testify before a committee. I stand on the same position there that every President has stood on."

CHAPTER 38

March 23, 1973

O N MARCH 4, *The New York Times* began a four-part series under a front-page headline:

NIXON'S PRESIDENCY:
EXPANSION OF POWER

SCHOLARS SEE A MAJOR IMPACT
ON GOVERNMENT'S OPERATION

The first article, by John Herbers, began: "Richard M. Nixon, in what he achieved in his first term and in what he has undertaken in his second, is attempting an expansion in Presidential powers that could have more impact on the national government than that of any other President since Franklin D. Roosevelt. . . . That is the opinion of historians, political scientists and other students of the Presidency who were interviewed during recent weeks."

It was a peak for Nixon. The *Times* said the President had contempt for Congress, and not without reason; that he was gaining control over the 2.5 million bureaucrats who made up the executive branch; that he was making fundamental changes in the ways Americans were educated, housed, and policed, and even in what they saw on television news. He had ended the United States' longest war, there was no draft, and the size of the military had been reduced from 3.5 million men to 2.2 million. He was pushing to balance the federal budget by fiscal year 1975. The gross national product was growing by 7 percent annually and personal income had risen by ten percent in just one year. Prices were still rising, but the President was still fighting, announcing, on March 6, new price controls on oil and gasoline. And if Watergate would not go away, at least Daniel Ellsberg, the purveyor of the Pentagon Papers, was on trial as a criminal in Los Angeles.

In his first 1973 meeting with his party's congressional leaders, Senator Hugh Scott and Representative Gerald Ford, the President listened for only a couple of minutes to Scott's tales of low morale among Republicans and the need for more White House meetings on congressional problems. Then he said: "Bring them down for cookies . . . ? Our Senators are nothing but a bunch of jackasses. . . . We can't count on them. Fuck the Senate!" He was gentler with Ford, but repeatedly asked exactly what help he could count on from the House. When Scott came back into the conversation, asking what he should do when senators felt they had to oppose the President, Nixon answered: "You can vote any way you want. No one gives a shit what the Senate does or how the Senate votes."

Nixon simply hated this Senate, which had harassed him with threats to cut off war funding for the past two years. Now, he had two great problems with the body. The first was the resistance of even the friendliest members to supporting economic aid to North Vietnam, which he saw as the last, best chance to induce the leaders in Hanoi not to push militarily into South Vietnam—and deeper into Laos and Cambodia. "Can you buy peace, Mr. President?" asked John McClellan, the Arkansas Democrat who had supported the war from beginning to end. "You have given them enough, you stopped bombing them."

Nixon's second big gripe with the Senate was that, in his mind, his enemies there were now substituting Watergate for Vietnam in trying to humble him. He resented Ervin's new Select Committee and was even angrier about the issuing of subpoenas by the Judiciary Committee in the confirmation hearings of L. Patrick Gray as FBI director. Democrats wanted to question White House aides beginning with Dean, who had received access to raw FBI interviews during the early investigation of the break-in. The President was also angry with Gray for revealing such things, telling Dean: "I want all communication with Gray cut off. I know the type. He's a nice guy, loyal in his own way. But he's panting after the goddamn job and is sucking up."

On March 12, the President sent a memo to Haldeman, asking:

"What happened to the suggestion that the IRS should run audits of all members of Congress? . . . What I have in mind is that the IRS run audits of all top members of the White House staff, all members of the Cabinet and all members of Congress. It could be said, if any questions are raised, that this is what we are doing because of letters we have received indicating that people in government do not get IRS checks because of their special position. . . . Give me an oral report."

The next day, Nixon met with Dean, who was sometimes spending more than an hour a day in the new Oval Office after Colson finally left the White House on March 10, and told him, confidently: "This is the last gasp of our hardest opponents. They've just got to have something to squeal about. . . . They got the hell kicked out of them in the election. . . . The basic thing is the establishment. The establishment is dying. . . ."

Dean responded: "There are dangers, Mr. President. I'd be less than candid if I didn't tell you." Dean was wary. He knew others in the White House were consulting criminal lawyers. Without telling the President, he began thinking he should hire one, too. Later that day he was told that Hunt was demanding more money and he went from wary to scared. He asked Haldeman for another meeting with the President the next day, March 21. Within a minute, Dean said: "I think that there's no doubt about the seriousness of the problem we're, we've got. We have a cancer within—close to the Presidency—that's growing. It's growing daily. It's compounding, it grows geometrically now, because it compounds itself. That'll be clear as I explain, you know, some of the details: 1) we're being blackmailed; 2) people are going to start perjuring themselves very quickly. There is no assurance—"

The President interrupted: "That it won't bust."

Assuming Nixon did not know much of what had happened, Dean began with Haldeman ordering the setting up of a campaign intelligence operation at CREEP early in 1972 and then sending Liddy over there—and then going on to Gemstone and the bugging of the Democratic National Committee offices in May. Then, he continued, the Liddy-Hunt team went in again, to fix the bug, and got caught. Then he listed the demands for money and the use of leftover campaign cash, with the amounts quickly running into the hundreds of thousands of dollars. More and more money was needed, so Kalmbach and others were sent out to get it.

"The blackmail is continuing," Dean said. "Hunt now is demanding another seventy-two thousand dollars for his own personal expenses; fifty thousand dollars to pay his attorneys' fees. . . . wanted it by the close of business yesterday . . . Hunt now has made a direct threat against Ehrlichman. He says, 'I will bring John Ehrlichman down to his knees and put him in jail. I have done enough seamy things for he and Krogh that they'll never survive it.' "

"What's that?" Nixon asked. "On Ellsberg?"

"Ellsberg and apparently some other things. I don't know the full extent of it."

"How much money do you need?" Nixon asked.

"I would say these people are going to cost a million dollars over the next two years."

"We could get that. . . . If you need the money, you could get the money. . . . You could get it in cash. I know where it could be gotten. . . . I mean it's not easy but it could be done."

After more talk on details, the President talked about the blackmail again and finally said: "I wonder if that doesn't have to be continued? Let me put it this way: Let us suppose that you get, you get the million bucks, and you get a proper way to handle it, and you could hold that side. It would seem to me that would be worthwhile—"

Haldeman came into the office then and Nixon repeated himself: "Now, let me tell you, it's no problem, we could get the money. There is no problem in that. We can't provide the clemency. The money can be provided. Mitchell could provide the way to deliver it."

"It's a very high risk," Dean said.

"All right. Fine," the President said, beginning to break up the meeting, after almost two hours. "I have no doubts about the right plan before the election. And you handled it just right. You contained it. Now after the election we've got to have another plan. . . ."

Haldeman answered: "John's point is exactly right, that the erosion here now is going to you, and that is the thing that we've got to turn off at whatever the cost and we've got to figure out where to turn it off at the lowest cost we can, but at whatever cost it takes."

After Dean left, the President walked out to meet with a group of Soviet Olympians, led by their teenage star, gymnast Olga Korbut. Then he called in Rose Mary Woods and asked her about amounts of money on hand, saying: "Let me ask you something I was checking. We at the present time may have a need for substantial cash for a personal purpose for some things. . . ."

"I don't know," she said. "I would have to look. I'd have to get in the safe. I don't remember. . . . Nobody here knows I have it. . . . I'm so worried. . . ." The amount was more than a hundred thousand dollars.

That night, seventy-five thousand dollars in cash was delivered to Hunt's home. The next morning, March 22, Mitchell told Haldeman, Ehrlichman, and Dean that Hunt would not be a problem anymore. Now the President wanted a report written, saying once again that no one on the White House staff was involved in Watergate or a cover-up. The idea was to give Nixon himself a way to say that he had ordered an internal investigation and that he had no cause for action after reading it. But he needed something on paper—it did not matter whether it was true, what mattered was he could say he believed it to be true—and he wanted Dean to write it. So that afternoon, he sent Dean to Camp David for a long weekend to write the thing. The President was already on his way to Key Biscayne.

While Dean was driving to Camp David with his wife the next day, Friday, March 23, Liddy was sentenced by Judge Sirica to from six years eight months to twenty years in federal prison. The four men from Miami were sentenced to forty years in prison and Hunt to thirty-five years, but Sirica pronounced those sentences "provisionary," indicating that they would be reconsidered if the men cooperated with government prosecutors. James McCord was also scheduled for final sentencing, but at 10 A.M. Sirica revealed that McCord's lawyer had delivered a sealed letter from his client to the court on Wednesday. The judge read McCord's words aloud:

> In the interest of justice . . . I will state the following to you at this time: 1. There was political pressure applied to the defendants to plead guilty and remain silent. 2. Perjury occurred during the trial. . . . 3. Others involved in the Watergate operation were not identified during the trial when they could have been. . . . 4. The Watergate operation was not a C.I.A. operation. The Cubans may have been misled by others into believing it was a C.I.A. operation. . . .
>
> Following sentence, I would appreciate the opportunity to talk to you privately in chambers. Since I cannot feel confident in talking with an F.B.I. agent, in testifying before a grand jury, whose U.S. attorneys work for the Department of Justice or in talking with other government representatives, such a discussion with you would be of assistance to me.

Ehrlichman called the President in Key Biscayne and gave him that news. "A bombshell," Nixon wrote in his diary that night. Nixon spent six hours with Haldeman on Sunday, talking only about Watergate. He said for the first time that if this continued, it would become impossible for him to govern.

THERE WAS MORE NEWS from Washington: Earl Silbert, the prosecutor, announced that he would reconvene the Watergate grand jury, and Samuel Dash, a Georgetown University Law School professor who was chief counsel to the Ervin committee, announced that he had talked to McCord for the past two days and now had the names of more participants in Watergate planning. The next day's edition of the *Los Angeles Times* carried the headline "McCord Says Dean, Magruder Knew of Bugging in Advance." The Watergate story was becoming more than just a contest between *The Washington Post* and *The New York Times*. Now there were packs of reporters watching who came and went in the grand jury room. Television crews staked out the homes of McCord and Dean, and then of Haldeman and Ehrlichman.

It was not just a Washington story now. The nation was ready to watch. The next day, Monday, March 26, the Senate Watergate committee voted to permit live television coverage of its hearings and Magruder resigned as assistant secretary of commerce, the job he was given after the campaign. On March 27, Hunt denied to the grand jury that he knew of involvement of higher-ups in Watergate, and that night Martha Mitchell called *The New York Times* to say: "I fear for my husband. I'm really scared. I can't tell you why. But they're not going to pin anything on him. . . ."

The President spent more than eight hours on Watergate that day, ordering Ehrlichman to make an independent investigation of the case. Dean had not delivered on the assignment. The President's lawyer was meeting secretly with his own lawyers, getting ready to testify before the Washington grand jury and meet with the staff of the Ervin committee in a closed session. Nixon spent an hour with Secretary of State Rogers. The subject was more Watergate. Rogers had told Haldeman that the White House Watergate stories were not credible: "Why did we get into the cover-up if we don't know what the real story is to begin with? . . . The attempts to cover up make the basic alibi of noninvolvement of the White House inconceivable."

In the Oval Office, the President gave Rogers this version: "I think Mitchell authorized it. I don't think he did it perhaps in a very conscious way but what happened here apparently was that they had this room over there, you know, these people and so forth, and they were supposed to get intelligence, and then they have this wild-eyed scheme involving Liddy. Apparently they discussed such a scheme. It was turned down. And then they discussed it a second time, and Dean was present on both occasions. . . . Dean said this won't go. You just can't go on this course. Then, at a later time, they went on and went ahead with it anyway, because they said they had to get information and so forth and so on and so on. Now the question is who triggered them to go forward with this cockeyed scheme. My view is Magruder. . . . Mitchell was all tied up in his Martha problems. Magruder would probably say that he had pressure from Haldeman, which he will claim, which is not true according to Haldeman. . . . It was Mitchell. He's never said. I've never asked him."

"That's been my guess," said Rogers.

"Why should I ask him? "Nixon continued. "Why should I now put him in the position of lying to me? He's already lied. . . ."

He stopped and then said: "I don't believe in just holding on and letting it come out drip by drip. . . . I am not getting a goddamn thing done. . . . I've got to get on to other things."

HE DID GET TO OTHER THINGS on March 29, in a prime-time television speech carried on all three networks. The event was an announcement that the last American military men and prisoners had left Vietnam: "For the first time in twelve years, no American military forces are in Vietnam. . . . We have prevented the imposition of a Communist government by force on South Vietnam."

Halfway through the twenty-minute speech, he switched to domestic affairs. Wholesale prices, dormant for months, were suddenly rising at the highest rate since 1951, jumping more than 2 percent a month, with food prices going higher than that. "Meat prices must not go higher," he said, and announced a freeze on the wholesale and retail prices of beef, pork, and lamb.

With that, the President went to San Clemente for a two-day meeting with President Thieu, who had chartered a Pan American Boeing 707 and repainted it with a South Vietnamese flag on the tail in the manner of *Air Force One.*

The visit, which Nixon had promised would formalize continuing American aid for Thieu's country, began with a small state dinner featuring large cuts of price-fixed filet mignon, a food Thieu had trouble eating. He took that as a sign that from now on the Americans intended to do things their way. "You can count on us," Nixon had told Thieu at a meeting before the dinner.

Outside, at a cocktail party by the pool, Kissinger pulled Hoang Duc Nha aside and said: "The past is behind us. I realize now that I moved too fast and that October was a mistake."

"I could make a lot of money if I released your admission of a mistake to the press right now," said Nha, who hated Kissinger. The men laughed, drawing attention. "I know you wouldn't do that sort of thing," said Kissinger.

Thieu was still taking Nixon at his word, telling Nha the next day: "I got the assurances. We're going to get economic aid. We're going to get military assistance and they will react strongly if the North Vietnamese violate the cease-fire."

"It is one thing to say and another thing to do," Nha said. "They have no legal ground to come back."

"The United States will fly out of Thailand and really pound the Communists," Thieu said. That was the plan. But Thieu did see how distracted Nixon seemed. The American President kept repeating himself. There was no ceremony when the South Vietnamese leader left California. Watching from his helicopter, Thieu saw that Nixon turned away as soon as the door closed and walked away, never looking back. In Washington for an official state visit, Thieu was greeted only by Vice President Agnew and the new secretary of labor, Peter Brennan. Everyone else found reasons not to come.

In San Clemente, the White House announced that it was withdrawing the nomination of Pat Gray as director of the FBI. Two possible nominees were mentioned in background briefings: Henry Petersen, a career civil servant who was the director of the Justice Department's criminal division (which meant he was overseeing Earl Silbert and other Watergate prosecutors); and a federal judge, Matthew Byrne of Los Angeles, who was presiding over the ongoing Pentagon Papers trial of Daniel Ellsberg. In fact, Byrne had been to San Clemente to confer with Ehrlichman about the possible appointment and had even exchanged a few words with the President.

The President returned to Washington on the evening of April 9. Now half of each day was filled with long and rambling Watergate conversations, mostly with Haldeman and Ehrlichman, focusing on who was talking to the District of Columbia grand jury, who was talking to the Ervin committee's closed sessions, what they were asked, what they answered. On one day, April 11, Dwight Chapin, the appointments secretary; Gordon Strachan, a Haldeman assistant; and Donald Segretti, the campaign trickster, were all called before the district grand jury.

In the middle of all that, Haldeman received a call from the Vice President, asking him to come over to his office in the Executive Office Building. Agnew said he had a problem: a former assistant of his named Jerome Wolff had been called before a grand jury in Baltimore to testify about campaign contributions and construction kickbacks while Agnew was governor of Maryland. The Vice President wanted Haldeman to call Senator J. Glenn Beall Jr. and see if he would exert pressure on the United States attorney involved, the senator's brother, George Beall. Agnew said there were never shakedowns, just collecting contributions from contractors getting state work. "But it will sound bad," he said. Haldeman refused.

The chief of staff was more than ever functioning as a kind of deputy president, handling anything and everything that the President did not want to do himself. Agnew was something Nixon did not want to deal with. So, often, was Kissinger. There was a bond and a certain trust between the President's two most powerful assistants. Two days later Kissinger was in Haldeman's office, asking if he knew that every time he was in the Oval Office alone, Nixon would ask him whether he thought he should dump Haldeman. Then Kissinger said that if Haldeman was pushed out, he would resign, too.

"Looks like we're nearing the moment of truth," wrote Haldeman that night, "and everybody's getting a little panicky in the crunch."

By April 14, the man in the crunch was Mitchell. A few days before, talking with Haldeman about the money going to Hunt and the burglars, Nixon had said, "Mitchell ought to step up and say he did it."

"Mitchell is sitting up in New York and pulling the covers over his head," Ehrlichman had said the next day.

"I can't believe Mitchell is so blind to this goddamned thing . . . ," the President had responded.

"He's blind in the emotional sense . . . ," Ehrlichman had said. "Mitchell has got to decide. . . . I don't think he's going to get all these guys to stand up there and lie, that's what it gets down to."

At 9 A.M. on April 14, Ehrlichman, who saw himself as the honest broker of Watergate information—there had still been no public mention of his involvement in the Fielding burglary—came into EOB 175 with the report of his investigation. He had worked on it almost full-time for three weeks before staying up most of the night and writing out seven long-hand pages. He was in the office for almost three hours—Haldeman was there, too—but he had trouble getting the President to focus on what he had to say.

"There's a go, no-go decision that has to be made," Ehrlichman insisted. "Here's your situation. Look again at the big picture. You now are possessed of a body of fact. . . . You can't just sit here—"

"That's right," Nixon said.

"You've got to make some decisions. . . . I want you to read this—"

The President started to interrupt, but Ehrlichman continued, talking about the hush money: "There were eight or ten people around here who knew about this, knew it was going on. Bob knew, I knew, all kinds of people knew—"

"Well, I knew it," Nixon said. "I knew it."

When Ehrlichman finally gave his handwritten notes to Nixon, the President handed them back, saying, "Read it to me." So Ehrlichman did, with the President interrupting him every few words, usually asking questions about Mitchell. The "report," really a long memo, read:

> Although JNM, JSM, GL and JDIII* met several times in early 1972 while JNM was still Attorney General to discuss "intelligence" activities, I believe these meetings ended without agreement by JNM as to the course or plan to be followed. JDIII says he expressly objected to GL's proposals as improper and even illegal. And so nothing happened. Sometime later, in the spring, Liddy and Hunt complained to Colson that JSM would not authorize the funds for them to do the work necessary to gather information requested by Colson. At about that time HRH and Colson wanted specific information about Democratic primary candidates, their schedules, speech content, etc. Apparently the material requested by them was pretty innocuous. When "intelligence" was said by Hunt and Liddy, they meant different information—harder, less properly come by. . . .
>
> Subsequently, JSM and GL conferred, and a memorandum was prepared and submitted to JNM asking him to "pick the targets" for electronic surveillance and other intelligence gathering. JNM did so in the belief that the operatives would be two or three people removed from any CREEP personnel. JSM then authorized Sloan to give GL funds to procure equipment and people.
>
> Watergate Democratic offices were first entered in May and bugs were planted. . . . When the plant was performing badly, Liddy was told to go back in and fix it, also to photograph some documents. Liddy advised Hunt they had to do it, in spite of Hunt's protests, because John Mitchell insisted. Of course they were apprehended in June. Thereafter began an effort to insure that the five burglars and Hunt and Liddy did not implicate anyone else.
>
> John Dean was enlisted by John Mitchell to seek help from the White House to pay subsistence and attorneys' fees. . . . A number of White House people became aware of JNM's effort, including Dean, HRH, Colson, Moore and me.
>
> Liddy prepared three rather obscure synopses of what was heard over the bugs. . . . JSM sent one carbon to Strachan. He, in turn, digested the contents of at least one for HRH. . . .
>
> I believe JSM, Hunt, Liddy (?) and Fred LaRue** are willing to

---

* John N. Mitchell, Jeb Stuart Magruder, (G.) Gordon Liddy, and John Dean III.
** A Mitchell assistant.

make full disclosures in the coming week. Hunt is, for sure, on Monday. Mitchell and Mardian still are not. Liddy apparently has remained silent on JNM's assurance that he would be given a pardon. If and when JSM is recalled, he will implicate JNM, Dean and Strachan, and probably others. Dean is also ready to testify and would involve JNM and JSM. . . . As he apparently has for literally months, JNM is the key to a full disclosure of the facts of the Watergate matter. . . .

Just after eleven o'clock, the President told Haldeman to call Mitchell in New York: "Ask him if he can come down."

"Mitchell's case is a killer," Nixon said. "Dean's case is the question. And I do not consider him guilty. Now that's all there is to that. Because if he, if that's the case, then half the staff is guilty. . . . And, frankly, then I have been since a week ago, two weeks ago. . . . The Mitchell thing is damn painful."

Then Nixon, who did not have the heart to face Mitchell, told Ehrlichman what to say, referring to himself in the third person: "You've got to say that this is the toughest decision he's made and it's tougher than Cambodia, May 8 and December 18 put together. And that he just can't bring himself to talk to you about it. Just can't do it. . . . You're suggesting he go in and say look, I'm responsible here. I had no knowledge but I'm responsible. And nobody else had—that's it. Myself . . . This thing has got to stop. Innocent people are being smeared in this thing. . . . We're going to prick this boil and take the heat. Am I overstating?"

Then Kissinger came into the office for a noon meeting. Nixon talked for only a couple of minutes with the national security adviser, saying the important thing was to save Haldeman, yet adding: "But if it's going to come out, then the question is whether once and for all to take some brutal measures."

Nixon said nothing was more brutal than sacrificing Mitchell.

Mitchell took the noon Eastern Airlines shuttle flight from New York and was in the White House by 1:30 P.M. Ehrlichman told Mitchell that Magruder and Dean were both talking to the prosecutors—that Magruder was confessing all, including his meetings in Mitchell's office—but he got nowhere. The former attorney general repeated again and again that he had done nothing wrong.

"All finished?" Nixon asked when he saw Ehrlichman after Mitchell left.

"Yes sir," said Ehrlichman, and characterized Mitchell's response: "He is an innocent man in his heart and in his mind and he does not intend to move off that position. He appreciated the message of good feeling between you and him. . . . His characterization of all this is that he was a very busy man and he wasn't keeping track of what was going on at the committee—and that this was engendered as a result of Hunt and Liddy coming to Colson's office and getting Colson to make a phone call to Magruder. . . ."

Frustrated and sarcastic, Ehrlichman summed up the Gemstone meetings by saying: "Dean says it was Mitchell and Magruder. It must have been the quietest meeting in history. Everybody's version is that the other two guys talked."

MITCHELL FLEW BACK to New York on the shuttle. Quite by accident, he sat down next to Daniel Schorr, the CBS correspondent he had once ordered investigated. Mitchell told him that he knew nothing about Watergate and that the country outside Washington did not care about Watergate.

At the same time, the President was dressing for the annual dinner of the White House Correspondents Association, timing his arrival at the Washington Hilton so that he got there after the presentations of the awards for outstanding Washington journalism. The top two awards went to Woodward and Bernstein of *The Washington Post* for their early Watergate revelations. Their editor, Barry Sussman, who was in charge of the paper's Watergate coverage, stood as the President entered to the music of "Hail to the Chief." He was surprised by how much better Nixon looked in person than in photographs. This was the first time he had ever seen the President.

Nixon got a couple of laughs, the biggest one at the beginning when he said, "It is a privilege to be here . . . I suppose I should say it is an executive privilege." When he got serious, he paid tribute to David Lawrence, the founder of *U.S. News & World Report*, who had recently died. Nixon said: "David Lawrence, who was a charter member of this club fifty-nine years ago, said to me a couple of years ago: 'There is only one more difficult task than being President of this country when we are waging war, and that is to be the President when we are waging peace.' "

"What did you think of the Lawrence quote?" he asked Haldeman later.

"Appropriate," was the answer.

"I made it up," Nixon said.

ATTORNEY GENERAL RICHARD KLEINDIENST was at the dinner, too. He got home at 1 A.M., Sunday. The phone was ringing. It was Henry Petersen of the criminal division, saying that he and Earl Silbert wanted to come over immediately to brief him on what they had learned from Magruder and Dean. The men from Justice talked until 5 A.M. At 8:30 A.M., Kleindienst telephoned the President, saying he had to see him immediately. Nixon told him to come to the White House church service and they could talk after that.

They sat down in EOB 175 a little after 1 P.M. The Attorney General began by saying: "Last night after the correspondents' dinner, Henry Petersen . . . and Earl Silbert, who is the Chief Assistant U.S. Attorney who tried the Watergate matter, and Henry Titus came over. Titus is the United States Attorney. . . . to give me the benefit of what had transpired on Thursday, Friday, and Saturday with Magruder, and then what had been transpiring for a week with John Dean and his attorneys."

Kleindienst told Nixon: "Magruder is going to plead guilty and he's going to tell everything he knows. That kind of information is not going to remain confidential." He said that the trail of indictments was leading to Mitchell, Haldeman, and Ehrlichman.

"Ehrlichman?" Nixon asked.

"He's hooked," Kleindienst said.

Dean had testified about the papers taken from Hunt's safe just after the break-in. The order to get rid of the papers—which Ehrlichman was denying—had been followed. On Christmas day, Pat Gray had burned the envelopes along with wrapping paper and ribbons in a fireplace at his home in Connecticut. The Attorney General also said he would have to recuse himself from the case because of his close relationship with Mitchell over the years. So, Henry Petersen, who was supervising the Silbert investigations, would report directly to the President.

"Keep me ahead of the curve," Nixon said, in his first meeting with Petersen. The next day, April 16, Petersen, who was reporting in to the White House every few hours, told the President that both Magruder and Dean wanted full immunity before testifying in detail, and that Dean had told prosecutors that unless he got immunity he was going to implicate the President in the cover-up, and in the bugging of journalists' phones back in 1969.

THAT NIGHT, AFTER 9 P.M., the President called Dean in for almost an hour. The conversation was both cordial and tense, two lawyers trying to make their points, speaking as if there was a court stenographer in the corner—or a tape machine. Dean said he was sorry that Petersen had delivered the news that he was talking to prosecutors, he had wanted to tell the President himself. Much of the first talk was about "executive privilege," with Nixon saying, "I don't want you talking about national-security matters . . . those newsmen wiretaps and things like that—those are privileged, John."

"I agree, Mr. President."

As Nixon stood up to end the meeting, he leaned over Dean and said: "You know, that mention I made to you about a million dollars and so forth as no problem. . . . I was just joking, of course, when I said that."

"Well, Mr. President, I'm not even getting into those areas. You can be assured of that."

Haldeman got home after midnight, but still managed to dictate into his diary: "Another all-Watergate day as they generally tend to be now."

The next morning, April 17, the President called in Dean before 10 A.M. He said there would have to be staff resignations and asked Dean for his thoughts on who had to go. "Well," was the answer, "I think it ought to be Dean, Ehrlichman and Haldeman."

"I thought Dean at this moment," the President said. He presented his counsel with two letters, asking him to sign both. One read:

> As a result of my involvement in the Watergate matter, which we discussed last night and today, I tender you my resignation effective at once.

The second read:

> In view of my increasing involvement in the Watergate matter, my impending appearance before the grand jury and the probability of its action, I request an immediate and indefinite leave of absence from my position on your staff.

Dean asked for a chance to rewrite them and the President did not press him. Dean said he thought Haldeman and Ehrlichman should be resigning at the same time he did. Nixon said he already had their resignations in hand. Then he proceeded to again make legal points or try to amend some of the things he had said to Dean over the past few weeks: "On this privilege thing—nothing is privileged that involves wrongdoing. . . . On your part or wrongdoing on the part of anybody else. I want you to testify, if you do, to say that the President told you that. Would you do that? . . ."

"Yes, sir."

"Tell the truth," said Nixon. "That is the thing I have told everybody around here. Tell the truth! . . . That son of a bitch Hiss would be free today if he hadn't lied. . . . You go to jail for the lie rather than the crime. . . . I could have told you to go to Camp David and concoct a story couldn't I? And you never have heard that said, have you?"

"No, sir."

Then Dean offered his rationale and position: "When history is written and you put the pieces back together, you will see why it happened. Because I triggered it. I put everybody's feet to the fire because it just had to stop."

But that was a role the President wanted for himself: "I would like for you to say, 'I told the President first there was no involvement in the White House. And the President said, 'Look, I want to get to the bottom of this thing, period.' . . . You continued your investigation, et cetera, and the President went out on his own. Which I have done, believe me. I put a little pressure on Magruder and a few . . . And as a result of the President's actions this thing has been broken. . . .'"

That was the new strategy: The President broke the case!

Immediately after his second meeting with Dean, the President sat down with Haldeman and Ehrlichman in the Oval office and asked: "How has the scenario worked out?"

"Well, it works out very good," began Haldeman. "You became aware some time ago that this thing did not parse out the way it was supposed to and that there were some discrepancies between what you had been told by Dean—"

"I would say that I was not satisfied that the Dean report was complete and also I thought it was my obligation to go beyond . . . ," the President said.

"Remember you had John Dean go to Camp David to write it up," Ehrlichman said. "He came down and said, 'I can't . . . ' That is the tipoff right then and you started to move."

Nixon asked, "How do I get credit for getting Magruder to the stand?"

"Well, it's very simple," Ehrlichman said. "You took Dean off the case right then. . . . So then we started digging into it and we went to San Clemente. While I was out there I talked to a lot of people on the telephone, talked to several witnesses in person, kept feeding information to you and as soon as you saw the dimensions of this thing from the reports you were getting . . . It culminated last week—"

"Right," Nixon said.

Ehrlichman picked it up again: "In your decision that Mitchell should be brought down here; Magruder should be brought in; Strachan should be brought in. . . . You should say, 'I heard enough that I was satisfied that it was time to precipitously move. I called the Attorney General. . . . ' "

Then the President saw Dean one more time. The counsel's proposed letter read:

> You informed me that Bob Haldeman and John Ehrlichman have verbally tendered their request to give them immediate and indefinite leave of absence from the staff. So I declare I wish also to confirm my similar request that I be given such a leave of absence from the staff.

That led to more hours of Nixon-Haldeman-Ehrlichman meetings. But the President was unwilling to push out Haldeman and Ehrlichman and afraid to do it to Dean alone. "There's no sense in aggravating Dean," Nixon said. "He'll do anything to save his own ass. He's pissing as high as he can get now. We can't let him piss higher"—because higher meant pissing on the President.

At 4:42 that afternoon, the President went over to the Briefing Room and read a three-page statement that began: "I have two announcements to make."

The first was an agreement with the Senate Watergate committee, which was scheduled to begin public hearings on May 15, on ground rules for invoking executive privilege. The second was the President's announcement that he had broken the case:

> On March 21, as a result of serious charges which came to my attention . . . I began intensive new inquiries into this whole matter. . . . I can report today there have been major developments in the case concerning which it would be improper to be more specific now, except to say that real progress has been made in finding the truth. . . .

He added that he had informed the Attorney General that no immunity from prosecution should be granted to high officials in the administration in return for their testimony. That was aimed at Dean. If Dean wanted to talk, he had to risk prison—and, Nixon thought, his enthusiasm for bringing down the White House might be tempered by the temptation of a possible presidential pardon. Dean's attorney, Charles Shaffer, telephoned his client about the President's moves: "For a guy who you say is sometimes a little loose upstairs, he looks pretty clever to me."

Briefing the press after the President's statement, Ron Ziegler said it was now "the operative statement on Watergate." Pressed by reporters on what the President had said in the past, he added: "Other statements are inoperative."

CHAPTER 39

April 30, 1973

O
N APRIL 17, the President hosted a state dinner for Prime Minister Giulio Andreotti of Italy. A famous Italian-American, Frank Sinatra, entertained, and a good time was had by all. Then, just before midnight, Nixon telephoned Henry Kissinger at home; he sounded close to tears. He talked about the pressure he was under to get rid of Haldeman and Ehrlichman. That was what Henry Petersen was urging him to do, and that night his old law partner Len Garment, who was acting as counsel to the President while Nixon tried to decide what to do about Dean, told him the same thing: he had to clean house, the White House.

"Goddamn, I think of these good men," Nixon said.

". . . who wanted to do the right thing," Kissinger completed the sentence.

"The real culprit is Mitchell, of course," the President said. "He's in charge of the whole goddamn thing, and John Mitchell should step up like a man and say, 'Look, I was in charge; I take the responsibility.' Period. . . . They're going to get him."

"I think to fire Haldeman would make him the villain."

"Well, in the end he probably will have to go, Henry. They're going to rip him up good. . . . I'm not going to fire a guy on the basis of a charge made by Dean, who basically is trying to save his ass and get immunity. . . ."

"Well, the major thing now, Mr. President, if I may say so, is to protect the presidency and your authority."

"That will be hard. . . . Well, if we can. If we can we will, and if we don't, what the hell. Maybe we'll even consider the possibility of, frankly, just throwing myself on the sword . . ."

"No!"

". . . and letting Agnew take it. What the hell."

"That is out of the question, with all due respect, Mr. President," Kissinger said. He had gone to a small party hosted by Sinatra after the dinner and was surprised when Vice President Agnew coolly told him that Haldeman and Ehrlichman were finished, then added: "The President can't save them. He'll be lucky to save himself."

Now when Nixon mentioned Agnew, Kissinger said: "That cannot be considered. The personality, what it would do to the presidency, and the historical injustice of it. Why should you do it, and what good would it do? Whom would it help? It wouldn't help the country."

They talked on for fifteen minutes. Winding down, Nixon said, "Well, don't you get discouraged."

"Mr. President, I'm not discouraged."

"You do your job. Two or three of us have got to stick around to hold the goddamn fort."

"You have saved this country, Mr. President. The history books will show that, when no one will know what Watergate means."

"Yup. Well, it'll be a great day on the other side for all of our enemies, won't it? The *Times,* the *Post,* the rest—shit."

"Mr. President. You have to gather the wagons and pull it through, as you've done so often."

In fact, Kissinger was discouraged, and then some. The President was no longer available for rambling, worldly conversations, throwing the fate of nations around like a football. Kissinger was having trouble getting Nixon to concentrate even on Vietnam. The North Vietnamese, according to intelligence sources, had sent at least thirty-five thousand fresh troops south since the signing of the settlement. As early as mid-March, Kissinger and the Joint Chiefs of Staff had recommended massive bombing of the Ho Chi Minh Trail, which was choked with trucks ferrying men and supplies into South Vietnam—and into Laos and Cambodia. At first, Nixon had decided against any action until all American prisoners were back home. Then, by the time that happened, he seemed incapable of focusing on anything but Watergate and his hours of strategizing with Haldeman and Ehrlichman and long telephone conversations with Petersen, who was providing Nixon with reports on the doings of investigators and the Washington grand jury. A month of heavy bombing was finally scheduled to begin in mid-April, but the President never gave the order. Kissinger blamed John Dean for that.

At home that night, Haldeman dictated: "Another major Watergate day . . . super-major."

The next morning, April 18, at his first morning meeting with Haldeman, the President told his chief of staff that he wanted him to take all of the tapes from closets around the White House—there were more than eight hundred five-inch tape reels, each holding six hours of conversation—and store them somewhere outside the building until they could be permanently stored in a Nixon library. The two of them had begun talking about the tapes a week earlier and at one point the President had said he wanted them destroyed. "I don't want to have in the record discussions we've had in this room on Watergate," he had told Haldeman on April 9. "You know, we've discussed a lot of that stuff."

A month before, on March 18, Nixon had ordered the removal of the taping system in Aspen Lodge at Camp David; it had been installed in May 1972. But there were still six stations in operation: in the Oval Office, EOB 175, and the Cabinet Room, and on the telephones in the Oval Office, EOB 175, and the Lincoln sitting room in the residence. All the stations had originally been voice-activated, but after the April 9 conversation, a switch was put inside the Wilson desk, and this allowed Nixon to turn the microphones on and off during conversations in the Oval Office.

That afternoon, April 18, Petersen called the President to tell him that investigators had learned, from Dean, about the burglary of Dr. Fielding's office.

"I know about that," the President said. "That's a national security matter. You stay out of that."

Petersen dutifully passed that as an order to Earl Silbert, the Washington prosecutor. Silbert angrily accused Petersen of being an agent of the President. The two of them shouted at each other, then went together to see Attorney General Kleindienst, who told them that he was going to withdraw from any involvement in the Watergate investigation because of his ties to Mitchell, to Dean, and to Robert Mardian. But he listened to their argument.

THE STONE WALL burst the next day, April 19. The lead headline across the top of *The New York Times* of April 20 read:

MITCHELL NOW SAYS HE HEARD BUGGING PLOT
AT THREE MEETINGS IN 1972, BUT REJECTED IT

Beneath those words and large photographs of Mitchell and Dean, the newspaper printed a two-column box four inches deep, a device last used to report the events in the many theaters of World War II. But this box was headed "Watergate at a Glance."

> • MR. MITCHELL has been subpoenaed to appear before the grand jury today. . . . Written plans for the bugging were hidden from the authorities last year. . . . Eight cartons of documents were reportedly removed from the White House. . . .

> • ATTORNEY GENERAL RICHARD KLEINDIENST confirmed that he had withdrawn from the case. . . .

> • E. HOWARD HUNT JR., one of the Watergate conspirators, testified for about two hours before the Federal grand jury. . . .

> • HERBERT W. KALMBACH . . . was seen entering the Federal Courthouse in Washington to consult with Government prosecutors. . . .

> • JOHN W. DEAN 3RD, the White House counsel, issued a statement declaring . . .

The Dean statement, which was the lead story in *The Washington Post,* had been telephoned to newspapers by his secretary: "Some may hope or think that I will become a scapegoat in the Watergate case. Anyone who believes this does not know me, know the true facts, nor understand our system of justice."

Inside the White House that morning, Haldeman recorded: "The P had me in first thing this morning. Read me a note Julie had written, talking about how great he is and the family all stand behind him. We had a quick discussion on Watergate, and the P then had to go into the head, and had me come in with him while standing in the hall, and we continued this discussion, mainly about the need to hunker down. . . ."

Then the President flew to Key Biscayne, leaving Haldeman and Ehrlichman behind. On Easter Sunday, he called each of them, telling Haldeman: "Remember, you're doing the right thing. That's what I used to think when I killed some innocent children in Hanoi." He also called Dean, wishing him "Happy Easter"—and Dean immediately called newspapers to say the President told him, "You're still my counsel."

Ziegler was with Nixon in Florida and called Haldeman on Monday, April 23, to say that the President believed he and Ehrlichman had to resign. Ziegler paraphrased what Nixon had said: "He must get this out of his mind. He has an obligation to run the nation and he cannot, as a human being, run the country with this on his mind."

Then the press secretary read from his notes:

There's no good way to handle this. It will in no way separate Ehrlichman and Haldeman from me.... They did no wrongdoing.... There's no way that this will not go down in history as a very bad chapter, that the Presidency is seriously hurt, and I must accept responsibility for this.... Haldeman and Ehrlichman are strong men, probably the strongest men in dedication who have ever served the Presidency. But as we look at the political forces, the forces against the Presidency, the country must have a president moving in a direction ... I'm still involved. Charges and claims are still made that I knew about it and was aware of it.... I believe in these two men, I love these two men. The White House can't respond and can't work with this force against us, though.

"I'VE GOT TO SEE YOU RIGHT AWAY," began Kleindienst in a call to the President on the afternoon of April 25. As soon as he walked into EOB 175 twenty minutes later, the Attorney General began to read from the April 16 memo from Silbert to Petersen about Dean's testimony to prosecutors: "This is to inform you that on Sunday, April 15, 1973, I received information that on a date unspecified Gordon Liddy and Howard Hunt burglarized the offices of a psychiatrist ..."

"That's correct," Nixon said. Kleindienst continued reading:

"... of Daniel Ellsberg to obtain the psychiatrist's files on Ellsberg."

Kleindienst told the President about the argument between Silbert and Petersen, then said the legal problem with the discovery of the Fielding burglary was not about Watergate, but about the trial of Ellsberg going on in Santa Monica. The prosecution, in this case the Justice Department, was obligated to inform the judge that it had come into possession of information that could impact on the rights of the defendant. Then the judge, Matthew Byrne, had to decide whether to advise the defendant and his attorneys.

"This is national security," the President said. But Kleindienst went on: "This is going to be out in the street tomorrow or two days from now, a week, and the law clearly dictates that we have to do—it could be another goddamn cover-up, you know.... We can't have another cover-up, Mr. President."

"I don't want any cover-ups of anything," Nixon said. "You know that."

"... I've got to do this, Mr. President," Kleindienst said.

"I know, I know ...," Nixon said. "Dean runs in there, let's see what his motive is for telling Silbert this?"

Kleindienst answered, "His motive is to create an environment whereby he will get immunity."

"Can it be given?"

"Sure, we can give him immunity. . . . Petersen has asked me the same question, and he even comes up to the point where a trump card of Dean would be that I'm going to implicate the President—and I told Henry at that point you have to tell Dean to go fuck himself. You're not going to blackmail the government of the United States and implicate the President in the Ellsberg matter."

Nixon talked twice more that day to Kleindienst, ending a telephone conversation after dinner by urging the Attorney General to make the Ellsberg prosecutors understand that the break-in was an important national security matter. Then he said: "Good luck. What the hell, you know. People say impeach the President. Well, then they get Agnew. What the hell?"

"There's not going to be anything like that, Mr. President," said Kleindienst.

In between conversations with Kleindienst, Nixon spoke for more than an hour with Petersen, aggressively trying to find out what Dean was telling prosecutors. Petersen told him that Dean had told Silbert about Pat Gray's destruction of the envelopes of material from Hunt's safe, saying again that it was done on Ehrlichman's "deep six" orders. The President, for the moment, was more interested in Dean's status, saying: "I've raised the problem with you very candidly about the question of immunity. That's your decision. But, Henry, he can't make the immunity thing on the basis of blackmailing the President."

"I agree, Mr. President."

"He says, look, I won't say that I talked to the President about the question of whether or not we could get this money and the President said, well, we can get the money et cetera, et cetera. I want you to know that he was told that this is a road you can't go down, and if you don't believe me on this—understand I don't ask you to believe me any more than anybody else. I don't lie to people."

"Neither do I, Mr. President. You may throw me out of here sometimes for what I say, but I'll never lie, Mr. President."

"I just wanted you to know that because if anything comes up, if he starts anything about the fact that there's any other discussion with the President, with regard to paying off Hunt and so forth . . . Because basically you'd be frankly letting him blackmail the President and we'd be living with that the rest of our lives. I'll be damned. . . . I would never approve the payoff of Hunt. . . ."

Nixon continued: "The Presidency has to go ahead here. I've got enormous problems. . . . I've got to meet with the Russians in June and Brandt next Tuesday, Pompidou on May the thirty-first, and deal with the economy and the rest. We cannot let this stinking damned thing kill the Presidency. . . . The second thing. Can you for these eyes only give me your evaluation, your case against Haldeman? . . . Give me a little sheet of paper. Would you do that for me? . . . I want to know what your case is. I haven't asked for that much. . . . When could you have that for me by? Today? Tomorrow? Today is Wednesday."

"By Friday evening."

"I don't want to rush you. . . . Do your best to give me an evaluation because I want to think about it and study about it and make the right decision at the right time. . . . I can assure you, goddamn, if they're in this thing, they're either indicted or named as non-indictable co-conspirators—*That's it!*"

In another conversation with the President that evening, Petersen began talking about his trust in him, saying: "My wife is not a politically sophisticated woman. . . . She said, 'Doesn't all this upset you?' and I said, 'Of course it does.' "

"She said, 'Why the hell doesn't the President do something? . . . Do you think the President knows?' And I looked at her and said, 'If I thought the President knew, I would have to resign.' "

"We've got to get it out. . . . I have wrestled with it. I've been trying to . . ." Nixon said.

"Mr. President, I pray for you, sir."

That night, Nixon again talked to both Petersen and Kleindienst. The subject was Gray and who had ordered him to destroy the Hunt documents, including the phony cables saying that President Kennedy ordered the assassination of South Vietnam's President Diem.

The Attorney General, with Gray in the next room, called the President at 7:44 P.M. to say: "Henry Petersen and I are down here at my office with Pat Gray. Let me give you his version. . . . Several days after the apprehension of the Watergate burglars, he was asked to come over and met in John Ehrlichman's office with him, and there was Dean. . . . John Dean says, 'Pat, here are some highly sensitive and very secret files that were in the possession of Howard Hunt that had nothing to do with the Watergate. They are of a very, very secret, sensitive nature. They should not be put in the FBI files and they should never see the light of day. Here, you take them.' . . . Ehrlichman said nothing about the documents. . . . That's Pat's story."

So, either Dean or Ehrlichman was lying—and the only witness to that conversation in June 1972, Gray, said the liar was Dean. Or perhaps Gray was lying, because he knew Nixon wanted to protect Ehrlichman and impugn Dean. The President told Kleindienst that Gray, still the act-ing FBI director, had to resign immediately. The Attorney General recom-mended that he be replaced by the bureau's number two man, Mark Felt.

"Another all day shot on the Watergate," Haldeman dictated into his diary.

Nixon rejected the Felt suggestion the next day, April 27: "I don't want him. I can't have him. I just talked to Bill Ruckelshaus and Bill is a Mister Clean"—he was director of the Environmental Protection Agency—"I want a fellow in there who is not part of the old guard."

That day began as what looked like an ordinary presidential day. Nixon flew to Meridian, Mississippi, with Senator John Stennis, to dedi-cate a naval air station that was being renamed the Stennis Center. On the way, *Air Force One* circled over flood damage in the Mississippi Valley and then landed to the cheers of more than twelve thousand local people. Stennis, a Democrat, praised the President for his work ethic and tough-ness, saying that was what got American prisoners back from Vietnam. On the way back to Washington, Ziegler told the pool reporters in the back of the plane that Gray was announcing his resignation as acting FBI director.

Back in Washington, by 4 P.M., the President resumed his conver-sations with Kleindienst and Petersen. Down the hall, Haldeman was lis-tening again and again to the recording of Nixon's meeting with Dean on March 21. After Petersen and Kleindienst left, Haldeman told the Presi-dent that the tape showed he had given no specific instructions to raise money to pay off Hunt.

By 8:30 the President was alone in EOB 175 with Ziegler. He was feeling sorry for himself: "The whole hopes of the whole goddamned world of peace, you know, Ron, you know where they rest, they rest right here in this damn chair. . . . The press has got to realize that. Whatever they think of me they've got to realize I'm the only one in the present time in this whole wide blinking world that can do a goddamn thing, you know. Keep it from blowing up. . . ."

"That's right. . . . Yes, Sir. . . . That's right. . . . That's right," said Ziegler. The dog, King Timahoe, barked. "King!" said the President. "Goddamn, get off of me!"

Then he continued: "And Bob made a point to me today, he said look, half of me is worth one of anybody else, and he is exactly right."

"But that isn't the point," Ziegler said.

"Half of him is damaged goods. That's what he doesn't realize, you see? He's damaged goods. Right?"

"That's right."

"You can't have damaged goods in the White House."

"That's right."

"If we went in sackcloth and ashes and fired the whole White House staff . . . that isn't going to satisfy those goddamned cannibals. They'd still be after us. Who are they after? Hell, they're not after Haldeman or Ehrlichman or Dean; they're after me, the President. They hate my guts!"

He told Ziegler to tell Ray Price, his chief speechwriter, to begin working on a statement about personnel changes: "Tell him make it strong, not cross, not apologetic. Just say this is the fact. I assume the responsibility. Be a president and not a peon. You tell him that. . . . The President can't come before the country and say, look, I made a horrible mistake and please forgive me, my friends. . . . You realize that if the President comes in and apologizes, and I'm very sorry—Kennedy didn't do that in the Bay of Pigs. He says I take responsibility, da, da, da, and I ask for your support. . . ."

Then—it was almost 9:30 P.M.—Nixon decided he wanted to go to Camp David, and away he went. The next morning's *Washington Post* reported: "The President cancelled a scheduled meeting today with his chief economic advisers, and flew off alone to his mountaintop Camp David retreat, where he decided apparently on short notice to spend the full weekend. It was clear that Mr. Nixon was planning to spend the weekend privately pondering what to do next."

"THAT'S QUITE A COLLECTION of headlines this morning, isn't it?" the President said to Ziegler in his first call the next morning, April 28, at 8:21.

The first paper he saw, *The Washington Post,* said across the top of its front page:

GRAY RESIGNS; RUCKELSHAUS HEADS FBI;
HUNT, LIDDY LINKED TO ELLSBERG CASE

The New York Times had a three-deck banner:

GRAY QUITS THE F.B.I., RUCKELSHAUS NAMED;
A JUSTICE DEPARTMENT MEMO SAYS LIDDY AND HUNT
RAIDED OFFICE OF ELLSBERG'S PSYCHIATRIST

There were two photographs on the *Times*'s front page. One showing Haldeman and Ehrlichman getting off *Air Force One* after the Mississippi trip. The other showed Ellsberg and his wife, happily meeting reporters after Judge Byrne released the Kleindienst-Petersen memo—and made it clear that the Pentagon Papers charges were about to be dismissed.

The President called Haldeman next. First, Haldeman confirmed that he and Ehrlichman were coming to Camp David—and that they understood that they would be leaving the White House. Nixon's next question was about his own vulnerability; he was wondering about the comments he had written on news summaries over the years and whether Dean might have a collection of them.

"I wanted to ask you a question," he said. "You know, I mark things in news summaries now and then, you know, to do this, Good God, check on this, what the hell's this guy doing, and so forth and so on. . . . It was not your practice to just make multiliths of those and send them to fellows like Dean and so forth? They don't have the verbatims of that stuff, do they?"

"No," Haldeman answered. "What they have is a memo from the staff secretary saying it's been requested that you check such and such."

"Does it indicate the President has requested?"

"No. . . . And it doesn't ask for a report back to the President. It says: Please report back to the staff secretary on your actions, or something, by April 15th. And then the originals of those go into your file. . . . That was standard procedure."

After his round of calls, the President walked into the living room and was surprised to see a fire burning in the fireplace. Then he saw his daughter, Tricia, sitting on the couch in front of the fire. There were tears in her eyes. She said that she had been up all night at the White House talking with her sister, Julie, and Julie's husband, David Eisenhower, and they all agreed that Haldeman and Ehrlichman must resign.

"You know," she said. "I never felt that the way they handled people served you well—but I promise you I made my decision carefully and objectively. . . . I am speaking for Julie, David and Mama as well. . . . If you decide not to take our advice, we will understand. Whatever you do, just remember we will support you, and we love you very much."

The next morning, the Sunday *Washington Post,* delivered to Camp David, carried seven Watergate stories. In the lead story, Bernstein and Woodward wrote: "Presidential counsel John W. Dean III intends to swear under oath that he gave regular reports on the progress of the cover-up to Haldeman and Ehrlichman at their direction, reliable sources reported yesterday."

Haldeman and Ehrlichman followed the Sunday papers to Camp David. Ziegler met them and said he had to talk to Haldeman. They walked along a path in the woods. The press secretary said the President had just told him that he had made a firm decision to resign. "That's not going to happen," Haldeman said. "He's just steeling himself to meet with us. He's creating a big crisis he can't meet, so that he can meet the lesser crisis of dealing with us."

Haldeman walked over to Aspen Lodge, carrying a book of the writings of Mary Baker Eddy, the founder of his faith, Christian Science. He was surprised at how bad the President looked. Nixon shook hands at the door, which he had never done before. The two of them stepped onto the porch, which overlooked the spring trees in the valley below and beds of tulips around the cabin. "I have to enjoy this," Nixon said, "because I may not be alive much longer." He told Haldeman that he prayed on his knees every night, as his mother had taught him. He said he had prayed long and hard that night and hoped he would not wake up in the morning.

Haldeman said he disagreed with Nixon's decision on the resignations, but he accepted it. "What you have to remember," Haldeman said, "is that nothing that has happened in the Watergate mess has changed your mandate in the non-Watergate areas. That is what matters. That is what you do best."

Haldeman came out after about forty minutes. He saw Ehrlichman, pointed toward Aspen Lodge, and said, "Your turn."

"How did it go?"

"About as we thought."

The President shook hands with Ehrlichman, too. He told him about praying and hoping he would not wake. "Don't talk like that," Ehrlichman said. "Don't think like that."

The President began to cry. "This is like cutting off my arms," he said, and cried more. "You and Bob, you'll need money; I have some— Bebe has it—and you can have it."

"That would just make things worse," said Ehrlichman. "You can do one thing for me though, sometime. Just explain all this to my kids, will you?"

Ziegler came into the lodge after Ehrlichman left. The lights were off and the President stood framed in the window, looking out over the mountains. He was surprised when Ziegler came up behind him. He turned and said, "It's all over, Ron, do you know that?"

Ziegler knew he meant his presidency. Nixon sat down and cried. Ziegler stood for a long time, looking at the floor in the dark. He thought of the days just after Nixon was elected, before the Inaugural. President Johnson had given the Nixons the use of *Air Force One*. The young press secretary—he was twenty-nine then—was on board but no one knew that or saw him there. The Nixons came up the stairway alone, looked into the plane, and Nixon put his arms around his wife's waist, picking her up, and they twirled around, laughing and laughing. Now this.

An hour later, Ray Price came in with final drafts of the statement. He was shocked by how Nixon looked. "Ravaged" was the word in his mind. He looked toward Ziegler, who was relieved to see him come in. The President said, "Maybe I should resign, Ray. If you think so just put it in."

Then Nixon walked outside, toward the heated swimming pool he had ordered built just outside his door. Price stayed a few steps behind. He was afraid the President might try to kill himself.

Haldeman and Ehrlichman stayed at Camp David until after dark, working on the wording of their resignation letters. As they left, the President went to their helicopter and said, "I wish I were as strong as you. God bless you both." Neither of them spoke on the trip back.

The next day, April 30, the President stayed at Camp David until 6 P.M., working on his first Watergate speech. Walking to the Oval Office, he passed an FBI agent guarding the door to Haldeman's office, then realized the man was there to prevent records from being destroyed or taken away. He turned, came back, and shoved the FBI man against the wall. "What the hell is this?" said the President. "These men are not criminals."

He went on national television from the Oval Office at 9 P.M., announcing the resignations of Haldeman and Ehrlichman, calling them "two of the finest public servants it has been my privilege to know." Then he announced the resignation of Attorney General Kleindienst and said his successor would be Elliot Richardson, the patrician Massachusetts Republican who had served just one hundred days as secretary of defense. Before the speech, Nixon had told Kissinger about the Richardson appointment, saying, "He's trusted by the so-called damned establishment. . . . first in his class at Harvard Law . . . I'm going to give him a free hand."

On television the President said: "I have given him complete authority to make all decisions bearing upon the prosecution of the Watergate case and related matters. I have instructed him that if he should consider it appropriate, he has the authority to name a special supervising prosecutor for matters arising out of the case."

He said, "The Counsel to the President, John Dean, has also resigned."

After the statement, the President walked into the press briefing room. There were only fifteen people there and without television lights on the room was dim. The President stood in the shadows behind Ziegler's lectern and said: "Ladies and gentlemen of the press, we have had our differences in the past, and I hope you give me hell every time you think I'm wrong. I hope I'm worthy of your trust."

Nixon went upstairs and waited for the telephone calls that always followed a television appearance. Only Caspar Weinberger called in the first hour. Then, at 10:16 P.M., the phone in the Lincoln sitting room rang again. It was Haldeman, who told him that the White House switchboard was turning away callers, saying they had orders not to let calls through. He did not know why.

"You're a strong man," Nixon said. "Godammit, and I love you."

Then he said: "I don't know whether you can call and get any reaction and call me back—like the old style. Would you mind?"

"I don't think I can. I don't . . . I'm in kind of an odd spot. . . ."

EPILOGUE

Amiddle

AFTER HIS TELEVISION APPEARANCE of April 30, President Nixon left Washington for Key Biscayne. From there, he named General Alexander Haig as his new chief of staff. During the next six months, until the end of November 1973, the President spent only thirty-two days in Washington, ten of them as a patient, with pneumonia, at Walter Reed Army Hospital. He stopped annotating daily news summaries and did not make a single diary entry for almost fourteen months. The first entry after April 30, 1973, was in June of 1974.

By the middle of May 1973, Richard Nixon's world had been turned upside down. John Mitchell and Maurice Stans were indicted on May 10 for perjury in testifying about campaign contributions. The next day in Los Angeles the charges against Daniel Ellsberg were dropped because of the break-in of his psychiatrist's office by the White House Plumbers. The hearings of the Senate Select Committee on Presidential Campaign Activities, chaired by Senator Sam Ervin, began on May 17. The next day, attorney general designate Elliot Richardson, under pressure during his confirmation hearings before the Senate Judiciary Committee, announced that he would name a Democrat as the Justice Department's special prosecutor for Watergate. His choice was Archibald Cox of Harvard Law School, who had served as solicitor general during the Kennedy administration. On July 16, Alexander Butterfield, testifying before the Ervin committee, publicly revealed the existence of the White House taping system.

The Senate Watergate committee recessed early in August after thirty-seven days of televised hearings. On August 15, the President, who had refused to testify, went on television to say: "Not only was I unaware of any cover-up, but . . . I was unaware of anything to cover up." Meanwhile, Vice President Agnew was also on television defending himself. "Damned lies," he called charges of bribery and extortion being heard by a Baltimore grand jury investigating construction contracts when he was a county executive and governor of Maryland. Then, on August 22, from San Clemente, in his first press conference in more than five months, the President announced that Secretary of State William Rogers was resigning and would be replaced by Henry Kissinger. He also said Kissinger would retain his position as national security adviser. "Al Haig is keeping the country together, and I am keeping the world together," Kissinger told someone that summer.

On September 11, 1973, with United States encouragement, but no proved American aid, generals in Chile, led by Augusto Pinochet, overthrew the government of the country's elected president, Salvador Allende. The Marxist politician was found dead in his office and the military announced he had committed suicide as tanks and air force planes bombarded the presidential palace in Santiago. On October 6, Yom Kippur, the Jewish Day of Atonement, Egyptian troops crossed the Suez Canal in an all-out attack on Israeli positions in the Sinai Peninsula, and Syrian planes and troops attacked Israeli positions to the north on the Golan Heights. The President was in Key Biscayne when the war began, and he stayed there for four days, consumed by Watergate and plotting an endgame to get Agnew quietly out of office. On the fourth day of the fighting, October 10, with the President back in Washington, the Vice President resigned after pleading nolo contendere to Justice Department income tax charges related to payoffs in his Maryland days. Forty-eight hours later, the President announced that he was submitting for Senate confirmation the name of House Minority Leader Gerald Ford as the first appointed vice president in the nation's history. Nine days later, on Saturday night, October 20, Nixon ordered Attorney General Elliot Richardson to fire Archibald Cox, the special prosecutor. Richardson refused and resigned. So did the deputy attorney general, William Ruckelshaus. Finally, Solicitor General Robert Bork signed the dismissal order and the press had another new crisis to name. "Saturday Night Massacre" was the chosen shorthand. Two days later, the House Democratic leadership ordered the Judiciary Committee to begin consideration of whether the President had committed impeachable offenses.

Meanwhile, the war in the Middle East was largely left to Kissinger, although Nixon did make the most important single decision.

The Israelis were prevailing on the ground but were taking large losses in men and equipment, as the Soviets continued to resupply the Egyptian and Syrian armies. In Washington, Kissinger and Defense Secretary James Schlesinger, conferring with Haig rather than with the President, were still debating how to aid Israel without worsening American relationships with Arab oil suppliers—worrying, as always, about provoking Soviet intervention. There were, after all, already lines of cars at American gasoline stations as gas supplies dwindled and prices doubled and doubled again because of oil embargoes aimed at the United States and other allies of Israel. On October 13, after a call from Schlesinger to Haig, the President took charge for a day. "Do it now!" he ordered the Defense Department. American transports began flying into Israel that day; so did fifty new Phantom jets for the Israeli air force. Huge United States transport planes flew 550 sorties, carrying more tons of equipment and ammunition into Israel in two weeks than had been delivered during the Berlin airlift of 1948 and 1949. Traffic stopped in the streets of Tel Aviv as the first transports began to land. People waved and sang "God Bless America."

Then it was back to Watergate. By the end of the year, there were stories told at the Georgetown dinners Nixon so hated that the President was in terrible shape, that he was drinking, that he was having a breakdown. But they were not printed or broadcast, because so few people actually saw Nixon as he restlessly moved between Camp David, Key Biscayne, and San Clemente. "President is acting very strangely," wrote one who did see Nixon in those days, the Speaker of the House, Tip O'Neill, in his notes of a meeting at the White House during the Yom Kippur War. Two months later, Senator Barry Goldwater wrote: "I have reason to suspect that all might not be well mentally in the White House. This is the only copy that will ever be made of this; it will be locked in my safe." There were also a couple of public incidents. In New Orleans for a speech to the Veterans of Foreign Wars convention, Nixon was seen pushing Ron Ziegler toward photographers and reporters, telling him to keep them away. In Orlando, Florida, editors at an Associated Press convention asked the President a series of questions about his personal finances and new IRS investigations of his income tax returns from 1969 to 1972. He said, finally: "I welcome this kind of examination, because people have got to know whether or not their President is a crook. Well, I am not a crook."

Four days after the Orlando appearance, it was revealed that there was an eighteen-and-a-half minute gap in the recording of an Oval Office conversation between Nixon and Haldeman on June 20, 1972, three days after the Watergate break-in. Rose Mary Woods said she had erased the tape accidently, but the White House was forced to deny speculation in Congress and the press that the President himself was destroying evidence. While Nixon was denying and denying, it was announced that Henry Kissinger and Le Duc Tho had jointly been awarded the Nobel Peace Prize.

The country's wholesale price index rose 18.2 percent during 1973. Some of that was because of the double-digit price increases in petroleum products, partly because of new embargoes imposed by the Organization of Petroleum Exporting Countries after the defeat of Egypt and Syria. But the consensus among American economists, liberal and conservative, was that Nixon's wage and price controls had effectively held back modest inflation in the election year of 1972 and created a significantly worse situation in 1973 and 1974. Gas station lines and reduced speed limits on highways were symbols of those troubles, but the reality was worse: the American economy was slipping into recession even as consumer prices were increasing as much as 2 percent per month.

On March 1, 1974, the federal grand jury in Washington announced the indictment of seven men from the White House, including Haldeman, Ehrlichman, John Mitchell, Charles Colson, and Robert Mardian. The charges were lying to the FBI and the grand jury, and conspiring to pay hush money to the Watergate burglars. By then, the men who came to the White House in 1969 with what they considered a moral mandate and high purpose, plea-bargainers now, were giving investigators from the Justice Department and the House Judiciary Committee, which was considering impeachment hearings, a rough idea of what had happened inside the Nixon White House. *Time* magazine that week summarized what the new Watergate special prosecutor, Leon Jaworski, a former president of the American Bar Association, was looking for in a round of new subpoenas:

> Tapes and documents related to: 1) the possible "sale" of ambassadorships to large contributors; 2) the Administration's settlement of an antitrust suit against ITT; 3) meetings at which Nixon and aides discussed increased dairy supports; 4) Nixon's notations from the summer and fall of 1972 on the White House News Summary; 5) the records of former White House aide John Ehrlichman on his dealings with Nixon's secret squad of plumber investigators; 6) other Nixon conversations with his aides relating to the Watergate cover-up conspiracy; 7) the location of the tape containing an 18½ minute gap during the period in which Nixon claimed all of the subpoenaed tapes were in his custody. . . .

On April 29, 1974, a year after he jettisoned H. R. Haldeman and John Ehrlichman, the President went on television, sitting before stacks of blue loose-leaf books that contained two hundred thousand words of heavily edited tape transcripts. "As far as the President's role with regard to Watergate is concerned," he said, "the entire story is there." But it was not. The transcripts released the next morning contained confusing versions of only eleven of the sixty-four conversations specifically cited in subpoenas and court orders. The President's swearing on the tapes surprised many—the phrase "expletive deleted" in the transcripts became a national joke. Senate Minority Leader Hugh Scott called the transcripts "deplorable, shabby, disgusting, and immoral." On June 6, the *Los Angeles Times* reported that a sealed addendum to the March 1 federal indictments named the President of the United States as "an unindicted coconspirator" in the Watergate cover-up. The actual wording of the finding, released on June 15, was: "There is probable cause to believe that Richard M. Nixon (among others) was a member of the conspiracy to defraud the United States and to obstruct Justice."

Five days later, on June 12, the same man was being seen and cheered by more than five million people. In Egypt.

Egyptian President Anwar Sadat had invited Nixon to the Middle East for what amounted to a victory lap after months of Kissinger shuttle diplomacy between Arab countries and Israel had brought an uneasy peace to the region. The huge crowds along the country's main rail line from Cairo to Alexandria chanted, "Nixon! Nixon!" under great banners showing pictures of the two presidents over the slogan, "TWO GREAT MEN DEDICATED TO PEACE AND PROGRESS." Then Nixon moved on to Saudi Arabia, Syria, Jordan, and Israel.

The personal triumph made it seem for a few days that he might survive Watergate. "Turned the corner" was the line pushed by the White House, or what was left of it. After he returned, it was revealed that Nixon had hidden the fact that he had phlebitis, a painful life-threatening vein inflammation, and that he could have died on the trip—a political warrior struck down at a peak.

The President was back for just five days before he took off for a Moscow summit meeting with Soviet leader Leonid Brezhnev. The two men talked for six days, modifying the ABM agreement, but were unable to agree on limitations of offensive missile construction. They did, however, agree to meet again in October or November—of 1974.

On July 24, with more than a dozen of the President's former aides already sentenced to prison for burglaries or for knowledge of the cover-ups and payment of hush money, the Supreme Court ruled unanimously that the President must release the tapes. Between July 27 and 30, the Judiciary Committee, after a month of public hearings, voted to submit three articles of impeachment of the President to the full House. On

August 2, subpoenaed tapes, including the June 23, 1972, conversations in which Nixon and Haldeman had talked about using the CIA and FBI to present the Watergate break-in as a matter of national security, were delivered to Judge John Sirica.

Inside the White House, the President's lawyers called that tape "the smoking gun," proof that the President knew about the burglary and had set out to keep the facts from the government's own investigators. Transcripts of the tapes were released on August 5 and the President went on television one more time, admitting that he had listened alone to the June 23 tape in May 1973, an admission that confirmed that he had knowingly lied—to the nation, to the courts, to Congress, to his staff and lawyers, to his family, and probably to himself day after day, month after month, for more than two years. "Whatever mistakes I made in the handling of Watergate," he said, "the basic truth remains that when all the facts were brought to my attention I insisted on a full investigation and prosecution of those guilty. I am firmly convinced that the record, in its entirety, does not justify the extreme step of impeachment and removal of a President."

That statement was not true. It also came too late. On August 8, Nixon went on television to announce that he would resign the next day at noon. The last news summary, was placed on the Wilson desk in the Oval Office on the morning of August 9. The desktop was otherwise empty except for a telephone. Steven Bull was placing the last boxes he had packed on *Marine One,* the helicopter that would carry Nixon to Andrews Air Force Base for his flight to California.

The five-page summary began with NBC News: "Well, one hardly knows what to say," said John Chancellor. "His speech was restrained and statesmanlike." Correspondent Tom Pettit was quoted, saying: "It was the best of Richard Nixon's farewells."

Notes

The first citation of a work lists the author, full title, and publication information. The texts of speeches, press conferences, and other public pronouncements are taken from the *Public Papers of the Presidents of the United States, Richard Nixon* (Washington, D.C.: U.S. Government Printing Office, 1971–1975). All memos are from the Nixon Presidential Materials Project at the National Archives II, unless otherwise noted. Memos to and from President Nixon are in Boxes 1 through 4 of the President's Personal Files, Boxes 1 through 28 of the President's Office Files, or in the presidential correspondence file of the relevant staff member. References to news the President received in his summary and his written reactions to it do not have source notes. These Annotated News Summaries are in POF Boxes 30 through 50.

Items found in the President's desk, which include many of the notes he wrote to himself on yellow legal pads, are filed in PPF boxes 185 through 188. References to the legal pads and other items in the desk will not receive a note.

The President's schedule can be found in the Daily Diary file of the Staff Member and Office File, or in *The Haldeman Diaries*.

"Nixon Tapes" will be the generic term for recordings made at the White House, Old Executive Office Building, and Camp David, and transcribed by Stanley Kutler in *Abuse of Power*, by William Doyle in *Inside the Oval Office*, and by the author; in books and news accounts by *The New York Times* and *The Washington Post*; and by the Nixon Library in Yorba Linda, California.

Abbreviations

The following abbreviations are used throughout the notes:

ANS   Annotated News Summary
ANS nd   Annotated News Summary (not dated)
HRHD   *The Haldeman Diaries*

HRHD (excised)	section was excised from the published Haldeman diaries (book and cd-rom) for national security, privacy, or other reasons
int.	interview (by author unless specified)
LC	Library of Congress
MemCon	Memorandum of Conversation
NA	National Archives
NSA	National Security Archives
NSC	National Security Council
NSDM	National Security Decision Memorandum
NSSM	National Security Study Memorandum
NT	Nixon Tapes
NYT	*The New York Times*
POF	President's Office Files
PPF	President's Personal Files
RN	Richard Nixon
SMOF	Staff Member and Office Files
WHSF	White House Special Files
WHCF	White House Central Files

Interviews

Administration Officials

Mort Allin, Pat Buchanan, W. Dewey Cloward, John Dean, John Ehrlichman, Robert Finch, Gerald Ford, Leonard Garment, Bill Gulley, Richard Helms, Lee Huebner, Arthur Klebanoff, Herb Klein, Henry Kissinger, Egil "Bud" Krogh, Anthony Lake, Winston Lord, John Mitchell, Roger Morris, Pat Moynihan, Richard Nixon, Leon Panetta, Stanley Pottinger, John Price, Ray Price, William Safire, Caspar Weinberger, Clay Whitehead, and Ron Ziegler.

Scholars, Reporters, and Others

Stephen Ambrose, Robert Sam Anson, Benton Becker, Robert Bartley, Carl Bernstein, Ben Bradlee, James Buckley, Clifford Case, Jess Cook, Elias Demetracopoulos, Joseph Di-Mona, Anatoly Dobrynin, Robert Dole, Susan Eisenhower, Max Frankel, Katharine Graham, Bill Josephson, Sultan Khan, Xandra Kayden, Scott Klososky, Flora Lewis, John V. Lindsay, Stuart Loory, Lawrence Malkin, Frank Mankiewicz, Chris Matthews, Thomas Monsell, Larry O'Brien, Herbert Parmet, Tully Plesser, Dan Rather, Nelson Rockefeller, Gus Schubert, Robert Semple, Jerrold Schecter, William Shawcross, John Taylor, Jerry TerHorst, Lester Toth, Theodore White, Tom Wicker, Bob Woodward, and Mohammad Zia ul-Haq,

Also useful were oral histories conducted by A. James Reichley, which can be found at the Gerald Ford Presidential Library. Among these are interviews with Arthur Burns, John Connally, Robert Finch, Milton Friedman, Alan Greenspan, Bryce Harlow, Jerris Leonard, Paul McCracken, Pat Moynihan, Richard Nixon (1967), Leon Panetta, Ray Price, Ronald Reagan, George Shultz, Herbert Stein, William Timmons, and Caspar Weinberger.

Introduction

12   *Prepared and comfortable:* Art Klebanoff int.

12   *John Price:* Price int.

12   *Ann Whitman:* Whitman's diary entry was published in Robert J. Donovan, *Confidential Secretary: Ann Whitman's 20 Years with Eisenhower and Rockefeller* (New York: Dutton, 1988).

12   *memorized hundreds of pieces of music:* Leonard Garment int.

12   *"I've found a way":* Hess int.

13   *"Firm instructions not to bother":* Harlow oral history, Miller Center, University of Virginia.

13   *Elliot Richardson:* Richardson oral history with James Reichley, Gerald Ford Library.

14   *"He arrived in my office":* Ehrlichman oral history, Miller Center, University of Virginia.

15   *"They deliberately mirrored adversaries":* Lord int.

Prologue: *August 9, 1974*

19   *Stephen Bull . . . pack away the things:* Bull int.

20   *"THE UNAUTHORIZED DISCLOSURE":* PPF Boxes 185–188. All materials from the President's desk referred to in this chapter and throughout the book are found in these four boxes at the National Archives and will not receive additional source notes. References to President Nixon's jottings on his yellow pads will not receive source notes for the same reason.

Chapter 1: *January 21, 1969*

26   *Irish setter, was a gift:* NYT, 1/29/69.

26   *Vickie . . . Pasha:* John Osborne, *The Nixon Watch* (New York: Liveright, 1970), p. 11. This was the first of five collections of Osborne's columns for *The New Republic,* each covering one year of the Nixon administration.

26   *"how adequately the records are being kept":* RN memo to Haldeman, date unknown, PPF Box 1.

26   *The schedule:* President Richard Nixon's Daily Diary, WHCF: SMOF: Daily Diary, Box RC-2. Future references to the President's schedule and movements will not receive source notes. *The Complete Multimedia Edition of the Haldeman Diaries* (Santa Monica, California: Sony Electronics Publishing, 1995) also includes a daily schedule.

26   *Wilson desk:* Safire int.

27   *simpler than it had been:* Richard Nixon, *RN: The Memoirs of Richard Nixon* (New York: Grosset & Dunlap, 1978) (henceforth: Memoirs), pp. 368–369; Hugh Sidey, *Life,* 1/31/69, p. 4.

27   *Patrick Buchanan:* Mort Allin int.

27   *gold-imprinted blue leather:* Fortune, 7/70, p. 105. Nixon received almost all his news from this digest. Unless otherwise indicated, any reference to Nixon receiving or reacting to news stories is taken from the Annotated News Summaries, and will not receive a source note. Likewise, uncited references to the news are taken from the news summary. The summaries are filed chronologically in POF boxes 30–50 at the National Archives.

28   *"major effort to reduce crime":* Buchanan memo to RN, 1/22/69.

28   *"One of our difficulties":* RN memo to Haldeman, 1/21/69.

28   *"with regard to RN's room":* RN memo to Mrs. Nixon, 1/25/69.

29   *a hideaway office:* HRHD, 1/20–21/69.

31   *cottage cheese . . . and a canned pineapple ring:* HRHD, 9/5/69; John Ehrlichman, *Witness to Power: The Nixon Years* (New York: Simon & Schuster, 1982), p. 161.

31   *Urban Affairs Council:* Ray Price memo for the staff secretary, 1/23/69, POF Box 77.

32   *Cabinet Committee on Economic Policy:* Safire memo to Haldeman, 1/24/69.

32   *creating the thing:* HRHD, 1/23/69.

33   *series of memos to John Ehrlichman:* RN memo to Ehrlichman, 1/25/69.

34   *demilitarized zone:* The DMZ defined in 1954 was the area on both sides of the seventeenth parallel dividing North and South Vietnam.

34   *with his party's congressional leaders:* Buchanan memo to RN, on minority leadership meeting, 1/28/69, POF Box 77.

34   *Irish setter named for the town:* NYT, 1/29/69.

34   *first strictly political meeting:* Haldeman memo to RN, 1/30/69.

34   *"He immediately starts":* HRHD, 2/2/69.

35   *in public, though, Haldeman realized:* HRHD, 1/31/69.

35   *dog biscuits . . . nick on the antique:* HRHD, 1/31/69, 2/4/69; Alexander Butterfield memo to RN, 2/5/69, POF Box 77.

35   *"No more landing at airports":* Safire int.

36   *"I want everyone fired":* ANS nd, 2/69, POF Box 30.

36   *"Remarkable ease and sense of pleasure":* Sidey, *Life,* 1/31/69, p. 4.

36   *"I think one point":* RN memo to Ehrlichman, 2/5/69.

37   *"I still have not":* RN memo to Ehrlichman, 1/5/69.

38   *Tkach:* HRHD, 2/9/69; Herbert G. Klein, *Making It Perfectly Clear: An Inside Account of Nixon's Love-Hate Relationship with the Media* (Garden City, New York: Doubleday, 1980), p. 149. Klein wrote: "Haldeman recognized validly, when he organized the 1968 campaign and eventually the White House operation, that Nixon has a highly sensitive energy tolerance point, and exhaustion can make a major difference in his performance and personality."

38   *"There is concern":* Harold Saunders to RN, Memorandum of Conversation (henceforth: MemCon), 2/13/69.

39   *Haldeman was dispatched:* HRHD, 2/15/69.

39   *moved into Rogers's house:* Richard M. Nixon, *Six Crises* (Garden City, New York: Doubleday, 1962), pp. 141–147.

39   *Robert Murphy:* Henry Kissinger, *The White House Years* (Boston: Little, Brown, 1979), p. 26.

39   *William Scranton:* Rowland Evans Jr. and Robert D. Novak, *Nixon in the White House: The Frustration of Power* (New York: Random House, 1971), p. 22.

40   *secret political fund:* RN memo to Haldeman, 1/8/69.

40   *Bebe Rebozo:* Charles Gregory Rebozo, who was the same age as Nixon, was the son of Cuban immigrants. A Florida businessman, Rebozo met Nixon in 1950 through Florida senator George Smathers, a high school classmate of Rebozo's. He graduated from Miami High School in 1930 and began a business career by making enough money to buy a laundromat, which he built into a chain. He was a founder of the Key Biscayne Bank. He had brought his friend, then a New York lawyer, into several land deals, which accounted for more than half of Nixon's net worth of eight hundred thousand dollars at the time of his election as president. Rebozo was a famously shy man, a loner who talked little. One Nixon aide said unkindly, "The President likes to be alone and with Bebe alone he is."

Chapter 2: *February 23, 1969*

41   *shower head pictures:* HRHD, 2/22/69.

41   *fire hose:* Nixon, *Memoirs,* p. 369.

41   *Williamsburg:* HRHD, 2/16/69.

41   *"5th grade teacher, and Mrs. Dargatz":* RN memo to Rose Mary Woods, 2/17/69, PPF Box 1.

41   *"Parker Pen":* ibid.

42   *"coffee table in front of the fireplace":* RN memo to Haldeman, 2/17/69, PPF Box 1.

42   *"artists and orchestra leaders":* RN memo to Woods, 2/17/69, PPF Box 1.

42   *"all the jazz greats"*: HRHD, 2/21/69.

43   *"our goal and the Soviet goal"*: Nixon, *Memoirs*, p. 477.

43   *"They must recognize"*: RN memo to Kissinger, 3/17/70. This memo was dictated a year later, during Israel's war with Egypt and Syria.

43   *"country could run itself"*: Theodore H. White, *The Making of the President, 1968* (New York: Atheneum, 1969), p. 147.

44   *Nixon's affections*: William Safire, *Before the Fall: An Inside View of the Pre-Watergate White House* (Garden City, New York: Doubleday, 1975), pp. 497–498.

44   *"Say one thing, say it again and again"*: Klebanoff int.

45   *blue blazers with insignia*: Melvin Small, *The Presidency of Richard Nixon* (Lawrence: University Press of Kansas, 1999), p. 53.

45   *his conversations with Moynihan . . . "Don't do it"*: Nixon, *Memoirs*, pp. 424–425.

45   *Benjamin Disraeli*: Safire, *Before the Fall*, pp. 533–535.

45   *"heavyweight . . . clean-up hitter"*: Price memo to RN, minutes of the Cabinet meeting, 12/21/70, POF Box 83.

45   *"I don't mind"*: Price memo for the President's File, minutes of the Urban Affairs Council meeting, 2/17/69, POF Box 77.

46   *Republican and Democratic leaders*: Buchanan memo to RN, 2/19/69, POF Box 77.

Chapter 3: *March 17, 1969*

48   *7:58 A.M.*: HRHD, 2/23/69.

48   *three hundred men and women*: Sidey, *Life*, 3/7/69, p. 22.

48   *maroon smoking jacket*: ibid.

48   *sat alone reading*: HRHD, 2/23/69.

48   *Cambodia*: Kissinger, *White House Years*, pp. 240–244.

48   *forty thousand North Vietnamese troops*: Nixon, *Memoirs*, p. 381.

49   *landed in Belgium*: Safire, *Before the Fall*, p. 125.

49   *watching his boss*: HRHD, 2/23/69.

49   *"I have come for work"*: Safire, *Before the Fall*, p. 125.

49   *went back into Air Force One*: HRHD, 2/24/69.

49   *guest list*: Kissinger, *White House Years*, pp. 76, 95.

50   *"a man of no principle"*: Time, 3/7/69, p. 20.

50   *Safire, whose wife . . . "new statesman"*: Safire, *Before the Fall*, p. 126.

50   *thumped the tables*: Nixon, *Memoirs*, p. 371.

50   *President met privately*: Safire, *Before the Fall*, pp. 126–127.

51   *"How long do you think"*: ibid.

51   *the Wall*: HRHD, 2/27/69.

51   *Kennedy's city*: Safire notes, 2/27/69, Safire papers courtesy of Safire, Manuscript Division, LC.

52   *"Battle Hymn of the Republic"*: ibid.

52   *photographs of himself*: Safire, *Before the Fall*, pp. 127–128.

52   *"Here we go"*: ibid.

52   *his host was wearing no coat*: Nixon, *Memoirs*, p. 371.

52   *Shriver*: Kissinger, *White House Years*, pp. 76–77.

52   *"a remote microphone"*: Ehrlichman int.

53   *forty-five minutes*: Sidey, *Life*, 3/14/69, p. 4.

53   *De Gaulle's words as recorded by Nixon*: Nixon, *Memoirs*, pp. 373–374.

54   *canceling the B-52 raids*: HRHD, 3/1/69.

54   *"Why don't you"*: Kissinger, *White House Years*, pp. 109–110.

54   *Air Force One . . . "get from there"*: Safire, *Before the Fall*, pp. 131–132.

54   *briefing the congressional leaders:* Buchanan memo to RN on second meeting with bipartisan leadership, 3/4/69, POF Box 77.

54   *only two or three hours of sleep:* Safire, *Before the Fall,* p. 132.

54   *Soviet Union and China:* NYT, 3/3/69.

56   *"press conference was a masterpiece":* Buchanan memo to RN, 3/4/69, POF Box 30.

56   *headlines over the next couple of days:* ANS nd, 3/69, POF Box 30.

56   *down again within forty-eight hours:* Osborne, *Nixon Watch,* p. 53; HRHD, 3/5/69.

57   *turning back internal reports:* HRHD, 3/20/69.

57   *"Good! (Predict it?)":* ANS, 3/13/69, POF Box 30.

57   *barred the use of the old word "mansion,":* HRHD, 3/6/69.

57   *Trezise:* HRHD, 3/12/69; ANS nd, 3/69, POF Box 30.

57   *thirty-three thousand Americans killed in Vietnam:* ANS, 3/25/69, POF Box 30.

57   *"Good . . . RN is for this":* ANS, 3/23/69, POF Box 30.

57   *"madman theory":* Seymour M. Hersh, *The Price of Power: Kissinger in the Nixon White House* (New York: Summit Books, 1983), p. 53. The "madman theory," introduced to Kissinger by Daniel Ellsberg while the two were at Harvard, is discussed in most books on Nixon and Vietnam. The idea was to seem irrational, violent, and afraid of losing face. Though Ellsberg's formulation was unrelated to U.S. foreign policy, Nixon appropriated the negotiating tactic to scare Hanoi into believing that he would rather obliterate the North Vietnamese than be seen as a weakling.

57   *wanted a domestic czar:* HRHD, 3/5/69.

58   *"President doesn't have a philosophy":* James Reichley oral history with Harlow, 11/3/77, Ford Library.

58   *bullies and liars:* Reichley int. with Burns, 9/21/77, Ford Library: Klein int.

58   *Kissinger was calling. . . . own resolve:* Kissinger, *White House Years,* pp. 263–264; HRHD, 3/9/69.

58   *The tension between Kissinger . . . "not to bomb":* Kissinger, *White House Years,* pp. 243–247; Nixon, *Memoirs,* pp. 380–382.

58   *"Execute Operation Breakfast":* Walter Isaacson, *Kissinger: A Biography* (New York: Simon & Schuster, 1992), p. 175.

58   *phony records:* Hersh, *Price of Power,* pp. 61–65. The deception of Congress in the bombing of neutral Cambodia was considered as an article of impeachment in 1974, but was voted down 26 to 12 by the House Judiciary Committee.

59   *Norodom Sihanouk, no reason to protest publicly:* Nixon, *Memoirs,* p. 382.

59   *Sixty B-52 bombers:* Isaacson, *Kissinger,* p. 175.

59   *"very productive!:"* HRHD, 3/18/69.

59   *the next Cabinet meeting:* HRHD, 3/20/69.

59   *Acheson:* Stephen E. Ambrose, *Nixon,* vol. 2, *The Triumph of a Politician, 1962–1972* (New York: Simon & Schuster, 1989), pp. 259–260.

59   *did call in congressional leaders:* Buchanan memo to RN, 3/14/69, POF Box 77; Kissinger memo to RN, "Talking Points for Meeting with Sen. Pastore, 3/24/69," 3/22/69.

61   *"talcum powder":* Safire diary, 3/14/69, Safire papers, Manuscript Division, LC.

61   *met alone with the Republican leaders:* Buchanan memo to RN, 3/18/69, POF Box 77.

61   *French Revolution:* HRHD, 5/28/69; Ehrlichman int.

61   *first state dinner:* H. R. Haldeman with Joseph Di Mona, *The Ends of Power* (New York: Times Books, 1978), p. 73. Soup was never again served in the Nixon White House.

62   *seen former president Eisenhower:* Butterfield memo for the President's File, 3/27/69, POF Box 77.
62   *better part of the next morning:* HRHD, 3/28/69.
62   *I Am Curious (Yellow):* ANS nd, 3/69, POF Box 30.
62   *"Rally for Decency":* Ibid.
62   *Newsweek:* ANS nd, 4/69, POF Box 30.
62   *Hair:* HRHD, 3/28/69.
63   *"Eisenhower just died":* HRHD, 3/28/69; Nixon, *Memoirs,* p. 375.

Chapter 4: *April 15, 1969*

64   *Camp David:* W. Dale Nelson, *The President Is at Camp David* (Syracuse, New York: Syracuse University Press, 1995), pp. 69–70.
64   *"I will return":* Julie Nixon Eisenhower, *Pat Nixon: The Untold Story* (New York: Simon & Schuster, 1986), p. 253.
64   *"Everybody loved Ike":* Nelson, *President Is at Camp David,* pp. 69–70.
65   *President met with one after another:* HRHD, 3/31/69, 4/1/69.
65   *a parade began:* ibid.
66   *Borguiba:* MemCon, 4/1/69, POF Box 77.
66   *Don Nixon and Donald Kendall:* HRHD (excised), 4/1/69. The last sentence of the quotation—"A real jerk and a real burden for P"—was excised from the published versions of Haldeman's diaries. Many of the sanitized sections involved the various schemes of Donald Nixon. On May 22, Haldeman wrote: "E. came in on way home to say report that Don N. had told Ogden he had 1 mill coming from H."—presumably Hughes Aircraft—"Bebe had checked and he is making this claim on basis of commissions due. Hard to believe." HRHD 5/22/69 (excised). Another running story excised from the diaries was the President's antipathy toward his wife's friend Helene Drown. When she was around, Nixon would arrange his schedule so that he did not have to go to the living quarters in San Clemente or in the White House itself. On March 10, 1969, for instance, Haldeman wrote: "P spent only a few minutes in the office—Helene has gone—so he can relax again. The stories of her incredible behavior . . ." In an interview, John Dean said, "Ehrlichman was Don Nixon's keeper."
66   *the first ball:* NYT, 4/8/69.
66   *King Hussein:* MemCon, 4/8/69, POF Box 77.
67   *"got to help the King":* Hersh, *Price of Power,* p. 214.
67   *Caulfield:* J. Anthony Lukas, *Nightmare: The Underside of the Nixon Years,* (New York: Viking Press, 1976), pp. 13–15; David Wise, *The American Police State: The Government Against the People* (New York: Random House, 1976), pp. 10–11.
67   *"around-the-clock surveillance":* HRHD (excised), 3/26/69.
67   *On April 15 . . . "honor.":* Nixon, *Memoirs,* pp. 382–384.
67   *"When . . . a fourth-rate military power":* Lewis Chester, Godfrey Hodgson, and Bruce Page, *An American Melodrama: The Presidential Campaign of 1968* (New York: Viking Press, 1969), p. 498.
68   *electronic intelligence intercepts:* Hersh, *Price of Power,* pp. 69–70.
68   *Bombing was what Nixon . . . invade the North:* Hersh, *Price of Power,* pp. 69–76; Nixon, *Memoirs,* pp. 382–385; Kissinger, *White House Years,* pp. 312–321; Haldeman, *Ends of Power* p. 110. Use of the word "weakling" was a regular Kissinger thrust. Ehrlichman int.
69   *"it could go nuclear":* Isaacson, *Kissinger,* pp. 180–181.
69   *The President considered. . . . cancelled them:* Kissinger, *White House Years,* pp. 317–318.
69   *slurring his words:* Hersh, *Price of Power,* p. 88.
69   *get rid of the two:* Kissinger, *White House Years,* p. 320.

69   *American Society of Newspaper Editors:* Hersh, *Price of Power,* p. 72.
69   *five days of planning:* HRHD, 4/19/69.
69   *"They got away with it":* Nixon, *Memoirs,* p. 385.
69   *moral decay:* HRHD, 4/19/69.
70   *secret one-page memo:* Nixon, *Memoirs,* pp. 390–392.
70   *"The maddening diplomatic style":* Kissinger, *White House Years,* pp. 259, 979; Isaacson, *Kissinger,* p. 251.
70   *retaliation for the EC-121:* Kissinger, *White House Years,* p. 320; HRHD, 4/18/69.
70   *Camp David for the rest of the weekend:* HRHD, 4/19–20/69.
70   *Mendel Rivers:* Harlow memo to the staff secretary, 4/22/69.
71   *wives of Cabinet members:* James Keogh memo to RN on Cabinet meeting, 4/15/69, POF Box 78.
71   *"Red" Blount:* John Whitaker memo for the President's File, 4/22/69, POF Box 78.
71   *regular meetings:* HRHD, 4/23/69.
71   *space council:* HRHD, 4/25/69.
71   *"Just keep them away":* HRHD, 4/23/69.
71   *"Your appointment is over":* Krogh int.
71   *"Even John Mitchell":* ibid.
72   *The President had . . . "bite them.":* Time, pp. 16–17.
72   *Wall Street Journal, Max Ascoli:* ANS, 5/28/69, POF Box 30.
72   *Columbia . . . Harvard . . . fires . . . City College:* NYT, 4/11/69, 4/19/69, 4/23–26/69.
72   *"Student Unrest in Brief":* NYT, 4/24/69.
72   *Cornell:* NYT, 4/20–24/69.
73   *de Gaulle:* Nixon, *Memoirs,* pp. 385–386.
74   *United States Information Agency reported:* USIA Special Report, 5/13/69, Safire Papers, Manuscript Division, LC.
74   *"K—pretty colorful!":* ANS, 5/19/69, POF Box 30.
74   *Ellington's seventieth birthday:* Nixon, *Memoirs,* p. 540; NYT, 4/30/69.
74   *CBS News:* CBS News Special: "The Correspondents Report: The First Hundred Days of Richard Nixon," transcript.
75   *Henry Kissinger was beside himself. . . . destroy whoever did this:* Isaacson, *Kissinger,* pp. 212–215.
75   *Kissinger asked Halperin:* Wise, *American Police State,* pp. 31–36.
75   *Haig, went to the FBI:* Alexander M. Haig Jr., with Charles McCrary, *Inner Circles: How America Changed the World: A Memoir* (New York: Warner Books, 1992), pp. 215–216.
75   *targets were Kissinger's assistants:* New York Times, *The End of a Presidency* (New York: Bantam Books, 1974), pp. 96–97.
75   *tapping . . . Kraft:* Lukas, *Nightmare,* pp. 64–65.
76   *sweep telephone lines:* Haldeman, *Ends of Power,* p. 104.
76   *Airborne Command Post:* HRHD (excised), 5/11/69.
76   *Kissinger called the two principal writers:* Safire notes, 5/12/69, Safire papers, Manuscript Division, LC.
76   *final discussions on draft reform:* Buchanan memo to RN, Legislative Leadership Meeting, 5/13/69, POF Box 78.
77   *group led by the Reverend Ralph Abernathy:* Price memo to RN, 5/13/69, POF Box 78.
78   *"pisses on the President":* Nixon, *Memoirs,* p. 436.
78   *President told Moynihan:* ibid.
78   *Committee on Economic Policy:* "Meeting of the Cabinet Committee on Economic Policy," 5/16/69, POF Box 78.

79 *"cooled off"*: "Meeting of the Cabinet Committee on Economic Policy," 4/10/69, POF Box 77.

80 *meeting of the Cabinet and the National Security Council*: James Keogh memo to RN, 5/15/69, POF Box 78.

Chapter 5: *June 19, 1969*

82 *At the end*: James Keogh memo to RN, 5/15/69, POF Box 78.

82 *Fortas*: NYT, 5/16/69.

82 *The President had followed*: HRHD, 5/7/69.

83 *Huston*: Huston memo to RN, 3/25/69, President's desk, PPF Box 185.

83 *"I noted that Howard Baker"*: RN memo to Mitchell, cc Harlow, 4/14/69, PPF Box 1 (contested).

83 *Nixon went to Camp David. . . . "with the press"*: HRHD, 5/18/69.

84 *Ohio State*: HRHD, 5/15/69, 5/17/69, 5/19/69.

84 *"He has a girl"*: HRHD, 5/26/69.

84 *Johnson*: Kissinger, *White House Years*, p. 272.

84 *compromised on a plan*: HRHD, 5/19/69.

84 *ban all communication*: HRHD, 5/20–21/69.

84 *choice for Chief Justice*: HRHD, 5/20/69; Nixon, *Memoirs*, p. 420.

85 *prime-time televison announcement*: HRHD, 5/21/69.

85 *governor of Florida*, Claude Kirk: Kirk letter to RN, 5/31/69, President's desk, PPF Box 188.

85 *Apollo 10*: NYT, 5/23/69.

85 *the weekend . . . bowl*: HRHD, 5/23/69.

86 *"Is this huge amount"*: Report on Summer 1969 Youth Programs, President's handwriting, 10/27/69, POF Box 3.

86 *Okinawa*: HRHD, 6/3/69; NYT, 6/3/69.

86 *anti-American sentiment*: Kissinger, *White House Years*, p. 325.

86 *new wire-taps*: HRHD, 6/3/69; New York Times, *The End of a Presidency*, pp. 96–97; Lukas, *Nightmare*, pp. 52–60.

86 *He was flying. . . . in secret*: HRHD, 6/4/69.

87 *"Put yourself in the Russians' position"*: Safire, *Before the Fall*, p. 141.

87 *fifteen minutes*: Nguyen Tien Hung and Jerrold L. Schecter, *The Palace File* (New York, Harper & Row, 1986), p. 32.

87 *five hundred assistants. . . . Honolulu meeting*: Kissinger, *White House Years*, pp. 272–273.

88 *Nixon's chair*: Hung and Schecter, *Palace File*, p. 32.

88 *acting on the recommendation*: Nixon, *Memoirs*, p. 392.

88 *inside the house*: Hung and Schecter, *Palace File*, p. 33.

88 *"before you go" . . . forty thousand men*: ibid., p. 33.

89 *Chiang Kai-shek*: ibid., pp. 34–35.

90 *"Before the inauguration"*: RN memo to Haldeman, 6/16/69.

90 *"the 'bitch' groups"*: RN memo to Ehrlichman, 6/16/69, PPF Box 1 (contested).

91 *John Osborne*: Osborne, *Nixon Watch*, pp. 79–83.

92 *among those who speculated*: Ehrlichman int.

92 *Hutschnecker*: Look, 7/15/69.

Chapter 6: *July 20, 1969*

94 *to visit Romania*: Kissinger, *White House Years*, p. 156.

94 *congressional leaders of both parties*: Buchanan memo to RN, 7/22/69, POF Box 78.

96   *"musical selections"*: RN memo to Haldeman, 7/9/69.

96   *"Chez Vito"*: RN memo to Ehrlichman, 6/16/69.

96   *"a stag dinner"*: RN memo to Rex Scouten, cc Ehrlichman, 7/9/69.

96   *Camp David:* Bill Gulley with Mary Ellen Reese, *Breaking Cover* (New York: Simon & Schuster, 1980), pp. 148–150, 158; Nelson, *President Is at Camp David,* pp. 71–72.

97   *"Duck Hook":* Hersh, *Price of Power,* p. 120.

97   *ultimatum for delivery to . . . . Ho Chi Minh:* Nixon, *Memoirs,* p. 394; Kissinger, *White House Years,* p. 278; Hersh, *Price of Power,* p. 120.

97   *Sainteny:* Kissinger, *White House Years,* pp. 277–278.

98   *Burns . . . Moynihan:* Ehrlichman, *Witness to Power,* p. 247.

98   *"Rogers feels that Kissinger is":* Nixon, *Memoirs,* p. 433.

98   *Ehrlichman . . . advance man . . . Seattle:* Ehrlichman, *Witness to Power,* p. 39.

98   *impressed Nixon:* HRHD, 4/7/69.

98   *Ehrlichman's takeover:* Ehrlichman, *Witness to Power,* p. 106.

98   *"The many departments involved":* Evans and Novak, *Nixon in the White House,* p. 237.

99   *"Domestic Council,":* HRHD, 7/12–18/69, 6/20/69; Ehrlichman, *Witness to Power,* pp. 247–248.

99   *Burns knew something was wrong:* Reichley int. with Burns, 11/3/77, Ford Library; Safire int.

99   *wean away from the Democratic Party:* ANS, 1/24/69, POF Box 30.

99   *The President asked Shultz:* Irwin Unger, *The Best of Intentions: The Triumphs and Failures of the Great Society under Kennedy, Johnson, and Nixon* (New York: Doubleday, 1996), pp. 115–116.

100   *accepting government help was demeaning:* RN memo to Buchanan, 2/9/71. This memo was to be sent to Peregrine Worsthorne of London's *Sunday Telegraph* after Worsthorne interviewed him.

100   *"What I am seeking":* Evans and Novak, *Nixon in the White House,* p. 224.

100   *"Workfare":* Ambrose, *Nixon,* vol. 2, p. 294.

100   *statistics like these:* Nixon, *Memoirs,* p. 425.

100   *"Wipe them out":* Vincent J. Burke and Vee Burke, *Nixon's Good Deed: Welfare Reform* (New York: Columbia University Press, 1974) p. 67.

100   *"The service-dispensing groups":* Nixon, *Memoirs,* p. 425.

100   *Chappaquiddick:* NYT, 7/20/69.

100   *every detail:* HRHD, 7/19/69.

100   *"hush this one up":* Safire, *Before the Fall,* p. 149.

100   *"He was obviously drunk." . . . Kalmbach:* HRHD 7/19–20/69; Lukas, *Nightmare,* p. 15.

101   *The original story . . . "Eagle Has Landed":* NYT 7/20–21/69.

101   *President watched Neil Armstrong:* Nixon, *Memoirs,* p. 429.

102   *Four days later:* NYT, 7/25/69; Nixon, *Memoirs,* p. 429.

104   *Time gave Nixon:* ANS nd, 8/69, magazine report, POF Box 30.

104   *Kennedy was on television:* HRHD, 7/26/69.

104   *Kissinger was stunned:* Kissinger, *White House Years,* pp. 223–224.

105   *renamed the "Nixon Doctrine":* ibid., p. 224. The idea for the Nixon Doctrine probably originated with Kissinger, who wrote this in 1968, before joining Nixon: "In the fifties and sixties, we offered remedies; in the late sixties and seventies, our role will be to contribute to a structure that will foster the initiative of others. . . . We must seek to encourage and not stifle a sense of local responsibility."

105   *the next morning:* HRHD, 7/30/69.

105   *"Put this on two pages":* Safire diary, 8/4/69, Safire papers, Manuscript Division, LC.

105   *Yahya Khan:* HRHD (excised), 8/2/69.

105   *Ceausescu:* Nixon, *Memoirs,* pp. 281–282, 395–396; Kissinger, *White House Years,* p. 156.

106   *The crowds . . . "Oora!":* *NYT,* 8/3/69.

106   *"Historic":* HRHD, 8/2–3/69.

106   *"Fat chance":* Haldeman, *Ends of Power,* p. 91.

106   *Xuan Thuy:* Kissinger, *White House Years,* pp. 278–282.

106   *stepped off Air Force One:* *NYT,* 8/4/69.

108   *"kick us in the teeth":* RN memo to Haldeman and Ehrlichman, 8/7/69.

108   *Kennedy:* HRHD, 8/4/69.

Chapter 7: *August 8, 1969*

109   *"Tory men with liberal policies":* Evans and Novak, *Nixon in the White House,* p. 213.

109   *"reverberate through society":* Burke and Burke, *Nixon's Good Deed,* p. 93.

109   *The liberal New Republic:* Osborne, *Nixon Watch,* pp. 141–143.

110   *Talking about welfare reform:* HRHD (excised), 4/28/69. There was an excision from the published version of Haldeman's diaries for this day, but it wasn't the blatant racism in the cited passage. Haldeman was more concerned about withholding the fact that Nixon was ready to fire his secretary of twenty-three years, Rose Mary Woods, because of a spat over seating at the Duke Ellington dinner.

110   *August 6, he assembled his Cabinet:* Keogh memo to RN, 8/6/69, POF Box 79. Most of the account of the meeting was drawn from this memo.

111   *Robert Patricelli:* Evans and Novak, *Nixon in the White House,* p. 229.

111   *"we can count on your vote":* Burke and Burke, *Nixon's Good Deed,* pp. 104–107.

111   *"If it is the President's object":* Harlow memo to Ehrlichman, 7/28/69.

111   *"E—in confidence":* Moynihan memo to RN, 4/25/69, POF Box 1.

112   *Gallup poll:* Ambrose, *Nixon,* vol. 2, p. 294.

113   *Ninety-five percent . . . Reston:* Irwin Unger, *Best of Intentions,* p. 319.

113   *the "Western White House":* Lukas, *Nightmare,* pp. 348–353; Gulley, *Breaking Cover,* pp. 156–159; *Life,* 9/5/69.

114   *"Washington Beat":* Lukas, *Nightmare,* p. 356.

114   *The White House press office . . . $1 million mortgage:* ibid., pp. 344–346.

115   *new housekeeping memo:* Haldeman memo to Larry Higby, 8/11/69, Haldeman Box 51.

115   *"For a rare moment":* Time, 8/29/69.

115   *"Good grief!":* HRHD, 9/2/69.

115   *that refused to follow orders:* NYT, 8/26/69.

116   *the old Confederacy:* In 1964, the Republican nominee, Barry Goldwater, had also carried five Southern states—Georgia, Mississippi, Alabama, Louisiana, and South Carolina—but as Nixon once said, they were the "wrong" southern states, meaning they were the states most alienated from the rest of the country, voting only on the issue of race. Of the five, all but South Carolina joined Arkansas in voting for the independent candidacy of Alabama governor George Wallace in 1968.

116   *closed meeting with southern delegates: Miami Herald,* 8/7/68. The story was broken by an enterprising reporter for the *Herald* who smuggled a tape recorder into the meeting on the person of a delegate.

117   *Five school districts:* Leon E. Panetta and Peter Gall, *Bring Us Together: The Nixon Team and the Civil Rights Retreat* (Philadelphia: J. B. Lippincott, 1971), p. 67.

117   *Thurmond issued a statement:* ibid., p. 77.

118   *"enough to make you vomit":* ibid., p. 222.

118   *"Cool it, Leon!":* Panetta int.
118   *"This line is to be used":* ANS nd, 9/69, POF Box 30.
119   *"The plan now proposed will":* Stennis letter to RN, 8/11/69, WHCF, HU2-1/ST24.
119   *appeal the desegregation order:* Panetta and Gall, *Bring Us Together* p. 254.
119   *argued the opposite. At least one quit:* ibid., pp. 260–262.
119   *Finch . . . wrote a letter:* ibid., pp. 255–256.
119   *The court granted the stay:* ibid., p. 263.
120   *Haynsworth:* Nixon, *Memoirs,* p. 420–421; *Time,* 8/29/69.
120   *Huston got another long memo through:* Huston memo to Haldeman, 8/12/69, HRH Box 51.
120   *seven million . . . students: Time,* 9/12/69, p. 50.
120   *"a little noisy outside":* MemCon, 8/21/69, POF Box 79.
121   *the two presidents met again:* MemCon, 8/22/69, POF Box 79.
121   *August 25, the Urban Affairs Council:* "Notes for the President's File," 8/25/69, POF Box 79; Price memo to RN, minutes of the Council for Urban Affairs, 8/25/69, POF Box 79.
122   *Alcatraz:* Safire papers, Manuscript Division, LC.
122   *Kraft: Washington Post,* 9/16/69.
122   *James David Barber: NYT,* 9/4/69; *Time,* 9/12/69.
123   *Canfield cartoon: Time,* 9/26/69.
123   *Miami Herald: Herald,* 9/9/69.
124   *Gulfport, Mississippi: Time,* 9/19/69; *Birmingham News,* 9/9/69; *New Republic,* 1/17/70.

Chapter 8: *October 15, 1969*

125   *September 12:* HRHD, 9/12/69, 9/25/69.
125   *"HEHK":* HRHD, 9/8/69, 9/12/69.
126   *Haynsworth:* Clark R. Mollenhoff, *Game Plan for Disaster: An Ombudsman's Report on the Nixon Years* (New York: W. W. Norton, 1976), pp. 49–65; Evans and Novak, *Nixon in the White House* pp. 161–162; *Time,* 9/26/69, p. 21.
126   *phone started ringing. . . . fodder for the antiwar types:* HRHD, 9/12/69.
126   *"How do you suppose" . . . "He's a sneak":* Ehrlichman, *Witness to Power,* pp. 95–96.
127   *The Green Berets:* The most complete narrative of the story is in *A Murder in Wartime by* Jeff Stein (New York: St. Martin's Press, 1992). Other sources used in this narrative include: *Life,* 11/14/69; *NYT,* 9/30/69–10/2/69, 10/6/69.
128   *Rothblatt:* ANS, nd, 9/69, POF Box 30.
128   *Hawk . . . National Student Association:* Tom Wells, *The War Within: America's Battle Over Vietnam* (Berkeley: University of California Press, 1994), pp. 294–295.
129   *Nixon did meet with student leaders:* Osborne, *Nixon Watch,* pp. 109–113.
129   *"Useless" . . . Bob Hope:* HRHD, 9/20/69.
129   *three men from politics . . . "We've got a tiger":* Ambrose, *Nixon,* vol. 2, *Triumph of a Politician,* p. 298.
130   *the White House press corps:* HRHD, 9/23/69.
130   *When Mendel Rivers:* Stein, *A Murder in Wartime,* p. 366.
131   *Daniel Ellsberg:* David Rudenstine, *The Day the Presses Stopped: A History of the Pentagon Papers Case* (Berkeley: University of California Press, 1996), p. 42; Wells, *War Within,* p. 364; Tom Wells, *Wild Man: The Life and Times of Daniel Ellsberg* (New York: St. Martin's Press, 2001), p. 322. On April 3, 1971, one of the Green Berets, angered over the conviction of Lieutenant William Calley for the murder of Vietnamese civilians at My Lai, told *The New York Times* that he shot and killed Chuyen on "very,

very clear" orders from the CIA. "He was my agent," Robert Marasco said, "and it was my responsibility to eliminate him with extreme prejudice."

132 *Republican leaders two days later:* Buchanan memo to RN, "Notes for Republican Leadership Meeting," 9/30/69, POF Box 79.

133 *Friday, October 3:* HRHD, 10/3/69.

133 *Kissinger sat with Bill Safire:* Safire, *Before the Fall,* p. 160.

134 *Time and Newsweek:* Nixon, *Memoirs,* pp. 400–401.

134 *U.S. News & World Report:* HRHD, 10/6/69.

134 *"birds seem to be plummeting":* Haldeman memo to Larry Higby, 10/17/69, HRH Box 53.

134 *Senator Griffin:* HRHD, 10/6/69.

134 *Republican congressional leadership:* Buchanan memo to RN, "Notes for Leadership Meeting," 10/14/69, POF Box 79.

134 *"Divert attention":* ANS nd, 9/69, POF Box 30.

134 *Ehrlichman:* Caulfield memo to Ehrlichman, 10/10/69.

135 *having overheard Nixon talking:* Kissinger, *White House Years,* p. 304.

135 *Duck Hook:* Kissinger, *White House Years,* pp. 284–286; Isaacson, *Kissinger,* pp. 246–249; Hersh, *Price of Power,* pp. 125–133; Roger Morris, *Uncertain Greatness: Henry Kissinger and American Foreign Policy* (New York: Harper and Row, 1977), pp. 164–167.

135 *"drunken friend":* Morris, *Uncertain Greatness,* p. 147.

136 *President himself leaked:* Nixon, *Memoirs,* p. 400.

136 *Strategic Air Command on full alert:* Hersh, *Price of Power,* p. 124.

136 *"The struggle of the Vietnamese":* Nixon, *Memoirs,* p. 402.

136 *"We must pause":* Life, 6/27/69.

136 *Randy J. Dicks:* WHCF, Human Rights Box 31.

137 *Student Monarchist Society:* Wells, The War Within, pp. 353–354.

137 *More than twenty thousand . . . views and goals:* NYT, 10/16/69; Wells, *War Within,* pp. 371–375.

137 *"A nothing":* Ambrose, *Nixon,* vol. 2, p. 325.

137 *Nixon ordered Haldeman to talk to the national security adviser:* HRHD, 10/13–15/69.

137 *in the bomb-shelter war room:* Wells, *War Within,* pp. 375–376.

137 *Two of Ehrlichman's children . . . their candles:* Wells, *War Within,* pp. 373–374.

138 *"The Moratorium was a success":* Moynihan memo to RN, 10/16/69, Haldeman Box 130.

138 *"The war in Vietnam will now be":* Buchanan memo to RN, 10/17/69, Haldeman Box 130.

138 *the "Middle America Committee":* Dent memo to RN, 10/16/69, POF Box 79.

139 *Agnew:* Osborne, *Nixon Watch,* pp. 126–128.

139 *"Don't Get Rattled":* Nixon, *Memoirs,* p. 403.

140 *Barber: Time,* 9/12/69; NYT, 9/4/69.

140 *twelve . . . drafts:* Associated Press, 1/22/99.

140 *Sir Robert Thompson:* Nixon, *Memoirs,* pp. 404–405; Ambrose, *Nixon,* vol. 2, p. 306.

140 *Mansfield:* Nixon, *Memoirs,* p. 408.

141 *Soviet ambassador, Anatoly Dobrynin:* Nixon, *Memoirs,* pp. 405–407; Kissinger, *White House Years,* p. 305.

141 *"I've described the back-channel communications":* Hersh, *Price of Power,* p. 42.

142 *"Well, that's all for today":* HRHD, 10/27/69.

142   *"I would like one brief paragraph"*: RN memo to Kissinger, 10/27/69.
142   *"wrong from the start"*: ibid.
142   *"let's see how they enforce it"*: HRHD, 10/30/69.
142   *"They can't defeat us"*: Nixon, *Memoirs*, p. 404.
143   *"The baby's just been born"*: HRHD, 11/1/69.
143   *he had memorized:* Garment int. Nixon normally used no notes in even minor meetings, committing briefing papers to memory, which meant that sometimes he did not listen carefully as he went through his script. Kissinger recounts a meeting where the gift of memorization caused the President a problem because the briefing paper was wrong: "The prime minister of Mauritius had been invited to Washington. Mauritius is a subtropical island located in the Indian Ocean. . . . its relations with the United States were excellent. Somehow my staff got the impression that the visitor was from Mauritania, an arid desert state in West Africa which had broken relations with us in 1967 as an act of solidarity with its Muslim brethren in the aftermath of the Middle East War . . . Coming straight to the point"—of the memorized memo—"Nixon suggested that the time had come to restore diplomatic relations . . . permitting resumption of American aid, and one of its benefits would be assistance in dry farming, in which Nixon maintained the United States had special capabilities. The stunned visitor tried to shift to a more promising subject. He inquired whether Nixon was satisfied with the operation of the space tracking station the United States maintained on the island. The President scrawled a note, slipping it to Kissinger: "Why the hell do we have a space-tracking station in a country with which we do not have diplomatic relations?" Henry Kissinger, *The Years of Renewal* (New York: Simon & Schuster, 1999), p. 72; Lord int.
143   *meeting with congressional leaders:* Buchanan memo to RN, "Notes for Leadership Meeting," 10/28/69, POF Box 79.
144   *"vicious, dirty ones"*: HRHD, 11/3/69.
144   *77 percent approval:* Nixon, *Memoirs*, p. 410.
145   *68 percent. Congressional resolutions:* ibid., p. 410.
145   *"When the lives of our young men"*: Time, 9/21/69, p. 17.
145   *fifty thousand telegrams . . . thirty thousand letters:* Nixon, *Memoirs*, p. 410.
145   *White House, with the help of:* Associated Press, 1/22/69.
145   *chairman of the Federal Communications Commission:* Time, 9/21/69, p. 22.
145   *Woodrow Wilson . . . Henry Wilson:* Safire, *Before the Fall*, pp. 105–106.

Chapter 9: *December 8, 1969*

146   *"he's got 'It' "*: NYT, 8/10/68; Jules Witcover, *The Resurrection of Richard Nixon* (New York: Putnam, 1970), p. 368; Ambrose, *Nixon*, vol. 2, p. 163.
146   *county executive and was elected governor:* Evans and Novak, *Nixon in the White House*, p. 307.
146   *"circuit-riding, Hanoi-visiting"*: ibid., p. 309.
147   *"Caligula named his horse"*: Washington Post, 9/25/68.
147   *talked to the man a couple of times:* Evans and Novak, *Nixon in the White House*, p. 308.
147   *"squishy-soft . . . one slum"*: ibid., p. 310; Ambrose, *Nixon*, vol. 2, p. 191.
147   *IQ of 135 . . . "not catching"*: Life, 1970. Profile of Agnew by Brock Brower.
147   *networks' live analysis:* James Keogh, *President Nixon and the Press* (New York: Funk & Wagnalls, 1972), appendix.
147   *"Let Agnew go after"*: Safire, *Before the Fall*, p. 352; Safire int; HRHD, 11/11–13/69.
148   *Buchanan wrote the speech and Nixon personally edited it:* Nixon, *Memoirs*, p. 411.

148   *The text*: Keogh, *President Nixon and the Press,* appendix.
149   *"flicks the scab"*: Safire, *Before the Fall,* p. 352.
149   *a second speech*: Keogh, *President Nixon and the Press,* appendix.
149   *"Counterattack on Dissent"*: Time, 11/21/69.
149   *"the Mobe"*: Wells, *War Within,* pp. 389–395; HRHD, 11/14–15/69; *NYT,* 11/15–16/69; Nixon, *Memoirs,* p. 413; *Time,* 11/28/69.
150   *My Lai*: *NYT,* 11/17/69; Hersh, Dispatch News Service, 11/13/69; Robert Jay Lifton, *Home from the War: Vietnam Veterans: Neither Victims nor Executioners* (New York: Simon & Schuster, 1973), pp. 47–50, 54; Hersh, *My Lai 4: A Report on the Massacre and Its Aftermath* (New York: Random House, 1970); *NYT,* 11/25/69.
151   *a joint meeting . . . "I'm sickened"*: *NYT,* 11/27/69.
151   *"dirty, rotten, New York Jews"*: Hersh, *Price of Power* p. 135.
151   *"The clown"*: John W. Dean, *Blind Ambition: The White House Years* (New York: Simon & Schuster, 1976), p. 42.
151   *a sixteen-page brief*: Rehnquist memo to Ehrlichman, 10/10/69, President's desk, PPF 185–188.
151   *call forty reporters into his office . . . most notable thing*: Osborne, *Nixon Watch,* pp. 114–119.
152   *revenge . . . against the seventeen*: HRHD, 12/2/69.
152   *"With regard to all those who opposed"*: RN memo to "HEHK," 11/24/69.
152   *"wires would really pour in from Harvard"*: HRHD, 11/26/69.
152   *Thanksgiving*: *NYT,* 11/28/69.
152   *The first lottery*: *NYT,* 12/2/69.
153   *"The Town House Project"*: Lukas, *Nightmare,* pp. 111, 114.
154   *horrific color photos*: ANS nd, 12/69, POF Box 31.
154   *CBS News polls*: ANS, 12/5/69, POF Box 31.
155   *David Broder*: ANS nd, 12/69, POF Box 31.
155   *"Nixon the President seems"*: Osborne, *Nixon Watch* p. 200.

Chapter 10: *January 22, 1970*

157   *auto racing*: Haldeman memo to Jeb Magruder, 1/9/70.
158   *"the miracle of this age"*: Dent memo to RN, "Report on Southern Chairmen's Meeting and Desegregation in the South," 1/13/70.
158   *"The nation is at a historic moment"*: Harlow memo to RN, meeting with speechwriters, 2/24/70, POF Box 80.
159   *"making Nero Christ"*: HRHD (excised), 3/25/70. This comment was made during a meeting two months later.
160   *an unsigned editorial*: ANS, 1/13/70; Haldeman memo to Price, 11/30/70; Price memo to Haldeman 12/3/70.
160   *Bartley stayed with the* Journal—winning a Pulitzer Prize—and became a leading voice of movement conservatives through the 1990s.
161   *Bud Krogh waved checks*: Klebanoff int.
161   *"abhorrent"*: NYT, 1/22/70.
161   *a boob, a dummy"*: Ehrlichman, *Witness to Power,* p. 126.
161   *"non-substantive areas"*: ibid., p. 266.
162   *"designing Walter Cronkite's lead story"*: ibid.
162   *"He spends as much time"*: HRHD, 4/15/70.
162   *fire alarm in the White House*: HRHD, 1/18/70.
162   *"prepared to answer so many questions"*: RN memo to Haldeman, 1/31/70.
162   *Jefferson quote*: Price int.
163   *several polls*: RN memo to Haldeman, 12/30/69, PPF Box 1; HRHD, 1/12/70.
163   *"smoke and jobs"*: Safire, *Before the Fall,* p. 592.

164   *"white Alabama coon-killer"*: HRHD (excised), 1/23/69. Nixon had Mayor Washington in to "put heat on him" over rising D.C. crime rates. He threatened to have him replaced unless the crime statistics were reversed by June. His "Alabama coon-killer" joke afterward was recorded, and excised, by Haldeman.

164   *"frank borrowing from decadent European"*: John R. Brown memo to Ehrlichman, re Trohan, 2/4/70. Description of the uniforms is from *NYT*, 1/28/70. Comments are from the ANS.

165   *the next Cabinet meeting*: Keogh memo to RN, Cabinet meeting, 2/19/70, POF Box 80.

166   *"golden-haired granddaughter"*: Ehrlichman, *Witness to Power*, p. 226.

167   *"must be a better way"*: RN memo to Ehrlichman, 2/5/70.

167   *Panetta got the word*: Panetta and Gall, *Bring Us Together*, pp. 250–255.

168   *"The poor bastard"*: Ehrlichman, *Witness to Power*, p. 226; Ehrlichman int.

169   *Soviet Union to invade China . . . "Chinese are less dangerous"*: HRHD (excised), 12/10/69, 12/12/69, 1/8/70. The warning of a Russian attack on China, as well as word of the Warsaw parley, was recorded by Haldeman on December 10. On December 12, Haldeman wrote more on the Warsaw meeting: "K's plans proceed apace. [Ambassador Walter] Stoessel met the Chinese at their embassy—first time for an American—and while no major breakthrough—it was at least a new step. And the Romanian is on his way to meet K here Tues. Then a feeler from North Vietnam—to meet K in Paris—which also may develop. K really in his element. Loves this." These passages were excised from the published diaries, as was the January 8 description quoted in the chapter.

170   *"This is unconscionable"*: HRHD, 2/26/70.

170   *"I'm going then"*: HRHD (excised), 2/17/70. The excised portion of the entry read: "P also crashed Lindsay and Rockefeller for their utter hypocrisy in snubbing Pompidou after 'slobbering' all over Kosygin who is direct cause of Mideast war."

170   *"Cut all Federal projects"*: John Brown memo to Ehrlichman, 3/3/69; Ehrlichman memo to RN, 3/24/69.

171   *"When I learned"*: *NYT*, 3/3/70.

171   *John B. Connally*: RN memo to Haldeman, 3/2/70.

171   *"I want Missouri, New York"*: RN memo to Ehrlichman, 3/2/70.

171   *"$100,000 or more"*: RN memo to Haldeman, 3/2/70.

171   *"telephone polls"*: ibid.

171   *"Billy Graham tells me"*: ibid.

171   *"After a great deal of consideration"*: RN memo to Haldeman, Ehrlichman, and Kissinger, 3/2/70.

173   *"I think interest"*: President's handwriting, PPF Box 5.

173   *"If important leaks do occur"*: Haldeman notes, 2/3/70, "Leaks."

Chapter 11: *April 8, 1970*

174   *more than two thousand Department of Health, Education, and Welfare employees*: *NYT*, 3/7/70.

174   *twenty-one civil rights leaders*: *NYT*, 3/6/70.

175   *"Operation O'Brien"*: HRHD, 3/4/70, 3/10/70.

175   *bomb factory for the Weathermen*: *NYT*, 3/7/70, 3/11/70.

176   *his daughter Julie's graduation*: On November 24, 1969, RN sent a memo to Haldeman: "For your long-range planning, it will be necessary for me to plan some sort of trip out of the country at the time of Julie's graduation. She insists that she does not want us to come to the graduation ceremony because of the attitude of the faculty and students, and I believe she is probably correct. However, we could not justify not being there unless we were gone at that time on some sort of special trip."

176   *"Forget them"*: HRHD, 12/15/69.

176   *the Gridiron Club:* Harold Brayman, *The President Speaks Off-the-Record: From Grover Cleveland to Gerald Ford* (Princeton, New Jersey: Dow Jones Books, 1976), pp. 11–13; HRHD, 3/14/70.

177   *Laos:* Hersh, *Price of Power,* pp. 168–171; Kissinger, *White House Years,* pp. 450–456; HRHD, 3/6–9/70.

178   *"Keep Henry out":* HRHD, 3/9–11/70.

178   *"psychopath about Rogers":* HRHD, 3/18/70.

178   *negotiations . . . with Le Duc Tho:* Kissinger, *White House Years,* pp. 478, 488, 520.

179   *"Stabbing me":* HRHD, 3/17/70.

179   *Cambodia:* Kissinger, *White House Years,* pp. 457–468; Isaacson, *Kissinger,* pp. 256–258; NYT, 3/19–31/70; William Shawcross, *Sideshow: Kissinger, Nixon, and the Destruction of Cambodia* (New York: Simon & Schuster, 1979), pp. 112–126.

181   *"hell do those clowns":* Nixon, *Memoirs,* p. 447.

181   *"Skip the argument":* HRHD, 3/20/70.

182   *"Fire them all!":* HRHD, 3/20/70.

182   *sorting stacks of mail:* NYT, 3/24/70.

182   *The next day . . . regular basis:* HRHD, 3/30/70, 4/1/70.

183   *Rogers announced:* NYT, 3/24/70.

184   *"Israel is relying on":* RN memo to Kissinger, 3/17/70.

184   *back to Southeast Asia:* NYT, 3/27–30/70, 4/4/70.

184   *By April 7:* Kissinger letter to RN, 4/7/70, PPF Box 10.

185   *Carswell:* Time, 4/20/70.

185   *"a demon":* HRHD, 4/9/70.

186   *Gallup . . . television:* HRHD, 4/2–3/70.

186   *"go see Patton":* HRHD, 4/7/70.

186   *as analyzed by Time:* Time, 4/20/70.

186   *one of the highest wage increases:* NYT, 3/28/70, 4/1/70, 4/3/70.

187   *Teamsters . . . tugboat operators:* NYT, 4/2–3/70.

187   *"Arthur has a way":* Keogh memo to RN, Cabinet meeting, 4/13/70, POF Box 80.

187   *"and great stupidity":* Keogh memo to RN, Cabinet meeting, 3/18/70, POF Box 80.

187   *"On monetary policy":* Keogh memo to RN, Cabinet meeting, 4/13/70, POF Box 80.

188   *Apollo 13:* NYT, 4/14–18/70; HRHD, 4/13–14/70.

Chapter 12: *April 30, 1970*

190   *Apollo 13:* NYT, 4/6–20/70; HRHD, 4/13—18/70. The investigation of what went wrong took more than two months. The result was reported in *Newsweek* on June 15, 1970: "The thermal switches are designed to safeguard a heating element inside the ship's oxygen tanks. Normally the switches are closed and carry electric current to the heater. But if the heater exceeds 80 degrees Fahrenheit, the switches—like circuit breakers in a household electrical system—are designed to pop open and shut off the system. The manufacturing specifications for the switches stipulate that the units should not be subjected to more than 30 volts. But during the pre-launch tests on the Apollo 13 spaceship at Cape Kennedy in late March, technicians using an approved checklist turned on the heating element, operating under printed instructions that called for 65 volts to be applied to the circuit. The overvoltage welded the switches shut before the heating element itself could get hot enough to trip them open. Once the switches were thus sealed, so was the fate of that oxygen tank, the Apollo 13 mission—and very nearly the astronauts themselves."

191   *GSA to clear all contracts:* HRHD, 3/31/70.

192   *President was drunk:* HRHD, 4/17/70 (excised). "E says by 4:15 he was loaded," reads the entry.

192   *photo opportunity with Diamond Head:* Gulley, *Breaking Cover,* pp. 198–99; Gulley int. The account in Gulley's book has this photo op taking place during Nixon's 1969 journey around the world, when he met the astronauts from Apollo 11. During that trip, however, there was no ceremony in Hawaii; the meeting took place on the USS *Hornet.* A five-column photo on the cover of *The New York Times* of April 19, 1970, depicts the ceremony Gulley describes. In an interview, Gulley confirmed that the photo op was for the astronauts of Apollo 13, not 11. One could object to twenty thousand dollars in bulldozing just for a photo. Haldeman objected to a mound of dirt marring a photo the President flew five thousand miles to have taken. And on this day, the demanding Haldeman was, for once, impressed. "Our guys did a spectacular advancing and logistics job," he noted that night. Front pages nationwide confirmed his PR judgment the next day.

192   *Admiral John S. McCain Jr.:* Shawcross, *Sideshow,* p. 136; Isaacson, *Kissinger,* p. 259; HRHD, 4/19/70.

193   *"what I've been waiting for":* NYT, 7/1/70.

193   *Snoul and Takeo: Look,* 8/11/70.

193   *four hundred thousand . . . Prasaut:* Shawcross, *Sideshow,* pp. 132–133.

193   *Bodies were floating:* NYT, 4/16/70.

193   *Jakarta:* Marshall Green telegram to American embassy in Jakarta, 4/24/70. This was the initial telegram from State encouraging Indonesian involvement. Several more followed as plans were made.

194   *"Psychological warfare":* Shawcross, *Sideshow,* p. 133.

194   *"Stocktaking in Indochina" . . . "certain revisions":* ibid., p. 137.

194   *Westmoreland cabled General Abrams:* Shawcross, *Sideshow,* p. 138.

194   *Moratorium, was announcing the end:* NYT, 4/20/70.

194   *"He's tickled":* HRHD, 4/20/70.

195   *"Cut the crap":* HRHD, 4/20/70.

195   *1:26 A.M.: Look,* 8/11/70. Over the next weeks and months, "tick-tock" accounts of the decision to invade Cambodia proliferated. The administration mobilized a leak offensive to create coverage as favorable as possible. The campaign included a chronology that listed the exact time of relevant meetings, if not always their exact content.

195   *"BURN AFTER":* RN memo to Haldeman, 4/21/70.

195   *letter from Doctor Hutschnecker:* ibid.

195   *"a freeze (orally, of course)":* ibid.

195   *"he was 'bitter' ":* RN memo to Klein and Ziegler, 4/21/70.

196   *"the exception of Sidey":* RN memo to Haldeman, 4/21/70.

196   *"silliness of youth":* RN memo to Buchanan, 4/21/70.

196   *"bold move in Cambodia":* RN memo to Kissinger, 4/22/70.

196   *Earth Day:* NYT, 4/23/70.

197   *"Playing Bismarck":* HRHD, 4/22/70.

197   *"stop this pussyfooting":* Isaacson, *Kissinger,* p. 261.

197   *"Don't let them intimidate you":* Nixon, *Memoirs,* p. 448.

197   *"Nodis/Khmer":* Watts memo to Kissinger, "State Department Handling of Sensitive Cambodian Messages," 4/24/70.

197   *"President has directed":* Kissinger memo to Laird, "Air Support for Vietnam," 4/17/70.

197   *"Laird's response ignores your memo":* Lynn memo to Kissinger, "Laird's Views on Air Support for Vietnam," 4/29/70.

198   *"inconsistent with above":* Rogers telegram to Phnom Penh and Saigon, 4/24/70. All telegrams and other materials related to Cambodia are found in National Security Council Files, Boxes 579–590, at the National Archives.

198   *"no additional comment"*: Rogers telegram to Rives, 4/20/70, NSC files.
198   *"Damn Johnson"*: HRHD, 4/23/70.
198   *thirty thousand tons*: Shawcross, *Sideshow*, p. 140.
198   *only as an adviser*: ibid., p. 140.
199   *Kissinger telephoned Laird*: ibid., pp. 140–141.
199   *Kissinger, alone now with Haldeman*: HRHD, 4/24/70.
199   *called together his young staff*: Isaacson, *Kissinger*, pp. 261–263.
199   *"it's your ass"*: Wise, *American Police State*, p. 92.
199   *"Your views represent"* . . . *"Fuck you, Al"*: Hersh, *Price of Power*, pp. 190–191; Isaacson, *Kissinger*, p. 275.
200   *Lake and Morris*: Shawcross, *Sideshow*, p. 145.
200   *Klebanoff, quit*: Klebanoff int.
200   *Patton again*: HRHD, 4/25/70.
200   *Laird and Rogers realized*: Isaacson, *Kissinger*, pp. 265–266.
201   *Laird and Rogers were in the President's hideaway*: HRHD, 4/27/70; Isaacson, *Kissinger*, pp. 265–267.
202   *Stewart Alsop*: Alsop papers, courtesy of Robert Merry.
204   *"positions taken by the Secretary of State and"*: Mitchell memo to RN, 4/28/70, POF Box 80.
204   *"Martha Mitchell"*: RN memo to Haldeman, 5/25/70, PPF Box 2.
204   *William Gulley*: Gulley int.
204   *"Higher authority has authorized"*: Shawcross, *Sideshow*, p. 145.
204   *"Avoid picturing this"*: Rogers telegram to Rives, 4/27/70, NSC files, Boxes 579–590. Robert Sam Anson int.
205   *"ferry at Neak Leung"*: Rives telegram to Rogers, 4/28/70, NSC files, Boxes 579–590.
205   *"Fire Rives"*: Kissinger, *White House Years*, p. 490.
205   *Rockefeller*: Rockefeller int.
206   *not to perform but to sell*: HRHD, 4/30/70.
206   *" 'Total Victory 42' "*: Safire papers, Manuscript Division, LC.
206   *"about your face"*: Look, 8/11/70.
206   *briefing in the Roosevelt Room*: Safire, *Before the Fall*, pp. 155–187.
208   *"Unable to discuss with Lon Nol"*: Rives telegram to Rogers, 5/1/70, NSC files, Boxes 579–590.
209   *first wave of calls*: Ambrose, *Nixon*, vol. 2, pp. 347–348.
209   *Ziegler began his briefing* . . . *Pentagon briefers*: NYT, 5/2/70; Isaacson, *Kissinger*, pp. 268–269.
209   *"Do you approve"*: Brennan memo to Woods, memo for the President's File, 5/4/70, POF Box 80.
210   *Patton again*: The President watched *Patton* twelve times, according to records in the White House Military Office, which provided projectionists to show films in the White House and at Camp David. He also arranged screenings for eleven Democratic senators, beginning with Senator Sam Ervin of North Carolina. China transcripts released on May 7, 2001, show that Chou En-lai brought up the film at least twice during their conversations when Nixon went to China in February 1972. *Patton*, however, was not the film Nixon viewed most often in the White House. He loved *Around the World in 80 Days*, according to Ehrlichman in *Witness to Power*, and knew the dialogue by heart. He would announce his favorite scenes, saying things like: "Watch, watch. Here comes the elephant!"

Chapter 13: *May 4, 1970*

211   *President Nixon was on the phone*: HRHD, 5/2/70.
211   *early on Sunday*: HRHD, 5/3/70.

212   *Before the Times. . . . Laos:* Hersh, *Price of Power,* pp. 319–324; Isaacson, *Kissinger,* pp. 216–221. The four taps remained on until February 10, 1971. The original source for Beecher's story was none of the above; the bombings had been reported by Radio Hanoi. In 1973, Beecher became assistant secretary of defense, appointed by a new defense secretary, Elliot Richardson.

212   *Kent State:* NYT, 5/4–6/70; *Time,* 5/18/70; *Newsweek,* 5/18/70; Wells, *War Within,* pp. 424–432; Safire int.

213   *"Something just came over the wires":* HRHD notes; 5/4/70; Nixon, *Memoirs,* pp. 455–457.

214   *brief written . . . Rehnquist:* "Constitutional Basis for United States Actions against Sanctuaries in Cambodia" stated: "The action in Cambodia should not be viewed as an independent use of U.S. armed forces involving the general question of the President's responsibility to Congress under the power to 'declare war.' It should be defended as a Presidential action to protect our troops. The Military Appropriations Act for fiscal 1970 prohibits the use of general Department of Defense funds for the introduction of ground troops into Laos or Thailand but says nothing about Cambodia."

214   *The columnist's notes:* Alsop papers, notes of May 6 meeting with Kissinger, courtesy of Robert W. Merry. Merry's biography of the Alsop brothers, *Taking on the World: Joseph and Stewart Alsop—Guardians of the American Century* (New York: Viking, 1996), is superb.

215   *the Dow . . . had dropped:* Allen J. Matusow, *Nixon's Economy: Booms, Busts, Dollars, and Votes* (Lawrence: University Press of Kansas, 1998), pp. 57–58, 69–72.

215   *78 percent of corporate executives:* NYT, 5/11/70.

215   *Muskie:* Wall Street Journal, 4/3/70.

216   *"It's heresy":* Ehrlichman notes, 9/11/69; Ehrlichman files, SMOF.

216   *White House tennis court:* HRHD, 5/7/70.

216   *hard-hats construction workers,* NYT, 5/9/71, 5/20/71.

216   *"Fire them all!":* Isaacson, *Kissinger,* pp. 269–270.

217   *James Lapham:* Time, 5/25/70.

217   *Wallace Butenhoff:* ibid.

217   *A true voice:* The New Yorker piece on Nixon was written by Richard N. Goodwin, a former aide to both John and Robert Kennedy, and a contributor to the magazine since 1964.

218   *soldiers were jumping:* Gulley int.

219   *In the Lincoln sitting room:* Safire, *Before the Fall,* pp. 201–204.

219   *Nancy Dickerson:* John Osborne, *The Second Year of the Nixon Watch* (New York: Liveright, 1971), p. 75.

219   *He even called:* Safire int.

219   *Nixon went to bed:* The account of Nixon's early-morning travels is based on his own thirteen-page dictated account; Haldeman's diary and his book, *The Ends of Power;* and interviews with Krogh, Ziegler, and Ehrlichman.

222   *commander in chief suddenly appeared:* Chapin memo for the President's File, 5/9/70.

Chapter 14: *June 30, 1970*

223   *"I can understand":* RN memo to Haldeman, 5/13/70.

224   *"He followed that call":* Nixon discussed violence, ignoring the press, Supreme Court nominations, and research funds at universities in another long taped memo to Haldeman on 5/13/70.

224   *"He's in love with the machine":* In a February 24, 1988, oral history for the National Archives, Jerrold Schecter, who toured parts of the living quarters of the White

House as part of *Time* magazine's reporting on a "Man of the Year" cover, described Nixon's bedroom: "He and Mrs. Nixon had separate bedrooms, and he had a brass bed that was bigger, but not much bigger, than the bed that Lenin had in the Kremlin. . . . He had a pad, a white pad, next to his bed, on which he would jot down ideas that came to him in the middle of the night. And he had a tape recorder, a Sony tape recorder, which he showed me. If he had an idea, he'd put it in the machine, so that he'd have it in the morning. . . . I sort of felt sorry for him at the end of it. Here was the President of the United States, and he was a man who didn't really seem to have much self-esteem, self-love. He spent a lot of time trying to impress me, for example, by saying that he picked the menus, that he would pick the wines. . . ."

224   *Nixon was also:* "Cambodia: Now It's 'Operation Buy Time,' " *Time,* 5/25/70.

225   *In Life magazine:* Sidey column, *Life,* 5/22/70.

227   *"Blue Heart":* HRHD, 5/18/70; Nixon, *Memoirs,* p. 466.

227   *the election of George Wallace:* Dan T. Carter, *The Politics of Rage: George Wallace, the Origins of the New Conservatism, and the Transformation of American Politics* (New York: Simon & Schuster, 1995), p. 370.

228   *$100,000 to Postmaster General:* Ehrlichman notes, 3/10/70; Ehrlichman files; Haldeman notes, 3/25/70; Haldeman files, Box 41; HRHD, 3/19/70.

228   *"Are you Mr. Jensen":* Carter, *Politics of Rage,* pp. 388–389.

228   *ordered Clark Mollenhoff:* Mollenhoff, *Game Plan for Disaster,* p. 113.

228   *Jim Bob Solomon:* Carter, *Politics of Rage,* pp. 391–392.

228   *Wallace dubbed:* ibid., pp. 395–396.

229   *the President met:* Lukas, *Nightmare,* pp. 31–32.

230   *The elevation of Huston:* Lukas, *Nightmare,* p. 33; Evans and Novak, *Nixon in the White House,* p. 243; Frank J. Donner, *The Age of Surveillance: The Aims and Methods of America's Political Intelligence System* (New York: Alfred A. Knoff, 1980; Vintage Books), p. 265.

230   *So the Nixons:* int. Susan Eisenhower; Julie Nixon Eisenhower, *Pat Nixon,* pp. 439–440.

230   *interested in domestic policy:* HRHD, 6/8–9/70. The personnel changes in this paragraph are discussed in Haldeman's diaries for these days and in Ehrlichman's *Witness to Power,* pp. 101–110, and, of course, were announced in the newspapers.

231   *"That does it:* Ehrlichman, *Witness to Power,* p. 102.

231   *The President's mind:* Stephen Bull, memo to President's File, 6/10/70.

231   *The candidates will be:* Stephen Bull memo to RN, 6/10/70.

231   *list . . . included:* Kalmbach memo to RN, 6/10/70. The entire list, with asterisks marking potential rather than continuing givers:

W. Clement Stone, Richard Pistell, John King, Robert O. Anderson, John Rollins, Willard F. Rockwell Jr., Sam Wyly and Charles Wyly, Dudley Swin, H. Ross Perot, Edgar W. Brown Jr., Walter Annenberg, Thomas Pappas, Richard Mellon Scaife, Loren Barry, David Parr, Clement Hirsch,* William Liedtke, Wayne Hoffman, Henry Ford II,* Albert H. Gorden, Vincent de Roulet, Roscoe Pickett Jr., Mrs. Blanche Seaver, Arthur Lipper, Henry Salvatori, David K. Wilson, Fred Russell, Ned Gerritty, Shelby Davis, William Casey, Arthur K. Watson, DeWitt Wallace, Kenneth Franzheim, Robert P. McCulloch, J. Howard Pew, Charles Luckman, Max Fisher, Frank K. Greenwall, Kent H. Smith, Benson Ford, Robert H. Abplanalp, Claude Wilde, Walter Davis, Jack Mills, Howard Newman, John M. Shaheen, Kingdon Gould, Foster McGaw, James Crosby, Bernard Johnson, Thomas J. Morrison, F. K. Weyerhauser, John P. Humes, A. C. Nielsen, Guilford Dudley, John Olin and Spencer Olin, J. William Middendorf II, Charles Payson, Robert Hill, John Hay Whitney, Mrs. Helen Clay Frick, Elmer Bobst, Willard W. Keith, William Lasdon.

232   *Jill St. John:* HRHD, 6/23/70.
232   *In San Clemente:* Background briefing 6/26/70, embargoed until 7/2/70, NSC files, boxes 579–590. Kissinger's backgrounder is also in this series.
234   *"The whole trick":* HRHD, 6/29/70.

Chapter 15: *September 23, 1970*

235   the *"Special Interagency":* Lukas, *Nightmare;* pp. 30–37; Huston memo to Haldeman, 7/10/70.
236   *"The recommendations you have proposed":* Haldeman memo to Huston, 7/14/70.
236   *beginning with the Brookings:* Colson memo to RN, 7/10/70. Nixon regularly talked about ways to neutralize the influence of the Brookings Institution, which he considered a safe haven for out-of-office liberals, a sort of government in exile. One idea that worked was the building up of a conservative rival. On June 23, 1970, the President met with John Swearingen to talk about making the American Enterprise Institute into what Nixon called a Republican "ammunition factory." Swearingen was president of the small business-oriented public policy group. Nixon assigned Colson to work with Swearingen in persuading conservative contributors to Brookings studies and programs to switch their support to AEI. The Scaife-Mellon Foundation gave $1 million to AEI and so did the Pew Family Trusts.
237   *"rough them up":* HRHD, 7/24/70.
237   *"How can you expect":* Kissinger, *White House Years,* p. 444; Isaacson, *Kissinger,* p. 253.
238   *"No comment":* HRHD, 7/10/70.
238   *"Our people have got to quit bragging":* Dent memo to RN, "memo for President's File," 7/22/70, POF Box 81; Edward Morgan memo to RN, 8/27/70; Ehrlichman, *Witness to Power,* p. 227. The President received detailed daily summaries with option boxes for each southern school district deemed "particularly volatile."
239   *"expel" the Soviets:* Hersh, *Price of Power,* pp. 227–228. Hersh's footnote explains how only one reporter, Murrey Marder of *The Washington Post,* came to report the "expel" remark. Kissinger used the word in a June 26 backgrounder that was embargoed until July 1. On June 27, in a second backgrounder, also embargoed, Kissinger recanted the word "expel." Marder wasn't at either backgrounder, but read a transcript of the first briefing on July 1 and wrote a story for the next day. Marder told Hersh that, at first sight, "Henry wasn't unhappy about it at all." After the European press began to criticize Kissinger for insensitivity to diplomatic language, he refused to speak to Marder for a year. Another factor was Rogers, who publicly denied plans for expulsion, and privately accused Kissinger of trying to undermine his negotiations in the Middle East, the only area in which he had any real power.
239   *SALT . . . had begun in Vienna:* Kissinger, *White House Years,* pp. 545–551.
240   *bargaining chip:* National Security Decision Memorandum 69, 7/9/70. The President's talking-points memo on the SALT talks in Vienna, drawn up by Buchanan, read: "Those who are recommending a unilateral and unconditional moratorium on American development of MIRV and ABM would throw away the only bargaining counter we have before negotiations begin—and throw away the only chance for success the SALT talks have. . . . the success of the talks hinges on the United States having something to trade to the Soviets in return for restraint in their ICBM program."
240   *"Why is it so difficult":* Kenneth BeLieu memo to RN, 7/23/70, POF Box 81.
241   *ambassador Rabin told:* Kissinger, *White House Years,* pp. 580–585.
241   *"Have you considered attacking":* Hersh, *Price of Power,* p. 223. This exchange was originally recounted in Rabin's memoir.
242   *"Henry thinks Bill":* Safire, *Before the Fall,* p. 406.

242   *"He's almost psycho"*: HRHD, 7/15/70.

242   *On July 23*: Kissinger, *White House Years*, pp. 576, 582–591; Nixon, *Memoirs*, p. 482; Isaacson, *Kissinger*, p. 286; Hersh, *Price of Power*, pp. 228–231; *Time*, 8/3/70.

243   *"The Soviets are massing"*: HRHD, 8/15/70; Kissinger int.

243   *"Weird"*: Haldeman notes, 8/16/70. Four days later Haldeman wrote: "Thinks K is deliberately trying to wreck the peace proposal—because it was proposed by Rogers—and K opposed it and now can't stand to see it work. . . . Israelis keep screaming about violations of the cease-fire by Egypt and P fears K is encouraging them. K also trying to get him to see Meir. . . . Thinks it's an Israeli trick." HRHD (excised) 8/20/70. Then: "P is convinced K is purposely trying to screw up the peace proposal—because Rogers gets credit for it, and because it's basically bad for Israel." HRHD (excised), 9/1/70.

244   *"Attacks on Henry Kissinger"*: Ehrlichman, *Witness to Power*, p. 299; Hersh, *Price of Power*, p. 227.

244   *organized for deception*: Kissinger memo to RN, 8/17/70.

244   *Navy yeoman . . . named Charles Radford*: The Radford story did not become public until mid-January of 1974, when elements of it were reported by the *Chicago Tribune*.

244   *There were double books*: Dent memo to RN, "memo for the President's File," 7/22/70, which includes: "Decisions were made with regard to financing of candidates. This information is considered sensitive for recordation in this report." A second memo, found in Dent's safe, carried an attachment saying: "Attached is a memorandum of understanding of the conclusions of our political meeting as this related to the dollar assistance program for key candidates." The second memo was the real one, and can be found in Harry Dent Box 15 (Special Files Unit). A carbon copy remains in his Box 15 (folder, 1970 Memos to Staff Secretary).

245   *Lenore Romney*: Also, in a September 24 political meeting recorded by Safire, Nixon noted that in Michigan Lenore Romney was "big trouble."

245   *"We are dropping"*: Safire notes on meeting with the President, 9/9/70, Safire papers, Manuscript Division, LC.

245   *Agnew*: Safire notes, political meeting in the Oval Office, 9/24/70, Safire papers, Manuscript Division, LC.

246   *"kike girl"*: Haldeman notes, 3/19/70, Haldeman Box 42.

246   *control his wife's drinking*: HRHD, 5/18/70.

246   *The Real Majority*: HRHD, 8/31/70.

247   *" 'Proper' family"*: Bull memo to RN, 8/18/70, "Greeting of One Millionth Visitor to the White House for Calendar Year 1970," POF Box 82.

248   *The "hijacking"*: The airlines involved were Pan American, Trans World Airlines, El Al, and Swissair. The Pan American Boeing 747 was destroyed by an explosion in Cairo after the passengers and crew had disembarked under Egyptian protection. The El Al hijackers were subdued by passengers and the plane landed safely in London. The three planes in the desert were emptied on September 13 and blown up.

248   *"Tom, I've gotten"*: Hersh, *Price of Power*, pp. 235–237; Isaacson, *Kissinger*, p. 286.

249   *Tough as he was*: Hersh, *Price of Power*, pp. 260, 266; Isaacson, *Kissinger*, p. 288.

249   *"I don't see why"*: Isaacson, *Kissinger*, pp. 288–291.

251   *Kissinger called Haldeman*: HRHD, 9/17/70.

251   *"It looks like the Soviets are"*: Kissinger, White House Years, pp. 614–617; Nixon, *Memoirs*, pp. 483–484; Isaacson, *Kissinger*, pp. 294–295; Hersh, *Price of Power*, pp. 237–240; Kissinger int.

252   *"Analysis of reconnaissance"*: Haldeman, *Ends of Power*, pp. 85–86; Kissinger memo to RN, 9/18/70. Kissinger was wrong about the soccer. Fidel Castro en-

couraged soccer playing in the 1960s and by the 1970s, Cuba had leagues and fields all over the country.

252   *"The Prime Minister said"*: Haig memo to RN, 9/18/70, meeting with Meir and Rabin, POF Box 82.

253   *talked with Kissinger about Cuba*: Kissinger int; HRHD (excised), 9/20/70; Isaacson, *Kissinger*, pp. 296–298; Kissinger, *White House Years*, pp. 638–639; Nixon, *Memoirs*, pp. 485–486; Hersh, *Price of Power*, pp. 250–254.

254   *Kissinger was more persuasive*: Isaacson, *Kissinger*, p. 299.

254   *Sunday, September 20*: Haig, *Inner Circles*, pp. 248–249; Isaacson, *Kissinger*, pp. 299–301; Kissinger, *White House Years*, pp. 617–626.

254   *"We are pissing"*: HRHD (excised), 9/17/70, 9/20/70. The "summit" remark is from the excised portion of 9/17; "patsy" from the excised part of 9/20.

255   *"Bomb the bastards"*: Hersh, *Price of Power*, p. 244.

255   *the next day*: HRHD (excised), 9/21/70; Isaacson, *Kissinger*, pp. 301–302; Kissinger, *White House Years*, pp. 625–628; Haig, *Inner Circles*, pp. 250–251.

255   *his men were driving*: The fifty-eight-thousand-man British-trained Jordanian army, most of them Bedouins noted for desert brutality, was an effective fighting force. It also had the help of foreign officers, contract soldiers from other Islamic countries. One of the commanders of a tank unit was a Pakistani major named Mohammad Zia ul-Haq, who would take power in his own country in 1977 and rule for more than ten years.

255   *"First, the tough"*: HRHD (excised), 9/23/70.

256   *"Mr. Sidey will have"*: Ziegler memo to RN, 9/25/70.

257   *German accent*: Klein int.

257   *On September 27*: NYT, 9/27–28/70.

257   *"The United States is fortunate"*: Isaacson, *Kissinger*, p. 307.

258   *On the eight-hour flight*: HRHD, 9/27/70.

258   *"Nasser is dead!"*: HRHD, 9/28/70.

258   *Dobrynin came to the White House*: Kissinger, *White House Years*, p. 649.

258   *On Friday, October 9*: Kissinger, *White House Years* p. 678; Hersh, *Price of Power*, pp. 283–284. Edward Korry, *"The Sellout of Chile and the American Taxpayer,"* Penthouse, 3/78.

260   *"It is firm and continuing"*: CIA cable to Santiago station chief, 10/18/70.

Chapter 16: *November 3, 1970*

261   *"Have you all read"*: Safire notes, 9/9/70, on President's meeting with Buchanan, Dent, Chotiner, Rumsfeld, Finch, Anderson, Dick Burress, and Harlow, Safire papers, Manuscript Division, LC. The exact quote is from a September 9 meeting, though the President discussed the book at virtually every political meeting throughout the fall, including the September 26 meeting.

263   *The United Auto Workers*: NYT, 9/20/70; CEA Annual Report, 1971, p. 35.

263   *"People don't want to be good"*: Safire memo, 9/9/70. Safire papers, Manuscript Division, LC.

264   *"notorious reputation in the trade"*: RN memo to Flanigan, 3/16/70, Haldeman Box 228 (contested).

264   *"For Democratic politicians"*: Wall Street Journal, 4/3/70.

264   *"I really want"*: Ehrlichman notes, 10/2/70, Ehrlichman files, WHSF.

264   *inflation*: Matusow, *Nixon's Economy*, pp. 57, 82.

264   *Mike Mangione*: NYT, 10/29/70.

264   *"The Democrats are trying"*: Safire notes, President's meeting with Buchanan, Dent, Chotiner, Rumsfeld, Finch, Anderson, Burress, and Harlow, 9/9/70; Safire papers, Manuscript Division, LC; Safire notes, 9/14/70, Safire papers, Manuscript Division, LC; Safire notes, 9/24/70, on the President's meeting with Agnew, Harlow, Art Sohmer, and Carl DeBloom, Safire papers, Manuscript Division, LC.

266   *"Our terrestrial god"*: Colson meeting memo to RN, 9/11/70, POF Box 82.
266   *"ostensibly endorses the radic-lib"*: Higby memo to John Brown, 9/30/70.
267   *Mulcahy, the master of Kilfrush*: HRHD, 10/3, 10/4, 10/5/70; Haldeman memo to Butterfield, 10/6/70; Haldeman memo to Colson, 10/6/70; Butterfield memo to Haldeman, 10/22/70. Mulcahy, a native of Ireland, was the inventor of an efficient oxygen-reduction steel furnace; his gifts to Nixon's 1972 reelection campaign were listed as $255,000 that year and then, in a revised statement made in response to a Common Cause lawsuit in 1973, as $599,595. That statement took into account contributions given secretly before April 1972, the effective date of the Campaign Finance Act of 1971. On those records, Mulcahy was ranked third among Nixon's 1972 givers, behind W. Clement Stone ($2.067 million) and Richard Mellon Scaife ($1.02 million.)
267   *"beaver patrol"*: Butterfield memo to Haldeman, 10/22/70.
267   *small loose-leaf binder*: President's desk, PPF Box 185.
268   *"Christine Jorgensen"*: Evans and Novak, *Inside the White House*, p. 334.
268   *"Have we misjudged"*: RN memo to himself, 10/10/70, President's desk, PPF Box 185. Usually, RN's yellow pad jottings receive no note, since they can be found chronologically filed in PPF Boxes 185–188. But the reader could have mistaken this for a memo.
268   *"BUCKLEY FOR SENATE"*: HRHD, 10/12/70.
268   *John Osborne*: Osborne, *Second Year of the Nixon Watch*, p. 163.
269   *killings at Kent State*: Ken Cole memo to RN, 10/23/70.
269   *United Nations*: Nixon had contempt for the UN. Late in 1969, Haldeman recorded: "Met with lady president of the General Assembly and then with U Thant. Really a useless bunch. K says U Thant"—the Secretary General—"told him he should replace Thieu with a stronger leader in South Vietnam. Some gall!" HRHD (excised), 9/18/69.
269   *Yahya Khan of Pakistan*: Kissinger memo to RN, 10/25/70.
269   *President Ceausescu*: Kissinger memo to RN, 10/26/70.
270   *San Jose*: Safire, *Before the Fall*, pp. 327–334.
270   *"The real blockbuster"*: HRHD, 10/29/70.
270   *"He's a war criminal"*: Wells, *War Within*, pp. 465–466.
271   *burned his own house*: HRHD, 10/29/70.
271   *Phoenix*: Safire, *Before the Fall*, pp. 335–340; HRHD, 10/31/70; Wells, *War Within*, p. 466.
271   *"My God, he looks"*: Safire int.
271   *"mackeral snappers"*: HRHD, 11/3/70.

Chapter 17: *December 31, 1970*

273   *"A missed opportunity"*: Ehrlichman notes, 11/7/70, Ehrlichman files, WHSF.
273   *Evans and Novak*: These points from their column are also on pp. 352–353 of their book *Nixon in the White House*.
274   *"Don't keep saying that"*: Ehrlichman notes, 12/11/70, Ehrlichman files, WHSF.
274   *He wanted to move Moynihan*: Moynihan, report to the President's File 11/17/70. Nixon believed that one way to forge a bipartisan foreign policy consensus was to have a Democrat in the United Nations job, a visible position with little real power. He had, beginning in January 1969, offered the job to Eugene McCarthy and R. Sargent Shriver, among others. He also, in November of 1970, toyed with the idea of naming a Democratic or liberal Republican senator to get that senator out of office and create the possibility of a conservative replacement. The names considered then included John Sherman Cooper, of Kentucky; Charles Percy, of Illinois; and Edward Brooke, of Massachusetts. Appointing Brooke might have had a double benefit, or so Nixon hoped. If Brooke left the Senate, the President hoped to persuade the Republican governor of Massachu-

setts, Francis W. Sargent, to appoint Transportation Secretary Volpe as his replacement, thereby getting Volpe out of the Cabinet.

274   *"Sink FAP"*: Ehrlichman notes, 11/17/70, Ehrlichman files, SMOF.

274   *value-added Tax:* HRHD, 11/7/70.

274   *"I never get to do":* HRHD, 11/12/70.

274   *Marquis Childs:* John Brown (staff secretary) memo to Klein and Ziegler, 11/16/70.

275   *Buckley and by Lloyd M. Bentsen:* HRHD, 11/16/70.

276   *Pearl Bailey:* Hullin memo to Ehrlichman, 11/16/70; Garment memo to RN, 11/16/70.

277   *Debra Jean Sweet:* HRHD 12/3/70, NYT, 12/4/70.

277   *Stewart Alsop:* Newsweek, 12/7/70.

277   *Treasury Secretary Kennedy:* HRHD, 12/8–9/70, 12/11/70.

277   *"He talks big":* HRHD, 11/13/70, 12/2/70.

277   *On Thanksgiving eve:* Ehrlichman memos to RN, 11/24/70, 11/25/70, and 12/17/70.

279   *We have people like Ed Brooke:* RN memo to Haldeman, 12/4/70.

279   *"Chapman's friend":* Memo to Murray Chotiner from Chapman's Friend, 12/15/70. Among the Chapman "friends" trailing Muskie were Seymour Friedin, a former *New York Herald Tribune* reporter, and Lucianne Goldberg, who became a literary agent in New York and, in 1999, a figure in the impeachment of President Clinton.

279   *And, as always, "warmth":* Halderman memo to Chapin; "anecdotalist" interviews with Price, Safire, and Huebner.

280   *The memo was part:* Andrew Rouse memo to RN, "Report on Meeting of President's Advisory Council on Executive Reorganization," 11/19/70, POF Box 83.

280   *"The President's in love":* Safire int.; Safire, *Before the Fall,* pp. 497–498.

280   *call Connally and persuade him:* HRHD, 12/4–5/70.

281   *"I've got to get rid":* Ehrlichman int., Miller Center, University of Virginia, The White House and Policymaking, p. 114.

281   *George Bush":* Haldeman memo to the President's File, 12/9/70; HRHD, 12/7/70

281   *Edward Kennedy:* HRHD, 12/5/70, 12/7/70.

281   *Nancy Dickerson:* HRHD, 12/9/70.

282   *Moshe Dayan:* Kissinger memo to RN, 12/10/70.

282   *Agha Hilaly:* Sultan Khan int.; Kissinger, *White House Years,* pp. 700–702.

283   *"Our leader has taken leave":* Haig, *Inner Circles,* p. 257.

283   *Deep inside, Kissinger thought:* Kissinger int.

284   *Stuart Loory and Jules Witcover:* Loory int. Nixon particularly disliked Loory and had ordered that he be barred from press pools. But in September 1970, the reporter was surprised to be named for the pool covering the President on his visit to the carrier USS *Saratoga* in the Mediterranean. "What happened?" a surprised Loory asked Ziegler. The press secretary answered, "I told him you get terribly seasick."

284   *Max Frankel:* NYT, 12/10/70.

284   *A first-time visitor:* Allen Drury, *Courage and Hesitation: Notes and Photographs of the Nixon Administration* (Garden City, N.Y.: Doubleday, 1971), p. 137. Nixon laid out his public view of the press in an interview with Drury on March 30, 1971: " 'The press?' His expression changed, became earnest, stubborn, close to contemptuous. 'I probably follow the press more closely and am less affected by it than any other President. I have a very cool detachment about it. . . . I never get mad. I expect I have one of the most hostile and unfair presses than any President has ever had, but I've developed a philosophical attitude about it. I developed it early. I have won all my political battles with 80 to 90 percent of the press against me. How have I done it? I ignored the press and went to the people."

285   *"prostitute attitude of the press"*: RN memo to Haldeman, 12/11/70.

285   *dictating long, intricate letters*: On November 24, 1969, the President sent a memo to Haldeman: "When I give an assignment in the PR field, I think it is important that you pass it on orally to Buchanan and Safire rather than through a memorandum from me. . . . I do not think it is a good idea for Safire to be able to tell people that I am trying to instigate letters to columnists, etc."

285   *The first was to John Osborne*: RN memo to Haldeman, 12/11/70.

285   *"Absolutely stunned"*: Reichley oral history with Burns, 9/21/77, Ford Library.

285   *Acting Secretary Connally*: Safire int.

286   *one of the grayest*: Ehrlichman notes, 12/15/70; Ehrlichman memo to RN, meeting with Burns, 12/15/70, POF Box 83.

287   *Milton Friedman*: Shultz memo to President's File, 11/19/70, POF Box 83.

288   *Elvis Presley*: Krogh int.; Chapin memo to Haldeman, 12/1/70; Krogh memo to RN, 12/21/70, meeting with Presley, POF Box 83; Egil "Bud" Krogh, *The Day Elvis Met Nixon* (Bellevue, Washington: Pejama Press, 1994).

290   *end-of-year Cabinet meeting*: Price memo to RN, 12/21/70, Cabinet meeting, POF Box 83.

291   *"Let Dr. Tkach"*: RN memo to Haldeman, 12/13/70

291   *Cronkite. . . . Sevareid*: CBS News transcript, 12/27/70, Safire papers, Manuscript division, LC.

292   *The President hosted*: Drury, *Courage and Hesitation*, pp. 243–246; HRHD, 12/31/70; Helen Thomas int.

292   *"highest IQs"*: Alan Greenspan, an economic adviser, said in an interview with James Reichley that he believed President Nixon had the highest IQ of any president since Woodrow Wilson and that the staff, particularly Haldeman and Ehrlichman, were extremely intelligent. "But," he added, "it was the type of intelligence that tended to block out people who disagreed. They did not tolerate dissent."

Chapter 18: *March 29, 1971*

293   *Jim Plunkett*: HRHD, 1/1/17.

294   *"Neither fish nor fowl"*: Buchanan memo to RN, 1/7/71. In a June 1972 memo to Buchanan, Nixon explained the difference between left-wing extremists and conservative true believers like Buchanan. "The right wing would rather lose than give up one iota as far as principle is concerned. The left wing's primary motivation is power. They are always willing to compromise their principles in order to get power because they know without power they cannot put their principles to work." For further discussion of the "neither fish nor fowl" polemic, see Safire, *Before the Fall*, pp. 543–551.

295   *I am now a Keynesian*: Ambrose, *Nixon*, vol. 2, p. 404; *NYT*, 1/7/71.

296   *Moore began*: Dick Moore memo to RN, 1/22/71, "President's Open Door," POF Box 84. Hugh Sloan went on to become treasurer of the Committee to Re-Elect the President, and a key source for Carl Bernstein and Bob Woodward in their Watergate reporting.

296   *State of the Union*: PPF, 1/22/71. "Revenue sharing" had originally been proposed in the 1950s by Mel Laird, when he was a young congressman from Wisconsin. In 1964, President Johnson considered making the proposal, but backed off because of opposition by organized labor. The specifics of Nixon's revenue sharing, as reported by John Osborne in *The New Republic* and reprinted in his *The Third Year of the Nixon Watch* (New York: Liveright, 1972).

The sharing would take two forms, one a genuine innovation and the other not so genuine. Federal revenue amounting to a fixed proportion (1.3 percent) of the nation's total taxable personal income would be returned each year to states and localities. The only conditions limiting its use would be that states and localities share it according to a federally set formula (on average, 52 percent to the states and 48 percent to localities) and that federal laws and regulations prohibiting racial and other discrimination be observed. The base percentage would produce $5 billion for "general sharing" in the first full year of operation, more in years when total personal income increases. The companion "special revenue sharing" would in fact be a sharing of funds that states and localities already get in the form of federal grants made according to predetermined federal criteria and expended under varying degrees of federal control. The aided governments would no longer have to match the federal money with their own (usually 10 to 30 percent of the total). With some extra money ($1 billion, the briefers said; $700 million, the 1972 budget message said), the conversion of these "categorical grants" to the more-or-less free grants proposed by the President would come to $11 billion for states and localities in the first complete fiscal year.

On the health care proposal, Osborne wrote:

The Nixon scheme deals separately with Americans who can afford to pay for their health care and with those who cannot. But it deals with the poor and the non-poor in the same way—by reliance upon privately provided health insurance. The federal government would buy the insurance for families with no or very low incomes (up to $3000 for a family of four). An official fact sheet supplementing the Nixon message said that 'all employers of one or more persons' would be required by law to provide 'minimum standard health insurance protection' for their employees, with the employers paying at least 65 percent of the cost initially and 75 percent later on. The employees would pay the rest, unless they or their unions obtained higher or total employer payment. The fine print limited the superficially inclusive mandate to employers 'engaged in interstate commerce,' a very broad but not totally embracing category. The 'minimum protection' to be required was not defined, leaving the impression that it could, with one generous exception, consist of the cheapest and most limited coverage available through Blue Cross and similar private insurance arrangements. The exception, insisted upon by the President, was the provision of coverage up to $50,000 for catastrophic illness of the kind that took the life of a tubercular older brother and burdened the Nixon family in Mr. Nixon's boyhood. Covered employees would get full maternity care and preventative care for children, but they would have to pay the first $100 to $208 of hospital costs and a vaguely indicated proportion of medical costs. The very poor would not have to meet these costs, but families of four with incomes above $3000 would have to pay some of the costs and, at income levels above $5000, all of them. Secretary Richardson guessed that employers in the first year would have to pay $7 billion a year more than employers now pay for health insurance. But he conceded that this and literally all other cost estimates, for the Nixon and rival programs, are no better than guesses and flimsy guesses at that.

297   "a holding action": HRHD, 3/6/71.
297   In a January poll: Jon Huntsman memo to Ehrlichman, 2/20/71.
297   lists of friends and enemies: Mort Allin memo to George Bell, 1/28/71. On November 30, 1970, the President dictated a memo to Haldeman: "On the political front, I would suggest that over the next few weeks, after consultation with those you consider to be our best political analysts, you should develop a list of those who are and will continue to be our major opponents between now and 1972. I refer not simply to press and TV, but the University community, religious organizations, finance, Eastern Establishment, the major Senate/House/Gubernatorial/Party leaders on the other side, and the special interest groups like Labor and Minorities." The first wave of enemies lists in-

cluded twenty academics; twenty-four businessmen; nine entertainers; twelve labor leaders; fifty-seven reporters, editors, and broadcasters; fifteen organizations; and thirty politicians.

298 *"I received a copy"*: Butterfield memo to Haldeman, "Opponents," 7/8/71, Staff Secretary Box 82.

298 *"To get out"*: Safire interview; Safire notes, 2/21/71, Safire papers, Manuscript Division, LC.

299 *When they finished working:* Safire memo to Butterfield, 2/24/71.

300 *Kissinger would fall on a sword:* HRHD, 3/3/71.

300 *"If the enemy fights"*: Haig memo to RN, meeting with Kissinger, Haig, and Moorer, 1/26/71, POF Box 84.

301 *Riland, manipulated:* HRHD, 2/3/71.

301 *"WARNING—NO U.S. PERSONNEL"*: NYT, 2/6/71.

301 *The operation in Laos was running. . . . political discussions:* Haldeman meeting notes, 2/4/70, HRHD, 2/4/71.

301 *the futures of J. Edgar Hoover:* HRHD, 2/4/71. One of the men pushing for Hoover's ouster was Buchanan, who wrote in a memo to the President on 2/12/71: "I think the President should give serious consideration to replacing Mr. Hoover as soon as possible—for his good, for our good, for the country's good. . . . he is increasingly becoming a villain; and he is totally tied to us."

302 *care and feeding:* HRHD, 2/6/71.

302 *"If Rogers doesn't knuckle"*: Safire, *Before the Fall*, p. 403.

303 *Lam Son 719:* Kissinger, *White House Years*, pp. 1002–1010; Hersh, *Price of Power*, pp. 307–313; NYT, 2/1/71–4/4/71.

303 *In the end, the President:* Haig, memo of the President's meeting with Admiral Moorer, 2/25/71.

304 *reported by Iver Peterson:* NYT, 3/24/71.

304 *"This building will blow up"*: NYT, 3/2/71.

305 *Haldeman turned the job over:* Lukas, *Nightmare*, pp. 372–378; William Doyle, *Inside the Oval Office: The White House Tapes from FDR to Clinton* (New York: Kodansha International, 1999), pp. 167–169; Klein, *Making It Perfectly Clear*, p. 327. The President was not the only one recording conversations. Ehrlichman had a complete taping system in his office. Colson taped phone calls. Kissinger had a secretary on an extension phone taking notes on his calls. In an October 5, 1993, interview with Christopher Matthews for his book *Kennedy & Nixon: The Rivalry That Shaped Postwar America* (New York: Simon & Schuster, 1996), Haldeman said: "It evolved out of a lot of things. . . . He was worried that in private head-to-head meetings he didn't want the burden on himself of having to be the only recorder of that meeting because that's a lot of work and he had to be thinking. . . . So we set up a lot of different processes. A guy to sit in, a fly on the wall. An automatic debriefing of both parties after the meeting by our staff. Nixon didn't like someone sitting in, especially if they were taking notes because that always bothers people. . . . The one solution we came up with was getting Vernon Walters in who had a photographic memory and have him just sit in the meetings as an aide. And we called him back from Europe to tell him that's what Nixon wanted him to do. Walters stood up and said, 'Mr. Haldeman, generals command troops, they are not secretaries,' and he stalked out of the room. . . . I asked Nixon at one point—the tapes were piling up—do you want me to start getting someone to transcribe these things? . . . He says absolutely not. He did not want anyone hearing them. He said to me, 'No one is ever going to hear those tapes but you and me.' "

306 *There had been separatist:* The account of the Indo-Pakistani War was drawn from interviews with Kissinger and with Sultan Khan and General Muhammad Zia al-Haq, when he was president of Pakistan. Also, some details are from Isaacson's *Kissinger*, pp. 371–373.

306 *Lieutenant William Calley, Jr. Guilty:* NYT, 3/30/71–4/5/71; HRHD,

3/30/71–4/2/71; Nixon, *Memoirs*, pp. 499–500; Evans and Novak, *Nixon in the White House*, pp. 394–399; Carter, *Politics of Rage*, p. 386. Buchanan followed the Calley story for the President, writing on April 5: "We should catch opinion as it shifts, get in front of it—not reaming Calley, but defending the Army, the process of law in this country, our belief that excesses in combat will not be tolerated—and giving a good scourging to the guilt-ridden, war-crime crowd that is on the other side of our fence, and of the national fence." Nixon replied in writing: "This is our position."

307   " 'Yes, sir' ": HRHD, 4/1/71.

308   *"I would like to leave"*: Drury, *Courage and Hesitation*, pp. 389–400.

308   *meetings with milk producers*: NT, 3/23/71, 11:00 A.M.; memo to RN, 3/23/71, "President's Meeting with 20 Key Dairy Industry Personnel, POF Box 84; HRHD, 3/23/71; Lukas, *Nightmare*, pp. 115–126. The AMPI actually delivered only $632,500. Connally was indicted—and later acquitted—on charges that the milk producers had also delivered $15,000 in cash to him personally. Nelson served four months in jail after conviction on bribery charges.

309   *Lieutenant Calley*: HRHD, 4/2/71.

310   *Captain Aubrey W. Daniel III*: Letter to the President, 4/3/71; NYT, 4/11/71; HRHD, 4/7/71.

Chapter 19: *June 12, 1971*

311   *"THIS MEMORANDUM"*: RN memo to Haldeman, 3/31/71.

311   *"He is so thoughtful"*: Drury, *Courage and Hesitation*, pp. 226–235.

312   *"in the Rose Garden"*: Andrews memo to RN, 4/19/71, color report, POF Box 84.

312   *"no special words"*: Butterfield memo to RN, 4/15/71, color report, POF Box 84.

313   *"sniffing device"*: Law Enforcement Alliance of America meeting memo, Denver, 8/3/70, POF Box 81.

313   *The Wall Street Journal*: WSJ, 4/14/71.

314   *"I think Rumsfeld"*: RN dictation, 4/14/71.

314   *He was a sentimental man*: "He had a feeling for the underdog. Remember Richard Nixon was a Mets fan," Klein said in an interview.

314   *"Thelma."* Ehrlichman int.

314   *Mrs. Nixon*: HRHD (excised), 1/8/70. Early in the administration, Haldeman, presumably on the President's orders, asked Julie Nixon Eisenhower to drop out of Smith College for a year to take over some of her mother's duties. HRHD (excised), 4/27/69.

314   *"When are we going to get"*: Gulley, *Breaking Cover*, p. 159.

315   *letter to Lester Maddox*: Maddox later became governor of Georgia.

315   *"humdrum existence"*: HRHD, 3/17/71.

315   *"diplomacy of smiles"*: ANS nd 4/71, POF Box 33.

315   *Chou En-lai, knew*: Chou told Nixon of Mao's role on February 22, 1973, in Peking, MemCon to President's File, 2/22/73.

315   *The visit of fifteen*: Time, 4/26/71.

316   *"Mr. Hoover has"*: Buchanan memo to RN, 2/12/71.

316   *Moynihan*: Moynihan letter to RN, 2/28/71.

317   *In private, he was still*: HRHD, 5/22/71.

317   *"Going to the bathroom"*: HRHD, 4/16/71.

317   *The early-morning session*: HRHD, 4/20/71.

317   *"If we can keep the liberal writers"*: Edward L. Morgan memo to RN, "Status of School Desegregation Matters," 5/24/71.

318   *"The incursion"*: Wells, *War Within*, pp. 471–472, 480–499.

319   *"crank the Vice President"*: HRHD, 4/23/71.

319   *"Seventy people died"*: Wells, *War Within*, pp. 498–500.

319   *Hilaly of Pakistan*: Kissinger, *White House Years*, pp. 713–717; HRHD, 4/28/71; Isaacson, Kissinger, pp. 339–340.

319   *Monday, May 3*: Wells, *War Within*, pp. 500–505.

320   *"Demostrators gathering"*: Dean memo to RN, 5/4/71.

321   *a crate of oranges*: Wells, *War Within*, pp. 504–505. Fred Fielding jokingly suggested sending the oranges, a Muskie trademark. Colson took it seriously. Also, the brass monkey remark came earlier.

321   *"Every one of the recipients"*: RN dictated memo to Haldeman, 5/4/71.

322   *obvious, roaring fag*: RN memo to Haldeman, 4/28/71.

322   *Kerry, who was invited to testify*: Wells, *War Within*, p. 495.

322   *"The returning men"*: Krogh int.; Michael Massing, *The Fix* (New York: Simon & Schuster, 1998), pp. 107–110. The minutes of a June 3 meeting on the drug problem stated: "The President expressed concern that some of the public, especially some employers, view the Vietnam veteran as a ruthless killer and junkie and therefore he cannot get a job. This image must be changed." Krogh was given two charges: To deal with drug use as a "national problem" to take the focus off Vietnam, and to find a way to clean up men before they left Vietnam for home.

With a presidential mandate, Krogh immediately brought in a thirty-seven-year-old Chicago psychiatrist named Jerome Jaffe. Dr. Jaffe had an idea and, suddenly, he was in the Oval Office explaining it to the President, who liked it. The psychiatrist said that most of the soldiers in question were not hard-core addicts but just users, dabbling, and that harsh military penalties would only bring more attention to the Vietnam problem— exactly what Nixon did not want—but there was a way to use a small but immediate penalty. "Like what?" the President asked. Like giving urine tests as men lined up for the planes taking them home from Vietnam. If his instant test showed "positive"—indicating drug use—a man was not allowed to leave until after a couple of weeks of detoxification. Nixon thought the idea was both brilliant and perfect for his purposes. The exposure and detox would stay offshore. On May 30th, he sent Dr. Jaffe to the Pentagon where generals and admirals said it would take five or six months to set up a system and servicemen would not cooperate. The doctor, unschooled in the ways of Washington, said: "Gentlemen, the White House wants something done about the problem a little sooner than that. . . . I cannot believe that the mightiest army on earth can't get its soldiers to piss in a bottle." They could and they did. A week later, the President created the $155 million Special Action Office for Drug Abuse Prevention—with both civilian and military responsibility—headed by Jerome Jaffe. Part of the reason he moved so quickly was that most of the money would come out of HEW drug programs (quipping in the office, "They're all on drugs over there anyway.") At the same time the President himself was seriously "staffing out"—a Haldeman phrase—a Moynihan brainstorm: buying the opium crop of Turkey and other drug-producing countries. The Vietnam screening began on June 17th—the urine was analyzed within thirty seconds by free radical assay technique machines—and of the first twenty-two thousand GIs tested, just under 5 percent showed evidence of having used opiates within seventy-two hours of departure. That percentage rapidly dropped. Most men preferred going home to using drugs.

323   *George Wallace was along*: Dan Carter, *Politics of Rage*, pp. 409–410.

323   *"give them Hartford . . . McLaren . . . Oh God, yes . . ."* Oval Office tape, 5/13/71.

324   *"bad, good, or indifferent"*: Lukas, *Nightmare*, pp. 130–132; NT, 5/13/71.

324   *"I'm tired of these kooks*: Carter, *Politics of Rage* pp. 409–410.

324   *meeting with Connally*: Haldeman memo for the President's File, 5/20/71.

324   *play a little joke*: HRHD, 5/20/71.

325   *"The thing is okay"*: HRHD, 5/18/71.

325   *dinner cruise on the Sequoia:* HRHD, 5/18/71; Isaacson, *Kissinger,* pp. 327–328; Charles W. Colson, *Born Again* (Old Tappan, New Jersey: Chosen Books, 1976), pp. 43–45, 57–59; Kissinger, *White House Years,* p. 820.

326   *"a laughingstock":* HRHD, 5/19/71; memo for the President's File, 5/19/71, "President's Talking Points for Meeting with Secretary Rogers," POF Box 85.

326   *MIRVs:* Hersh, *Price of Power,* pp. 341–342.

326   *a joint meeting of the Cabinet and Congressional leaders:* MacGregor memo to RN, 5/20/71, POF Box 85.

327   *a Republican leadership meeting:* Ken BeLieu memo to RN, 4/20/71, "Meeting with Senate Republican Loyalists," POF Box 84.

328   *The full message from the Chinese:* Kissinger, *White House Years,* pp. 726–727; Nixon, *Memoirs,* pp. 551–552; Hilaly int.

328   *"This is the most important":* Nixon, *Memoirs,* pp. 552–553.

329   *On Saturday, June 12:* Nixon, *Memoirs,* pp. 504–508.

329   *foolish during a dinner cruise:* HRHD, 6/10/71, 6/12/71.

329   *Fifty-nine million:* Colson memo to Haldeman, 6/15/71.

Chapter 20: *June 30, 1971*

331   *Nixon told Haldeman:* HRHD, 6/13–18/71.

331   *"Top Secret" classification:* Haig memo to RN, security clearance review, 6/30/71.

332   *Nixon thought Gelb:* Rudenstine, *Day the Presses Stopped;* pp. 31, 252; Sanford Ungar, *The Papers & the Papers: An Account of the Legal and Political Battle over the Pentagon Papers* (New York: Columbia University Press, 1989), pp. 40–42.

332   *Kissinger thought:* Bernard and Marvin Kalb, *Kissinger* (Boston: Little, Brown, 1974), p. 242; Rudenstine, *Day the Presses Stopped,* pp. 33–35, 72–73.

333   *"you're a weakling":* Haldeman, *Ends of Power,* p. 110.

333   *At 7:30 P.M.:* Rudenstine, *Day the Presses Stopped,* pp. 67–71, 102–103; Ungar, *Papers & the Papers,* pp. 108, 120–124; HRHD, 6/14/71.

333   *At 4:09 P.M.:* Ehrlichman memo to RN, 6/15/71, POF Box 85.

334   *When Mitchell left:* Kissinger memo to RN, meeting with Dobrynin, 6/15/71, POF Box 85.

334   *When Daniel Ellsberg's name:* Ehrlichman, notes of meeting with RN, Kissinger, and Haldeman, 6/17/71; Hersh, *Price of Power,* pp. 384–385.

334   *Haldeman was taken aback:* Haldeman, The Ends of Power, p. 110.

335   *You can blackmail Johnson:* NT, 6/17/71, 5:17 P.M.

335   *argue the case himself:* HRHD, 6/17/71.

336   *The next afternoon:* NYT, 6/14–29/71; Rudenstine, *Day the Presses Stopped,* pp. 2–4, 169, 252, 289–290; Ungar, *Papers & the Papers,* pp. 168–174, 193–194. The chronology of public facts in the Pentagon Papers case is, of course, available in *The New York Times* for the period, and in other newspapers.

336   *President invited Senate Majority Leader:* HRHD, 6/23/71.

337   *since World War II:* Nixon, *Memoirs,* p. 552; HRHD, 6/28/71.

337   *Chinese were afraid:* HRHD, 6/22/71.

337   *lord high executioner:* HRHD, 6/29/71.

338   *Bedell Smith:* Haldeman notes, 6/29/71. Haldeman files, SMOF.

338   *Nixon called in:* Haldeman dictated notes 6/22/71, Haldeman files, SMOF.

339   *Brookings was:* NT, 6/30/71, 7/1/71. These passages are from tapes made throughout these two days. Also, see Haldeman, *Ends of Power,* p. 115.

339   *"kind of a tiger":* Hunt first appears in White House records in a January 12, 1971 memo from Colson to George Bell: "Put in a request immediately for Mr. and Mrs. Howard Hunt, Witches Island, Potomac, to be afterdinner guests at the dinner for Juan

Carlos. Hunt was the head of all of our intelligence operations in Spain. His wife is presently the Spanish Ambassador's secretary. Howard is a staunch Republican who is now in PR business on the outside and is beginning to take on a number of special assignments for us of a very sensitive nature. It is very important politically that we let him know he is in the family and this happens to be a unique occasion as far as he and his wife are concerned."

Chapter 21: *August 12, 1971*

340   *Peter Peterson:* Matusow, *Nixon's Economy,* pp. 131–141.

341   *meeting of the Productivity Commission:* Safire memo to RN, 6/29/71, POF Box 85; Safire notes, 6/29/71, Safire papers, Manuscript Division, LC.

343   *largest drops ever:* Stein memo to RN, "June Unemployment and Employment," 7/1/71.

343   *Harold Goldstein:* HRHD, 2/6/71, 6/29/71, 7/2/71; NT, 7/3/71. In the same conversation with Haldeman and Ehrlichman, Nixon asked about a former Kissinger assistant: "Is Tony Lake Jewish?. . . . He looked it." Lake, who is not Jewish, became national security adviser under President Clinton. At the same time, Nixon, who did not consider himself to be anti-Semitic, said, according to Ehrlichman, *Witness to Power,* p. 258: "You know, I think Connally is anti-Semitic. It probably troubles him to deal with Herb Stein and Arthur Burns and Henry Kissinger and Safire and Garment. Too bad."

343   *"Most Jews are disloyal":* *Washington Post,* 10/6/99. The article cites a Nixon tape from the summer of 1971. The tapes are riddled with similar remarks.

344   *"Thirteen of the 35":* Malek memo to Haldeman, 7/27/71, Alpha Name file; Malek, Haldeman files.

344   *leave secretly:* HRHD, 7/7/71. Haldeman was no sinologist. That night, referring to Kissinger visiting Mao and Chou, he wrote: ". . . it's possible he'll see the old man, as well as the guy who he originally was going to see."

344   *called in Rogers:* HRHD, 7/8/71.

344   *"three-in-four chance":* HRHD, 7/9/71. This conversation took place the day after the initial RN-Rogers meeting.

344   *"Eureka":* Nixon, Memoirs, p. 553; Kissinger, *White House Years,* p. 756.

344   *Radford:* Senate Armed Services Committee Hearing, 2/20–21/74, "Transmittal of Documents from the National Security Council to the Chairman of the Joint Chiefs of Staff"; Lukas, *Nightmare,* p. 105–106; Isaacson, *Kissinger,* p. 348.

345   *"We have laid the ground":* Kissinger, *White House Years,* pp. 754–758. Kissinger memo to RN, 7/13/71; Nixon, *Memoirs,* pp. 553–554; HRHD, 7/13–14/71.

346   *"follow the Stennis line":* Clark MacGregor memo to RN, re bipartisan leadership meeting, 7/19/71, POF Box 85.

346   *the briefing of White House staff:* Memo to RN (unsigned), re staff briefing on RN's China trip announcement, 7/19/71, POF Box 85.

346   *jawboning of television executives:* Colson memo to Haldeman, 7/20/71, Colson Box 15; HRHD, 7/20/71.

347   *"One effective line":* RN memo to Kissinger, 7/19/71.

348   *"new arrogance of the young":* Colson meeting memo to RN, 7/21/71, POF Box 85.

349   *Plumbers:* Lukas, *Nightmare,* pp. 72–80, 86, 87; Krogh int; Ehrlichman int.

349   *fallback positions:* Some thought the leaker was Richard Perle, the national security expert on the staff of Senator Henry Jackson. Krogh int.

350   *Agnew returned:* NYT, 9/19/96.

351   *The problems of Coach Nixon:* These economic data and quotations are taken from Matusow, *Nixon's Economy,* pp. 112–117, 146–149; John Connally, with Mickey Herskowitz, *In History's Shadow: An American Odyssey* (New York: Hyperion,

1993), pp. 238–241; Wyatt C. Wells, *Economist in an Uncertain World: Arthur F. Burns and the Federal Reserve, 1970–1978* (New York: Columbia University Press, 1994), pp. 73–76; and issues of *The New York Times, The Wall Street Journal, Time,* and *Newsweek* for the period.

351   *Fort Knox:* Until March 1968, governments, central banks, corporations, and individuals could exchange dollars for Fort Knox gold, but that changed on March 18, 1968, when corporations and speculators took out $3 billion in gold in anticipation of a rise in its price. After that, only governments and their central banks had the actual right to demand United States gold.

353   *Krogh reported:* Krogh int.; Lukas, *Nightmare,* p. 93.

353   *"Tell Krogh he should":* ibid., p. 94. Nixon defenders emphasize that Ehrlichman could have been lying when he said he was passing on orders from the President.

353   *sent Ehrlichman a two-page memo:* Krogh and Young memo to Ehrlichman, re Pentagon Papers, 8/11/71, courtesy of Bud Krogh.

353   *secret letter to the Kremlin:* Anatoliy Fedorovich Dobrynin, *In Confidence: Moscow's Ambassador to America's Six Cold War Presidents, 1962–1986* (New York: Times Books, 1995), pp. 226–233.

354   *Speechwriter Bill Safire:* Safire, *Before the Fall,* pp. 491–496.

354   *"the most important weekend":* Safire papers, Manuscript Division, LC; Safire, *Before the Fall,* pp. 509–510.

Chapter 22: *August 15, 1971*

355   *a circle in the living room of Aspen:* Safire notes, 8/13/71; Safire papers, Manuscript Division, LC; Safire, *Before the Fall,* pp. 510–518; HRHD, 8/13/71. Since the end of World War II, the stability of currencies around the world had been based on rigid exchange rates. The value of other major currencies around the world was calculated against an unchanging dollar and, since 1934, an unchanging, official price of gold— thirty-five dollars per ounce. The central banks of most countries held huge amounts of dollars as reserve assets—stable money in the bank—guaranteed, in effect, by the convertibility of other currencies into dollars, and the convertibility of dollars into gold at the official rate. That had been true for thirty-seven years. Most world currencies revolved around the steady gold-backed dollar. This new idea was to let the dollar float like any other currency, its value going up and down based on how many marks or francs or pounds foreigners were willing to pay for dollars.

359   *"Fortunes could be made":* HRHD, 8/13/71; Safire, *Before the Fall,* p. 518.

359   *At 3:15 A.M.:* HRHD, 8/14/71; Safire, *Before the Fall,* pp. 519–520.

359   *an IBM Executary: Life,* 12/72.

359   *the presidential sauna:* HRHD, 8/14/71. Safire erred in his book by placing the officer in the pool. He was in the sauna, as evidenced by Haldeman's diary and Safire's own notes.

359   *"another speechwriter":* Safire notes, 8/14/71; Safire papers, Manuscript Division, LC.

359   *"Following is a rough":* Safire, *Before the Fall,* p. 520.

359   *Nixon called Haldeman:* HRHD, 8/14/71.

360   *"hell of a spot":* HRHD, 8/14/71.

360   *"Stop high prices":* Safire diary, 8/11/70; Safire papers, Manuscript Division, LC. This diary entry is dated a year previously, but is with the current subject matter; it may have been misdated.

360   *"bugaboo of devaluation":* Safire, *Before the Fall,* p. 523. The so-called bugaboo was certainly more complicated than Nixon cared to admit. A devaluation of the dollar discourages imports, as some foreign companies no longer find it profitable to operate in the American market. For any market that includes imports, this decrease in supply will allow the price of domestic goods to increase.

361 *"a noble motive"*: Safire, *Before the Fall*, p. 524.

361 *Stein had written*: Stein and Dening memo to RN, "Next Steps in Anti-Inflationary Policy," 3/24/71.

361 *last shared meal*: *Newsweek*, 8/30/71.

361 *"try to be Number One"*: HRHD, 8/14/71.

361 *"Nixon Acts Boldly"*: Nixon, *Memoirs*, p. 520.

364 *"This makes Nixon's"*: *Time*, 8/30/71. All reaction and commentary is taken from *Newsweek* and *Time* magazines of 8/30/71, unless otherwise specified.

364 *Sindlinger poll*: *Wall Street Journal*, 8/17/71.

365 *cover of Newsweek*: *Newsweek*, 8/30/71.

Chapter 23: *September 8, 1971*

367 *Knights of Columbus*: NYT, 8/18/71.

367 *national monument, Haldeman told*: HRHD, 8/18–19/71; Lukas, *Nightmare*, p. 17; Safire, *Before the Fall*, pp. 354–355.

367 *In California*: HRHD, 8/23–24/71.

368 *"Delusions of grandeur"*: HRHD, 9/8/71.

368 *note from Rose Kennedy*: President's desk, PPF Boxes 185–188.

368 *"If I'm assassinated"*: HRHD, 9/9/71.

368 *On September 8*: NT 9/8/71, 3:36 P.M.

369 *breaking into the office*: Lukas, *Nightmare*, pp. 97–101.

370 *"a lot of hanky-panky"*: NT, 9/10/71, 3:03 P.M.

370 *"don't give a damn"*: NT, 9/18/71.

370 *"Billy Graham tells me"*: NT, 9/13/71, 4:36 P.M.

370 *"satanic Jews"*: HRHD, 2/1/72. Graham later denied ever using the phrase.

370 *ideas he had*: NT, 9/14/71, 9/17/71, 9/18/71.

371 *fabricated a cable*: Lukas, *Nightmare*, pp. 83–84.

371 *Black . . . Harlan*: Ehrlichman, *Witness to Power*, pp. 133–134.

372 *getting rid of Hoover*: Ehrlichman, *Witness to Power*, pp. 165–167; HRHD, 4/13/71, 7/12/71; Lukas, *Nightmare*, pp. 60–62.

372 *"It was a no-go"*: HRHD, 9/20/71.

372 *"What happened?"*: Ehrlichman, *Witness to Power*, pp. 166–167.

372 *Supreme Court nominees*: ibid., pp. 134–139.

373 *auto racing*: Andrews memo to the staff secretary, "Color Report on President's Reception for Auto Racing Figures," 9/24/71 (meeting was 9/21), POF Box 86.

373 *"Lest you think"*: Haldeman memo to Chapin, re Racing Plan, 9/20/71, Haldeman Box 197.

374 *Andrei Gromyko*: HRHD, 10/12/71.

Chapter 24: October 21, 1971

375 *John Andrews was the designated anecdotalist*: Andrews resigned in December 1973 and four months later wrote an essay published in *Newsweek* (3/4/74): "As a conservative Republican and long-time admirer of Richard Nixon, deeply indebted to him for my start in Washington, the hardest and saddest thing I have ever had to do in my life has been to break publicly with the President over his crisis of integrity. . . . To forbear from personal condemnation of the man, however, is not to accept the misgovernment over which he has presided. In the absence of any hint of willingness on the President's part to bear voluntarily the consequences of his acts either by starting over or stepping down, impeachment must go forward."

375 *Richard H. Poff*: HRHD, 9/24/71, 10/2/71.

376 *"He's a real reactionary"*: HRHD, 10/2/71.

376   *The outline of Phase II:* Stein memo to RN, 10/5/71.
376   *George Meany:* Colson meeting memo to RN, 7/21/71, POF Box 85; HRHD, 7/21/71.
376   *"Philadelphia Plan":* NYT, 10/13/71.
377   *"The Congress gave the President":* NYT, 10/5/71.
377   *The consumer price index . . . Hourly wage rates:* Matusow, *Nixon's Economy,* p. 159.
377   *"labor cooperation":* HRHD, 8/13/71.
377   *he was so angry about an Immigration:* NT, 10/7/71.
378   *Buchanan had sent Nixon an article:* Buchanan memo to RN, 8/26/71, POF Box 13 (contested).
378   *Moynihan sent back eleven pages:* Moynihan memo to RN, 9/20/71, POF Box 13 (contested).
379   *"a Jew or a Catholic":* HRHD, 10/7/71.
379   *satisfy Meany:* Osborne, *Third Year of the Nixon Watch,* pp. 151–157; NYT, 10/9/71.
381   *"I don't think anybody should have":* Price memo to RN, meeting of the Cabinet, 10/12/71.
381   *"Triangular diplomacy":* Kissinger int.
381   *Vietnam . . . news:* ANS nd, 10/71, POF boxes 34–35.
382   *"Administratively Confidential":* Haldeman memo to Ziegler, re *Time's* "Man of the Year," 10/12/71.
382   *"Haig remind Henry":* HRHD, 10/20/71.
382   *"Ostpolitik":* NYT, 10/21/71.
383   *Attorney General Mitchell . . . Chief Justice Burger:* HRHD, 10/15/71.
383   *Osborne wrote . . . Ehrlichman immediately dispatched:* Osborne, *Third Year of the Nixon Watch,* pp. 162–167.
383   *Osborne's best sources:* Ehrlichman, *Witness to Power,* p. 275.
383   *9 A.M. He called at 9:30:* HRHD, 10/21/71; Dean, *Blind Ambition,* p. 42.
384   *"two hard-right conservatives":* Washington Post, 10/30/71.
384   *"Boy, is she mad":* HRHD, 10/21/71.

Chapter 25: *December 16, 1971*

385   *"he can't stay" . . . "Will he rat":* NT, 10/25/71.
386   *United Nations General Assembly:* NYT, 10/26/71.
386   *"Win it!":* Life, 11/5/71.
386   *abide by UN votes:* HRHD, 10/26/71.
386   *Senator James Buckley issued a statement:* NYT, 10/26/71.
386   *"We just have to ride this out":* HRHD, 10/26/71; NT, 10/30/71.
387   *persuade the Senate to restore:* HRHD, 10/30/71–11/10/71; memos to the President's File re congressional leadership meetings, POF Box 86.
387   *The Washington Post published:* Safire, *Before the Fall,* pp. 354–357; HRHD, 8/17–8/19/71.
388   *an angry letter:* RN memo to Burns, 11/4/71.
389   *"Bill, remind the people":* Safire int.; Safire, *Before the Fall,* pp. 492–496.
389   *Bernard J. Lasker:* Matusow, *Nixon's Economy,* p. 175.
389   *Hundreds of thousands:* Sultan Khan int.
389   *"Our government has failed":* Hersh, *Price of Power,* pp. 444–445.
389   *"idle spectator":* Sultan M. Khan, *Memories and Reflections of a Pakistani Diplomat* (London: London Centre for Pakistan Studies, 1997), pp. 268–269.
390   *L. K. Jha:* Hersh, *Price of Power,* pp. 451–454.
391   *the military balance:* ANS, 11/4/71.

391   "To all hands": Kissinger, *White House Years*, p. 856.
391   "tilt toward Pakistan": The January 5, 1972, *Washington Post* printed the "memorandum for the record" of this WSAG meeting on India/Pakistan. The original documents were obtained by Jack Anderson, and copies were turned over to several newspapers. Anderson won the Pulitzer Prize for his coverage.
391   *Prime Minister Gandhi*: MemCon for the President's File, 11/4/71; MemCon 11/5/71, POF Box 86.
391   *Nixon thought Mrs. Gandhi was lying . . . "bitch"*: Hersh, *Price of Power*, p. 447; Isaacson, *Kissinger*, p. 374; Kissinger int.
392   "Isn't that right, Henry?": Isaacson, *Kissinger*, p. 374.
392   "the alternative was to lose East Pakistan": Sultan Khan int.; Khan, *Memories and Reflections*, p. 360.
392   *price freeze . . . four hundred thousand*: Matusow, *Nixon's Economy*, pp. 161–164.
393   "Daniel in the Lions' Den." . . . *throw away the text*: HRHD, 11/17/71.
393   *no "Hail to the Chief"*: HRHD, 11/19/71; NYT, 11/20/71.
394   "Let me tell you something": RN memo for Colson, 11/20/71 (contested).
394   "the Hoffa move right now": HRHD, 11/20/71.
394   *releasing Jimmy Hoffa*: HRHD, 11/1/71.
395   *In Life*: Life, 12/3/71.
396   *1959 aid treaty*: Kissinger, *White House Years*, pp. 894, 1488.
396   "no idle threat": HRHD, 11/30/71.
396   *full-scale war*: Kissinger, *White House Years*, pp. 894–902; Hersh, *Price of Power*, pp. 454–460.
397   *Farland then told Foreign Secretary Sultan Khan*: Khan int.
397   *Charles Yeager*: Yeager was the first man to break the sound barrier, hitting Mach 1 in his Bell X-1 aircraft in 1947 and later became celebrated as a character in Tom Wolfe's book *The Right Stuff* and a film of the book.
397   *the Washington Special Action Group*: Washington Post, 1/5/72.
398   *The WSAG met the next day*: ibid.
399   *The President's television day*: NBC summary of program; Timmons memo for the President's File, re meeting with congressional leadership, 12/6/71; HRHD; Ziegler int.
399   *no "old friend"*: Woods memo to Hoopes, re report for the President's File 12/6/71.
400   *Off camera*: Washington Post, 1/5/72.
400   "a friend of Russia's": ibid.
401   *announce his resignation in December*: HRHD, 12/7/71.
401   *Kissinger was delegated*: Washington Post, 12/7/71.
401   "Can we allow": WSAG meeting memo, 12/8/71, NSC Box 572.
401   "He's tired": HRHD, 12/8/71.
401   *Pakistan problem was his own fault . . . Jimmy Hoffa*: HRHD, 12/9/71.
401   "What I want to suggest": Kissinger memo for the President's File, re meeting with Matskevich 12/9/71, POF Box 86.
402   *Much different messages to China*: Kissinger, *White House Years*, pp. 905–906; Lord int.
403   "We have received": William Burr, ed., *The Kissinger Transcripts: The Top Secret Talks with Beijing and Moscow* (New York: New Press, 1998), pp. 48–59.
404   *meeting with President Pompidou*: HRHD, 12/12/71.
404   "Don't push your luck, Henry": HRHD, 12/13/71.
405   *Nixon celebrated by staying up*: HRHD, 12/14/71.
405   *solarium by himself*: HRHD, 12/14/71.
405   *A. M. Malik*: Time, 12/27/71.

405   *"On the price front"*: Safire memo for the President's File re bipartisan leadership meeting, 12/15/71, POF Box 87.

406   *the Group of Ten*: The Group included the finance ministers and central bankers of the leading industrial nations: the United States, Germany, Japan, Britain, Canada, France, Italy, Belgium, Sweden, and the Netherlands.

406   *Kissinger kept calling to talk*: HRHD, 11/11/71.

406   *source of a Jack Anderson column*: Lukas, *Nightmare,* pp. 104–105.

406   *unconditionally surrendered*: NYT, 12/17–19/71; Khan, *Memories and Reflections,* pp. 386–395.

407   *"Mr. Bhutto stated"*: Haig memo for the President's File, re President's meeting with Z. A. Bhutto, 12/18/71, POF Box 87.

408   *"I hope it lasts three months" . . . changed the estimate*: Matusow, *Nixon's Economy,* pp. 178–179. The devaluation was accomplished by increasing the price of gold at Fort Knox from thirty-five dollars per ounce, the price since 1934, to thirty-eight dollars per ounce—even though the United States was no longer converting gold at any price.

Chapter 26: *January 2, 1972*

409   *Anderson had made a revealing mistake*: Issacson, *Kissinger,* pp. 380–386; Hersh, *Price of Power,* pp. 465–477.

411   *Ehrlichman, with Haldeman*: Ehrlichman, *Witness to Power* pp. 306–308; Ehrlichman int.

411   *the President called in Ehrlichman*: Ehrlichman, *Witness to Power,* pp. 306–307.

412   *"I had a long talk"*: HRHD, 12/13/71.

413   *year-end decisions and statements*: These news stories were taken from news summaries and newspapers from December.

413   *"Haldeman's fellows"*: RN dictation, 12/1/71.

414   *Willy Brandt*: Haig meeting memo to RN, 12/28/71, POF Box 86.

416   *With Heath*: Kissinger memo to RN, 12/21/71, "The President's Private Meeting with British Prime Minister Edward Heath," POF Box 86.

417   *The meetings with Chancellor Brandt*: Haig memo to RN, 12/28/71, POF Box 86.

418   *On the second day of 1972*: *Public Papers of the Presidents of the United States, Richard Nixon* (Washington, D.C.: U.S. Government Printing Office, 1971–1975).

420   *"That'll suck out"*: HRHD, 1/3/72.

Chapter 27: *January 25, 1972*

421   *John Osborne offered*: Osborne, *Third Year of the Nixon Watch,* pp. 204–208.

422   *Hallett focused*: Hallet memo to Colson, 1/3/72; Colson memo to RN, 1/6/72. The Hallet memo to Colson was passed on to Nixon, who marked it up.

422   *Herbert Stein*: Stein memo to RN, 1/3/72.

422   *Arthur Burns*: RN, "Eyes Only" letter, 1/28/72.

423   *"Now More Than Ever"*: Garment int.

424   *A retired Washington taxi driver*: Lukas, *Nightmare,* pp. 14, 86–87, 162, 170.

424   *Action Memo P-1957*: Colson memo to RN, 1/12/72.

424   *George Wallace*: Carter, *Politics of Rage,* pp. 412, 423.

425   *Writing from Alabama's capital*: ibid., pp. 412–413.

425   *Then Haldeman met*: HRHD, 1/10/72, 2/3/72.

426   *On Sunday, January 16*: Safire, *Before the Fall,* p. 398, Safire int.

426   *"After reading the proposed text"*: RN memo to Safire, 1/6/72.

426   *"I was reading about Disraeli"*: Safire, *Before the Fall*, p. 406; Safire int.

428   *Antiwar members*: ANS nd, 1/72, POF Box 38.

429   *President's permission*: HRHD, 1/28/72.

429   *"Operation Gemstone"* . . . *"We need preventive action"*: Lukas, *Nightmare*, pp. 171–173; Dean, *Blind Ambition*, pp. 74–76.

430   *Mitchell, puffing his pipe . . . Suddenly, Dean said*: Dean, *Blind Ambition*, pp. 76–79.

431   *O'Brien had been getting*: O'Brien's name often came up in Oval Office conversation. After one session, on January 14, 1971, Haldeman sent a memo to Dean: "The time is approaching when Larry O'Brien should be held accountable for his retainer with Hughes. . . . Bebe has some information on this, although it is, of course, not solid. But there is no question that Hughes' people did have O'Brien on very heavy retainer for 'services rendered' in the past. I believe Nofziger has been doing some work here. Please check into this and give me a report."

431   *Richard Scammon*: Colson meeting memo to RN 1/27/72, POF Box 87. Nixon once drew the same diagram for me, during an interview in the early 1980s.

Chapter 28: *February 22, 1972*

432   *The President began his journey*: Nixon, *Memoirs*, pp. 559–560; HRHD, 2/17/72; Kissinger, *White House Years*, pp. 1053–1054.

432   *Senator James Buckley*: Tom C. Korologos memo to RN, 2/14/72, MemCon, POF Box 87.

433   *Malraux was another matter*: Kissinger meeting memo to RN, 2/14/72, 4 P.M.–5:30 P.M., POF Box 87; Kissinger memo to RN, 2/14/72, "Dinner in Honor of M. André Malraux," POF Box 87; John Scali memo to RN, 2/14/72, "Summary and Analysis of Andrew Malraux's comments"; Nixon, *Memoirs*, pp. 557–558; Sidey, *Life*, 2/25/72. Malraux also offered his interpretation of the "Cultural Revolution" that had racked China for the past three years: "The communist party that Mao had known in the past was made up of cadres who knew how to read, and they were not his friends. What he wanted to do was to teach young people to read who would become the Maoist youth, unlike the former youth. And Mao won." Malraux also said that China actually had no foreign policy, that the Chinese and Mao cared only about China. Kissinger and Scali, however, were not as impressed as Nixon was and Scali ended his report of the conversations: "I felt I was listening to the views of a romantic, vain, old man who was weaving obsolete views into a special framework for the world as he wished it to be."

434   *Stephen Bull*: Bull int.,

434   *"any non-Jews"*: Ziegler int.; Haldeman notes, 2/17/72; Haldeman files, SMOF.

435   *"This will probably show"*: Ziegler int.

435   *"Risks for them"*: President's notes, 2/15/72, China Notes folder, PPF Box 7. Notes Nixon took during his China trip are filed separately from his other notes, so they will receive citations.

435   *"These people are"*: Kissinger memos to RN, "Your Encounter with the Chinese," 2/5/72; "Mao, Chou and the Chinese Litmus Test," 2/19/72.

436   *"What they want"*: President's notes, 2/18/72, China Notes folder, PPF Box 7.

436   *"The crucial factor"*: Kissinger memo to RN, 2/19/72.

436   *The plane landed*: Kissinger *White House Years*, pp. 1054–1056; Nixon, *Memoirs*, pp. 559–561; Eisenhower, *Pat Nixon; The Untold Story*, pp. 506–511; HRHD 2/21/72; *The President's Trip to China: A Pictoral Record . . . with Text by Members of the American Press Corps* (New York: Bantam Books, 1972), pp. 12–20; Sidey, *Life*, 3/3/72, p. 12.

438   *"Face clean"*: Harrison Salisbury, *The New Emperors*, p. 314.

438   *At 2:30:* Nixon: *Memoirs,* pp. 559–564; Kissinger, *White House Years,* pp. 1057–1063; Winston Lord int.; MemCon, Mao-Nixon meeting, 2/21/72, POF Box 87. This memo was declassified on January 6, 1998, and later published by the National Security Archive. Most of the memos for the other meetings between the leaders were not declassified until 1999, 2000, and 2001.

441   *cut Winston Lord out:* Lord int.

441   *the first order:* MemCon, 2/21/72, 5:58 P.M.–6:55 P.M.

441   *first plenary session . . . welcoming banquet:* Nixon, *Memoirs,* pp. 564–566; HRHD, 2/21/72; *Public Papers of the Presidents,* Richard Nixon, 1972, pp. 368–370.

443   *February 22, Nixon and Chou:* MemCon, Great Hall of the People, 2/22/72, 2:10 P.M.–6:00 P.M., POF Box 87; Lord int.

443   *"Principle one. There is one China":* In fact, Kissinger, with the President's approval, had, on July 9, 1971, promised that the United States would not support the Taiwan Independence Movement. James Mann, "China's Invisible Weapon" *Los Angeles Times,* 6/16/94, p. 1.

445   *"the wild horse":* President's notes to himself, 2/15/72, China Notes folder, PPF box 7.

446   *"Why not give this up . . . Be bold":* In fact, however, the Chinese did attempt to exert some pressure on the North Vietnamese. North Vietnam's foreign minister, Nguyen Co Thach, in a March 6, 1982, interview with *De Volkescrant* in Amsterdam, said: "After Nixon's visit to China, Mao Tse-tung told Prime Minister Pham Van Dong that his broom was not long enough to sweep Taiwan and ours was not long enough to get the Americans out of South Vietnam. He wanted to halt reunification and force us to recognize the puppet regime in the South. He had sacrificed Vietnam for the sake of the United States."

447   *Sidey described it in a cable:* Sidey cable to *Time,* New York, 2/22/72.

447   *"Your people expect":* RN note 2/23/72, China Notes folder. PPF Box 7.

448   *The second day of the Nixon-Chou:* MemCon, 2/23/72, Great Hall of the People, 2 P.M.–6 P.M., POF Box 87.

449   *Capital Gymnasium:* HRHD 2/23/72. Rogers recorded an incident at the sports exhibition: A woman with a sheaf of papers came up to Chou during the gymnastics exhibition. The Premier looked at the papers, said a few words softly, and nodded his head. When the Secretary asked an interpreter what was going on, the Chinese official said that Chou was checking the headlines and layout of the next morning's *People's Daily.* Listening to the story, Nixon muttered, "I'd like to rearrange a front page now and then."

450   *"deepest secret diplomacy":* Sidey cable to *Time,* New York, 2/23/72.

450   *"Eat your lunch!":* Kraft int.

450   *John Osborne: The Fourth Year of the Nixon Watch* (New York: Liveright, 1973), pp. 20–33.

451   *The third session:* MemCon, Great Hall of the People, 2/24/72, 5:15 P.M.–8:05 P.M., POF Box 87.

452   *The next morning:* Nixon, *Memoirs* pp. 570–571; Kissinger, *White House Years,* pp. 1077–1081; HRHD, 2/25/72.

453   *"You can say more":* MemCon, 2/25/72, The President's Guest House, Peking, 5:45 P.M.–6:45 P.M., POF Box 87.

453   *"It's a victory":* Nixon, *Memoirs,* pp. 570–577; HRDH, 2/25/72; Lord int.

454   *"I have found a shortcoming":* Kissinger, *White House Years,* pp. 1080–1081.

454   *"What the hell are you taking about?":* Film by Haldeman, inserted into CD version of HRHD 2/26/72. MemCon, Peking Airport, 9:20 A.M.–10:05 A.M., POF Box 87.

455   *"Canucks":* Later stories indicated that the "Canucks" letter was fabricated, probably in the White House. Ken Clawson told a friend on *The Washington Post* he had

written it, and this became a story by Carl Bernstein and Bob Woodward. Others thought they saw the handiwork of Chuck Colson.

455   *"Tell him I'm asleep,"*: HRHD, 2/27/72; Haldeman memo for the President's File, 3/8/72.

457   *"If Chou can stay up all night,"*: HRHD, 2/27/72.

457   *Political time was the subject:* MemCon, Ching Kiang Guest House, Shanghai, 2/28/72, 8:30–9:30 A.M., POF Box 88.

457   *On the ride to the airport:* Price notes on Cabinet meeting, 2/29/01, POF Box 88.

Chapter 29: *April 7, 1972*

458   *"The most fundamental point"*: Korologos memo to RN, 2/29/01, 10 A.M., "Meeting with Bipartisan Leadership," POF Box 88; Price memo to RN, 2/29/01, "Cabinet Meeting," POF Box 88; Safire notes on Cabinet meeting, 2/29/01, Safire papers, Manuscript Division, LC.

459   *an antibusing bill:* NYT, 3/1/72.

459   *the schools of Richmond: Life,* 3/3/72. U.S. District Court Judge Robert R. Merhige Jr. ruled that the city was "identifiably black," and the suburbs "identifiably white," and that it was the state of Virginia's duty to dismantle the two systems.

459   *political attention of the country:* Richard Reeves, "Eleven Alligators in Florida's Political Swamp," *New York Times Magazine,* 3/12/72.

460   *awaiting confirmation:* Kleindienst was finally confirmed as attorney general by a 64–19 vote on June 8, 1972. A year later he pleaded guilty to charges that he had not been fully responsive to Senate questions and was sentenced to a month in prison. The former lieutenant governor of California, Ed Reinecke, was found guilty of perjury and sentenced to fifteen months. Both sentences were suspended.

460   *called Bill Safire to Camp David:* Safire, *Before the Fall,* pp. 481–485; Safire int., Stanley Pottinger int.

461   *"Edward J. Hamilton"*: Lukas, *Nightmare,* pp. 182–184.

462   *"The total was $915,037.68:* Lukas, *Nightmare,* pp. 138–143; *Life,* 4/72, editorial: "Speak up, Republicans"; Sloan testimony before the Senate Select Committee on Watergate, LC.

463   *Moving the money around:* Liddy memo to Mitchell, 3/15/72, "Democratic National Convention Finance Investigation." This memo can be found in the records of the Senate Watergate hearings, and in Bruce Oudes's *From the President: Richard Nixon's Secret Files* (New York: Harper and Row, 1989), pp. 390–391.

463   *Sloan had more:* Lukas *Nightmare,* p. 145.

463   *The press secretary said that there was a problem:* Ziegler int.; NT, 3/23/72, 5:33 P.M. The tape of this telephone conversation was released in October, 1999, with other "abuse of power" tapes previously restricted for national security reasons.

464   *"What we have to realize"*: RN memo to Haldeman and Ziegler, 4/14/72; Edward Morgan memo to RN, 3/6/72, "Meeting with the Cabinet Committee on Busing," POF Box 88.

Chapter 30: *May 1, 1972*

465   *spring offensive:* Jeffrey Kimball, *Nixon's Vietnam War* (Lawrence: University Press of Kansas, 1998), pp. 302–304; Hersh, *Price of Power,* pp. 503–508.

466   *"The Air Force isn't worth a shit"*: HRH notes, 4/4/72. Haldeman files, SMOF.

466   *"Defeat is not an option"*: Nixon, *Memoirs,* p. 588.

466   *the President was in despair:* ibid.

467   *"McGovern's the One"*: Buchanan/Ken Khachigian memo to Mitchell and Haldeman, 4/12/72.

467   *"1. Peace and foreign policy"*: RN memo to Haldeman, 4/11/72.

467   *"Ehrlichman has got to understand"*: ibid.

467   *writing to Ehrlichman*: RN memos to Ehrlichman, 4/12/72.

468   *In an April 12 briefing*: Memo for the President's File, re congressional leadership meeting, 4/12/72, POF Box 88.

468   *The United States struck*: Kimball, *Nixon's Vietnam War,* pp. 304–305; Hersh, *Price of Power,* pp. 508–512.

469   *"Well, we really left them our calling card"*: Nixon, *Memoirs,* p. 590; HRHD, 4/16/72.

469   *"Brezhnev wants a summit"*: Isaacson, *Kissinger,* pp. 407–414.

470   *"You will be able to sign"*: Nixon, *Memoirs,* p. 592. Isaacson, *Kissinger,* p. 414.

470   *"Haig emphasized"*: Isaacson, *Kissinger,* p. 415.

471   *"What else does he say?"*: Nixon, *Memoirs,* p. 594. Isaacson, *Kissinger,* p. 416.

471   *"Forget the domestic reaction"*: RN memo to Kissinger, 4/30/72; Nixon, *Memoirs,* p. 593–594.

472   *Haldeman received a telephone call*: HRHD, 5/2/72.

472   *his way back home*: Isaacson, *Kissinger,* p. 417.

472   *"we cannot lose this war"*: Haldeman notes, 5/2/72. Haldeman files, SMOF; HRHD 5/2–3/72.

472   *That same day; James McCord*: Lukas, *Nightmare,* p. 193.

473   *Julie argued*: Nixon, *Memoirs,* p. 602.

473   *The last . . . meeting*: HRHD, 5/8/72.

473   *"They spit in our eye"*: Life, "How the President Made Up His Mind," 5/19/72.

474   *"I cannot emphasize too strongly"*: RN memo to Kissinger, "Eyes Only," 5/9/72; Nixon, *Memoirs,* p. 606; Kissinger, *White House Years,* p. 1199.

474   *"military strategy"*: RN memo to Kissinger and Haig, 5/15/72.

475   *"Protest activity"*: John Dean hourly report to RN, 5/15/72, 11 A.M.

476   *"This is to advise you"*: Colson memo to Dean, 5/14/72.

476   *"grim scene"* . . . *"The President must not have a free hand"*: Kissinger, *White House Years,* p. 1191.

477   *Patolichev*: ibid., p. 1194.

477   *"A Cadillac"*: Dobrynin, *In Confidence,* p. 256.

Chapter 31: *May 15, 1972*

478   *"We just got word"*: HRHD, 5/18/01.

478   *"I was distressed to learn from Don Kendall"*: RN memo to Haldeman, 5/18/72.

479   *"Do they understand"*: Haldeman notes, 5/16/72, Haldeman files, SMDF.

479   *The guy was named Arthur Bremer*: The account of the investigation of Bremer and the search of his apartment is taken principally from Carter's *Politics of Rage.* This incident is covered in pp. 435–441. Also, see "The Shooting of George Wallace," *Life,* 5/20/72.

480   *Beginning at 7:30 P.M.* HRHD, 5/16/72; Colson memo to the files 5/16/72 Colson Box 18, SMDF.

480   *"Is he a left-winger?"* NT 5/15/72, 9:30 P.M.

480   *"Hey world! Come here!"*: Carter, *Politics of Rage;* pp. 418–455.

481   *"Fantastic!"* HRHD, 5/17/72.

481   *Nixon went over to the crowd*: Nixon, *Memoirs,* p. 608.

481 *"The Connally trip is vitally important"*: RN memo to Kissinger, 5/19/72.

482 *"I am thoroughly disgusted"* . . . *"Finally, I have told Henry"*: RN memos to Kissinger and Haig, 5/19/72.

482 *"The problem is the CIA"*: RN dictation to Haldeman, 5/18/72.

483 *"quit recruiting"*: Buchanan was among the staffers who played on the President's hatred of the Ivy League. Buchanan sent him the results of a survey of the universities attended by the sixty-five United States ambassadors to countries listed alphabetically, from Afghanistan to Morocco: "Ivy League: Harvard—9, Yale—8, Princeton—8, Brown—2, Wesleyan—1, Amherst—1, U. of Penn.—2, Williams—3, Columbia—1; State and City Universities—14; Private Non-Denominational—13; Black—1; Catholic—1."

483 *Nixon had gone with Dr. Lukash:* RN diary; Nixon, *Memoirs*, p. 608.

483 *"We hope to negotiate an ABM treaty"*: memo for the President's File, 5/19/72, Congressional leadership meeting, POF Box 88.

484 *"The situation in Canada"*: RN dictation to Haldeman, 5/20/72.

484 *"There should be a minimum of 1200 sorties"*: RN to Haig, 5/20/72.

484 *"Something is now terribly askew"*: Life, 5/19/72.

Chapter 32: *June 17, 1972*

486 *"This has got to be one of the great"*: Nixon, *Memoirs*, p. 609.

486 *ICBMs:* Small, *Presidency of Richard Nixon*, pp. 109–111.

487 *"Bullshit!"*: Gerard C. Smith, *Doubletalk: The Story of the First Strategic Arms Limitation Talks* (Garden City, New York: Doubleday, 1990), p. 376.

487 *Roosevelt, Churchill, and Stalin:* Nixon, *Memoirs*, p. 609.

488 *"He might as well be in Siberia"*: Safire int.

488 *At 4:30 in the morning:* Safire, *Before the Fall*, p. 446.

488 *"I know that my reputation"*: Nixon, *Memoirs*, p. 611

489 *"You obviously cooked up this deal"*: HRHD, 5/23/72.

489 *"The rest of us"* . . . *"It is my opinion"*: J. V. Brennan memo to Haldeman, 5/23/72; William Duncan, Secret Service report, 5/23/72.

490 *"Nazi-like"*: Nixon, *Memoirs*, p. 613; Harold Evans, *The American Century* (New York: Knopf, 1998), p. 582.

490 *the President was lying naked:* Safire, *Before the Fall*, p. 450; Safire int; Nixon, *Memoirs*, p. 615.

491 *Smith was almost incoherent:* Hersh, *Price of Power*, pp. 544–546.

491 *Kissinger and Smith presided:* Safire, *Before the Fall*, p. 454; HRHD, 5/26/72.

491 *"What good will that accomplish?"*: HRHD, 5/26/72.

491 *In Washington, it was just past:* The Watergate account in this chapter is primarily from Lukas, *Nightmare*, pp. 197–224.

492 *Parker ballpoint . . . a witness unseen:* Hugh Sidey, *Life*, 6/72.

492 *The papers were, in effect:* Washington Post, 5/27/72, p. 1.

493 *the Tomb of the Unknown Soldier:* Nixon, *Memoirs*, p. 616; Safire, *Before the Fall*, p. 454.

493 *"You have my commitment"*: Nixon, *Memoirs*, p. 617.

494 *"He should not be punished"*: Kissinger, *White House Years*, p. 1215.

494 *"spear-carriers"*: HRHD, 5/31/72.

494 *"Not bad for a couple of Jewish boys"*: Safire, *Before the Fall*, p. 459.

494 *"The President is riding"*: Colson memo to Haldeman, 5/31/72.

494 *John Osborne:* Osborne, *The Fourth Year of the Nixon Watch* (New York: Liveright, 1973), p. 88.

495 *"We were not present at the creation"*: memo for the President's File, 6/2/72, Congressional leadership meeting, POF Box 88.

497 *"One of the factors that brought Goldwater"*: RN memo to Mitchell, 6/6/72.

498   *"our left-wing friends:"* RN memo to Kissinger, 6/6/72.
498   *"The Eastern Establishment media"*: Nixon memo to Buchanan, 6/10/72.
498   *"If you cut the defense budget"*: HRHD, 6/13/72.
499   *"Jews can check out of Israel"*: Buchanan, GOP Leadership memo for the President's File, 6/13/72.
499   *"Find a good young reporter"*: NT, 6/13/72, 4:17 P.M.
499   *He called Billy Graham:* HRHD 6/17/72.
499   *In his diary:* RN *Memoirs,* p. 609. It has so far been impossible to determine when Nixon first learned of the June 17 burglary—or if he knew of the plan itself. Alex Butterfield, for one, believes that Nixon did not know in advance—but did know beforehand about the May 28 break-in when bugs were first planted but did not work well. See Butterfield essay in *Nixon: An Oliver Stone Film* (New York: Hyperion, 1995).

Chapter 33: *June 23, 1972*

501   *The five men arrested:* Hunt called a lawyer named C. Douglas Caddy in the early hours of the morning, according to Lukas, *Nightmare,* p. 211. Chapter 8 of that book is the principal source for the activities of Hunt, Liddy, and other administration and CREEP figures over the next few days.
501   *"Security consultant"*: Bob Woodward and Carl Bernstein, *All the President's Men* (New York: Simon & Schuster, 1974), pp. 18–25.
502   *The Post had found . . . Hunt:* ibid., pp. 22–24.
502   *the contents of Hunt's office safe:* Dean, *Blind Ambition,* pp. 108–117.
503   *"Exotic"*: Newspaper, magazine, and television reports of Watergate in this chapter are taken from the President's news summaries.
503   *"Horrors"*: NT, 5/16/73; *Washington Post,* 2/26/99, p. A-9.
503   *possible break-ins:* One possible break-in, revealed later, was a November 1971 burglary of the office of Mrs. Daniel Ellsberg's psychiatrist in Manhattan.
503   *President began a series of one-on-one:* NT, 6/20/72. Quotations for this day are from the Nixon Tapes.
506   *cover story idea with Colson:* NT, 6/21/72.
506   *"We've got another thing"*: NT, 6/22/72.
508   *Kenneth Dahlberg, a Republican fundraiser:* Lukas, *Nightmare,* pp. 142, 229–235.
508   *"Mitchell came up with the plan yesterday"*: NT, 6/23/72.
510   *"It's getting pretty big"*: NT, 6/26/72.
510   *"He said that Kay Graham"*: Nixon, *Memoirs,* p. 684. On July 1, the tapes picked up Nixon calling Graham "that terrible old bag."
511   *"Go back to Mitchell"*: NT, 6/28/72.
511   *"He's afraid she'll jump"*: NT, 6/29/72.
512   *"Without Martha"*: Nixon, *Memoirs,* p. 649.
512   *"I don't need to know anything"*: NT, 6/29/72.
513   *That night, alone with history:* Nixon, *Memoirs,* p. 646.
513   *"Let McGovern sink himself"*: Safire int.
513   *The night of July 13:* HRHD, 7/13/72.
514   *the President sent a memo:* RN dictation, 7/19/72 and 7/20/72.

Chapter 34: *August 22, 1972*

515   *"Give me an update"*: NT, 7/19/72, 12:45 P.M.
516   *"Dean is watching it"*: NT, 7/20/72, 3:16 P.M.
517   *Monthly economic statistics:* "The power of prayer, slightly assisted by seasonal adjustment, is revealed by the CPI for June," wrote Herb Stein in a 7/20/72 memo to the President. "Herb—brilliant!" Nixon wrote across the numbers.

517   *Wallace was in no shape:* HRHD, 7/20/72.
517   *persuade Agnew to resign:* HRHD, 7/20/72.
517   *"No, no, no":* Haldeman memo to RN, 7/21/72, re meeting with VP and Mitchell, with RN annotation.
517   *"Play them as suckers":* RN memo to Haldeman, 8/12/72.
517   *"On a personal side":* RN memo for Tricia and Julia, 7/24/72.
518   *"They're going to keep, keep, keep":* NT, 7/25, 11:14 A.M.
518   *he had been hospitalized:* Nixon, *Memoirs,* p. 663; Ambrose, *Nixon,* vol. 2, p. 609.
518   *"They nominated a crazy man":* HRHD, 07/25/72.
518   *"so you don't get a swelled head":* Shultz memo to Haldeman, re Meany golf game, 7/28/72.
519   *"The American leader class:"* Nixon, *Memoirs,* p. 670.
519   *"they can go to hell":* Rumsfeld memo to RN, 08/10/72, re 1973 automobile price increases, with RN annotation.
519   *Woodward and Bernstein:* Woodward and Bernstein, *All the President's Men,* pp. 41–47.
519   *Sargent Shriver said yes:* Time, 8/16/72.
519   *"Everybody's satisfied":* NT, 8/1/72, 11:03 A.M.
520   *"What in the name of God":* 8/3/72, 9:44 A.M.
520   *Kimmelman had sat next to Pat Moynihan:* Buchanan memo to Haldeman, 08/16/72.
521   *"Everybody thinks George":* NT, 8/3/72, 9:44 A.M., 5 P.M.
521   *"We've got his files":* NT, 8/7/72, 11:24 A.M..
522   *"We have gotten closer":* Ambrose, *Nixon,* vol. 2, p. 621.
523   *intensive bombing:* Life, 8/25/72.
523   *"kind of thing you expect under a person like Hitler":* Ambrose, *Nixon,* vol. 2, p. 615.
523   *Nixon, 64 percent; McGovern, 30 percent:* HRHD, 8/29/72. The one convention vote not for Nixon was for Pete McCloskey, the antiwar congressman from California. In the official record it was set down as "Others."
523   *his thirteen-year-old son, Terry:* Nixon, *Memoirs,* p. 644. Nixon also wrote gracious letters to Caroline Kennedy and her brother, John, after they visited the White House with their mother in February 1971. He sympathized with Caroline's complaints about a history teacher, but urged her to continue to read history and biography. To young John, he wrote of how much his dogs loved playing with the boy. On March 16, Jacqueline Kennedy wrote to the President: "I am embarrassed to continue our correspondence. You have had a surfeit of letters from 1040 5th Avenue. But I was so touched by your letters to Caroline and John. One is most vulnerable where one's children are concerned—so I must thank you for such extraordinary kindness. You wrote so charmingly to each child, in the idiom of its age, pinpointing for each what was most memorable about that special day. They were thrilled. There are no words to thank you and Mrs. Nixon for your thoughtfulness, so please forgive me for just saying thank you again. Most sincerely, Jackie."
523   *"When you've got a fellow":* NT, 8/3/72, 9:44 A.M.

Chapter 35: *November 7, 1972*

524   *"three big Nixon contributors":* NT, 9/13/72, 11:40 A.M.
525   *Theodore H. White:* White, letter to the President, the President's desk, PPF Boxes 185–188.
525   *"I'm not going into the states";* White, *The Making of the President, 1972* (New York: Atheneum, 1973), pp. 209–234.
525   *twenty-five thousand dollars that ended up in Barker's Miami account:* Lukas,

Nightmare, p. 142. *Life* magazine revealed that the source of the money was Dwayne Andreas.

526   *"Nelson, let me fill you in":* NT, 9/14/72. 10:03 A.M.

526   *The governor had his own theory:* Reeves interviews with Rockefeller in 1970, 1971, and 1972.

526   *I had a rather curious dream":* Nixon, *Memoirs,* p. 686.

526   *"Is the line pretty well set":* NT, 9/15/72, 9:12 A.M.

527   *"Well, you had quite a day":* NT, 9/15/72, 5:27 P.M.

527   *"Do you really want":* HRHD, 9/16/72.

527   *"the American people are no longer":* Kissinger, *White House Years,* p. 1331.

528   *Thieu had asked Kissinger:* Hung and Schecter, *Palace File,* pp. 65–67.

528   *"Insolent":* Isaacson, *Kissinger,* p. 444.

528   *Gif-sur-Yvette . . . "We shall be obliged":* Hung and Schecter, *Palace File,* pp. 71–72.

529   *"there are serious disagreements":* RN to Thieu, 10/6/72. Hung and Schecter, *Palace File,* appendix A, p. 376.

529   *"Are we making a race":* Kissinger, *White House Years,* p. 1141.

530   *"We've done it":* Lord int.

530   *That night Kissinger cabled:* Kissinger, *White House Years,* p. 1357.

530   *Kissinger knew that Haig:* Isaacson, *Kissinger,* p. 442.

531   *"We have decided to stay":* Kissinger, *White House Years,* p. 1357.

531   *discovered Donald Segretti:* HRHD, 10/10/72.

531   *"Segretti, just so you know":* NT, 10/15/72, 9:16 A.M.

532   *John Connally called:* HRHD, 10/11/72; NT, 10/17/72, 3:03 P.M.

532   *"Mark Felt":* NT, 10/19/72, 1:48 P.M.

533   *"we've got three out of three":* HRHD, 10/12/72.

533   *the deal:* Nixon, *Memoirs,* pp. 691–693; Isaacson, *Kissinger,* pp. 451–452; Kissinger, *White House Years,* pp. 1361–1362; HRHD, 10/12/72.

534   *Kissinger arrived at the Presidential Palace:* The best source for the October 1972 Kissinger-Thieu meetings is Hung and Schecter, *Palace File,* pp. 85–90, 98–106.

535   *"a typographical error":* Isaacson, *Kissinger,* p. 455.

536   *Thieu was going to reject:* Haig memo to RN, 10/20/72, "Meeting with General Westmoreland and General Haig," POF Box 40.

536   *"a shotgun marriage":* Isaacson, *Kissinger,* p. 454.

536   *telephoned Haldeman:* HRHD, 10/22/72.

537   *editorials supporting:* Klein memo to RN: 10/23/72.

537   *"may I read you":* Hung and Schecter, *Palace File,* p. 101.

537   *"We have fought for four years":* Isaacson, *Kissinger,* pp. 439, 456.

537   *What Kissinger told Nixon:* Isaacson, *Kissinger,* p. 457.

538   *"The press still thinks":* Hung and Schecter, *Palace File,* p. 105.

539   *Sloan . . . had told:* HRHD, 10/25/72.

539   *"We're going to screw them":* NT, 10/25/72, 12:29 P.M.

540   *"Peace is at hand":* Isaacson, *Kissinger,* p. 459.

540   *"No Amnesty":* Remarks of the President, Surrogate Briefing, 10/29/72.

541   *he and Ehrlichman should resign:* HRHD, 11/7/72.

542   *reading Robert Blake's Disraeli:* HRHD, 11/8/72; Klein, *Making It Perfectly Clear,* p. 378.

542   *"start pissing on the party":* HRHD, 11/8/72.

Chapter 36: *December 19, 1972*

543   *Eighty of eighty-nine members:* HRHD, 11/8/72.

543   *give the house and grounds to the government:* HRHD, 11/10/72.

544   *his 117th visit since he took office:* Life, 12/1/72.
544   *distribute an action memo:* Haldeman action memo, 4/24/72, Haldeman Box 112.
545   *"After Christmas, it will be too late":* Haldeman, *Ends of Power*, p. 174.
545   *"Your continuing distortions":* RN letter to Thieu, 11/8/72, Hung and Schecter, *Palace File*, appendix A, p. 383.
545   *"A true executive":* Ehrlichman notes, 11/14/72, Ehrlichman files, SMOF.
545   *"You, General Haig":* Hung and Schecter, *Palace File*, p. 123.
546   *check off and sign a . . . fifteen-item list:* Klein's list, 11/27/72, Ehrlichman files, SMOF.
547   *"Not brains, we want loyalty":* Ehrlichman notes, 11/20/72, Ehrlichman files, SMOF.
547   *based first on loyalty:* HRHD, 11/18/72.
547   *"Fewer people talk to the President":* Ehrlichman notes, 11/14/72, Ehrlichman files, SMOF.
547   *"too many Jews":* Ehrlicman notes, nd, Ehrlichman files, SMOF.
547   *"Genius needs to be recognized":* Ehrlichman notes, 11/14/72, Ehrlichman files, SMOF.
547   *Haldeman had made the main room off-limits:* Eisenhower, *Pat Nixon*, p. 363.
547   *"Henry, in his view, is completely paranoid":* HRHD, 11/29/72.
548   *"There is no point in going on television":* Haldeman notes, 11/20/72, Haldeman files, SMOF.
548   *let Kissinger know that there was a complete taped record:* HRHD, 11/19/72.
548   *"The President is very disappointed":* Haldeman cable to Kissinger, 11/22/72.
548   *"Not a directive":* Hersh, *Price of Power*, p. 614.
248   *"My evaluation is that":* RN memo to Kissinger, 11/24/72, "Backchannel Message."
549   *Texan wanted a year to make money:* HRHD, 11/16/72.
549   *Rogers was scheduled to leave on June 1:* HRHD, 11/17/72.
550   *John Scali was named to replace Bush:* HRHD, 12/15/72.
550   *"Henry is concerned":* Haldeman notes, 12/2/72, Haldeman files, SMOF.
551   *thought Kissinger had a suicidal complex:* HRHD, 12/8/72.
551   *What happened here":* Nixon, *Memoirs*, p. 731.
551   *an airplane crash:* Lukas, *Nightmare*, p. 260.
551   *"Do they have any reading":* NT, 12/11/72, 11:07 A.M.
552   *"the final stage has been reached":* ANS, 12/13/72. POF Box 46.
552   *"Tawdry, filthy shits":* Nixon, *Memoirs*, p. 733.
552   *"Gray had the idea":* NT, 12/13/72, 5 P.M.
552   *Kissinger said he never saw Osborne:* HRHD, 12/14/72.
552   *"I don't want any more of this crap":* Nixon, *Memoirs*, p. 734
552   *Nixon was limping:* HRHD, 12/14/72.
553   *order Kissinger not to speak with anyone:* HRHD, 12/15/72.
553   *"I have asked General Haig":* Nixon, *Memoirs*, pp. 736–737.
554   *"there will be no peace":* Hung and Schecter, *Palace File*, p. 141.
554   *"I must get away from the thought":* Nixon, *Memoirs*, p. 739.
554   *a half-dozen phone calls each day:* RN memo to Haldeman, 12/27/72.
555   *"The North Vietnamese have agreed":* Nixon, *Memoirs*, p. 741.
555   *"The President was alone on New Year's Eve":* ibid., p. 742.

Chapter 37: January 23, 1973

556   *logging all calls:* NT, 1/1/73, 9:40 A.M.
556   *"wouldn't talk to that son-of-a-bitch":* Hersh, *Price of Power*, p. 630.

556   *President and Colson talked about Watergate:* NT, 1/2/73, 4:51 P.M.

557   *"Even though Colson's going to be missed":* NT, 1/3/73, 11:30 A.M.

558   *"Hunt's is a simple case":* Lukas, *Nightmare*, pp. 263–264.

558   *"We celebrated the President's birthday":* Kissinger cable to RN, 1/9/73, PPF Box 82, Ford Library.

558   *"Henry's probably overoptimistic":* HRHD, 1/9/73.

559   *Agnew said he wanted to go to Egypt:* HRHD, 1/11/73.

559   *"Rockefeller and Connally":* HRHD, 1/25/73.

559   *"best interests of my country":* NYT, 1/12/73.

560   *Nancy Maginnes:* HRHD, 1/12/73.

560   *far corner of the airport:* Kissinger, *White House Years*, p. 1468.

560   *"I told him the country":* Nixon, *Memoirs*, pp. 747–748; Kissinger int.

560   *"I have irrevocably decided":* Hung and Schecter, *Palace File*, p. 148.

561   *"I'm sorry, but I don't believe you":* NYT, 1/16/73.

561   *McCord, though, was a different story:* Lukas, *Nightmare*, pp. 265–269.

562   *Thieu and Nixon:* Hung and Schecter, *Palace File*, pp. 145, 149–155.

562   *five hundred steps in place:* Nixon, *Memoirs*, p. 752.

563   *legalized abortion:* Newsweek, 2/5/73; Time, 2/5/73.

563   *Testimony in the Watergate trial resumed:* NYT, 1/24/73.

564   *nine "chapters":* The wording was: "In pursuance of its traditional policy, the United States will contribute to healing the wounds of war and to post-war reconstruction of the Democratic Republic of Vietnam and throughout Indochina." Nixon's original proposal estimated the five-year cost of reconstruction at $7.5 billion, with $2.5 billion of that going to North Vietnam. In his oral history of 2/24/88, Jerrold Schecter talked of the research for his book, written with Nguyen Tien Hung, *The Palace File,* and said: "It seemed to me, and I think the record will bear this out, that Nixon was more concerned about the fall of South Vietnam than Kissinger was. Nixon saw it as part of the geopolitical overview of Asia. Kissinger, I think, was more willing to let South Vietnam go; this idea of decent interval.... If you look at the record, both Nixon and Kissinger carried on a secret policy, which in the end destroyed our relationship with our ally and has still not allowed us to assimilate the Vietnam war experience.... We had these secret committments which we totally backed out on."

564   *back upstairs ... "talking to me":* Nixon, *Memoirs*, pp. 756–757; Kissinger, *White House Years*, p. 1475.

564   *"remained a small junta":* Life, 9/1/72.

564   *"Cocoon of Power":* Newsweek, 1/22/73.

565   *"the lonely man in the White House" ... fourteen references:* HRHD, 1/27/73, 1/30/73.

565   *"Peace with Honor" ... public relations points:* RN memo to Haldeman, 1/25/73.

565   *taking all the credit:* HRHD, 1/30/73.

566   *birthday calls ... receiving credentials:* HRHD, 12/7/72, 1/16/73; Dean int.

566   *"hold out for a year and a half":* Ehrlichman, *Witness to Power,* p. 316.

566   *leather-bound calendars:* Nixon, *Memoirs*, p. 758.

566   *no new programs and eliminated or cut one hundred:* ibid., pp. 761–762.

567   *Watergate trial ended:* NYT, 1/31/73; Lukas, *Nightmare,* p. 269.

568   *"What the hell is the strategy":* NT, 2/3/73, 11:05 A.M.

569   *"Sindlinger indicated":* W. Richard Howard memo to RN, "Meeting with Albert Sindlinger," 2/5/73, POF Box 91.

569   *Lieutenant Colonel William Nolde:* NYT, 2/6/73, HRHD, 2/5/73, 2/8/73.

569   *Nixon's reaction was a sarcastic comment:* The President had contempt for Sulzberger, who was called "Punch," writing in a 8/12/72 memo to Haldeman: "Punch is Punch to even his dearest friends—is considered to be about a 14-year old moron in his mental capabilities."

570   *"You hear the same old crap"*: NT, 2/7/73, 10:25 A.M.

570   *long Cabinet breakfast:* Safire notes, 2/8/73, Safire papers, Manuscript Division, LC; HRHD, 2/8/73.

570   *Nobel Peace Prize:* HRHD, 2/8/73. In Haldeman Box 179, there's an action memo of 2/12/73 reading: "The President wants a letter drafted from him to the Nobel Committee saying in effect that it is his practice as President not to accept honors and awards for doing what he considers to be his duty. He therefore requests that he not be considered this year for the Nobel Peace Prize, and wants the committee to know that he would not be able to accept the award if it were to be given to him. He wants Price to take a stab at a draft on this. It should not be widely discussed, however."

570   *talk about his schedule:* HRHD, 2/9/73.

571   *"Colonel Risner, sir"*: HRHD, 2/12/73.

571   *Captain Jeremiah Denton:* NYT, 2/13/73.

571   *They thanked the President:* ANS nd, 2/73.

571   *"A Celebration of Men Redeemed":* Time, 2/26/73. Accounts of the POWs' return were taken from *Time* and *Newsweek* of February 26, as well as the Annotated News Summaries for the period.

572   *orchid corsages:* Nixon, *Memoirs,* p. 861.

572   *"K—This kind of story":* ANS (contested), 2/14/73.

572   *"The President told Scali":* General Brent Scowcroft memo to RN, "The President's Meeting with Ambassador John Scali," 2/13/73, POF Box 91.

573   *"Nobody knows I'm here":* NT, 2/22/73, after 4:04 P.M.

573   *President met with John Dean:* Dean, *Blind Ambition,* pp. 182–183; NT, 2/28/73, 9:12 A.M.

574   *"knowledge of the Watergate matter":* In fact, Nixon knew, and five days later, on March 7, he spoke briefly with one of the men supplying cover-up money—$250,000, according to Dean—Thomas Pappas, a Greek immigrant who ran an import business in Boston and was a friend of both Agnew and the generals of the military junta ruling his native country. "I am aware of what you're doing to help out on some of these things that Maury's people and others are involved in," Nixon said. "I won't say anything further, but it's very seldom you find a friend like that, believe me." Pappas also delivered $549,000 to the 1968 Nixon-Agnew campaign, money believed to have come from the military government of Greece, according to a respected dissident Greek journalist, Elias Demetracopoulos. The correspondent, a resident alien living in Washington, gave records involving such transactions to Larry O'Brien of the Democratic National Committee—and there were some who believed a search for those records might have been the reason for the Watergate break-in of 1972. Demetracopoulos said that he was told by Murray Chotiner, "Lay off Pappas . . . You could get in trouble. You could be deported. You know Tom Pappas is a friend of the President." According to John Dean: "There was cash all around. We thought it came from the Greeks, Pappas." Dean interview. On May 23, 1972, Nixon said to Rose Mary Woods: "Good old Tom Pappas, as you probably know or heard, if you haven't already heard, it is true, helped at Mitchell's request, fund-raising for some of the defendants."

Chapter 38: *March 23, 1973*

576   *reduced from 3.5 million:* HRHD, 3/9/73.

576   *new price controls:* By January 1973, the United States with 6 percent of the world's population, was consuming 33 percent of the world's energy, a daily per capita equivalent of 46 pounds of coal or 9.5 gallons of oil products. (*Newsweek,* 1/22/73). The U.S. Geological Survey reported that American proven recoverable reserves amounted to: oil, thirteen years; natural gas, eleven years; uranium, thirteen years; coal, five hundred years.

576   *"Fuck the Senate":* HRHD, 3/6/73.

576   *"Can you buy peace"*: Korogolos meeting memo to RN, 3/8/73, POF Box 91.
576   *"communication with Gray cut off"*: NT, 3/7/73, 8:53 A.M.
577   *"the last gasp"*: NT, 3/13/73, 12:42 P.M.
577   *"a cancer within"*: NT, 3/21/73, 10:12 A.M.
578   *"need for substantial cash"*: NT, 3/21/73, 1:06 P.M.
578   *seventy-five thousand dollars*: Lukas, *Nightmare*, pp. 299–300.
579   *Liddy was sentenced*: NYT, 3/24/73.
579   *"a bombshell"*: Nixon, *Memoirs*, p. 803.
580   *"Why did we get into"*: HRHD, 3/26/73.
580   *"I think Mitchell authorized it"*: NT, 3/27/73, 3:27 P.M.
581   *meeting with President Thieu*: Hung and Schecter, *Palace File*, pp. 161–164.
582   *kickbacks while Agnew was governor*: HRHD, 4/10/73.
583   *dump Haldeman*: HRHD, 4/13/73.
583   *"moment of truth"*: HRHD, 4/11/73.
583   *"Mitchell ought to step up"*: HRHD, 3/26/73.
583   *"pulling the covers over his head"*: NT, 4/10/73, 12:48 P.M.
583   *seven longhand pages*: WHSF, Ehrlichman papers, Box 8, Ford Library; HRHD, 4/14/73.
583   *"a go, no-go decision"*: NT, 4/14/73, 8:55 A.M.
585   *"Ask him if he can come down"*: NT, 4/14/73, 8:55 A.M.
585   *"take some brutal measures"*: NT, 4/14/73, 12:02 P.M.
585   *Ehrlichman told Mitchell*: HRHD, 4/14/73.
585   *"All finished?"*: NT, 4/14/73, 2:24 P.M.
586   *next to Daniel Schorr*: Safire int.
586   *Barry Sussman*: Sussman, *The Great Coverup: Nixon and the Scandal of Washington*, 3rd, ed. (Arlington, Virginia: Seven Locks Press, 1992), pp. 182–183.
586   *"the Lawrence quote"*: HRHD, 4/14/73.
586   *Kleindienst*: Lukas, *Nightmare*, pp. 319–320.
587   *"after the correspondents' dinner"*: NT, 4/15/73, 1:12 P.M.
587   *papers taken from Hunt's safe*: Lukas, *Nightmare*, pp. 227–228.
587   *Petersen, who was supervising*: NT, 4/15/73, 8:14 P.M., 8:25 P.M., 9:39 P.M., 11:45 P.M.
587   *after 9 P.M., the President called Dean*: Dean, *Blind Ambition*, pp. 260–264.
588   *President called in Dean before 10 A.M.*: NT, 4/16/73, 10:00 A.M.; Dean, *Blind Ambition*, pp. 266–268.
589   *with Haldeman and Ehrlichman*: NT, 4/16/73, 10:50 A.M.
590   *"a leave of absence"*: NT, 4/16/73, 4:07 P.M.
590   *"He's pissing as high"*: HRHD, 4/17/73.

Chapter 39: *April 30, 1973*

591   *Nixon telephoned Henry Kissinger*: NT, 4/17–18/73, 11:45 P.M.
592   *party hosted by Sinatra*: Kissinger, *The Years of Upheaval* (Boston: Little, Brown, 1982), pp. 90–91.
593   *"I don't want to have"*: NT, 4/9/73, 9:47 A.M.
593   *turn the microphones on and off*: NT, 4/9/73, 2:05 P.M.
593   *"I know about that"*: Lukas, *Nightmare*, p. 329; HRHD, 4/18/73.
593   *two of them shouted*: Lukas, *Nightmare*, pp. 331, 333.
594   *"killed some innocent children,"* HRHD, 4/22/73.
594   *Ziegler . . . called Haldeman*: HRHD, 4/23/73.
595   *Kleindienst in a call to the President*: NT, 4/25/73, 3:14 P.M.; NT, 4/25/73, 3:35 P.M.
596   *an hour with Petersen*: NT, 4/25/73, 5:37 P.M.

597   "My wife is not": NT, 4/27/73, 6:04 P.M.
597   called the President at 7:44: NT, 4/26/73, 7:44 P.M.; NT, 4/27/73, 4:14 P.M.
The "Mister Clean" remark was made the following afternoon in another conversation
with Kleindienst.
598   Meridian, Mississippi: Washington Post, 4/28/73; ANS, 4/28/73.
598   "The whole hopes of the whole": NT, 4/27/73, 8:22 P.M.
599   "That's quite a collection": NT, 4/28/73, 8:21 A.M.
600   called Haldeman next: NT, 4/28/73, 8:43 A.M.
600   Tricia, sitting on the couch: Nixon, Memoirs, pp. 845–846.
600   path in the woods: HRHD, 4/29/73.
601   Haldeman walked over to Aspen Lodge: HRHD, 4/29/73; Haldeman, Ends of
Power, pp. 292–294; Nixon, Memoirs, p. 847.
601   "Your turn": Ehrlichman, Witness to Power, p. 392; Nixon, Memoirs, pp.
847–848.
601   "It's all over": Nixon, Memoirs, p. 848.
601   Ziegler knew: Ziegler int.
602   "Ravage" . . . kill himself: Price int.
602   "God bless you": Nixon, Memoirs, p. 848.
·602   shoved the FBI man: Klein, Making It Perfectly Clear, p. 354. Klein int.; NYT,
5/2/73. The order to the FBI came from Leonard Garment, who replaced Dean as White
House counsel.
602   "trusted by the so-called": NT, 4/29/73, 10:19 P.M.
603   Weinberger . . . It was Haldeman: NT, 4/30/73, 10:16 P.M.; HRHD, 4/30/73.

Epilogue

604   did not make a single diary entry: Ziegler int.
605   "Al Haig is keeping the country together": Fawn Brodie int. with Mel Elfin,
Brodie papers, UCLA.
606   "Do it now!" Isaacson, Kissinger, p. 522.
606   "President is acting": Anthony Summers with Robbyn Swan, The Arrogance
of Power: The Secret World of Richard Nixon (New York: Viking, 2000), p. 458.
606   "I have reason": ibid., p. 463.
607   Time magazine: Time, 4/1/74.
608   "TWO GREAT MEN": Nixon, Memoirs, pp. 1027–1034; Time, 6/24/74.
609   Stephen-Bull was placing: Bull int.
609   five-page summary: Unmarked news summary, 8/9/74, POF Box 76.

Bibliographic Essay

For more than twenty years, historians were teased by the irony of the papers and tapes of President Richard Nixon: that a record so extensive should be so frustratingly inaccessible. From his resignation in 1974 until his death in 1994, Nixon suffered only one major defeat in his effort to keep private the forty million pages and thirty-seven hundred hours of tape documenting his presidency: the 1987 release of the Special Files unit. Even this release of the most sensitive White House documents was not a total defeat for him. He contested the opening of 42,191 of these documents, delaying their release for another decade.

Nixon fought to protect what remained of his reputation, just as he had clung to a diminished presidency. In both battles, he fought long after he knew defeat was inevitable. Like his other accomplishments, Nixon's success at protecting his papers was a triumph of will. With his death, that force is gone, and the papers are coming to light, slowly.

For most of American history, chance determined what became of a president's papers. Abraham Lincoln's papers, for example, did not become public until 1949. When Franklin Delano Roosevelt donated his records and part of his Hyde Park estate to the government in 1939, he set a pattern that would be codified by Congress in 1955. The Presidential Libraries Act established the system of privately constructed and publicly maintained presidential libraries. The Presidential Recordings and Materials Preservation Act of 1974, Congress's ad hoc response to an agreement Nixon signed with the head of the General Services Administration mandating the destruction of his tapes, allowed the exigent, yet ex post facto, expropriation of Nixon's records. A new policy was set later with the Presidential Records Act of 1978, stating that all records documenting the official exercise of the presidency were government property.

The 1974 law requires the Nixon Presidential Materials Project at the National Archives to process materials related to "abuse of government power" as quickly as possible, and to separate and return to the Nixon estate all personal material. The best known of the abuse-of-power materials are the 60 hours of tapes used for the Watergate trial. The remaining 204 hours of abuse-of-power tapes were opened in 1996 due to the settlement of a lawsuit jointly filed in 1992 by Professor Stanley Kutler of the University of Wisconsin and Public Citizen. The new tapes were transcribed by Kutler in his book *Abuse of Power,* published in 1997. (In the abuse-of-power category, a few dozen snippets of tape previously deleted for national security reasons were declassified and opened in February 1999.) The remaining tapes are divided into five chronological segments, scheduled to be released one each year. The first two, comprising 870 hours of conversation spanning February to December, 1971, were released in 1999 and 2000. There is an extensive guide to this material, but no official transcript.

The complete tapes cover approximately twenty-eight hundred hours of conversation recorded over thirty-seven hundred hours. Taping began with the installation of a few Oval Office microphones in February 1971, and ended in July 1973, when Alexander Butterfield revealed the existence of the taping system to the Senate Watergate committee. As a tool for the lone historian, the tapes are useful primarily as a record of important meetings and conversations. Their sheer volume makes systematic exploration of the tapes impractical.

"The tapes can be very misleading," Henry Kissinger told Richard Reeves. "Nixon was a man of writing. The real Nixon can be found on paper." The incoherence of the taped Nixon—the stammers and fragments—can seem almost deliberate. The taped Nixon shows little evidence of his brilliance. Nixon on paper is a more compelling figure.

Of the forty million pages of documents of the Nixon administration, seven million are open to the public. The most important of these are the Special Files, opened in 1987. These files, culled in September 1972 from the White House Central Files because of their sensitive nature, comprise the papers of Nixon and his key domestic and political assistants. Though Nixon contested opening 42,191 of these documents, 28,035 were released in October 1996. Researchers should know that the contested documents were not refiled with the rest of the Special Files. Instead, they are a shadow file. The contested documents, considered the most sensitive of the sensitive by Nixon, are fascinating. They include, for example, a Nixon memo to John Mitchell and Bryce Harlow on April 14, 1969, concerning Senate patronage: "I noted that Howard Baker is concerned that his Tennessee candidate for a vacancy on the 6th Circuit Court of Appeals is being pushed by a candidate from Kentucky sponsored by Cooper and Cook. . . . Unless we can get Cook to swing over to us on ABM, the appointment should go to Baker's man. . . ." Or a March 16, 1970, memo to Peter Flanigan on price-fixing of meat: "I think you will find that the chain stores who generally control those prices nation-wide are primarily dominated by Jewish interests. These boys, of course, have the right to make all the money they want, but they have a notorious reputation in the trade for conspiracy."

This shadow file of contested documents is the most obvious place to look for documents missing from their Special File folders. But there are other ways to find them. When looking for a restricted or missing document, researchers should check all relevant chronological and subject files, as well as those of all parties. Companion documents, or copies, can turn up in unexpected places. For example, National Security Council transcripts of Nixon's conversations with Chou En-lai were opened, with media notification, in April 2001. But transcripts of the same conversations were declassified a few years earlier, and sat unnoticed in Nixon's regular meeting file. Also, documents that were subpoenaed for the Watergate trials are available in public court records, though they may still be restricted at the National Archives. In this category is the memo in which John Ehrlichman authorized Bud Krogh and David Young to burglarize the offices of Daniel Ellsberg's psychiatrist; it is unavailable in the Archives but available in federal court records.

Other series in the Special Files are of obvious importance: H. R. Haldeman's files, which contain many of the President's orders in the form of action memos, and thousands of pages of notes on Haldeman's meetings with the President; John Ehrlichman's files, also filled with memos and meeting notes; the Office of the Staff Secretary files; Charles

Colson's files; the President's Personal Files, where his dictated memoranda can be found; and the President's Office Files, which include his meeting memos and the news summaries. The importance of the news summaries may not be self-evident, but thousands of presidential orders issued from Nixon's notations on the summaries. The marginalia also reveal a relentlessly calculating mind. After reading of a martial artist who broke his hand punching bricks for a failed charity fund-raiser, Nixon scrawled an order to send one hundred dollars to the cause. The response stands out for its sentimentality. More typical would be his reaction to a report that a Housing and Urban Development official said the administration was "encouraging and perpetuating racial discrimination." "Good," Nixon wrote.

Until now, studies of Nixon's foreign policy were based primarily on memoirs, interviews, and, occasionally, documents from other countries. State Department documents are available, but the department was not Nixon's principal vehicle for foreign policy; the National Security Council was. The Foreign Relations of the United States series does not yet cover the Nixon administration, though completion of these studies is required within thirty years of the events they cover. Kissinger's papers are in the Library of Congress, largely sealed until five years after his death. The Kissinger papers that are unclassified may be searched with his permission, but access to classified documents is contingent upon authorization of the relevant agency, as well as Kissinger's permission. When the National Archives has opened a copy of a Kissinger document, the original is available at the Library of Congress. But documents too sensitive to copy are sealed in the Library of Congress. The handful of NSC folders available at the National Archives cover POW matters and, for some reason, relations with Sudan.

The famine ended in March 1998 with a major release of NSC documents. This was followed by the opening of 130,000 pages in April 2000, and another 100,000 pages a year later. These include cables and memos dealing with the India-Pakistan crisis and the Cambodia incursion, and the long-awaited memoranda of conversations for Kissinger's Paris negotiations and the China and Moscow summits.

The National Archives is the main source for primary documents, but other collections are also useful. The Nixon Library and Birthplace Foundation in Yorba Linda, California, contains his pre- and postpresidential materials. The National Security Archive in Washington, D.C., gathers extensive documentation for researchers, libraries, and its own publications. The Gerald Ford Library at the University of Michigan has several collections of interest to Nixon researchers, especially the oral histories of administration officials conducted by James Reichley. California State University at Fullerton also has an extensive collection of oral histories concerning Nixon's early years. Chuck Colson gave his papers to the Billy Graham Center at Wheaton College in Illinois. William Safire's papers are at the Library of Congress. Stanley Pottinger's papers at the University of Wyoming were also of help. The Hoover Institution at Stanford University has the papers of a number of administration officials. The Nixon Library has information on where papers of other administration officials can be found.

Hundreds of books have been written on Nixon, his politics, policies, scandals, and times. Most of them were read, either in their entirety or for their relevant sections, during seven years of work on this project. This essay will discuss the most notable of them. For an exhaustive treatment of sources, see the bibliographic essay in Melvin Small's judicious and readable study, The Presidency of Richard Nixon (Lawrence: University Press of Kansas, 1999).

Haldeman's astonishingly frank diaries—published in book form as The Haldeman Diaries: Inside the Nixon White House (New York: Putnam, 1994) and on CD-ROM as The Complete Multimedia Edition of the Haldeman Diaries (Santa Monica, California: Sony Electronic Publishing, 1994)—are perhaps the most valuable record of Nixon's presidency. Haldeman was a sounding board as much as an administrative conduit, and his diaries often reflect Nixon's thought on a subject as it developed. The diaries were pared extensively to fit inside a book cover, but the CD-ROM is considerably more complete. Excisions previously made for national security and privacy reasons are published for the first time in this book. These segments show Nixon ruminating on replacing the mayor of Washington, D.C., with a "white Alabama coon-killer," and celebrating the safe landing of Apollo 13 by getting drunk and passing out in the middle of the afternoon. But they also add to the understanding of policy. In them, Kissinger is certain early in 1970 of an imminent Russian invasion of China. During Israel's confrontation with Syria and Egypt in August 1970, we see Kissinger bent on sabotaging Secretary of State William Rogers's peace process, and Nixon wary of an "Israeli trap." Haldeman had a unique role in the relationship between Nixon and Kissinger. When they were fighting, he would mediate. When they were suspicious of each other, he would try to restore trust. Because of this, his depictions of a Kissinger near hysteria gain real credibility. Haldeman's diaries make up for his sloppy memoir, written with Joseph DiMona, *The Ends of Power* (New York: Times Books, 1978).

RN: The Memoirs of Richard Nixon (New York: Grosset & Dunlap, 1978) is essential reading. At times it is frank, and offers depth or insight concerning important events, for example, his trip to China. However, much of it is self-serving or suspect, particularly some critical "diary" entries that could have been written or rewritten long after the events covered. Its treatment of lesser occurrences, some of them significant, is abbreviated. Nixon's *Six Crises* (New York: Doubleday, 1962) offers particularly valuable insight into the man, though his eight later works also should be read.

Henry Kissinger's memoirs, *The White House Years, The Years of Upheaval* (Boston: Little, Brown, 1979, 1982), and *The Years of Renewal* (New York: Simon & Schuster, 1999) are indispensable. For this study, *The White House Years* was most important because it covers the administration up until Watergate. All are "memoir history," self-serving, but providing unique context. The style is literary and digressive with great detail that can confuse rather than clarify.

The third member of Nixon's administrative troika, domestic policy czar John Ehrlichman, took a different tack with his recollections. *Witness to Power: The Nixon Years* (New York: Simon & Schuster, 1982) is more tabloid in content—gossipy detail written by an embittered man. Kissinger may have lied to suit his purposes and direct history; Ehrlichman seemed to lie for the hell of it.

Considering the volume of Nixoniana, there are remarkably few comprehensive studies of the man's career. Most notable is the three-volume history by Stephen E. Ambrose, *Nixon: The Education of a Politician, 1913–1962; The Triumph of a Politician, 1962–1972;* and *Ruin and Recovery, 1973–1990* (New York: Simon & Schuster, 1987, 1989, 1991). The second volume made good use of the White House Special Files, which had just been released. Ambrose recognized the importance of the news summary, and found a lot of new material. Few administration papers were available when these volumes were written, so some events aren't thoroughly covered.

Nixon granted Jonathan Aitken, a former British defense minister and member of Parliament, interviews for his book *Nixon: A Life* (Washington D.C.: Regnery, 1993), which Aitken claimed was the first objective biography of the man. It has a little insight into aspects of Nixon's character, but is a blatant apologia, and hardly discusses the presidency.

In addition to Small's book, another scholarly work worth reading is Michael A. Genovese's *The Nixon Presidency: Power and Politics in Turbulent Times* (Westport, Connecticut: Greenwood Press, 1990). The view of American power in decline—which was in minor vogue when this was written—is in evidence, as Genovese sees the Nixon Doctrine as the start of a continuing loss of American hegemony in the world. Among contemporary histories, one of the best is *Nixon in the White House: The Frustration of Power* (New York: Random House, 1971), by Rowland Evans Jr. and Robert D. Novak. It is top-notch reporting by one of the best duos ever. As contemporary history, it is light on dialogue and a step removed from the action, but still a perceptive picture of the first half of the administration.

William Safire's *Before the Fall: An Inside View of the Pre-Watergate White House* (Garden City, New York: Doubleday, 1975) is terrific—perhaps the best-written memoir of the Nixon White House. Safire may not have been at every important meeting, but he offers a great sense of place and character. His book includes detailed accounts of some key moments, along with telling and funny anecdotes. His papers also are useful. His fellow speechwriter Raymond Price recounts in *With Nixon* (New York: Viking Press, 1977) his journey from writing the *New York Herald Tribune*'s endorsement of Lyndon Johnson to writing Nixon's resignation speech, and all the highs and lows in between.

John Osborne wrote the influential "Nixon Watch" column for *The New Republic,* and in hindsight, he was the most perceptive of White House chroniclers. His columns were gathered in yearly compendiums, called *The Nixon Watch, The Second Year of the Nixon Watch,* and so on. (New York: Liveright, 1970–1975). He had better sources than most, Ehrlichman among them, an eye for Freudian detail, and a strong sense of atmosphere.

Research into foreign policy and the administration's conduct of the Vietnam War should start with two works (aside from Kissinger's own): Seymour M. Hersh's *The Price of Power: Kissinger in the Nixon White House* (New York: Summit Books, 1983), and Walter Isaacson's *Kissinger: A Biography* (New York: Simon & Schuster, 1992). Hersh uncovered a tremendous amount of what is now known about Kissinger. In tone, his book is something of a counterweight to Kissinger's memoirs. It is relentlessly negative, but his interpretations are usually well grounded. Hersh is careful to note shortcomings in some of his arguments. Isaacson is balanced, tilting toward favorable. His work should stand as the authoritative account until Kissinger's papers and the rest of the NSC papers are released. Roger Morris's attack on his old boss, *Uncertain Greatness: Henry Kissinger and American Foreign Policy* (New York: Harper & Row, 1977), is written like a long essay, and is not up to the level of his justifiably acclaimed biography of young Nixon, *Richard Milhous Nixon: The Rise of an American Politician* (New York: Henry Holt, 1990). Much of the best material in *Uncertain Greatness* was taken by later works, so the book is best read for views on foreign policy. Bernard and Marvin Kalb's *Kissinger* (Boston: Little, Brown, 1974) represents Kissinger as he saw himself at the time. Its best reporting, too, has been taken by later volumes.

The memoirs of Alexander M. Haig Jr., written with Charles McCarry, *Inner Circles: How America Changed the World* (New York: Warner Books, 1992), fill out the picture of some historical events. There is noteworthy work on Jordan, and on the operations of the NSC. Also, McCarry brings a nice style to the book.

For a fuller understanding of the Cold War, Soviet ambassador Dobrynin's memoirs should be consulted. *In Confidence: Moscow's Ambassador to America's Six Cold War Presidents, 1962–1986* (New York: Times Books, 1995), by Anatoliy Fedorovich Dobrynin, explains the extraordinary way in which the first Moscow summit came about. After getting nowhere going through Andrei Gromyko, Nixon sent a private feeler to Leonid Brezhnev on August 5, 1971, and five days later had an invitation to visit Moscow in May or June of 1972.

A valuable account of the U.S.-Vietnamese relationship was written by Nguyen Tien Hung and Jerrold L. Schecter. *The Palace File* (New York, Harper & Row, 1986) details the commitments the United States made and broke, and the secret correspondence and meetings between Nixon and President Thieu. Hung served President Thieu and later interviewed him and almost everyone else involved in deciding South Vietnamese policy. This book also offers new understanding of the efficacy of the Christmas bombings and the mining of Haiphong.

Jeffrey Kimball's *Nixon's Vietnam War* (Lawrence: University Press of Kansas, 1998) is the only major work devoted exclusively to Nixon's conduct of the war. The prose is a bit workmanlike, and long sections of the book rely heavily on secondary material. This is largely because almost no NSC files had been released until March 1998, which was fairly late in this project. Still, there is considerable new material gathered here from NSC files and foreign archives; available sources were consulted carefully, and the final product is well organized and useful. Stanley Karnow's *Vietnam: A History* (New York: Viking Press, 1983) accompanied a TV documentary and is worthwhile reading, but has less than a hundred pages on the Vietnam War under Nixon. William Shawcross's *Sideshow: Kissinger, Nixon, and the Destruction of Cambodia* (New York: Simon & Schuster, 1979) is the leading account of the bombing of Cambodia.

For information on the overthrow of Salvador Allende, see the report of the Senate Select Committee to Study Governmental Operations with Respect to Intelligence Activities, *Alleged Assassination Plots Involving Foreign Leaders* (Washington, D.C.: U.S. Government Printing Office, 1975).

The best comprehensive look at the Vietnam War protest movement is Tom Wells's *The War Within: America's Battle over Vietnam* (Berkeley: University of California Press, 1994). It is well written and well researched, if a bit one-sided. But it captures the zeitgeist in presenting the turmoil as a low-grade civil war. The stories of both protesters and government officials are told, with much new material from interviews.

Watergate generated enough literature to form its own subgenre. Of the hundreds of titles, a few were of particular use on events up through April 30, 1973. *Blind Ambition: The White House Years* (New York: Simon & Schuster, 1976), by John W. Dean III is an indispensable if self-serving account by one of the chief players, but is, of course, at odds with other accounts. Charles W. Colson's *Born Again* (Old Tappan, New Jersey: Chosen Books, 1976), like the man himself, is something of a paradox. It is both defiant and contrite. Jeb Stuart Magruder's book, *An American Life: One Man's Road to Watergate* (New York: Atheneum, 1974), also bears reading, as he was another principal in the scandal.

If "the exception that proves the rule" meant what people thought it did, J. Anthony Lukas's book is the exception to the rule about contemporary history. *Nightmare: The Underside of the Nixon Years* (New York: Viking Press, 1976) is by far the best work on the Nixon administration's abuses of power. Even one inured to the scandals through long years of research can be shocked by the contents of a forgotten page. Lukas's initial reporting was for three stories that filled entire issues of *The New York Times Magazine*. He talked to everyone he should have, read everything he could, and set the bulk of Watergate abuses to the page in 1976. Another excellent book is *The Wars of Watergate: The Last Crisis of Richard Nixon* (New York: Alfred A. Knopf, 1990), by Stanley D. Kutler. Kutler's *Abuse of Power: The New Nixon Tapes* (New York: Free Press, 1997) is a transcription of the Nixon tapes demonstrating "abuse of governmental power," whose release he won through a lawsuit. William Doyle's *Inside the Oval Office: The Secret White House Tapes from FDR to Clinton* (New York: Kodansha International, 1999) is a history of White House taping. It does not have a lot on Nixon, but there is some original transcription. Extensive transcription is available in *The White House Transcripts,* by the staff of *The New York Times* (New York: Viking Press, 1974) and *The Presidential Transcripts,* by *The Washington Post* (New York: Delacorte Press, 1974).

Silent Coup: The Removal of a President (New York: St. Martin's Press, 1991), by Len Colodny and Robert Gettlin, was widely dismissed when it was released. Libel suits stemming from its publication are still working their way through the courts. Perhaps there is something to the authors' conspiracy theories, but their strands of argument quickly become tangled. Worse, the book treats conclusions arrived at by Rube Goldberg syllogisms as facts for later arguments. The gist is that Watergate was actually about uncovering a sex-for-hire ring involving Maureen Dean, John Dean's wife. Unreconstructed Nixon-haters will enjoy *The Arrogance of Power: The Secret World of Richard Nixon* (New York: Viking, 2000), by Anthony Summers, with Robbyn Swan, which is an anthology of malfeasance real and imagined.

David Wise revealed extensive detail on several of the Watergate abuses in *The American Police State: The Government against the People* (New York: Random House, 1976). Much of its content has been summarized or ignored by later works, so it is well worth a read. *All the President's Men* (New York: Simon & Schuster, 1974), the classic by Bob Woodward and Carl Bernstein, is an obvious must-read. It offers a sense of the time, and its reporting has essentially held up after years of more detailed accounts of the events of the middle 1970s. Clark R. Mollenhoff recounted his time in the White House in *Game Plan for Disaster: An Ombudsman's Report on the Nixon Years* (New York: W. W. Norton, 1976), a useful book on Watergate and other troubles. The director of the White House Military Office, Bill Gulley, worked with Mary Ellen Reese on *Breaking Cover* (New York: Simon & Schuster, 1980), his report on the waste and extravagance in the White House. The book is great fun. Jack Anderson's *Confessions of a Muckraker: The Inside Story of Life in Washington During the Truman, Eisenhower, Kennedy, and Johnson Years* (New York: Random House, 1979), written with James Boyd, recounts some of the scandals broken by a major player of the day.

For all topics, a handy book is *From the President: Richard Nixon's Secret Files* (New York: Harper & Row, 1989), edited by Bruce Oudes. It is a collection of memos both important and quirky, and saves endless hours of photocopying.

Allen J. Matusow wrote a valuable study in *Nixon's Economy: Booms, Busts, Dollars, and Votes* (Lawrence: University Press of Kansas, 1998). Rarely has a book on economics been so pleasant to read. Matusow rolled up his sleeves and pulled out a lot of great material from the National Archives, as well as gathering the relevant economic studies and secondary material. He twines the political and economic together, adding much to the understanding of a historic time.

For the Family Assistance Plan, three works should be consulted: Daniel P. Moynihan's *The Politics of a Guaranteed Income: The Nixon Administration and the Family Assistance Plan* (New York: Random House, 1973); Vincent J. Burke's and Vee Burke's groundbreaking *Nixon's Good Deed: Welfare Reform* (New York: Columbia University Press, 1974); and Irwin Unger's *The Best of Intentions: The Triumphs and Failures of the Great Society under Kennedy, Johnson, and Nixon* (New York: Doubleday, 1996).

On the Pentagon Papers, see David Rudenstine, *The Day the Presses Stopped: A History of the Pentagon Papers Case* (Berkeley: University of California Press, 1996), and Sanford J. Ungar's *The Papers & the Papers: An Account of the Legal and Political Battle over the Pentagon Papers* (New York: Dutton, 1972). Ellsberg's own story is told at great length by Tom Wells in *Wild Man: The Life and Times of Daniel Ellsberg* (New York: St. Martin's Press, 2001).

Leon E. Panetta recounts his experience in civil rights enforcement at the Department of Health, Education, and Welfare in *Bring Us Together: The Nixon Team and the Civil Rights Retreat* (Philadelphia: J. B. Lippincott, 1971), with Peter Gall. This excellent account of the civil rights struggle demonstrates first hand the efficacy of Nixon's strategic ambiguity on civil rights. Also in this general category is *The Politics of Rage: George Wallace, the Origins of the New Conservatism, and the Transformation of American Politics* (New York, Simon & Schuster, 1995), by Dan T. Carter. This is one of the best books encountered during years of research for this project. One would use the index to look for a particular fact, and twenty minutes later look up and realize he had to get back to work.

Michael Massing's *The Fix* (New York: Simon & Schuster, 1998) is an interesting look at American drug policy under Nixon. On drugs, Nixon wasn't easy to stereotype. Though he raged about government officials who were publicly soft on drugs, he drew fine distinctions that were lost on contemporary demagogues. For example, in one memo he worried that a tough new law on pushers would be unfairly harsh to those who sold just to support their habit. Massing's book shows that current policy makers could learn a lot from Nixon's realpolitik.

The most requested photograph at the National Archives is of Nixon shaking hands with Elvis Presley. For those who want the full story of that summit written by the assistant who arranged it, read Egil "Bud" Krogh's *The Day Nixon Met Elvis* (Bellevue, Washington: Pejama Press, 1994).

Theodore H. White's *The Making of the President, 1968* (New York: Atheneum, 1969), wasn't quite up to the standards he earlier set for the genre. White's chronicle was challenged by *An American Melodrama: The Presidential Campaign of 1968* (New York: Viking Press, 1969) by Lewis Chester, Godfrey Hodgson, and Bruce Page, staffers of the London *Sunday Times;* Joe McGinniss's *The Selling of the President* (New York: Trident Press, 1969); and Jules Witcover's *The Resurrection of Richard Nixon* (New York: Putnam, 1970). Though he missed the mark again in 1972, White atoned for the errors of his earlier judgment with *Breach of Faith: The Fall of Richard Nixon* (New York: Atheneum) in 1976.

There are many worthwhile accounts of Nixon's relationship with the press. Herbert G. Klein, who was with Nixon for nearly thirty years, offers his unique perspective in *Making It Perfectly Clear: An Insider's Account of Nixon's Love-Hate Relationship with the Media* (Garden City, New York: Doubleday, 1980). For the personal side, see Julie Nixon Eisenhower's *Pat Nixon: The Untold Story* (New York: Simon & Schuster, 1986), which is also very much about her father.

A. James Reichley's extraordinary *Conservatives in an Age of Change: The Nixon and Ford Administrations* (Washington, D.C.: Brookings Institution, 1981), based on extensive interviews with leading officials and conservative thinkers, explains what conservatives believed and did during the Nixon and Ford administrations.

JONATHAN CASSIDY
Washington, D.C.
April, 2001

Acknowledgments

Whatever else he accomplished, Richard Nixon produced more paper and tape than any president before or since. Because of that, I owe a great deal to the men and women who helped me try to manage all that information, beginning with Jonathan Cassidy, who was a student in my "Press and the Presidency" class at the Annenberg School of Communication at the University of Southern California. He gave up the sun to toil in the grayer atmosphere of Washington and the National Archives II in College Park, Maryland, and I and this book are better for his labors. My own labors were encouraged and enhanced greatly by my editor, Alice Mayhew of Simon & Schuster. This is our fifth book together. I don't know whether I'm getting better with age, but she certainly is, and she has all my gratitude.

Others who worked on the book with me include: Peter Keating, who was my principal assistant on *President Kennedy: Profile of Power* and helped me start this one before going on to his own career as one of the best young political writers around these days; Taylor Lincoln, Megan Chaney, Kirsten Marie Frese, Julie Gammill Gibson, Maggie Laurie, Ken Hughes, Nasim Moalem, Michael Ianni, and David Huebner. Alexandra Truitt did the picture research.

I am grateful, too, for the assistance I received at libraries and archives across the country. At the National Archives: Pat Anderson, Byron Parham, Kathleen Grant, and Bill Joyner. At the Library of Congress: John Earl Haynes. At the Nixon Library in Yorba Linda, California: John Taylor. At the National Security Archives: Kevin Simons. At the Billy Graham Center Archives, Wheaton College, Wheaton, Illinois: Wayne Weber. At the Annenberg School:

Stella Lopez. Reese Cleghorn and Christopher Callahan of the University of Maryland School of Journalism provided me with office space and introduced me to some of the people I later worked with on archival research. The staffs at the Gerald Ford Library in Ann Arbor and Grand Rapids, Michigan, and the Nixon Oral History Collection at California State University at Fullerton were also helpful. Bruce Stark walked and talked me through endless computer crises.

I am personally indebted, too, to a number of friends, some of them former assistants to President Nixon: Arthur Klebanoff, John Price, Raymond Price, Lee Huebner, William Safire, Leonard Garment, Stanley Pottinger, Tom Wicker, Sidney Harman, Iqbal Riza, Jerrold Schecter, Lawrence Malkin, Scott Armstrong, Bob Woodward, Robert Semple, Walter Isaacson, Jess Cook, Carl Bernstein, Robert Scheer, William Shawcross, and Strobe Talbott. I also owe a great deal to the late J. Anthony Lukas, whose 1976 book *Nightmare* is still the best single volume on the events we call Watergate.

My lawyer, Robert Barnett, made a lot of this happen. So did Roger Labrie at Simon & Schuster.

Finally, I got a kick out of working for the first time with a typist named Fiona O'Neill Reeves, my youngest daughter. And most every good thing in my life depends on the woman I was lucky enough to marry, Catherine O'Neill.

RICHARD REEVES
Washington, D.C.
June 2001

Index

Photo Credits

About the Author

RICHARD REEVES is the author of *President Kennedy: Profile of Power*, acclaimed as the authoritative volume on that presidency and named the Non-Fiction Book of the Year by *Time* magazine in 1993. He is a syndicated columnist and winner of the 1998 American Political Science Association's Carey McWilliams Prize. His documentary films have won Emmy, Columbia DuPont, and Peabody awards.